ESCAPE FROM NEW YORK

THE NEW NEGRO
HAS NO FEAR
CHOP SUEY
Edwin's
CIGAR
STORE
EDWIN'S CIGARS

ESCAPE FROM NEW YORK

THE NEW NEGRO RENAISSANCE BEYOND HARLEM

**Davarian L. Baldwin and
Minkah Makalani, Editors**

Foreword by Robin D. G. Kelley

University of Minnesota Press
Minneapolis
London

An earlier version of chapter 5 was published as Yuichiro Onishi, "The New Negro of the Pacific: How African Americans Forged Solidarity with Japan, 1917–1922," *Journal of African American History* 92, no. 2 (2007): 191–213; reprinted with permission of the *Journal of African American History*. An earlier version of chapter 6 was published as Emily Lutenski, "'A Small Man in Big Spaces': The New Negro, the *Mestizo*, and Jean Toomer's Southwestern Writings," *MELUS: Multiethnic Literature of the United States* 33, no. 1 (2008): 11–32; reprinted with permission of *MELUS*.

Published by the University of Minnesota Press
111 Third Avenue South, Suite 290
Minneapolis, MN 55401-2520
http://www.upress.umn.edu

Library of Congress Cataloging-in-Publication Data

Escape from New York : the New Negro Renaissance beyond Harlem
Davarian L. Baldwin and Minkah Makalani, editors.
  Includes bibliographical references and index.
  ISBN 978-0-8166-7738-2 (hc)
  ISBN 978-0-8166-7739-9 (pb)
1. Blacks—Race identity—History—20th century. 2. African
Americans—Race identity—History—20th century. 3. Blacks—
Social conditions—20th century. 4. African Americans—Social
conditions—20th century. 5. Blacks—Intellectual life—20th
century. 6. African Americans—Intellectual life—20th century.
7. Harlem Renaissance—Influence. 8. Harlem Renaissance—Social
aspects. I. Baldwin, Davarian L., author, editor of compilation.
II. Makalani, Minkah, author, editor of compilation.
  GN645.E79 2013
  305.896'073—dc23
                    2013021788

Printed on acid-free paper

The University of Minnesota is an equal-opportunity educator and employer.

Contents

Foreword

ROBIN D. G. KELLEY

"We, the soldiers of the national liberation front of America, in the name of the workers and all the oppressed of this imperialist country have struck a fatal blow to the racist police state!" So declared a young female revolutionary in the 1981 dystopian thriller *Escape from New York,* as she hijacked Air Force One with the president on board. The year is 1997. Manhattan had been turned into a maximum security prison, and our erstwhile rebel aims to bring the plane down on the beleaguered island so that the president can "perish in the inhuman dungeon of his own imperialist prison." Feeding off the revolutionary movements and political scandals of the 1970s, *Escape from New York* is a story of political corruption, empire, repression, rebellion, and the dark side of modernity. It anticipates the neoliberal security state, predicts a future that is now our present nightmare, and imagines a new generation who resists the status quo and recognizes that the real criminals are those in power.

Although Minkah Makalani and Davarian L. Baldwin adopted the film's title as a not-so-subtle critique of the New York–centric focus of studies on the "New Negro," I suspect there is more being invoked here than meets the eye. The "New York" to which the film refers is not a city but a metaphor for the whole U.S. empire—its brutal, repressive regime, its racial character, its centrality to finance capital, its global reach. The dialectics of Empire also breeds its own gravediggers: movements that reject racial hierarchy, refuse victimization, and declare the humanity of the ruled while exposing the inhumanity of the rulers.

Herein lies the book's most critical insight, that is, *that the New Negro was the product of a particular historical convergence*—the expansion of U.S. and European empires, settler colonialism, an increasingly industrialized racial capitalism, and their attendant processes: expropriation, proletarianization, massive migration, urbanization, rapid technological development, and war. The New Negro, in other words, was not exceptional but a manifestation of the same forces that produced revolutionary upheavals in Mexico, Russia, Ireland, China, Germany, India, Algeria, Egypt, the Arab world under the Ottoman Empire, South Africa,

Nicaragua, Brazil, and Trinidad, to name but a few. From the green corn rebellion in Oklahoma to the Tuareg rebellion in Niger, from the workers and intellectuals in Turin, Italy, to the workers and intellectuals in republican Spain, the entire world was on the move in this period: demanding democracy, challenging social norms and laws defining appropriate behavior, fighting for the repossession of indigenous lands and rights, finding new modes of expression that reveal modern anxieties as well as the hidden world of the folk. These movements were diverse and distinctive, often at odds with one another or simply not in conversation. But they all were trying to come to terms with what it means to live as human in a modern, increasingly interconnected, rapidly industrializing capitalist world. Though military conscription, travel, and print capitalism helped catapult American New Negroes and their ideas around the world, the global character of the movement owes more to the global reach of Empire.[1]

The essays collected in *Escape from New York* are not escaping anything so much as placing the New Negro movement within a larger, global trajectory. As Baldwin points out in his deft introduction, the new scholarship explores in greater depth what the so-called New Negroes understood about their own historical epoch and their place in it. Alain Locke himself compared the New Negro movement with "those nascent movements of folk-expression and self-determination, which are playing a creative part in the world to-day. The galvanizing shocks and reactions of the last few years are making, by subtle processes of internal reorganization, a race out of its own disunited and apathetic elements. A race experience penetrated in this way invariably flowers. As in India, in China, in Egypt, Ireland, Russia, Bohemia, Palestine and Mexico, we are witnessing the resurgence of a people."[2]

But Locke was only partly right. The New Negro represented a *political* expression, or better yet, *expressions*. As the essays here demonstrate, some New Negroes fought for fundamental rights and dignity within a constitutional framework. Others sought to "escape" from the United States, or the West altogether, and find a new promised land. And still others chose a third, more radical path. Rejecting both emigration and appeals for inclusion, some New Negroes aimed to *transform* the nation's social, cultural, political, economic, and juridical institutions to the core. They sought to build a new society in which the notion of rights, privileges, commitments, and social relationships would be radically reformulated—not just for black folk but for everyone.

Why revisit the New Negro now? Why does it matter? Because we are still grappling with the consequences of settler colonialism and racial capitalism. Because we are still witnessing struggles to bring an end to these forms of domination. Because the specter of the New Negro is still upon us. We can point to post-Katrina New Orleans, a key battleground in neoliberalism's unrelenting war on black working people. Out of this neoliberal disaster rose twenty-first-century New Negroes leading multiracial coalitions that continue to resist the privatization of schools, hospitals, public transit, public housing, and dismantling public sector unions. We see it in the current generation of immigrant rights activists fighting Immigration and Customs Enforcement raids and racist legislation in Arizona and Alabama, in the undocumented workers and students organizing trade unions and fighting for the Dream Act. The book's contributors reveal with stunning clarity the specter of the New Negro behind today's movements, in excavation of Jazz Age New Orleans, in the black solidarity movements with Mexicans, Japanese, and Filipinos, in Cuba's Garveyites and London's black Marxists.

But I also see the dialectics of empire and the specter of the New Negro in Occupied Palestine—the embattled territory from which I write these words. Being here profoundly shaped my perspective, not unlike those New Negroes who came to see their country with greater clarity from a battlefield in the Philippines or a salon in Paris or a dock in Liverpool. I read these essays in a land still ruled by settler colonialism, where Palestinians have produced at least four or five generations of "New Negroes"—from the Arab resistance of the 1930s, the 1948 war, and the formation of the Palestine Liberation Organization, to the first and second intifadas, to the current Boycott, Divestment, and Sanctions campaign. Many came from refugee camps and built social movements and cultural institutions under surveillance and bombardment by the third most powerful military in the world. They created and sustained universities, wrote histories, and sustained at least a seven-decade-long cultural renaissance, all under a system of apartheid that makes U.S. segregation look benign. Many were forced into exile, died or were maimed, lost limbs, or pulled their own children or parents from piles of rubble that were once homes, schools, mosques, churches, or community centers. But they stand up to home demolitions, the uprooting of Palestinian olive trees, the construction of a massive apartheid wall to keep them penned in and policed. Eyeing the landscape from East Jerusalem to Bethlehem, I immediately think of Claude McKay, the poet laureate of the New Negro movement: "Pressed to the wall, dying, but fighting back!"

If we learn anything from *Escape from New York,* it is that each generation that refuses to remain pressed to the wall, that refuses to accept dispossession as a natural occurrence, that claims first-class citizenship as a natural right, will fight back. How they fight, how they express their discontent, how they see life after occupation and subordination, may differ dramatically. But it is in the fight itself, it is in the struggle, that we can begin to understand how the last century came to be, what might become of this century, and what is at stake.

Ramallah, Palestine, January 2012

NOTES

1   Of course, my characterization of the historical convergence that gave birth to the New Negro is not new. Robinson made the same point far more eloquently in his masterful *Black Marxism*.

2   Locke, *New Negro*, 4.

BIBLIOGRAPHY

Locke, Alain. *The New Negro*. 1925. Reprint, New York: Touchstone, 1997.

Robinson, Cedric. *Black Marxism: The Making of the Black Radical Tradition*. Chapel Hill: University of North Carolina Press, 2000.

Introduction: New Negroes Forging a New World

DAVARIAN L. BALDWIN

"The Bogy-men Will Get You If You Don't Look Out"
—*Chicago Defender,* March 6, 1915

"THE DARKER MILLIONS"

On a balmy Wednesday in October 1921, President Warren Harding stood before a racially mixed crowd of over one hundred thousand residents jam-packed into Birmingham, Alabama's, Capital Park. What was supposed to be a simple speech commemorating the semicentennial of the city's founding turned into an address haunted by the specter of the "race problem." Harding stunned white listeners into silence and black onlookers into rapturous applause when he declared, "The negro is entitled to full economic and political rights as an American citizen." The president certainly made an unexpected and important declaration, but his stance on political equality was hardly a benevolent one. Offering the southern Negro economic and political rights addressed what he saw as a matter of national security. From the outset, Harding soundly dismissed the strivings of social equality—racial mixing in social settings—as "a dream." Yet he opined that racial antagonisms in the South had encouraged "its colored population" to be "drained away by the processes of migration." Harding soberly acknowledged that the South's "industrial dependence on the labor of the black man" must force the region into a new set of race relations. It was clear to the president that the Negro's decision to "quit the South" could undermine the vital agricultural base of the entire country. A new Negro consciousness was in the air.[1]

As Harding discussed the national implications of this new Negro, he emphasized that "our race problem here in the United States is only a phase of a race issue that the whole world confronts." For confirmation, the president implored the crowd to read the work of Lothrop Stoddard. In his best-selling books *The Rising Tide of Color* and *The Re-forging of America,* Stoddard outlined an intensifying self-consciousness among the "darker races" that threatened to undermine white

1

world supremacy. According to Stoddard, the rise of Japan, Russia's Bolshevism, and anticolonial resistance in the Middle East, Asia, and Africa brought to life what he called the "phantoms of internationalism." Yet Stoddard found the "most chronic and most acute" dangers of this rising racial tide festering in America's "great negro problem." For Stoddard, the First World War created a tectonic shift in race relations. The influences of global agitation, the growth of the Negro press, and the influx of southern migrants and returning black veterans converged on American cities. He described the "great negro quarters of New York, Chicago, and other Northern cities" as "cauldrons seething with ideas and emotions." Stoddard warned that a "radical negro movement" had arisen in cities stimulated by "foreign-born negroes," most notably one centered around the black radical group the African Blood Brotherhood and Moscow leaders hoping to "Bolshevize America." He further elaborated that this new Negro found expression in "urban riots" and "agrarian disturbances" alongside political agitation and the "cultural forms" of Negro arts and letters.[2]

While rejecting Lothrop Stoddard's call to reassert white supremacy, black scholars and newspapers agreed that a racial armageddon—a day of racial reckoning—was near. W. E. B. Du Bois had long argued that American race relations were "but a local phase of a world problem." The great West Indian American intellectual and "father of Harlem radicalism" Hubert Harrison was so impressed with *Rising Tide*'s analysis of worldwide revolt among the darker races that he began a correspondence with Stoddard. But Harrison made clear, "Naturally, since I am a Negro, my sympathies are not at all with you: that which you fear I naturally hope for." A *Chicago Defender* cartoon mocked white anxieties about a new Negro more broadly, threatening "The Bogy-men Will Get You If You Don't Look Out" (see Figure I.1). The paper went on to poke fun at Stoddard directly: "The tide that has started will continue to rise in spite of all Mr. Stoddard and the white races can do. Might as well try to stop the tide from flowing or the sun from setting!"[3]

For President Harding, Lothrop Stoddard, and throngs of white and black citizens alike, the rising tide of a new Negro had emerged. And this new Negro was found in both culture and politics with a race consciousness that spoke to the strivings of the darker races across the globe. Therefore one must ask why such a dynamic outpouring of New Negro expression has remained relatively confined, in our memory, to the arts and letters of the Harlem Renaissance. *Escape from New York* takes seriously the insight of poet Sterling Brown that Harlem was merely the "show-window, the cashier's till" for a much broader "New Negro experience" that took place outside of Harlem and across the globe. This collection of essays marks the first attempt to assemble the latest scholarship in what might profitably be called a "renaissance" in New Negro studies. Here the more well-known literary and visual art expressions most associated with Harlem are

FIGURE I.1. "The Jungles of Prejudice," *Chicago Defender,* March 16, 1915.

situated within a broader range of social movements, popular culture, and public behavior that spanned the globe from New York and New Orleans to Paris, the Philippines, and beyond.[4]

It has certainly become axiomatic to state that the New Negro movement exceeded Harlem while finding expression in not only arts and letters but also the popular cultures of sport, music, film, protest, public behavior, and so on. Yet there have been few rigorous studies of this social and cultural movement in other physical locations.[5] Alongside a wider array of cultural expressions, this collection will also position the New Negro experience in the United States as just one nodal point within a dynamic and uneven circuit of black internationalism. But to be clear, *Escape from New York* does not initiate the process of mapping the global sites of early-twentieth-century black internationalism so much as it draws attention to how New Negroes and their global allies already lived.[6] Our work stresses the need for scholarship to "catch up to history," to create studies that match the breadth and depth of the actual New Negro experience.

Besides perhaps a handful of monographs, it is primarily at the dissertation and early manuscript stage where we find any substantial treatment of the New Negro experience beyond the traditional boundaries of genre and location. Most of the pioneering scholars in New Negro studies are in fact assembled in this collection. Here parallel developments in the scholarship are finally brought together for more direct conversation with each other. *Escape from New York*, in fact, constitutes *a field in formation*. Therefore this anthology announces the New Negro as an analytic—the notion of an analytic highlights how we have not assumed a prefigured definition of the New Negro. Our method in this collection has been to let the New Negro's meanings emerge from the research process through the acts of critical investigation collectively employed in these essays. Such an approach charts broadly the New Negro experience as an overlapping and contested architecture of race consciousness that moved around the United States, traveled along a range of expressive frequencies, and was translated (or not) in other languages and frames of local and global discourse.

A more comprehensive vision of the New Negro experience provides better understanding of what we identify as a global modernity by pinpointing the relationship between industry and empire, migration and social movements, and cultural renaissance and mass consumption in the early twentieth century. Decentering Harlem, both as a physical space and as the model for an appropriate "renaissance," helps to insist on this moment's both geographical and expressive reach. *Escape from New York* takes us beyond national boundaries, across broader fields of activity, and through unconventional modes of cultural expression, attending to the rough edges and fine grains of the period. To be sure, the historical record reveals a range of New Negroes who were more than just the objects of black modernist art and writings waiting for aesthetic construction. New Negroes were subjects whose unexpected existence would forever alter the course and shape of the modern world.

"THE NEW NEGRO IS HERE"

The term *New Negro* goes as far back as the era of chattel slavery, designating those who had just come from Africa. During Reconstruction, the term referred to the assertiveness and defiance of the first generation of free black people. But the notion of New Negroes or a New Negro movement is most commonly framed by the racial assertiveness found in the last decade of the nineteenth century and the more pronounced convergence of politically leftist and black radical internationalisms in the mid- to late 1930s. Many, in fact, scoffed at the very idea of a "new" racial assertiveness in the first four decades of the twentieth century. But to be sure, black people, many in solidarity with the darker races all over the world, engaged in a collective outpouring of political protest, cultural expression, and intellectual debate—or what they commonly described as the forging of a *New* Negro.[7]

At the turn of the twentieth century, New Negroes largely represented those within intellectual circles who debated various strategies for solving the "race problem" of social integration, which still plagued the United States after the end of slavery. The National Association of Colored Women's Clubs was becoming the most powerful black organization in the country. Booker T. Washington, N. B. Wood, and Fannie Barrier Williams's 1900 edited collection *A New Negro for a New Century: An Accurate and Up-to-Date Record of the Upward Struggles of the Negro Race* highlighted the individual achievements of black citizens, including the military valor of Spanish–American War soldiers. That same year, the initial London Pan-African Conference convened in partial response to Europe's scramble to carve up and colonize Africa after the 1884–85 Berlin Conference. This early Pan-Africanism did not demand the elimination of empire but called for better treatment under colonial rule. And still it was in London where W. E. B. Du Bois first announced, "The problem of the twentieth century is the problem of the color line." Black professionals and intellectuals, including Du Bois and organizations such as T. Thomas Fortune's Afro-American League, countered what many saw as Washington's "separate but equal" approach to integration with an alternate set of demands for immediate civil rights and equal protection in the age of Jim Crow. From this arm of the New Negro elite came J. Max Barber's Atlanta journal *Voice of the Negro,* with its 1904 "Rough Sketches" of the New Negro man and woman. Intellectuals and clergy in Washington, D.C., produced the African Methodist Episcopal *AME Review* and supported Alexander Crummel's American Negro Academy. Boston added *Colored American* magazine, edited by writer Pauline Hopkins and supported by the Colored Co-operative Publishing Company, foreshadowing later New Negro economic strategies for a combined racial and economic self-determination.[8]

Yet even at this early stage, elite clergy, intellectuals, and professionals did not fully control the meaning of a New Negro experience. While *New Negro for a New Century* focused on the loyal patriotism of Spanish–American War soldiers to the United States, some hoped that disenfranchised black people could resettle in Cuba and the Philippines, creating their own black colony. Others protested the oppression of any "people of color" in America's expanding empire, even if it benefited African Americans. Some went as far as to celebrate the exploits of black soldier David Fagen and others who left the U.S. military to join Philippine *insurectos* fighting American imperialism. At the same time, professional actors were transforming Broadway and, in the process, literally setting the stage for the emerging New Negro consciousness. Behind the caricatured masks of blackface comedy, figures including Bob Cole, Aida Overton, George Walker, and Bert Williams "corked up" to revolutionize American dance and song. Shows, including *Clorindy* (1898), *In Dahomey* (1903), and *Abyssinia* (1906), fed white America's desire for the master–slave relations of the plantation days, while America's cities were now being transformed by modern and urbane black folk. But these shows also inserted subtle political commentary about African redemption, intraracial class divisions, and white supremacy. Blackface artists also publicly put their ample resources behind expressions of black self-determination and race pride, including Bob Cole's powerful "Colored Actor's Declaration of Independence" (1898) and the racially controversial sporting exploits of boxer Jack Johnson in the early decades of the twentieth century.[9]

The year 1910 is noted as a significant New Negro signpost because it marks the official naming of the National Association for the Advancement of Colored People and the start of its landmark magazine *The Crisis*. But at the same time, a young Marcus Garvey began cutting his transnational organizing teeth, helping to rally black workers in Central America against inhumane treatment by the United Fruit Company. Still, most remember this year as the moment when Jack Johnson, the "Negro's Deliverer," trounced the "Great White Hope," Jim Jeffries, to retain the heavyweight championship of the world. Black communities all over the country took to the streets talking back to Jim Crow in both impromptu parades and gun battles with white soldiers on leave, setting off possibly the first ever nationwide race riots in U.S. history. Soon after, Johnson touched down in Mexico, where he perhaps joked but still promised that if the United States and Mexico went to war, black people would stand with their Mexican brothers against the gringo invaders. Yet even the "Johnson affair" was just the beginning.

Various strands of imperial expansion and anticolonial resistance would come to an apocalyptic head during World War I in ways that transformed the political and cultural concerns associated with the New Negro. Cultural critics, activists, and laborers saw the Great War as part of a thirty-year-old European scramble for materials and men in Africa, hoping to satisfy the growing demands of working-class citizens at home. Both Du Bois's 1915 *Atlantic Monthly* piece "The African Roots of War" and Hubert Harrison's essay "Our International Consciousness" (1920) highlighted how this white-on-white violence on the world stage exposed the dark underside of European "civilization," undermining a blind faith in the racial supremacy of the so-called Western world. Du Bois recalled, "In the awful cataclysm of World War, where from beating, slandering, and murdering us the white world turned temporarily aside to kill each other, we of the Darker Peoples looked on in mild amaze."[10]

Postwar armistice brought a particular urgency to the 1919 Pan-African Conference in Paris, while a number of organizations tried to get to the Versailles peace treaty meetings. Of particular note was the short-lived International League of Darker Peoples that included pan-Africanist Marcus Garvey, New York politician and pastor Adam Clayton Powell Sr., labor organizer A. Philip Randolph, and beauty culturist Madam C. J. Walker. This international league made a direct appeal to the Japanese delegation in the "spirit of race internationalism" to place Negro grievances on the platform of the Versailles agenda. Meanwhile, all over the world, members of the darker races took to stage show, sermon, and social protest, scoffing at Woodrow Wilson's fork-tongued tales of worldwide self-determination, made infamous in his "Fourteen Points" speech.

Wilson's "Fourteen Points" address was scrutinized amid the U.S. occupation of Haiti in its own backyard. Some argued that Haiti had become America's Ireland and India as it exported Jim Crow labor practices and social codes to the region. But the contradictions of a League of Nations built on racial supremacy also ignited an international network of globe-trotting race radicals, including Haitian writer Jacques Roumain. While back in the United States, a postwar New Negro consciousness was even made audible through James Reese Europe's 369th U.S. Infantry Band the "Hell Fighters"—known both for their battlefield bravery and as early exporters of jazz to France during the war. When Europe released the song "How 'Ya Gonna Keep 'Em on the Farm after They've Seen Paree," it was one of the biggest hits in 1919, partly because it touched on the larger wartime implications of "bringing the boys into town," just as millions of black people had quit the South and descended on global cities.

World War I and the Great Migration catapulted the New Negro onto the world stage in new ways. The migration of over one million African Americans into the North and West followed the flow of immigrants from southern and eastern Europe and from the colonial outposts of Asia and the Caribbean to U.S. cities. These population shifts spoke to larger processes, including the growth of industrial capitalism searching for new labor and markets alongside the continual resistance of the darker races against both Jim Crow and the "New Colonialism." Wartime suspicions of "the West" now placed images of the "exodus from Dixie" alongside dispatches from anticolonial rebellions in Ireland, China, and Trinidad, the Mexican Revolution, and even the imperial advance of Japan against European expansion. Radicals in the United States and abroad interpreted the Bolshevik Revolution of 1917 as a "slave movement," while V. I. Lenin himself saw direct parallels between the conditions of Russian peasants and black sharecroppers. The convergence between migration and anticolonial social movements helped shift the New Negro consciousness toward a direct and transnational challenge to Euro-American visions of the modern world.

The North was not even the final destination for many. A distinct segment of migrants made merely momentary stops in U.S. cities. Some went to Moscow to test the new Soviet Union's claims to be a republic without racism and enrolled at the Communist University of Toilers of the East, served as agricultural experts, or joined the cast and crew of the never completed film *Black and White*. Others headed to Paris to study at the Sorbonne, attended literary salons with the Nardal sisters, worked and played in Montmarte, caught Josephine Baker's *Revue negre* shows, or heard Ho Chi Minh and Lamine Senghor's anticolonial reformulation of communist ideals in their Union Intercoloniale. The 1927 League against Imperialism Conference in Brussels would build on the Union Intercoloniale challenge to traditional political analysis by announcing that the racial organization of the colony, as much or more than the class consciousness of industrial cities, was the central fulcrum on which capitalism rests. This conference marked arguably the first description of the U.S. black community as an "internal colony." From Sao Paulo to London to Bloemfontein, the darker races were crisscrossing the world, remapping the meanings of racial solidarity and economic relations.[11]

But those migrants who did not travel abroad transformed urban industrial landscapes all across the country. In sheer numbers, between 1910 and 1930, New York City's black population more than tripled, while Chicago's exploded from 44,130 to 233,903. At the same time, forty thousand Caribbean immigrants joined with African Americans to forge the "ethnic amalgam" of black diversity that became Harlem. Some started protests on campuses as part of the collegiate arm of New Negro activism in Washington, D.C. (Howard), Nashville (Fisk), and Atlanta, among other places, protesting the racial paternalism of white "headmasters" and their black proxies, while black soldiers came home with a Pan-African sense of New Negro militancy. Du Bois pointed out in his 1919 packed-to-capacity speech at Chicago's Wendell Phillips High School that returning black soldiers "will never be the same again. You need not ask them to go back to what they were before. They cannot, because they are not the same men anymore." Upon return, one soldier boldly confirmed, "We were the first American regiment on the Rhine. . . . We fought for democracy, and we're going to keep on fighting for democracy 'til we get our rights here at home. The black worm has turned."[12]

Though President Woodrow Wilson could not imagine reasons for a domestic brand of race militancy, it is telling that he worried returning black soldiers would be "our greatest medium in conveying bolshevism to America." Most were not "Bolshevik," but many soldiers quickly "return[ed] fighting" alongside newly arriving migrants and established residents in the struggle against long-standing white restrictions on black life. An early racial upheaval erupted in East St. Louis, Illinois (1917), and black New Yorkers took to the streets in a mass silent protest parade down Fifth Avenue. But white angst and annoyance with a growing black presence most notably exploded into what writer James Weldon Johnson termed the "Red Summer" of 1919, with over twenty race-rioting hot spots as far away as Liverpool, England. From one angle, it was clear that Confederate Americanism was becoming the national antidote. Others argued the other way around, that in fact, the seeds of white discontent sown in *northern* factories were bearing fruit in places farther south. In Elaine, Arkansas—also dubbed the "American Congo"—black observers called white attackers the American "hun" (a term used to describe wartime Germans) who sought to repress black sharecroppers who dared attempt to join labor unions. However, as white mobs attacked, black people all over the world fought back, adding global resonance to Claude McKay's timely poem "If We Must Die."[13]

In the September 1919 issue of *The Crisis,* Du Bois announced that the strategy of "Passive Resistance" had to be laid down in favor of the "terrible weapon of Self-Defense" in the struggle for "Freedom or Death." In two 1919 cartoons, black leftist *The Messenger* magazine criticized the "'Old Crowd' Negro" leadership for supporting both black military patriotism during the war and black nonviolence during the riots (see Figure 1.2), whereas the "'New Crowd' Negro" was depicted as a group of gun-toting black men seeking retribution for racial violence (see Figure 1.3). The black radical *Crusader* journal made direct links between local and global events across the "darker" world, declaring, "Whether the caucasian reads the news dispatches from Egypt or from West Africa, from the Capital of the United States or from the West Indies, from Chicago or from Panama, it must be dawning upon his junker mind that his self-constituted lordship of the world is at an end."[14]

This international and riot-induced New Negro spirit injected new life into older black organizations, including the National Association of Colored Women. At the same time, new "race" groups emerged, from the labor-focused Brother-hood of Sleeping Car Porters and Maids to the religious Moorish Science Temple. A "fighting spirit" even emerged in Los Angeles's small black community, where residents were members of both the integrationist NAACP and Marcus Garvey's Pan-Africanist Universal Negro Improvement Association (UNIA), in the battle to stop Jim Crow from winning the city. Of special note was a group of black radical trade unionists in the Hampton Roads, Virginia, cities of Norfolk, Portsmouth, and Newport News, who, with the National Brotherhood Workers of America, made clear that political consciousness did not erupt at the point of leaving the South. Abroad this race consciousness found form in the Parisian Ligue Universelle de

FIGURE I.2. "Following the Advice of the 'Old Crowd' Negro," *Messenger,* June 1919.

Defense de la Race Noire, the *Diario de la Marina* newspaper in Havana, London's West African Student Union, the renamed African National Congress, and general expressions of Negro entitlement in factories, in nightclubs, and on streetcars.[15]

As black people descended on global cities, white demands for black containment took physical shape when new urban policies buttressed anonymous fire bombings and the intimate assaults of white working-class "athletic clubs." Municipal leaders from Baltimore to Louisville to San Francisco even momentarily enacted racial zoning laws that cordoned off "undesirables" into specific areas of the city. Other metropoles, including Chicago and New York, followed suit by infamously rezoning citywide vice directly and exclusively into black neighborhoods. After racial zoning was deemed unconstitutional, racially restrictive covenants came to prominence as legally binding agreements between buyers and homeowners associations to prevent the renting or sale of housing to African Americans with threat of civil action. This convergence between black community making and racially restrictive urban policy turned urban "black belts" into the

FIGURE I.3. "The 'New Crowd' Negro Making America Safe for Himself," *Messenger*, July 1919.

nation's good-time zones but also materialized the already general assumption that black culture embodied vice, leisure, and entertainment.

Fear of black culture, however, soon turned to fascination. Many white artists, intellectuals, and Bohemians who witnessed white-on-white violence on the World War I stage grew critical or anxious about the transformation of Western civilization into a "modern machine-ridden and convention-bound society."[16] As an alternative, some turned to (in their minds) the premodern vitality, spirit, rhythm, and communalism of Africa and its now urban descendants. Many thought that the heartbeat of a premodern Africa could still be found in the sights and sounds of black work songs, jazz clubs, and storefront churches. Such black primitive traces were "discovered," excavated, and then civilized through the "Western" forms of canvas, compositional notation, and written verse. The Negro became en vogue, celebrated but trapped in a caricature, as the essence of all that Western modernity was not.[17]

The Negro, as vogue, remained a tangled web of interracial solidarity and fascination with blackness as primitive. In such spaces, Pablo Picasso showcased African sculptural forms in his revolutionary cubist style but had little interest in black artists beyond placing their physical bodies on canvas. Charlotte Mason served as a wonderful patron to black colleges and the writers Langston Hughes and Zora Neale Hurston, but her support was premised on the degree to which these authors' writings embodied the "primitive." White slummers largely looked right past social struggles and strivings to gawk and gaze at the grand drag balls, cotton clubs, and plantation cafes. These urban spaces became destinations for those seeking the perceived black primitivism of emotional excess and bodily release found in performances of the Old South or the concrete jungle. And yet black and white artists and entertainers managed to form sincere bonds while never fully undoing the racial constraints that shaped dance floors, stages, literary salons, and storefronts.[18]

Still, a legion of black cultural producers, critics, and reformers understood the Negro vogue as one of the few opportunities to seize the realm of urban culture and transform it into a vehicle for race pride, profit, and politics. Out of this vogue, the literary and visual arts of the Harlem Renaissance were pushed up as the signature showpiece of New Negro cultural production, and *The New Negro: An Interpretation* was presented as the "definitive bible." This auspicious collection came together when Charles Johnson, editor of the National Urban League magazine *Opportunity,* brought white patrons and black artists together for a 1924 Civic Club dinner. Johnson organized the event to celebrate the publication of *Crisis* editor Jessie Fauset's first novel, *There Is Confusion.* Fauset, however, was quickly pushed aside when the night's master of ceremonies and Howard University philosophy professor Alain Leroy Locke captured the attention of *Survey* magazine editor Paul Kellogg. Not even a year later, this journal devoted to social work and philanthropy released the arts-focused special number "Harlem: Mecca of the New Negro," edited by Locke. That same year, Locke expanded the special issue into the landmark anthology *The New Negro.*[19]

From the start, *The New Negro* announced the rebirth or renaissance as a racial awakening that had made great effort to push past "the watch and guard of statistics," where the Negro had become "a chronic patient for the sociological clinic, the sick man of American Democracy." Locke positioned arts and letters as the vehicle for racial self-expression and accurate portrayal beyond the caricature of social science and the minstrel stereotype. For such an ambitious task, Locke enlisted the illustrations of Winold Reiss, Aaron Douglas, and Miguel Couvarrubias, while under one umbrella he brought together a range of literary styles, from the "nonnegro" work of Jean Toomer to the genteel poetry of Countee Cullen and Georgia Douglas Johnson, alongside Langston Hughes's and Zora Neale Hurston's more explicitly blues and folklore musings. Social science contributions included an historical essay by historian and bibliophile Arturo Schomburg and both the African retention thesis of anthropologist Franz Boas's student Melville Herskovits and the racial assimilation focus of sociologist E. Franklin Frazier. Finally, Du Bois rounded out the collection with a view toward the larger world of the darker races.[20]

Some dismissed Locke's focus on the arts, especially given the much broader political history of the New Negro. But the captivating caricatures of the race in social science textbooks, on minstrel stages, and in D. W. Griffith's *Birth of a Nation* made the case that cultural representation was a central site of struggle within the larger New Negro experience. Locke's particular framing of the collection, however, revealed that he upheld a particular brand of New Negro arts and letters that could best guarantee appropriate contact "between the more advanced and representative classes" of the races. Writer George Schuyler called Locke the "high priest of intellectual snobbocracy," while younger writers rebelled with a more provocative exploration of sexuality and the realities of everyday black life through the short-lived literary magazine *Fire!* But whether it comprised learned prose or a "blues poem," the New Negro cultural world was never fully contained within the realm of arts and letters.[21]

The Harlem Renaissance may now be the most celebrated expression of the New Negro world, but in the moment, Marcus Garvey's magisterial parades and vitriolic defiance against white supremacy captured the imagination of thousands (see Figure I.4). In fact, it is more than curious that Locke waxed poetic about the "race question as a world problem" but remained obscenely silent concerning the over twenty-five thousand delegates from around the world assembled at Madison Square Garden for Garvey's 1920 UNIA convention. For most who did not want to follow Garvey and the UNIA "back" to Africa, his ideas of black self-determination still resonated with Chicago's "metropolis" paradigm. Advocates of a black metropolis remained skeptical of the Harlem Renaissance's focus on white philanthropy and instead sought to convert urban segregation into a coordinated network of black producers and consumers. Local people believed that a focused consumption could help secure community control over ideas, industry, politics, popular culture, *and* the arts. This black metropolis ideal was reproduced in more modest form all over the country.[22]

Therefore most ignored cultural critic J. A. Rogers's suggestion that popular music be lifted "into nobler channels" and still flocked to the hot jazz of Louis Armstrong, the stomp blues of Bessie Smith, and the driving rhythms of Son Cubano. The Black Broadway musical *Shuffle Along* and Oscar Micheaux's controversial "photo-plays" overshadowed the more serious work of Harlem's Lafayette players or the Chicago Ethiopian Theater. A significant but select group read the black radical and literary magazine *The Messenger* or Charles Johnson's post-riot

FIGURE I.4. "The New Negro Has No Fear," slogan displayed at a Universal Negro Improvement Association parade in Harlem, 1924, corner of 135th Street and Lenox Avenue. Photographs and Prints Division, Schomburg Center for Research in Black Culture, New York Public Library.

sociological study *The Negro in Chicago,* while Pullman Porters carried the defiant *Chicago Defender* all over the country as imperial officials banned the UNIA's *Negro World* throughout various colonial outposts across the globe. In the end, most discussions of black self-determination or race enterprise could point to the illicit lottery system of "policy" or "numbers" that underwrote black-owned churches, cabarets, coastal resorts, financial institutions, and import–export interests. This informal economy also sponsored Garvey's UNIA, national Negro League baseball, and even the landmark *New Negro* anthology: More than Harlem's arts and letters, the very notion of a New Negro consciousness was produced and consumed through the various race protests, race papers, race records, race films, race sporting leagues, and race enterprises that circulated across the country and around the world.[23]

Most scholars mark the end of the Harlem Renaissance with the onslaught of the Great Depression. To be sure, the notion of an exceptional, even magical, black world deflated under the weight of soup kitchens and the collapsing dreams of an independent black capitalism. Even Locke began to recast the relations between white patrons and black artists as "exploitation." Still, the New Negro movement's focus on race-conscious cultural production and political agitation did not cease. But the literal bankruptcy of capitalist advance found most exploring the economic texture of racial experiences or what was called the "proletarian turn." In the world of arts and letters, the patronage system shifted from the coiffeurs of wealthy white philanthropy to New Deal dollars or support from the Communist International (Comintern). In fact, Depression-era preoccupations with the plight of the "common man" continued the Negro vogue of interest in a largely working-class black population. The Federal Writer's Project employed over twenty-five thousand white-collar workers to collect local histories and create the American Guide Series as well as a range of side projects, which included a Negro Studies Project and a Slave Narrative Project. At the same time, the Comintern began to aggressively support the arts and ideas of Negroes after their 1928 black belt thesis envisioned black America as an oppressed nation within a nation with the right to political, cultural, and territorial self-determination within the U.S. South.[24]

As part of the "proletarian turn," Harlem Renaissance writers Langston Hughes, Claude McKay, and Zora Neale Hurston produced even more, while black communities helped locally shape New Deal arts projects and Communist-sponsored writing groups. This new convergence between the African diaspora and Marxist ideals gave life to Richard Wright's *Lawd Today* as well as the interests of black francophone students in Paris that became the Negritude arts movement. Even the seemingly apolitical gospel sound was a product of this moment, where its call-and-response structure and barrelhouse blues improvisations gave a voice to the voiceless against the rigid religious respectability that was governing black sacred music at that point. Black culture moved from romantic renderings of an exotic folk to more literary "naturalist" and pulp fiction portrayals of a largely working-class experience.[25]

At the same time, an already established black radical critique shaped both the global left and a growing trend in race-specific economic activism. In cities all over the country, fellow travelers fought to join labor unions and unemployed councils, instigated rent strikes, and attacked lynch law and urban "slave markets" where black women domestics waited to be picked up for day labor. Race and class powerfully converged in Chicago's 1929–30 "Don't Spend Your Money Where You Can't Work" campaign. The "Don't Spend" movement was an important urban mass protest and boycott strategy initiated with varying levels of success all over the country, whereas the "Young Turks" at Howard University, including social scientist E. Franklin Frazier, political scientist Ralph Bunche, writer Sterling Brown, and librarian Dorothy Porter, generally preferred an economic analysis over a race-based perspective. Still a varied race consciousness persisted, especially as white supremacy pervaded the New Deal state and various communist parties across the globe. New Negroes grew more convinced that race profoundly shaped economic realities throughout an imperial world. In fact, as the darker peoples of the world grew closer, the galvanizing call was as much antifascism as it was anticapitalism.[26]

When the NAACP failed to fully support the case of nine black teenagers falsely accused of rape in Scottsboro, Alabama, in 1931, the Comintern's International Labor Defense went into action. Protests and support groups erupted in cities all over the world to support the "Scottsboro Boys," making the fight against racism, imperialism, and a looming fascism all part of the same struggle. A few years later, black fair-housing activists in Chicago and Los Angeles began to use the specifically Jewish notion of "ghetto" to shed light on the racist, New Deal state–sponsored, and hence *fascist,* conditions of residential and economic segregation. But housing was just one plank when the 1936 National Negro Congress convened in Chicago, creating a Black Popular Front across class and status to fight, as they said, fascism in all its forms.[27]

An "Abyssinian International" of protest and agitation best crystalized the link between racism, imperialism, and a global fascism. Many from the darker races jumped to action after both the League of Nations and the Comintern remained silent when fascist Italy invaded Ethiopia in 1935. Though many, especially radicals, were critical of Emperor Haile Selassie's monarchal regime, New Negroes fought to defend one of the few countries that had pushed back against the European scramble after the Berlin Conference. In the name of Ethiopia, thousands of men sought to join the royal army, defense committees raised money, dockworkers blocked shipments, and many more took to the streets. Some who couldn't get to

Ethiopia joined up with the Comintern's military forces fighting against fascist leader Francisco Franco in Spain. Even as part of the Comintern, a race consciousness would persist. One soldier boldly wrote about Spain, "This ain't Ethiopia, but it'll do." Finally, the political left and even mainstream nationalists caught up just in time to cheer on this larger vision of antifascism when boxer Joe Louis defeated both the Italian Primo Carnera and the German Max Schmeling.[28]

Ultimately, the Great Depression did not bring the New Negro movement to an end. A New Negro brand of race consciousness became less relevant by the 1940s, when the darker races had effectively pushed to situate domestic racism and colonial policies within a larger understanding of global fascism. In their grand tome *Black Metropolis,* St. Clair Drake and Horace Cayton discuss in detail what they call the "New Negro mentality" of the 1930s:

> The Negro became more international-minded than the rest of the population. His sympathy with other colored peoples had been aroused long before the general population had begun to question America's policy of isolationism, especially during the Italio-Ethiopian war.

The New Negro mentality pushed Western states to turn from white supremacy, at least officially, for fear of looking like Hitler and alienating "colored peoples" throughout the colonial world who were on the verge of independence. The racism that had been so central to the normal functioning of Euro-American nations was being creatively sidestepped with a claim that racial justice had always been at the foundation of democratic (vs. fascist) principles. Democratic nations were falsely celebrated as spaces of color-blind inclusion, and therefore the racial justice culture and politics of New Negroes were eventually denounced as not only divisive but also archaic. Swedish economist Gunnar Myrdal's *An American Dilemma: The Negro Problem and Modern Democracy* focused on U.S. race relations and came to serve as the bible for the American version of this new political liberalism at mid-century. Myrdal went so far as to argue that race consciousness, as much or more than racism, was the problem. America presented itself as a color-blind nation, while racial identity was caricatured as a wrong turn along the inevitable road of uniting all under the big tent of democratic law and order. In an ironic sense, the race consciousness of New Negroes had been too successful.[29]

"THE NEW NEGRO—WHAT IS HE?"

In the August 1920 edition of *The Messenger* magazine, A. Philip Randolph and Chandler Owen posed the question, "The New Negro—What Is He?" And we can respond that New Negroes were more than "a metaphor, a trope." To be sure, the literary and visual arts explosion known as the Harlem Renaissance was central but must be situated within a much broader field of political resistance and cultural revolution that extended far beyond Harlem. The same year as *The Messenger* essay, America's "race" paper, the *Chicago Defender*,[30] immediately dismissed the adjective *new* as a misnomer but recognized that "the same old tainted individual was roused into self-consciousness" and "awakened . . . with new desires, new hopes for the future." *Defender* editor Robert Abbott eschewed the term *Negro* altogether, and for him black people were no longer a race but understood as "*the* race." Still the term *New Negro* did take hold, while also exposing the exceptionally American nature of the reference point. New Negroes were identified by the explicit, and sometimes competing, principles of racial uplift, race consciousness, self-determination, and even self-defense as part of a larger international that described themselves as the "darker races." Fellow travelers in Africa, Asia, the Caribbean, the Middle East, and even Ireland shared with the American Negro a desire to break from, or at least initiate a rupture within, the global order of white supremacy. What became local expressions of race consciousness were the product of multidirectional conversations and collective actions that crisscrossed the globe.

But of course, not every individual within the diaspora of the darker races always embodied the ideals of the New Negro during the first half of the twentieth century. As an ideal of race consciousness and self-determination, the New Negro represents a moment in time more so than a discrete collection of individuals who thought and acted the same way. In this moment, there were critical points when individual desires lined up but also could never match up with the collective aims of the New Negro moment. Ida B. Wells held on dearly to Victorian ideals of respectability and decorum while supporting the brash displays of black beauty culture and race films. Booker T. Washington both publicly advocated the Atlanta Compromise and privately funded self-defense initiatives in the Jim Crow South. Du Bois was heavily critical of Marcus Garvey's brand of black economic nationalism, but by the 1930s, he pushed for the creation of consumer networks to drive a semiautonomous black economic system. Even writer George Schuyler vocally celebrated Jack Johnson's 1910 boxing victory as a showcase of the race, while provocatively lampooning the very idea of racial identity through his satirical 1931 novel *Black No More*. And in the end, the interests, ambitions, and well-being of the anonymous folk may have been the canvas but could never be fully captured when crafting the collective tapestry that was called the New Negro experience.

At best, we are expanding the frame of the New Negro experience temporally, geographically, and conceptually in specific ways. Here the New Negro moment spanned the period between the turn of the twentieth century and the start of World War II. Those we identify through the New Negro analytic asserted a new race consciousness that was sometimes explicit but was also felt through individualized rebukes or reimaginings of long-held traditions and even new expectations. This new race consciousness was profoundly shaped by class position, gender identity, geographical location, and sexual orientation. Ultimately, a wide range of political and cultural mediums brought the New Negro to life, from the pages of literary magazines and stepladder protests to storefront churches and military battlefronts, touching down and taking off from points all over the world.

New Negroes emerged at the turn of the twentieth century to combat the physical constraints of Jim Crow and colonial relations that were made common sense through both the "coon songs" of popular culture and the Anglo-Saxon civilization theories driving the new social sciences. On the ground, intellectuals, entrepreneurs, artists, and activists understood that the cultural and political constraints of a variably termed "Old Negro" had been propped up by the power of white "masters." Any possibility of constructing a new racial self required a break—some level of independence from what had been the controlling hand of white patriarchy, patronage, and philanthropy. Self-determination was the key word here and would mean many things, from struggles to control the image of the race in literary salons and even beauty salons to demands for civil rights or a desire for territorial independence. Members of the American Negro Academy, the Universal Negro Improvement Association, national Negro League baseball, and the Negritude movement all fit under the larger New Negro umbrella of those who sought control over the cultural, political, and economic future of the darker races. The New Negro became obsolete by the 1940s, when race-conscious political and cultural expressions that traipsed the globe were superseded by the democratic myth of color-blind inclusion within nations, amid the Second World War.

However, even in commemoration, we must be careful to remember that desires for self-control, self-definition, and self-determination were continually struggled over, as various interest groups asserted and debated dynamic visions of who or what a New Negro could possibly be. Black Spanish–American War soldiers saw Cuba and the Philippines as spaces of both black colonial occupation and anticolonial solidarity. Few African delegates attended the 1900 Pan-African Conference because Western Negroes appointed themselves the advanced guard of the race. Most famously, Locke's *New Negro* anthology and Charles Johnson's *Opportunity* magazine largely ignored New Negro social movement protests and popular cultures, preferring an image of sophisticated cosmopolitanism. Many New Negroes asserted an exclusively urban vision of racial modernity, posing a sharp and overblown contrast between modern Western cities and a premodern U.S. South or primitive colonial outposts. Richard Wright's "Blueprint for Negro Writing" was openly critical of the Harlem Renaissance and its cultural elitism, while ignoring the Harlem Renaissance–era radical prose and popular culture that foreshadowed his insights.

Finally, the New Negro movement, and the mostly male intellectuals who defined it, worked within explicit gender exclusions. The previously mentioned *Messenger* article reveals that the New Negro was largely assumed to be a "he" from the start. On one hand, a romance with gun-toting militants battling race riots or the upright race man intellectual shaping public opinion relegated women to the mantle of matronly temperance or domestic respectability. On the other hand, the masculine focus of the New Negro ignored black women's resistance against the markers of both mammy to the white world and helpmate for the race. Moreover, the masculine New Negro can't even begin to help us work through the meaning of the black women who physically fought back during the Jack Johnson race riots or the fabulous cross-dressing displays of songstress Bessie Smith. Still, such fissures and contestations don't mark the failures of solidarity but provide a window into the daily negotiations of cultural and social movements in continual formation. We can and must look back with the luxury of hindsight and remain critical. But at the same time, Lothrop Stoddard should have been afraid. It was with good reason that President Harding looked on with fear. The "bogy-men" (and women) were coming. New Negroes were on the rise and traipsing the globe, initiating moments of solidarity, collective action, and personal desire—a legacy that has forever changed the world.

With this collection, we invite you to explore the larger New Negro landscape. *Escape from New York* comprises sixteen essays and three concluding commentaries. The six headings of "The Diasporic Outlook," "New (Negro) Frontiers," "The Garvey Movement," "Engendering the Experience," "Consumer Culture," and "Home to Harlem" give shape to the anthology. These collected essays survey varied thematic, geographic, and temporal aspects of the New Negro experience. The contributors to this volume explore a wide array of New Negro expressions, including the intimate space of black middle-class marriages; the transnational routes of black activists, artists, and war veterans; the fight against police brutality in the city; and the pleasures and politics of various forms of both popular and elite cultural production, from music making and literature to boxing and coastal resort ownership.

The essays in this anthology are held together by a collective engagement with rethinking the Harlem Renaissance within its New Negro movement context. By covering so many aspects of the New Negro movement, this collection actually lends itself to greater use by the widest audience possible. Furthermore, the collection works on multiple levels. The actual essays present the lay reader with a set of well-known but also a wider range of narratives now situated within a global New Negro context. At the same time, the breadth of essays will help teachers who want to ensure that their students have access to a broad set of questions or content materials from the period without needing to assign multiple texts. The introduction provides a thematic and scholarly road map for undergraduates being introduced to the field. Finally, the commentaries draw out still more aspects and questions about the field that serve the interests of graduate students and established scholars.

In *Escape from New York,* we ask you to reconsider but remain excited about the Harlem Renaissance from a new vantage point. This is a meditation on the growing efforts of a new generation of scholars to challenge and expand our understanding of the New Negro experience. Here aesthetic concerns and popular cultural formations are inseparable from political interests and personal desires within Harlem, across the country, and throughout the world.

NOTES

1   "Harding Says Negro Must Have Equality in Political Life," *New York Times,* October 27, 1921.

2   "Harding Says Negro"; Stoddard, *Rising Tide of Color* and *Re-forging America,* vii, 305, 276, 277, 306, 283. Also see Guterl, *Color of Race in America,* 51–56, 131–34.

3   Du Bois, "Color Line Belts the World," 330, and "The Rising Tide of Color," *Chicago Defender,* July 2, 1927.

4   Brown, "New Negro in Literature," 185. In the same passage, Brown points out that "most of the writers were not Harlemites; much of the best writing was not about Harlem."

5   The limited understanding of the Harlem or New Negro Renaissance as a project of literary and visual art begins with Locke's *New Negro.* Also see Hutchinson, *Harlem in Black and White*; Baker, *Modernism and the Harlem Renaissance*; Lewis, *When Harlem Was in Vogue*; Huggins, *Harlem Renaissance.* The larger New Negro scholarship includes Lamothe, *Inventing the New Negro*; Sherrard, *Portraits of the New Negro Woman*; Gates and Jarrett, *New Negro*; Goesser, *Picturing the New Negro*; Carroll, *Word, Image, and the New Negro*; Nadell, *Enter the New Negroes*; Levine, "Concept of the New Negro"; Gates, "Trope of a New Negro." Projects that focus on Harlem but engage a wider range of cultural production include Ogbar, *Harlem Renaissance Revisited*; Vogel, *Scene of Harlem Cabaret*; Anderson, *Deep River*; Fabre and Feith, *Temples for Tomorrow*; Marks and Edkins, *Stylemakers and Rulebreakers of the Harlem Renaissance*; Davis, *Blues Legacies and Black Feminisms*; Krasner, *Resistance, Parody, and Double Consciousness*; Powell, *Rhapsodies in Black*; Spencer, *New Negroes and Their Music*; Floyd, *Black Music in the Harlem Renaissance.* Works that push to interrogate new modes (and sites) of New Negro experience include Chapman, *Prove It on Me*; Wintz and Glasrud, *Harlem Renaissance in the American West*; Curwood, *Stormy Weather*; Baldwin, *Chicago's New Negroes*; Foley, *Spectres of 1919.* Forthcoming books include Emily Lutenski, *Beyond Harlem: New Negro Cartographies of the American West.*

6   For work that attempts to catch up with or attend to the historical experience

of a New Negro internationalism, see Runstedtler, *Jack Johnson, Rebel Sojourner*; Makalani, *In the Cause of Freedom*; Guridy, *Forging Diaspora*; Jones, *In Search of Brightest Africa*; Luis-Brown, *Waves of Decolonization*; Wilks, *Race, Gender, and Comparative Black Modernisms*; Stephens, *Black Empire*; Edwards, *Practice of Diaspora*; Leininger-Miller, *New Negro Artists in Paris*; Kelley, "But a Local Phase of a World Problem"; Brock and Fuertes, *Between Race and Empire*.

7   Gates and Jarrett, *New Negro*.

8   Mitchell, *Righteous Propagation*. Also see Baldwin, *Chicago's New Negroes* and "New Negro." From here on, the general history of the New Negro has been pulled from the two works by Baldwin, unless otherwise noted.

9   Brown, "African American Soldiers and Filipinos"; Sotiropoulos, *Staging Race*, and Krasner, *Resistance, Parody, and Double Consciousness*.

10 Du Bois, *Darkwater*, 20.

11 Mukherji, "Anticolonial Imagination"; Baldwin, *Beyond the Colorline and the Iron Curtain*; Edwards, "Shadow of Shadows"; Makalani, *In the Cause of Freedom*.

12 Hart, "New Negro."

13 Wilson, as quoted in Foglesong, *America's Secret War*, 42; Kornweibel, "*Seeing Red.*" See Du Bois, "Returning Soldiers." The reference to the Congo was meant to compare the racial violence found in this African country and the U.S. South. See Woodruff, *American Congo*.

14 "Following the Advice of the 'Old Crowd' Negro," *The Messenger*, June 1919; "The 'New Crowd' Negro Making America Safe for Himself," *The Messenger*, July 1919, and "Our Far-Flung Challenge," *Crusader* 1 (September 1919): 8.

15 Flamming, *Bound for Freedom*. Also see Claudrena Harold's amazing manuscript in progress *No Ordinary Sacrifice: New Negro Politics in the Jim Crow South, 1914–1929*.

16 J. A. Rogers, "Jazz at Home," in Locke, *New Negro*, 217.

17 Locke, *New Negro*, 217.

18 Blake, *Le Tumulte Noir*, and Kramer, *Harlem Renaissance Re-examined*.

19 Fabre and Feith, *Temples for Tomorrow*.

20 Locke, *New Negro*, 3 and 11.

21 Ibid., 10; Fabre and Feith, *Temples for Tomorrow*, xix.

22 Locke, *New Negro*, 14.

23 Ibid., 224.

24 Hirsch, *Portraits of America*; Mangione, *Dream and the Deal*; Kelley, *Race Rebels*.

25 Jackson, *Indignant Generation*; Mullen, *Popular Fronts*; Naison, *Communists in Harlem*.

26 Holloway, *Confronting the Veil*.

27 Pennybacker, *From Scottsboro to Munich*; Kelley, *Race Rebels*; Hirsch, "Containment on the Home Front"; "A Subversive Covenant," *Chicago Defender*, July 10, 1937, 16; "Building Ghettoes," *Chicago Defender*, October 2, 1937; Gellman, *Death Blow to Jim Crow*.

28 Makalani, *In the Cause of Freedom*; Kelley, *Race Rebels*; Plummer, *Rising Wind*; Harris, *African American Reactions*.

29   Drake and Cayton, *Black Metropolis*.

30   "The Old and the New," *Chicago Defender,* January 3, 1920.

BIBLIOGRAPHY

Anderson, Paul. *Deep River: Music and Memory in Harlem Renaissance Thought*. Durham, N.C.: Duke University Press, 2001.

Baker, Houston. *Modernism and the Harlem Renaissance*. Chicago: University of Chicago Press, 1987.

Baldwin, Davarian. *Chicago's New Negroes: Modernity, the Great Migration, and Black Urban Life*. Chapel Hill: University of North Carolina Press, 2007.

———. "The New Negro." In *Encyclopedia of the Great Black Migration of the Twentieth Century,* edited by Steven Reich, 610–14. New York: Greenwood Press, 2006.

Baldwin, Kate. *Beyond the Colorline and the Iron Curtain: Reading Encounters between Black and Red, 1922–1963*. Durham, N.C.: Duke University Press, 2002.

Blake, Jody. *Le Tumulte Noir: Modernist Art and Popular Entertainment in Jazz-Age Paris, 1900–1930*. University Park: Pennsylvania State University Press, 1999.

Brock, Lisa, and Digna Castañeda Fuertes, eds. *Between Race and Empire: African-Americans and Cubans before the Cuban Revolution*. Philadelphia: Temple University Press, 1998.

Brown, Scott. "African American Soldiers and Filipinos: Racial Imperialism, Jim Crow, and Social Relations." *Journal of Negro History* 82, no. 1 (1997): 45–53.

Brown, Sterling. "The New Negro in Literature, 1925–1955." In *A Son's Return: Selected Essays of Sterling A. Brown,* edited by Mark Sanders, 184–205. Boston: Northeastern University Press, 1996.

Carroll, Anne. *Word, Image, and the New Negro: Representation and Identity in the Harlem Renaissance*. Bloomington: Indiana University Press, 2007.

Chapman, Erin. *Prove It on Me: New Negroes, Sex, and Popular Culture in the 1920s*. New York: Oxford University Press, 2012.

Curwood, Anastasia. *Stormy Weather: Middle Class African Americans Marriages between the Two World Wars*. Chapel Hill: University of North Carolina Press, 2010.

Davis, Angela. *Blues Legacies and Black Feminisms*. New York: Pantheon Books, 1998.

Drake, St. Clair, and Horace Cayton. *Black Metropolis: A Study of Negro Life in a Northern City*. Vols. 1 and 2. New York: Harper and Row, 1945.

Du Bois, W. E. B. "The Color Line Belts the World." In *W. E. B. Du Bois: A Reader,* edited by David Levering, 42–43. New York: Henry Holt, 1995.

———. *Darkwater: Voices from within the Veil*. 1920. Reprint, Mineola, N.Y.: Dover, 1999.

———. "Returning Soldiers." *The Crisis,* May 1919, 13.

Edwards, Brent. *The Practice of Diaspora: Literature, Translation, and the Rice of Black Internationalism*. Cambridge, Mass.: Harvard University Press, 2003.

———. "The Shadow of Shadows." *positions* 11, no. 1 (2003): 11–49.

Fabre, Genevieve, and Michel Feith. *Temples for Tomorrow: Looking Back at the Harlem Renaissance*. Bloomington: Indiana University Press, 2001.

Flamming, Douglas. *Bound for Freedom: Black Los Angeles in Jim Crow America.* Berkeley: University of California Press, 2005.

Floyd, Samuel. *Black Music in the Harlem Renaissance.* New York: Greenwood Press, 1990.

Foglesong, David. *America's Secret War against Bolshevism.* Chapel Hill: University of North Carolina Press, 1995.

Foley, Barbara. *Spectres of 1919: Class and Nation in the Making of the New Negro.* Urbana: University of Illinois Press, 2003.

Gates, Henry Louis, and Gene Jarrett, eds. *The New Negro: Readings on Race, Representation, and African American Culture, 1892–1938.* Princeton, N.J.: Princeton University Press, 2007.

———. "The Trope of a New Negro and the Reconstruction of the Image of the Black." *Representations,* Fall 1988, 129–55.

Gellman, Erik. *Death Blow to Jim Crow: The National Negro Congress and the Rise of Militant Civil Rights.* Chapel Hill: University of North Carolina Press, 2012.

Goesser, Caroline. *Picturing the New Negro: Harlem Renaissance Print Culture.* Lawrence: University Press of Kansas, 2007.

Guridy, Frank. *Forging Diaspora: Afro-Cubans and African Americans in a World of Empire and Jim Crow.* Chapel Hill: University of North Carolina Press, 2010.

Guterl, Matthew. *The Color of Race in America, 1900–1940.* Cambridge, Mass.: Harvard University Press, 2001.

Harris, Joseph. *African American Reactions to the War in Ethiopia, 1936–1941.* Baton Rouge: Louisiana State University Press, 1994.

Hart, Rollin Lynde. "The New Negro, When He's Hit, He Hits Back!" *Independent* 15 (January 1921): 59–60, 76.

Hirsch, Arnold. "Containment on the Home Front: Race and Federal Housing Policy from the New Deal to the Cold War." *Journal of Urban History* 26, no. 2 (2000): 159–89.

Hirsch, Jerrold. *Portraits of America: A Cultural History of the Federal Writers' Project.* Chapel Hill: University of North Carolina Press, 2003.

Holloway, Jonathan Scott. *Confronting the Veil: Abram Harris Jr., E. Franklin Frazier, and Ralph Bunche, 1919–1941.* Chapel Hill: University of North Carolina Press, 2001.

Huggins, Nathan. *The Harlem Renaissance.* New York: Oxford University Press, 1972.

Hutchinson, George. *Harlem in Black and White.* Cambridge, Mass.: Harvard University Press, 1996.

Jackson, Lawrence. *The Indignant Generation: A Narrative History of African American Writers and Critics, 1931–1960.* Princeton, N.J.: Princeton University Press, 2010.

Jones, Jeanette. *In Search of Brightest Africa: Reimagining the Dark Continent in American Culture, 1884–1936.* Athens: University of Georgia Press, 2010.

Kelley, Robin D. G. "'But a Local Phase of a World Problem': Black History's Global Vision, 1883–1950." *Journal of American History* 86, no. 3 (1999): 1045–77.

———. *Race Rebels: Culture, Politics, and the Black Working Class.* New York: Free Press, 1994.

Kornweibel, Theodore, Jr. *"Seeing Red": Federal Campaign against Black Militancy: 1919–1925.* Bloomington: Indiana University Press, 1998.

Kramer, Victor, ed. *The Harlem Renaissance Re-examined*. New York: AMS Press, 1987.

Krasner, David. *Resistance, Parody, and Double Consciousness in African American Theater, 1895–1910*. New York: St. Martins Press, 1997.

Lamothe, Daphne. *Inventing the New Negro: Narrative, Culture, and Ethnography*. Philadelphia: University of Pennsylvania Press, 2008.

Leininger-Miller, Theresa. *New Negro Artists in Paris: African American Painters and Sculptors in the City of Light, 1922–1934*. New Brunswick, N.J.: Rutgers University Press, 2001.

Levine, Lawrence. "The Concept of the New Negro and the Realities of Black Culture." In *The Unpredictable Past: Explorations in American Cultural History*, 86–106. New York: Oxford University Press, 1993.

Lewis, David Levering. *When Harlem Was in Vogue*. New York: Knopf, 1981.

Locke, Alain. *The New Negro: Voices of the Harlem Renaissance*. New York: Albert and Charles Boni, 1925.

Luis-Brown, David. *Waves of Decolonization: Discourses of Race and Hemispheric Citizenship in Cuba, Mexico, and the United States*. Durham, N.C.: Duke University Press, 2008.

Makalani, Minkah. *In the Cause of Freedom: Radical Black Internationalism from Harlem to London*. Chapel Hill: University of North Carolina Press, 2011.

Mangione, Jerre. *The Dream and the Deal: The Federal Writers' Project, 1935–1943*. Boston: Little, Brown, 1972.

Marks, Carole, and Diana Edkins, eds. *Stylemakers and Rulebreakers of the Harlem Renaissance*. New York: Crown, 1999.

Mitchell, Michelle. *Righteous Propagation: African Americans and the Politics of Racial Destiny after Reconstruction*. Chapel Hill: University of North Carolina Press, 2004.

Mukherji, S. Ani. "The Anticolonial Imagination: Exilic Productions of American Anticolonialism in Interwar Moscow, 1919–1939." PhD diss., Brown University, 2009.

Mullen, Bill. *Popular Fronts: Chicago and African American Cultural Politics, 1935–1946*. Urbana: University of Illinois Press, 1999.

Nadell, Martha. *Enter the New Negroes: Images of Race in American Culture*. Cambridge, Mass.: Harvard University Press, 2004.

Naison, Mark. *Communists in Harlem during the Depression*. Urbana: University of Illinois Press, 1983.

Ogbar, Jeffrey, ed. *The Harlem Renaissance Revisited: Politics, Arts, and Letters*. Baltimore: Johns Hopkins University Press, 2010.

Pennybacker, Susan. *From Scottsboro to Munich: Race and Political Culture in 1930s Britain*. Princeton, N.J.: Princeton University Press, 2009.

Plummer, Brenda Gayle. *Rising Wind: Black Americans and U.S. Foreign Affairs, 1935–1960*. Chapel Hill: University of North Carolina Press, 1996.

Powell, Richard. *Rhapsodies in Black: Art of the Harlem Renaissance*. Berkeley: University of California Press, 1997.

Runstedtler, Theresa. *Jack Johnson, Rebel Sojourner: Boxing in the Shadow of the Global Color Line*. Berkeley: University of California Press, 2012.

Sherrard, Cherene Johnson. *Portraits of the New Negro Woman: Visual and Literary Culture in the Harlem Renaissance*. New Brunswick, N.J.: Rutgers University Press, 2007.

Sotiropoulos, Karen. *Staging Race: Black Performers in Turn of the Century America*. Cambridge, Mass.: Harvard University Press, 2006.

Spencer, Jon Michael. *The New Negroes and Their Music: The Success of the Harlem Renaissance*. Knoxville: University of Tennessee Press, 1997.

Stephens, Michelle. *Black Empire: The Masculine Global Imaginary of Caribbean Intellectuals in the United States, 1914–1962*. Durham, N.C.: Duke University Press, 2005.

Stoddard, Lothrop. *Re-forging America: The Story of Our Nationhood*. New York: Charles Scribner's Sons, 1927.

———. *The Rising Tide of Color against White World-Supremacy*. New York: Charles Scribner's Sons, 1920.

Vogel, Shane. *The Scene of Harlem Cabaret: Race, Sexuality, Performance*. Chicago: University of Chicago Press, 2009.

Wilks, Jennifer M. *Race, Gender, and Comparative Black Modernisms: Suzanne Lacascade, Marita Bonner, Suzanne Césaire, Dorothy West*. Baton Rouge: Louisiana State University Press, 2008.

Wintz, Cary, and Bruce Glasrud, eds. *The Harlem Renaissance in the American West: The New Negro's Western Experience*. London: Routledge, 2011.

Woodruff, Nan. *American Congo: The African American Freedom Struggle in the Delta*. Cambridge, Mass.: Harvard University Press, 2003.

I

THE DIASPORIC OUTLOOK

1

"Brightest Africa" in the New Negro Imagination

JEANNETTE EILEEN JONES

In 1894, Reverend W. E. C. Wright declared, "We are making a new Negro." This Negro would differ from the "American Negro of thirty years ago [who] was a product of African paganism and American slavery that called itself Christian." A prominent clergyman from Cleveland, Ohio, Wright gave credit to missionary schools for educating a new generation of African Americans that would challenge the images of the Negro forged during slavery and Reconstruction that justified the political disenfranchisement and social segregation of the "race." His "New Negroes" would contribute to the capitalist economy, participate in the "nation's life," and help propagate the Gospel around the world.[1] Six years later, Booker T. Washington, Norman Barton Wood, and Fannie Barrier Williams would echo Wright's sentiments in their book *A New Negro for a New Century*. The text catalogs the struggles of African Americans and their most important achievements made since emancipation and includes several portraits of distinguished men and women who exemplified the qualities of the New Negro for the twentieth century: educated, Christian, refined, business savvy, patriotic, and proud of their heritage. The volume highlights "the superb heroism" of soldiers who served in the Spanish–American War, male and female educators, clergymen, and club-women. Collectively, the essays in the volume discuss the roles that black men and women should play in uplifting and regenerating "the race" in the coming century. Arguably, the New Negroes featured are, for the most part, presented as apolitical. The women are noted for their dedication to education and "social betterment," the soldiers for their duty to the United States (perhaps the most political stance), the clergy for propagating the Gospel, and men like W. E. B. Du Bois for furthering the higher education of "Afro-Americans."[2]

Of particular significance to this essay is the image of Africa that both fin de siècle visions of the New Negro described previously engage. For Wright, Africa is a site of "paganism" and, as such, one source of the "Old Negro's" backwardness. Although not stating so outright, his essay alludes to a worldwide Christian evangelization that will include New Negro missionary work in Africa. *A New Negro for a New Century* confines its discussion of Africa to historical explications of the transatlantic slave trade, American slavery, colonization and emigration, missionary activities, and European imperialism. The various essays in the text assert that the New Negro's relationship to Africa is remote, except for his duty to spread the Gospel and prevent the importation of rum onto the continent. However, as this essay will demonstrate, for a cadre of self-fashioned New Negroes in the late nineteenth and early twentieth centuries, their relationship to Africa was anything but "remote." This New Negro consciousness and identity that directly engaged Africa was both international and transnational in character. It involved people of African descent from across the diaspora, and within the United States, those New Negroes who occupied spaces outside Harlem, which had become the iconic site of the 1920s and 1930s New Negro movement and black activism.

Henry Louis Gates Jr. and Gene Andrew Jarrett point out that the trope of the New Negro emerged in the nineteenth century and was inextricably linked to debates about the destiny of African Americans postemancipation. Indeed, much of the discussion of the New Negro in late-nineteenth-century literature reads the New Negro against the Old Negro supposedly benighted as a result of centuries of enslavement. Declaring that they were free New Negroes was to some extent a rhetorical move to reject rationales for Jim Crow legislation and white supremacy based on the logic of the Old Negro mythology. However, this should not distract us from the real political and social expressions of New Negro-ness that emerged during that same time period, particularly among blacks committed to Negro liberation *and* invested in Africa as a site of both redemption and black colonization. If we use their experiences as lenses through which to reinterpret the New Negro, we are forced not only to expand New Negro studies back into the late nineteenth century but to continue extending our discussions of the New Negro beyond that of a "movement" and consciousness associated with the Harlem Renaissance.

One can locate the transnational New Negro preoccupation with Africa in the aftermath of the Berlin Conference (Kongokonferenz) in 1884. When Europeans met in Germany to carve up Africa into spheres of influence, colonies, and protectorates, they ushered in a new era of Western imperialism. Of course, Africans themselves responded in myriad ways ranging from attempts to negotiate with the colonizers to outright warfare. Persons of African descent outside the continent also articulated an array of responses that reflected their own national and regional concerns as well as the transnational debates regarding the color line, free labor, capitalism, and empire.[3] Black journalists, intellectuals, clergymen, leaders, and nonelites decried the speed with which the continent fell under European dominance. By the turn of the century, African Americans, West Indians, Africans, and Afro-Europeans mobilized politically and joined domestic and transnational social movements that imagined Africa free from colonial rule. Some went as far as to proclaim it the "American Negro's burden" or the "black man's burden" to uplift his racial brethren in Africa and, in so doing, help them take the continent back from the colonizers. For some, this meant embarking on their own colonial "civilizing mission" by promoting industrial education, missionary activity, and capitalist-driven commerce in Africa. Others maintained that the black diaspora must assume the position of an advance guard or support troops in the war against imperialism so that the leading forces of Africans could emancipate themselves. This latter viewpoint rejected any attempts by nonindigenous Africans to spearhead the redemption of Africa.

In responding to the colonization of Africa, New Negroes contributed to a growing body of knowledge about Africa in several ways that informed what I term the "discourses of Brightest Africa." Intellectuals and historians sought to dispel the myth of "Darkest Africa" by claiming that Africa was never dark, pointing to the precolonial history of Africa that boasted of empires, kingdoms, and powerful city-states. Clergymen prophesied that the Dark Continent would one day disappear under Christianization and a racial uplift program imported from blacks in the West. Journalists and ordinary citizens wrote articles and editorials that debated whether the continent could be redeemed without the aid of "enlightened" Negroes. New Negro political activists convened pan-African conferences to discuss the intertwining fates of Africans and "their brethren." Ultimately, the "Brightest Africa" discourses expressed at these conferences would help shape an anticolonial New Negro consciousness, which included a range of political orientations but shared a belief in the ties of consanguinity between all persons of African descent.

Tracing the polyvalent discourses of Brightest Africa, this essay explores not only the work of familiar pan-Africanist figures like W. E. B. Du Bois, Marcus Garvey, and members of the African Blood Brotherhood but also Booker T. Washington and other New Negroes who engaged Africa in their everyday politics. The persons of African descent in this study are New Negroes not simply because they wielded the trope of the New Negro but because they began making themselves over as "modern" men and women invested in the ever-changing world for Negroes. They understood that their very lives and experiences were touched by the forces of modernity—industrialization, migration, urbanization, and expanding capitalism—and responded accordingly. As modernization unfolded, New Negroes began asserting a new political and social consciousness that rejected Jim Crow–style legislation and efforts to curtail their economic independence and freedom of movement. For many New Negroes, becoming modern thus meant embracing a new identity that placed them both within and outside the confines of Western nationalist experiences. These New Negroes often claimed their special relationship with Africa as descendants of enslaved Africans in the Americas, even as they affirmed their rights as Americans, Frenchmen, Jamaicans, Trinidadians, and so on. In this sense, modern New Negroes' emerging cosmopolitan sensibilities found congruence with pan-Africanism. Responding to new European attacks on their "Motherland," these men and women embraced a new solidarity with Africans premised not only on blood ties but also on political commitments to African independence. In the process of imagining an independent, modern Brightest Africa, New Negroes dismantled images of Africa as a Dark Continent at multiple sites of critical engagement.

As V. Y. Mudimbe has argued, the pan-Africanist "invention of Africa" in the late nineteenth century involved an intricate melding of Christian values, Western political theory, racial myths of blackness and personality, and anthropological readings of "primitive" cultures projected onto Africa as a promised land for African Americans and West Indians in search of political enfranchisement. Indeed, African Americans and West Indians, predominantly from Trinidad, Jamaica, and the Francophone Caribbean, exhibited increasing interest in Africa during the latter half of the nineteenth century, often looking to it as a panacea for the economic and political marginalization that they faced in the western hemisphere. Edward W. Blyden, considered by many scholars to be the father of pan-Africanism, was the preeminent pan-African intellectual of the period, who fashioned diaspora blacks as the principal actors in culturally and politically modernizing Africa. Blyden, along with black leaders such as Alexander Crummell, Henry Highland Garnet, Bishop James Holly, Martin Delany, and Bishop Henry McNeal Turner, imagined a Brightest Africa uplifted through black-styled Christianity and Western civilization. As David Levering Lewis states, these men were "forerunners of the Pan-Africanism and black nationalism that would expand early in the next century."[4]

New Negro identities and pan-Africanism intersected in black anticolonialist and emigrationist (so-called Back-to-Africa) movements as part of a larger phenomenon of black internationalism discussed by Brent Hayes Edwards, Kate A. Baldwin, Robin D. G. Kelley, and other scholars. While Edwards focuses on black internationalist initiatives in the early twentieth century (particularly during the interwar years) and the significance of Paris to pan-African, literary, and anticolonial enterprises, he acknowledges that the linking of blacks in the diaspora began before the 1900 Pan-African Conference. However, 1900 signaled a new era, particularly in African American politics and engagement with Africa as a physical, geographical, and intellectual construct. Brenda Gayle Plummer notes that the Pan-African Conference constituted an international response to the new imperialism of the late nineteenth century, the disenfranchisement of African Americans, the political unrest in the Caribbean colonies, and the declining status of persons of African descent in Latin America. Although pan-Africanism involved a good deal of myth making and the reimagining of Africa as a new Canaan, real political commitments to anticolonialism and black self-determination stimulated rural, working-class, and elite blacks alike. Stirred by W. E. B. Du Bois's proclamation that "the problem of the twentieth century is the problem of the colour line," which he first articulated at the 1900 Pan-African Conference and then in *The Souls of Black Folk* in 1903, elite pan-Africanists embarked on what Lewis describes as "an inherently revolutionary Pan-African idea" that was "bound to take on a life of its own."[5]

IN DEFENSE OF THEIR BRETHREN ACROSS THE DEEP

In 1887, an editorial titled "The Negro's 'Peculiar Work'" appeared in the *New York Freeman* (later the *New York Age*)—the premier and authoritative black newspaper of Harlem, New York. The article summarized a speech delivered by Reverend J. C. (Joseph Charles) Price, a faculty member of the Zion Wesley Institute of the African Methodist Episcopal (AME) Zion Church in North Carolina, to commemorate the Emancipation Proclamation. Price's address spoke not of the situation of Negroes in America but of the status of the newly divided Africa. Price stated, "The whites found gold, diamonds, and other riches in Africa. Why should not the Negro? Africa is their country. They should claim it: they should go to Africa, civilize those Negroes, raise them morally, and by education show them how to obtain the wealth which is in their own country, and take that grand continent as their own." Price offered a counterpoint to the "white man's burden"—the "American Negro's burden" to uplift his racial brethren and oust the European usurpers. He also claimed that Africa belonged to the Western Negro, who could best redeem the continent for future use, that is, make it "bright" for Africans and their descendants. This pan-Africanist vision circulated commonly among African American missionaries and clergymen, who inextricably linked proselytizing in Africa to the continent's political and economic independence.[6]

Price's speech received favorable reviews from the *Freeman*'s white-owned contemporary, the *New York Sun*. A politically conservative paper, the *Sun* (1887) held that the "civilization of the native Africans by American Africans" might be the best method for developing the continent. However, the newspaper urged African Americans to take up their burden immediately as "a tremendous stream of Europeans" poured into the "fertile and valuable African lands, threatening eventually to overrun the whole continent for their own benefit." The *Sun* speculated that whether African Americans or Europeans "civilized" Africa, perhaps one day, "there may be there a Negro State that will rank with the great nations of the world." The *New York Freeman*'s editorialist conceded that "colored people all over the world" held a vested interest in the development of Africa as it might one day provide a site for their own liberation, believing that it might take centuries for African Americans to achieve heightened status in the United States. Nevertheless, African Americans were in the United States and had to "make the very best of the situation." The paper assured its readers, however, that in the interim, "thoughtful" African Americans would pay close attention to occurrences in Africa, as these events would determine both the continent's and their own futures.[7]

Indeed, over the next decade, the *New York Freeman/Age* and other prominent black newspapers increased their coverage of African affairs, in the process helping to shape the image of Africa in the black community and among self-proclaimed New Negroes.[8] Letters to the editor of the *Age* revealed that Africa held great importance for blacks across the United States, not just in Harlem. In March 1888, William A. Peete, a resident of Tyler, Texas, addressed the "problem of Liberia"—the alleged inability of Americo-Liberians to transform the country into a leading state on the continent and to "civilize" the indigenous peoples. Peete complicated the prevailing civilizationist currents in Brightest Africa discourses during this period. Rejecting arguments that African American immigrants were the cause of the country's downfall, Peete dismissed observers who generally regarded Liberia as a failure and those who placed the blame on the inefficiency of black self-government and lack of "enterprise . . . in civilizing and developing a country." He held Christianity liable for Liberia's failure, arguing that Christians had a long history of standing aside while blacks fought against prejudice and political persecution. At best, Christians remained content with joining the battle after it had already begun, or they "led the assault" in "Quixotic skirmishes against the devil." Peete argued that the increase in the African Muslim population in west central Africa suggested that the providential mission of Christianity was not a foregone conclusion. Unless missionary efforts in Liberia worked toward the benefit of the Africans by investing capital instead of Bibles and hymnals, he saw no immediate resolution to the "Liberia problem."[9] In the same 1888 issue of the *Age,* B. Bowser of Hartford, Connecticut, commented on his fifteen-year (1860–75) residence in Liberia, in light of the "considerable interest manifested of late about the condition of that country, its people, and climate." Bowser dispelled assertions that Liberians (of American origin) prospered and Liberia College thrived. He argued that if it were not for the "aborigines," the immigrants would starve. As for the acclaimed university, it had no significant student body. Bowser painted a less flattering picture of black immigration to and "civilizing" efforts in Liberia, noting that the average immigrant Liberian demonstrated little initiative and patience in cultivating the land. As Michele Mitchell has noted, "by the mid-1890s, a number of women and men . . . were becoming 'dissatisfied' with emigration" to Liberia. "Swindles" and scandals undermined "Liberia fever." Perhaps more important, while readers of black newspapers that promoted and covered emigration, including the Indianapolis *Freeman,* may have been attracted to the "idea of an all-black nation" and criticized European imperialism in Africa, black professionals and elites showed little interest in permanently settling in Africa. They focused their efforts on Christianizing Africans.[10]

Liberia became contested ground for African Americans interested in promoting republicanism, Christianity, and commerce in Africa, that is, realizing a Brightest Africa. In 1888, Reverend Price had declined President Grover Cleveland's appointment of him as minister resident and consul general of the United States at Liberia. Price explained that he needed to dedicate his energies to the "work of Negro education in the South." However, he offered this caveat: "My interest . . . in Africa must not be measured by my refusal to this position; for while my work here has for its primary object the education of the Negroes, and the bringing about of a better state of things in the South generally, still it also has in view, as an ultimate object, the enlightenment of Africa and the final redemption of the Dark Continent, which will be greatly advanced by the Christian education and the industrial development of the Negroes in this country."[11] Price made explicit the connection between his efforts to uplift African Americans in the South—to create "new" Negroes, as it were—and the redemption of Africa. He believed that only Christian, educated American blacks could go to Africa and enlighten its masses. Brightest Africa would emerge as a result of intraracial Christian cooperation between Africans and their American descendants.[12]

The perceived urgency, according to some New Negroes, for African Americans to intervene in African affairs, especially those of Liberia, led to the assembling of various conferences on Africa. In 1893, the Chicago Conference on Africa convened with attendees including Henry McNeal Turner, Alexander Crummell, Yakub Pasha (from Egypt), and AME Zion church bishop Alexander Walters. Held at the same time as the World's Columbian Exposition, the conference covered a range of topics focusing on the situation of African Americans, the present and future of Liberia, and African Americans' duties to their African "kin." Two years later, the Congress on Africa assembled in Atlanta, Georgia, under the auspices of the Stewart Missionary Foundation for Africa. This conference differed from the 1893 gathering in that it brought together an interracial and international delegation to discuss the Christianization of Africa. While those blacks who attended the conference did not refer to themselves as pan-Africanists, it is clear from the published proceedings that they couched their interest in Africa in terms of consanguinity—shared blood ties between Africans on the continent and Negroes in the diaspora. Their discourse emphasized the duty of African Americans to their African brethren. Whites attending the conference believed that they had a spiritual duty to help African Americans in the providential mission to redeem Africa and Africans. While the delegates at the Chicago conference included religious leaders, evangelism was not their sole concern.[13]

Religious pan-Africanism reflected the convictions of African American missionaries from the African Baptist, black Baptist (National Baptist Convention), and AME churches who had already begun missions in Africa. However, for example, when they arrived in South Africa in the 1890s, they discovered an incipient independence–church movement called "Ethiopianism." In 1892, Reverend Mangena Makke Mokone left the Wesleyan Methodist church in the Transvaal and founded the Ethiopian Church of South Africa. This church became affiliated in 1898 with the AME Church as its fourteenth district so that the Ethiopian Church could operate legally under the freedom of religious expression extended to American missionaries. In the first decade of the twentieth century, this alliance came under increasing suspicion by the South African government, with whites arguing for the deportation and/or "disbarring" of African Americans from the country.[14]

The top-down approach to Christianizing Africa ignored the autonomy of African Christians like Mokone, who sought out Bishop Turner to align his church with the AME denomination. While religious arguments for pan-African interaction dominated much of the late-nineteenth-century discourse on Africa, New Negro organizations emerged that offered alternative visions of Brightest Africa premised first on ameliorating the conditions of colonized Africans and ultimately on dismantling imperialism. Key to this transformation was the prominence of Caribbean radicals in early-twentieth-century pan-African movements.

"A NEW ERA FOR THE COLORED RACE THROUGHOUT THE WORLD"

S. E. F. C. C. Hamedoe, writing for *Colored American* magazine, declared that "a new era for the colored race throughout the world" began on July 23, 1900, when people from all over the African diaspora convened the first Pan-African Conference in London "with the object of discussing and improving the condition of the colored race."[15] Organized by lawyer and Trinidadian transplant H. Sylvester Williams and AME Zion bishop Alexander Walters, the conference was attended by several African Americans, including W. E. B. Du Bois, Anna Julia Cooper, Mrs. Jones of Kansas, former slave Henry "Box" Brown, and author D. Tobias Walters. Walters was a former slave from Kentucky who pastored the Mount Zion Church in New York City and cofounded the National Afro-American Council with T. Thomas Fortune in 1898, serving as its first president. The conference participants discussed the global black population as being "deserved" and "worthy" of freedom. They called attention to the lack of equal rights granted African Americans, the political and social discrimination faced by blacks in the British Empire, and the harsh labor conditions for black workers in South Africa, among other topics, arguing that the "future of the race must be in the hands of the race itself." Instead of looking at whites to lead the way, the attendees argued that blacks should take additional initiative to secure freedom and equality for all people of African descent. Nevertheless, they petitioned Queen Victoria and the British Colonial Office to take up their resolutions, which included allowing Africans access to education and participation in the colonial government, while also calling for the end of racial discrimination and labor exploitation in the colonies.[16]

The conference closed with H. F. Downing stating that the "black race" sought freedom by "deserving it" and not by violent means. As Hamedoe noted, never before had that many people of African descent from around the world gathered together to discuss their political and social status as citizens of democratic republics or as imperial subjects. Convened on the basis of black brotherhood, the conference added to existent discourses among Africans in the diaspora about the political significance of Africa to their lives and the need for Africa to emerge as a bright continent in the twentieth century. The conference speakers convincingly pointed out the parallels between the lives of Africans under colonial rule and blacks in the Caribbean, Americas, and Great Britain. More important, they asserted that there existed a global threat to black autonomy that respected no national boundaries. Though they did not directly call for an immediate end to imperialism, they hoped to intervene on behalf of Africans by negotiating with colonial governments. As Edwards notes in "The Uses of Diaspora," the pan-Africanism that emerged after 1900 arose "as a discourse of internationalism aimed generally at the cultural and political *coordination* of the interests of peoples of African descent around the world."[17]

The newly formed Pan-African Association planned to convene a conference in the United States in 1902 and one in Haiti in 1904; however, the Pan-African Association disbanded after Williams returned to the Caribbean in 1901. Yet, as historian Minkah Makalani notes, "the spirit of the Pan-African Conference and the Pan-African Association would continue in various parts of the African Diaspora." He credits this conference with inspiring John Edward Bruce and Arturo Schomburg to form the Negro Society for Historical Research (NSHR) in 1911 in Harlem. Both had been members of Alexander Crummell's American Negro Academy (ANA), founded in 1897 in Washington, D.C. Through its occasional papers, the ANA hoped to "raise the standard of intellectual endeavor among American Negroes."[18] Whereas the ANA limited its membership to graduate students, professors, writers, and artists—mostly from the United States—Bruce and Schomburg opened their organization to Africans and blacks residing in the Americas. The

NSHR would publish and collect "data, pamphlets, [and] books" that attested to the "history and achievement of the Negro race," including continental Africans.[19] One goal was to demonstrate that Africa was at one time a bright continent.[20]

It was not until 1912 that another major pan-African conference convened—the International Conference on the Negro, held at Tuskegee Institute. Attended by representatives from missionary societies and several countries from the western hemisphere, Europe, and eight "states or provinces" from Africa, including Liberia and South Africa, the conference represented the first pan-Africanist gathering of the new century held on American soil. In 1911, Washington issued an official announcement for the conference, in which he stated that his goal was to foster dialogue among not only blacks but also government representatives of African colonies to discuss methods for educating and "upbuilding Negro peoples." According to the *Chicago Defender,* Washington called the conference to "bring about an exchange of ideas among those who are working for the uplift of the black race throughout the world." Like self-proclaimed pan-Africanists, Washington viewed the situation of African Americans and West Indians as related to "the problems of Africa." Though he did not call for deliberations on African independence, he invited the participation of missionaries, workers, and anyone who could bring empirical knowledge of the African diaspora to bear on the conference proceedings. Washington received enthusiastic responses from many Africans, including members of the Ethiopian Church in South Africa who planned to attend the conference. The South African delegate praised him as a "race man" with a vision for uplifting Africans.[21]

Since the 1895 conference, Washington had been working to "civilize" Africa. In 1899, he negotiated with the German Empire to embark on a cotton cultivation and vocational training project in Togoland. What resulted was a coercive labor regime that subverted Togolese autonomy and gender relations. Unapologetic of his role in propping up German imperialism in Togo, Washington went on to publish "Industrial Education in Africa" (1906), an essay in which he speculates as to whether the curricula taught at Tuskegee and Hampton could aid in the uplift of Africans, particularly those under colonial rule. The 1912 conference must be contextualized in Washington's continued engagement with European imperialism. During the proceedings, Washington demonstrated a marked consistency in his promotion of industrial education for the New Negro and Negroes in Africa.[22]

The conference issued several declarations emphasizing the need for intraracial cooperation and establishing a committee to work on the second conference, scheduled for 1915 (the year that Washington died). Noting the urgent need to address the "Negro race and its problems," the document claimed that the meeting's importance was "obvious" as Europeans had colonized tropical regions with considerable black populations. Even as the participants acknowledged the impact of imperialism on "native races," they did not critique it as the source of Negro degradation in Africa. The declarations neither mentioned African republicanism as a panacea for the problems of Africa nor imagined a united African continent under black leadership. However, black missionaries continued to refer to the "redemption of the Dark Continent," that is, their duty to make Africa bright.[23] The 1912 conference revealed that Washington's New Negroes for the new century had not strayed far from religious pan-Africanism, as the majority of the attendees were, in fact, missionaries.

Washington's ideology of racial uplift and the industrial education philosophy wedded to his own brand of pan-Africanism resonated with many blacks in and outside of the United States, including Marcus Garvey. Garvey revered Washington but rejected accommodating white imperialist sensibilities. He would fashion a separatist pan-Africanism purportedly based on black terms and militant in its denunciation of imperialism in Africa. Garveyism idealized Africa as the "Motherland of all Negroes," a "vast continent" whose treasures were stolen by unscrupulous Europeans. As Mary Rolinson argues, "Garvey undoubtedly shared a romanticized image of Africa with many African Americans, who like the UNIA leader, had never been there."[24] In reinventing Africa as "Ethiopia, Thou Land of Our Fathers" (the title of the organization's Negro anthem), the UNIA discursively extracted the continent from the annals of Darkest Africa.[25]

When Garvey formed the UNIA in Jamaica in 1914, he hoped to mobilize West Indians to fight for self-determination and freedom from British rule. He was a member of Jamaica's National Club, founded in 1906 by Sandy Cox and Robert Love. A nationalist organization promoting Jamaican independence and identity, the club disbanded shortly after Cox immigrated to the United States. For Garvey, the quest for his native Jamaica's independence was part of broader struggles for black autonomy around the globe. Garvey believed that a sense of race pride and a "Universal Confraternity among the race" had to serve as the foundation of any collective action to dismantle white rule over people of African descent. Unable to establish a large following in the West Indies, Garvey came to the United States to raise money for his organization and also to meet Booker T. Washington. However, Washington died before Garvey could make the trip. The East St. Louis Riot of 1917 inspired Garvey to come to Harlem to "re-form" the UNIA.[26]

Within two years, Garvey had amassed such a following in the states outside of New York that other pan-Africanists (including Du Bois) had to contend with his charismatic style and ability to get rank-and-file black folk excited about Africa. Du Bois once remarked, "Garvey is an extraordinary leader of men. Thousands of people believe in him. He is able to stir them with singular eloquence and the general run of his thought is of a high plane. He has become to thousands of people a sort of religion."[27] Indeed, Garvey struck many of his admirers and critics as messianic in his message of black deliverance. He evoked an image of black men waging battle to liberate Africa and envisioned a "new Negro race" asserting its manhood and womanhood around the globe. His nationalist rhetoric and plans to establish an African Republic captivated and emboldened his followers to dream of Brightest Africa.[28]

Garvey warned "man and nation" not to stand in the way of diaspora Africans as they strove to "make Africa a republic." Identifying the white man as the obstacle to African republicanism and democracy, Garvey emphasized that members of the UNIA were "not Bolshevik, I.W.W. Democratic, Republican, or Socialists" but unwaveringly "pro-Negro." He disavowed any connection to political parties and labor unions dominated by whites but did not discard the idea that republican government and democratic political processes could best uplift Africa. Garvey believed that blacks in the West would emerge as formal political leaders in Africa. Prophesying a judgment day when the world would have to account for its treatment of peoples of African descent, he imagined a "new Toussaint L'Ouverture" (most likely himself) carrying "the sword and banner of the new African Republic"[29] to the court of judgment. He believed bloodshed would prove necessary for the New Negro bent on claiming his Motherland, as the imperial powers would never willingly surrender control over their African colonies. He demanded the restoration of black political autonomy and bolstered this political discourse of militaristic nation building with images of Africa as a bright continent of riches. Rejecting images of Africa as poverty ridden, he proclaimed, "Today the richest people of the world are the Negro peoples of Africa. Their minerals, their diamonds, their gold and their silver and their iron have built up the great English, French, German and Belgian Empires."[30] He reminded his audience that the wealth of the European superpowers derived from natural resources that belonged rightfully to Africans (and their Negro brethren), who could reclaim these riches upon the ousting of Europeans' imperial power. Contribution to the UNIA's African Redemption and Colonization Fund would further this cause.[31]

When the UNIA issued its "Declaration of Rights of the Negro Peoples of the World," at its first international convention in 1920, it demanded "Africa for the Africans at home and abroad." Its members enumerated several complaints and demands with respect to Africa, foremost among them their objection to the European partition of the continent and colonial policies that treated Africans as slaves. In a bold statement of racial solidarity, the organization declared all persons of African descent to be free citizens who enjoyed the right to claim Africa as their nation and to "reclaim the treasures" and land seized by "open aggression or secret schemes." At the Second UNIA International Convention in 1921, Garvey echoed his call to arms, protesting the League of Nations's decision to divide the former German African colonies between France and England without asking "the civilized [New] Negroes of the world"[32] how to dispose of their homeland. When Du Bois organized the Pan-African Congress in 1919, he, too, believed that the Versailles Conference's deliberations on the status of Germany's African colonies offered a forum for European nations and the United States to reject the imperialism that, he argued, impelled the West into the Great War. In this sense, Du Bois proved equally as convinced as Garvey that the redemption of Africa required leadership from peoples of African descent living in the West. In other words, for Africa to emerge from its darkness, it needed help from its diaspora.[33]

Declaring that "the handwriting is on the wall," Garvey announced that UNIA members would return to their communities resolved that Africa would become free at whatever cost. He advised his followers to preach "the doctrine of universal emancipation for Negroes, the doctrine of a free and a redeemed Africa."[34] In contrast to missionary pan-Africanists, who spoke solely of redeeming Africa from its own "savagery" and "superstition," Garvey used the term *redeem* to mean the rescue of Africans from European "unrighteousness" *and* from their own "backwardness." In declaring himself provisional president of Africa, he argued that Africans lacked the culture, education, and civilization at that time to assume leadership over the continent. In this sense, Europeans were guilty of "inhuman, unchristian, and uncivilized" behavior in Africa, contributing to the darkness emanating from the continent.[35] Garvey's rewriting of the white man's burden in Africa as the white man's iniquity appealed to black audiences, who felt victimized by white injustice.

Garvey's faith in the African capacity for instant self-government under the counsel of enlightened blacks from the United States, the West Indies, and Europe and his nonnegotiable stance on European imperialism aligned his pan-Africanism with that of Du Bois. Like Garvey, Du Bois's initial image of Brightest Africa was not of the continent immediately free from the European colonial system. In his 1915 essay "The African Roots of War," Du Bois argued that the Dark Continent was "in a very real sense . . . a prime cause of this terrible overturning of civilization which we have lived to see."[36] The Great War was a contest between European imperialist nations, whose antagonism toward each other continued to build after the partition of Africa. Rewriting "this most marvelous of continents" back into "world-history," Du Bois identified three needs for imperial subjects that would have to be satisfied if the war were to end: land, training in "modern civilization," and home rule. Like Garvey, he predicted that Africans would one day rise up and demand their freedom from foreign authority and that the "War of the Color Line" (what Garvey called the "conflict between the races") would ensue, causing more death and destruction than the Great War had seen thus far. However, he believed that this could be forestalled, if not prevented entirely, if Europeans gave up their monopoly on African land, Africans sought to become "modern men," and colonial powers allowed Africans to participate in the political process. Du Bois envisioned an Africa where educated modern Africans, in a way similar to New Negroes, participated in democracy and held high positions in state government. Summoning the figure of Queen Nefertari as a black woman who became pharaoh and protected her people from outside invaders, Du Bois called for a "new peace and new democracy" that would defend the equality of all peoples and end the despotic reign of imperialism.[37]

Demonstrating his leftist politics, Du Bois called for the common ownership of land and "the socialization of income," the latter for which the state would provide social services, establish wages, and convert private wealth into public wealth to ensure the economic stability of the nation. The calling of the 1919 Pan-African Conference was timely, but the momentum for Du Bois's brand of pan-Africanism came from the 1921 conference, which met in Paris, London, and Brussels, with forty-one African participants among over one hundred white and black delegates from Europe and the Americas. However, Du Bois faced opposition from conservative French delegates opposed to the London resolution criticizing Belgium and French colonialism. Despite their objections, the *statutes* issued by the conference reflected Du Bois's commitment to cooperative action in fostering the economic and political development of Africa—to rid the continent of its "Darkest Africa" moniker.[38]

As early as 1918, St. Croix–born intellectual Hubert Harrison had urged "Negroes of sense" (arguably New Negroes) to go to Africa, "live among the natives and LEARN WHAT THEY HAVE TO TEACH US." Instead of listening to "ignorant missionaries" and looking for white "generosity," Harrison encouraged New Negroes to learn about Africa before attempting to "do them any good" at the Peace Conference. Harrison called for American Negroes "to establish friendly relations and correspondence" with Africans. In his essay "The White War and the Colored Races," he concluded that African colonies turning to themselves instead of to European metropoles for help would undermine the privileges afforded white workers and make them turn to the colonies for solidarity, thus undermining capitalism. Harrison represented a new vanguard of anti-imperial, internationalist pan-Africanists who rejected the notion that Westernized Negroes had any right to speak for "their brothers" in Africa.[39]

The African Blood Brotherhood (ABB), founded in 1918 by Cyril Briggs, while not exclusively a pan-Africanist organization, drew parallels between the oppression of blacks in America and Africans under colonial regimes. In 1922, the ABB issued its most comprehensive pan-Africanist program, in which it committed itself to defending Africans from imperialist aggression. Published in the *Communist Review*, the organ of the Communist Party of Great Britain, the ABB outlined a plan for the liberation of all people of African descent based on the premise that their struggle was primarily economic, the result of white capitalist exploitation of black labor around the world. The organization explained that it looked toward Soviet Russia for inspiration not solely because of its political system but also because it opposed "the imperialist robbers who have portioned our motherland and subjugated our kindred." Briggs and his followers maintained that the Soviets instilled fear in capitalists and imperialists alike, and thus communism offered the best solution for liberating blacks.[40]

The ABB called for a "Negro Federation" led by "the more able and developed Negroes" on the coasts of Africa and African organizations in the colonies to work with Africans in the interior "barely touched by predatory Capitalism." This federation would ally with Arabs, Egyptians, and revolutionary groups in Europe and America to organize African workers, create a secret pan-African army, smuggle modern arms onto the continent, and map the geography of the interior. Reemphasizing their contempt for "the white man's religion," the ABB suggested that comrades travel to Africa in the "guise of missionaries," as the colonial authorities appeared to favor their presence as a civilizing force. Like Garvey and Du Bois, the ABB viewed blacks in America as saviors of the race worldwide, stating, "The Negroes resident in America—whether native or foreign born— . . . are destined to assume the leadership of our people in a powerful world movement for Negro liberation," as they lived in a "great empire" with access to modern technology, warfare, and industry. However, the ABB did not believe that Western Negroes would redeem Africa and lead Africans. Rather, they constantly emphasized united global movements, with Africans leading their own struggles. Their insistence on African independence and rejection of an African capitalist economy were major planks in their criticism of Garvey and his vision of an African empire. Finally, the ABB called for an end to rhetoric, public performances of Africanisms, and "other tomfoolery" and urged the adoption of "proper tactics" to defeat capitalists and imperialists oppressing African peoples. The program called for an alliance with the Third International, criticizing the tactics of the UNIA and Pan-African congresses. Ultimately, the ABB's Brightest Africa would be a continent run by Africans who embraced their indigenous religions, rejected capitalism, and adopted communism.[41]

The transnational scope of the Pan-African congresses and the UNIA helped blacks renegotiate the significance of Africa to New Negro consciousness, identity, and liberation. As Plummer argues, "pan-Africanism expanded Afro-American consciousness by rescaling questions of racial justice to global dimensions." Du Bois's and Garvey's movements effectively placed African American enfranchisement and African independence (or a least self-determination) in a discursive relationship with global events and foreign policy issues such as World War I and the redistribution of German colonies. Pan-Africanism evaded the seemingly parochial politics of the American "Negro problem" by insisting on a global solution and perspective to localized black struggles. This internationalist framework for addressing racial injustice influenced New Negroes, who embraced more radical visions of Brightest Africa.[42] The pan-Africanist platform of the ABB offered a counterpoint to pan-Africanist rhetoric that emphasized the necessity for Africans to unite to form a republic or empire based on democratic values and capitalism, or a requisite conversion to Christianity.

CONCLUSION: BRIGHTEST AFRICA FOR BRIGHT AFRICANS

Du Bois's seminal 1933 essay "Pan-Africa and the New Racial Philosophy," and his subsequent writings on the "theory of colonial imperialism," encapsulated the new marriage of traditional pan-Africanism, anti-imperialism (in a global context), and workers' rights. Du Bois argued that the so-called Negro problem had to be approached not from a "narrow, provincial, or even national background, but in relation to the great problem of the colored races of the world and particularly those of African descent." Although he had made a similar argument in *The Souls of Black Folk,* Du Bois had yet to articulate his concept of the "color line" in the framework of a radical pan-Africanism influenced by radical leftist political philosophies. Du Bois implored African Americans to cease thinking of themselves "as belonging to the white race." He argued that despite the fact that by birth, African Americans were "American," in reality, their experiences resonated more with those of "the dark people outside of America" than with their "white fellow citizens." Citing "color caste," discrimination, and labor exploitation as experiential links between African Americans and the "colored peoples" of Latin America, the Caribbean, Africa, and Asia, he called for "spiritual sympathy and intellectual co-operation" in working toward the "freedom of the human spirit . . . incased in dark skin" and dismantling the economic and political systems that deprived these persons of their humanity.[43]

Du Bois believed that New Negroes had to take the lead in addressing the problems of "the colored peoples of the world" first by embracing pan-Africanism—an "intellectual understanding and co-operation among all groups of Negro descent in order to bring about at the earliest possible time the industrial and spiritual emancipation of the Negro peoples." In explaining the new racial philosophy for pan-Africanists, he returned to the idea of black self-governance and the need to reject stereotypes of savage Africans and Darkest Africa. He asked African Americans to conduct a "spiritual housecleaning" where they "cease to think of Liberia and Haiti as failures in government; of American Negroes as being engaged principally in frequenting Harlem cabarets and Southern lynching parties; of West Indians as ineffective talkers; and of West Africans as parading around in breech-clouts."[44] Du Bois's emphasis on race pride served as a rallying cry for African Americans to move beyond their color and nationalist prejudices (supposedly inherited from white Americans) to embrace their mission to help emancipate the colored peoples of the world. Du Bois postulated that the championing of Africa required not only political action but a reimagining of the black self as a proud descendant of Brightest Africa—the motherland.

The transition from the missionary and emigrationist pan-African movements of the late nineteenth century to the Pan-African Conferences of the early twentieth century to the Garveyism in the 1920s and finally to the radical pan-Africanism and internationalism of the 1930s is critical to understanding the polyvalence of New Negro discourses on Brightest Africa. Initially concerned with modernizing Africa, New Negroes like Booker T. Washington imagined an Africa uplifted by Western-styled Christianity, commerce, and "civilization" as well as industrial education. Their vision of pan-African cooperation amounted to the black man's burden to "redeem" the continent, not from unscrupulous European imperialists, but from the supposed savagery of Africans. However, as New Negroes expanded their political and intellectual horizons, they began to see their own fates intertwined with those of Africans on the continent. While they maintained a sense of duty to their African brethren, many rejected the idea that diaspora blacks had a providential mission to save Africa. Increasingly, they imagined an independent Brightest Africa, freed by African initiatives and intraracial cooperation.

NOTES

1   W. E. C. Wright, "A New Negro" (1894), in Gates and Jarrett, *New Negro*, 23–26.

2   Washington et al., *A New Negro for a New Century*.

3   Zimmerman, *Alabama in Africa*, 3–9.

4   Mudimbe, *Invention of Africa*, 88–91, 114–17, 130–33; Lewis, *W. E. B. Du Bois*, 161–62.

5   Edwards, *Practice of Diaspora*, 1–3, 10; Plummer, *Black Americans*, 13–14; Lewis, *W. E. B. Du Bois*, 248; Baldwin, *Beyond the Color Line*, 2–4; Sundiata, *Brothers and Strangers*.

6   "The Negro's Peculiar Work," *New York Freeman*, January 15, 1887. See "A Cry from Africa," *Virginia Star*, December 23, 1882, and Mitchell, *Righteous Propagation*, 53–54.

7   "Negro's Peculiar Work."

8   Williams, "Black Journalism's Opinions," 224–35.

9   William A. Peete, "The Problem of Liberia," *New York Age*, March 17, 1888.

10   B. Bowser, "More about Liberia," *New York Age*, March 17, 1888; Mitchell, *Righteous Propagation*, 47–48.

11   Price, "Price's Rejection of Position," 234.

12   Clegg, *Price of Liberty,* 301.

13   Bowen, *Africa and the American Negro*; Makalani, "Pan-Africanism"; Shepperson, "Pan-Africanism and 'Pan-Africanism,'" 353.

14   "The African Baptist Foreign Mission Convention at Xenia, Ohio," *National Baptist World,* November 9, 1894; Chirenje, *Ethiopianism and Afro-Americans,* 1–5, 63–65; "Ethiopianism's Menace in Africa," *New York Age,* March 15, 1906; "Relation of England to the Natives of South Africa," *New York Age,* August 16, 1906.

15   Hamedoe, "First Pan-African Conference of the World."

16   Ibid.; Edwards, *Practice of Diaspora,* 1; Lewis, *W. E. B. Du Bois,* 250; Plummer, *Black Americans,* 14.

17   Hamedoe, "First Pan-African Conference of the World"; Lewis, *W. E. B. Du Bois,* 248–51; Edwards, *Practice of Diaspora,* 1; Plummer, *Black Americans*; Edwards, "Uses of Diaspora," 46.

18   Moss, *American Negro Academy*, 23.

19   Ibid., 192–93.

20   Makalani, "Pan-Africanism."

21   "An Announcement of a Conference at Tuskegee Institute," March 1911; Isaiah Goda Sishuba, Queenstown, South Africa, to Booker T. Washington, July 25, 1911; "The Opening Address of the International Conference on the Negro," April 17, 1912, in the Booker T. Washington Papers Online, 72, 273, 520–22; Evans, "International Conference on the Negro," 420–23.

22   Evans, "International Conference on the Negro," 417, 420–23; Lewis, *W. E. B. Du Bois,* 248; "International Conference at Tuskegee Institute," 1; *Southern Workman,* "Future of Tropical Africa," 353–72; Zimmerman, *Alabama in Africa,* 45–53.

23   "Declarations of the First International Conference on the Negro," in Evans, "International Conference on the Negro," 425–27.

24   Rolinson, *Grassroots Garveyism,* 151.

25   Marcus Garvey, "Declaration of the Rights of the Negro Peoples of the Word," in Wintz, *African American Political Thought,* 208–14.

26   Stein, *World of Marcus Garvey,* 273–77; Rolinson, *Grassroots Garveyism,* 150–51.

27   W. E. B. Du Bois, "Marcus Garvey," in Wintz, *African American Political Thought,* 123.

28   W. E. B. Du Bois, "Marcus Garvey: Information Exclusively from the Files of the Military Intelligence Division and State Department," in Wintz, *African American Political Thought,* 194; Martin, *Race First,* 280.

29   Marcus Garvey, "Address to the UNIA Supporters in Philadelphia, October 21, 1919," in Wintz, *African American Political Thought,* 194, 199, 200–204.

30   Ibid., 206.

31   Du Bois, "Marcus Garvey: Information Exclusively from the Files of the Military Intelligence Division and State Department," and Garvey, "Address to UNIA Supporters in Philadelphia, October 21, 1919"; Rolinson, *Grassroots Garveyism,* 154–60.

32 Marcus Garvey, "Address to the Second UNIA Convention, New York, April 31, 1921," in Wintz, *African American Political Thought*, 208–14, 218–23

33 Campbell, *Middle Passages*, 231; Contee, "Du Bois, the NAACP, and the Pan-African Congress of 1919," 15–16; "Declaration of the Rights of the Negro Peoples of the World"; Stein, *World of Marcus Garvey*, 86–87.

34 Garvey, "Address to the Second UNIA Convention," 220–21.

35 Ibid.

36 Du Bois, "African Roots of War," 707.

37 Campbell, *Middle Passages*, 230–31; Lewis, *W. E. B. Du Bois*, 59–60.

38 Campbell, *Middle Passages*, 231; Contee, "Du Bois, the NAACP, and the Pan-African Congress of 1919," 15–16.

39 Hubert Harrison, "Africa at the Peace Table," in *A Hubert Harrison Reader*, 210–12; Harrison, "The White War and the Colored Races," in ibid., 204–8.

40 African Blood Brotherhood, "Programme of the African Blood Brotherhood," 1; Robin D. G. Kelley, "'Afric's Sons with Banner Red': African American Communists and the Politics of Culture, 1919–1934," in *Race Rebels*, 106, 108.

41 African Blood Brotherhood, "Programme of the African Blood Brotherhood," 2–3, 5; Martin, *Race First*, 72.

42 Plummer, *Black Americans*, 12; Edwards, *Practice of Diaspora*, 243–44.

43 W. E. B. Du Bois, "Pan-Africa and the New Racial Philosophy," in Wintz, *African American Political Thought*, 152–53; Lewis, *W. E. B. Du Bois*, 335–36.

44 Du Bois, "Pan-Africa and the New Racial Philosophy," 154–55; Lewis, *W. E. B. Du Bois*, 335–36.

BIBLIOGRAPHY

African Blood Brotherhood. "Programme of the African Blood Brotherhood." *The Communist Review* 2, no. 6 (1922). http://www.marxists.org/.

Baldwin, Kate A. *Beyond the Color Line and the Iron Curtain: Reading Encounters between Black and Red, 1922–1963*. Durham, N.C.: Duke University Press, 2002.

Bowen, John Wesley Edward, ed. *Africa and the American Negro: Addresses and Proceedings of the Congress on Africa: Held under the Auspices of the Stewart Missionary Foundation for Africa of Gammon Theological Seminary in Connection with the Cotton States and International Exposition December 13–15, 1895*. http://docsouth.unc.edu/church/bowen/menu.html.

Campbell, James T. *Middle Passages: African American Journeys to Africa, 1787–2005*. New York: Penguin Books, 2006.

Chirenje, J. Mutero. *Ethiopianism and Afro-Americans in Southern Africa, 1883–1916*. Baton Rouge: Louisiana State University Press, 1987.

Clegg, Claude A., III. *The Price of Liberty: African Americans and the Making of Liberia*. Chapel Hill: University of North Carolina Press, 2004.

Contee, Clarence G. "Du Bois, the NAACP, and the Pan-African Congress of 1919." *Journal of Negro History* 57, no. 1 (1972): 13–28.

———. "The 'Statuts' of the Pan-African Association of 1921: A Document." *African Historical Studies* 3, no. 2 (1970): 409–17.

Du Bois, W. E. B. "The African Roots of War." *Atlantic Monthly* 115, no. 5 (1915): 707–14.

Edwards, Brent Hayes. *The Practice of Diaspora: Literature, Translation, and the Rise of Black Internationalism*. Cambridge, Mass.: Harvard University Press, 2003.

———. "The Uses of *Diaspora*." *Social Text* 19, no. 1 (2001): 45–73.

Evans, Maurice S. "International Conference on the Negro." *Journal of the Royal African Society* 11, no. 44 (1912): 416–29.

Garvey, Marcus. *Philosophy and Opinions of Marcus Garvey*. Edited by Amy Jacques-Garvey. 1923. Reprint, New York: Arno Press, 1963.

Gates, Henry Louis, Jr., and Gene Andrew Jarrett, eds. *The New Negro: Readings on Race, Representation, and African American Culture, 1892–1938*. Princeton, N.J.: Princeton University Press, 2007.

Hamedoe, S. E. F. C. C. "The First Pan-African Conference of the World." *Colored American Magazine*, no. 4 (1900): 223–31.

Harrison, Hubert. *A Hubert Harrison Reader*. Edited by Jeffrey B. Perry. Middletown, Conn.: Wesleyan University Press, 2001.

Jones, Jeannette Eileen. *In Search of Brightest Africa: Reimagining the Dark Continent in American Culture, 1884–1936*. Athens: University of Georgia Press, 2010.

Kelley, Robin D. G. *Race Rebels: Culture, Politics, and the Black Working Class*. New York: Free Press, 1994.

Lewis, David Levering. *W. E. B. Du Bois: The Biography of a Race, 1868–1919*. New York: Holt, 1993.

———. *W. E. B. Du Bois: The Fight for Equality and the American Century, 1919–1963*. New York: Holt, 2000.

Makalani, Minkah. *In the Cause of Freedom: Radical Black Internationalism from Harlem to London, 1917–1939*. Chapel Hill: University of North Carolina Press, 2011.

———. "Pan-Africanism." In *Africana Age: African and African Diasporan Transformations in the 20th Century*. http://exhibitions.nypl.org/africanaage/essay-pan-africanism.html.

Martin, Tony. *Race First: The Ideological and Organizational Struggles of Marcus Garvey and the Universal Negro Improvement Association*. Westport, Conn.: Greenwood Press, 1976.

Mitchell, Michele. *Righteous Propagation: African Americans and the Politics of Racial Destiny after Reconstruction*. Chapel Hill: University of North Carolina Press, 2004.

Moss, Alfred A., Jr. *The American Negro Academy: Voice of the Talented Tenth*. Baton Rouge: Louisiana State University Press, 1981.

Mudimbe, V. Y. *The Invention of Africa: Gnosis, Philosophy, and the Order of Knowledge*. Bloomington: Indiana University Press, 1988.

Perry, Jeffrey B. *A Hubert Harrison Reader*. Middletown, Conn.: Wesleyan University Press, 2001.

Plummer, Brenda. *Black Americans and U.S. Foreign Affairs, 1935–1960*. Chapel Hill: University of North Carolina Press, 1996.

Price, J. C. "Price's Rejection of Position." *Journal of Negro History* 63, no. 3 (1978): 234.

Rolinson, Mary G. *Grassroots Garveyism: The Universal Negro Improvement Association in the Rural South, 1920–1927*. Chapel Hill: University of North Carolina Press, 2007.

Shepperson, George. "Pan-Africanism and 'Pan-Africanism': Some Historical Notes." *Phylon* 23, no. 4 (1962): 346–58.

Southern Workman. "The Future of Tropical Africa." 41 (1912): 353–72.

Stein, Judith. *The World of Marcus Garvey: Race and Class in Modern Society*. Baton Rouge: Louisiana State University Press, 1986.

Sundiata, Ibrahim. *Brothers and Strangers: Black Zion, Black Slavery, 1914–1940*. Durham, N.C.: Duke University Press, 2003.

Washington, Booker T., Norman Barton Wood, and Fannie Barrier Williams. *A New Negro for a New Century*. New York: Arno Press, 1990.

Williams, Walter L. "Black Journalism's Opinions about Africa during the Late Nineteenth Century." *Phylon* 34, no. 3 (1973): 224–35.

Wintz, Cary D., ed. *African American Political Thought, 1890–1930: Washington, Du Bois, Garvey, and Randolph*. Armonk, N.Y.: M. E. Sharpe, 1995.

Zimmerman, Andrew. *Alabama in Africa: Booker T. Washington, the German Empire, and the Globalization of the New South*. Princeton, N.J.: Princeton University Press, 2012.

2

Cuban *Negrismo*, Mexican *Indigenismo*: Contesting Neocolonialism in the New Negro Movement

DAVID LUIS-BROWN

Alain Locke's foreword to the "Harlem: Mecca of the New Negro" (1925) issue of *Survey Graphic* situates the "Negro Renaissance" among "nascent movements of folk-expression and self-determination" in countries like Mexico.[1] Indeed, a year earlier, "Mexico: A Promise" appeared in the same journal. This earlier issue announces an exuberant "New Mexico" following the Mexican Revolution (1910–17). Contributors included the anthropologist Manuel Gamio, the artist Diego Rivera, President Plutarco Calles, and the Mexican secretary of education and essayist José Vasconcelos, best known for his manifesto on *mestizaje* (race mixing), *La raza cósmica* (*The Cosmic Race,* 1925). The white U.S. intellectuals Carleton Beals, a leftist journalist, and Katherine Anne Porter also contributed. This issue captures the postrevolutionary resurgence of pride in indigenous Mexico—*Indigenismo*—a time of cultural foment that an editorial compares to the "Italian renaissance."[2] It is likely, then, that "Mexico: A Promise" served as the model for Locke's landmark New Negro issue.

That possibility points toward the interrelations among three such movements in the Americas in the 1920s that called for a recognition of the rights and cultural achievements of blacks and indigenous groups: the New Negro movement, Cuban *Negrismo,* and Mexican *Indigenismo.*[3] Many scholars now know that an interest in black diasporic vernacular expression, particularly the blues and the *son,* was common to Nicolás Guillén, a founder of Cuban *Negrismo,* and Langston Hughes, the leading poet of the New Negro movement. But few know that Cuba's *Revista de Avance* (1927–30) published U.S. writers, including Hughes, Eugene O'Neill, and Countee Cullen.[4] Even fewer have heard that intellectual currents also crossed between Mexico City and New York—as did the Mexican Miguel Covarrubias, whose illustrations adorned *The Weary Blues* (1926) by Hughes, *Blues: An Anthology* (1926) by W. C. Handy, and *Mules and Men* (1935) by Zora Neale Hurston.[5] Such evidence of continuities among arts movements in Havana,

Mexico City, Chicago, and New York provides merely a slice of their converging interests and multiple collaborations. A comparative and transnational approach to these 1920s nationalisms serves to unsettle their sedimented histories, allowing one to perceive their broader significance and shared political projects.[6]

Each of these three nationalisms featured *primitivism,* a cultural discourse that sought to explain racial identities and hierarchies as well as geopolitical inequalities by contrasting primitive and modern cultures to varying degrees. As early as the 1830s, romantic racialists in the United States, typically antislavery in their politics, argued that Negroes were a primitive people who were more highly endowed with emotions than with intellect and therefore were more religiously devout and artistic than white people.[7] In 1918, the Chicago School sociologist Robert E. Park updated this tradition by arguing that the Negro was the "lady among the races," linking blacks and women in their allegedly heightened emotionality.[8] By the 1920s, primitivism was a fixture of popular culture common to social scientific, artistic, and literary discourses in Europe and the Americas, and artists and writers at every conceivable point on the political spectrum deployed the vocabularies of primitivism to address questions of race and empire.

Although many have associated primitivism with a naive racial essentialism that simplified complex political dynamics by alternately celebrating or condemning the allegedly precivilized culture of the so-called darker races, its political meanings varied widely. Some used primitivism to try to rationalize existing racial hierarchies and the imperial might of the Jim Crow United States; others found themselves lured by primitivism into the traps of racial discourse; while still others deployed primitivism to criticize racial hierarchies and U.S. imperialism in the Americas.

Protean in its uses, primitivism was perhaps the chief discursive commonality linking the nationalisms and transnationalisms of those whom W. E. B. Du Bois and others termed the "darker peoples" in the Americas. My hemispheric Americas approach to the New Negro movement, Cuban *Negrismo,* and Mexican *Indigenismo* reveals their common use of primitivist discourses, their shared institutional and discursive spaces, and the broad alliances that artists and writers constructed among the poor and racially oppressed.[9] Conventional accounts of these interwar nationalisms have occluded their hemispheric ties. Moreover, up until recently, scholars such as Michael Fabre and Paul Gilroy have emphasized U.S.–European routes of black culture in the 1920s, while ignoring equally compelling trends in the Americas.[10]

Here I use *primitivism* in a counterintuitive manner, emphasizing its deployment as a distinctly transnational discourse that could be used in critiques of U.S. neocolonialism. I replace the common disparaging notion of primitivism with a historically grounded analysis to construct a more nuanced account of the politics of 1920s primitivist nationalisms. Primitivist discourses in the post–World War I era fall into three broad categories: residual, dominant, and alternative.[11] Opposing the primitive to the civilized, residual primitivisms opt for the European. In 1934, Samuel Ramos argued that Mexico was not yet civilized: Mexico "wanted to jump to the heights of the older European civilizations in one bound, and then the conflict erupted between what one wants and what one can achieve."[12] In keeping with such a preference for European civilization, Miguel Angel Menéndez's novel *Nayar* (Mexico, 1940) implicitly endorses *mestizaje* (race mixture) as a homogenizing project of national unity that would "de-Indianize" Mexico.[13] By contrast, dominant primitivist discourses oppose the primitive to the modern to point out the faults of the modern. U.S. scholar Edward Sapir's "Culture, Genuine and Spurious" (1924) argues that "genuine culture" is more likely to be present at "a lower level of civilization."[14] Similarly, in "The Characteristics of Negro Expression" (1934), Hurston argues that like other "primitive communities," Negroes "think in hieroglyphics" and therefore have "done wonders to the English language."[15]

Whereas dominant primitivism romanticizes the primitive, alternative primitivism exposes oppressive social forces and dispenses with the idea that the primitive embodies a throwback to an earlier stage of history.[16] In a 1924 report from Africa, Du Bois gestures toward such a historicizing strategy by pointing out multiple historical "paths": "Primitive men are not behind us in some swift foot race. Primitive men have arrived. . . . They have used other paths."[17]

Departing from the transnational collaborations of writers like Beals, Guillén, and Hughes, I assess the utility of alternative primitivist discourses in terms of their ability to sharpen critical perspectives on U.S. and Latin American racisms and the "stretched out" social relations of U.S. neocolonialism.[18] *Colonialism* refers to direct territorial rule, whereas *neocolonialism* refers to a combination of indirect political and economic rule.[19] Following the devastation of Europe in World War I, U.S. investment in Latin America exceeded that of Europe for the first time, and the U.S. State Department aggressively intervened in Latin America to protect U.S. corporate interests.[20] U.S. racism against the darker peoples shaped this neocolonialism: the U.S. press had justified imperial aggression in the Spanish–American War of 1898 and the subsequent wave of neocolonialism in Latin America by representing Latin American countries like Cuba, Mexico, and Puerto Rico as black children, thereby linking the Jim Crow era of racial segregation to imperialism.[21] Writers such as Cuba's Guillén responded by portraying the U.S. racial order as the anathema of the hemisphere in his "The Road to Harlem" (1929).[22]

Neocolonialism in Cuba and Mexico differed according to the degree of U.S. control. Neocolonialism in Cuba emerged with the ratification of the Platt Amendment in 1903, inaugurating U.S. control of Cuba's sovereignty.[23] By contrast, the impetus for neocolonialism in Mexico developed from within the country, as presidents Alvaro Obregón and Plutarco Calles curtailed the land distribution and nationalization of resources that the Constitution of 1917 had mandated.[24]

In addition, U.S. military and business interests sought to repress egalitarian movements. In Cuba, U.S. corporations bankrolled politicians and repressed organized labor from the 1900s through the 1930s.[25] U.S. businesses owned 22 percent of Cuban land by 1926.[26] Similarly, the United States commenced occupations of Haiti in 1915 and the Dominican Republic in 1916.[27] And in Mexico, the threat of a U.S. invasion postponed the nationalization of oil for over a decade.[28]

In chronicling U.S. neocolonialism, writers such as Hughes and Beals—both of whom deployed primitivist discourse—informed readers about how neocolonialism deprived Latin Americans of their citizenship rights. Hughes condemned the racist "white shadows" of the U.S. military occupation of Haiti, and Beals attacked the U.S.-supported "despotism" of the Machado dictatorship in Cuba. In so doing, they joined the Guillén of "The Road to Harlem" in devising discourses of hemispheric citizenship.[29] Discourses of hemispheric citizenship expose a gray zone of citizenship, in which U.S. imperialism denies rights to neocolonized subjects, and dissenters, including the darker peoples, respond by reasserting rights on a hemispheric scale and by criticizing the U.S. neocolonial center that is calling the shots. Thus, however one assesses its contradictory politics, primitivism can expose conflicts over racism and U.S. neocolonialism in the Americas, thereby creating the conditions for discourses of hemispheric citizenship, which recognize that the issue of rights crosses national boundaries.

This essay examines the uses of primitivism in discourses of hemispheric citizenship. Primitivism readily lends itself to discourses of hemispheric citizenship because it is an interethnic and transnational discourse that is already embedded in debates over race and imperialism. Even as primitivist nationalisms inevitably deploy racial discourses in ways that at times contradict their aims of antiracist politics, they have the virtue of assessing transnational formations of culture under the shadow of neocolonial capitalism.

THE CAGE OF CIVILIZATION IN HUGHES AND BEALS

Hughes and Beals both developed alternative primitivisms—and hence discourses of hemispheric citizenship—by traveling through Latin America. During the course of these travels, Hughes and Beals illustrated the perils and potential of primitivist discourses. At times they romanticized nonwhite cultures, thereby evacuating historical specificities, but at other times they used primitivism to critique the precise conditions of life under neocolonialism. The travel writings of Hughes and Beals exemplified and stimulated cross-fertilizations among 1920s nationalisms in the Americas.

Hughes composed "The Negro Speaks of Rivers" (1921) while pondering his father—a resident of Mexico—and his "strange dislike for his own people" on a train headed to Mexico.[30] On his second trip to Mexico, Hughes befriended Carlos Pellicer, a poet who exalted indigenous cultures, much as Hughes's poetry romanticized ancient Africa.[31] The narrator of Hughes's "The Negro Speaks of Rivers" is not only a poetic visionary but also a worker, exposing a continuity between his early work that emphasized racial pride and later work that focused on capitalist exploitation, such as "Advertisement for the Waldorf Astoria" (1931), but also signaling Hughes's enduring transnational commitment to "dark-peoples."

The wisdom of the "dark-peoples" similarly takes center stage in "Mexican Market Woman" (1922), in which Hughes implicitly links workers and the racially oppressed across national identities:

> This ancient hag
> Who sits upon the ground
> Selling her scanty wares
> Day in, day round,
> Has known high wind-swept mountains,
> And the sun has made
> Her skin so brown.[32]

In these two poems, "Negro" and "brown" identities, equally revered, form the basis for a primitivist discourse of pride that indulges in generalities but also forms the basis for alternative histories. On one hand, Hughes maintains racialist terms while reversing their values; both "brown" and "Negro" become signifiers of pride countering allegations of inferiority. On the other hand, Hughes's romanticization of nonwhite cultures exposes commonalities among "Negro" and "brown" workers who would otherwise exclude one another from their political projects based on national or ethnic identities.

Hughes's later travel writings grew more sophisticated as he confronted various discrepancies in processes of racialization in the Americas. Returning from Mexico, Hughes ordered his ticket in Spanish at a San Antonio train station, thereby assuming a mestizo or mulatto identity.[33] Hughes attempted to elude the indignities of southern U.S. segregation with this racial masquerade. His cosmopolitan awareness of variations in racialization coexisted in tension with his implicitly biologically based definitions of blackness as epitomized by the vitality of Africa—as he wrote in *The Weary Blues* (1926), "all the tom-toms of the jungle beat in my blood."[34]

Hughes's experiences in Mexico set the groundwork for subsequent trips to

Latin America, in which he further developed his critique of U.S. racism and imperialism. In his essay "White Shadows in a Black Land" (1932), Hughes shows how U.S. neocolonialism impinges on the "darker world" of Haiti:

> To a Negro coming directly from New York . . . [Haiti] is like stepping into a new world, a darker world . . . where the white shadows are apparently missing, a world of his own people. . . . Even the president of the Republic will have a touch of color in his blood. . . . The dark visitor from America will feel at home and unafraid.[35]

Haitians in positions of political authority embody the hopes of the New Negroes to achieve equality. Yet Haiti is haunted by what Hughes calls the "white shadows" that overwhelm initial impressions once the traveler understands the realities of U.S. neocolonialism, which subjects the Haitian people to "a sort of military dictatorship backed by American guns."[36] Indeed, U.S. Marines massacred three thousand peasants in the U.S. occupation of Haiti.[37] The U.S. occupation, led by southern soldiers who were ironically thought to have been experts on Negroes, also suspended the Haitian constitution and introduced segregation, forced labor, and censorship.[38] The white shadows, then, figure an alignment between U.S. racism and neocolonialism.

Like Hughes, Beals traveled to both Mexico and Cuba in the 1920s. And like Hughes, Beals published in journals that constituted major threads in the journalistic fabric of the New Negro movement: the *Survey Graphic,* the *New Masses,* the *New Republic,* and the *Nation.* Beals soon grew famous through his leftist journalism in Mexico, where he lived from 1923 to 1928.[39] He moved through intellectual circles that exemplified binational U.S.–Mexican cultural foment. In Mexico, Beals defended his friend Diego Rivera's murals against critics offended by their sympathetic portrayals of the dark-skinned poor.[40] Beals also associated with U.S. exiles in Mexico City and contributed to the *Survey Graphic* special issue on Mexico in 1924.[41] Living in Mexico turned Beals into an anti-imperialist—he opposed the 1927 U.S. intervention in Mexico.[42] Beals's parents had raised him to be supportive of egalitarian ideals: they participated in the populist movement in Kansas in the 1890s, and his father helped to organize Mexican beet workers in southern California in the early 1900s.[43]

Beals's sympathy for leftist causes led him to travel to Cuba in the early 1930s to investigate President Gerardo Machado's violent suppression of leftist labor and student movements. Despite Machado's indiscriminate assassinations of political opponents, U.S. ambassador Henry Guggenheim supported the Machado regime.[44] While in Cuba, Beals interviewed Gustavo Urrutia and met with anthropologist Fernando Ortiz, both key players in *Negrismo.*[45] Horrified by the 1929 murder in

Mexico of his friend Julio Antonio Mella, an exiled communist leader of Cuban student protests, Beals castigated U.S. neocolonialism in *The Crime of Cuba* (1933):[46]

> The Machado despotism has overthrown the constitution . . . has destroyed free press . . . and has ruled by force and murder. During this period that despotism was publicly praised by our highest officials. . . . What right have we to get exercised about Hitler when we helped to maintain a protectorate at our very doorstep?[47]

Beals's anger is informed by his knowledge of U.S. neocolonialism. Cuba's protectorate status consisted of a dual economic and political dominance by U.S. business interests.[48] By 1927, U.S. businesses owned up to 82 percent of Cuban sugar production.[49] U.S. corporations contributed to the dire economic straits of the majority of Cubans by making massive campaign contributions to corrupt presidential candidates who were then able to rig elections.[50] Antonio Machado won the election of 1924 by exploiting nationalist sentiment.[51] But when he illegally extended his mandate in 1927, students responded with demonstrations, which Machado repressed.

The Crime of Cuba by Beals contributes to the dissident Afro-Cubanism of writers like Alejo Carpentier and Guillén by combining journalism, history, and a "photographic essay" with photographs of the poor, imprisoned students, and murdered dissenters. Beals was shocked to discover that a Cuban was assassinated the day he was scheduled to interview him.[52] The text presents an unrelentingly grim picture of Cuba that undermines, as did Guillén's poetry, the tourists' idealization of "Old Havana." Beals's Cuba is instead ruled by U.S. landowners who make life "an elementary, savage struggle for survival."[53] A "thin Negro" tells Beals that with the advent of U.S. neocolonialism, "we merely changed masters."[54]

Beals's angry, impassioned critique of U.S. neocolonialism in Cuba coexists uneasily with sexist and racially essentialist language in his passage on Fela, an "octaroon" dancer in a Havana cabaret. The octoroon's body is this activist intellectual's sexual and ideological weak spot, which threatens to undermine his political critique with stark oppositions between whites and nonwhites. As Fela dances, her body becomes "an instrument of racial purpose quite beyond itself," a potent racial signifier.[55] Watching her, he finds "rhythms—so far from commercialized tunes—locked in her lovely tan and gold body," reiterating Sapir's romanticization of allegedly vibrant nonwhite cultures that were throwbacks to a premodern world.[56]

Fela's performance, then, coincides with another performance, that of the accomplished primitivist who attempts to have it both ways: to revel in racial essences while dreaming of their elimination. For Beals, witnessing Fela's dance makes accessible a "primitive force":

> Mind and will had been melted away in that quiver, slide and wheel of the flesh-covering . . . that stripped off, even in us clumsy beholders, all civilized layers, and left some primitive force deeper, more important even, than symbolic orgy. It thrusts us, more than naked, into kinship with elemental attraction and repulsion of ions.[57]

Here Beals recasts the common 1920s notion that civilization is a cage (as in Hughes's "Lament for Dark Peoples") and that white regeneration is possible by observing a primitive Other. Beals claims that the seduction of Fela's "flesh-covering" has penetrated "cultural barriers," creating a cross-racial "kinship."[58] However, Beals's desire for such a cross-racial "kinship" is undermined by his own participation in the sexualized tourist economy of the cabaret and by the racial discourses he deploys.

In his descriptions of Fela, Beals constructs an opposition between whiteness, associated with the intellect, and blackness, associated with the body and sexuality. So while Hughes and Beals transcend narrow racial ideologies by aligning themselves with the struggles of nonwhites from Latin America, they part ways in their differing valuations of blackness. Both Hughes and Beals contest U.S. neocolonialism through primitivist representations of nonwhite Latin American women. However, each deploys primitivism with significantly different consequences for racial and gender politics. Hughes's alternative primitivist discourse figures Mexican "brown" and black identities as aligned against the white shadows of U.S. racist neocolonialism. The "Mexican Market Woman" figures a transnational "brown" collectivity as much through economic exploitation—"selling her scanty wares"—as through her position as a Republican Mother. Similarly, Beals's career brings together the egalitarian impulses of the New Negro movement, the Mexican Renaissance, and Afro-Cubanism. But Beals's dominant primitivist discourse betrays his own participation within a sexualized tourist economy, as he figures Fela's female flesh as uniting men across social divides. Moreover, Beals's descriptions of biological racial difference distract from his critique of neocolonialism.

In Hughes and Beals's primitivist alliance, politics oscillates between a detailed specifying of the social production of racial difference and ahistorical appeals to racial difference. Primitivist discourses, then, must be evaluated according to their ability to signify racial pride while not erasing the historical construction of racial groups. By challenging U.S. foreign policy in Mexico and the Caribbean, U.S. citizens like Beals and Hughes practiced a kind of hemispheric citizenship, one that called for the restoration of the rights of those suffering under neocolonialism.

The following sections expose the "vaster reality" of U.S. neocolonialism and its effects on lives seemingly remote from those of U.S. citizens yet bound together by transnational cultural and political–economic threads that bring together the Americas in unexpected ways.[59]

THE "CONTENTED ANIMAL" AND DECOLONIZATION IN CLAUDE MCKAY

I now turn to an analysis of two novels that address U.S. neocolonialism in the Caribbean: Claude McKay's *Home to Harlem* (Haiti) and Jesús Masdeu's *La raza triste* (Cuba). McKay and Masdeu represent the violence committed by state-sponsored nationalism as a homogenizing project that suppresses self-determination by the marginalized. Identifying primitivist folk expression not with the state-based citizen but with the black diasporic "proletariat" (McKay) and "peon" (Masdeu), these writers expose racism and demonstrate how neocolonial control deploys the exploitative force of capitalism through the U.S. control of foreign markets.[60]

Much like Hughes and Beals, McKay, a Jamaican migrant, narrated neocolonialism in Latin America and the Caribbean alongside the plight of Negroes in Harlem, sites joined through the friendship between his characters Ray, a Haitian immigrant, and Jake, a working-class black Harlemite. McKay conceptually ties together the stretched out social relations that allowed U.S. business elites to thwart the rights of citizens in the Caribbean, especially in Haiti. In contrasting Ray and Jake, McKay constructs a discourse of hemispheric citizenship in which critiques of class and racial subordination unseat narratives of national and racial loyalty, creating the conditions for a politics of alliance among the oppressed of different nations.

Traveling from his homeland of Jamaica to New York, McKay encountered the workers whose lives would inspire his "proletarian novel."[61] Indeed, the rise of the Harlem Renaissance coincided with the emergence of Harlem as a slum. Primitivist nationalisms of the 1920s emerged amid frustrated economic expectations: the thwarting of land redistribution in Mexico and the early advent of the depression in Cuba and Harlem.[62] The Great Migration of blacks to the North ran parallel to the ghettoization of Harlem, which grew by more than one hundred thousand between 1920 and 1930.[63] Moreover, most black men worked in the service industry—Hughes worked as a busboy—and 70 percent of black women in Manhattan worked as domestics, as did Hurston.[64] Therefore New Negro representations of the black poor did not merely constitute a counterpart to fascination with the primitive "folk" but also exposed the economic plight of blacks in the modern world. McKay's pairing of Ray and Jake reveals an educational disparity—Ray is university educated whereas Jake is not—and an economic parity, highlighting the anomalous class position of black intellectuals that he emphasized in *The*

Negroes in America (1923).[65] McKay knew this from personal experience as well: he worked as a railroad porter and waiter.[66]

Despite their similarly dim economic prospects, a key tension between Ray and Jake emerges from differences in gender ideologies, which are central to McKay's decolonizing vision—McKay places his critique of gender on equal standing with his assessment of race and empire. An opposition between sexuality and respectability and the ultimate collapse of that opposition drive the plot in *Home to Harlem*: Jake's search for the black woman Felice who, he believes, slept with him not for money but for love. Hazel Carby has shown how "sexist" representations in McKay grew out of the widespread "moral panic" over the alleged sexual mores of black migrant women.[67] In her argument, facing limited economic opportunities, black female migrants either turned to sex work or to marriage.

It is indeed true that Jake, a longshoreman who fought in World War I, expresses sexist views.[68] However, contrary to Carby, other characters criticize Jake's sexism in this multivoiced narrative. While working on the Pennsylvania Railroad, Jake meets Ray, who is reading a novel titled *Sapho*. He explains to Jake that the historical Sappho was a lesbian. When Jake remarks that lesbians are "ugly women" and "bulldykers," Ray asks Jake not to disparage them.[69] Rather than construing McKay's text as sexist, as Carby does, I regard his representation of gender roles as developing the text's project of educating readers about another moral panic over what was then termed sexual "degeneracy."[70]

It is precisely Ray's friendship with Jake—with all its complexities of class and gender—that defines the novel's alternative decolonizing primitivism. McKay implicitly defines a decolonizing primitivism by pairing an anticolonial politics with a broadly radical vision that refuses to hierarchize differing oppressions: racial, gender, and class oppression all matter. Indeed, McKay's speech to the Fourth Congress of the Third Communist International in Moscow in 1922 places racial subordination on par with class hierarchies by castigating Communists for their racism.[71] In the early 1920s, McKay joined the African Blood Brotherhood—whose very name suggests it didn't adopt a progressive agenda on gender—which proposed racial equality and higher wages and later merged into the Communist Party.[72] McKay's claim to fame was his protest poem "If We Must Die," published in the July 1919 edition of *The Liberator*. With that celebrated poem, McKay became the black voice of the Red Summer, in which whites attacked blacks in twenty-five urban race riots. *Home to Harlem* adds a new element to McKay's work by emphasizing gender politics alongside communism, antiracism, and antimperialism.

In the novel, McKay repeatedly and implicitly calls for a broader political vision that emphasizes gender and imperialism alongside problems of race and class. The character Ray introduces the problem of imperialism into what McKay described as a "proletarian novel." Ray tells Jake that his father was imprisoned and that his brother died while fighting the brutal U.S. military occupation of Haiti (1915–34). The country's promise as an independent black republic stirs Jake's imagination: "it was incredible to Jake that a little island of freed slaves had withstood the three leading European powers."[73] Ray's history lesson about Haiti helps Jake grow out of his ethnocentric hatred toward "foreign niggers."[74]

In Ray's analysis of oppression, anti-imperialism, antiracism, and a Marxist analysis of economic exploitation converge:

> Ray felt that as he was conscious of being black and impotent, so correspondingly, each marine down in Haiti must be conscious of being white and powerful . . . all perfect Occidentals and investors in that grand business called civilization. That grand business in whose pits sweated and snored . . . all the black and brown hybrids and mongrels, simple earth-loving animals, without aspirations toward national unity and racial arrogance.[75]

With bitter irony, Ray undermines the racialist vocabulary of residual primitivism ("hybrids and mongrels") through a critique of the racialized political economy. Although Ray attempts to educate Jake on imperialism in Haiti and the importance of a feminist perspective, Ray stands to learn much from Jake. Ray's abhorrence of European civilization leads to self-hate instead of Jake's resilient optimism.

While Ray criticizes race and empire, Jake shows how the "common people," McKay's somewhat patronizing term for Jake and his lover Rose, thrive despite oppression.[76] McKay's description of how African American youth have taken over the street life of the "Block Beautiful," the sole remaining white enclave in Harlem, reveals how he constructs black joie de vivre as constituting a strategy of survival against racial oppression. By strolling the Block Beautiful, African American youth stake claim on an exclusive neighborhood despite blacks' widespread exclusion from home ownership. As Felice says when her favorite club is shut down by the police, "white folks can't padlock niggers outa joy forever."[77] Indeed, for Ann Douglas, the black reclaiming of Harlem as a "homeland" marks its renaissance as "the 'post-colonial' phase of African-American culture."[78] If the New Negro movement can be viewed as constructing a postcolonial sensibility, McKay searches for the methods of decolonization among the black proletariat, allegedly endowed with the imprimatur of racial authenticity, "simple, raw emotions and real."[79]

The friendship between Ray and Jake signals the text's effort to construct a progressive class, gender, anticolonial, and antiracist politics rejecting black middle-class notions of uplift with a Marxist, black Atlantic—and black hemispheric—vision.[80] *Home to Harlem* thus contributes to what Cary Nelson has identified as "an emergent alliance politics of resistance" within a constellation of black, feminist, and leftist publications in the 1920s, a scene in which McKay participated as an associate editor of Max Eastman's *Liberator* beginning in 1921.[81] McKay further expands the scope of this coalition by criticizing U.S. imperialism in Haiti.

"TO BE AN INTELLIGENT BLACK IS A CRIME": MASDEU AND CUBAN NEGRISMO

Like the New Negro movement, Cuban Negrismo paired a focus on the racial violence inherent to the nation-state with a critique of U.S. imperialism. The Negrismo movement first found expression in "Danzarina africana" ("African Dancer," 1917–18), a poem by Luis Palés Matos of Puerto Rico. In Cuba, Negrismo took root with Fernando Ortiz's *Glosario de afronegrismos* (Glossary of Afro-Cuban terms, 1924) and Gustavo Urrutia's "Ideales de una Raza" (The ideals of a race) series in Havana's *El Diario de la Marina* (1926–31), followed by the poetry of Guillén and the Chinese-Afro-Cuban Regino Pedroso. This movement also took shape in visual culture with Eduardo Abela's *El triunfo de la rumba* (1928) and Carlos Enríquez's *Tocadores* (1935). In popular music, Afro-Cubanism dominated with various Afro-Cuban *conjuntos de son* as well as the work of the white composer Ernesto Lecuona, the Afro-Cuban singer Rita Montaner, and the mulatto singer and composer Bola de Nieve (Ignacio Villa), said to be the Cuban Louis Armstrong.[82]

Negrismo emerged during a tumultuous decade of activist organizing, which witnessed the founding of the Cuban Federation of Women's Associations in 1921 and the Communist Party of Cuba in 1925. At a time when race-blind discourses prevailed, writers such as Alejo Carpentier, in his novel *¡Ecue-Yamba-O!* (May the Lord be praised!, 1933), Guillén, and Pedroso courageously foregrounded the predicaments and longings of Afro-Caribbeans as epitomizing Cuba's aspirations.[83] Chief among these national problems were dramatic economic and social disparities exacerbated by U.S. neocolonialism.

U.S. neocolonialism was a key ingredient in Negrismo's representations of the political scene. But for Negrismo, racial oppression was equally important to combat. In his essay "El Camino de Harlem" (1929), Guillén argued that Cuban racial oppression was coming to resemble that of the United States, setting Cuba on the "road to Harlem":

Is it possible that after the two great revolutions against Spain and after the installation of the *patria libre* (independent republic) . . . there could be one population of Cubans . . . who feel differentiated from the other? . . . *Sí, señores,* the *raza de color* still has problems in Cuba. . . . We must continue combating innumerable prejudices.[84]

Thus Negrismo both participated in the activism that swept across Cuba in the 1920s in response to the dire economic plight of the majority and insisted on the specificity of racial oppression, particularly what Alejandra Bronfman has identified as the discourse of the allegedly violent and irrational "black barbarian," a discourse that was homegrown and not simply an import from the United States.[85] In Negrismo, as in the New Negro movement, antiracist, anti-imperialist, and nationalist discourses could converge with global primitivism.

The publication of Masdeu's *La raza triste* (The sad race, 1924) was delayed for over ten years, perhaps as a result of the chilling effect of the massacre of thousands of Afro-Cubans with the collusion of the U.S. Marines in the Race War of 1912, a war that created the conditions for the travails of the mulatto protagonist. In his preface, Masdeu does not reveal his own racial identity, but he does claim that he conceived of the book while working in cane fields alongside blacks:

> I wrote *La raza triste* . . . to vent my sadnesses as a slave, a vagabond pariah, a rebel against the justice that condemned me to an inferior position among human refuse.[86]

Regardless of his racial identity, Negrismo allowed Masdeu to transform his experience of laboring alongside black workers into a critique of neocolonialism and racial inequality in Cuba.

This as yet untranslated novel focuses on the tragic love between Miguel Valdés, a mulatto doctor, and the white Gabriela Estrada y Céspedes. With the financial aid of two white men, Don Antonio, Gabriela's father, and Don Epicuro, Miguel is able to study in the United States. However, upon his return, he discovers the limits to their generosity: both turn against him under the influence of the ex–slave owner Don Enrique Reyes and his son Armando. The pair persuades the newspaper *El Demócrata* to smear Miguel's reputation. With his clientele gone, Miguel loses hope, becoming an alcoholic. By the end of the novel, Miguel has become the naturalist archetypal "brute": he has murdered his friend, the mulatto Edmundo, having mistaken him for the editor of the paper that had libeled him.[87]

The title of the novel—*La raza triste*—points to its use of naturalist social determinism: the idea that social conditions fully dictate life's outcomes. Miguel's scholastic career begins auspiciously when he shows great talent as an orator but then ends in frustration when he can't find employment as a doctor in Cuba as a result of racism. Miguel's experience was representative: in 1907, only 4 out of 1,345 lawyers were Afro-Cuban.[88]

Such hopes and frustrations of Afro-Cubans are epitomized by two contradictory poles in Cuban history shaping the novel's plot. On one hand, the interracial War for Independence (1895–98), in which Afro-Cubans composed 85 percent of the troops and 40 percent of the officer corps, epitomizes ideals of racial egalitarianism.[89] As Don Antonio says to the father of Miguel, "Nos hermanó la guerra" ("the war made us brothers").[90]

On the other hand, the Aponte slave rebellion of 1812 and the Race War of 1912 loom as evidence of enduring racial conflict. By insisting that scholarships for studying abroad be given only to whites, Don Enrique invokes the Aponte conspiracy, arguing that Miguel wants "to give wings to blacks . . . and blacks are going to cause us quite a few headaches. Remember Aponte."[91] The Aponte conspiracy was an antislavery rebellion involving free people of color and slaves in Havana in March 1812 that was spearheaded by Afro-Cuban *cabildos* or mutual-aid societies.[92] On March 14, 1812, spurred on by rumors that military leaders from the Haitian Revolution were offering to spread their revolution to Cuba, a group of free Afro-Cubans and slaves burned down the Peñas Altas plantation and killed the whites there; the rebellion then spread to three nearby plantations. The Cuban army spent months hunting down the insurgents in the countryside.[93] The presumed leader of these rebels, José Antonio Aponte, was a free Afro-Cuban sculptor who was a member of the Batallón de Morenos (free black militia), and some scholars speculate that he was a member of the Cabildo Chango-Tedum.[94]

The Race War of 1912 erupted when the Partido Independiente de Color (Independent Party of Color or PIC) organized strikes throughout Cuba, pressing the government to rescind the Morua Act (1909), which sought to perpetuate the myth that racial oppression didn't exist in Cuba by outlawing the organization of race-based political parties. The PIC stood for a democratized Cuba: it called for free education and expanded employment opportunities.[95] The specter of the PIC arises when the newspaper wrongly attributes Don Antonio's death to Miguel's "atavisms" as a mulatto in the same issue that it describes the PIC's uprising of ten thousand Afro-Cubans.[96]

The novel reveals that the public discourses constructing those two poles of Cuban history severely limit the scope of debates on race and nation. On one hand, what Aline Helg has called the "myth of Cuban racial equality" asserts color-blind democracy at the cost of downplaying racial oppression: "all that has ended," as Don Antonio claims.[97] On the other hand, the Reyes family scapegoats blacks for all social conflicts. These two seemingly opposed political positions actually emerge out of a shared discursive field. The scapegoating of blacks is made possible by the myth of Cuban racial equality, which, from the time of revolutionary leader José Martí onward, held that any assertion of racialized particularity by blacks was racist. The newspaper *El Demócrata* makes just this claim about a meeting

Miguel calls among "the race of 'color'" to discuss widespread poverty.[98] Thus the dominant racial discourse avoids confronting oppression.

Setting this text apart from most novels dealing with race in Cuba is the fact that its critique of the United States, evident in Miguel's expulsion from twenty-two universities in the United States due to being mulatto, joins a fierce critique of internal Cuban racism. Indeed, it is Armando, who attends a U.S. college along with Miguel, who repeatedly exposes Miguel's mulatto identity, forcing him to study at a Negro college in Atlanta. Vera Kutzinski's argument that Negrismo typically targeted U.S. imperialism to the exclusion of domestic conflicts points out the rarity of Masdeu's contribution.[99] At first, Miguel serves as a spokesperson for the myth of racial equality when he remarks, upon returning to Cuba, "In Cuba the black is a companion of the white, in the United States, the black is a dog."[100] However, Miguel soon changes his mind on the matter, even before don Enrique refers to him as "that black dog" and espouses southern U.S.-style segregation.[101] After Armando's libelous article in *El Demócrata* accuses Miguel of fomenting rebellion in a "racist" meeting of Afro-Cubans, Miguel fumes, "Hace falta una revolución, un cataclismo" (We need a revolution, a cataclysm).[102] Numerous incidents follow in which *El Demócrata* libels Miguel, depriving him of his livelihood. Cuba, Miguel finds, is a country where "to be an intelligent black is a crime."[103] His critique deflates claims that Cuba was a racially egalitarian nation.

My analysis of Masdeu shifts attention away from the primitivist racial stereotypes that crop up in the novel, instead emphasizing how primitivism coincides with the novel's firm commitment to a truly democratic Cuba, freed from the dual ills of racial oppression and neocolonialism. Indeed, as Alejandro de la Fuente has argued, Afro-Cubans were able to appropriate the "myth of racial equality" to their advantage by insisting that Cuba should live up to its egalitarian ideals.[104]

CONCLUSIONS: PRIMITIVISM AND NEOCOLONIALISM IN THE AMERICAS

My comparative approach to texts from the New Negro movement and Negrismo shows that alternative modes of primitivism focus attention on local political conditions and the transnational reach of neocolonial politics to create a litterature engagée. While no coherent strategy linked these two movements, both constructed alternative primitivisms that focused on the resistance of racialized subjects in the face of U.S. neocolonialism both within and beyond the country's national borders. Hughes, Beals, McKay, and Masdeu construct "cognitive maps" of neocolonialism and racial oppression through transnational ties based on political affinity (communism and socialism), diasporic African popular cultural forms such as the blues and the *son* (Hughes and Guillén), and other common artistic and political milieus.[105]

While Hughes, Beals, and McKay construct transnational alliances crossing the divide of uneven development in the Americas, Masdeu emphasizes the internal fractures of nationalism and race in Cuba and the United States. These 1920s nationalisms in Cuba, Mexico, and the United States—the Negrismo of Masdeu, the socialism of Beals, and the Marxist pan-Africanism of Hughes and McKay—all devised critiques of U.S. neocolonialism by adopting the perspectives of those whom McKay called the "black and brown" workers.

I have argued that we should read the transnational travels and imaginings of U.S. writers such as Beals, Hughes, McKay, and Masdeu as contributing to the practice of hemispheric citizenship—a critique of racism and the repressive social consequences of U.S. foreign policy and capital in the Caribbean and Latin America and the attempt to redress the consequent loss of citizenship rights. Adopting such a revisionary approach would offer an important transnational and intercultural perspective on the New Negro movement. Rather than analyzing racial conflict in the terms of the more familiar black–white axis, such an approach would force us to understand the simultaneous construction of the domestic and foreign in discourses of race. Such a convergence is evident in Hughes's alignment between black and brown in his poem "Mexican Market Woman" but is also revealed in a National Foreign Trade Council special report from 1924: "Foreign trade is an absolute necessity if the development of American life is to continue along the lines of which it has proceeded ever since the first white man landed on these shores."[106] The Foreign Trade Council tells a story of U.S. triumph whereby modernization is made synonymous with whiteness. If U.S. capitalists and policy makers viewed neocolonialism in Latin America as the engine of white prosperity, Beals, Hughes, and McKay took the radical approach of attempting to understand neocolonialism's devastating consequences on the majority of citizens in Cuba, Haiti, and Mexico. A transnational and multilingual approach to the New Negro movement could follow their cue by focusing comparatively on cultural production in Spanish-speaking Latin America, the Francophone Caribbean, and/or Portuguese Brazil, following the circuits of capitalism, empire, social repression, and resistance.

NOTES

1   Locke, foreword to *New Negro,* xxvii.

2   *Survey Graphic,* May 1, 1924, 186.

3   Given constraints of space, I have not been able to discuss Indigenismo in great detail here. For a fuller discussion, see my *Waves of Decolonization,* chapters 3 and 4.

4   See Masiello, "Rethinking Neocolonial Aesthetics."

5 For a survey of U.S.–Mexico cultural relations, see Delpar, *Enormous Vogue of Things Mexican*. See also, more recently, Vaughan and Lewis, *Eagle and the Virgin*; López, *Crafting Mexico*.

6 For recent work on the New Negro movement that moves beyond New York, see Edwards, *Practice of Diaspora*; Baldwin, *Chicago's New Negroes*; Guridy, *Forging Diaspora*; Stephens, *Black Empire*.

7 On romantic racialism, see Fredrickson, "Uncle Tom and the Anglo-Saxons."

8 Park, "Education in Its Relation to the Conflict and Fusion of Cultures," 280.

9 For a critique of comparativism in historiography, see Seigel, "Beyond Compare."

10 See Fabre, *From Harlem to Paris*; Gilroy, *Black Atlantic*. Earlier studies only mentioned in passing such transnational dimensions. See Huggins, *Harlem Renaissance*; Lewis, *When Harlem Was in Vogue*; Hutchinson, *Harlem Renaissance in Black and White*. See also Gates, "Trope of a New Negro."

11 Here I am adapting Raymond Williams's analysis of residual, dominant, and emergent forms of culture in *Marxism and Literature*, 121–27.

12 Ramos is cited in Bartra, *La jaula de la melancolía*, 109.

13 On de-Indianization, see Bonfil Batalla, *México Profundo*.

14 Sapir, "Culture, Genuine and Spurious," 318.

15 Hurston, "Characteristics of Negro Expression," 49, 50, 51.

16 I thank Davarian Baldwin for lending his phrasing to this sentence.

17 Du Bois, as quoted in Lively, "Continuity and Radicalism in American Black Nationalist Thought," 228.

18 Massey, *Space, Place, and Gender*, 22.

19 Baumgart, *Imperialism*, vi.

20 Halperín Donghi, *Contemporary History of Latin America*, 254.

21 See Johnson, *Latin America in Caricature*.

22 Nicolás Guillén, "El Camino de Harlem," quoted in Augier, *Nicolás Guillén*, 89.

23 See Pérez, *Cuba under the Platt Amendment*.

24 Halperín Donghi, *Contemporary History of Latin America*, 185.

25 See Benjamin, *United States and Cuba*.

26 Pérez, *Cuba under the Platt Amendment*, 258.

27 On U.S. intervention in Haiti, see Farmer, *Uses of Haiti*. On U.S. intervention in the Dominican Republic, see González, *Harvest of Empire*, chapter 3.

28 Aguilar Camín and Meyer, *In the Shadow of the Mexican Revolution*, 80–81.

29 For a more extensive definition of discourses of hemispheric citizenship, see the introduction to my *Waves of Decolonization*.

30 Hughes, *Big Sea*, 54.

31 Mullen, *Carlos Pellicer*.

32 Hughes, *Collected Poems*, 25.

33 Hughes, *Big Sea*, 50.

34 Langston Hughes, "Poem" (1923), in *Collected Poems*, 32.

35 Langston Hughes, "White Shadows in a Black Land" (1932), in Mullen, *Langston Hughes in the Hispanic World and Haiti*, 90.

36   Ibid., 91.

37   Plummer, "Afro-American Response to the Occupation of Haiti," 125–43.

38   I am indebted to Davarian Baldwin for reminding me of the use of southern white soldiers in the occupying forces.

39   Britton, *Carleton Beals,* 44–66.

40   Ibid., 61.

41   Beals, "Obregon Regime," 136–37.

42   Britton, *Carleton Beals,* 59.

43   Ibid., 6.

44   Ibid., 106.

45   Ibid.

46   Mella (1903–29) cofounded Cuba's Communist Party in 1925. For a brief biography of Mella, see Liss, *Marxist Thought in Latin America,* 243–47.

47   Beals, *Crime of Cuba,* 6–7.

48   Benjamin, *United States and Cuba,* 13.

49   Kutzinski, *Sugar's Secrets,* 135.

50   On the Race War of 1912, see Helg, *Our Rightful Share.*

51   Benjamin, *United States and Cuba,* 50.

52   Beals, *Crime of Cuba,* 38.

53   Ibid., 22.

54   Ibid., 34.

55   Ibid., 42.

56   Ibid., 40.

57   Ibid., 42.

58   Ibid., 42, 44.

59   The term *vaster reality* is Antonio Cornejo Polar's ("El indigenismo y las literaturas heterogéneas: su doble estatuto socio-cultural," 9).

60   I borrow phrasing from Davarian Baldwin here.

61   McKay, as quoted in Cooper, *Claude McKay,* 247.

62   On economic depression in Cuba and Harlem, see Kutzinski, *Sugar's Secrets,* 136; Greenberg, *"Or Does It Explode?,"* 39.

63   Greenberg, *"Or Does It Explode?,"* 15.

64   Ibid., 21, 24.

65   McKay, *Negroes in America,* 18.

66   Cooper, *Claude McKay,* 77–78.

67   Carby, "Policing the Black Woman's Body," 738–55.

68   McKay, *Home to Harlem,* 40.

69   Ibid., 129.

70   In Harlem, the police arrested cross-dressers for "degeneracy," as the *Amsterdam News* reported on February 8, 1928, and on November 16, 1929, the *New York Age* printed a story about minister Adam Clayton Powell's denunciation of "sex degeneracy and sex perverts." Wilson, "Bulldykes, Pansies, and Chocolate Babies," 149, 165.

71 McKay, "Speech to the Fourth Congress." See also Maxwell, *New Negro, Old Left,* chapters 1 and 2.

72 Cooper, *Claude McKay,* 106.

73 McKay, *Home to Harlem,* 132.

74 Ibid., 2–3, 134.

75 Ibid., 154–55.

76 Ibid., 114.

77 Ibid., 336.

78 Douglas, *Terrible Honesty,* 304, 312.

79 McKay, *Home to Harlem,* 338.

80 The *black Atlantic* is Gilroy's term—see his *Black Atlantic.*

81 Nelson, *Repression and Recovery,* 234.

82 On the Negrismo movement, see Kutzinski, *Sugar's Secrets,* chapters 5 and 6, and more recently, Guridy, *Forging Diaspora,* chapter 3. On painting focusing on Afro-Cuban themes, see Martínez, *Cuban Art and National Identity;* on musicians' participation in Negrismo, see Moore, *Nationalizing Blackness,* chapter 5.

83 Carpentier, *¡Ecue-Yamba-O!* For a literary biography of Carpentier, see González Echevarría, *Alejo Carpentier.* See also Guillén, *Obra Poetica.* Regino Pedroso's early poetry, some of which has been translated into English by Langston Hughes, is collected in *Nosotros.*

84 Nicolás Guillén, "El Camino de Harlem," as quoted in Augier, *Nicolás Guillén,* 89.

85 Bronfman, *Measures of Equality,* chapter 3.

86 Masdeu, *La raza triste,* 7.

87 Ibid., 304.

88 Moore, *Nationalizing Blackness,* 35.

89 Benjamin, *United States and Cuba,* 21; de la Fuente, "Race, National Discourse, and Politics in Cuba," 54.

90 Masdeu, *La raza triste,* 31.

91 Ibid., 32.

92 Childs, *1812 Aponte Rebellion,* 122.

93 Ibid., 141–42.

94 Ibid., 145.

95 Helg, "Race in Argentina and Cuba," 55.

96 Masdeu, *La raza triste,* 287.

97 On "the myth of Cuban racial equality," see Helg, *Our Rightful Share,* 6–7, 16, 106. For a persuasive critique, see de la Fuente, "Race, National Discourse, and Politics in Cuba," 45.

98 Masdeu, *La raza triste,* 81.

99 Kutzinski, *Sugar's Secrets,* 181.

100 Ibid., 69.

101 Ibid., 101.

102 Ibid., 84.

103 Ibid., 208.

104   de la Fuente, "Race, National Discourse, and Politics in Cuba," 45.

105   Jameson, "Cognitive Mapping," 347–60.

106   Pérez, *Cuba under the Platt Amendment*, 182.

BIBLIOGRAPHY

Aguilar Camín, Héctor, and Lorenzo Meyer. *In the Shadow of the Mexican Revolution: Contemporary Mexican History, 1910–1989: Contemporary Mexican History, 1910– 1989*. Translated by Luis Alberto Fierro. Austin: University of Texas Press, 1993.

Augier, Angel. *Nicolás Guillén*. Havana: Unión de Escritores y Artistas de Cuba, 1984.

Baldwin, Davarian. *Chicago's New Negroes: Modernity, the Great Migration, and Black Urban Life*. Chapel Hill: University of North Carolina Press, 2007.

Bartra, Roger. *La jaula de la melancolía: identidad y metamorfosis del mexicano*. Mexico City: Grijalbo, 1987.

Baumgart, Winfried. *Imperialism: The Idea and Reality of British and French Colonial Expansion, 1880–1914*. New York: Oxford University Press, 1982.

Beals, Carleton. *The Crime of Cuba*. Philadelphia: J. B. Lippincott, 1933.

———. "The Obregon Regime." *Survey Graphic* 52, no. 1 (1924): 136–37.

Benjamin, Jules Robert. *The United States and Cuba: Hegemony and Dependent Development, 1880–1934*. Pittsburgh, Pa.: University of Pittsburgh Press, 1977.

Bonfil Batalla, Guillermo. *México Profundo: Reclaiming a Civilization*. Translated by Philip A. Dennis. Austin: University of Texas Press, 1996.

Britton, John A. *Carleton Beals: A Radical Journalist in Latin America*. Albuquerque: University of New Mexico Press, 1987.

Bronfman, Alejandra. *Measures of Equality: Social Science, Citizenship, and Race in Cuba, 1902–1940*. Chapel Hill: University of North Carolina Press, 2004.

Carby, Hazel. "Policing the Black Woman's Body in an Urban Context." *Critical Inquiry* 18, no. 4 (1992): 738–55.

Carpentier, Alejo. *¡Ecue-Yamba-O!* Buenos Aires: Editorial Xanadú, 1968.

Childs, Matt D. *The 1812 Aponte Rebellion in Cuba and the Struggle against Atlantic Slavery*. Chapel Hill: University of North Carolina Press, 2006.

Cooper, Wayne. *Claude McKay: Rebel Sojourner in the Harlem Renaissance*. Baton Rouge: Louisiana State University Press, 1987.

Cornejo Polar, Antonio. "El indigenismo y las literaturas heterogéneas: su doble estatuto socio-cultural." *Revista de Crítica Literaria Latinoamericana* 7–8 (1978): 7–21.

de la Fuente, Alejandro. "Race, National Discourse, and Politics in Cuba: An Overview." *Latin American Perspectives* 100, no. 25 (1998): 43–69.

Delpar, Helen. *The Enormous Vogue of Things Mexican: Cultural Relations between the United States and Mexico, 1920–1935*. Tuscaloosa: University of Alabama Press, 1992.

Douglas, Ann. *Terrible Honesty: Mongrel Manhattan in the 1920s*. New York: Farrar, Straus, and Giroux, 1995.

Edwards, Brent Hayes. *The Practice of Diaspora: Literature, Translation, and the Rise of Black Internationalism*. Cambridge, Mass.: Harvard University Press, 2003.

Fabre, Michel. *From Harlem to Paris: Black American Writers in France, 1840–1980.* Urbana: University of Illinois Press, 1991.

Farmer, Paul. *The Uses of Haiti.* Monroe, Maine: Common Courage Press, 1994.

Fredrickson, George. "Uncle Tom and the Anglo-Saxons: Romantic Racialism in the North." In *The Black Image in the White Mind: The Debate on Afro-American Character and Destiny, 1817–1914,* 97–129. Middletown, Conn.: Wesleyan University Press, 1987.

Gates, Henry Louis, Jr. "The Trope of a New Negro and the Reconstruction of the Image of the Black." In *The New American Studies,* edited by Phillip Fischer, 319–45. Berkeley: University of California Press, 1991.

Gilroy, Paul. *The Black Atlantic: Modernity and Double Consciousness.* Cambridge, Mass.: Harvard University Press, 1993.

González, Juan. *Harvest of Empire: A History of Latinos in America.* New York: Viking, 2000.

González Echevarría, Roberto. *Alejo Carpentier: The Pilgrim at Home.* Ithaca, N.Y.: Cornell University Press, 1977.

Greenberg, Cheryl Lynn. *"Or Does It Explode?": Black Harlem in the Great Depression.* New York: Oxford University Press, 1991.

Guillén, Nicolás. *Obra Poetica, 1922–1958.* 2nd ed. Havana: Editorial Letras Cubanas, 1980.

Guridy, Frank. *Forging Diaspora: Afro-Cubans and African Americans in a World of Empire and Jim Crow.* Chapel Hill: University of North Carolina Press, 2010.

Halperín Donghi, Tulio. *The Contemporary History of Latin America.* Translated by John Charles Chasteen. Durham, N.C.: Duke University Press, 1993.

Handy, W. C. *Blues: An Anthology.* Illustrated by Miguel Covarrubias. New York: A. and C. Boni, 1926.

Helg, Aline. *Our Rightful Share: The Afro-Cuban Struggle for Equality, 1886–1912.* Chapel Hill: University of North Carolina Press, 1995.

———. "Race in Argentina and Cuba, 1880–1930." In *The Idea of Race in Latin America, 1870–1940,* edited by Richard Graham, 37–70. Austin: University of Texas Press, 1990.

Huggins, Nathan Irvin. *Harlem Renaissance.* New York: Oxford University Press, 1971.

Hughes, Langston. *The Big Sea.* New York: Thunder's Mouth Press, 1986.

———. *The Collected Poems of Langston Hughes.* Edited by Arnold Rampersad. New York: Vintage, 1994.

———. *The Weary Blues.* Illustrated by Miguel Covarrubias. New York: Knopf, 1926.

Hurston, Zora Neale. "The Characteristics of Negro Expression." In *The Sanctified Church,* 41–78. Berkeley, Calif.: Turtle Island Press, 1981.

———. *Mules and Men.* Illustrated by Miguel Covarrubias. Philadelphia: J. B. Lippincott, 1935.

Hutchinson, George. *The Harlem Renaissance in Black and White.* Cambridge, Mass.: Harvard University Press, 1995.

Jameson, Fredric. "Cognitive Mapping." In *Marxism and the Interpretation of Culture,* edited by Cary Nelson and Lawrence Grossberg, 347–60. Urbana: University of Illinois Press, 1988.

Johnson, John J. *Latin America in Caricature.* Austin: University of Texas Press, 1980.

Kutzinski, Vera. *Sugar's Secrets: Race and the Erotics of Cuban Nationalism.* Charlottesville: University of Virginia Press, 1994.

Lewis, David Levering. *When Harlem Was in Vogue.* New York: Oxford University Press, 1981.

Liss, Sheldon B. *Marxist Thought in Latin America.* Berkeley: University of California Press, 1984.

Lively, Adam. "Continuity and Radicalism in American Black Nationalist Thought, 1914–1929." *Journal of American Studies* 18, no. 2 (1984): 207–35.

Locke, Alain. Foreword to *The New Negro.* 1925. Reprint, New York: Atheneum, 1992.

López, Rick. *Crafting Mexico: Intellectuals, Artisans, and the State after the Revolution.* Durham, N.C.: Duke University Press, 2010.

Luis-Brown, David. *Waves of Decolonization: Discourses of Race and Hemispheric Citizenship in Cuba, Mexico, and the United States.* Durham, N.C.: Duke University Press, 2008.

Martínez, Juan A. *Cuban Art and National Identity: The Vanguardia Painters, 1927–1950.* Gainesville: University Press of Florida, 1994.

Masdeu, Jesús. *La raza triste.* Havana: Rambla, Bouza, 1924.

Masiello, Francine. "Rethinking Neocolonial Aesthetics." *Latin American Research Review* 28, no. 2 (1993): 3–32.

Massey, Doreen. *Space, Place, and Gender.* Cambridge: Polity Press, 1994.

Maxwell, William J. *New Negro, Old Left: African American Writing and Communism between the Wars.* New York: Columbia University Press, 1999.

McKay, Claude. *Home to Harlem.* 1928. Reprint, Boston: Northeastern University Press, 1987.

———. *The Negroes in America.* Translated by Robert J. Winter. Port Washington, N.Y.: National University Publications, 1979.

———. "Speech to the Fourth Congress of the Third Communist International, Moscow." In *The Passion of Claude McKay,* edited by Wayne Cooper, 91–95. New York: Schocken Books, 1973.

Menéndez, Miguel Angel. *Nayar.* Mexico City: Editorial Porrúa, 1978.

Moore, Robin. *Nationalizing Blackness: Afrocubanismo and Artistic Revolution in Havana, 1920–1940.* Pittsburgh, Pa.: University of Pittsburgh Press, 1997.

Mullen, Edward. *Carlos Pellicer.* Boston: Twayne, 1977.

———, ed. *Langston Hughes in the Hispanic World and Haiti.* Hamden, Conn.: Archon, 1977.

Nelson, Cary. *Repression and Recovery: Modern American Poetry and the Politics of Cultural Memory.* Madison: University of Wisconsin Press, 1989.

Park, Robert E. "Education in Its Relation to the Conflict and Fusion of Cultures." In *Race and Culture.* 1918. Reprint, New York: Free Press, 1950.

Pedroso, Regino. *Nosotros.* Havana: Editorial Trópico, 1933.

Pérez, Louis A., Jr. *Cuba under the Platt Amendment, 1902–1934.* Pittsburgh, Pa.: University of Pittsburgh Press, 1986.

Plummer, Brenda. "The Afro-American Response to the Occupation of Haiti, 1915–34." *Phylon* 43, no. 2 (1982): 125–43.

Sapir, Edward. "Culture, Genuine and Spurious." In *Selected Writings of Edward Sapir,* edited by David Mandelbaum, 308–31. Berkeley: University of California Press, 1958.

Seigel, Micol. "Beyond Compare." *Radical History Review* 91 (2005): 62–90.

Stephens, Michelle. *Black Empire: The Masculine Global Imaginary of Caribbean Intellectuals in the United States, 1914–1962.* Durham, N.C.: Duke University Press, 2005.

Vasconcelos, José. *The Cosmic Race: A Bilingual Edition.* Baltimore: Johns Hopkins University Press, 1997.

Vaughan, Mary Kay, and Stephen E. Lewis, eds. *The Eagle and the Virgin: Nation and Cultural Revolution in Mexico, 1920–1940.* Durham, N.C.: Duke University Press, 2006.

Williams, Raymond. *Marxism and Literature.* New York: Oxford University Press, 1977.

Wilson, James F. "Bulldykes, Pansies, and Chocolate Babies: Performance, Race, and Sexuality in the Harlem Renaissance." Ph.D. diss., City University of New York, 2000.

3

An International African Opinion: Amy Ashwood Garvey and C. L. R. James in Black Radical London

MINKAH MAKALANI

Late in summer 1935, as Italy began amassing its forces in Eretria along the Ethiopian border, activists, intellectuals, and laypeople throughout the African diaspora voiced their protest against this most recent act of European imperialist aggression. Alongside protests throughout the African diaspora, black anticolonial activists in London joined the International African Friends of Ethiopia (IAFE) to address what was quickly becoming known as the Abyssinia crisis. Founded by the storied Trinidadian activist–intellectual Cyril Lionel Robert (C. L. R.) James, together with Amy Ashwood Garvey (a central figure in the early Universal Negro Improvement Association [UNIA] and Marcus Garvey's first wife), the IAFE aimed "to assist by all means in their power, in the maintenance of the territorial integrity and the political independence of Abyssinia."[1] At a mid-August rally in Trafalgar Square, Ashwood, noting the failure during World War I to extend Wilsonian self-determination to Africa, declared that although "no race has been so noble in forgiving," it was "now the hour . . . for our complete emancipation." Ashwood's prevailing concern with black liberation did not stop her from highlighting what many considered the broader significance of Abyssinia, that black people now stood "between [Europe] and fascism." When James spoke at this rally, he assured the largely white crowd that they were not attending "an antiwhite demonstration," though he was clear that it was "pro-Negro." More provocative, though, was his claim that "Abyssinia is a backward nation" in need of "Western civilization," just not the barbaric civilization of Italian fascism.[2]

Students of James will note the dissonance between his declaration of backward Ethiopia's need for Western civilization and his relentless critique of imperialism over the span of his lifetime. James later described his 1932 arrival in London as a case of "the British intellectual . . . going to Britain."[3] His political activities in Trinidad had been limited to writing in local periodicals and working with Arthur A. Cipriani's Trinidad Workingmen's Association. He came to

England with a manuscript for a biography of Cipriani, a portion of which was published as the pamphlet *The Case for West Indian Self-Government*. As a moderate appeal for British Caribbean autonomy rather than complete independence, James presented Caribbeans as a uniquely modern people compared to those in colonized Africa and India. "There is in these colonies today," James noted of the West Indies, "no conflict between freshly assimilated ideas of modern democracy and age-old habits based on tribal organisation or a caste system."[4] However, by 1938, when he published his history of the Haitian revolution, *The Black Jacobins,* his intent, as he recalled years later, was "to stimulate the coming emancipation of Africa."[5] Within a brief six-year period, James had come to see Caribbean modernity less as a testament to its fitness for self-governance than as a mark of its limited revolutionary potential. It would seem that the Caribbean's *problem,* indeed, was that it was thoroughly rooted in Western civilization—that Caribbeans were, in fact, a thoroughly modern people.

Political organizing among Caribbeans and Africans in 1930s London provided a context in which James could break with this modernist notion of New Negroes as a race vanguard. The years between James's arrival in England and the appearance of *The Black Jacobins* represent a shift far more complex than merely an evolving radicalism. In coming to see the Caribbean's limitations and stressing Africa's importance to global emancipation, James turned toward coloniality as a basis from which to theorize liberation. Modernity as a regime of knowledge and rationality orders social life according to a European social model and is "presented as a rhetoric of salvation," but it "hides coloniality, which is the logic of oppression and exploitation." James explored the self-activity of the colonial masses as a response to oppression and exploitation, which provided him an angle from which to initiate a critique of modernity, even though he remained committed to modernity through his (heretical) engagement with Marxism.[6] Such a tension, such an unresolved element in his thinking in 1930s London, should not obscure that James was at odds with his contemporaries, who believed that Western blacks, because of their proximity to Western power, were a vanguard who would redeem the race and civilize Africa. Alain Locke, in his anthology *The New Negro,* called American blacks the "advanced-guard of the African peoples in their contact with twentieth century civilization,"[7] a sentiment echoed by W. E. B. Du Bois in the same anthology when he declared that for the African diaspora, "the main seat of their leadership is to-day the United States."[8] Such views created deep fissures among diasporic populations. In Europe, Caribbeans hailed their education and grasp of Western cultural norms as sanctioning their leadership. This view among Caribbeans in Paris led the radical Guadeloupean lawyer Joseph Gothon-Lunion to conclude that Africans lacked "the prestige and education needed to lead" race organizations. Similarly, James recalled that in London, "there was a definite cleavage between the two groups," with most Caribbeans considering themselves uniquely modern, while Africans often disparaged Caribbeans as "white black men."[9]

James's interactions with Africans in the social institutions and political movements of black London challenged his basic assumptions about African "backwardness." That his views did change was due in part to his meeting Africans who fit the mold of the New Negro. Many were students at university studying law, history, philosophy, and anthropology, endeavors that would have impressed someone of James's considerable intellect and elite Trinidadian background.[10] This turn, then, neither entailed a romantic, idealized Africa nor an argument for an authentic, primitive African culture that one might position against European modernity. James's encounter with African New Negroes tilted his analytic compass toward Africa, and thus toward coloniality.

This essay explores the anticolonial networks established by C. L. R. James, Amy Ashwood Garvey, and George Padmore in 1930s London. In a collection rethinking the New Negro movement, a focus on anticolonial London aims to broaden the historical lens beyond Harlem, but also beyond the United States, to stress a geographic expanse that would include the Caribbean, Africa, and key metropolitan nodes in Europe as well as extend its temporal range into the 1930s. To be sure, shuttling a term like *New Negro* from its U.S. black activist–intellectual context to frame the experiences of Caribbeans and Africans in England tempts a kind of diasporic hegemony. I want to stress, however, the term's heuristic utility in capturing a range of black cultures throughout the African diaspora that were similarly concerned with racial progress, uplift, and modernity and that were in dialogue with one another. Rather than an epistemic privileging of African Americans, this holds out an opportunity to break with a periodization scheme for the New Negro that U.S. scholars have based either on the ebb and flow, the beginning and end of key moments in African American political struggles, or more narrowly on the successes and failures of African American artistic and literary production.[11] Put another way, to consider blacks in 1930s London through the frame of the New Negro offers an opportunity to rethink the frame itself, to consider the New Negro experience beyond the confines of civil rights, racial uplift, black migration and community formation, *and* modernity in which U.S.-based scholarly discussions tend to be rooted.

Black activists and intellectuals were always concerned with situating African diasporic liberation within a global context as they pursued international connections and networks that might place New Negro politics on a world stage. It was in this context that important figures in early-twentieth-century black radical thought, such as James, made gestures toward coloniality. This is important for thinking about the hinge on which much New Negro thought turned: racial progress; fitness for citizenship and self-government; the nation as the ultimate goal of black liberation. Within both U.S. civil rights struggles and anticolonial nationalist projects, many believed that participation in Western empire—as civil servants in West Africa, as members of American military forces in the Caribbean and the Philippines—would substantiate the race's manhood, redeem Africa, and demonstrate the New Negro's political maturity.[12]

Italy's invasion of Abyssinia and the response of African diasporic peoples and organizations the world over, but especially in London, provided James an opportunity to contemplate colonial Africa's role in world revolution, which marked the beginning of his turn from the Caribbean and toward Africa as a source of world revolution. This was not purely an intellectual turn. An important narrative strand in this story concerns how the diasporic community James encountered in London informed his politics. Another narrative strand involves a central figure in London's black anticolonial circles, Amy Ashwood Garvey. Ashwood's intellect, organizing skills, and political associations drew into her orbit an assemblage of African and Caribbean activist–intellectuals who, along with Ashwood, challenged James's views about Africa. Black London was, as one contemporary put it, the "seething African pot" in which James thought out class struggle, world revolution, and the importance of Africa to each.[13] This was the context in which James rethought African "backwardness," questioned Caribbean modernity, and began thinking about the meaning of race in socialist revolution. Put differently, to understand how James approached socialist revolution is to understand the context of his response to Abyssinia.

ANTICOLONIAL LONDON

C. L. R. James came to England in 1932 ready to measure the metropole against the lore he had learned in Trinidad. In his initial observations of London, published in Trinidad's *Port of Spain Gazette,* he noted the grandeur of the British Museum and the character of London's intellectual debate and life; he also wrote of the racialized sexual politics of the empire and showed an oddly gendered sense of racism as the sole province of white men. What is remarkable about his articles, however, is what they reveal about James's sense of the limitations of the metropole. Though he found London's robust public intellectual life stimulating, he was astonished that so few Londoners took part in it. In fact, James found London and Western Europe more generally utterly unimpressive, convinced he already knew what Britain had to teach him before he had arrived. Rather than the jubilation of a British intellectual homecoming, he grew more confident in the Caribbean's modernity and coevality with Western civilization.

James moved effortlessly in London's intellectual and political circles, lecturing widely on such topics as poetic form, American literature, British imperialism, the Bolshevik Revolution, sex, Abyssinia, and the Indian question. At summer's end, he made his way to Nelson, where he stayed with the famous Trinidadian cricketer Learie Constantine, who had encouraged him to come to England. By this time, he had already begun taking note of Britain's Labour Party, which he joined briefly before entering the Revolutionary Socialist League. In the town of Nelson, James covered cricket matches for the *Manchester Guardian* and embarked on an intense study of Marxism. He also began collecting material for a study of Toussaint Louverture, which resulted in his classic, *The Black Jacobins*. It was also around this time that he likely began to meet black radicals in Europe. Arthur Cipriani was in London earlier in 1932 and had been in contact with British Communists and the Labour Party's James Maxton (also of the Independent Labour Party) about a ban in Trinidad of *Negro Worker*, the organ of the International Trade Union Committee of Negro Workers (ITUCNW). It may have been from Cipriani that James first heard the name George Padmore, the black Communist running the ITUCNW. Unfortunately, James had missed Padmore when he was in London in 1932.

Based in Hamburg, Germany, the ITUCNW was the Communist International's first sustained anticolonial organization focused on Africa, the Caribbean, and black workers the world over. It proposed to organize black workers around the world, and many black radicals came to see in the ITUCNW a vehicle for building an international movement. George Padmore stood at the fore of this effort. Padmore had left his native Trinidad for the United States in 1924 to attend Fisk University, and in 1927, he joined the Communist Party USA's Harlem branch. Rising quickly up the party's ranks and within the corridors of international communism in Moscow, he assumed leadership of the ITUCNW in late 1931.[14] Padmore focused the group's energies on organizing black workers in the British Isles, French and German ports, the Caribbean, and most importantly West Africa, and he envisioned the group's monthly journal, *Negro Worker*, as his main organizing tool. *Negro Worker* focused on the "day to day problems of the Negro toilers," in the hope of connecting these "with the international struggles and problems of workers" and non-African anticolonial movements.[15] Within a year, *Negro Worker* boasted a distribution network whose offices in New York, Paris, and Cape Town, South Africa, ensured that it circulated throughout the diaspora.[16] Reflecting on *Negro Worker* and Padmore's importance several decades later, James recalled that "tens of thousands of black workers in various parts of the world received their first political education from the paper [Padmore] edited, *The Negro Worker*. It gave information, advice, guidance, ideas about black struggles on every continent," providing a "consciousness among blacks that they were part of an international movement."[17] Not a year after taking control of the ITUCNW, Padmore cultivated a network of black workers and activists that surpassed anything seen previously in the Comintern. It was in this capacity that Padmore began working with the Barbadian Communist Arnold Ward, head of the London-based Negro Welfare Association, and turned his attention to anticolonial organizing in the metropole.[18] Whereas Ward envisioned Padmore helping to reshape the Communist Party of Great Britain and its white cadre, for Padmore, London came to represent an independent site of activism outside the corridors of organized communism.

Within two years of taking the helm of the ITUCNW, Padmore had grown thoroughly frustrated with the lack of support coming from Communist officials in Europe, and he grew increasingly critical of Moscow's policies. His attention turned increasingly to African and Caribbean liberation struggles, and he began to argue that the push for West Indian self-government and federation "arises from the widespread mass movement against the disgraceful exploitation of the workers and peasants . . . by British imperialism." He continued to emphasize class struggle but urged Communists to "give more attention, more concrete assistance, more material aid, support and advice, to the colonial victims of British Imperialism." Yet such aid seemed unlikely, as Communist parties in England and France gave the ITUCNW only nominal support.[19] Matters only got worse with Hitler's rise to power, as the Nazis arrested Padmore and deported him to England early in 1933.[20]

Padmore settled initially in Paris, where he resumed ITUCNW work and publication of *Negro Worker*. Shuttling between Paris and London, he claimed to have over a thousand contacts throughout the diaspora, to have helped establish trade union committees in places like Guadeloupe, Haiti, Senegal, Cameroon, Liberia, Panama, St. Lucia, and Madagascar, and reported that *Negro Worker* had nearly five thousand subscriptions. Yet despite such gains, by August, Moscow decided it was time to deemphasize anticolonial struggle. Entering its Popular Front phase, where the Soviet Union sought rapprochement with England and France in the face of fascism's rise in Germany, the Kremlin sent Padmore instructions to stop agitating against British and French imperialism. But Padmore refused to follow this line and resigned his position, deciding to pursue anticolonial struggle outside organized communism. Soviet efforts to "appease the British Foreign Office, which was raising hell because the Blacks in Africa were beginning to wake up," he admitted privately, had led to his departure. "Stalin has given up the idea of support to those who are still under the row."[21] He viewed the new Soviet Popular Front policy as "a betrayal of the fundamental interests of my people, with which I could not identify myself."[22]

These developments corresponded with the period of James's own move to Marxism and British Trotskyism. So when, back in London, as during his first

visit, he continued to hear the name George Padmore, he decided that it was time
to go hear this fellow speak and made his way to Grey's Inn Road. "One day,"
James recalled years later, "I had heard a lot about George Padmore . . . organising
black people all over the world, so I said I would go." Whatever James's expectations, he had not anticipated that Padmore would turn out to be his childhood
friend Malcolm Nurse. But now Padmore "was tied up with Moscow, I was headed
away from Moscow; I was a Trotskyist, but that didn't trouble us." Rather than
respond to one another as sectarian adversaries (as had been both their habits),
their interaction reflected a supervening anticolonial preoccupation. Indeed,
they talked almost until dawn after Padmore's speech. One exchange stood out
for James. When Padmore asked, "You came here in 1932?" James replied, "Yes,
March 1932. I was here and I stayed about here in London for about three months."
Taken aback, Padmore remarked, "My God, man, I was here in 1932 looking for
people to carry to Moscow to help to train them to organise blacks. If I had seen
you I would have asked you." James admitted that had they met, he would have
gone. "That was how we just missed one another," James recalled. "What would
have happened to me I don't know," James pondered, "because by 1935 Padmore
broke with them, and I remember that day very well."[23]

ABYSSINIA AND THE SOCIAL SPACE OF BLACK ANTICOLONIALISM

The British Left certainly represents an important moment for James's anticolonial Marxist thought. What has gone little noticed, though, is how London's
uniquely diasporic black community shaped what became his challenge to the
colonialist notion of historical time that deemed Africa and the Caribbean (along
with Asia and India) as lagging behind the modern West and thus not yet suited
to independence. To be sure, when he returned to London, James spent much of
his time in the Communist League, which had formed in the hope of transforming
the Independent Labour Party (ILP) into a revolutionary party. James was among
the Communist League members who, in 1934, formed the Marxist Group, and
he emerged as one of its most important thinkers. But it was the Abyssinia crisis
that provided him an occasion to rethink the racial logic of capital.

The ILP had debated whether to support League of Nations sanctions against
Italy. Like Lenin, who dubbed the League of Nations a "Thieves Kitchen," James
considered the question of sanctions a ruse for imperialist war. Instead, he proposed "workers sanctions" as an internationalist response to the Italian invasion
and the rise of fascism more generally, where workers would refuse to load ships
bound for Italy or the African horn and refuse to work on any projects supporting imperialist war. Writing in the ILP's paper, *New Leader,* James implored the
"workers of Europe, Peasants and workers of Africa and of India, sufferers from

Imperialism all over the world, all anxious to help the Ethiopian people," rather than support their governments in war, "organise yourselves independently, and by your own sanctions, the use of your own power, assist the Ethiopian people."[24]

Within the British Trotskyist movement, James garnered widespread support for this position, which for him had everything to do with the colonial question.[25] He traveled throughout the British Isles to South Wales and Dublin as well as Norwich, Coventry, and Nottingham in England, making appeals to support Ethiopia against Italian imperialism and putting forward the case for workers' sanctions. By fall 1935, he chaired the ILP's Finchley branch in North London, leading a sizable group that supported his position. It is therefore important to note that in James's view, workers' sanctions would allow Africans to use the crisis among imperial powers to liberate themselves. Theirs was not an isolated struggle; it was central to anticolonial and workers' struggles.[26]

If James found room in the British Left to elaborate his ideas about black liberation, London's black institutions provided fertile, if at times contentious, grounds on which to build a movement. One of the early arenas of his black public activism was Harold Moody's League of Coloured Peoples (LCP), a black-led organization with a sizable white membership committed to improving race relations. James met Moody in 1933 through Constantine, a LCP member and financial supporter. And while James was critical of the LCP's liberalism, he still lectured at its first summer weekend conference and occasionally wrote for its journal, *The Keys*[27] (Figure 3.1). On the Abyssinian crisis, London-based black radicals were agreed on the country's importance to African diasporic liberation and the future of the British empire, though they hardly agreed on what should be done.

Matters were complicated further by tensions between Africans and Caribbeans in London. With Caribbeans focused on the need for self-government in the Caribbean and Africans insisting on the importance of Africa to the diaspora, at times these differences appeared debilitating. When, in 1936, the West African Student Union (WASU) put on a debate on what advantages might come from "greater cooperation between Africans and West Indians," the focus turned to what many Africans experienced as Caribbean hubris. In a lively debate, Africans criticized Caribbeans for imitating whites and "their ignorance of the cultures of their forefathers . . . and their blindness to the advantages of mutual understanding." Participants agreed that Caribbeans needed to discard "the anti-African propaganda with which their educational system is saturated" and to "re-establish contact with the civilizations in which they have their roots."[28] James understood the points made that night, and it was likely in the orbit of Amy Ashwood Garvey that they made most sense.

If James was one of the more important black radical intellectuals to emerge from 1930s London, Amy Ashwood Garvey, a formidable intellectual herself, did

FIGURE 3.1. C. L. R. James speaking on the platform at Speaker's Corner, Hyde Park, London, circa 1935. Constance Webb Papers, Box 14, Folder 3, Rare Book and Manuscript Library, Columbia University Library.

the heavy lifting and toiled the loam that nurtured such a politics. Ashwood's abilities and considerable intellect propelled her involvement in the founding and early growth of the UNIA. In addition to the UNIA, while living in London in 1924, she helped the young Nigerian law student Ladipo Solanke establish the Nigerian Progress Union, a forerunner to WASU. Yet those same qualities made her ill suited to the role of the domesticated New Negro woman who enabled the New Negro man's political activities. Although Ashwood was involved in building the UNIA alongside Marcus Garvey, her refusal to accept a subservient role, not to mention their divergent political views, led to their divorce in 1922. After a brief return to Jamaica, she settled in London in 1930, taking up residence at 62 New Oxford Road and opening both the Florence Mills Social Parlour and the International Afro-Restaurant below her flat. Ashwood quickly became a major figure in London's black anticolonial circles, and to many, her businesses provided a welcome respite from a damp, strange country (see Figure 3.2).[29]

Ashwood's male peers respected her immense energy as an activist, though much of their praise betrayed the gendered structures of early-twentieth-century black radicalism. Hubert Harrison saw in her "a well-spring of ambition and inspiration" and privately lamented, "If I could get her for *my* helpmeet . . . I should rise to giddy heights of achievement!"[30] Former students remembered Ashwood as "a mother of African and West Indian students" who was always "concerned about their behaviour." More important, though, her establishments were centers of activism. According to the British Guiana–born radical T. Ras Makonnen, one could go to Florence Mills "after you'd been slugging it out for two or three hours at Hyde Park . . . and get a lovely meal, dance and enjoy yourself."[31] James, who spent a great deal of time there because he could not stand English food, recalled that Ashwood was a "militant anti-imperialist . . . of tremendous force of personality." While James found her historically uninformed, he considered her "an extremely acute woman, able to see what was taking place in conversation and people's orientation—one of the brightest women I have known."[32]

Florence Mills provided a political and social venue where black people could find familiar food, see familiar faces, and relax away from the gaze of white Londoners. The need for such places cannot be underestimated, for the metropole exacted quite a toll on black immigrants separated from friends, family, and familiar settings. It was therefore natural for political discussions to thrive at Florence Mills. As a *London Sunday Express* article noted of Ashwood's parlor, "race intellectuals from all parts of the world [were] wont to gather" there.[33] For James, Ashwood's political appeal was immediate, especially considering the radicals in her social network, including Solanke, as well as Solanke's friend Jomo Kenyatta, an anthropology student at the London School of Economics. When news came of Mussolini's activities in the African horn, it was at Ashwood's restaurant and with her help

FIGURE 3.2. Amy Ashwood Garvey with three of the sons (in white pants) of Dr. A. Workneh Martin, the Ethiopian ambassador to London, at an IFE rally, Trafalgar Square, London, August 25, 1935. Bettman/Corbis.

that James established the International African Friends of Ethiopia in July 1935.[34]

From various segments of the African diaspora, the response to the Abyssinia crisis revealed the anticolonial orientation of black internationalism. The IAFE captured the sentiments of many in the diaspora when it announced that it aimed "to assist by all means in their power, in the maintenance of the territorial integrity and the political independence of Abyssinia."[35] The IAFE worked with a range of groups that either had formed or turned their attention to Ethiopia. Anticolonial radicals in West Africa viewed Italian aggression against Ethiopia as evidence of the continued view among European powers that Africa existed merely to strengthen colonial empires and home markets. For many in West Africa, the situation "could only be interpreted in terms of racial strife, cynicism, and power politics," leaving many to conclude that a "war with Abyssinia is our war."[36] The WASU passed a resolution condemning Italian aggression and British collusion and established ties with the Paris-based Ethiopian Defense Committee and the African American–led, Washington, D.C.–based Ethiopian Research Council. African Americans writing to the Ethiopian Research Council volunteered for military service, and black people in the United States and the Caribbean boycotted Italian businesses. The Trinidadian Negro Welfare Social and Cultural Association declared that "only the united action of all Negroes and oppressed peoples can stop this horrible mass murder," and Trinidadian and South African maritime workers refused to service Italian ships. If some on the British Left remained committed to League of Nations sanctions, black workers were actively pursuing workers' sanctions.[37]

The IAFE claimed an unprecedented number of anticolonial radicals as members. Alongside James as chair were vice chairs Peter Milliard from British Guiana and T. Albert Marryshow from Grenada (who had headed the Grenada Worker's Association and was later one of the architects of the West Indies Federation); Kenyatta held the title of honorary secretary, and Ashwood was honorary treasurer. Others included George Moore, Samuel Wood, and Joseph B. Danquah from Gold Coast; Samuel Manning from Trinidad; and Mohammed Said from Somalia. Most of these figures had come to the IAFE through their contact with Padmore when he headed the ITUCNW.[38] Indeed, James credited this moment of metropolitan black anticolonialism to Padmore's extensive network of contacts and his spreading reputation among African and Caribbean colonial subjects of the British Crown.[39]

It would be hard to overstate IAFE's importance for understanding James's evolving critique of Caribbean modernity. Though he came to England concerned with West Indian self-government, he was now "meeting a lot of black people and African people in London."[40] And what must James have thought when, at Ashwood's restaurant and parlor, he met Africans such as Nigeria's Adetokunbo Adegboyega Ademola, who had studied law at Cambridge, and Joseph B. Danquah, WASU's first president, who studied philosophy and law? Had Ashwood challenged James's considerable hubris?

London was James's uniquely diasporic moment. His interactions with African students, intellectuals, and activists informed his political activities, as was evident in the name he gave his first organization, the International *African* Friends of Ethiopia. "Gradually," he later recalled of his time in London, "I began to gain in England a conception of black people which I didn't possess when I left the Caribbean."[41]

If the IAFE's work reflected James's evolving racial consciousness, it was Ashwood who thrust the group to the center of public discussions about Ethiopia. Headquartered at Ashwood's restaurant, Friends produced pamphlets calling on all peoples of African descent to pledge their support to Ethiopia. Ashwood soon emerged as the organization's central figure, speaking at London rallies of both the Labour Party and the Communist-controlled League against Imperialism and connecting the IAFE to various organizations. A tireless organizer, she assumed much of the responsibility for the group, and while James devoted his attention to struggles among British Socialists, she built the organization into an international network. Ashwood made sure that Friends had representatives at any demonstration on Ethiopia. And when Italy finally invaded in October 1935, she ratcheted up the work. With Padmore and Mohammed Said, and in conjunction with the New York–based Friends of Ethiopia, she planned a fund-raising trip to New York to buy medical supplies for Ethiopia. Although the trip never materialized, she continued to press for financial support, urging WASU to create the Ethiopian Defense Fund, which likely utilized contacts from IAFE's members to establish ties to various Ethiopian defense committees in West Africa.[42]

By 1936, when Padmore was back in London working with Ashwood in the IAFE, he found a well-organized, diverse black anticolonial movement. And his timing could not have been better. Ashwood's pace as an organizer and the daily demands of running two businesses began to take their toll. Initially Padmore worked alongside Ashwood, traveling throughout England speaking about Ethiopia. In Liverpool, they drew several hundred longtime residents from the maritime-based African community, who supported a resolution demanding that Britain allow arms shipments to Ethiopia and permit black people "to volunteer to fight in defence of Abyssinia's independence." However, Ashwood slowly receded into the background of the IAFE, and with James engrossed in the British Socialist movement, Padmore emerged as the glue holding the group together. James, by his own account, recalled that he and Padmore "were leaders of the black movement" but that he remained on the "outside as a Marxist, Trotskyist." Padmore regularly chaired IAFE meetings and worked tirelessly to build support among white progressives. The Friends' platform on Sundays at Hyde Park's Speaker's Corner and in Trafalgar Square soon included British members of Parliament Stafford Cripps and Ellen Wilkinson. Padmore also built ties to Indian radicals and, along with James, at one point discussed with Krishna Menon, founder of the India League, organizing a Colonial Marxist League.[43]

Padmore's expansive knowledge of Africa and the array of colonial radicals in London led many in Friends to begin thinking beyond Abyssinia. Ashwood believed, and James agreed, that the IAFE could easily broaden its focus to the entire continent. Thus, during the month of April 1937, Padmore held a series of meetings with Ashwood, James, Kenyatta, Makonnen, Akiki Nyabongo, the West African labor organizer I. T. A. Wallace-Johnson, Nigerian Louis Nwachukwu Mbanefo, and African American intellectual Ralph Bunche to discuss creating a new organization focused on Africa. All agreed that the new group should adopt a socialist program and publish a journal to disseminate information on African problems and the problems of all black people. On Thursday, April 29, this group announced that they would call their organization the International African Service Bureau. Succeeding the now defunct IAFE, they immediately began raising money to rent office space and publish a journal.[44]

The IASB captured the growing attention to coloniality among black activist–intellectuals in the metropol. In a gesture that implicitly rejected the prevailing claims of colonial regimes of knowledge production about Africa and the Caribbean as backward, the IASB adopted as its motto "Educate, Co-operate, Emancipate. Neutral in nothing affecting the African people." Moreover, the bureau refused the role of a diasporic vanguard that would direct colonial struggles, announcing instead that it would support "the demands of Africans and other colonial people for democratic rights, civil liberties and self-determination" and represent "progressive and enlightened public opinion among Africans and peoples of African descent." In one of its earliest press releases, the IASB declared that one of the greatest hindrances to progress remained "the lack of direct . . . contact between the colonial peoples, the British public and interested friends, and peoples of African descent." An early pamphlet announced that the bureau would work with "English friends and subject races" to help "enlighten public opinion." Equally important, it would provide a "link between the Africans at home (in Africa) and the Africans abroad" through the transmission of messages, information, and views "from one to another." For IASB radicals, the most suggestive approach entailed pursuing "a theory of colonial emancipation" that would chart a course for proletarian revolution outside the realms of organized Marxism. It would thus balance theorizing imperialism and colonial struggle with facilitating intercolonial exchanges and engagements.[45]

The IASB exhibited an ideological ecumenicalism and organizational pragmatism that served it well in courting the support of white leftists and progressives. The labor organizer and Sierra Leonean Communist I. T. A. Wallace-Johnson used his connections to the League against Imperialism's British Section to secure the IASB office space, and much of the group's early financial support came from the Communist Party of Great Britain, though British Communists hardly appreciated the bureau's political independence. James, Padmore, and other bureau members openly criticized the Communist Party as well as Soviet Russia's policies under Stalin, which, along with several other conflicts, led the Communist Party to end its support by 1938.[46] Rather than fall in line behind Stalin or party dogma, Padmore turned to the Independent Labour Party (ILP), moving the bureau's offices into an ILP building in west London. He grew steadily closer to the ILP, lecturing regularly at its summer school in Glasgow and writing articles for the *New Leader* praising the ILP's "correct theoretical approach on . . . imperialist war and colonies." Still, Padmore maintained his and the IASB's independence. When he decided to put out a new monthly journal, *International African Opinion,* and convinced the ILP to help finance it, he made C. L. R. James its editor—a brazen show of independence given that the ILP had expelled James in 1935.[47]

Work in the IASB brought James back into the center of black anticolonial struggles in London, and his editorial tenure over *International African Opinion* revealed a decided focus on Africa—quite apart from his earlier preoccupation with West Indian self-government. James worked to shape *Opinion* into "the mouthpiece of the black workers and peasants," presenting it as a vehicle for sharing information and coordinating action in Africa and throughout the diaspora. Mirroring the *Negro Worker*'s format under Padmore, *Opinion* did not pose as a "literary journal or giver of advice from the mountain-tops" of the colonial metropole but rather sought to "stimulate the growing consciousness of the blacks" by drawing "from the black masses the lessons of the profound experiences that they accumulate in their daily toil" and helping them mobilize "whatever assistance there is to be found in Europe for the cause of African emancipation." *Opinion* would serve as "a living weapon in the struggle, a reflection of the everyday demands of the masses as they fight their way to the larger goal." With articles on Ethiopia and labor activities in West Africa and the Caribbean, letters from workers in the colonies, and coverage of various IASB activities, *Opinion* quickly gained the attention of colonial authorities. After only two issues, the Colonial Office placed *Opinion* on its list of periodicals banned from the colonies.[48] James appeared to have found his form.

C. L. R. JAMES AND AN ANTICOLONIAL MARXISM

As C. L. R. James surveyed the political field of 1930s London, he discussed with British publisher Frederic Warburg the need for "books that were Marxist but not CP."[49] Warburg agreed and provided James the necessary support to write *World Revolution.* James envisioned a history that explained how "Moscow [had] shifted from the '*revolutionary*' policy" of self-determination and abandoned proletarian struggle and, most importantly for James, Abyssinia. At the same time, he was carrying out research for his magisterial work, *The Black Jacobins. World Revolution* thus constituted a detour—of sorts.

With *World Revolution,* James proposed a survey of the Comintern's rise and "collapse as a revolutionary force," claiming that "the ideas on which the book are based are the fundamental ideas of Marxism," where James sought to explain "the present crisis in world affairs." That crisis involved the Soviet Union's Popular Front policy, which urged workers to align with their national bourgeoisie to defend Russia against German fascism and led it to abandon Abyssinia. He assailed the Comintern's failed commitment to revolution and noted of Abyssinia, toward the end of the penultimate chapter, "The Revolution Abandoned," that "thoughtful revolutionaries . . . realise how the [Third] International, following Stalin, missed the greatest opportunity in years of at best striking a powerful blow against the colonial policy of imperialism, and at worst rallying round itself the vanguard of the working-class movement." James argued that the Comintern "from the first moment could have pointed out that nothing but working-class action could have saved Abyssinia," which he believed would have "driven home nail after nail into the coffin of the League" of Nations.[50] It was not for literary effect or simply a rhetorical gesture that James located a major part of Stalin's abandonment of the world proletariat in the Comintern's failure to seize on Abyssinia as a conflict demanding proletarian struggle.

James engaged in what political theorist Anthony Bogues describes as a black heretical practice of engaging Western radical thought yet critiquing it on encountering its limits around race and colonialism. A committed Socialist, James saw his work serving black anticolonial politics and the Trotskyist struggle against Stalinism, though he rejected any hint of disentangling the two. Years later, when told that his old acquaintance Reginald Reynolds had once complained that he had turned his back "on the problems of his own people to follow the barren cult of Trotskyism," James replied curtly, "It was not narrow confines. *The Black Jacobins* was not conceived within narrow confines, and neither was . . . *The History of Negro Revolt,* which was not limited to a Trotskyist position."[51] Rather, James had been rethinking Marxism precisely through his growing attention to coloniality. His critique of the Comintern hinged on Moscow's failure to recognize the potential for proletarian revolution represented by Abyssinia—a theoretical horizon that lay beyond an imagination fixated on the European proletariat and the Western nation-state.

In James's intellectual work, *World Revolution* is of a piece with *The Black Jacobins* and his larger intellectual output of the time, a robust period of intellectual activism that announced a burgeoning critique of modernity and enlightenment thought. Taken together in the context of the IASB, and of 1930s black anticolonial London more generally, *World Revolution* and *The Black Jacobins* reflect the moment and milieu in which James and Padmore began to argue that Africa was the launching pad for world revolution. In Trinidad, James had grown tired of hearing about Caribbean backwardness and inferiority and decided he would "write a book which showed the West Indians as something else." But ironically, by the time he started to write *The Black Jacobins,* he had "reached the conclusion that the center of the Black revolution was Africa, not the Caribbean."[52] Allusions to this realization suffuse the text and are particularly evident in the final two pages of the 1938 edition. Like the French rulers who would have scoffed at the idea of Saint Domingue slaves emancipating themselves, James was convinced that British colonial officials would never accept that their black subjects could lead successful revolutions. But "the blacks of Africa," James warned, "are more advanced, nearer ready than were the slaves of San Domingo."[53]

James was here thinking through coloniality, not the modernity of Western imperialism or Marxism. Taking this heretical orientation in *The Black Jacobins,* rather than following Marxism's stagist approach to history and characterizing slavery as a precapitalist holdover, and thus slaves as non- or preproletarian, James called the Saint-Domingue slaves "working and living together in gangs of hundreds on the huge sugar-factories closer to a modern proletariat than any group of workers in existence at the time." He considered the Haitian revolution "a thoroughly prepared and organised mass movement" in which "Voodoo was the medium of the conspiracy. . . . The slaves travelled miles to sing and dance and practise the rites and talk . . . and make their plans."[54] James thus entered into what literary theorist Walter Mignolo calls Marxism's colonial fracture, the gap or lack in Karl Marx's work representing his failure to take up "the colonial mechanism of power underlying the system he critique[d]."[55] Indeed, the elegance of James's prose makes it easy to miss the double critique in which he is engaged. On one hand, he is theorizing Marxism beyond its initial articulations to fully explore the complexities of slavery. James's treatment of slavery as a modern capitalist institution, and his casting the Saint Domingue slaves as the most modern proletariat of the late eighteenth century, insists on the centrality of race to capitalism and, in turn, antiracist and anticolonial struggle to socialism. Still, as Bogues points out, James framed the Haitian revolution through Marxism's modernist lens and therein missed that "there was a different African worldview which was central to their revolutionary upsurge."[56] But in highlighting how slave rebellion undercut a major pillar of modern European empire, and in pointing to slave cultural and religious practices as essential to their revolutionary consciousness, identifying Voodoo as the medium of the conspiracy, James was invoking, even if incompletely, the coloniality (what one might call the decolonial orientation) of that uprising and gesturing at the possibility of understanding it in terms other than modernity.[57]

London's diasporic, African and Caribbean community fostered the initial offerings in what one might call James's decolonial thought. As James recalled in a series of lectures in the 1970s in the United States, London was where he first read Marx, the circumstances requiring that he "thoroughly master . . . Marxism" to write *World Revolution*. "At the same time," he was also "meeting a lot of black people and African people in London," who impressed him immensely. "I began to see these Africans around me," Africans one might describe as modern Negroes—sharply dressed, studying at university, well read in the Western canon. *The Black Jacobins* thus was no accident: "it didn't just fall from a tree." James "had in mind writing about the San Domingo Revolution as the preparation for the revolution that George Padmore and all of us were interested in, that is, the revolution in Africa."[58]

While James and Padmore worked to reshape Marxism, and while Marxism was reshaping how James viewed history, London's diasporic community and anticolonial ferment helped James abandon notions of African backwardness and question the value of Caribbean modernity. But James was also pointing out the coloniality of knowledge dominating the Caribbean. This was apparent in his discussion of Toussaint Louverture's failures in Haiti. If Toussaint's successor, Jean-Jacques Dessalines, "could see so clearly and simply" the path to full emancipation where Toussaint could not, "it was because the ties that bound this uneducated soldier [Dessalines] to French civilisation were of the slenderest." For Toussaint, whom James situated within the train of European Enlightenment thought, his "failure was the failure of enlightenment, not of darkness." Similarly, the failing of the Caribbean was its modernity. Caribbeans "were and had always been Western-educated," he noted in the 1963 appendix to *The Black Jacobins*. For those in the Caribbean, James believed "the first step to freedom was to go abroad." The second, far more complex step involved getting "clear from [their] minds the stigma that anything African was inherently inferior and degraded. The road to West Indian national identity lay through Africa."[59] The insistence on racial consciousness in Caribbean colonial liberation reflected an abiding belief in the decisive role that Africa would play in the coming global upheavals, and coloniality as a site of struggle.

CONCLUSION

Padmore and Ashwood remained key figures in London black anticolonial politics, both playing central roles in the 1945 Fifth Pan-African Congress held in Manchester, England. James would leave London at the end of 1938 for a brief tour of the United States before ultimately meeting Leon Trotsky in Mexico City. It was there that James proposed the IASB as a model for a new, global organization focused on "full economic, political, and social rights for all Negroes," national independence for African and Caribbean colonies, opposition to imperialist war, and the organization of black workers and peasants for their own liberation.[60] Although this never materialized, what is important to point out is that the model James proposed, one reflecting the possibilities that he, Padmore, and Ashwood saw in London, served as a guide for his work on and thinking about black liberation and proletarian revolution over the next several decades.

London in the 1930s is therefore suggestive for rethinking the New Negro movement beyond Harlem and the United States, its attendant civil rights logic, and the concern with images of a modern Negro. To be sure, black anticolonial activists in the colonial metropole were equally concerned to substantiate their modernity in calling for an end to colonial rule. Yet in London, black activist–intellectuals also offered a robust and radical critique of modernity, which would not occur in the United States for some time. It is thus in the international nodes of the New Negro that we find challenges to the modes of governance, nation-state formation, and progress that were critical elements in thinking about a black modernity.

C. L. R. James took from the intradiasporic conflicts between Caribbeans and Africans in London a new challenge to the very colonialist logic that parceled self-rule based on the historical proximity of non-Western peoples to the "developed" West. From the parliamentarian radical convinced of West Indian modernity to the radical black internationalist who saw the Caribbean's modernity as a fatal flaw, James carried this view into his political and cultural work and writing the remainder of his life. If the Caribbean's failing was one of modernity, a failure of enlightenment, not darkness, it would be in black cultural practices, such as calypso, Caribbean cricket, or Rastafari, that he would find inspiration for imagining a future beyond the nation-state and envisioning forms of governance beyond prevailing notions of representative democracy.[61] For James, the masses offered a model for heretical thinking about ways to draw on received knowledges, modern forms, and Western reason and find what was born of the colonial context, and develop that into a distinctively new form. One even sees in James's time in London, in his intellectual work, the basis for what later became his conflict with Trinidad and Tobago's first prime minister, Eric Williams (a former student of James). His sense of the postcolonial failures of the Caribbean in the 1960s grew out of a process of rethinking modernity that had begun for James in the International African Friends of Ethiopia and later the International African Service Bureau. That diasporic moment is testament to the capaciousness of the New Negro experience for a global political vision and critique to which scholars are just now turning their attention.

NOTES

1   J. M. Kenyatta, "Hands off Abyssinia," *Labour Monthly,* September 1935, 532.

2   *Daily Herald,* August 26, 1935, 3; Martin, *Amy Ashwood Garvey,* 142–44, 150; Adi, *West Africans in Britain,* 68. Wilsonian self-determination references U.S. president Woodrow Wilson's notion of self-determination that, during World War I and after, with the founding of the League of Nations, conceptualized independence for European nations.

3   James, *Beyond a Boundary,* 111.

4   James, *Life of Captain Cipriani,* 16; Høgsbjerg, "A Thorn in the Side of Great Britain," 27.

5   James, *Black Jacobins,* vii.

6   Mignolo, "Introduction: Coloniality of Power," 162; Mignolo, *Local Histories/Global Designs,* 69; Dussel, "Eurocentrism and Modernity," 66; Quijano, "Coloniality of Power." Equally important to my thinking here is the discussion of black heretical and prophetic practices and thought in Bogues, *Black Heretics, Black Prophets.*

7   Locke, *The New Negro,* 14.

8   W. E. B. Du Bois, "The Negro Mind Reaches Out," in ibid., 411.

9   Spiegler, "Aspects of Nationalist Thought," 115, 120; James, "Notes on the Life of George Padmore," 31a–32.

10 Although it is generally assumed that James had an average middle-class background, interviews with family members reveal that the family was of rather elite standing in terms of colonial black Trinidadian social circles. Though not possessing the money of white colonial elites, they nonetheless possessed an expansive library (rare for colonials of any racial or class standing at the turn of the twentieth century), dressed formally for dinner, and had servants; James's father, a headmaster, had enough standing that James's mother was a woman of leisure, as was his sister Olive James. Minkah Makalani, interview with Erica James and Henry James, June 11, 2012, Brooklyn, New York.

11 I am drawing here on Wall's discussion of how prevailing periodization schemes excluded women from the New Negro renaissance (see *Women of the Harlem Renaissance*) and on Mitchell's history of black uplift politics in Liberia and the Philippines (see *Righteous Propagation*).

12 On the belief that black involvement in empire helped redeem Africa, see Mitchell, *Righteous Propagation,* 51–75; Blyden, *West Indians.*

13 See Makonnen, *Pan-Africanism from Within,* 147.

14 The African American Communist James Ford initially headed the ITUCNW.

15 *International Negro Workers' Review,* January 1931, 3.

16 Adi, "Pan-Africanism and Communism," 249; Weiss, *Road to Hamburg,* 124–25; *The International Negro Workers' Review,* January 1931 and February 1931; mass mailing addressed to Dear Friend, n.d., Crusader News Agency letterhead, LP/ID/CI/36/39ii, Labour Party Papers, Labour History Archive and Study Center, Manchester, England (hereinafter Labour Party Papers).

17   James, "Notes on the Life of George Padmore," 290.

18   Russian State Archive of Socio-political History (RGASPI) 538/1/12/77–78. RGASPI materials found at Library of Congress, Manuscript Reading Room, and European Reading Room, International Committee for the Computerization of the Comintern Archive Project, Washington, D.C. Citations follow the Russian archival organizational structure, which gives *fond* (collection), *opis* (index), *delo* (file), and *listok* (page).

19   George Padmore, "Nationalist Movement in West Indies," *Negro Worker,* November–December 1932, 6–7; Padmore, "Negro Toilers Speak at the World Congress of ILD," *Negro Worker,* February–March 1933, 4.

20   RGASPI 534/3/754/21; RGASPI 534/3/754/20; Hooker, *Black Revolutionary,* 24; Turner, *Caribbean Crusaders,* 195; Pennybacker, *From Scottsboro to Munich,* 72.

21   George Padmore, "Au Revoir," *Negro Worker,* August–September 1933, 18; George Padmore to Cyrill Ollivierre, July 28, 1934, George Padmore Letters, Schomburg Center for Research in Black Culture, Manuscript, Archives, and Rare Books Division, New York Public Library; Turner, *Caribbean Crusaders,* 213.

22   Quote in Hooker, *Black Revolutionary,* 31.

23   James, *At the Rendezvous,* 254.

24   Richardson et al., *C. L. R. James*; C. L. R. James, "Is This Worth War?" *New Leader,* October 4, 1935, 5; Alexander, *International Trotskyism,* 442–43; Upham, "History of British Trotskyism."

25   Trotskyism was an organized international Marxist movement, the Fourth International, led by exiled Bolshevik Leon Trotsky, and was presented as an alternative to the Soviet-led Communist (Third) International. While Trotskyism remained marginal in U.S. left political culture, in Britain, it formed a major leftist movement. For a good, if polemical, account of British Trotskyism, see Upham, "History of British Trotskyism."

26   Richardson, *C. L. R. James*; Archer, "C. L. R. James and Trotskyism in Britain," 61–63.

27   "Conference Report," *The Keys,* July 1933, 3–8; "'*The Keys*' Disclose," ibid., 9; Killingray, "To Do Something for the Race," 62–63; Bush, *Imperialism,* 220; Ralph Bunche Diary, April 12, 1937, box 279, folder 1, Ralph J. Bunche Papers, Department of Special Collections, Charles E. Young Library, University of California at Los Angeles (hereinafter Bunche Diary).

28   *The Keys,* December 1936, 16, as quoted in Matera, "Black Internationalism," 160–61.

29   Martin, *Amy Ashwood Garvey,* 136–41; Adi and Sherwood, *Pan-African History,* 69–70.

30   Hubert Henry Harrison Diary, March 5, 1925, box 6, folder 2, Rare Book and Manuscript Library, Columbia University, New York.

31   Makonnen, *Pan-Africanism from Within,* 130.

32   James, as quoted in Martin, *Amy Ashwood Garvey,* 140–42, 144.

33   *Sunday Express,* as quoted in Martin, *Amy Ashwood Garvey,* 140.

34   Ibid., 141; James, "Black Intellectuals," 160; Asante, *Pan-African Protest,* 45.

Originally the group was called the International African Friends of Abyssinia. Padmore, *Pan-Africanism or Communism?*, 144–45; Bush, *Imperialism*, 222; Martin, *Amy Ashwood Garvey*, 141.

35 Kenyatta, "Hands off Abyssinia," 532.

36 Langley, *Pan-Africanism*, 326–37.

37 Adi, *West Africans in Britain*, 68–69; Padmore, *Pan-Africanism or Communism?*, 144–45; Edwards, *Practice of Diaspora*, 298; Bush, *Imperialism*, 222–23; *Daily Herald*, September 2, 1935, 7; Kelley, *Race Rebels*, 123–58. The IAFE also worked with white Ethiopian support groups, including the Abyssinian Association, and Sylvia Pankhurst's *New Times and Ethiopian News*. Harris, *African-American Reactions*, 26, 25–28.

38 Asante, "Neglected Aspects," 34–35; Rohdie, "Gold Coast Aborigines," 397–402.

39 MacKenzie, "Radical Pan-Africanism," 72.

40 James, "Lectures on *The Black Jacobins*," 69.

41 Ibid., 71, 72.

42 Martin, *Amy Ashwood Garvey*, 144–45; Harris, *African-American Reactions*, 65–66; Adi, *West Africans in Britain*, 68; Adi and Sherwood, *Pan-African History*, 71.

43 Hooker, *Black Revolutionary*, 45–47; Owen, *British Left and India*, 203–39; Surveillance Report, June 29, 1938, KV 2/1824, 28A, Public Records Office, National Archives, Kew Gardens, London Colonial Office Metropolitan Police; Metropolitan Police Report, September 12, 1938, KV 2/1824, 34A, National Archives of the UK, Kew, Surrey, England (hereinafter TNA).

44 Bunche Diary, April 5, 12, 18, 23, 24, 29, 1937; Mbinga Koinange to Ralph Bunche, April 23, 1937, box 10b, folder 14, Ralph J. Bunche Papers, General Correspondences, Schomburg Center for Research in Black Culture, Manuscript, Archives, and Rare Books Division, New York Public Library (hereinafter Bunche Correspondences); Asante, *Pan-African Protest*, 206; Matera, "Black Internationalism," 159.

45 International African Service Bureau Press Release, n.d., and "The International African Service Bureau for the Defense of Africans and Peoples of African Descent," pamphlet, both in box 10b, folder 13, Bunche Correspondences; "Our Policy," *African Sentinel*, October–November 1937, 1; Edwards, *Practice of Diaspora*, 303.

46 M. M. Milne-Thomson to R. J. D. Lamont, May 8, 1938, CO 323/1610/2, 29, TNA; D. J. Jardine to O. G. R. Williams, May 12, 1938, CO 323/1610/2, 31, TNA; Surveillance Report, June 8, 1938, KV 2/1824, 24A, TNA.

47 George Padmore, "Fascism in the Colonies," *Controversy*, February 1938; George Padmore, "Hands Off the Colonies!," *New Leader*, February 25, 1938, 5; Hooker, *Black Revolutionary*, 46; E. B. Boya to R. H. Drayton, n.d., CO 323/1610/2, 43, TNA.

48 "Editorial," *International African Opinion*, July 1938, 2–3; H. R. Oke to Malcolm MacDonald, July 1, 1938, and Colonial Sir Vernon Keel to F. J. Howard, September 1938, TA: PRO CO 323/1610/2, 51, 55.

49 Richardson et al., *C. L. R. James*; Reynolds, *My Life and Crimes*, 116, 141; Warburg, *Occupation for Gentlemen*, 185, 211.

50 James, *World Revolution*, 386–89.

51 MacKenzie, "Radical Pan-Africanism," 70.

52 Ibid.

53 Bogues, *Black Heretics, Black Prophets*; James, *Black Jacobins*, 376–77.

54 James, *Black Jacobins*, 85–86.

55 Mignolo, "Delinking," 483.

56 See Bogues, *Black Heretics, Black Prophets*, 80–81.

57 On the decolonial project, see Maldonado-Torres, "Enrique Dussel's Liberation Thought," 17, 18; Mignolo, *Darker Side of Western Modernity*, chapter 1.

58 James, "Lectures on *The Black Jacobins*," 69, 71, 72.

59 James, *Black Jacobins*, 197–98, 239–40, 288, 402.

60 C. L. R. James to unknown, February 28, 1939, Leon Trotsky Exile Papers (MS Russ 13.1), Series I:2069, Houghton Library, Harvard University.

61 James, *At the Rendezvous*, 163–65.

BIBLIOGRAPHY

Adi, Hakim. "Pan-Africanism and Communism: The Comintern, the 'Negro Question,' and the First International Conference of Negro Workers, Hamburg 1930." *African and Black Diaspora Journal: An International Journal* 1, no. 2 (2008): 237–54.

———. *West Africans in Britain, 1900–1960: Nationalism, Pan-Africanism, and Communism*. London: Lawrence and Wishart, 1998.

Adi, Hakim, and Marika Sherwood. *Pan-African History: Political Figures from Africa and the Diaspora since 1787*. London: Routledge, 2003.

Alexander, Robert Jackson. *International Trotskyism, 1929–1985: A Documented Analysis of the Movement*. Durham, N.C.: Duke University Press, 1991.

Archer, John. "C. L. R. James and Trotskyism in Britain: 1934–1938." *Revolutionary History* 6, nos. 2/3 (1996): 58–73.

Asante, S. K. B. "The Neglected Aspects of the Activities of the Gold Coast Aborigines Rights Protection Society." *Phylon* 36, no. 1 (1975): 32–45.

———. *Pan-African Protest: West Africa and the Italo-Ethiopian Crisis, 1934–1941*. London: Longman, 1977.

Blyden, Nemata Amelia. *West Indians in West Africa, 1808–1880: The African Diaspora in Reverse*. Rochester, N.Y.: University of Rochester Press, 2000.

Bogues, Anthony. *Black Heretics, Black Prophets: Radical Political Intellectuals*. New York: Routledge, 2003.

Bunche Papers. General Correspondences. Schomburg Center for Research in Black Culture, Manuscript, Archives, and Rare Books Division, New York Public Library.

Bush, Barbara. *Imperialism, Race, and Resistance: Africa and Britain, 1919–1945*. London: Routledge, 1999.

Edwards, Brent Hayes. *The Practice of Diaspora: Literature, Translation, and the Rise of Black Internationalism*. Cambridge, Mass.: Harvard University Press, 2003.

George Padmore Letters. Schomburg Center for Research in Black Culture, Manuscript, Archives, and Rare Books Division. New York Public Library.

Harris, Joseph E. *African-American Reactions to War in Ethiopia, 1936–1941*. Baton Rouge: Louisiana State University Press, 1994.

Høgsbjerg, Christian. "'A Thorn in the Side of Great Britain': C. L. R. James and the Caribbean Labour Rebellions of the 1930s." *Small Axe* 35 (2011): 24–42.

Hooker, James R. *Black Revolutionary: George Padmore's Path from Communism to Pan-Africanism*. New York: Praeger, 1967.

Hubert Henry Harrison Diary. Rare Book and Manuscript Library, Columbia University, New York.

James, C. L. R. *At the Rendezvous of Victory*. London: Allison and Busby, 1984.

———. *Beyond a Boundary*. 1963. Reprint, Durham, N.C.: Duke University Press, 1993.

———. "Black Intellectuals in Britain." In *Colour, Culture, and Consciousness: Immigrant Intellectuals in Britain*, edited by Bhikhu Parekh, 154–63. London: Allen and Unwin, 1974.

———. *The Black Jacobins: Toussaint L'Ouverture and the San Domingo Revolution*. New York: Vintage, 1989.

———. *The Case for West Indian Self-Government*. London: Hogarth Press, 1933.

———. "Lectures on *The Black Jacobins*." *Small Axe* 8 (2000): 65–112.

———. *The Life of Captain Cipriani: An Account of British Government in the West Indies*. Nelson, U.K.: Coulton, 1932.

———. "Notes on the Life of George Padmore." Typescript on Microfilm, Schomburg Center for Research in Black Culture, New York.

———. *World Revolution, 1917–1936: The Rise and Fall of the Communist International*. 1937. Reprint, Atlantic Highlands, N.J.: Humanities, 1993.

Kelley, Robin D. G. *Race Rebels: Culture, Politics, and the Black Working Class*. New York: Free Press, 1996.

Killingray, David. "'To Do Something for the Race': Harold Moody and the League of Coloured Peoples." In *West Indian Intellectuals in Britain*, edited by Bill Schwarz, 51–70. Manchester, U.K.: Manchester University Press, 2003.

Labour Party Papers. Labour History Archive and Study Center. Manchester, England.

Langley, J. Ayodele. *Pan-Africanism and Nationalism in West Africa: A Study in Ideology and Social Classes*. Oxford: Clarendon Press, 1973.

Leon Trotsky Exile Papers. Houghton Library, Harvard University.

Locke, Alain, ed. *The New Negro*. 1925. Reprint, New York: Touchstone, 1997.

Mackenzie, Alan J. "Radical Pan-Africanism in the 1930s: A Discussion with C. L. R. James." *Radical History Review* 24 (1980): 68–75.

Makonnen, T. Ras. *Pan-Africanism from Within*. London: Oxford University Press, 1973.

Maldonado-Torres, Nelson. "Enrique Dussel's Liberation Thought in the Decolonial Turn." *Transmodernity* 1, no. 1 (2011): 1–30.

Martin, Tony. *Amy Ashwood Garvey: Pan-Africanist, Feminist, and Mrs. Marcus Garvey no. 1; or, A Tale of Two Amies*. Dover, Mass.: Majority, 2007.

Matera, Marc. "Black Internationalism and African and Caribbean Intellectuals in London, 1919–1950." PhD diss., Rutgers University, 2008.

Mignolo, Walter D. *The Darker Side of Western Modernity: Global Futures, Decolonial Options*. Durham, N.C.: Duke University Press, 2011.

———. "Delinking: The Rhetoric of Modernity, the Logic of Coloniality, and the Grammar of De-coloniality." *Cultural Studies* 21, nos. 2–3 (2007): 449–514

———. "Introduction: Coloniality of Power and De-colonial Thinking." *Cultural Studies* 21, nos. 2–3 (2007): 155–67.

———. *Local Histories/Global Designs: Coloniality, Subaltern Knowledges, and Border Thinking*. Princeton, N.J.: Princeton University Press, 2000.

Mitchell, Michelle. *Righteous Propagation: African Americans and the Politics of Racial Destiny after Reconstruction*. Chapel Hill: University of North Carolina Press, 2004.

National Archives of the UK, Kew, Surrey, England.

Owen, Nicholas. *The British Left and India: Metropolitan Anti-imperialism, 1885–1947*. Oxford: Oxford University Press, 2007.

Padmore, George. *Pan-Africanism or Communism? The Coming Struggle for Africa*. 1956. Reprint, New York: Doubleday, 1971.

Pennybacker, Susan. *From Scottsboro to Munich: Race and Political Culture in 1930s Britain*. Princeton, N.J.: Princeton University Press, 2010.

Quijano, Aníbal. "Coloniality of Power, Eurocentrism, and Latin America." *Napantla: Views from South* 1, no. 3 (2000): 533–80.

Ralph J. Bunche Papers. Department of Special Collections. Charles E. Young Library, University of California at Los Angeles.

Reynolds, Reginald. *My Life and Crimes*. London: Jerrolds, 1956.

Richardson, Al, Clarence Chrysostom, and Anna Grimshaw. *C. L. R. James and British Trotskyism: An Interview with C. L. R. James*. June 8 and November 16, 1986, South London. http://workersrepublic.org/Pages/Ireland/Trotskyism/clrjames.html.

Rohdie, Samuel. "The Gold Coast Aborigines Abroad." *Journal of African History* 6, no. 3 (1965): 389–411.

Spiegler, J. S. "Aspects of Nationalist Thought among French-Speaking West Africans, 1921–1939." PhD diss., Nuffield College, Oxford University, 1968.

Turner, Joyce Moore. *Caribbean Crusaders and the Harlem Renaissance*. Urbana: University of Illinois Press, 2005.

Upham, Martin Richard. "The History of British Trotskyism to 1949." PhD diss., University of Hull, 1980. http://www.socialist.net/the-history-of-british-trotskyism-to-1949-part-1.htm.

Wall, Cheryl A. *Women of the Harlem Renaissance*. Bloomington: Indiana University Press, 1995.

Warburg, Frederic. *An Occupation for Gentlemen*. 1959. Reprint, Boston: Houghton Mifflin, 1960.

Weiss, Holger. *The Road to Hamburg and Beyond: African American Agency and the Making of a Radical African Atlantic, 1922–1930, Part Three*. Comintern Working Paper 18. https://www.abo.fi/student/media/7957/cowopa18weiss.pdf.

II

NEW (NEGRO) FRONTIERS

4

The New Negro's Brown Brother: Black American and Filipino Boxers and the "Rising Tide of Color"

THERESA RUNSTEDTLER

In November 1899, the Eleventh U.S. Cavalry reportedly found a pair of boxing gloves made by Sol Levinson of San Francisco abandoned in the Luzon village of San Mateo. According to the apocryphal story, Filipino prisoners of war claimed that a renegade soldier of the African American Twenty-Fourth Infantry had not only supplied them with boxing gloves but had even given them fighting lessons.[1] Many of the first boxers on the islands were black Americans because the all-black Ninth and Tenth U.S. Cavalry, the Twenty-Fourth and Twenty-Fifth U.S. Infantry, and the Forty-Eighth and Forty-Ninth U.S. Volunteer Infantry composed a sizeable proportion of the U.S. forces from 1899 to 1902. Decades later, in the 1930s, a photographer captured an image of Jack Johnson, the first black world heavyweight champion (1908–15), giving pointers to the Philippine fighter "Young Tommy" (also known as Fernando Opao) in a California gym[2] (Figure 4.1). Over the years, the boxing ring had emerged as an important cultural "contact zone" in which black Americans and Filipinos not only learned of each other's plight but also built a sense of racial solidarity.[3]

Suggestive rather than exhaustive, this essay uses the sport of boxing as a vector through which to trace the underlying connections between the New Negro renaissance and the development of Filipino consciousness from the Spanish–American War to the 1930s. I argue that the rise of the New Negro was just one part of a much wider political current that the white American political scientist Lothrop Stoddard once lamentingly coined "the rising tide of color." Writing in 1920, Stoddard warned that in the wake of the Great War, the darker races, "long restive under white political domination," were developing "a common solidarity of feeling against the dominant white man." Yet this "rising tide of color" was more than just a consequence of the "frightful weakening of the white world during the war."[4] It also grew out of a tenacious tradition of countercultural exchange between subaltern peoples—one ironically aided and accelerated by the expansion

FIGURE 4.1. Former world heavyweight champion Jack Johnson giving pointers to Philippine fighter Fernando Opao ("Young Tommy"), circa 1930s. Reproduced from the original held by the Department of Special Collections of the Hesburgh Libraries of the University of Notre Dame.

of Western imperialism and capitalism in the late nineteenth and early twentieth centuries. Even though Stoddard's alarmist assertions were grounded in the pseudoscience of eugenics (and ultimately led him to advocate for the separation of the races), he was right in characterizing this growing colored consciousness as a collective challenge "against white world-supremacy."

Viewing the New Negro within the context of global cultural flows reveals that the so-called Harlem Renaissance was by no means just an isolated, local phenomenon. Instead, the New Negro movement and other examples of anticolonial agitation in the early twentieth century came together in the undercurrents and eddies of Western imperial military and political power, commerce, and culture. While black studies scholars have begun to emphasize the transnational, anticolonial, and radical leftist character of New Negro politics during the interwar years, many remain focused on the Atlantic World.[5] However, even a cursory look at the transpacific travels of African Americans along the burgeoning routes of U.S. empire suggests that we need to expand our geographic scope and imagination of the black renaissance.[6] Although historian Michelle Mitchell contends that some black elites eagerly joined the United States' project of "benevolent assimilation" in the Philippines as a means to reinforce their own racial manhood, many of the black soldiers and boxers who traveled to the archipelago during the Spanish–American and Philippine–American wars and subsequent U.S. occupation were troubled by their nation's imperialist designs.[7] Much like Frank Guridy demonstrates in his study of early-twentieth-century African American and Afro-Cuban encounters, regardless of their opinions on U.S. expansion, black Americans and Filipinos from across class and ideological lines "often chose to use the imperial structure toward their own ends," as the everyday interactions of empire building ironically opened up subversive spaces for transnational racial affiliation.[8] The New Negro was as much a product of these multiple and often contradictory lines of cross-national connection as it was the brainchild of black artists and intellectuals based in the United States.

Indeed, the popular movements that composed the so-called "rising tide of color" against white world supremacy developed as much from below as from above in the quotidian activities of regular people of color across the globe. The rank and file of these movements shared a special interest in reconfiguring colored subjectivity on their own terms, not just in the traditional Renaissance media of literature or the high arts but in the realm of popular culture, and boxing in particular. As a sport that involved hand-to-hand combat between two male competitors, boxing resonated with the "rising tide's" growing sense of racial militancy—a militancy that remained decidedly masculine in its orientation and focused on the public recuperation of colored manhood. Building on the spirit of C. L. R. James's *Beyond a Boundary,* in which he argues that cricket had already introduced him to the subtleties of race, class, and colonialism in Trinidad long before he became overtly "political," I argue that pugilism helped lay the imaginative groundwork for the budding race-based and anticolonial movements of the 1920s and 1930s.[9]

Although U.S. servicemen initially brought the sport to the Philippines as a mode of military and colonial discipline, boxing soon provided a forum for countercultural resistance and colored collaboration. Moments of solidarity coalesced as Filipino insurgents learned the manly art of pugilism from black soldiers in the midst of the Philippine–American War, as Filipino nationalists embraced the black heavyweight Jack Johnson's 1910 triumph over the white American Jim Jeffries as their own, and as the 1920s Filipino flyweight Francisco "Pancho Villa" Guilledo transgressed racial boundaries during his short but successful run in the United States. Through the unlikely vector of boxing, the masculine politics of the New Negro and his Brown Brother converged, as they bolstered each other in their fight against white supremacy.

When Admiral George Dewey entered Manila Bay aboard the USS *Olympia* in 1898, boxing followed the flows of U.S. empire. Many of Dewey's men were fans of the former white world champion John L. Sullivan, and during the Philippine–American War and U.S. occupation, many soldiers, both white and black, continued to carry boxing gloves with them. Faced with troubling rates of desertion (especially among African Americans), suicide, venereal disease, and substance abuse among the troops, U.S. military officials encouraged boxing to prevent servicemen from degenerating and "going native" in the tropics. Boxers in training were supposed to avoid tobacco, alcohol, and sexual activity to help fortify their bodies for battle.[10] In the eyes of many U.S. officials, pugilism and the practice of imperialism went hand in hand.

However, the apocryphal tale of the black American deserter providing Filipino POWs with boxing gloves and fighting lessons not only poses an alternative story of pugilism in the archipelago but points to the subversive camaraderie and racial consciousness shared by people of color on both sides of the conflict. Hinting at this subterranean connection, Filipino boxing trainer Johnny Samson later maintained that "when American soldiers were sent to the Islands to hoist the Stars and Stripes there, they took with them a few pairs of boxing gloves just for the benefit of their health, without dreaming those same gloves would take active part in shaping the history of the Philippines."[11] As Samson recalled, "Our first teachers in English, boxing or anything else, were American soldiers. . . . In its early stage, boxing was taught and learned privately due to the rather suspicious attitude of the natives at that time. American instructors of the art of self-defense were satisfied to give domicile service to those who were not so superstitious."[12] Although it is unclear to which American soldiers (white and/or black) Samson was referring, many of them were likely black, since the record shows that black servicemen tended to develop closer relationships with the Filipino people, whereas white Americans routinely discriminated against them.

Moreover, the apocryphal tale of pugilistic rebellion also suggests a different trajectory for the rise of the New Negro, as a militant mode of political thinking forged in the heat of black soldiers' experiences and revelations on the front lines of U.S. imperial expansion. Their everyday interactions with colonial peoples fighting for sovereignty and self-determination, which they shared through the black American press, undoubtedly shaped their generation's conceptions of, and approaches to, the "Negro problem." It is a confluence of interests nearly erased from history classrooms and popular memory in both the United States and the Philippines.

African American studies scholars usually point to *A New Negro for a New Century* (1900), an anthology of racial progress edited by Booker T. Washington, Fannie Barrier Williams, and N. B. Wood, as an earlier, albeit less bold, iteration of the New Negro. This turn-of-the-century New Negro was mostly focused on gaining public respectability and upward mobility through education, cultural sophistication, patriotic duty, and wealth accumulation.[13] Washington's compendium spends much time reconstructing black American men as brave and loyal soldiers, particularly in the recent U.S. imperial interventions abroad.[14] Yet what is missing from this interpretation of the initial thrust of the New Negro is that many of the black soldiers who served in the Philippines were ambivalent about, if not opposed to, U.S. control of the islands. In their contacts with pro-independence Filipinos, one can see the beginnings of the New Negro as a critique of black accommodation to white supremacy at home and abroad, grounded in a kind of militant masculinity.

This militant masculinity on the colonial battlefield melded well with the gendered politics surrounding black boxers in the late nineteenth century. In an era characterized by antiblack violence, racial segregation, and political disfranchisement, the boxing ring was one of the few social spaces in which black men could publicly assert their manhood and equality vis-à-vis their white counterparts. Boxing was part of an underground culture that prized black masculine bravado, conspicuous consumption, and the open display of physical and sexual prowess, at a time when black people were expected to remain meek and subservient in their assigned racial place. In this way, the performative aspects of boxing, both in and out of the ring, held a special appeal for the black masses. Through their pugilistic icons, black people gained a form of control over the black body and its gendered representation at a time when popular ideals of citizenship and the nation remained tightly entwined with images of white manhood. Moreover, at a moment of renewed imperial expansion, they used boxing to speak back to the racial and gendered logic of social Darwinism, which argued that the darker races were less "fit" for civilization and political self-determination because they were less manly.[15] Though pugilism may have arrived in the Philippines on the heels of Dewey and the U.S. imperial machine, the many black soldiers who served there also brought their gloves, along with their own interpretations of the sport's insurgent political and cultural significance. Boxing opened up a space for collaboration between black renegade soldiers and Filipino Insurrectos.

Certainly there were many black American soldiers who continued to hope that their work in the archipelago on behalf of the white man's burden would prove their manhood and garner them full citizenship rights at home. Yet, as the military went to battle against Philippine nationalists, the African American community as a whole had become increasingly hesitant about what they saw as a war of conquest. Many black observers had already seen that the United States had no real intention of granting their colored cousins in Cuba full independence. Faced with a similar situation, the Filipino Insurrectos led by General Emilio Aguinaldo chose to stand their ground. As early as mid-1898, Aguinaldo had emerged as a masculine hero in the black American press, referred to as "kinsman" and celebrated for his "spunk." According to historian Willard B. Gatewood, "the image of the Filipino leader was not only that of a bold colored leader, but also of one manfully holding his own against the whites who were oppressing colored people in the United States."[16] When the United States refused to recognize Aguinaldo's authority as the president of an independent Philippine Republic in January 1899, he declared war on the U.S. forces in the islands. Back home, African Americans could not help but see the convergence of their interests when filmmakers such as Thomas Edison used black performers to play the conquered Filipinos in their popular reenactments of the Philippine–American War.[17] Many black American soldiers also began to seriously reconsider their role in suppressing the Filipino insurgency. As Patrick Mason of the Twenty-Fourth Infantry wrote from Corregidor in November 1899, "I have not had any fighting to do since I have been here and don't care to do any. I feel sorry for these people and all that have come under the control of the United States. I don't believe they will be justly dealt by."[18]

The rise of a secret fellowship in the boxing ring was just one part of a broader cultural exchange between black American servicemen and the Philippine people. Not only did African American newspapers make their way to the archipelago but black soldiers also sent back stories of their experiences—a convenient solution to the black press's lack of funds for foreign correspondents.[19] Thus reports of the brutalities of Jim Crow traveled to the Philippines at the same time that black soldiers' observations of white American racism against both themselves and Filipinos circulated back home. It is by no means a stretch to imagine that black newspapers were sometimes left behind in U.S. encampments in the midst of the guerilla war, thereby making their way into the hands of the Insurrectos. Given the many reports of black soldiers' fond encounters with civilians, some may have even given these newspapers to their Filipino friends. Although there was definitely a language barrier, some African American soldiers took up the task of learning Spanish and native dialects, while many Filipinos expressed an interest in speaking English.[20]

The racial thrust of Philippine propaganda illustrates that the Insurrectos were keenly aware of white American discrimination against African Americans. Posters and flyers actively encouraged black soldiers to imagine their domestic plight as intertwined with that of the Filipino revolutionaries. The Philippine foreign minister and master propagandist Apolinario Mabini followed the latest news of the U.S. "Negro problem," and it is likely that he got at least some of his information from black renegade soldiers and black publications.[21] As Michael H. Robinson Jr. of the Twenty-Fifth Infantry wrote to the *Colored American*,

We have been warned several times by insurgent leaders in the shape of placards, some being placed on trees, others left mysteriously in houses we have occupied, saying to the colored soldier that while he is contending on the field of battle against people who are struggling for recognition and freedom, your people in America are being lynched and disfranchised by the same who are trying to compel us to believe that their government will deal justly and fairly by us.[22]

In November 1899, the *Richmond Planet* printed the text from one of these placards for its black American readers:

To the Colored American soldier: It is without honor that you are spilling your costly blood. Your masters have thrown you into the most iniquitous fight with double purpose—to make you the instrument of their ambition and also your hard work will soon make the extinction of your race. Your friends, the Filipinos, give you this good warning. You must consider your situation and your history, and take charge that the blood of Sam Hose proclaims vengeance.[23]

These placards appeared in the months after the horrific lynching of Sam Hose in Newnan, Georgia. On April 23, 1899, a mob of white vigilantes had killed and mutilated Hose in front of a crowd of several thousand white spectators. Knowing that this lynching had become a cause célèbre in the black press, the Insurrectos used it in their efforts to gain the support of black American servicemen.

Black soldiers' letters to the black press also point to their ongoing communication with Philippine civilians. Their everyday encounters with Filipinos, along with their observations of U.S. imperialism in action, often convinced them of the two groups' shared oppression at the hands of Jim Crow America. John W. Galloway of the Twenty-Fifth Infantry recounted several conversations with educated Filipinos for the benefit of black readers in the United States. He had learned that despite the fact that white Americans had done their best to demonize African Americans in the eyes of the Philippine people, many Filipinos had still developed an "affinity of complexion" with black servicemen in the islands.[24] "The colored soldiers do not push them off the streets, spit at them, call them damned 'niggers,' abuse them in all manner of ways, and connect race hatred with duty," one Filipino physician had told Galloway. Given the maltreatment and exploitation that Galloway had already witnessed in Manila, he worried about the long-term implications of white American control in the Philippines. "The future of the Filipino," he feared, "is that of the Negro in the South."

Not content simply to go along with prevailing white American justifications for the pacification of the Philippine rebels, some black American servicemen tried to find out as much as they could about the real roots of the insurrection. Having "mingled freely with the natives" and initiated "talks with American colored [business] men" living in the archipelago, one black soldier admitted, "I must confess they [Filipinos] have a just grievance. All this never would have occurred if the army of occupation would have treated them as people."[25] This soldier claimed that as soon as the Filipinos started to agitate for complete independence, white American servicemen "began to apply home treatment" to them, cursing them as "niggers," stealing from and ravishing them, kicking those who complained, and even desecrating their churches and graves. White American soldiers remained remarkably blind to the racial hypocrisy underlying their "liberation" of the Philippines. "They talked with impunity of 'niggers' to our soldiers," the black serviceman explained, "never once thinking that they were talking to home 'niggers' and should they be brought to remember that at home this is the same vile epithet they hurl at us, they beg pardon and make some effiminate [sic] excuse about what the Filipino is called." As the black soldier lamented, "Expansion is too clean a name for it."

Over the course of the Philippine–American War, approximately twenty black soldiers chose to desert to the opposing side, the most famous being Private David Fagen of the Twenty-Fourth Infantry, who served on the island of Luzon starting in summer 1899. This type of desertion was unprecedented in the history of black American service in the U.S. military. Some of the black renegades secretly taught the Insurrectos marksmanship skills and boxing moves, while others fought alongside them in combat. Even before Fagen abandoned his company, he was known for butting heads with his white officers. His official dossier characterized him as "rowdy" and constantly "bucking" the orders of his commanders. In a matter of five months, Fagen managed to rack up seven convictions for insubordination. As his company broke camp to move to a new post in November 1899, he gathered up as many pistols as he could conceal and calmly walked out of his barracks. The fact that a saddled horse awaited him suggests that he had previously notified the guerillas of his defection. Fagen soon became an officer in Aguinaldo's army, and there were rumors that he even became a general.[26]

The insurgent legend of Fagen and the subversive significance of pugilism during the war come together in the aforementioned apocryphal story of the black renegade who supplied Filipino Insurrectos with boxing gloves and lessons. After all, the timing and location of the tale coincide with Fagen's well-publicized exploits. Ironically, even though the black press remained lukewarm in its coverage of the black deserter, Fagen emerged as an iconic figure of black defiance thanks to the many reports circulated by the U.S. Army and the white mainstream press regarding his military prowess and his uncanny ability to elude capture. As historians Michael C. Robinson and Frank N. Schubert argue, the army and the press "created a public image not unlike Nat Turner's [the leader of an 1831 slave rebellion in Virginia]. The myth became larger than the man, as stories of the rebel officer's brutality, cunning, and audacity spread."[27] The white American-owned

Manila Times vividly described an encounter between two white civilians and the smartly dressed Fagen in a Philippine brothel:

> [He wore] a crash blouse, similar to those of the native police, with a broad white trimming such as officers wear. The insignia on the shoulder straps were a pair of Spanish bugles. His trousers were dark in color, neat fitting, and topped a pair of patent leather shoes. A brown soft felt hat completed his apparel.[28]

As the white Americans approached, Fagen reputedly jumped up from his chair, "grasping his concealed revolver in his right [hand] and a small sword or bolo in his left."[29] Such descriptions of Fagen, the anticolonial rebel, were not unlike the masculine images of black American prizefighters as heroic and dapper New Negroes sticking it to white America in the boxing ring. Thanks to the black press, the boxing ring, and other sites of informal communication, black Americans and Filipinos found common racial ground in the midst of war.

Even though President Theodore Roosevelt declared the official end of the Philippine–American War on July 4, 1902, U.S. authorities continued to worry about the racial affinity and close relationships between Filipinos and black American servicemen. Consequently, William Howard Taft, the first civil governor of the Philippines, pushed for the rapid withdrawal of black troops in 1902.[30] Despite this effort at removal, over twelve hundred black soldiers opted to stay during the occupation. Many found work as civil servants and professionals, while others went into business.[31]

Much like during the Philippine–American War, boxing remained a double-edged sword throughout the U.S. occupation. While boxing provided an apt forum for triumphant U.S. narratives of benevolent assimilation, it also offered Filipinos a subversive means to flip the gendered scripts of white supremacy. The U.S. military was still invested in maintaining the health and discipline of its largely white soldiery. By 1902, army major Elijah Halford had requested two hundred thousand dollars of philanthropic funds to build a YMCA training gym for U.S. servicemen in Manila, and in 1909 a facility was opened.[32] Boxing also retained its popularity among U.S. Navy men, and when the U.S. Pacific Fleet began hiring Filipino cooks and mess stewards in 1903, many of them learned the sport on board the ships.[33] At the same time, white American fight promoters arrived ready to claim the Philippines as their new commercial arena. They often used the paternalistic and civilizationist language of the white man's burden to describe their pugilistic ventures in the islands. However, boxing took on very different meanings for Filipinos, particularly poor and working-class men. It not only brought them into close contact with Americans, both white and black, but also provided them with a means to publicly affirm their own manhood, modernity, and readiness for political self-determination.

A group of white American promoters—Frank Churchill, the Tait brothers (Bill and Eddie), and Joe Waterman—controlled the fight game in Manila, and in many respects, their sporting ventures mirrored the power dynamics of U.S. conquest. As Filipino-American boxing trainer Johnny Samson noted, "these men saw that the Philippine Islands furnished fertile soil for producing first class fighters and didn't regret their toils and troubles for a few years later they reaped handsome financial returns."[34] Waterman, a chief petty officer in the U.S. Navy stationed at Cavite, became a prominent referee, announcer, and promoter. Churchill started out as a customhouse employee and then moved into the business of fight promotion.[35]

They saw their work in the pugilistic realm as an integral part of the United States' broader efforts to modernize the Philippines. Under the banner of benevolent assimilation, U.S. colonial officials endeavored to use public education, English-language instruction, and Christianization to suppress indigenous cultures and to remedy the Filipinos' supposedly natural tendency for vice. In 1915, the YMCA finally opened a facility for Filipinos in Manila. U.S. authorities welcomed this institution, hoping that its mix of physical and spiritual training would improve the strength and moral fiber of Filipino, particularly male, youth.[36] Using similar language, Waterman later boasted, "The native is manlier, cleaner and healthier because of his interest in boxing."[37] He claimed that Filipinos had learned how to fight in a stand-up manner using their fists, in contrast to their savage custom of stabbing people in the back with their bolo knives. "The Filipino as a boxer has done more in 2 years for Philippine independence and to eradicate the cock fighting evil, than insurrectos and propaganda politicians have done in 12 times the length of time," Waterman declared.[38] A popular pastime in the Philippines for centuries, cockfighting had become synonymous with the backwardness and barbarity of Spanish colonial rule. Thus the decline of cockfighting and the rise of boxing seemed to signal the triumph of U.S. neocolonial stewardship.

One of the physical manifestations of white American modernity in Manila was the Olympic Stadium and Athletic Club, established by Churchill and the Tait brothers in 1909. It housed up to eighty-five hundred people, and in the words of *Ring* magazine correspondent Bill Miller, the Olympic was "better equipped than 90 per cent of the American fight-clubs I had been in."[39] It had a signature mahogany bar managed by white American Mike Toomey and serviced by Filipino bartenders in clean, white jackets. Miller described, "It was a colorful scene. Soldiers and sailors in uniform, mingling with American civilians in snow-white duck suits, and Filipinos in silk-striped mohair and palm-beach togs; with here and there a red-trousered Filipino tao, or laboring man, headed for the gallery."[40] While the Olympic's founders envisioned it as a marker of white American civilization, the interracial mixing that took place inside it was also suggestive of the potential for Philippine modernity.

Indeed, the boxing ring was one of the few cultural spaces in which white Americans tolerated some disruption of prevailing racial and imperial hierarchies. Many Filipino fighters traveled to the Olympic to get "discovered," for the club held a "bargain bill" every Wednesday night that gave "all the would-be champions and amateurs a chance" to showcase their skills.[41] Churchill recollected, "There were a great many ambitious Filipino lads who craved ring glory. . . . These boys would storm the [Olympic] club on Wednesday night, begging for a chance to go on. Many of them didn't have money enough to buy an outfit of ring togs, so we always kept a supply of trunks, shoes, etc., available for them."[42] At first Filipinos fought each other on the undercards, but it was not long before they began to monopolize the main events. According to *Ring* magazine writer Carroll Alcott, "then a dangerous experiment was tried. A Filipino was matched with an American and the Filipino won."[43] To meet the growing demand for prizefights, promoters began to import professional boxers from the United States and Australia. Yet Filipino spectators were not necessarily interested in watching white men fight each other; they preferred matches featuring Filipino boxers.

The sport quickly took on a life of its own among Philippine youth. As Waterman recalled, "every Filipino youngster and his brother was seen daily in the streets 'practicing' with the gloves."[44] Much as it did for their black American counterparts, boxing held a special appeal for Filipino laborers, who used the sport to assert their masculinity at a moment when white Americans cast them as childish and feminine "Little Brown Brothers" desperately in need of white male tutelage. In an effort to emphasize their manhood, early Filipino fighters often refused "to wear cups that protected their genitalia, considering that American practice to be effeminate."[45]

Beyond Manila, an underground prizefight scene also thrived due to the heavy regulations surrounding military boxing. The War Department prohibited military boxers from fighting civilians until 1923, while both the army and navy offered free admission to matches and discouraged gambling on the bases. As a result, promoters organized bootleg prizefights near the U.S. bases at Corregidor and Subic Bay, where by the late 1910s mixed crowds of spectators swelled to thousands of people.[46] It was in these alternative spaces that the co-mingling of Americans and Filipinos challenged prevailing imperial mores.

Filipino support for black American success in the ring further underscored the racial significance of Philippine boxing. Many were longtime fans of black pugilists thanks to the laudatory reports contained in African American newspapers that made their way to black soldiers living in the archipelago. Moreover, catering to growing demand, local newspapers also began to publish reports on the U.S. boxing scene. In 1908, when Jack Johnson defeated the white Canadian Tommy Burns in nearby Sydney, Australia, to become world heavyweight champion, his victory and its moving picture reportedly caused a sensation in the islands. According to the fight's promoter, Hugh McIntosh, Filipinos, alongside other "coloured peoples of the earth," began to show a greater interest "in the personality, life, and career" of the new black champion.[47] They had doubtless heard about his infamously brazen lifestyle, including his penchant for conspicuous consumption, his love of urban nightlife, his public displays of masculinity and virility, and most of all, his many relationships with white women.

Two years later, when Johnson defended his world title against the white American Jim Jeffries in Reno, Nevada, Filipinos once again embraced his racial triumph as their own, using it as a rallying cry for self-determination. Local newspapers provided front-page stories of the Jeffries–Johnson fight. The white American-owned *Manila Times* had even promised to post the fight results as soon as they arrived by telegraph from Reno.[48] Hoping for their own chance to witness this historic match, Johnson's Filipino fans had looked forward to the arrival of the moving picture. Fearing racial unrest, Manila's municipal council had quickly banned its exhibition. The large numbers of *muchachos* or male house servants in the capital city, along with the recent rise of the Nacionalista Party for Philippine independence, likely influenced the council's decision.[49] Johnson's victory resonated with Filipinos from across class lines. As one Filipino writer declared, "the punches thrown in Reno by the black boxer Johnson have reverberated in Manila, wounding the delicate eardrums of our Municipal Council." The reason for the ban was simple: "The victor is a black man. The vanquished is not."[50]

Thanks to the numerous postfight reports, Filipino fans were well aware of the violent white American backlash against Johnson's victory. Pedro Quinto of the *Renacimiento Filipino* argued that this backlash fit within a much longer history of white supremacy in the United States, dating back to the days of the Founding Fathers. "Even [George] Washington did not see in the black man anything other than a hunted slave in the African deserts and a trafficked object on the plantations of the new world," Quinto declared. "If in those days the black was a man in the United States, he was certainly not considered and treated as a man."[51] Evidently "the equality of men was not written for the unfortunate black man." Instead, as Quinto emphasized, "the mere idea of a man of this [black] race raising his hand against a white man was considered a monstrosity, and it is the same even today."[52] With U.S. forces still occupying the Philippines, the nationalist Quinto was not only commenting on the unfair treatment of African Americans but also critiquing the lowly status of Filipinos under the repressive regime of benevolent assimilation.

Whether or not the fight film ever made it to Manila, Quinto hoped that John-son's resounding defeat of Jeffries would help to overturn the "tyranny" of white supremacy, thereby promoting "civilization" and "social justice" throughout the world. In Quinto's estimation, the black American champion had provided "a service to Humanity" by "showing how far effort and 'training' can take indi-viduals and peoples."[53] Johnson's historic victory had provided Filipinos with a public platform from which to argue for political autonomy.

Throughout the 1910s, black American fighters continued to make their way to the Philippines in a number of ways. From 1913 to 1917, the U.S. Army stationed the Twenty-Fourth Infantry at Camp McGrath in Batangas and at Fort Mills in Corregi-dor, where black fighters such as Joe Blackburn, "Craps" Johnson, and "Demon" White made a name for themselves. The boxing scene in Manila also expanded, opening up new opportunities for black pugilists looking to dodge the Jim Crow color line in the U.S. boxing scene. African American lightweight Rufus Turner arrived in the capital in July 1914. A professional boxer since 1893, Turner was a veteran hoping for a chance to extend the life of his pugilistic career. He worked for Churchill as a trainer, a referee, and a prizefighter. Over the course of seven years, he fought against numerous American, Australian, and Filipino opponents.[54]

By the early 1920s, the Philippine legislature had passed a law legalizing and regulating twenty-round contests.[55] Philippine universities also began to intro-duce pugilism into their sporting programs. As medical student Pablo Anido told *Ring* readers in 1923, boxing tournaments at the University of Manila were a great success, attracting students, women, and even professors as fans. At a campus meeting, Governor-General Leonard Wood expressed his desire to see the "Filipino youth master the manly arts of self-defense—wrestling and boxing"—because he realized that both sports helped to "develop he-men who become high class citizens."[56] Boxing promoters echoed Governor-General Wood's sentiments. For instance, Churchill claimed to have a larger political purpose for his Philippine boxing business. He told *Ring* magazine,

> Before I am through here I mean to prove that whatever the Filipinos can do in a prize ring they can do in politics, in commerce, and in finance. I know the Filipino people about as well as anybody knows them. And I know those Filipinos as a hard-working, courageous and intelligent people who not merely are worthy and competent of independence and control of their affairs, but a nation of people which, if given a chance, will rise up within a generation to ranking as one of the most important in any part of the world.[57]

Educated Filipinos like Anido used these comments for their own purposes, call-ing for a physical revival in the Philippines, especially among the elite. Anido declared, "The time when it was popular to be a top and dandy—when it was considered as a sign of good breeding to be able to show delicate and well mani-cured, effeminate hands—is past. One cannot be successful in life unless one is in constant 'fighting trim.'" With boxing, they could fortify themselves physically, mentally, and morally for the challenges of political self-government. Whereas Governor-General Wood and other U.S. officials saw the sport as an effective means to refashion the Philippine people into good colonial subjects, for Filipinos of all walks of life, boxing had come to represent a path toward independence.

In the 1920s, white American promoters such as Frank Churchill started taking their best young charges to the United States to cater to the growing population of mostly male Filipino laborers on the West Coast, who worked in the fields as agricultural workers, in white Americans' homes as domestics, and in other service-oriented jobs. Faced with backbreaking labor and daily humiliations, Filipino migrants embraced boxing as both a momentary escape and an expression of national pride. Even after long days of work, they drove for hours in cavalcades, packing boxing arenas in Los Angeles, San Francisco, and Stockton whenever Filipinos were on the fight card. News of Filipino fighters also filled the pages of ethnic newspapers such as the *Philippines Review,* right alongside discussions of politics and current affairs in the Philippines.[58] As historian Linda España-Maram contends, "commuting between the United States and the Philippines, fighters became a force that bridged the Filipino and Filipino American experiences. As athletes, they challenged the stereotypes of the 'little brown brother' uttered by the colonizers in their homeland and the image of the dirty, lazy 'brown monkey' deployed in the racist language of their adopted country."[59]

New Negro boxers were important models for many of the Filipino fighters who began arriving in the United States in the 1920s. Francisco Guilledo was part of this pugilistic migration. In a few short years, he went from being a virtual unknown to world flyweight champion. In his prime, Guilledo stood just five foot one and weighed between 110 and 115 pounds.[60] Despite his small stature, he had a no-holds-barred boxing style. Filipino fans nicknamed the whirlwind fighter after the famous Mexican revolutionary Pancho Villa, "whose name and deeds were on every tongue in Manila in those days."[61]

Moreover, the Philippine "Pancho Villa" was just as fearless outside the ring, for he embraced the same urban culture of the dandy long popularized by auda-cious black American pugilists like Jack Johnson. Villa enjoyed the underground nightlife of the city, the art of ostentation, and the company of white women. He reportedly possessed an "extravagant wardrobe" complete with a "collec-tion of silk shirts, and natty hats, his pearl buttons and gold cuff links." Much like Johnson, he also had a retinue responsible for dressing and grooming him, including "a servant to massage him, another to towel him, a valet to put on his shoes, another to help him put on his trousers, still another valet to comb his hair, powder his cheeks, and spray him with the most expensive perfume."[62] While in the United States, Villa openly cavorted with white women, lavishing his winnings on a Ziegfield dancer and other Broadway performers. He reportedly carried a one thousand dollar bill in his pocket and bought his jewelry at Cartier.[63] Villa became an ethnic icon for the many Filipino agricultural workers who lived hand to mouth in California and Washington State. Back home in the Philippines, Villa also emerged as a national hero, gracing the covers of vernacular magazines such as *Lipang Kalabaw* and *Telembang*. Not only did he express his masculine prowess through conspicuous consumption and relationships with white women but he showcased his elevated status through his use of servants at a time when many Filipinos spent their lives toiling in service to white Americans.

Although in some respects Villa's biography read like the ultimate story of U.S. colonial uplift (and his manager Churchill promoted him as such), his Filipino fans from across the diaspora embraced him as testament to their tenacity in the face of white American oppression. Born in 1901 to a peasant family in the sugarcane-producing province of Iloilo, Villa had wandered to Manila as a young boy in search of work. One of Churchill's assistants claimed to have discovered the young boxer, and Villa began training at the Olympic.[64] Fighting in the Philippines from 1919 to 1920, Villa was often matched against much larger men; however, he only suffered three losses, while managing to gain two Filipino titles. His battleground may have been the boxing ring, but the Philippine Pancho Villa was, nonetheless, a figurative revolutionary in the same vein as Johnson. Still, as if to undermine Villa's masculinity and his broader political significance, white American sportswriters called him the "Living Doll." His small stature, along with his management's efforts to cloak him in narratives of colonial stewardship, made him much less of a threat to prevailing ideas of white supremacy.

On September 14, 1922, just five months after his arrival in the United States, Villa won an eleven-round knockout over Johnny Buff in Brooklyn, New York, to gain the American flyweight title. Although the Italian-American fighter Frankie Genaro took back the title on March 1, 1923, after winning a fifteen-round decision over Villa, many commentators believed Villa had won the fight. When the British flyweight champion Jimmy Wilde came to New York seeking a world title match, the wildly popular Villa got the contract instead of Genaro because promoters considered him to be a better box-office draw. On June 18, 1923, at New York City's Polo Grounds, Villa triumphed over Wilde in the seventh round to become the first Filipino ever to win a world title. Throughout the fight, Villa had punished Wilde until the British fighter was unable to see, his face swollen and bloodied from all the punches. As Carmelo Jacinto, one of the *Ring*'s Filipino correspondents, described, Villa's victory "was celebrated with great enthusi-asm and joy throughout the Philippines. Eleven million Filipinos are singing his yet-unequalled triumph over the Mighty Atom."[65] When the Villa–Wilde fight film arrived in Manila, it did brisk business.[66] "No words can describe the gladness that is reigning in the islands," Jacinto exclaimed. "The long-wished-for dream of the Philippines to have one of her sons as a world's champion has been realized."[67]

When Villa died suddenly in 1925, the white American press shaped the story of his demise into a warning about the dangers of Philippine independence. As the story went, Villa fought in a nontitle bout against Jimmy McLarnin on July 4 in Oakland, California. Weakened by the extraction of a wisdom tooth, he lost by decision. After the fight, Villa visited a dentist, who discovered an infection in his mouth. Ignoring the dentist's instructions to rest and return for a follow-up visit, Villa chose instead to party recklessly for a week, exacerbating the infection. By the time his trainer, Whitey Ekwert, rushed him to the hospital, it was too late. On July 14, Villa died of Ludwig's angina caused by the unchecked infection.[68] In contrast, Filipino migrant workers fashioned an alternative memory of his death. In their version, the weakened Villa had refused to cancel his bout with McLarnin because he did not want to disappoint his hardworking Filipino fans.[69] He had sacrificed his well-being for his people and his nation.

The Philippines mourned the loss of its sporting hero. Around one hundred thousand people attended Villa's public funeral in Manila, and stores closed to pay homage to the late world flyweight champion.[70] So important was Villa in the collective imagination of the Philippine people that they erected a monument to the prizefighter in the Cemetery del Norte. As sportswriter Carroll Alcott described, "there by the side of Dr. Jose Rizal, the Abraham Lincoln of the archipelago, and the great men of the Philippines, this boy who was formerly a boot-black on the Luneta and who lived like the squirrels under the trees, rests his head under a slab as pretentious as that of a millionaire's or general's."[71] Despite the obvious paternalism of his statement, Alcott was right in gesturing to (even if inadvertently so) the emancipatory effect of boxing for both Filipinos and African Americans.

Villa's success inspired the so-called Filipino boxing invasion of the next few decades, which brought New Negro pugilists into close contact with more of their Brown Brothers. Henry Armstrong, a successful black American fighter of the 1930s, and the only fighter ever to hold three world titles simultaneously (welterweight, lightweight, and featherweight), honed his talents in the multira-cial fight scene of Los Angeles's Main Street Gym. As Armstrong later recalled in his autobiography, "the gym was big inside, but bustling with activity. Fighters went through their paces—Mexican, Filipino, Negro, and white."[72] Armstrong claimed that the success of Philippine bantamweight Speedy Dado (Diosdado

Posadas) had "inspired [him] to go in for boxing seriously."[73] While lying in bed one night as a young man in East St. Louis, Armstrong had decided to move to California to become like his Filipino idol:

> Why, Dado was drawing super-gates that netted him as much as $5,000 every two weeks! And on the ceiling over [my] staring eyes appeared a vision of Speedy Dado, just as he'd looked on the cover of the recent issue of *Knockout* . . . smiling, dressed in elegant, expensive clothes. A large diamond ring flashed insistently on one hand.[74]

Armstrong eventually had a chance to train with his hero Dado in the Main Street Gym, and from 1933 to 1934, he fought against the Filipino Kid Moro three times; in 1938, he beat the "Bolo Puncher" Ceferino Garcia in a world welterweight title bout. The militant and self-assured stance of the New Negro had come full circle, by way of Manila. Indeed, the photo of the elder pugilistic statesman Jack Johnson sparring in a California ring with Young Tommy in the 1930s underlines the existence of this vibrant and subversive cultural connection—a connection often overlooked in conventional histories of the black renaissance. Yet it was arguably in these underground spaces of convergence that the "rising tide of color" against white world supremacy found much of its revolutionary power. Ironically set in motion by the process of empire building, the multiple routes of everyday exchange connecting the New Negro and his Brown Brother helped give rise to their masculine politics of resistance in the years to come.

NOTES

1 Damon Runyon, as quoted in Svinth, "Origins of Philippines Boxing."

2 "Jack Johnson and Young Tommy," Harry E. Winkler Photographic Collection, http://www.library.nd.edu/rarebooks/exhibits/winkler_boxing/images/JohnsonJ.710-18-77.jpg.

3 I borrow the term *contact zone* from Pratt, *Imperial Eyes*, 6–7. Whereas Pratt uses the phrase to describe spaces where cultures collide in the context of highly unequal power relations, such as colonialism or slavery, I am using it to describe the cultural spaces in which subaltern peoples meet, negotiate, and forge new visions of freedom.

4 Stoddard, *Rising Tide of Color*, vi, 9. Stoddard was just one of a cohort of eugenicists who decried the weakening of the white race alongside the increasing militancy of nonwhite peoples. See Lake and Reynolds, *Drawing the Global Colour Line*, 310–31; Guterl, *Color of Race in America*, 14–67.

5 E.g., Gilmore, *Defying Dixie*; Stephens, *Black Empire*; Edwards, *Practice of Diaspora*;

Badiane, *Changing Face of Afro-Caribbean Cultural Identity*; Philipson, "Harlem Renaissance as Postcolonial Phenomenon."

6 Scholars are beginning to uncover the many subversive strands of Afro-Asian political and cultural alliance against white supremacy in the twentieth century. See Taketani, "Cartography of the Black Pacific"; Onishi, "New Negro of the Pacific"; Ho and Mullen, *Afro Asia*; Prashad, *Karma of Brown Folk*; Prashad, *Everybody Was Kung Fu Fighting*; and Prashad, *Darker Nations*.

7 According to Vincente Rafael, "Benevolent Assimilation . . . amounted to a sentimental reworking of manifest destiny. Instead of annihilation, it called for the domestication of native populations and their reconstruction into recognizable modern political subjects. . . . Filipinos were infantilized as racial others in need of nurturance and tutelage in the fundamentals of Anglo-Saxon democracy." Rafael, *White Love,* 54. Also see Mitchell, *Righteous Propagation*.

8 Guridy, *Forging Diaspora*, 13.

9 James, *Beyond a Boundary*.

10 Svinth, "Origins of Philippines Boxing."

11 Samson, "History of Boxing in the Philippines," 146–47. Samson was part of the Filipino middle class living in Los Angeles, California. He was a boxing trainer in the 1930s and the chairman of the local Filipino Unity Council. España-Maram, *Creating Masculinity in Los Angeles's Little Manila,* 86.

12 Ibid.

13 Gates, "Trope of the New Negro," 136–37.

14 Even Washington had some misgivings about the annexation of the Philippines: "My opinion is that the Philippine Islands should be given an opportunity to govern themselves. They will make mistakes but will learn from their errors." *Indianapolis Freeman,* September 24, 1898, as quoted in Gatewood, *Black Americans and the White Man's Burden,* 187.

15 On the connection between whiteness, manhood, civilization, and self-determination in this period, see Bederman, *Manliness and Civilization*.

16 Gatewood, *Black Americans and the White Man's Burden,* 186.

17 Gems, *Athletic Crusade,* 48; Streible, *Fight Pictures,* 129.

18 Quoted in Gatewood, *"Smoked Yankees" and the Struggle for Empire,* 257. Also see chapters 8–10 in Gatewood, *Black Americans and the White Man's Burden*.

19 On the presence of black American newspapers in the Philippines, see Galloway, *Richmond Planet,* December 30, 1899, as quoted in Gatewood, *"Smoked Yankees" and the Struggle for Empire,* 251.

20 On black American soldiers' close relations with Filipino civilians, especially Philippine women, see Brown, "African-American Soldiers and Filipinos," 46–51.

21 Ontal, "Fagen and Other Ghosts," 125.

22 *Colored American,* March 17 and 24, 1900, as quoted in Gatewood, *"Smoked Yankees" and the Struggle for Empire,* 268.

23 *Richmond Planet,* November 11, 1899, as quoted in ibid., 258.

24 All quotations in this paragraph are from John W. Galloway, *Richmond Planet,* December 30, 1899, as quoted in ibid., 253.

25 All quotations in this paragraph are from *Wisconsin Weekly Advocate,* May 17, 1900, as quoted in ibid., 280–81.

26 Ontal, "Fagen and Other Ghosts," 125–26.

27 Robinson and Schubert, "David Fagen," 77.

28 *Manila Times,* February 26, 1901, as quoted in ibid.

29 Ibid.

30 Gatewood, *"Smoked Yankees" and the Struggle for Empire,* 243.

31 Brown, "African-American Soldiers and Filipinos," 49.

32 Svinth, "Origins of Philippines Boxing"; Gems, *Athletic Crusade,* 60.

33 Svinth, "Origins of Philippines Boxing."

34 Samson, "History of Boxing in the Philippines," 149.

35 Miller, "Boxing's 'Mosquito Fleet.'"

36 España-Maram, *Creating Masculinity,* 75, 83–84.

37 Waterman, "Boxing Replaces Cock Fighting."

38 Ibid.

39 Miller, "Boxing's 'Mosquito Fleet.'"

40 Ibid.

41 Miller, "Stranger Than Fiction."

42 Churchill, as quoted in Svinth, "Origins of Philippines Boxing."

43 Alcott, "Boxing in Philippines."

44 Waterman, "Boxing Replaces Cock Fighting."

45 Gems, *Athletic Crusade,* 56.

46 Svinth, "Origins of Philippines Boxing."

47 Hugh D. McIntosh, "The Pride of the Blacks," *Boxing,* September 24, 1910. For more on Johnson's popularity in the Philippines, see Runstedtler, *Jack Johnson, Rebel Sojourner,* 69, 88–89.

48 "From the Far Off Philippines," *Chicago Defender,* August 20, 1912; "$101,000 Purse for the Fight Is Now Up," *Manila Times,* July 4, 1910; Gems, *Athletic Crusade,* 56; Kramer, *Blood of Government,* 298.

49 Gems, *Athletic Crusade,* 50, 53–54.

50 "A través de siete días," *Renacimiento Filipino,* July 11, 1910.

51 Pedro Quinto, "El bofeton de Reno," *Renacimiento Filipino,* July 11, 1910.

52 Ibid.

53 Ibid.

54 Svinth, "Origins of Philippines Boxing."

55 Fleischer, "As We See It." The Olympic Athletic Club had taken on the boxing rules of New York State's Walker Law. The only major difference was the Filipinos' inattention to weight categories.

56 Anido, "Boxing in Manila."

57 Menke, "Man Who Put the Philippines on the Map."

58 España-Maram, *Creating Masculinity,* 79–80, 97.

59 Ibid., 75–76.

60 Svinth, "Origins of Philippines Boxing."

61 Dorgan, "Grim Reaper Removes Two Fistic Stars."

62 Villegas, "Before Pacquiao and Elorde, There Was Pancho Villa."

63 Gems, *Athletic Crusade,* 62.

64 España-Maram, *Creating Masculinity,* 77. Also see "Villa Unknown in U.S. Year Ago—Champion Today"; Dorgan, "Grim Reaper Removes Two Fistic Stars."

65 Jacinto, "Philippine Boxing Notes."

66 Anido, "Boxing in Manila."

67 Jacinto, "Philippine Boxing Notes."

68 International Boxing Hall of Fame, "Pancho Villa."

69 España-Maram, *Creating Masculinity,* 102.

70 Miller, "Boxing's 'Mosquito Fleet.'"

71 Alcott, "Boxing in Philippines."

72 Quoted in España-Maram, *Creating Masculinity,* 87.

73 Quoted in ibid., 99.

74 Quoted in ibid.

BIBLIOGRAPHY

Alcott, Carroll D. "Boxing in Philippines Got Big Impetus with Villa's Victory over Jimmy Wilde." *The Ring,* October 1928.

Badiane, Mamadou. *The Changing Face of Afro-Caribbean Cultural Identity: Negrismo and Negritude.* Lanham, Md.: Lexington Books, 2010.

Bederman, Gail. *Manliness and Civilization: A Cultural History of Gender and Race in the United States, 1880–1917.* Chicago: University of Chicago Press, 1995.

Brown, Scot. "African-American Soldiers and Filipinos: Racial Imperialism, Jim Crow and Social Relations." *Journal of Negro History* 82, no. 1 (1997): 42–53.

Dorgan, John L. "Grim Reaper Removes Two Fistic Stars." *The Ring,* September 1925.

Edwards, Brent Hayes. *The Practice of Diaspora: Literature, Translation, and the Rise of Black Internationalism.* Cambridge, Mass.: Harvard University Press, 2003.

España-Maram, Linda. *Creating Masculinity in Los Angeles's Little Manila: Working-Class Filipinos and Popular Culture, 1920s–1950s.* New York: Columbia University Press, 2006.

Gates, Henry Louis, Jr. "The Trope of the New Negro and the Reconstruction of the Image of the Black." *Representations,* no. 24 (Autumn 1988): 129–55.

Gatewood, Willard B. *Black Americans and the White Man's Burden, 1898–1903.* Urbana: University of Illinois Press, 1975.

———, ed. *"Smoked Yankees" and the Struggle for Empire: Letters from Negro Soldiers.* Urbana: University of Illinois Press, 1971.

Gems, Gerald R. *The Athletic Crusade: Sport and American Cultural Imperialism.* Lincoln: University of Nebraska Press, 2006.

Gilmore, Glenda. *Defying Dixie: The Radical Roots of Civil Rights, 1919–1950.* New York: W. W. Norton, 2008.

Guridy, Frank. *Forging Diaspora: Afro-Cubans and African Americans in a World of Empire and Jim Crow.* Chapel Hill: University of North Carolina Press, 2010.

Guterl, Matthew Pratt. *The Color of Race in America, 1900–1940*. Cambridge, Mass.: Harvard University Press, 2001.

Ho, Fred, and Bill V. Mullen, eds. *Afro Asia: Revolutionary Political and Cultural Connections between African Americans and Asian Americans*. Durham, N.C.: Duke University Press, 2008.

International Boxing Hall of Fame. "Pancho Villa." http://www.ibhof.com/pages/about/inductees/oldtimer/villa.html.

James, C. L. R. *Beyond a Boundary*. 1963. Reprint, Durham, N.C.: Duke University Press, 1993.

Kramer, Paul. *Blood of Government: Race, Empire, the United States, and the Philippines*. Chapel Hill: University of North Carolina Press, 2006.

Lake, Marilyn, and Henry Reynolds. *Drawing the Global Colour Line: White Men's Countries and the International Challenge of Racial Equality*. Cambridge: Cambridge University Press, 2008.

Mitchell, Michelle. *Righteous Propagation: African Americans and the Politics of Racial Destiny after Reconstruction*. Chapel Hill: University of North Carolina Press, 2004.

Onishi, Yuichiro. "The New Negro of the Pacific: How African Americans Forged Cross-Racial Solidarity with Japan, 1917–1922." *Journal of African American History* 92, no. 2 (2007): 191–213.

Ontal, Rene G. "Fagen and Other Ghosts: African-Americans and the Philippine–American War." In *Vestiges of War: The Philippine–American War and the Aftermath of an Imperial Dream, 1899–1999,* edited by Angel Velasco Shaw and Luis H. Francia, 118–33. New York: New York University Press, 2002.

Philipson, Robert. "The Harlem Renaissance as Postcolonial Phenomenon." *African American Review* 40, no. 1 (2006): 145–60.

Prashad, Vijay. *The Darker Nations: A People's History of the Third World*. New York: New Press, 2007.

———. *Everybody Was Kung Fu Fighting: Afro-Asian Connections and the Myth of Cultural Purity*. Boston: Beacon Press, 2001.

———. *The Karma of Brown Folk*. Minneapolis: University of Minnesota Press, 2000.

Pratt, Mary Louise. *Imperial Eyes: Travel Writing and Transculturation*. New York: Routledge, 1992.

Rafael, Vincente. *White Love and Other Events in Filipino History*. Durham, N.C.: Duke University Press, 2000.

Robinson, Michael C., and Frank N. Schubert. "David Fagen: An Afro-American Rebel in the Philippines, 1899–1901." *Pacific Historical Review* 44, no. 1 (1975): 68–83.

Runstedtler, Theresa. *Jack Johnson, Rebel Sojourner: Boxing in the Shadow of the Global Color Line*. Berkeley: University of California Press, 2012.

Samson, Johnny. "History of Boxing in the Philippines." In *The Making of Champions in California,* edited by DeWitt Van Court (Los Angeles, Calif.: Premier, 1926).

Stephens, Michelle. *Black Empire: The Masculine Global Imaginary of Caribbean Intellectuals in the United States, 1914–1962*. Durham, N.C.: Duke University Press, 2005.

Stoddard, Lothrop. *The Rising Tide of Color against White World-Supremacy.* 1920. Reprint, New York: Charles Scribner's Sons, 1922.

Streible, Daniel. *Fight Pictures: A History of Boxing and Early Cinema.* Berkeley: University of California Press, 2008.

Svinth, J. R. "The Origins of Philippines Boxing." *Journal of Combative Sport* (July 2001). http://ejmas.com/jcs/jcsart_svinth_0701.htm.

Taketani, Etsuko. "The Cartography of the Black Pacific: James Weldon Johnson's *Along This Way.*" *American Quarterly* 59, no. 1 (2007): 79–106.

Villegas, Dennis. "Before Pacquiao and Elorde, There Was Pancho Villa." *Philippine Online Chronicles,* March 23, 2010. http://www.thepoc.net/thepoc-features/buhay-pinoy/buhay-pinoy-features/5075-the-first-filipino-boxing-champ-ever.html.

5

The New Negro of the Pacific:
How African Americans Forged
Solidarity with Japan

YUICHIRO ONISHI

Hubert Harrison (1883–1927), an African Caribbean immigrant from St. Croix of the Dutch West Indies and more famously known as the "father of Harlem radicalism," knew very well why Japan mattered to African America and the darker world during and after World War I. Writing for the *Negro World* in November 1921, the organ of Marcus Garvey's Universal Negro Improvement Association (UNIA), Harrison explained that "Japan" was only relevant insofar as it served as "an index" to advance the ends of black liberation.[1] Unpacking the symbolic significance of Japan in relation to the upcoming Washington Conference on disarmament, where Japan, in the end, relinquished much of what it had gained at the 1919 Paris Peace Conference to secure a position as an imperialist equal to "white" polities of the West, Harrison carefully crafted his rhetorical stance to remind peoples of African descent in New York and beyond of the meaning of Japan.

For Harrison, the image of a defiant Japan challenging the dominance of Anglo-American powers was not an idol with which to engage in wishful thinking about the world without the color line but rather a springboard from which to translate African American democratic aspirations into concrete engagements at the grass roots. Japan was, after all, an ambitious imperialist and an aggressive colonizer—not a champion of "darker races." Yet, it was not entirely devoid of a use value. *Japan* was a metaphor of sorts that could function as an incubator of what Harrison called "race-consciousness." Jeffery B. Perry, Harrison's biographer, interpreted it as "a necessary corrective to white supremacy" and "a strategic component in the struggle for a racially just and socialist society."[2] Starting in 1915, as Harrison directed his organizing energies toward African Americans in Harlem to mold a more militant, dynamic, and internationalist mass movement for black emancipation and equality, he steadfastly adhered to this principle of "race-consciousness" to quicken the currents of Harlem radicalism.[3]

When writing for such periodicals as the *Voice,* the organ of the Liberty League

(Harrison's own organization), and the *Negro World,* all the while doing agitational work from soapboxes on street corners in Harlem, Harrison so often instructed African Americans to keep the horizon of political possibility open to manifest race-consciousness. To reiterate, "Japan is only a index," Harrison wrote. He meant not just to look for Japan, which was struggling to hold on to its tenuous status as one of the great powers in the world dominated by "white" polities. Equally important were self-conscious efforts on the part of African American masses and leaders in Harlem to identify with, and, in so doing, achieve unity among, diverse peoples of African descent within their own communities locally as well as across the "colored world" in Asia and Africa. In "The Line-Up on the Color Line," published in the *Negro World* on December 4, 1920, Harrison declared,

> In the face of these facts the first great international duty of the black man in America is to get in international touch with his fellows of the downtrod-den section of the human population of the globe. . . . We need to join hands across the sea. We need to know what they are doing in India; we need to know what they are doing in China; we need to know what they are doing in Africa, and we need to let ["make" has been crossed out] them know what we are doing over here. We must link up with the other colored races of the world, beginning with our own, and after we have linked up the various sections of the black race the black race will see that it is in its interest and advantage to link up with the yellow and the brown races.[4]

An emphasis Harrison placed on the need to "link up" through the collective practice of self-teaching was what was at the core of his invocation concerning Japan. He defined the very labor of linking up as a way of bringing together theory and practice to make the space of resistance within Harlem's Afrodia-sporic everyday life productive for an insurgent politics and articulation of black internationalism.[5]

In essence, to register Japan as "only an index" was to rework the shape of black freedom. Not merely a pronouncement, it was the praxis of black radical-ism. Indeed, the manner in which he constructed in his narrative writing the figuration of Japan as defiant but outmatched against global white supremacy, as well as other images of "colored majority" across Africa and Asia "flying their own flags and dictating their own internal and foreign policies," as he put it, did "furnish a background for" Harlem-based intellectual–activists of varying political orientations to set in motion racial struggles for a new society that moved not only in scales that exceeded national boundaries but also across the "colored world." This formation of Harlem radicalism was historically contingent, and Harrison knew it; his indexical modality punctuated prevailing pro-Japan thinking among

African Americans to think otherwise. It was designed to animate acute advances on the front of the black freedom struggle. The construction of the iconography of Japan was a part of a thrust that gave form to the space of resistance that aided New Negro movement mobilization during the World War I period.[6]

All that said, however, such genius of what I call Harrison's "pro-Japan provocation" does not make a strong showing in the following essay I wrote, which was originally published in the spring 2007 issue of the *Journal of African American History*. For this reason, as an exercise in self-criticism, I present this "opening" to reset the context of my analysis, although to do so without revising the essay can invite criticism. In this prolegomenon, my modest objective is to set the following record straight concerning the relationship between Hubert Harrison and the place of Japan in New Negro movement mobilization in the years between 1917 and 1922: Harrison was the main vector that constituted the "New Negro" as a political category of struggle among Harlem-based intellectual–activists. He was the "voice of Harlem radicalism," as Jeffrey Perry reminds us, principally responsible for communicating the categorical imperatives of the New Negro to reach out, within, across, and beyond myriad Afrodiasporic experiences and communities.[7] An outcome was that Harrison placed "Harlem" on the cognitive map of international racial struggles and transformed it to become a wellspring of New Negro aspirations and inspirations. His voice—a pacesetter—guided the currents of Harlem radicalism in multiple directions, and one of the routes crossed the Pacific.

In late 1918, William Monroe Trotter, finding President Woodrow Wilson's Fourteen Points to be Jim Crow writ large, called for the inclusion of a "Fifteenth Point"—the abolition of race-based polities in all nations. He was determined to make white supremacy a global issue at the upcoming Paris Peace Conference. Throughout Wilson's presidency, Trotter, the founder of the Niagara Movement (1905) and National Equal Rights League (1909), denounced the administration's refusal and resistance to resolve racial injustices against African Americans and fought hard for black equality. In his mind, as long as Jim Crow remained at the core of the American polity, there was no hope for postwar democracy and internationalism, especially because both were used as principles with which to create the new structure of world governance called the League of Nations. At the time, while the 1917 East St. Louis race riots still horrified and enraged many African Americans, Trotter insisted that peace and justice would never materialize for African Americans and colonized people all over the world if the white supremacist conception of Wilsonian liberal democracy was legitimated.[8]

Trotter's opinions about war, peace, democracy, white supremacy, and Wilsonian foreign policy resonated loudly in the black public sphere as the Paris Peace Conference approached. To project a new political mood, intellectuals and prominent leaders mobilized around the image of a determined, assertive, and militant African American—the New Negro. However, those who identified with the movement informed by the idea of the New Negro were various. The New Negro movement enlisted support from the icons of African America with diverse ideological tendencies such as W. E. B. Du Bois, Marcus Garvey, Ida B. Wells-Barnett, Madam C. J. Walker, and James Weldon Johnson, as well as leading voices of black radicalism, including Hubert Harrison, A. Philip Randolph, Chandler Owen, Cyril V. Briggs, and Harry Haywood. These constituents of the New Negro movement were individuals whose lives, political identities, and global visions were transformed by rampant racial violence and state repressions, labor radicalism, Caribbean and southern black migration, the First World War, the Russian Revolution, Irish nationalism, and prospects for African liberation. Through grassroots organizing, political writings, soapbox oratory, and public meetings, despite differences in political orientations, they converged at various moments, especially in the years surrounding World War I. The participants of the New Negro movement cultivated a political space that was informed by black nationalism, vindicationism, and Marxism and presented a sharp critique of white supremacy.[9]

Although Wilson's vision of a "new world order" appealed to a wide audience and certainly influenced prominent African American leaders, New Negro intellectuals and activists' political outlooks were markedly different. During the years between 1917 and 1922, they were challenging the very dominant categories that were used to communicate universal human experience, such as freedom and democracy, and were at work in fashioning their own distinct idioms within the black public sphere. Indeed, the formation of a new politics was strategic and historically contingent, and the application of the concept of the New Negro showed remarkable flexibility and creativity, transgressing boundaries of class and nation as well as myriad strains of the African American intellectual tradition. What is most striking about New Negroes' call for a new politics during the wartime and immediate postwar periods was that it animated diverse political actors to navigate the politics of race at local and global levels to carve out *a space of resistance*. Specifically, I argue in this essay that the New Negro discourse helped create a new form of human struggle based in what political theorist Cedric J. Robinson calls the "Black radical tradition." The participants of this new movement stepped into a "culture of liberation," as Robinson states, and "crossed the familiar bounds of social and historical narrative" emerging out of shared historical experience with racial capitalism.[10] "This was a revolutionary consciousness that proceeded from the whole historical experience of Black people," Robinson emphasizes, "and not merely from the social formations of capitalist slavery or the relations of production of colonialism."[11] At the core of this revolutionary consciousness was,

according to historian V. P. Franklin, "the cultural objective of black self-determination, which operated in a dialectical relationship with white supremacy"[12]

This essay is concerned with the emergence of such a revolutionary consciousness in the midst of political mobilization around the concept of the New Negro
and how the long-standing intellectual tradition of black protest intersected
in an unlikely fashion with Japan's struggle to achieve racial equality with the
"white" nations. During and after the Paris Peace Conference, the diverse constituents of the New Negro movement utilized the case of Japan's race-conscious
defiance against the United States, the British Empire, and the French Empire.
They projected the image of Japan as a race rebel and a racial victim and helped
construct the iconography of Japan as the New Negro of the Pacific. Such a work
of political imagination proved effective in nurturing the distinct ethos of black
self-determination among intellectuals and activists with varying ideological
and political orientations who worked with concepts of race and nation and enabled the black public sphere to become productive for the articulation of black
radicalism. Indeed, this forging cross-racial solidarity with Japan was all about
politics. The trans-Pacific alliance was based on seeing Japan as "a racialized political group rather than a biologically determined racial group."[13] As historian
Nikhil Pal Singh brilliantly argued in Black Is a Country, "black intellectuals and
activists recognized that racial belonging operates at scales that are both smaller
and larger than the nation-state, and voiced visions of communal possibility that
consistently surpassed the conceptions available in the prevailing idioms of U.S.
political culture."[14]

In recent years, Reginald Kearney, Ernest Allen Jr., Gerald Horne, Robin D. G.
Kelley, Elizabeth Esch, George Lipsitz, Penny M. Von Eschen, Vijay Prashad, Sudar-
shan Kapur, and other historians have established the theoretical foundation for the
trans-Pacific study of black radicalism. These scholars emphasize the importance
of Asia in the formation of the black radical tradition in the twentieth century
and explore how African Americans' imagined and real solidarities with peoples
of Asia produced an uncompromising critique of white supremacy.[15] All of them
exhibit sensitivity toward African Americans' determination to struggle for freedom and advancement—as Cedric Robinson has observed, "the raw material of the
Black radical tradition, the values, ideas, conceptions, and constructions of reality
from which resistance was manufactured."[16] However, the existing literature does
not elaborate the precise role that the Japanese played in shaping a new form of
struggle based in the black radical tradition in the World War I era, even though,
in the margins of the discourses of leading New Negroes such as Marcus Garvey,
Hubert Harrison, Andrea Razafinkeriefo (Andy Razaf), Cyril V. Briggs, Chandler
Owen, and A. Philip Randolph, the symbolic significance of Japan often crops
up. Moreover, the analysis of the location of Japan in black liberation theory and

practice receives scant attention in the recent study of New Negro radicalism.[17] Although Japan never occupied these leaders' and intellectuals' political imaginations for a sustained period of time, it did inform their creative ruminations on the radical possibilities and transnational dimensions of the black freedom struggle.

NEGOTIATING THE COLOR LINE INTERNATIONALLY

During the 1919 Paris Peace Conference, as Woodrow Wilson set out to ensure that the League of Nations was modeled after his Fourteen Points, William Monroe Trotter's demand for global racial justice, the inclusion of a "Fifteenth Point," was included in the negotiations. However, it was the Japanese delegation that put the issue on the table in Paris and demanded that the antidiscrimination clause be included in shaping the new international community. Acknowledging that diplomacy at the conference, especially its deliberations, negotiations, and decisions, would be dictated by Anglo-American powers, Japan sought to attain equality with the imperial powers of the West and did so by invoking the language of racial equality. Yet, however much Trotter's "Fifteenth Point" resembled, at the level of semantics, the racial equality clause submitted by the Japanese delegation at the Paris Peace Conference, the Japanese government was only remotely interested (at best) in attacking the stronghold of white supremacy. It pursued its own imperial ambitions and colonial interests by demanding the control of the islands in the South Pacific, especially the Marshalls, the Marianas, and the Carolines, and the German concessions in Shantung, China. Nonetheless, Japan's race-conscious diplomatic maneuver did shake up the nature of the debate and incited strong opposition from the British Empire and American delegations.[18] In fact, as the debate unfolded and became contentious, the racial equality clause ironically became an effective tool to strengthen Japan's position within the global racial polity in attaining "white" imperial power status.

At the Paris Peace Conference, the demand for racial equality was defined as one of Japan's key issues, although some of the political leaders back home felt apprehensive about asserting power on the international stage. It became a salient issue for the Japanese government as public opinion became ever more critical of the dominance and arrogance of Anglo-American powers. The leaders of the Japanese delegation, Baron Makino Nobuaki and Viscount Chinda Sutemi, thus, took this issue to Colonel Edward M. House, President Wilson's most trusted advisor, to figure out a way to accommodate the Japanese concern. In talks with Makino and Chinda in early February 1919, House remained attentive to the Japanese demand and expressed that the problem of the color line was "one of the serious causes of international trouble, and should in some way be met."[19] In the end, both parties decided to introduce the racial equality clause by way of seeking an amendment to the religious freedom article (Article 21) of the covenant of the League of Nations. On February 13, 1919, the Japanese presented the following draft:

> The equality of nations being a basic principle of the League of Nations, the High Contracting Parties agree to accord as soon as possible to all alien nationals of states, members of the League, equal and just treatment in every respect making no distinction, either in law or in fact, on account of their race or nationality.[20]

The delegates representing the British Empire and the United States opposed the amendment. They interpreted that Japan's demand for racial equality was directed at achieving unrestricted Japanese immigration to countries such as Britain, Australia, Canada, and the United States. Lord Robert Cecil of the British Empire and Australian prime minister William Morris Hughes organized strong opposition. Cecil declared on the floor that the proposal was divisive and would lead to "interference in the domestic affairs of State members of the League." For the same reason, he added that the International Council of Women's demand for gender equality would not be considered in drafting the Covenant of the League of Nations.[21]

After repeated negotiations and revisions, the Japanese delegation dropped all the referential connections between "race" and "equality" and presented a revised version that endorsed "the principle of equality of nations and just treatment of their nationals." Italy and France as well as other countries, including China, Greece, Serbia, Brazil, and Czechoslovakia, all voted for this revised amendment on April 11, 1919. By 11–6, it was passed. However, Wilson, presiding as chair of this session, did not honor the result. He declared that "in the present instance there was, certainly, a majority, but strong opposition had manifested itself against the amendment and under these circumstances the resolution could not be considered as adopted." The Japanese did not pursue the fight for racial equality at the last session of the League of Nations Commissions.[22]

When the racial equality clause was introduced in Paris, it took a life of its own within the context of imperialist diplomacy. It generated Anglo-American apprehension and their determination to protect the system of white supremacy. While Lord Robert Cecil cast Japan as a troublemaker of the international community for introducing the contentious race question, Woodrow Wilson insisted that the issues of race and racism should "play no part in the discussions connected with the establishment of the League."[23] The response of the delegates from the white-dominated nations was aimed to dissemble. Their determination to reject the racial equality clause was intertwined with their unwillingness to give up domestic and colonial interests in the maintenance of white supremacy. During the Paris Peace Conference in May 1919, *The Messenger*'s A. Philip Randolph and Owen Chandler, leading New Negro activist–intellectuals and socialists, explained the logic of colonial and racial domination in this way: "Those who hold vested property interests and privileges under a given social system will resist with desperate determination any assault upon that system by the advocates of a new, a different social doctrine."[24]

Although these Western leaders sought to suppress the debate surrounding the problem of the color line, the global nature of racial discourse was a social and political fact that could not be denied. Amid contradictions, the great powers had vested interests in shaping the discourse of race, especially because they were all interested in rationalizing their claims to control Germany's former colonies in Africa and Asia. Even when they eschewed a direct reference to the language of racial equality, the debate was *racial* at every turn because of colonialism and imperialism.

Certainly the Japanese were responsible for introducing the racial equality proposal, but in reality, it had no interest in trumpeting the right of colonized and racially oppressed people for self-determination. While the Japanese delegation raised the banner of racial equality, the Japanese colonial government suppressed Koreans' struggle for self-determination and tightened the grip of colonial rule. Moreover, the Japanese government was concerned with the future of Germany's former colonies and eager to spread its political, military, and economic influences in China. When the Chinese learned that the German concessions in Shantung had come under Japanese control, intellectuals and students gathered at the Gate of Heavenly Peace in Peking on May 4, 1919, and challenged the legitimacy of Japanese and Western imperialism. Commonly known as the May Fourth movement, an outburst of political and intellectual activities awakened the people struggling to seek radical approaches to create a new nation. Nationalist China debated the crisis of modernity and struggled to define its own path toward peoplehood and nationhood. The anti-imperialist Chinese nationalists opposed the decisions made at the Paris Peace Conference and mobilized protests locally and internationally. On the day of the signing of the Versailles Treaty, Chinese students in Paris took direct action. They blocked the Chinese delegates from entering the signing ceremonies. Consequently, the treaty was signed without their presence on June 28, 1919.[25]

AFRICAN AMERICANS AND THE PARIS PEACE CONFERENCE

Like the Japanese, African American intellectuals and leaders also looked to the Paris Peace Conference as a political opportunity in the ongoing struggle for peace, racial justice, and self-determination in Africa and throughout the African diaspora. W. E. B. Du Bois was one of the leaders determined to make the presence of peoples of African descent known in the international arena. Convinced that the Pan-African Congress would be an ideal vehicle to communicate the desire of Africans and peoples of African descent for political representation to great powers participating in peace talks, he worked tirelessly to organize this historic conference. With the help of Blaise Diagne, a Senegalese leader and a high commissioner of French West Africa, who was a close friend of French prime minister Georges Clemenceau, the organizers of the Pan-African Congress acquired permission to hold the conference in Paris. Diagne presided as president, while Du Bois served as a secretary. The Pan-African Congress attracted fifty-seven delegates from fifteen countries and discussed the future of Africa on February 19, 1919.[26] However, the Pan-African Congress did not challenge colonialism, imperialism, and racism head-on to demand the right of Africans to struggle for self-determination and self-government, as promised in the Wilsonian program of internationalism. The adopted resolutions simply asked great powers to "establish a code of laws for the international protection of the natives of Africa, similar to the proposed international code for labor." Moreover, they urged great powers to oversee "the application of these laws to the political, social and economic welfare of the natives" through a permanent organization. As historian Manning Marable noted, "nowhere in Congress' demands were Europeans asked to grant Africans the right to complete self-determination."[27]

Meanwhile, leading voices of the New Negro movement at home, namely, A. Philip Randolph, Chandler Owen, Cyril V. Briggs, Hubert Harrison, and Andrea Razafinkeriefo, all based in Harlem, developed strategies to place the local and global problems of the color line on the table of peace talks. At public meetings and on street corners, these activist–intellectuals continuously discussed the future of colonialism in Africa, the imperialist scramble for colonial possessions, and the hypocrisy of Wilsonian liberal internationalism. They showed interest in the outcome of the Paris Peace Conference and interpreted events abroad through their own distinct race-based system of explanation. On the eve of the conference, many of them identified with powerful states and interest groups that could challenge global white supremacy. In particular, they were deeply influenced by the revolutionary moment precipitated by the First World War, especially the 1917 Russian Revolution. They absorbed the energies of Bolshevism and anticolonial nationalist struggles elsewhere and looked for an alternative route to struggle for black self-determination. In their writings, many articulated an anticapitalist perspective on world politics and synthesized it with an anticolonial outlook.[28]

Shortly after the armistice in November 1918, Hubert Harrison, a socialist intellectual from St. Croix, and one of Harlem's most important orators, writers, activists, and leaders in the black metropolis during the World War I era, offered a critique of the system of international diplomacy and peacemaking based on race and class:

> When Nations go to war, they never openly declare what they WANT. They must camouflage their sordid greed behind some sounding phrase like "freedom of the seas," "self-determination," "liberty," or "democracy." But only the ignorant millions ever think that those are the real objects of their bloody rivalries. When the war is over, the mask is dropped, and then they seek "how best to scramble at the shearers' feast." It is then that they disclose their real war aims. . . . Africa's hands are tied, and so tied, she will be thrown upon the peace table.[29]

Harrison aptly pointed out the relevant underpinnings of the Paris Peace Conference and the League of Nations: colonialism in Africa and the racial politics of imperialism. An editorial in *The Messenger,* published in March 1919, also shared Harrison's critique of imperial ambition and the workings of colonial power relations in world affairs, arguing, "If the peace conference does not break up in a war, it will be followed by wars, at no distant date." With sarcasm, the editorial noted, "There are *peace* conferences and *piece* conferences."[30] What characterized the politics of New Negro leaders and intellectuals was their refusal to accept Wilsonian prescriptions for the creation of a new international civil society.

Unlike the participants of the Pan-African Congress in Paris who adopted modest resolutions, New Negro activist–intellectuals echoed the uncompromising antiracist and anti-imperialist position of the revolutionary black organization called the African Blood Brotherhood, whose members included activists such as Cyril V. Briggs, W. A. Domingo, Richard B. Moore, and Grace Campbell.[31] In December 1918, the African Blood Brotherhood presented the following demands on the eve of the Paris Peace Conference: "that the full rights of citizenship be granted to all people of Color, that all discrimination because of Color be made illegal, that self-determination be extended to all nations and tribes within the African continent and throughout the World, and that the exploitation of Africa and other countries belonging to people of Color herewith cease."[32] When the Japanese delegation introduced the question of "Color" on the international stage, this action took on powerful meaning among Harlem war critics and politically conscious leaders. As Paris prepared to host the peace conference in late 1918, Marcus Garvey declared that Africans and peoples of African descent "hope Japan will succeed in impressing upon her white brothers at the Peace Conference the essentiality of abolishing racial discrimination."[33]

Indeed, throughout late 1918 and early 1919, numerous New Negro intellectuals looked to Japan approvingly. On January 5, 1919, retired Major Walter Howard Loving, an African American informer who worked for the U.S. Army's military intelligence branch, recognized the political radicalization in Harlem and reported that "New York 'soap box orators' are beginning to invade this city, and their presence carry some significance."[34] Loving's observation was not an overstatement. Despite ideological and political differences, African American and African Caribbean activists busily organized meetings and converged at various points. They participated in each other's local projects and frequently shared the same stage to articulate their perspectives on peacemaking in the immediate aftermath of World War I. Many of them entered the debates over war, peace, disarmament, and global racial justice and communicated their commitment to help establish what Marcus Garvey called the "Racial League" to counter Wilson's plan for the League of Nations.[35]

At the National Race Congress for World Democracy, held in Washington, D.C., in December 1918, for instance, William Monroe Trotter, Ida B. Wells-Barnett, Madam C. J. Walker, Reverend M. A. N. Shaw of Boston, and seven other leaders were elected to represent the African American peace delegation, although participants of this meeting, in the end, excluded women from taking part in the delegation.[36] Marcus Garvey's UNIA organized a delegation of its own, which included A. Philip Randolph, Ida B. Wells-Barnett, and Eliezer Caddet.[37] Moreover, on January 2, 1919, with Marcus Garvey in attendance and financial assistance from Madam C. J. Walker, Harlem's prominent black leaders formed a short-lived organization called the International League of Darker Peoples (ILDP).[38] Among the elected officers for the ILDP were Reverend Adam Clayton Powell, president; Isaac B. Allen, first vice president; Lewis G. Jordan, second vice president; Madam C. J. Walker, treasurer; A. Philip Randolph, secretary; and Gladys Flynn, assistant secretary. They agreed to submit an African American peace proposal, and Randolph drafted it.[39] In the March 1919 issue of *The Messenger,* Randolph described the overall thrust of their peacemaking strategy in an editorial titled "Internationalism":

> Carry the Negro problem out of the United States, at the same time that you present it in the United States. The mere fact that the country does not want the Negro problem carried out to Europe is strong evidence that it ought to be carried there. William Monroe Trotter has caught the point and gone to Europe to embarrass the President of the United States, who has been making hypocritical professions about democracy in the United States which has not existed and does not exist. . . . The international method of dealing with problems is the method of the future.[40]

The U.S. government closely monitored New Negro leaders' political activities in Harlem and noted, in particular, cross-racial solidarity between black America and Japan in proposed projects. According to the Bureau of Investigation report, Garvey allegedly "preached that the next war will be between the negroes and the whites unless their demands for justice are recognized and that with the aid of Japan on the side of the negroes they will be able to win such a war."[41] Indeed, UNIA members paid close attention to the mainstream media's view of Japan's role in the upcoming peace conference, citing a *New York Times* article that reported that "Japanese newspapers are suggesting that Japan and China raise the race question . . . with the object of seeking an agreement to the effect that in the future there shall be no further racial discrimination throughout the world." The *Negro World,* Garvey's weekly newspaper, also cited the comments of the U.S. ambassador in Tokyo, who said that "plans are being seriously discussed for an immediate alliance with China so that the two nations may work in harmony at the (Peace) Conference."[42]

The Garveyites welcomed Japan's assertiveness and interpreted it as a hopeful sign:

This report is very suggestive. In it can be seen immediate preparation by the yellow man of Asia for the new war that is to be [waged]—the war of the races. This is not time for the Negro to be found wanting anything. He must prepare himself, he must be well equipped in every department, so that when the great clash comes in the future he can be ready wherever he is to be found.[43]

The UNIA rallied behind the coming "war of the races" and at times invited Japanese speakers to their meetings to reinforce the idea of a race war. Indeed, as Gerald Horne and Reginald Kearney argue, such a vision of "a coming of racial Armageddon" enabled them to express their desire for liberation from white supremacy.[44] John Edward Bruce, a journalist and a pan-Africanist who later worked closely with Marcus Garvey, for instance, wrote a short story in which Japan and the United States were at war with each other and Japan triumphed. Bruce wrote, "The Philippines and Hawaii . . . were lost to America and the flag of Japan waved proudly from the fortifications lately occupied by American troops."[45]

The real and imagined encounters between Japan and African America heightened the concerns of U.S. authorities. Officials in the Bureau of Investigation commented that some members of the International League of Darker Peoples were actively propagating ways "to unite with the darker races, such as the Japanese, Hindus, etc.," while imagining the "broader movement," where "Japan may come to their aid in their struggle for [e]mancipation." Madam C. J. Walker, too, had come under the surveillance of the army's intelligence branch because she played an important role in the International League of Darker Peoples. She was especially instrumental in arranging a meeting with S. Kurowia, publisher of the Tokyo newspaper *Yorudo Chobo* and one of the Japanese representatives selected to participate in the Paris Peace Conference.[46] The report of the Bureau of Investigation indicated that the International League of Darker Peoples held a conference on January 7, 1919, "in honor of S. Kurowia, of the Japanese Peace Conference," during which the participants resolved to demand "the abolition of colored discrimination, freedom of immigration, revision of treaties unfavorable for Africa, abolition of economic barriers, [and] self-determination for Africa."[47] In 1918–19, supporters of the African American campaign to organize the world for peace and global racial justice converged politically, even though many did not necessarily share the same politics.

A. Philip Randolph and Chandler Owen, of *The Messenger,* did not always agree with the race-conscious worldview of Garveyites and some of the other New Negro intellectual–activists. However, they, too, interpreted the problem of the existing world system in racial terms and globalized the race question to challenge the international politics of racial discrimination. Both Randolph and Owen were especially incensed with the imperialists' use of systematic suppression of the race question at the Paris Peace Conference to consolidate their empires, which enabled them to solidify what Hubert Harrison once described as the "international Color Line."[48] In one editorial, published in March 1919, they expressed their indignation in this way: "There must be no more Belgiums. There may be Congo massacres of innocent Africans by Belgians, though. There may be Memphis and Waco [Texas] burnings of Negroes. Hush! Don't raise the race issue!"[49] Here the editors commented on the absence of a serious discussion about the problem of global white supremacy. What they presented, by way of linking the genocide in the Belgian Congo with the campaigns of white terror in the United States, however, was not only, as Amy Kaplan explains, "a counter-map of the United States"[50] that condemned the role of the United States as an imperial power but also a map of anticolonialism. When lines were drawn from one locale to another, their cognitive map revealed the nexus of race and empire.

Thus, when Japan introduced the racial equality clause during the League of Nations Commissions meeting in early 1919, Randolph and Owen responded with enthusiasm and engaged in the anticolonial and anti-imperialist practice of cartography. For them, mapmaking was a kind of intellectual activity that involved an ability to expose the arrogance of the white race.[51] They wrote in March 1919,

> Japan raised the race issue and threw a monkey wrench into the league of white nations which well nigh knocked the peace conference to pieces. It was successfully side-tracked, however. This question would not bear the slightest examination by the American peace commission which has its vexatious Negro problem and which excludes Japanese immigrants by a gentleman's agreement. Nor could Great Britain face the issue with her West

Indian colonies and her India. Australia, a British dominion, excludes both Negroes and Asiatics.[52]

Randolph and Owen integrated the symbolic significance of Japan's struggle for the racial equality proposal to develop a countermap of Wilsonian liberal internationalism, rendering visible the white supremacist underpinnings of debates and discussions that ensued at the Paris Peace Conference. In their political imagination, Japan functioned as a device and possessed "the cartographic power"[53] to communicate and represent the interconnectedness of the problems of racism, colonialism, and the racial politics of immigration.

Although Randolph and Owen identified with Japan in the wake of the appearance of the racial equality clause at the Paris Peace Conference, that did not mean that they looked to Japan as the leader of the "colored world" in the future race war, as some of the Garveyites did. Inspired by a Marxist interpretation of the world capitalist system, both were grounded in the class analysis and well armed with theoretical insights to scrutinize the Japanese imperialist state and colonial projects in Asia. Even as they expressed enthusiasm for Japan's diplomatic strategy, which exposed the real face of colonial powers and the white supremacist elements in Wilsonian internationalism, they remained critical, arguing that Japan was not interested in challenging the "international Color Line," let alone in putting pressure on the United States to end the practice of Jim Crow. In the May–June 1919 issue of *The Messenger,* Randolph and Owen included a lengthy cautionary note to explain the significance of Japan's race-conscious intervention in world politics:

> A word of warning, however, to the unsuspecting and to those not thoroughly versed in social science. The Japanese statesmen are not in the least concerned about race or color prejudice. The smug and oily Japanese diplomats are no different from Woodrow Wilson, Lloyd George or Orlando. They do not suffer from race prejudice. They teach in the Rockefeller Institute, wine and dine at the Waldorf Astoria, Manhattan or Poinciana, divide financial melons in Wall Street, ride on railways and cars free from discrimination. They care nothing for even the Japanese people and at this very same moment are suppressing and oppressing mercilessly the people of Korea and forcing hard bargains upon unfortunate China.[54]

Hubert Harrison, likewise, understood that what concerned Japan was the attainment of a "white" imperial power status. Japan was no different from other great powers of the West. He explained, "The secret of England's greatness (as well as of any other great nation's) is not bibles but bayonets—bayonets, business and brains. Ask Japan: she knows."[55] Many of the New Negro activist–intellectuals critically assessed the significance of Japan's invocation of the race question on the world stage, unlike Marcus Garvey, who rallied the masses to prepare for the imminent race war between the United States and Japan. Harrison, Randolph, and Owen eschewed such rhetoric and instead placed the political guarantee in the socialist struggle. Although socialists Randolph and Owen generally did not cast themselves with the communist camp and the supporters of revolutionary Marxism, nor with Garveyites, to expose the imperialist and white supremacist underpinnings of Wilsonian internationalism, their political position during this critical juncture was undeniably formulated and refined at the nexus of socialism and black nationalism.

DISARMAMENT DISSENTERS

New Negro intellectuals' internationalist outlook and revolutionary consciousness remained salient in the aftermath of the 1919 Paris Peace Conference, and their commentary on Japan continued to appear in the margins of their political discussions. When great powers of the West and Japan congregated to set the general framework for a new diplomacy in the Asia-Pacific during the Washington Conference of 1921–22, these writers developed sharp criticisms of the underlying imperialism and white supremacy of the new international system.

At this conference, the United States, Great Britain, Japan, and France, along with other nation-states such as Italy, the Netherlands, Belgium, and China, held a series of talks to establish the terms of disarmament and the basis of a new order in the Asia-Pacific. As in the 1919 Paris Peace Conference, the United States assumed world leadership and challenged the old structure of power diplomacy. Its primary objective was to abrogate the foundation of imperialist "scramble" for territories, resources, and colonies and replace it with a U.S.-led open door policy, which would guarantee great powers' access to the market in China. The U.S. government called on world leaders to organize a consortium that would foster international cooperation and enable the Western nations to derive power and wealth from the trade with China. Meanwhile, the Western powers excluded the new Soviet Union from participating in this consortium and forced Italy, Japan, Germany, and China to fall in line and accept subordinate roles within this newly reorganized international system.[56]

The Washington Conference reminded Japan of its tenuous status as a great power. The combination of diplomatic pressures, the need to secure foreign markets for domestic economic growth, and the desire to retain great power status influenced Japan's decision to concede to the U.S.-led reorganization of East Asian affairs. By the end of the conference, Japan had come to accept the new era of imperial diplomacy and gave up much of its wartime gains, including its control of the

Shantung Peninsula in China. The American and British diplomats also pressured the Japanese into accepting an unequal ratio of capital ship tonnage in the name of disarmament, which subsequently weakened Japan's naval power in the Asia-Pacific. In the end, the Japanese agreed to the liquidation of "all existing treaties between the powers and China [and] replaced them with the Open Door principles so long espoused by the United States."[57] Contrary to Western leaders' rhetoric of liberal internationalism, the main purpose of the conference was not to guarantee peace in the postwar Asia-Pacific but to figure out ways to exploit China. This new diplomacy in the Asia-Pacific intensified the contest for supremacy in the region, and Japan struggled to maintain its status within this globalized racial polity.

Throughout the period of the Washington Conference, Chandler Owen, A. Philip Randolph, Cyril V. Briggs, and Andy Razafinkeriefo were vocal critics of the terms of disarmament and international agreements to institute a new order in the Pacific. They argued that imperialists' pursuit of power and property interests encouraged the drive toward aggressive militarism and the reconstitution of global white supremacy in the Asia-Pacific. In particular, they emphasized that the combination of militarism and international capitalism strengthened the colonial system of exploitation and subjugation based on race and class. In a poem published in the January–February 1922 issue of *The Crusader,* a magazine published by the communist-influenced African Blood Brotherhood, Andy Razafinkeriefo condemned the white supremacist objectives of the conference on disarmament through the creative use of carefully plotted rhymes:

THE REASON

The conference is quite ill at ease
In regards to their friends, the Chinese.
There's no country finer
To exploit than China—
The Japs must not get all the cheese.[58]

Razafinkeriefo showed understanding toward the ways in which the Anglo-American alliance vied for white supremacy in the Asia-Pacific. His poem simultaneously mocked and exposed the arrogance and anxiety of the white world. The resistance expressed toward Japan's demand for racial equality, especially Western nations' militantly defensive posture toward Japan's assertiveness in the international system, served the New Nero intellectuals well. It enabled them to offer an analysis of the role of race in the reconstitution of white supremacy in the Pacific and its implications for African-descended people in the wider world.

Unlike Razafinkeriefo's poem, which relied on the creative use of language,

The Messenger's December 1921 editorial went straight to the Marxist critique of imperialism and colonialism. Randolph and Owen explained that an emphasis on "scrapping of some battleships" among the "Five Powers"—the United States, Great Britain, Japan, France, and Italy—at the Washington Conference concealed the real aims of international capitalist states—the exploitation of the resources and people of China in the name of the open door policy:

> Our readers should understand that this conference is not called to disarm. It was called to parcel out, divide up and emasculate China with a sort of gentlemen's agreement as to the spheres of influence. That is all which is meant by the "open door" and the Far East or Pacific question. Open the door to America, Great Britain, France and Japan to go into China and rob the helpless people of their iron, coal and oil.[59]

Moreover, Randolph and Owen argued that the conference on disarmament was, in fact, designed to arm the world in a new way. They specifically pointed to the proliferation of weapons of mass destruction: "What about poison gas, airplanes, submarines and torpedo boats? These are the modern, more deadly instruments of war. A ton of Lewisite gas is more deadly than the entire American navy."[60] The editorial explicitly stated that conditions for disarmament could never be found in the world capitalist system as long as a "bone of contention in trade routes, commerce, concessions, spheres of influence, underdeveloped territories, weaker peoples, cheap land and cheap labor will ever exist."[61]

Above all, Andy Razafinkeriefo's poem best represented the black commentary on the dangers of militarization and the absence of real disarmament throughout the world. Like other creative writings that appeared in *The Crusader,* Razafinkeriefo's voice not only contained the energies of New Negro radicalism but also the internationalist perspectives of black intellectuals. In the following poem published in the January–February 1922 issue, he used a complex system of rhyme patterns to produce particular sound and literary effects:

DISARMAMENT

O, Gentlemen! why not disarm
The hordes who daily do us harm,
Who ply their trade relentlessly
On suffering Humanity?

Disarm the bed-bug,
Disarm the flea,

> Disarm the mosquito,
> The cootie and bee.
> Disarm the barbers of their tongues
> And back-yard songsters of their lungs.
>
> But while there's money to be got
> By sending folks off to be shot;
> Just keep your side-arms at your hips
> And hold on to those battleships.
> For, my last pair of socks, I'll bet
> That we are booked for more wars yet.[62]

In this poem, Razafinkeriefo adopted complex musical forms and styles and used humor to communicate the dangers of continued armament and how it threatened world peace. He was a master at capturing the ethos of ordinary black working people. Instead of naming weapons of mass destruction and explicitly criticizing Western powers for making the world unsafe for people of color, he named insects, especially those that bite, sting, and suck and that cause ill feelings, harm, and pain, to convey the grievances of black people. The lyrics showed evidence of musical styles of slave songs, especially work songs, which were composed by enslaved and free black workers as they performed daily activities.[63]

The poem avoided denouncing the imperialist and white supremacist underpinnings of the Washington Conference directly in politicized language, as Randolph and Owen did. Instead, it relied on what historian Lawrence W. Levine called "black laughter," which "provided a sense of the total black condition not only by putting whites and their racial system in perspective but also by supplying an important degree of self and group knowledge."[64] The humor embedded in his poem possessed an explanatory power much like the street corner oratory that many of the leading New Negro leaders and activists, especially Hubert Harrison, performed and perfected during this period. The poem syncopated the rhythm, especially through carefully plotted rhymes, and projected African Americans' desire to disassociate from aggressive militarism, which buttressed the relentless expansion of colonial and white supremacist powers.

New Negro intellectual–activists' protest against the disarmament conference also emphasized the impact of militarization on the home front. They emphasized that imperialist clubs' obsession with world domination severely damaged the civic sector of the U.S. economy and contributed to an increase in living costs and taxes, which burdened ordinary working people and especially racially aggrieved populations. Chandler Owen, for instance, explained that the "apparent desire for peace, however, is not found to be the motivating cause of the conference by students of world politics. We find, on the contrary, that the burdens of taxation for maintaining armies and navies have soared so high that it is no longer possible to shift all of those loads on the working people, but any further assessment must, as they will, fall upon wealth. This, to say the least, is not a rosy anticipation." Owen concluded that "if each of them [imperialist powers] continues to pile up this huge burden upon the tired and bending backs of the working people, it must plan to face civil war at home—the revolt of the people—a revolt which may metamorphose into a revolution and sweep away the very foundations of the old order of society—the tottering system of capitalism, and its foster child, a dogged but doddering imperialism."[65]

Like Owen, Cyril V. Briggs of *The Crusader* and the African Blood Brotherhood dreamed of "the revolt of the people," especially of the black working class. However, Briggs's position was qualitatively different from the positions of Randolph and Owen. As an advocate of revolutionary Marxism, his position was characterized by unwavering commitment to black self-determination locally and globally, to anticolonialism, and to African liberation.[66] Moreover, Briggs looked beyond national borders, recognizing that the coming unity between and among Germany, Mexico, and Japan could be used as a weapon, as historian Gerald Horne argued, "to exploit the natural security weaknesses of white supremacy."[67] While the U.S. authorities repeatedly expressed their fears that Jim Crow and rampant racial violence at home could erode support among African Americans and in turn strengthen their ties with "allies" abroad—Mexico and Japan—Briggs presented a different option. During the period of "gathering war clouds" between the United States and Japan, as well as between the United States and Mexico, he emphasized that instead of waiting for the coming of "a war to force acceptance of the doctrine of white superiority upon Japan" or the "eventuality of war between white United States and colored Japan," Briggs presented the following statement: "*Not to fight against Japan or Mexico, but rather to fill the prisons and dungeons of the white man (or to face his firing squads) than to shoulder arms against other members of darker races.*"[68] As a leader of the militant and revolutionary black organization, whose aims were to abolish white supremacy and capitalism through armed resistance and establish the foundation for independent black states in the African diaspora, Briggs demanded an uncompromising struggle against racism, imperialism, and colonialism in the postwar world.

Writing in the wake of the "Red Scare" and "Red Summer" of 1919, Briggs, Harrison, and other New Negro leaders consistently communicated the internationalist conception of black freedom. They were convinced that the anti-imperialist struggle started at the local level and regarded the merging of black nationalism and revolutionary socialism as the motor of revolutionary change. With this in mind, in December 1922, Briggs presented the antiwar, antiracist, and anti-imperialist position of New Negro radicalism, urging them not to be accomplices in the white supremacist project:

> The Negro who fights against either Japan or Mexico is fighting for the *white man* against himself, for the *white race* against the darker races and for the perpetuation of *white domination of the colored races,* with its vicious practices of *lynching, jim-crowism, segregation and other forms of oppression* in opposition to the principle advocated by Japan of Race Equality, and there are things that, we are convinced, *no loyal Negro* will do.[69]

Briggs noted that those who would fight on behalf of the U.S. imperial power against Japan or Mexico compromised the principle of racial equality, the very issue that Japan helped to internationalize during the 1919 Paris Peace Conference. His gesture of affinity toward Japan, however, did not mean that he was blind to Japan's imperial ambitions and colonial projects. What he advocated was the war of black liberation on the home front, not a race war on a global scale.

NEW NEGRO FEMINISM

In the immediate aftermath of the First World War, the iconography of Japan as the New Negro of the Pacific helped to open another space to critique white supremacy. However, those who identified with the New Negro of the Pacific did so within a gendered framework and relied heavily on the tropes of war and militarism to articulate a masculinist vision of black freedom. Such a vision embraced traditional gender roles and consequently failed to elucidate the roles that African Caribbean and African American women played in the making of the black radical tradition. New Negro leaders' and writers' commentary on Japan was imbued with gendered assumptions that perceived international and domestic politics as male-dominated spheres.[70] During the years between 1917 and 1922, however, African American women, including Grace Campbell, Ida B. Wells-Barnett, and Jessie Fauset, shaped the antiwar, antiracist, and anti-imperialist politics of the New Negro movement in significant ways. Although issues of women's rights did not appear in the pages of *The Crusader,* women figured prominently in the African Blood Brotherhood. Grace Campbell in particular occupied a position of leadership in the group, and her home was used as a meeting place and an office. Moreover, Ida B. Wells-Barnett, a towering crusader for racial justice and a veteran antiracist and feminist activist, was nominated twice to represent the African American delegation to the 1919 Paris Peace Conference, even though she was, like Trotter, unable to secure a passport to travel abroad.[71]

Indeed, recent scholarship shows that African Caribbean and African American women's political activism gained momentum in the international context during this period. The first and second wives of Marcus Garvey, Amy Ashwood-Garvey and Amy Jacques-Garvey, for instance, were especially instrumental in rallying black women to challenge imperialism. According to historian Ula Y. Taylor, Jacques-Garvey's work as the associate editor of the *Negro World* shows that she not only helped build the black nationalist and pan-African movements but also constructed a distinct black feminist tradition, which Taylor calls "community feminism." Jacques-Garvey made feminism central to the UNIA and interpreted women as both helpmates and leaders capable of playing a leading role in community and nation building.[72]

Other women leaders, though revolutionary Marxism did not inform their politics as with Grace Campbell, considered women's active participation in world affairs important to the project of racial advancement. Madam C. J. Walker's role in the formation of the short-lived International League of Darker Peoples was a case in point, as noted in this essay earlier. Moreover, as Michelle Rief shows, the leaders of the club movement—Mary Church Terrell, Mary Talbert, Addie Hunton, and Margaret Murray Washington—participated in international organizations, such as the Women's International League for Peace and Freedom, and organized the International Council of Women of the Darker Races to synthesize the causes of racial justice and peace locally and globally.[73] For some, the so-called Japanese question entered into political discussions and was taken up as the topic of analysis among the membership.[74]

Above all, Jessie Fauset, then literary editor of *The Crisis* magazine, straddled diverse intellectual traditions during the New Negro era.[75] Writing in the wake of the 1917 East St. Louis race riots, Fauset articulated African Americans' determination to defend democracy in the face of white terrorist actions leveled against them. Although Fauset's following narrative did not make any reference to Japan, it did reflect the mood of New Negro radicalism. In it Fauset described the nature of white mobs' assault against African American women, babies, and families as a global trend and evoked the motif of the rape of black women, rather than emphasizing African American men as the victims of racial terror. Historian Robin D. G. Kelly noted the symbolic significance of Fauset's narrative strategy that "carried specific historical resonance in light of the history of sexual terrorism visited upon black women in slavery and freedom."[76] Fauset declared,

A people whose members would snatch a baby because it was black from its mother's arms, as was done in East St. Louis, and fling it into a blazing house while white furies held the mother until the men shot her to death—such a people is definitely approaching moral disintegration. Turkey has slaughtered its Armenians, Russia has held its pogroms, Belgium has tortured and maimed in the Congo, and Turkey, Russia, Belgium are synonyms for anathema, demoralization and pauperdom. We, the American Negroes, are the acid test for occidental civilization. If we perish, we perish. But when we fall, we shall fall, like Samson, dragging inevitably with us the pillars of a nation's democracy.[77]

Moreover, Fauset's narrative conveyed just how the black freedom struggle represented the only hope for democratic renewal in America and the world at large. She was convinced that cornerstones of democratization locally and globally were found in African Americans' struggles for freedom and that they were the vehicles for rescuing colored humanity from white supremacy. Certainly she was acutely aware of the "white problem" and interpreted it as a sign of the moral and political bankruptcy of so-called Western civilization. The repeated patterns of racial pogroms in the United States and abroad were clear evidence of the white world's "descent to Hell," as Du Bois once put it.[78] According to literary critic Jane Kuenz, Fauset's works of fiction, especially *There Is Confusion* (1924), emphasized "the theme that black cultural practices and black *people* are surpassing or even replacing white practices and people in the role of defining national progress."[79] During this period, Fauset was indisputably one of the sharpest critics of the white supremacist underpinnings of imperialism and colonialism.

Such a radical critique, however, went unmentioned in the pages of leading New Negro publications. What dominated instead were idealized images of African American women. The editors constructed narratives of race progress and race pride that emphasized Victorian gender conventions. These publications, as Kevin K. Gaines noted, "sought a new standard of feminine beauty as part of the New Negro cultural aesthetic."[80] African American women's cultural and political space for self-representation was narrow, and their long-standing struggles against institutional violence were often rendered invisible.[81]

In the context of war and revolution, colonialism and imperialism, and state-sanctioned white terrorism, the symbolic significance of Japan's fight for racial equality in the international system found its way into New Negro leaders' political imagination and intellectuals' narratives of antiwar, antiracist, and anti-imperialist struggles, even as their counterarticulations remained undeniably male centered. Appearing in the margins of black political discourse, the trope of Japan as the New Negro of the Pacific aided activist–intellectuals' efforts to smear the paint of the black radical imagination in the face of Wilsonian liberal and international democracy. More important, the attitudes of New Negro intellectual–activists toward Japan were multifaceted and best characterized as heterogeneous. They all defined their political positions variously and strategically. Even as they showed differing ideological and political orientations, they converged at critical conjunctures.

Randolph and Garvey, for instance, offered similar arguments, although the Garveyites generally failed to acknowledge Japan's imperialist aims and activities in the international community. Other New Negro activist–intellectuals, including Owen, Harrison, Briggs, and Razafinkeriefo, recognized Japan's imperial ascent and expansion but still used the symbolic significance of Japan's race-conscious defiance against white supremacy to bring the scope and methods of struggles for black self-determination at local and global levels into sharper focus. Race functioned as the mainspring of unpredictable creativity that made the space of black resistance productive for a new politics. Although these New Negro activist–intellectuals' commentary on Japan was not central to the formation of the ontological category called the New Negro during this period between 1917 and 1922, the spectacle of Japan's struggle with global white supremacy proved useful as a reference point to convey the visions and tactics of black radicalism.

NOTES

1   Hubert Harrison, "The Washington Conference," in Perry, *A Hubert Harrison Reader,* 230.

2   Perry, *Hubert Harrison,* 233–38, 278; Hubert Harrison, "Race Consciousness," in Perry, *A Hubert Harrison Reader,* 116–17. Jeffrey Perry promises to elaborate Hubert Harrison's "race-consciousness" in action in a much-anticipated second volume with the subtitle *Race Consciousness and the Struggle for Democracy, 1918–1927.*

3   Perry, *Hubert Harrison,* 243–395.

4   Harrison, "The Line-Up on the Color Line," in Perry, *A Hubert Harrison Reader,* 219.

5   Brent Hayes Edwards refers to this work of "linking up" as "the practice of diaspora." It sustained creative impulses among intellectuals and artists of African descent in Harlem and Paris and aided the coeval formation of black internationalism during the period commonly referred to as the Harlem Renaissance. Edwards, *Practice of Diaspora.*

6   Harrison, "The White War and the Colored World," in Perry, *A Hubert Harrison Reader,* 203; Harrison, "Race Consciousness," 117.

7   The characterization of Harrison as the "voice of Harlem radicalism" appears in the subtitle of Perry's first volume of Harrison's biography.

8   Fox, *Guardian of Boston,* 217.

9   Allen, "New Negro," 48–68. Also see Foley, *Spectres of 1919,* 1–69; Franklin, *Living Our Stories, Telling Our Truths,* 122–25, 147–58.

10 Robinson, *Black Marxism,* xxxi–xxxii; on the formation of racial capitalism, see ibid.

11 Ibid., 169.

12 Franklin, *Black Self-Determination,* 6.

13   I have turned to Minkah Makalani's analysis of Cyril V. Briggs's pan-Africanism to understand black intellectuals' trans-Pacific solidarity with Japan. Makalani, "For the Liberation of Black People Everywhere," 75–82. Also, Robin D. G. Kelley's most recent work has sharpened my overall analysis of the political imagination of what Kelley calls "renegade black intellectuals/activists/artists." Kelley, *Freedom Dreams,* 6.

14   Singh, *Black Is a Country,* 44.

15   For recent scholarship that explores the nexus of Japan and the black radical tradition, see Kearney, *African American Views of the Japanese*; Kearney, "Afro-American Views of the Japanese"; Kearney, "Pro-Japanese Utterances of W. E. B. Du Bois," 201–17; Allen, "When Japan Was 'Champion of the Darker Races,'" 23–46; Allen, "Waiting for Tojo," 38–55; Horne, "Tokyo Bound," 16–28; Horne, *Race War!,* esp. chapter 2; Lewis, *W. E. B. Du Bois: The Fight for Equality,* chapter 11; Koshiro, "Beyond an Alliance of Color," 183–215; Furukawa and Furukawa, *Nihonjin to Afurikakei Amerikajin*; Onishi, "Giant Steps of the Black Freedom Struggle." Also, for the theoretical and analytical discussion of the dynamics of Afro-Asian unities, see Prashad, *Everybody Was Kung Fu Fighting*; Lipsitz, "Frantic to Join . . . the Japanese Army," 324–53; Von Eschen, *Race against Empire*; Kelley and Esch, "Black Like Mao," 6–41; Edwards, "Shadow of Shadows," 11–49; Mullen, *Afro-Orientalism.*

16   Robinson, *Black Marxism,* 309.

17   For the analysis of New Negro radicalism, especially its relationship with revolutionary Marxism, see James, *Holding Aloft the Banner of Ethiopia*; Stephens, "Black Transnationalism and the Politics of National Identity," 592–608; Stephens, *Black Empire*; Maxwell, *New Negro, Old Left.*

18   Macmillan, *Paris 1919,* 312–16.

19   Quoted in Shimazu, *Japan, Race, and Equality,* 17; Gallicchio, *African American Encounter with Japan and China,* 21–24.

20   Quoted in Shimazu, *Japan, Race, and Equality,* 20.

21   Quoted in ibid., 28. Also see ibid., 20–21, 23–27; LaFeber, *The Clash,* 122–24; Gallicchio, *African American Encounter with Japan and China,* 24.

22   Quoted in Shimazu, *Japan, Race, and Equality,* 30; Gallicchio, *African American Encounter with Japan and China,* 24.

23   Quoted in Shimazu, *Japan, Race, and Equality,* 30.

24   "The Negro—A Menace to Radicalism," *The Messenger,* May–June 1919, 20.

25   Spence, *Gate of Heavenly Peace,* 154–59.

26   Lewis, *W. E. B. Du Bois: The Biography of Race,* 567–69, 576–78; Contee, "Du Bois," 13–28; Marable, "Pan-Africanism of W. E. B. Du Bois," 199–202; Du Bois, "Negro in Paris," 127–29; Du Bois, *World and Africa,* 6–13.

27   Marable, "Pan-Africanism of W. E. B. Du Bois," 201.

28   The clash between capitalist and anticapitalist ideological perspectives among members of the African American intelligentsia is highlighted in Franklin, *Living Our Stories, Telling Our Truths,* 165–83 passim.

29   Hubert Harrison, "Africa at the Peace Table," in Perry, *A Hubert Harrison Reader,* 211–12.

30 "Peace Conference," *The Messenger,* March 1919, 5. Also see Andrea Razafkeriefo, "Just Thinking," *The Crusader,* January–February 1922, in *The Crusader,* vol. 6, 1352. Razafkeriefo wrote, "The trouble with all Peace Conferences has been that they have always talked about 'pieces' instead of Peace."

31 Perry, introduction to *A Hubert Harrison Reader,* 1–30; James, *Holding Aloft the Banner of Ethiopia,* 122–134; Allen, "New Negro," 54–60; Makalani, "For the Liberation of Black People Everywhere," chapter 2.

32 "Negroes of the World Unite in Demanding a Free Africa," *The Crusader,* December 1918, in *The Crusader,* vol. 1, 113.

33 Marcus Garvey, "Race Discrimination Must Go," *Negro World,* November 30, 1918, in Hill, *Marcus Garvey and Universal Negro Improvement Association Papers,* 305; Lauren, *Power and Prejudice,* 79.

34 "Maj. W. H. Loving to the Director, Military Intelligence Division," in Hill, *Marcus Garvey and Universal Negro Improvement Association Papers,* 338.

35 Marcus Garvey, "Advice of the Negro to Peace Conference," in ibid., 302–4; "Bureau of Investigation Reports," in ibid., 288; "Announcement in the *New York Call,*" in ibid., 284; Allen, "New Negro," 54; Bundles, *On Her Own Ground,* 254–56.

36 Bundles, *On Her Own Ground,* 253–54.

37 "Bureau of Investigation Reports," in Hill, *Marcus Garvey and Universal Negro Improvement Association Papers,* 305–6; Lewis, *W. E. B. Du Bois: The Fight for Equality,* 59; Fox, *Guardian of Boston,* 223–24.

38 For an overview of the International League of Darker Peoples, see Bundles, *On Her Own Ground,* 257–65.

39 "Maj. W. H. Loving to the Director, Military Intelligence Division," in Hill, *Marcus Garvey and Universal Negro Improvement Association Papers,* 344–46.

40 "Internationalism," *The Messenger,* August 1919, 5–6. Also see "Peace Terms," *The Messenger,* March 1919, 11.

41 "Bureau of Investigation Reports," in Hill, *Marcus Garvey and Universal Negro Improvement Association Papers,* 305–6.

42 Marcus Garvey, "Race Discrimination Must Go," in ibid., 305.

43 Ibid., 304. Also see "Bureau of Investigation Reports," 309–10.

44 Kearney, *African American Views of the Japanese,* 59; Horne, *Race War!,* 46–47.

45 Quoted in Kearney, *African American Views of the Japanese,* 59.

46 Bundles, *On Her Own Ground,* 255, 258.

47 New York State Legislature, *Revolutionary Radicalism,* 1517.

48 Hubert Harrison, "Two Negro Radicalisms," in Perry, *A Hubert Harrison Reader,* 103.

49 "Peace Conference," 5.

50 Kaplan, *Anarchy of Empire,* 196. For the analysis of how W. E. B. Du Bois developed the discourse of anticolonialism in *Darkwater,* see ibid., 190–97.

51 On the definition of cartography, see ibid., 180–81.

52 "Peace Conference," 5.

53 Kaplan, *Anarchy of Empire,* 180.

54 "Japan and the Race Issue," *The Messenger,* May–June 1919, 6.

55 Harrison, "Africa at the Peace Table," 211.

56 LaFeber, *The Clash,* 128–43.

57 Hata, "Continental Expansion," 283; Iriye, *After Imperialism,* 13–21; LaFeber, *The Clash,* 128–43.

58 Andrea Razafkeriefo, "The Reason," *The Crusader,* January–February 1922, in *The Crusader,* vol. 6, 1358.

59 "The Disarmament Conference," *The Messenger,* December 1921, 298.

60 Ibid.

61 "Labor and Disarmament," *The Messenger,* February 1922, 352.

62 Andrea Razafkeriefo, "Disarmament," *The Crusader,* January–February 1922, in *The Crusader,* vol. 6, 1358.

63 Levine, *Black Culture and Black Consciousness,* 195–96.

64 Ibid., 320.

65 Chandler Owen, "Disarmament," *The Messenger,* November 1921, 279–80.

66 Foner, *American Socialism and Black Americans,* 309–11.

67 Horne, *Black and Brown,* 175. See esp. chapter 8 for the analysis of how both the "Zimmerman Telegram" and "The Plan of San Diego" helped to strike a major blow to the stronghold of white supremacy at home.

68 "The Gathering War Clouds," *The Crusader,* December 1920, in *The Crusader,* vol. 3, 942.

69 Ibid.

70 Kelley, *Freedom Dreams,* 25–59; James, *Transcending the Talented Tenth.*

71 On Grace Campbell, see James, *Holding Aloft the Banner of Ethiopia,* 174–77, and Makalani, "For the Liberation of Black People Everywhere," 120–30; on Ida B. Wells-Barnett, see James, *Transcending the Talented Tenth,* 46–53, 76–81.

72 Taylor, "Intellectual Pan-African Feminists"; Taylor, "Negro Women Are Great Thinkers As Well As Doers," 104–26; Taylor, *Veiled Garvey.*

73 Rief, "Thinking Locally, Acting Globally," 203–22.

74 Ibid., 215–16.

75 Kuenz, "Face of America," 89–111. Also see McDowell, "Neglected Dimension of Jessie Redmon Fauset," 33–49.

76 Kelley, *Freedom Dreams,* 27.

77 Jessie Fauset, "Letter to the Editor," *Survey,* August 8, 1917, 448.

78 Du Bois, "The Souls of White Folk," 186.

79 Kuenz, "Face of America," 100.

80 Gaines, *Uplifting the Race,* 243.

81 Makalani, "For the Liberation of Black People Everywhere," 121–23; Gaines, *Uplifting the Race,* 243–45.

BIBLIOGRAPHY

Allen, Ernest, Jr. "The New Negro: Explorations in Identity and Social Consciousness, 1910–1922." In *1915, the Cultural Moment: The New Politics, the New Women, the New Psychology, the New Art, and the New Theatre in America,* edited by Adele Heller and Lois Rudnick, 46–68. New Brunswick, N.J.: Rutgers University Press, 1991.

———. "Waiting for Tojo: The Pro-Japan Vigil of Black Missourians, 1932–1943." *Gateway Heritage* 15 (Fall 1995): 38–55.

———. "When Japan Was 'Champion of the Darker Races': Satokata Takahashi and the Flowering of Black Messianic Nationalism." *The Black Scholar* 24 (Winter 1994): 23–46.

Bundles, A'Lelia. *On Her Own Ground: The Life and Times of Madam C. J. Walker.* New York: Scribner, 2002.

Contee, Clarence G. "Du Bois, the NAACP, and the Pan-African Congress of 1919." *Journal of Negro History* 57 (January 1972): 13–28.

Du Bois, W. E. B. "Negro in Paris." In *Writings by W. E. B. Du Bois in Periodicals Edited by Others,* compiled and edited by Herbert Aptheker, 127–29. Millwood, N.Y.: Kraus-Thomson, 1982.

———. "The Souls of White Folk." In *Black on White: Black Writers on What It Means to Be White,* edited with an introduction by David R. Roediger, 184–99. New York: Schocken Books, 1998.

———. *The World and Africa: An Inquiry into the Part Which Africa Has Played in World History.* Enlarged ed. New York: International, 1996.

Edwards, Brent Hayes. *The Practice of Diaspora: Literature, Translation, and the Rise of Black Internationalism.* Cambridge, Mass.: Harvard University Press, 2003.

———. "The Shadow of Shadows." *positions* 11 (Spring 2003): 11–49.

Fauset, Jessie. "Letter to the Editor." *Survey,* August 8, 1917.

Foley, Barbara. *Spectres of 1919: Class and Nation in the Making of the New Negro.* Urbana: University of Illinois Press, 2003.

Foner, Philip S. *American Socialism and Black Americans: From the Age of Jackson to World War II.* Westport, Conn.: Greenwood Press, 1977.

Fox, Stephen R. *The Guardian of Boston: William Monroe Trotter.* New York: Atheneum, 1970.

Franklin, V. P. *Black Self-Determination: A Cultural History of African-American Resistance.* Foreword by Mary Frances Berry. Brooklyn, N.Y.: Lawrence Hill Books, 1992.

———. *Living Our Stories, Telling Our Truths: Autobiography and the Making of the African-American Intellectual Tradition.* New York: Scribner, 1995.

Furukawa, Hiromi, and Tetsushi Furukawa. *Nihonjin to Afurikakei Amerikajin: Nichibei-kankeishi niokeru sono Shoso* [Japanese and African Americans: Historical Aspects of Their Relations]. Tokyo: Akashi Shoten, 2004.

Gaines, Kevin K. *Uplifting the Race: Black Leadership, Politics, and Culture in the Twentieth Century.* Chapel Hill: University of North Carolina Press, 1996.

Gallicchio, Marc. *The African American Encounter with Japan and China: Black Internationalism in Asia, 1895–1945.* Chapel Hill: University of North Carolina Press, 2000.

Hata, Ikuhiko. "Continental Expansion, 1905–1941," translated by Alvin D. Cox. In *The Cambridge History of Japan,* vol. 6, edited by Peter Duus, 271–314. New York: Cambridge University Press, 1988.

Hill, Robert A. *The Crusader.* 6 vols. New York: Garland, 1987.

———, ed. *The Marcus Garvey and Universal Negro Improvement Association Papers.* Vol. 1. Berkeley: University of California Press, 1983.

Horne, Gerald. *Black and Brown: African Americans and the Mexican Revolution, 1910–1920.* New York: New York University Press, 2005.

———. *Race War! White Supremacy and the Japanese Attack on the British Empire.* New York: New York University Press, 2004.

———. "Tokyo Bound: African Americans and Japan Confront White Supremacy." *Souls* 3 (Summer 2001): 16–28.

Iriye, Akira. *After Imperialism: The Search for a New Order in the Far East, 1921–1931.* Cambridge, Mass.: Harvard University Press, 1965.

James, Joy. *Transcending the Talented Tenth: Black Leaders and American Intellectuals.* New York: Routledge, 1997.

James, Winston. *Holding Aloft the Banner of Ethiopia: Caribbean Radicalism in Early Twentieth-Century America.* New York: Verso, 1998.

Kaplan, Amy. *The Anarchy of Empire in the Making of American Culture.* Cambridge, Mass.: Harvard University Press, 2002.

Kearney, Reginald. *African American Views of the Japanese: Solidarity or Sedition?* Albany: State University of New York Press, 1998.

———. "Afro-American Views of the Japanese, 1900–1945." PhD diss., Kent State University, 1991.

———. "The Pro-Japanese Utterances of W. E. B. Du Bois." *Contributions in Black Studies* 13/14 (1999): 201–17.

Kelley, Robin D. G. *Freedom Dreams: The Black Radical Imagination.* Boston: Beacon Press, 2002.

Kelley, Robin D. G., and Betsy Esch. "Black Like Mao: Red China and Black Revolution." *Souls* 1 (Fall 1999): 6–41.

Koshiro, Yukiko. "Beyond an Alliance of Color: The African American Impact on Modern Japan." *positions* 11 (Spring 2003): 183–215.

Kuenz, Jane. "The Face of America: Performing Race and Nation in Jessie Fauset's *There Is Confusion.*" *Yale Journal of Criticism* 12 (Spring 1999): 89–111.

LaFeber, Walter. *The Clash: A History of U.S.–Japan Relations.* New York: W. W. Norton, 1997.

Lauren, Paul Gordon. *Power and Prejudice: The Politics and Diplomacy of Racial Discrimination.* Boulder, Colo.: Westview Press, 1998.

Levine, Lawrence W. *Black Culture and Black Consciousness: Afro-American Folk Thought from Slavery to Freedom.* New York: Oxford University Press, 1977.

Lewis, David Levering. *W. E. B. Du Bois: The Biography of Race, 1868–1919.* New York: Henry Holt, 1993.

————. *W. E. B. Du Bois: The Fight for Equality and the American Century, 1919–1963*. New York: Henry Holt, 2000.

Lipsitz, George. "Frantic to Join . . . the Japanese Army." In *The Politics of Culture in the Shadow of Capital,* edited by Lisa Lowe and David Lloyd, 324–53. Durham, N.C.: Duke University Press, 1997.

Macmillan, Margaret. *Paris 1919: Six Months That Changed the World*. New York: Random House, 2001.

Makalani, Minkah. "For the Liberation of Black People Everywhere: The African Blood Brotherhood, Black Radicalism, and Pan-African Liberation in the New Negro Movement, 1917–1936." PhD diss., University of Illinois at Urbana-Champaign, 2004.

Marable, Manning. "The Pan-Africanism of W. E. B. Du Bois." In *W. E. B. Du Bois on Race and Culture: Philosophy, Politics, and Poetics,* edited by Bernard W. Bell, Emily Grosholz, and James B. Stewart, 193–218. New York: Routledge, 1996.

Maxwell, William J. *New Negro, Old Left: African-American Writing and Communism between the Wars.* New York: Columbia University Press, 1999.

McDowell, Deborah E. "The Neglected Dimension of Jessie Redmon Fauset." *Afro-Americans in New York Life and History* 5 (July 1981): 33–49.

Mullen, Bill V. *Afro-Orientalism*. Minneapolis: University of Minnesota Press, 2004.

New York State Legislature. *Revolutionary Radicalism: A Report of the Joint Legislative Committee of New York Investigating Seditious Activities.* Vol. 2. Albany, N.Y.: J. B. Lyon, 1920.

Onishi, Yuichiro. "Giant Steps of the Black Freedom Struggle: Trans-Pacific Connections between Black America and Japan in the Twentieth Century." PhD diss., University of Minnesota, 2004.

Perry, Jeffrey B., ed. *A Hubert Harrison Reader*. Middletown, Conn.: Wesleyan University Press, 2001.

————. *Hubert Harrison: The Voice of Harlem Radicalism, 1883–1918*. New York: Columbia University Press, 2009.

Prashad, Vijay. *Everybody Was Kung Fu Fighting: Afro-Asian Connections and the Myth of Cultural Purity.* Boston: Beacon Press, 2001.

Rief, Michelle. "Thinking Locally, Acting Globally: The International Agenda of African American Clubwomen, 1880–1940." *Journal of African American History* 89 (Summer 2004): 203–222.

Robinson, Cedric J. *Black Marxism: The Making of the Black Radical Tradition.* Foreword by Robin D. G. Kelley, with a new preface by the author. Chapel Hill: University of North Carolina Press, 2000.

Shimazu, Naoko. *Japan, Race, and Equality: The Racial Equality Proposal of 1919.* London: Routledge, 1998.

Singh, Nikhil Pal. *Black Is a Country: Race and the Unfinished Struggle for Democracy.* Cambridge, Mass.: Harvard University Press, 2004.

Spence, Jonathan D. *The Gate of Heavenly Peace: The Chinese and Their Revolution, 1895–1980.* New York: Viking Press, 1981.

Stephens, Michelle. *Black Empire: The Masculine Global Imaginary of Caribbean Intellectuals in the United States, 1914–1962.* Durham, N.C.: Duke University Press, 2005.

————. "Black Transnationalism and the Politics of National Identity: West Indian Intellectuals in Harlem in the Age of War and Revolution." *American Quarterly* 50 (September 1998): 592–608.

Taylor, Ula Y. "Intellectual Pan-African Feminists: Amy Ashwood-Garvey and Amy Jacques-Garvey." In *Time Longer Than Rope: A Century of African American Activism, 1850–1950,* edited by Charles M. Payne and Adam Green, 179–95. New York: New York University Press, 2003

————. "'Negro Women Are Great Thinkers As Well As Doers': Amy Jacques-Garvey and Community Feminism in the United States, 1924–1927." *Journal of Women's History* 12 (Summer 2000): 104–26.

————. *The Veiled Garvey: The Life and Times of Amy Jacques-Garvey.* Chapel Hill: University of North Carolina Press, 2002.

Von Eschen, Penny M. *Race against Empire: Black Americans and Anticolonialism, 1937–1957.* Ithaca, N.Y.: Cornell University Press, 1997.

6

"A Small Man in Big Spaces": The New Negro, the Mestizo, and Jean Toomer's Southwest

EMILY LUTENSKI

> Taos is an end-product. It is the end of the slope. It is an end-product of the Indians, an end-product of the Spaniards, an end-product of the Yankees and puritans. It must be plowed under. Out of the fertility which death makes in the soil, a new people with a new form may grow. I dedicate myself to the swift death of the old, to the whole birth of the new. In whatever place I start work, I will call that place Taos.
>
> —Jean Toomer, "A Drama of the Southwest (Notes)"

A photograph of Jean Toomer taken by noted photographer Marjorie Content, his second wife, shows him posed at a table, his typewriter—replete with sheet of paper—before him (Figure 6.1). The portrait seems deliberately constructed, with the posed look of a book jacket. The ream of paper next to the typewriter and the books on the shelf in the background are perfectly placed. The writer sits pensive, hand under his chin, contemplating his work. Words are barely visible on the sheet of paper exiting the typewriter; the distance from which the photograph has been taken obscures them. They are faint, apparitional, and illegible.

The year is 1935, more than a decade after the publication of Toomer's opus, *Cane* (1923). *Cane* has long been considered the harbinger of New Negro literature. The letters and memoirs of well-known actors in the Harlem Renaissance, such as Wallace Thurman and Arna Bontemps, often reach back to *Cane*'s publication as the moment in African American literary history when an experimental, modernist, New Negro aesthetic was born. Often these writers lament that *Cane* was both Toomer's first and last published piece of avant-garde creative writing—and, many have argued, his first and last piece of New Negro writing. After *Cane*, he distanced himself both figuratively and geographically from the foment of black political, artistic, and cultural self-determination that tended to characterize

FIGURE 6.1. Jean Toomer in Taos, by Marjorie Content (circa 1935). Photograph courtesy of Jill Quasha on behalf of the Estate of Marjorie Content. Copyright the Estate of Marjorie Content.

the movement in Harlem, throughout the United States, and internationally.[1]

Toomer, indeed, fell notoriously silent after the publication of *Cane*. The mystery of this silence has long perplexed literary critics. When viewed in light of this literary biographical narrative, Content's 1935 photograph of Toomer thoughtfully pondering his next phrase seems almost pathetically contrived, little more than a fantasy of authorship for a writer who had already failed by this date. Yet the possibility of the photograph as documentary evidence remains—a compelling possibility, given the brief assertion by scholars Charles Scruggs and Lee VanDemarr that it was 1935 when Toomer reengaged with "a radical analysis of the politics of his time," albeit "not . . . an open discussion of racial matters."[2]

In essence, Content's photograph—and Toomer scholarship—represents the artist dichotomously. On one hand, Toomer is the writer of *Cane* and as such is conceived of as politically engaged, racially conscious, and aesthetically experimental. This Toomer—like many of the New Negro writers who came after him—looks back to the southern past, the history of slavery, and black folk tradition as sources for emergent, modernist, New Negro sensibilities. Yet, on the other hand, there is a less celebratory Toomer who lurks post-*Cane*. He is thought not to be a poet but to be a psychologist or a philosopher who falls hopelessly under the spell of his spiritual mentor, George Gurdjieff, making Toomer less a "race man" and more a mouthpiece for the "harmonious development of man" described by Gurdjieff's psychological system. After *Cane,* Toomer is said to have left the New York literary scene behind. In doing so, he distanced himself from white avant-gardists, such as Waldo Frank or the editors of the literary magazine *Broom,* who fostered his early work under the auspices of a primitivist fascination with black culture. This was a period when (as Langston Hughes puts it in *The Big Sea* [1940]) "the Negro was in vogue" as a salve to soothe the ills of white overcivilization. And he also leaves the burgeoning literary movement in Harlem behind—protesting his inclusion in Alain Locke's *The New Negro* and refusing permission to reprint his work in James Weldon Johnson's revised *Book of American Negro Poetry*. Toomer thereby absents younger black writers of a model and mentor and becomes depicted as increasingly reactionary, not only disclaiming New Negro writing but rejecting an empowered, transnational black identity politics on the rise during his historical moment, and perhaps even (particularly when he marries white women) passing as white. The nexus of Toomer's adherence to Gurdjieffian teachings, rejection of black heritage, and "escape from New York" creates the perfect storm for interpretations that see him as never again achieving the literary merit of *Cane,* leaving critics like Charles R. Larson wondering "why Jean Toomer failed as a writer after the publication of that one brilliant work. What diminished whatever potential there was in his later works?"[3]

While these oppositional narratives of Toomer's life and career have remained relatively untroubled, they are complicated by a closer look at Content's photograph. This image does more than raise the question of whether and what Toomer was writing after *Cane*—it also expands an understanding of Toomer's "escape from New York" by showing where he was writing. The setting is not among the familiar locations of *Cane* or of Toomer's biography. It is not the lush interior of his childhood home in Washington, D.C., its propriety mimicked in the stifling, feminized, and bourgeois domestic realm of Mrs. Pribby in "Box Seat." It is not the dorms where he lived and studied at Chicago's American College of Physical Training or at the University of Wisconsin–Madison, perhaps models for Paul's room in "Bona and Paul." Nor is it the eerie, gothic South woven through *Cane*'s first and third sections, beset by the terror of white supremacist violence and inspired by Toomer's eight weeks as substitute principal at a black school in Sparta, Georgia. Instead, Toomer's books are stacked neatly on the imperfectly curved shelves of a hand-built adobe house. He writes by the warmth of a semicircular kiva fireplace, a fixture of Pueblo architecture in New Mexico. The graceful, rounded pottery of southwestern tribal artisans is displayed on the mantle.

For Toomer, place matters. And thus an "escape from New York" serves as a methodology that provides new narratives complicating Toomer scholarship and, indeed, understandings of the New Negro literary culture that longed to see him as an elder. When Content's photograph relocates Toomer to the Southwest, in an adobe house near Taos, it places Toomer in a space articulate with yet distinct from the sites that inform *Cane* and the Harlem scene within which he is usually read, however uncomfortably. Always informed by location, Toomer's writings about race differ depending on the locales they engage, within which they are produced, and where they are distributed and read. Despite his tenuous biographical association with the Harlem scene (his activity in Harlem was largely limited to leading a short-lived Gurdjieffian group there), *Cane* is often read as presaging Harlem Renaissance efforts to depict modern black urban life as well as to mobilize folk traditions. *Cane,* with its tripartite structure, defines a New Negro against the old by juxtaposing a presumably northern modernity against a presumably southern history of slavery. Caught up in these geographical circuits are questions about racial ambiguity and passing (such as in "Fern" or "Bona and Paul")—topics rife in Harlem writing and outgrowths of widespread anxiety about codifying black identity. This racial codification could work in two ways: as a strategy among New Negroes, it could cohere the black community in the United States or even transnationally to make political gains. Yet among white-dominated institutions (such as the law), racial categorization was used to police the color line and maintain white supremacy and Jim Crow. Nurtured and produced by the New York publishing scene and literati such as Waldo Frank, *Cane* falls in line with these classificatory impulses and uses geography as a mechanism to do so. Although critics like Scruggs and VanDemarr have claimed that *Cane* is a cosmopolitan text, unyoked from static racial identification, the book relies on the construction of a binary between northern and southern spaces and the black and white races that are mapped onto them. This is embedded in the text's formal qualities (such as when the sections are organized in accordance with their southern or northern settings) and is also evident thematically. For example, when *Cane* presents mixed-race characters like Paul (in "Bona and Paul"), they are eventually rendered legible within the contours of tidy black or white scripts. Although Paul appears racially ambiguous (which provides the fetishistic allure and hint of danger that attracts his white date, Bona), he is ultimately pinpointed as black via the juxtaposition of Bona and a black doorman.

In the Southwest during this period, however, racial codification operated differently. The borderlands region saw the proliferation of racial discourses that focused not on codification but on indeterminacy. *Mestizaje*, racial mixing, and the modern invention of a futuristic *raza cósmica* developed as the dominant racial discourses. Toomer's southwestern writing follows in kind. Whereas in *Cane*, he had defined a New Negro against the past and the legacy of slavery, in the Southwest, he redefines the past to imagine a "new American race" of the future.

By the time Content took her photograph of Toomer in 1935, he was already a well-versed New Mexican traveler. He lived in the Southwest in sporadic and intermittent stints from 1925 to 1947. Like many artists and writers, Toomer was invited to Taos, New Mexico, for the first time by art patron, socialite, and memoirist Mabel Dodge Luhan, who encouraged him to consider founding a Gurdjieffian center for spiritual development there. Although his work on behalf of Gurdjieff brought him to Taos, Toomer continued to visit New Mexico long after they severed ties, believing, perhaps, that New Mexico could provide the fulfillment that Gurdjieff ultimately could not. When Toomer arrived in Taos, it was already a landscape crowded with artists and writers. Realist painters, such as those involved with the Taos Society of Artists, had been active in the region since well before World War I, and the area opened up to modernists after Luhan's arrival in 1917, when she began promoting it among figures such as Willa Cather, D. H. Lawrence, Georgia O'Keeffe, and Andrew Dasburg. Many of these figures represent the Southwest as dehistoricized and timeless and often construct it in opposition to paradigmatically modern urban spaces—in particular, New York. Creating nostalgic, primitive renderings of the landscape and of Native and Mexican Americans, they represent the Southwest, and particularly Pueblo Indians, as untouched by modernism's directive to "make it new." Needless to say, the primitivism of these writers and artists was similar to that of whites who sought contact with black culture in New York. Charlotte Osgood Mason, one of the most well known white patrons of Harlem Renaissance writers such as Zora Neale Hurston and Langston Hughes, had earlier been fascinated with Native Americans.

Although Toomer was the only writer of African descent who made his way into the Mabel Dodge Luhan circle, he was not the only writer associated with the New Negro movement who lived in New Mexico, and he was certainly not the only one in Greater Mexico. New Mexican Anita Scott Coleman published in notable New Negro magazines such as *The Crisis* and *Opportunity,* both based in Harlem, and in the middlebrow *Half-Century Magazine,* based in Chicago. Later in her life, she moved to Los Angeles, where she partook in a budding literary scene that was fostered by Charles S. Johnson, editor of the National Urban League's *Opportunity* magazine, which, along with the NAACP's *The Crisis* and the Brotherhood of Sleeping Car Porters' *The Messenger,* became a major outlet for the publication of New Negro literature. Chandler Owen, editor of *The Messenger,* also visited Los Angeles, proclaiming the Central Avenue district a "veritable little Harlem" as early as 1922. The growth of the Central Avenue district had already captured the imagination of figures such as Bontemps, whose family had arrived in Watts from Louisiana when he was a toddler. He lived in the Los Angeles area until he departed for Harlem in 1924. Wallace Thurman, too, was in Los Angeles. He studied at the University of Southern California while he published a short-lived magazine titled *The Outlet* in 1925. Originally from Salt Lake City, Utah, in 1925, Thurman also moved to Harlem. There he and Bontemps would meet Hughes, who had arrived for the first time in 1920, after departing his father's home in Toluca, Mexico. Clearly the intersection between the New Negro and Greater Mexico was not unique to Toomer's biography—not only was Greater Mexico on the biographical and often literary maps of these well-known Harlem Renaissance writers but it was home to numerous lesser-known artists, vibrant black communities, and their attendant publications. Indeed, not all aspiring black writers left the borderlands West—many, such as Coleman, remained.[4]

Toomer's geographical trajectory, however, stands in contrast to those of Bontemps, Thurman, Hughes, or Coleman—when they left the lands of Greater Mexico for Harlem, Toomer's travels were (rather circuitously) the other way around. And Toomer's vision of how race and place inform each other also diverges from the visions of these other writers—both before and after their engagements with Harlem. While his ideas may not have been influential to the wider New Negro movement, their relative lack of appeal reveals some of the limitations as well as the possibilities of the New Negro as both an aesthetic practice and a political and cultural ideology. In addition, the status of Harlem as the New Negro's home-place is a site both inadequate to accommodate the racial perspective of someone like Toomer and powerful in the imaginations of a diverse range of blacks nationally and transnationally.

Like the words faintly visible on Toomer's manuscript in Content's portrait, the published footprint of his time in New Mexico exists only lightly. His New Mexican writing went largely unpublished during his lifetime and has rarely been republished in collections since. The bulk of it—and the evidence of Toomer's time in New Mexico—remains archived. To read Toomer's archived work and explore his time in the Southwest complicates previous understandings of him as a writer who never, after *Cane*, returned to "an open discussion of racial matters." The Toomer archive shifts the critical optic from *Cane*'s fragmented formal qualities, its treatment of the connections between a postslavery, folk South and a bustling Great Migration North, and its modernist and New Negro sensibilities. While these are all qualities that continue to define Toomer and his literary worth, his southwestern writings move us toward a more nuanced understanding of the matrix of race, location, and the modern as it proliferated in the contexts of both the New Negro movement and the interwar period United States more generally. This archive reveals that Toomer did continue to discuss race but that his discussion takes a different shape when emerging from the U.S.–Mexico border region than it did in the locales that informed *Cane* and its reception history: the rural South, the urban North, and the New York publishing milieu, with its burgeoning attention to black texts.[5]

When Toomer moves from New York to the Southwest, his interest in the intersection between geography and racial identity remains. Like other modernists, there are times when Toomer constructs New Mexico in relation to the "man-made canyons of New York," such as with his essay "New Mexico after India." This essay suggests that the Southwest can take on different meanings, depending on from where one approaches it. Toomer writes,

> In times past, I had always come to New Mexico from the eastern states of America. I had greeted Raton Pass and the land extending southwestward and beyond, having in the background of my mind the low soft country of the eastern seaboard, the prairies of the middle west, commerce, industry, and of course the man-made canyons of New York. New Mexico had always looked grand, open, sunlit, a summit of ancient earth and historic peoples.

From the East, Toomer suggests, New Mexico can be conceived of as home to the primitive. His phrase "the man-made canyons of New York" sets the modern construction of towering buildings and poured concrete against the natural, prehistoric canyons of the Southwest, which, in contrast to New York's glossy, reflective skyscrapers, evoke the ancient in the depth of their sedimentary layers.[6]

In setting the Southwest against New York, Toomer describes the Southwest as atavistic and prelinguistic. It becomes a place where he is stripped of language:

> I have never tried to put into words the unique gift of New Mexico to me. It is enough that I feel it, I know it, that I recognize it without need of words. Something of New Mexico came to me for the first time fifteen years ago. It was a penetration deep under the skin. Ever since then there has existed a special polarization between this human being and the people and earth of the Southwest.

The Southwest, which "retains its hold upon [Toomer's] heart as home," exists not as a linguistic but as a physical connection. He describes embodiment rather than "words" and suggests that the Southwest issues physical sensation: "I feel it," he writes, as "a penetration deep under the skin" and "in the heart." To return to Content's photograph, location—in particular, the adobe house in Taos—is more recognizable than the ghostly traces of language barely visible on the page exiting Toomer's typewriter. Of course, this tension between language and embodiment is paradoxical given that Toomer describes wordlessness in the context of a written document. Nevertheless, this description of Toomer's silence deepens the narrative of Toomer's failure as a writer post-*Cane* by appealing to the nexus of language, geography, and racial belonging. When Toomer recognizes the Southwest as a "penetration deep under the skin," he also describes a location where he can reconcile, or get "deep under," the complexities of his racial identity as he experienced it in New York. Although the Southwest as "home" is described as having a "hold" on Toomer, his identity, by contrast, becomes far more flexible than it had been before his arrival there.[7]

Toomer's discussion of the prelinguistic, then, is divorced from the type of modernist primitivism that sees the prelinguistic as a sign of essentialized racial otherness. It makes more sense, then, to read Toomer's wordlessness not as an expression of timeless primitivism but as an effect of his biographical circumstance and historical situation—his struggles to publish after *Cane,* revealed by his expectant letters to acquaintances that insist his next publication is just around the corner. His "Unidentified Draft" issues another treatment of this silence:

> Furthermore I am a writer. In any case, that is what I am supposed to be. I, descendant of magicians, am supposed to use words with magical effects. But what words can I use that affect these mountains? Besides, as I have said, this country takes words away from me. Not only do the important words of my vocabulary go, but also the little words of everyday use. Sometimes I can't call to mind the word for some simple thing. Silence is grand, but writers are voluble folk. Who ever heard of a silent writer?

Although Toomer's writing of linguistic absence smacks of the kind of primitivism that other southwestern modernists cultivated to inspire aesthetic newness in a world they saw as otherwise lacking vigor, Toomer's writing of the Southwest takes a different tack. Instead of participating in racial reification in the form of primitivism, he provides an alternative to it.[8]

In "New Mexico after India," Toomer describes an attachment to place—a feeling of home—that remains unsatisfied in *Cane,* where both the North and the South cannot accommodate the racially ambiguous. This essay creates a sense of belonging not through codification but through deconstruction; it abandons a racial binary in favor of a network of geographical and corresponding racial locations that interlock in an idealized New Mexican landscape. Written after a 1939 trip to India that had failed to provide the spiritual renovation that Toomer was seeking, "New Mexico after India" uses the disappointment of India to heighten the experience of actualization that New Mexico provided him. If Toomer had imagined the Southwest only in conjunction with New York, his vision might be more similar to those of modern primitivists. Instead, Toomer insists on viewing the Southwest as an intermediary location, situated between New York and India. He writes, "Compared to New York the Southwest may seem slow and unchanging. Compared with the interior of India, the Southwest is in rapid change." He argues that the experience of arriving in New Mexico from India instead of from the eastern United States reveals a much more modern place than he had previously realized. As a result, his essay at first appears to be little more than a ranking of primitivisms, in which the voyage from India to New Mexico reveals that the latter is more modern than India but less modern than New York. This trip, Toomer writes, was built on "a background of experiences in India, Ceylon, Hong Kong, Shanghai, and Japan," and it exposes that "by contrast even the pueblos seemed to have a touch of the modern world, the Mexican villages seemed to be growing and changing as young things grow, and Taos and Santa Fe seemed to be altering under the same impulse that had created Chicago in some fifty years." Yet this liminal position between the ancient and the modern is what enables Toomer to theorize racial multiplicity.[9]

"New Mexico after India" describes a multiethnic coterie and the possibility of racial mixing: "The Indian is upstanding. The Mexican is upstanding. The Negro is upstanding. The White is upstanding. Let us continue to upstand, and at the same time bend towards each other on the basis of a common humanity, and we would become one people in spirit and fundamental aim." The Southwest functions as the nexus for this multiracial network, largely because of its position between New York and India. India, Toomer claims, is ruled by the caste system, which he feels is so ancient and deeply embedded that it would be impossible to resolve. In comparison, he suggests, "the Southwest is young," a condition that results in a challenge to "our own complexities, taboos, classes if not castes, racial prejudices, and knotty problems." Toomer imagines racial mixture made possible by the southwestern locale.[10]

Contrary to static images of an eternal primitive, to enter the Southwest is to enter a place with real and palpable racialized histories of colonial intervention. The discursive outgrowths of these histories, like *mestizaje,* run contrary to the impulses toward racial classification that proliferated elsewhere in the United States such as New York or the Jim Crow South. Toomer's notes reveal a keen interest in learning about these southwestern histories and discourses; he consulted a wide variety of sources. He read New Mexican tour guide, writer, and folklorist Erna Fergusson's *Our Southwest* (1940), which defines the Southwest as, above all, mestizo place. He read *Forgotten People: A Study of New Mexicans* (1940), by George I. Sánchez, a Mexican American writer and academic who would become the president of the League of United Latin American Citizens from 1941 to 1942. He read anthropology, such as Adolph F. Bandelier and Edgar L. Hewett's *Indians of the Rio Grande Valley* (1937), and regional literature, such as Frank Waters's novel *The Man Who Killed the Deer* (1942). One cannot help but wonder if some of these books appear on the shelf in Content's photograph, ready for consultation should Toomer need a reference or allusion as he writes the Southwest as a site for a de-essentialized and flexible racial newness, rather than as a site for a reified primitive to be utilized by modernist aesthetes in the name of regeneration.[11]

There are such allusions in "Sequences," a series of short impressionistic sketches that describe the southwestern landscape interspersed with rambling philosophical musings characteristic of the late Toomer. In "Sequences," Toomer refers obliquely to the colonial history of Greater Mexico, mentioning Bartolomé de las Casas and a "certain Spanish priest" in the eighteenth century who, he claims, followed in his tradition (likely Miguel Hidalgo). Toomer writes that these figures "came upon a vision of what human life in the new world should be, but . . . never journeyed far enough to see this particular [New Mexican] sky and earth." Though this passage may appear rife with the kind of vague spirituality that, claims Rudolph P. Byrd, "wasted [Toomer's] great talent," its historical references are not merely spiritual ones. They are also references to a liberatory racial ideology, as both Hidalgo and Las Casas have been mythologized as antiracist and anti-imperialist icons, temporal bookends to the Spanish colonial period and voices of resistance.[12]

Toomer's attention to regional history resonates with other theorizations of race emerging from Greater Mexico during this period, which also reflected on colonial history and subsequent racial mixing. The voice of Mexican intellectual José Vasconcelos dominated many of these conversations; he published *La Raza Cósmica* in 1925, the same year Toomer first visited Taos. *La Raza Cósmica* would become perhaps Vasconcelos's most influential work and a foundational articulation of *mestizaje*. Though it is possible that Toomer knew of Vasconcelos through newspaper accounts of his lectures and political activities (including a 1929 bid for the Mexican presidency), through translations of his writings, or through news of Waldo Frank's extensive Latin American tours, there is no clear evidence that Toomer used Vasconcelos as a source when studying Greater Mexico. Regardless, there are clear parallels between Toomer's writings and Vasconcelos's. In a discussion of *Cane,* for example, Tace Hedrick claims that both Toomer and Vasconcelos relied on the image of a graft or hybrid as a trope to explain their racial theories. When Toomer's writings from the Southwest are taken into account, such parallels become even easier to see, existing not only in similar theories of racial mixing but also in similar engagement with places marked by Spanish colonialism and U.S. imperialism. Both writers were also concerned with the processes and products of modernity, and both evince opaque, premonitional spiritual gestures.[13]

Like Toomer, Vasconcelos roots a theory of race mixing in Spanish colonialism, which he interprets not as an annihilation of the indigenous but as the promise of a harmonious, empowered future. In *La Raza Cósmica,* for example, he suggests, "Although [the Spanish] may have thought of themselves simply as colonizers, as carriers of culture, in reality, they were establishing the basis for a period of general and definitive transformation." Colonization unwittingly set into motion an epoch of racial mixing through which the cosmic race is born of a postcolonial modernity: "The days of the pure whites," he insisted, "the victors of today, are as numbered as were the days of their predecessors. Having fulfilled their destiny of mechanizing the world, they themselves have set, without knowing it, the basis for a new period: The period of the fusion and mixing of all peoples." This is *mestizaje*—for Vasconcelos, the mixture of "the Black, the Indian, the Mongol, and the White," an outgrowth of modernization only possible after "mechanizing the world."[14]

To read Toomer in the mestizo context of Greater Mexico departs from the usual critical practice of placing him within the Harlem milieu and the wider New Negro movement. This relocation finds Toomer in a place where racial boundaries disintegrate instead of becoming reified. As George Hutchinson remarks,

> Indeed, the great irony of Toomer's career is that modern American racial discourse—with an absolute polarity between "white" and "black" at its center—took its most definite shape precisely during the course of his life. The United States would be more segregated at the time of Toomer's death than it had been at the time of his birth, despite the dismantling of some of the legal bulwarks of white supremacy.

Legislation like the 1924 Virginia Racial Purity Act was one aspect of this racial codification, but aesthetic production and literary publication also served this cultural imperative. Narratives of Toomer's career are intimately connected to this desire to firm up, rather than break down, racial categories. When Toomer opposed his inclusion in Alain Locke's *New Negro* anthology, for example, he rejected the collection's mission to, as Arnold Rampersad points out, "document the New Negro culturally and socially,—to register the transformations of the inner and outer life of the Negro in America that have so significantly taken place in the last few years" and to enable him to "speak for himself" in an empowered and cohesive voice. Toomer was notoriously uncomfortable with efforts to define a monolithic African American identity—his letters to publisher Horace Liveright regarding the marketing of *Cane* as an African American text serve as an excellent example of his discomfort. As Toomer biographers Cynthia Earl Kerman and Richard Eldridge claim, the "new American did not want to be a New Negro," and Toomer thusly insisted that Locke had included his portrait and poem in the volume without his permission—effectively rejecting New Negro identity.[15]

Toomer's rejection of the New Negro both within and beyond Harlem has resulted in a pervasive set of regret among more recent academics as well as among Toomer's New Negro contemporaries. In Langston Hughes's autobiography, *The Big Sea,* he recalls that after *Cane,*

> the next thing Harlem heard of Jean Toomer was that he had married Margery Latimer, a talented white novelist, and maintained to the newspapers that he was no more colored than white—as certainly his complexion indicated. When the late James Weldon Johnson wrote him for permission to use some of his poems in the *Book of American Negro Poetry,* Mr. Johnson reported that the poet who, a few years before, was "caroling softly souls of slavery" now refused to permit his poems to appear in an anthology of *Negro* verse— which put all the critics, white and colored, in a great dilemma. How should they class the author of *Cane* in their lists and summaries? . . . Nobody knew exactly, it being a case of black blood and white blood having met and the individual deciding, after Paris and Gurdjieff, to be merely American.

Hughes's lament that Toomer became "merely American" and "Harlem is sorry he stopped writing" reveals that the New Negro movement participated in constructing a unitary black identity that Toomer undermined. Although the New Negro movement both within and beyond Harlem disrupted racist assumptions about blacks and refigured black identity for the modern moment, it also enforced a paradigm that could not delimit Toomer.[16]

For Toomer, the New Negro was restrictive because it participated in hegemonic racial discourses that insisted on an essentialist black identity as drops of blood. Such discourses can be seen in, for example, the 1930 U.S. Census, when "mulatto" was removed, becoming an untenable category. This forces identification as black or white and obscures the history of racial mixture in the United States. Interestingly, the same year that the United States removed "mulatto" from the classificatory nomenclature of its census, Mexico removed racial demarcations from its census altogether—a move that seems to refuse, rather than reinforce, racial borders. Notably, the 1930 U.S. Census also saw the first—and only—appearance of the category "Mexican."[17]

According to New Negro writers such as Hughes, or even recent critics such as Rudolph P. Byrd and Henry Louis Gates Jr., when Toomer refuses this essentialism, he begins "passing." Arna Bontemps became one of the first to suggest that Toomer passed as white, writing that Toomer "faded completely into white obscurity." He continues, "The rumor that Toomer had crossed the color line began circulating when his name stopped appearing in print" and suggests that "[Toomer] is on record as having denied later that he was a Negro. . . . At that point, it seems, Jean Toomer stepped out of American letters." The discourse of passing contributes to a strict demarcation between black and white racial formations. While the act of passing appears to disrupt a binary construction of race by demonstrating its permeability, it also tends to show that one can perform blackness or whiteness, but not both simultaneously. In Nella Larsen's Harlem Renaissance novel *Passing* (1929), Clare Kendry is fluently black and fluently white in separate racial spheres, but when these worlds are brought together, she risks exposure as black (in accordance with the principles of hypodescent) among whites or as a race betrayer among blacks. The severe consequences of this exposure can be delivered by the black community as well as by whites, as the ambiguous conclusion of the novel indicates. In *Cane,* passing characters are also exposed and punished. Paul of "Bona and Paul" starts as a paragon of racial multiplicity, entirely enfolded by the mystery of his physiognomy: "What is he, a Spaniard, an Indian, an Italian, a Mexican, a Hindu, or a Japanese?" the text asks. Yet when his blackness is exposed, his ambiguity dissipates; as punishment for his transgressions, he is both mocked by the black doorman and abandoned by his white date. Paul suffers for both his racial betrayal and his racial subversion.[18]

After the publication of *Cane,* Toomer (like his character Paul) could not pass as white. His pubic persona as *Cane*'s author always hailed to his black heritage. Rather than pass, Toomer again and again insisted on his membership in what he described as a new American race. At times Toomer's avowal of this identity seems an impotent protest against the publishing industry, which was determined to market an African American writer, against a mass media wracked with pathological fears of miscegenation, and against a New Negro milieu betrayed by Toomer's literary failure. Furthermore, there are persistent questions about Toomer's ability to pass as black as well as white. Recall that Hughes attests that "certainly [Toomer's] complexion indicated" that he was *other* than black.

Critics such as Larson buttress this view by suggesting that "Toomer was raised as a white person" and could never convincingly perform blackness. This is despite Toomer's childhood, raised largely by his grandfather, P. B. S. Pinchback (the first—and, to date, only—black governor of Louisiana, a position in which he served for thirty-five days during Reconstruction), who was active in black political circles. In *Terrible Honesty: Mongrel Manhattan in the 1920s,* Ann Douglas sustains this description of Toomer's racial performance, describing briefly Toomer's 1922 journey to South Carolina with Waldo Frank, during which both writers, ostensibly, passed as black:

> This was a culture to which well-bred Toomer, raised in cosmopolitan Washington D.C., was almost as great a stranger as Frank. . . . In an extension of the minstrel tradition of impersonation, the two men posed in South Carolina as "blood brothers." Frank was accepted by blacks as one of them, just as Toomer would "pass" in later decades and be accepted by whites as white.

Terrible Honesty boldly claims that New York was the cultural capital of the United States—and, indeed, the world—mainly because of its "mongrelization" of culture in the period that saw the rise of the New Negro. Arguably, however, Douglas's "mongrel Manhattan" is not a space for racial hybridity but rather a space of collaboration and mutual influence between blacks and whites. She sees passing as "emblematic of a wider pattern of trans-race needs and debts," yet suggests that Toomer's blackness was also a form of passing, calling this into question. What does "trans-race" mean in a context where blackness was as foreign to Toomer as it was to Frank?[19]

Unlike Clare Kendry's fluency with racial performance in Larsen's *Passing,* which enables her to access (at times) both the black and the white community—at least until her exposure and punishment for her transgressions—Toomer is equally illegible as black and as white. As a result, Douglas's New York and the northern and southern spaces of *Cane* where binary racial classification guides racial formations require Toomer's passing. To defy this dualistic system, then, he had no recourse but to create a new American race more suited to him. He had no option but to find a racial landscape distinct from the one in New York and dominant throughout most of the United States. It became necessary for him to invent a modern paradigm not of passing but of mixing—a paradigm complicit with the discourses about race emerging from Greater Mexico. As Toomer himself penned in his untitled notebook about New Mexico, "If you are between two worlds, which way?" asking a similar question about location and belonging.[20]

Larson explains, "There were speculations that [Toomer] had chosen to pass as a white person after his second marriage (to a white woman) in 1934." More recently, through an interpretation of Toomer's first marriage certificate (to writer Margery Latimer), Byrd and Gates have also contended that Toomer's passing was inspired by an interracial marriage. Hughes's comments in *The Big Sea* laid the groundwork for these allegations when he cuttingly refers to the Toomer–Latimer marriage as the moment when Toomer "maintained to the newspapers that he was no more colored than white." These 1931 nuptials did, indeed, provide the occasion upon which Toomer most famously announced the birth of the new American race. In an oft-quoted pronouncement that was represented in the media as more grandiose than revolutionary, more eccentric than deliberate, he stated,

> There is a new race in America. I am a member of this new race. It is neither white nor black nor in-between. It is the American race, differing as much from white and black as white and black differ from each other. It is possible that there are Negro and Indian bloods in my descent along with English, Spanish, Welsh, Scotch, French, Dutch, and German. This is common in America; and it is from these strains that the American race is being born. But the old divisions into white, black, brown, red, are outworn in this country. They have had their day. Now is the time of the birth of a new order, a new vision, a new ideal of man. I proclaim this new order. My marriage to Margery Latimer is the marriage of two Americans.

In this passage, Toomer is clearly not attempting to pass. Instead, he is theorizing a modern, multiple identity that he characterizes as American—perhaps even transnationally so. He envisions his marriage as the starting point for this racial redefinition. But rather than using his statement to clarify his position, the press used it to decry the evils of miscegenation.[21]

Story after story contorted Toomer's statement by focusing on the language he himself used—the language of birth. According to Kerman and Eldridge, the "culmination of this unwanted publicity was in an article in *Time* under 'Races.' Entitled 'Just Americans,' the article focused by innuendo on miscegenation and belittled what appeared to be Toomer's elaborate rationalization for marrying a white woman." Needless to say, articles focused not only on Toomer's black heritage but also on Latimer's whiteness. Even reports of her death during childbirth merely one year after her marriage not only insist on disclosing that Toomer is "part Negro" but also that Latimer was a descendant of poet Anne Bradstreet and Puritan clergyman John Cotton, rendering her not just white but ultra-white, with a purity of racial lineage dating to the colonization of the United States. Such articles titillate their readership by emphasizing childbirth, and Latimer's death becomes an allegory for the threat of miscegenation when the new American race becomes literalized in the figure of Toomer's and Latimer's child.[22]

Although Kerman and Eldridge claim that black publications, on the contrary, viewed the Toomer–Latimer marriage as "a form of race pride," comments like Hughes's or Bontemps's have a different tenor. Rather than seeing the marriage as an accomplishment, as a challenge to the color line in Jim Crow America, writers like these express a sense of regret, lamenting Toomer's fate from the perspective of the New Negro. This is not a sentiment unique to the New Negro; interracial origin stories in the Americas have often led to dual interpretations. For example, although Vasconcelos reframed Mexican *mestizaje* as a source of empowerment, the mestizo origin story has long been told as a story of racial betrayal. As Marilyn Grace Miller notes, the mythology of *la Malinche* has polarized discussions of *mestizaje*. On one hand, this figure has been interpreted as a traitor to the Indian people, and assimilation and cultural decimation have been attributed to her. Yet, on the other hand, this figure has been reworked as a radical hybrid, a cultural bridge—often by feminist thinkers. Toomer's story works similarly—aligning him, once again, with the Greater Mexican borderlands.[23]

The New Negro laments the loss of Toomer for literature, and for the race, when Hughes writes, "Harlem is sorry he stopped writing." When Hughes makes this assertion, he—ironically, a consummate internationalist of the New Negro movement—paints Harlem as synonymous with black identity. If this is the case, when Toomer moves to the Southwest, he commits a spatial betrayal as well as a racial one. Far earlier than *The Big Sea,* Hughes had seen the Southwest as a site for racial mixing in his poem "A House in Taos" (1927). Bontemps, among others, has insinuated that this poem was even based on rumors of an affair between Jean Toomer and Mabel Dodge Luhan, who was married to a Pueblo Indian, Antonio (Tony) Lujan. Hughes disputes this claim in *The Big Sea.* The poem, however, does characterize Taos as a place where interracial desire is enacted, describing a triangulation of "red, white, yellow skins." Whether the decimation of racial boundaries is lauded as progressive or frowned on as traitorous, the Southwest is a site for this border crossing. The Toomer–Latimer story is its epitome and the exemplification of Toomer's new American race. Their story, however, was disciplined by a mass media under the influence of white supremacist visions of black male predation and white female purity. Their union was regulated by notions of racial infidelity undergirded by bifurcated racial systems guided by the principle of hypodescent and which signaled essentialist visions of race.[24]

Critiques of Toomer's new American race thus assume that his turn away from blackness is a turn toward whiteness. But much like Vasconcelos's cosmic race, Toomer's vision is not one of passing. It is not a strategy of deracination but a radical reenvisioning of mixed-race identity as enabling and constructive rather than destructive and degenerate. Positioning Toomer in the Southwest alongside discourses of *mestizaje* allows a rereading of race mixing as more than a reversal of a binary system—instead, it subverts such a system. Perhaps surprisingly, Latimer herself participates in this subversion. In an October 1931 letter, she discusses her role in developing the new American and even describes Toomer, as he would in "New Mexico after India," in relation with India:

> People in Portage [Wisconsin, Latimer's hometown and the site of their wedding] think J. is East Indian. He looks very much like one, that color—beautiful rich skin, gold shade, fine features, and bones, very tall and slender, beautiful mouth, very sleek hair and fine hands. My mother knew about the racial thing and for a time felt quite agitated. Then when she saw that he really is the right person for me she jumped that hurdle and now we are enormously happy. . . . You don't know how marvelously happy I am and my stomach seems leaping with golden children, millions of them.

Latimer's letter calls into question the dominant black–white binary by buffering it with India: people think Toomer is Indian, which leads to a subversion of—in her rather flippant phrasing—the "racial thing" and a humanistic (and perhaps sweetly naive) lauding of Toomer as simply the "right person." Yet Latimer also sees herself as an agent and places herself alongside Toomer as progenitor of a mixed race, populating the world with "millions" of "golden children."[25]

Toomer certainly envisions such fecundity. He hints at it in his pronouncement on the occasion of his marriage when he notes that his "marriage to Margery Latimer is the marriage of two Americans," since for him "America" signifies racial mixing. And he expands on this vision in his New Mexican writing:

> I am one. Here I am I. In these grand spaces I feel grand, with largeness in me, and my body in the world. I tell myself that this geography must in the future as it has in the past produce a great race. I see this future, mountains beyond mountains, and then the sun. I buy land, a large tract. I build a big house and smaller ones. I have fields and cattle. My children grow up. Their children grow up. With my friends and workers I inhabit it, building in New Mexico my world of man.

In this passage, Toomer imagines the Southwest as an ideal homeland for a mixed-race subject, much as he does in "New Mexico after India." Place is connected to his racial vision. His "great race" has, as it does in Latimer's letter, humanistic overtones and is also connected to the southwestern geography: "Here I am I," he writes. The new American race is imagined as springing from the earth—from Toomer's large tract of land—much as Latimer imagined it "leaping" from her womb as "millions of golden children." This imagery circumvents renderings of the Southwest as a barren, desert landscape.[26]

Such optimism and emphasis on futurity are undercut, however, by ambivalence. Although in "New Mexico after India," Toomer had claimed that New Mexico "retains its hold upon [his] heart as home," he never permanently settled there. This is foreshadowed in "A Drama of the Southwest," where his dramatic double, Lewis Bourne, weighs the pros and cons of buying land in Taos—the same land linked to the harvest of the new American race. Bourne's ambivalence is based on his suspicions—which are shared by Toomer in his first-person essays—that the Southwest might become too modern, too soon. In other words, he fears that New Mexico might one day become like New York, with its racial bifurcation, among other characteristics. In his "Unidentified Draft," Toomer describes the endless deferral of his southwestern land purchase: "My wife [at the time he wrote this essay, Content, who he married in Taos in 1934] and I are looking at land. We looked last year. We will look the next. We will look every time we come until we buy." Although southwestern land is crucial to Toomer's racial project, he could never commit to finding the perfect tract.[27]

In the same essay, he writes, "I am attracted and repelled, attracted by the actual magnificence of physical New Mexico, attracted by my visions of the potentialities of life here, yet repelled by a number of trivial matters, all of which I know to be trivial, nevertheless they pester and obsess me as expressions of some deep undiscovered protest." This language of attraction and repulsion resonates with other modernist writing emerging from the Southwest, especially the work of Luhan and D. H. Lawrence. Both describe the Southwest as imbued with a seemingly magnetic energy, frequently using words like *polarization* to describe the impact of the region on white moderns. *Polarization* is a word also utilized by Toomer in "New Mexico after India."[28]

This language is carefully chosen, and in the New Mexican context, it carries specific meaning, particularly toward the end of Toomer's time there in the 1940s. *Polarization* hearkens to positive and negative charges, terminology that describes subatomic particles, which were being identified and characterized by physicists in the early twentieth century. This scientific language explains some of Toomer's ambivalence about New Mexico, for this is what threatens the regenerative possibilities of this site. The Southwest quickly becomes too modern, too soon—emblematized by the building of Los Alamos National Laboratory in 1943, with the specific project of creating a nuclear bomb. In "Sequences," Toomer returns to his image of the sloping New Mexican landscape as a metaphor. This time, however, he links it to a discussion of the bomb: "Until men are strong in their ascent up the spiritual slope, the existence of atomic energy will block the spiritual climb and enforce still more 'progress' up the material slope. Given men as they now are, its use in society would be an unqualified disaster. It should not be used, except in medicine." At the time "Sequences" was written, the Manhattan

Project—its name signifying and spatializing its relation to the paradigmatic site of U.S. modernity—was under way a mere sixty-five miles from Taos. The atomic bomb erupts in doomsday visions in the otherwise pristine landscape that Toomer constructs. In his notebook on New Mexico, Toomer writes,

> "The mountain will smoke, great winds will come up, the world will be destroyed by fire." So say the old men of the pueblo, some of whom may have true vision and gift of prophecy. Do we not hear the same prediction in different terms from scientists who know the fearful potency of the atomic bomb?
>
> What I do not know is—Do the elders of Taos vision the coming destruction as the end of man, or as the matrix of a new birth? Will resurrection follow this death? And, if so, who will be resurrected? White men? Red men? Black men? An entirely new race?

Despite his apocalyptic tone, Toomer insists, "new men and women are as possible as war. I will hold to the faith that we will be reborn until I see destruction sweep the earth and I am knocked to smithereens." Yet although he expresses such "faith," the fact remains that Toomer never made New Mexico his permanent home. He never purchased the parcel of New Mexican land he envisioned as the foundation for the new American race.[29]

Instead, Toomer lived the last years of his life in Bucks County, Pennsylvania, where he was asked to define his race at an "inquiry" (as Larson describes it) into whether his daughter could attend an all-white school. During the course of this inquiry, Toomer convinced his audience that he was not black. He did not, however, pass as white. Instead, he was positioned, once again, in relation to India. A resident of Bucks County interviewed in Larson's *Invisible Darkness* recalled that when he moved there, he had been "told . . . with a straight face, that Mrs. Toomer was married to an East Indian" because "the farmers around here are very narrow. If they thought Mrs. Toomer, white, was married to a Negro, they would make life miserable for both of them. An East Indian they can live with, so, remember, Jean Toomer is East Indian." In Bucks County, Toomer's mixed new American race is disabled, and he is forced to pass—although not as white. This creates a fissure between Bucks County and New Mexico. In New Mexico, Toomer had described the new American race as arising from the southwestern soil, made fertile through regional history and its cultural crosscurrents. In Bucks County, it is the farmers, the tillers of the land themselves, who are "narrow"—so different from the vast southwestern earth.[30]

The consistent mentions of India in Toomer's biography and southwestern writing are often vague and frustrating, yet also revealing. For they not only reinforce the ways in which racial identities—modern figurations like the New Negro and the mestizo—become mapped onto locations but they also remind us that these locations, be they Harlem, New Mexico, or India, exist in complicated networks. These networks defamiliarize the geographies of modernism and destabilize notions of race. By examining these relational sites, the Southwest, so often considered antithetical to the modern and racialized in kind, is shown to be engaged in the processes of modernization and racialization that exist not only in the place Toomer inhabits as "a small man in big spaces . . . between Taos and Santa Fe" but also in Harlem and Greenwich Village; Chicago and Sparta, Georgia; Portage, Wisconsin, and Washington, D.C.; Mexico and India—the complex routes revealed in Toomer's southwestern archive.[31]

NOTES

1   Bontemps, introduction to *Cane,* vii–xvi; Thurman, "Letter to Langston Hughes (c. July 1929)," 121–24; Thurman, "Letter to William Jourdan Rapp (c. July 1929)," 152–55.

2   Scruggs and VanDemarr, *Jean Toomer and the Terrors of American History,* 219.

3   Hughes, *Big Sea,* 223; Larson, *Invisible Darkness,* xiii.

4   On black literary societies such as the Ink Slingers, which Anita Scott Coleman attended in Los Angeles, see McHenry, *Forgotten Readers,* 293; Chandler Owen, as quoted in Flamming, "A Westerner in Search of 'Negro-ness,'" 91; for more on the New Negro and the American West, see Glasrud and Wintz, *Harlem Renaissance in the American West;* Allmendinger, *Imagining the African American West;* and Johnson, *Black Masculinity and the Frontier Myth in American Literature;* on Coleman, see Coleman, *Western Echoes of the Harlem Renaissance.*

5   Toomer's published New Mexican writing can be found in the following: Toomer, "To the Land of the People," "Rainbow," "The Dust of Abiquiu," "Taos Night," "New Mexico after India," "Part of the Universe," "Santa Fe Sequence," 238–58; Quirk and Fleming, "Jean Toomer's Contributions to the *New Mexican Sentinel,*" 65–73; Toomer, "Blue Meridian," 50–75; Toomer, "Lost Dancer," 39; and Toomer, "Imprint for Rio Grande," "I Sit in My Room," "Rolling, Rolling," "It Is Everywhere," 81–87. Toomer's major archival repository is the Jean Toomer Papers, James Weldon Johnson Collection, Beinecke Rare Book and Manuscript Library, Yale University. These include the following Southwestern writings: "A Drama of the Southwest," series II, box 44, folder 917; "A Drama of the Southwest (Notes)," series II, box 44, folder 913; "New Mexico after India: Notes and Drafts," series II, box 48, folder 1011; "Noises at Night," series II, box 48, folder 1012; "Notebook: Contains Notes about New Mexico," series II, box 15, folder 1482; "Sequences: Notes and Drafts," series II, box 48, folder 1013; and "Unidentified Draft," series II, box 48, folder 1014.

6 Toomer, "New Mexico after India," 249–50.

7 Ibid., 252–53.

8 Toomer, "Unidentified Draft," 8–9.

9 Toomer, "New Mexico after India," 250.

10 Ibid., 250–51.

11 Notes on these books are contained at the end of Toomer, "Notebook: Contains Notes on New Mexico."

12 Toomer, "Sequences: Notes and Drafts," 4; Byrd, *Jean Toomer's Years with Gurdjieff*, xv.

13 Vasconcelos, *La Raza Cósmica*; Hedrick, "Blood-Lines That Waver South," 47.

14 Vasconcelos, *La Raza Cósmica*, 9–10, 16.

15 Hutchinson, "Identity in Motion," 53–54; Rampersad, introduction to *The New Negro*, xxv; Toomer, "Letter to Horace Liveright," 156–57; Kerman and Eldridge, *Lives of Jean Toomer*, 112.

16 Hughes, *Big Sea*, 242–43.

17 Schor, "Mobilizing for Pure Prestige?," 91–92.

18 Byrd and Gates, introduction to *Cane*, lxx; Bontemps, "Commentary on Jean Toomer and *Cane*," 186–92; Larsen, *Passing*; Toomer, "Bona and Paul," 74–78.

19 Larson, *Invisible Darkness*, 201; Douglas, *Terrible Honesty*, 79.

20 Toomer, "Notebook: Contains Notes on New Mexico," 19.

21 Larson, *Invisible Darkness*, xii; Byrd and Gates, introduction to *Cane*, lxvii–lxx; Hughes, *Big Sea*, 242–43; Toomer, "A New Race in America," 105.

22 Kerman and Eldridge, *Lives of Jean Toomer*, 202; "Margery Toomer," *New York Times*, August 18, 1932, 19; "Woman Novelist Called by Death," *Los Angeles Times*, August 18, 1932, 3.

23 Miller, *Rise and Fall of the Cosmic Race*, 23–24. For feminist renovations of *la Malinche*, see Anzaldúa, *Borderlands*, or Alarcón, "Traddutora, Traditora."

24 Hughes, *Big Sea*, 242–43; Hughes, "A House in Taos," 80–81.

25 Latimer, as quoted in Kerman and Eldridge, *Lives of Jean Toomer*, 199.

26 Toomer, "A New Race in America," 105; Toomer, "Unidentified Draft," 1; Latimer, as quoted in Kerman and Eldridge, *Lives of Jean Toomer*, 199.

27 Toomer, "New Mexico after India," 253; Toomer, "A Drama of the Southwest," 37–44; Toomer, "Unidentified Draft," 3.

28 Toomer, "Unidentified Draft," 1; Toomer, "New Mexico after India," 252.

29 Toomer, "Sequences: Notes and Drafts," 63; Toomer, "Notebook: Contains Notes on New Mexico," 6–9.

30 Larson, *Invisible Darkness*, 156.

31 Toomer, "New Mexico after India: Notes and Drafts," 2.

BIBLIOGRAPHY

Alarcón, Norma. "Traddutora, Traditora: A Paradigmatic Figure of Chicana Feminism." *Cultural Critique* 13 (Fall 1989): 57–87.

Allmendinger, Blake. *Imagining the African American West*. Lincoln: University of Nebraska Press, 2008.

Anzaldúa, Gloria. *Borderlands/La Frontera: The New Mestiza*. 3rd ed. San Francisco: Aunt Lute, 2007.

Bontemps, Arna. "Commentary on Jean Toomer and *Cane*." In *Cane*, by Jean Toomer, edited by Darwin T. Turner, 186–92. New York: W. W. Norton, 1988.

———. Introduction to *Cane*, by Jean Toomer. New York: Perennial, 1969.

Byrd, Rudolph P. *Jean Toomer's Years with Gurdjieff: Portrait of an Artist, 1923–1936*. Athens: University of Georgia Press, 1990.

Byrd, Rudolph P., and Henry Louis Gates Jr., eds. Introduction to *Cane*, 2nd ed., by Jean Toomer. New York: W. W. Norton, 2011.

Coleman, Anita Scott. *Western Echoes of the Harlem Renaissance: The Life and Writings of Anita Scott Coleman*. Edited by Cynthia Davis and Verner D. Mitchell. Norman: University of Oklahoma Press, 2008.

Douglas, Ann. *Terrible Honesty: Mongrel Manhattan in the 1920s*. New York: Noonday, 1996.

Flamming, Douglas. "A Westerner in Search of 'Negro-ness': Region and Race in the Writing of Arna Bontemps." In *Over the Edge: Remapping the American West*, edited by Valerie J. Matsumoto and Blake Allmendinger, 85–104. Berkeley: University of California Press, 1999.

Glasrud, Bruce A., and Cary D. Wintz, eds. *The Harlem Renaissance in the American West*. New York: Routledge, 2011.

Hedrick, Tace. "Blood-Lines That Waver South: Hybridity, the 'South,' and American Bodies." *Southern Quarterly* 42, no. 1 (2003): 39–52.

Hughes, Langston. *The Big Sea: An Autobiography*. New York: Knopf, 1940.

———. "A House in Taos." In *The Collected Poems of Langston Hughes*, edited by Arnold Rampersad, 80–81. New York: Vintage, 1995.

Hutchinson, George. "Identity in Motion: Placing *Cane*." In *Jean Toomer and the Harlem Renaissance*, edited by Geneviève Fabre and Michel Feith, 38–56. New Brunswick, N.J.: Rutgers University Press, 2001.

James Weldon Johnson Collection, Beinecke Rare Book and Manuscript Library, Yale University.

Johnson, Michael K. *Black Masculinity and the Frontier Myth in American Literature*. Norman: University of Oklahoma Press, 2002.

Kerman, Cynthia Earl, and Richard Eldridge. *The Lives of Jean Toomer: A Hunger for Wholeness*. Baton Rouge: Louisiana State University Press, 1987.

Larsen, Nella. *Passing*. Edited by Carla Kaplan. New York: W. W. Norton, 2007.

Larson, Charles R. *Invisible Darkness: Jean Toomer and Nella Larsen*. Iowa City: University of Iowa Press, 1993.

McHenry, Elizabeth. *Forgotten Readers: Uncovering the Lost History of African American Literary Societies*. Durham, N.C.: Duke University Press, 2002.

Miller, Marilyn Grace. *The Rise and Fall of the Cosmic Race: The Cult of Mestizaje in Latin America*. Austin: University of Texas Press, 2004.

Quirk, Tom, and Robert E. Fleming. "Jean Toomer's Contributions to the *New Mexican*

Sentinel." In *Jean Toomer: A Critical Evaluation,* edited by Therman B. O'Daniel, 65–73. Washington, D.C.: Howard University Press, 1988.

Rampersad, Arnold. Introduction to *The New Negro: Voices of the Harlem Renaissance,* edited by Alain Locke. New York: Touchstone, 1997.

Schor, Paul. "Mobilizing for Pure Prestige? Challenging Federal Census Ethnic Categories in the USA (1850–1940)." *International Social Science Journal* 57, no. 183 (2005): 89–101.

Scruggs, Charles, and Lee VanDemarr. *Jean Toomer and the Terrors of American History.* Philadelphia: University of Pennsylvania Press, 1998.

Thurman, Wallace. *The Collected Writings of Wallace Thurman: A Harlem Renaissance Reader.* Edited by Amritjit Singh and Daniel M. Scott III. New Brunswick, N.J.: Rutgers University Press, 2003.

———. "Letter to Langston Hughes (c. July 1929)." In *The Collected Writings of Wallace Thurman,* edited by Amritjit Singh and Daniel M. Scott III, 121–24. New Brunswick, N.J.: Rutgers University Press, 2003.

———. "Letter to William Jourdan Rapp (c. July 1929)." In *The Collected Writings of Wallace Thurman,* edited by Amritjit Singh and Daniel M. Scott III, 152–55. New Brunswick, N.J.: Rutgers University Press, 2003.

Toomer, Jean. "The Blue Meridian." In *The Collected Poems of Jean Toomer,* edited by Robert B. Jones and Margery Latimer Toomer, 50–75. Chapel Hill: University of North Carolina Press, 1988.

———. "Bona and Paul." In *Cane,* 2nd ed., edited by Rudolph P. Byrd and Henry Louis Gates Jr., 70–78. New York: W. W. Norton, 2011.

———. *Cane.* Edited by Darwin T. Turner. New York: W. W. Norton, 1988.

———. *Cane.* 2nd ed. Edited by Rudolph P. Byrd and Henry Louis Gates Jr. New York: W. W. Norton, 2011.

———. *The Collected Poems of Jean Toomer.* Edited by Robert B. Jones and Margery Latimer Toomer. Chapel Hill: University of North Carolina Press, 1988.

———. "The Dust of Abiquiu." In *A Jean Toomer Reader: Selected Unpublished Writings,* edited by Frederik L. Rusch, 240–48. New York: Oxford University Press, 1993.

———. "Imprint for Rio Grande." In *The Collected Poems of Jean Toomer,* edited by Robert B. Jones and Margery Latimer Toomer, 81–82. Chapel Hill: University of North Carolina Press, 1988.

———. "I Sit in My Room." In *The Collected Poems of Jean Toomer,* edited by Robert B. Jones and Margery Latimer Toomer, 83. Chapel Hill: University of North Carolina Press, 1988.

———. "It Is Everywhere." In *The Collected Poems of Jean Toomer,* edited by Robert B. Jones and Margery Latimer Toomer, 85–87. Chapel Hill: University of North Carolina Press, 1988.

———. *A Jean Toomer Reader: Selected Unpublished Writings.* Edited by Frederik L. Rusch. New York: Oxford University Press, 1993.

———. "Letter to Horace Liveright." In *Cane,* edited by Darwin T. Turner, 156–57. New York: W. W. Norton, 1988.

———. "The Lost Dancer." In *The Collected Poems of Jean Toomer,* edited by Robert B.

Jones and Margery Latimer Toomer, 39. Chapel Hill: University of North Carolina Press, 1988.

———. "New Mexico after India." In *A Jean Toomer Reader*, edited by Frederik L. Rusch, 249–53. New York: Oxford University Press, 1993.

———. "A New Race in America." In *A Jean Toomer Reader*, edited by Frederik L. Rusch, 105. New York: Oxford University Press, 1993.

———. "Part of the Universe." In *A Jean Toomer Reader*, edited by Frederik L. Rusch, 253–57. New York: Oxford University Press, 1993.

———. "Rainbow." In *A Jean Toomer Reader*, edited by Frederik L. Rusch, 240. New York: Oxford University Press, 1993.

———. "Rolling, Rolling." In *The Collected Poems of Jean Toomer*, edited by Robert B. Jones and Margery Latimer Toomer, 84. Chapel Hill: University of North Carolina Press, 1988.

———. "Santa Fe Sequence." In *A Jean Toomer Reader*, edited by Frederik L. Rusch, 257–58. New York: Oxford University Press, 1993.

———. "Taos Night." In *A Jean Toomer Reader*, edited by Frederik L. Rusch, 249. New York: Oxford University Press, 1993.

———. "To the Land of the People." In *A Jean Toomer Reader*, edited by Frederik L. Rusch, 238–39. New York: Oxford University Press, 1993.

Vasconcelos, José. *La Raza Cósmica* [The Cosmic Race]. Translated by Didier T. Jaén. Baltimore: Johns Hopkins University Press, 1997.

III

THE GARVEY MOVEMENT

7

Making New Negroes in Cuba: Garveyism as a Transcultural Movement

FRANK GURIDY

> Three cheers for the Hon. Marcus Garvey, three cheers for the Universal Negro Improvement Association, viva Antonio Maceo, viva Cuba, and viva la raza Negra!
>
> —John Daniels, UNIA member, Guantánamo, Cuba, 1921

John Daniels's salute to Marcus Garvey, the Universal Negro Improvement Association (UNIA), the Cuban republic, and Antonio Maceo, the iconic Afro-Cuban patriot, took place during a meeting in Guantánamo, Cuba, held on the occasion of Marcus Garvey's 1921 visit to the island. Daniels bellowed his "cheers" after Luisa Raymond, a local UNIA leader, presented Garvey with a bouquet of flowers at the close of the meeting. The salute reveals the making of a New Negro transnational affiliation that was produced by the cultural encounters between Anglophone Caribbeans, African Americans, and Afro-Cubans during the 1920s. These New Negro cultures were created and re-created by the carrying out of the UNIA's elaborate performance rituals and symbolic repertoire, which drew on the diverse histories and cultural backgrounds of its members. By honoring the presence of Garvey and the memory of Maceo, the UNIA was able create a new pantheon of black male heroes that galvanized black people throughout the Americas and re-created the population Garveyites called the "Negro Peoples of the World."

This essay highlights the role of the Garvey movement in the making of New Negro cultures that came about as a result of the cultural engagements of diverse African-descendants during the 1920s. It centers on the Garveyite experience in Cuba to show the ways New Negroes emerged out of the interaction of Cubans and Anglophone Afrodescendants on the island in this period. Thus the term *New Negro* can be seen as more than a political slogan or shorthand description of the artistic and cultural movements of the era; it can also be a term that highlights the making of new transcultural Afrodiasporic subjects.[1] Garveyism, along with the mass migration and transformations engendered by U.S. empire building in the circum-Caribbean, helped create new Afrodiasporic cultures produced by the ongoing interaction of diverse Afrodescendants throughout the Americas and Africa. Characterizing Garveyites as "African American," "West Indian," and "Cuban" misses the ways mobility created transcultural subjects with multiple self-identifications. The UNIA's transnational reach and its cross-class constituency transformed diasporic politics and created new black diasporic cultures that cannot be adequately captured by Harlem-centric (or nation-based) perspectives on the New Negro phenomenon.

The UNIA was both a product and a catalyst of these transformations. Following the movements of Garveyites throughout the U.S. eastern seaboard, the Caribbean, and Central America enables us to see the emergence of black transnational communities linked together by translocal networks of capital, labor, and ideas. Cuba's geographic position at the center of this imperial formation made it an important cultural crossroads between Afro-Cubans and English-speaking African descendants from the United States, Central America, and the Caribbean. Indeed, Cuba had the largest number of UNIA branches outside the United States by the mid-1920s.[2] Thus it is a particularly apt location to examine the process of New Negro cultural formation among diverse Afrodescended peoples. The result of these changes was a mass movement that created a new transcultural understanding of the African diaspora. If the history of national formation in the Americas is a history of "intermeshed transculturations," so, too, is the history of the distinct yet interconnected populations that compose the African diaspora.[3]

The UNIA's centrality to the New Negro movements of the 1920s stemmed in part from its "race first" ideology. In a period when the dominant images of Afrodescended peoples were steeped in racist caricature, the Garveyite program of self-reliance and race pride galvanized people of African descent throughout the diaspora. However, Garveyism was also based on patriarchal models of nationhood, in which the message of "race first" was coded language for "men first." Moreover, the militaristic thrust of the UNIA, influenced both by World War I and the movement's appropriation of the combative Zionism of the Old Testament, ensured that the project of African redemption would be based on discipline and hierarchy. Discipline and hierarchy were important because Garvey self-consciously patterned the movement after Euro-American empires, with its own elaborate titles, military, and steamship line—in short, an "imperial model of diaspora," as Michelle Stephens has argued. Therefore the ideological underpinnings of the movement illustrate the contradictions embedded in the Garveyite effort to unite the "Negro peoples of the world."[4]

An analysis of Garveyite ideology, whether one characterizes it as black nationalism or black fascism, only partially explains the significance of the movement.

The UNIA's appeal across linguistic and cultural differences was due to its relentless effort to use performance to enact an imagined community of New Negroes. The notion of performance posited here understands it in its broadest sense, as not simply formal theatrical events but as any embodied practice that involves the witnessing and/or participation of an audience. This includes activities such as parade processions, speeches, bodily gestures, and the printed word itself. As Elin Diamond has argued, performance is both a process—"a doing"—and a product, a "thing done."[5] In the Garveyite world, embodied activities, such as elocution, marching, singing, and uniform-wearing, were designed to enact their vision of an African diaspora. UNIA embodied activities could reinforce already existing Garveyite ideologies, but the unstable character of performance always presented the possibility for their alteration.[6] A performance-attentive analysis allows us to account for the ways Garveyites could deviate from their scripts and assert their agency even within the most codified structures of performance. Rather than overlook these performances in a quest for documenting more "tangible" evidence, the analysis of Garveyism put forth here makes the supposed "ephemeral" a central part of the UNIA's history in Cuba. In this sense, Garveyism redefined "movement" in more ways than one by showing how bodily movement could function as a crucial element in self-making.

GARVEYISM IN THE U.S.–CARIBBEAN WORLD

The UNIA emerged within a regional imperial formation I have called the *U.S.–Caribbean World,* a particular transborder zone that emerged out of the intertwined processes of U.S. expansionism and the massive migration of Afrodescendants throughout the United States and circum-Caribbean during the first few decades of the twentieth century.[7] U.S. American economic and political expansionism created a complex imperial formation that included the circum-Caribbean and U.S. coastal communities in the South and Northeast. Moreover, the massive migration of Afrodescended peoples, particularly those from the British Caribbean colonies, dramatically changed the demographic complexion of the region. Hundreds of thousands of Afro-Caribbean migrants left their homelands to work for U.S.-controlled industries in Panama, Costa Rica, Guatemala, Cuba, and New York City, among other places.[8] Cuba was a major site of Afro-Caribbean migration in this period. An estimated 130,000–140,000 British West Indians migrated to Cuba to work in the island's sugar industry during the first three decades of the century, many of them prompted by the completion of the Panama Canal and the temporary decline of the banana industry in Central America. They were joined by approximately 183,000 migrants from Haiti. As black migrants moved throughout the circum-Caribbean, other black bodies were moving on a massive scale within the United States. During the era of the Great Migration in the United States, hundreds of thousands of people of African descent relocated from the U.S. South to various urban centers in the North.[9] Thus what we see emerging during these decades was a U.S.–Caribbean transcultural Afrodescended population that was a product of their engagement with U.S. expansionism throughout the region. By the late 1910s and early 1920s, this historic transformation was having a profound effect on the ways people of African descent in the U.S.–Caribbean World navigated the structures of racialized imperial power and imagined themselves and each other.

Garveyism has been primarily an Anglophone story, one that is usually centered on the UNIA's home base in Harlem and the English-speaking Caribbean. However, more recent studies of Garveyism have documented its influence in the Spanish-speaking Caribbean and Central America. Yet, like the other movements examined in this volume, the UNIA in these areas was not simply an outpost of a New York–based movement; rather, it was intricately connected to the activities of the association's parent body in Harlem.[10] English-speaking African Americans and West Indians were not the only constituents of the Garvey movement—so were Afro-Caribbeans who spoke both English and Spanish and, sometimes, French. In Cuba, Garveyism became a transcultural phenomenon because West Indian migrants did not stay confined to the company towns controlled by foreign sugar companies in the eastern provinces of the island. West Indian migrants maintained their language and their allegiance to the British Empire, but they did not live an isolated existence in Cuba, settling in various locales throughout the island, including urban areas such as Havana, Santiago de Cuba, and Sagua la Grande.[11] Furthermore, the racial segregation of leisure practices in Cuba compelled them to develop relationships with Afro-Cuban communities on the island. As this essay shows, the UNIA often worked with Afro-Cuban associations, the dominant cultural force in the lives of people of African descent on the island, even in moments when their aims and objects diverged ideologically. In fact, UNIA Liberty Hall meetings were often held within the headquarters of Afro-Cuban organizations. It was in these spaces where West Indian, African American, and Afro-Cuban cultural practices began to collide and transform.

The UNIA's transcultural membership is clear in the biographies of many of its members, many of whom were shaped by their experiences of movement across borders. Garvey's well-known radicalization process, engendered by his travels throughout the Caribbean and Central America, is strikingly similar to that of more obscure UNIA members. An illustrative example of the impact of migration and cultural transformation on Garveyites was Eduardo Morales. Morales was born in Cuba but raised in Panama, where he developed his racial awareness and his political activism. Like so many other Afrodescendants in the Americas, Morales was inspired by Booker T. Washington's example. In 1910, he wrote the Tuskegee Principal, inquiring about translations of the school's literature in Spanish.[12] Nine years later, Morales was one of the more vocal leaders of the UNIA in the Canal Zone. Along with William Preston Stoute, the Barbadian-born leader of the United Brotherhood labor union, Morales led the famous canal workers' strike of 1920. For Morales, the strike was an opportunity for the divided black population to overcome the cultural differences that had stifled racial organizing. Morales's rousing speeches never failed to extol the virtues of Garvey's masculinist "race first" philosophy, themes that he would continue to preach a short while later as a UNIA leader in Cuba. In a meeting in Panama, Morales asked his fellow male canal workers, "Do you want to prevent, when you get up in the morning and go one way in search of work [that] your wife is compelled to go to those white people and beg them for permission to scrub their floors? You will prevent that if you join the union." For Morales, unionism was merely the first step on the road to pan-African nationhood. Rejecting national identities, Morales declared, "I am a Panamanian but I do not call myself one." He insisted, "We should all be one and call ourselves negroes." In another speech, the UNIA leader attacked skin colorism among the local Afrodiasporic population: "Our direct object is Racial Success; physically, morally, intellectually and financially. In order to achieve Racial Success, we must first realize that however fair our complexion may be, however straight our hair may be, as long as we possess the minimum amount of Negro blood in our veins, we are considered Negroes." Morales's explicit racial–diasporic consciousness, which was informed by his travels throughout the U.S.–Caribbean World, disrupted prevailing understandings of comparative race relations models that differentiate the Anglophone race–conscious black person from the unconscious Latin American Afrodescendant.[13]

It was in Cuba where the diverse background of Morales converged with those of thousands of other Afrodescendants from the Caribbean, the United States, and Central America, giving the UNIA a distinctive transcultural quality. But the UNIA's uniqueness in Cuba, which distinguished it from the Garveyite experience in Panama and Costa Rica, rested with the fact that Cuba already possessed a large native-born Spanish-speaking population of African descent with its own race-based organizing traditions. Afro-Cubans were among the largest Spanish-speaking Afrodescended populations in the circum-Caribbean region. Although they suffered from racial discrimination like all other black peoples in the region, their undeniable participation in the founding of the Cuban nation gave them a prominent status in the national imagination. If the UNIA was to be successful in Cuba, it needed to develop strategies to appeal to Afro-Cubans. What they found was a population and its own understanding of their position vis-à-vis the Cuban nation and the larger "colored race."[14]

RACIAL UPLIFT AND BLACK ASSOCIATIONAL LIFE IN CUBA

The cultural encounters between the Anglophone Caribbeans and Cubans of African descent were shaped by their parallel organizational experiences, which were rooted in common understandings of racial improvement. Racial improvement, or racial uplift, posited the notion that the "colored race" could pull itself out of the vestiges of slavery by pursuing education and thrift and by adopting the dominant Western values of the day. Since the postemancipation period, the project of racial uplift had been central to Afrodiasporic social, cultural, and political organization. Like other black benevolent and fraternal organizations founded by upwardly mobile classes in the African diaspora, the UNIA was specifically dedicated to racial "improvement." While historians have shown the similarities between African American and West Indian conceptions of racial improvement, they have not yet documented their striking parallels with Afro-Cuban understandings of racial elevation. Indeed, Afro-Cubans also had their own conceptions of racial improvement, which were born out of their own experiences in a postemancipation society as well as their encounters with uplift discourses abroad.

The UNIA's vision of racial elevation and all its class and gendered contradictions have been well documented by historians. Garveyism's project for pan-African nationhood was rooted in, yet departed from, preexisting versions of racial uplift. Like many Afrodiasporic organizations of the time, the UNIA was preoccupied by the politics of respectability. The UNIA's brand of respectability was an eclectic blend of Victorian notions of morality with the traditions of black prophetic Christianity. Article V, section 39 of the association's constitution and "Book of Laws" required all UNIA officers to "maintain a high order of respectability."[15] Garveyite organizers translated their culture of respectability into a Cuban ambiance. The UNIA division in Sagua la Grande, a town on the northern coast of Las Villas province, for example, prohibited the drinking of rum "or any other beverage that contains alcohol in the halls of the association."[16] The UNIA put major emphasis on possessing "culture" and demonstrating it through elocution, Victorian dress and decorum, and "refined" cultural practices.

Afro-Cuban understandings of racial improvement were articulated in terms such as *superación* (overcoming), *regeneracíon* (regeneration), and, more frequently, *mejoramiento* (improvement).[17] At the core of the project of racial improvement during this period were three basic tenets. First, the Cuban of African descent was in a state of backwardness because of the experience of slavery. This notion of racial backwardness, or as one Afro-Cuban journalist put it, "our racial decadence," was based on the dominant positivist racial thinking of the day, which posited a social Darwinist notion of survival of the fittest among the "races."[18] Second, the primary responsibility for bringing the colored race out of this state of backwardness belonged to the "youth," those young men (and some women) who were more removed from slavery and would lead the colored race to a glorious future. Third, the guiding light of racial improvement was education. As Epifanio Calá, a leading member of the Afro-Cuban elite, argued in 1923, "the press and the school" were the levers for making the men of the colored race into an "entirely regenerated, respected citizen, who is respected for his virtues and his talent, a factor in civilization, and an exponent of national dignity!"[19]

Afro-Cuban associations, the *sociedades de instrucción y recreo* (educational and recreational societies), commonly known as the *sociedades de color* (colored societies), were concrete expressions of the Afro-Cuban notions of racial elevation. These societies were a network of associations that served mutual aid, educational, and recreational purposes for persons of African descent in Cuba that emerged in the late colonial period.[20] After the inauguration of the Cuban Republic in 1902, these organizations continued to proliferate throughout the island. Afro-Cubans formed many sport clubs, literary societies, recreational societies, and feminist organizations. These associations were important social centers for persons of African descent, not only because they provided needed functions for their members and the community at large but also because they instilled a sense of accomplishment among people of African descent. Thus, like African Americans in the United States, Afro-Cubans transformed the meaning of racial segregation by creating organizations that served as important centers of social interaction and collective empowerment. Though always fraught with tensions along the lines of class, gender, and color, these Afro-Cuban institutions were centers of social life during a period in which most leisure activity on the island remained racially segregated.[21]

While resonances clearly existed between Afro-Cuban and Garveyite understandings of racial improvement, there were also some clear differences. The most obvious dissimilarity was Garveyism's explicit "race first" transnationalist vision of diaspora that foregrounded an identification with the larger colored race rather than with a particular nation-state. Unlike Afro-Cuban associations, and most African American organizations, the UNIA's explicit projection of an Afrodiasporic imagined community skillfully drew from the diverse histories of its transcultural membership. The UNIA embraced its membership's diversity in the ways in which Garveyites routinely situated themselves as descendants of black revolutionary heroes from different parts of the diaspora. Garvey's Black Star Line ships were named after such prominent historical figures as Frederick Douglass, Phyllis Wheatley, and Antonio Maceo. Highlighting the exploits of military figures such as Maceo and Toussaint L'Ouverture was a routine rhetorical strategy in the Garveyite repertoire of speeches. During a speech to Garveyites in May 1920, UNIA leader Edward Smith-Green reported his desire to honor the memory of black soldiers who served in the War of 1898 during his trip to Cuba. He went to the Peace Tree in Santiago de Cuba, the monument to the Rough Riders, because "I thought it would have been a sin not to visit the spot where members of my race had made such a glorious past." During the same trip, he commemorated the achievements of Antonio Maceo. Like the African American soldiers who were stationed in Cuba in 1898, Smith-Green paid tribute to Maceo because he was "a man who shed his blood so that Negroes should be liberated."[22]

Garveyism's aggressive program of black enterprise also made it stand out from other black organizations in Cuba. Central to the UNIA's effort to establish transnational linkages was the Black Star Line, the steamship company founded in 1919 that sought to pursue "free and unfettered commercial intercourse with all the Negro people of the world." Despite the ultimate financial failures of the company, the UNIA's black capitalism program generated enormous enthusiasm among Afrodescended peoples in the early years of the movement. It was this enthusiasm for black enterprise that enabled Garveyism to make inroads into Cuba. As UNIA members from the parent body in New York sought to attract members on the island, they utilized their full arsenal of performance practices and tactile accoutrements to convince Cubans of the worthiness of their cause.

PERFORMANCE AND THE UNIA'S MOVEMENT CULTURE

On Sunday, July 24, 1927, members of the UNIA and interested spectators packed the Liberty Hall in Ciego de Avila, Cuba, to witness a special visit from Henrietta Vinton Davis, the prominent UNIA leader from the association's parent body in New York City. Davis was in the middle of an island-wide tour that was designed to generate support for the organization during Garvey's imprisonment. As the association's international organizer, Davis frequently found herself traveling throughout the circum-Caribbean to rally support for the movement. In the hours leading up to her visit, news spread throughout the town that illness would keep the UNIA leader from attending the meeting held in her honor. Undeterred, she managed to arrive at 8:15 P.M., fifteen minutes after the appointed hour of most UNIA meetings. Davis was escorted into the local Liberty Hall by the Black Cross Nurses and the African Police as the "congregation pealed forth the hymn 'Shine on Eternal Light,'" the customary hymn sang at the beginning of UNIA meetings. Davis, who was known as one of the association's most charismatic speakers, often drew from her own theater background to give rousing speeches at UNIA gatherings. However, her illness forced her to give a shorter address than usual on this particular day. Soon thereafter, Rafaela Thomas, Davis's private secretary, took over, giving a "stirring" speech in English and Spanish. Thomas's oratory inspired the *Negro World* reporter who attended the event to write, "Miss Thomas is one of the rising geniuses of our race and in an oratorical manner she kept the huge gathering spellbound for thirty-five minutes."[23]

This report of the Ciego de Avila meeting in the *Negro World* reveals the performative character of the UNIA's movement culture. The singing of "Shine on Eternal Light" during Davis's entrance into the Liberty Hall illustrates the centrality of music and especially religious hymns in Garveyite meetings. The participation of the Black Cross Nurses and the so-called African Police highlights the prominence of uniformed UNIA auxiliary groups in UNIA rituals in Cuba.[24] Moreover, the account of Rafaela Thomas's "stirring" address in English and Spanish shows the emphasis Garveyites placed on oratorical performance practices at UNIA events. Transcultural subjects such as Thomas, whose bilingualism makes it difficult to identify her as either Cuban or West Indian, played key roles in communicating the Garveyite message to the island's diverse Afrodescended population.

Mundane *Negro World* accounts of UNIA meetings such as this one provide glimpses into the performative world of Garveyites. Within the context of the Garvey movement, the performances were designed to create meanings and provoke responses from spectators. The association's performance culture comes through in the ways that contributors and editors of the *Negro World* sought to translate it onto the page. This is clear in the transcriptions of the speeches of UNIA leaders published in the *Negro World*. Many articles contained the insertion "cheers," "loud cheers," or "laughter" to communicate the approval of audiences and to underscore the significance of a particular point. These insertions are evocative of theatrical scripts with their attendant stage directions, thereby highlighting the performative nature of Garveyite events. The recording of audience participation conveyed the interactive character of UNIA meetings between performers and spectators, even as it sought to project the fantasy of absolute unanimity and agreement among Garveyites. Despite their limitations, the division reports in the *Negro World* provide glimpses of UNIA men and women *in performance*. They offer accounts of Garveyites giving speeches, carrying out UNIA rituals, and singing songs. In short, we get a hint of how these Garveyites became New Negro subjects through their engagement with diverse Afrodiasporic cultures in Cuba and other parts of the Americas in this period.

An analysis of UNIA performances in the *Negro World* can enhance our understanding of the messy process of transculturation among Afrodescendants in Cuba. Reports from divisions on the island contain numerous examples of Garveyite reporters trying to make sense of speeches or recitations made by Cuban participants in Spanish. For example, a *Negro World* report of the UNIA archbishop Alexander McGuire's visit to Cuba in March 1921 illustrates the linguistic challenges that occurred at Garveyite meetings. After detailing the rituals that opened the meeting, the reporter identified "the next speaker being a Cuban by the name of Elacio Espino who delivered himself most eloquently in Spanish." While the writer noted that "each and every word of his address were not understood by the audience," Espino's "warm feeling" was evidenced by "the impression that his address took on the several other Cubans present and the cheers given by them." Such accounts show how Garveyites sought to manage the challenges of establishing connections across linguistic differences by relying on bodily gestures as a means of translation. One can imagine Spanish-speaking listeners similarly stretching their limited knowledge of English to the limit in their attempts to understand West Indian and African American speakers at UNIA Liberty Hall events.[25]

The UNIA's role as a transcultural agent in Cuba was in part due to the fact that its performance culture appropriated preexisting performance traditions. As Robert Hill has pointed out, UNIA parades and royalty rituals were clearly inspired by carnival processions in the Anglophone Caribbean. Moreover, the UNIA's emphasis on elocution is also reminiscent of what Roger Abrahams has called the "man of words" tradition.[26] Such patterns of performance are not only prevalent among West Indians, however, but in fact, similar patterns are seen in other parts of the African diaspora. One can argue that the UNIA's appeal to non-Anglophone Afrodescended peoples was also based on its ability to draw on preexisting cultural practices. Afro-Cuban societies, like the UNIA, put a great premium on elocution as a way to demonstrate their vision of racial uplift. Indeed, Afro-Cuban associations often showcased their own "men of letters" by organizing readings and lectures. Such practices were not dissimilar to the UNIA's emphasis on elocution.[27]

Indeed, mastering elocution, oratory, and singing was a central activity of UNIA members. As was stipulated in the association's bylaws, Garveyites were expected to recite UNIA prayers and hymns at every meeting. Following the lead of Garvey himself, UNIA members, both male and female, were encouraged to engage in the art of speech giving. Division reports in the *Negro World* always highlighted members' ability to give "stirring" speeches and recitations. Oratory practice was one way the UNIA tried to bring members together across cultural and linguistic differences in Cuba. A report from a UNIA meeting in Cuba, for example, highlighted a recitation given by "J. Parris," one member of the association. Parris's recitation was a direct call for the island's black population to unite across its cultural and linguistic differences:

> Africa's sons and daughters, we
> Cubans, Jamaicans, small Islanders we be,
> Cast in your lot with us and tell me not nay,
> For your destiny is enveloped in our UNIA.[28]

If the Garveyite emphasis on elocution resonated with Afro-Cuban gendered understandings of racial uplift, the practice of wearing UNIA uniforms was a significant departure from the traditions of black-identified organizations in Cuba. UNIA auxiliaries had their own uniforms, and members were required to wear them at major associational functions.[29] The uniforms of the Universal African Legion (UAL) and the African Motor Corps, two of the more prominent UNIA auxiliaries, were patterned after military attire worn by British and U.S. military officials. Garveyite uniforms, as historian Robert Hill has persuasively argued, reflected Caribbean folk traditions of mimicry that simultaneously emulated and satirized Euro-American symbols of power.[30] For many Garveyites, wearing the uniforms was a transformative experience. "We wore this uniform everywhere," Virginia Collins, a former UNIA member from New Orleans, declared to interviewers for the 2001 documentary *Marcus Garvey: Look for Me in the Whirlwind*. "That was a physical statement . . . that we are Garveyites, and proud of it!"[31] Similarly, Frances Warner, the daughter of former UNIA member Jacob Samuel Mills, echoed the empowering effects of the uniform. After getting off work from his job as a janitor, Warner recalled, Mills would put on his uniform. "He felt very proud when he would wear that uniform," she remembered. "He would wear it on the trolley car. People would look at him and talk if they wanted to talk, but that was Captain Mills!"[32] Wearing uniforms and marching in UNIA parades enabled black male Garveyites to exhibit the so-called manly attributes of military generals: erect posture, discipline, and composure.

The sight of black men and women in uniform not only inspired people of African descent to feel a sense of belonging to a diasporic collective but also alarmed governments throughout the U.S.–Caribbean World. On a number of occasions, government officials expressed concern about the presence of uniformed black men marching in UNIA parades and engaging in militaristic practices.[33] Though there are no available images of uniformed Garveyites in Cuba, the *Negro World* accounts hint at the reactions of Cuban authorities to UNIA members in organizational attire. One account reported that UNIA male members were "interested in the Legions of Honor, and are anxious to wear the uniform of the Legion, but dare not do so on account of the Cuban officials, who frown down upon anything savoring of drilling or military training." Although the Cuban government generally tolerated the UNIA throughout most of the 1920s, this report indicates that it was probably less than enthusiastic about the prospect of Afrodescended men mimicking state power in a uniform that did not belong to the Cuban Army or police.[34]

Like Garveyites elsewhere, members in Cuba derived pleasure from recounting the responses of non-UNIA members (usually whites) when they wore their UNIA regalia. During his March 1921 speech to the Havana division, Eduardo

Morales described the reactions of others to the sight of him wearing the UNIA African Cross on his lapel. "This evening I was coming on the train and there were a number of spectators looking at me in amazement," Morales claimed. "They were at a loss to see a black man wearing a medal (pointing to African Cross)," he concluded. With typical Garveyite flourish, Morales proclaimed to his listeners, "As England has her cross and Germany have this cross, so have we got our medals."[35] While Morales's speech underscores the desire of the UNIA to mimic the symbolism of European nations, it also illustrates the power with which Garveyites imbued their paraphernalia, echoing Virginia Collins's claim that wearing Garveyite uniforms was "a statement." Moreover, the division reporter's reference to Morales's gesture of "pointing to the African Cross" illustrates the UNIA's textual attempts to capture the bodily movements of its members and their effects.

Aside from the uniforms and other paraphernalia, the most dramatic symbol of the UNIA's viability was the presence of Black Star Line ships at Cuban ports. By all accounts of the *Yarmouth*'s voyages, frenzied crowds converged at ports throughout the U.S.–Caribbean World to see the ship "entirely owned and operated by colored men." During the *Yarmouth*'s monthlong stay in Cuba in March 1920, UNIA leaders used the physical presence of the ship to stage their notion of a powerful commercial diaspora-in-the-making. The fact that the *Yarmouth* was an aging vessel that barely survived its voyage to Cuba did not matter once the ship pulled into the Havana harbor. As the ship lay at anchor for five days because of a longshoreman strike, Hugh Mulzac, the ship's chief officer, remembered how Cuban Garveyites and sympathizers "came out when we arrived, showering us with flowers and fruit." When the ship finally docked at the port, it was "overrun with visitors from dawn until sunset," recalled Mulzac. The black seaman underscored the symbolic power of the *Yarmouth* when he recalled with awe how the decaying ship had "become such a symbol for colored citizens of every land."[36]

The skillful use of paraphernalia and symbolism allowed Garveyites to do more than stage an Afrodiasporic imagination for the public. These embodied practices were also central to the ways the UNIA engaged in politics. In Cuba, UNIA performances were designed by African American, West Indian, and Cuban leaders to convey the organization's legitimacy to the wider Cuban public. This was a difficult task because Garveyites needed to contend with the banning of race-based political parties and a history of repression of Afro-Cuban collective mobilization.[37] For example, on August 31, 1924, the UNIA division in the town of Camagüey organized a Negroes' Day to commemorate the conclusion of the association's annual International Convention of the Negro Peoples of the World in Harlem. The fact that this event took place in Camagüey is not unimportant. Aside from it being a center of extensive West Indian settlement, the city was one of the more notorious centers of racial segregation during this period. Since the dawn of the Cuban Republic, Camagüey's central park was divided into white and black zones. People of African descent were not allowed to walk and socialize in the center of the park, the space reserved exclusively for people defined as white. This was a custom that required no signs to communicate its meaning. The movements of Cubans of African descent were routinely policed by Cuban authorities and white citizens during social hours at the park, and at times, they encountered violence when they crossed into the designated white spaces.[38]

How did the UNIA confront this practice of racial segregation? They did not hold a rally demanding the local authorities put an end to racial segregation. Instead, they organized their Negroes' Day march to the city's central park. In fact, somewhat remarkably, the Camagüeyan division secured permission from the local authorities to hold its ceremony in the park. All the UNIA's auxiliaries were present in the procession, including the Black Cross Nurses, the Motor Corps, and the UNIA Juveniles. "For the first time in Cuban history," the Negro World reported, "an assembly of Negroes, united under the one, true, and sublime cause of the UNIA, paraded the principal streets of the city." The division then held a meeting in the plaza, where the mayor and governor were in attendance. In an act that highlights the UNIA's multilingual membership, A. Corbin, a local UNIA division leader, gave an address in Spanish. Corbin's speech was followed by "rousing cheers" of "viva Cuba libre" from the audience on behalf of the governor and mayor. According to Ernest Provost, a Negro World reporter, UNIA local leaders spoke and held the audience "spellbound." Provost's claim of a "spellbound" audience reveals the criteria Garveyites often used to gauge the success of their movement. While the UNIA's stated objective was pan-African nationhood, the primary criteria they often used to gauge their effectiveness was how well their members spoke, sang, and marched at their events.

The ceremony concluded with the UNIA band playing the Cuban national anthem and the Garveyite "Ethiopian National Anthem." Provost reported that he "felt proud when our National Anthem was played for the first time on the platform of the historical park of Camaguey." To Provost, the procession "left a great impression on the minds of the Cuban public" and brought "greater respect to our race in Camaguey than ever before."[39] Thus, to Garveyites themselves, this performance, which featured the participation of the transcultural, multilingual members, and the audience's reaction to it, was clear evidence of the "greater respect" accorded to their race. Here we can see Diana Taylor's notion of performance as an "act of transfer" that can transmit social knowledge, cultural memory, and identificatory practices. The acts of marching and shouting "viva Cuba libre" alongside UNIA chants and songs illustrate the ways these rallies could communicate meanings across linguistic differences. At the same time, the insertion of Cuban nationalist rituals also highlights the ways such performances were never simply carbon copies of the originals conceived of by the parent body in Harlem precisely because of the agency of the historical actors who participated in these codified scenarios. The procession allowed spectators and participants to declare their loyalty to both the Cuban nation and the UNIA. Here we can see the stuff of transculturation, in which UNIA performance practices were enacted alongside Cuban public rituals.[40]

The *Negro World* account of the UNIA parade in Camagüey illustrates the centrality of music to Garveyite movement culture. UNIA members were expected to engage in musical practices, and the UNIA constitution stipulated that each division was required to have "a band of music or orchestra which shall be used at all meetings or gatherings of the organization in whole or in part, as also a well-organized choir."[41] Like UNIA divisions elsewhere, branches in Cuba had their own bands that were responsible for playing Garveyite anthems and hymns at every meeting. Programs from the UNIA's Division 24 in Havana, seized by the Cuban government in 1929, document the music performed at meetings. "De Heladas Cordilleras" (From Greenland's icy mountains) was played at the beginning of every session, while the "Himno Ethiópico Nacional" (Ethiopian national anthem) was performed at the end of meetings. Another program documents the playing of a "classical selection" by the "Universal Trio," which featured O. Pérez de Galindo, the wife of division president Rogelio Galindo, on the piano, A. Rivera on the violin, and A. N. Bustamante on the flute. These documents, along with the division reports published in the *Negro World,* show how music was part of every Garveyite activity, from weekly meetings to mass parades. Music occurred not only at public events but also at private *veladas* for the edification of members.[42]

Music's centrality to UNIA functions emerges in subsequent accounts of Garveyite activities on the island. This is clear in María "Reyita" de los Reyes Castillo Bueno's memoir, *Reyita*. In the narrative recorded by her daughter Daisy Rubiera Castillo, Reyita describes her participation in Garveyite activities as an adolescent woman growing up in Oriente Province on the eastern end of the island. Reyita learned about the movement from Molly Clark and her husband, Charles, who were the leaders of the UNIA local. After listening to Clark's speeches and getting acquainted with Miss Molly, Reyita concluded that the UNIA presented an opportunity to go back to Africa and escape the racism that victimized her family in Cuba. The Garveyite message of African redemption resonated with her grandmother's stories about Africa. Soon thereafter, she began to recruit other Cubans of African descent into the movement.[43]

Not surprisingly, Reyita's recollections of her experience with Garveyites centered on the music and performances at UNIA meetings. "The parties were great fun, lots of people came," Reyita recalled. These parties were significant because "there weren't very many places where poor—and especially black—people could go to enjoy themselves." Moreover, she remembered the music at the division's parties: "The music they played to liven up the atmosphere was from both countries; for this they had to reach an agreement: as the Cubans wanted their music and the Jamaicans wanted theirs, they decided to draw lots and play the music of the winners. And what commotion from whoever won!"[44]

Reyita's comments not only highlight the role of music in UNIA gatherings but also reveal the process of translation, negotiation, and cultural exchange that was embedded in these Afrodiasporic encounters. Her recollections of UNIA parties suggest a competition between multiple Afrodiasporic peoples, one that acknowledged the cultural distinctiveness of West Indians and Cubans of African descent. At the same time, her testimony also reveals a moment of congregation, created in part by the limited opportunities for leisure for all poor persons of African descent in Cuba, irrespective of their national and cultural backgrounds. Thus the UNIA provided an important space of congregation for people of African descent on the island, one that they used to fulfill their desires for socializing and belonging.

CONCLUSION

Garveyism in Cuba was a transcultural phenomenon that was driven by the participation of Afrodiasporic subjects from a wide range of cultural backgrounds. While the association was rooted primarily in Anglophone Caribbean cultural practices, it drew on a diverse array of Afrodiasporic cultures and histories, including those of Cubans of African descent. Part of its success was due to the ability of its members to perform their vision of the African diaspora. Whether it was by staging black enterprise with its less-than-functional ships, by marching in UNIA processions, or by giving speeches, the UNIA's presence within the associational lives of black people in Cuba was based on its ability to move (literally and metaphorically) black people across borders. An account of Afro-Cuban participation in the UNIA revises our understanding of the New Negro period. A full accounting of the interactions between English- and Spanish-speaking peoples of African descent in the UNIA experience challenges the assumptions that inform Anglophone-centric accounts of the New Negro movement (and African diasporic history in general), which rely on the notion that English-speaking blacks have possessed greater racial awareness than their Spanish-speaking counterparts. Furthermore, focusing on the supposed failures of Garveyism as a political project not only discounts the material effects of UNIA's performance culture but also ignores how Garveyites themselves evaluated the effectiveness of the movement. For Garveyites, mastering elocution and UNIA rituals was just as important as investing their meager resources in the Black Star Line. Taking the power of performance seriously allows historians of the African diaspora to enhance our understanding of the making of Afrodiasporic cultures and the wider New Negro phenomenon during the 1920s and beyond.

NOTES

1   As the editors of this volume argue, the voluminous literature on the New Negro era is dominated by studies of literary and artistic production, starting with Alain Locke's *The New Negro*.

2   The UNIA had over fifty divisions on the island by the mid-1920s. See McLeod, "Sin dejar de ser cubanos"; McLeod, "Garveyism in Cuba"; Giovannetti, "Black British Subjects in Cuba," 113–23, 193–201; Giovannetti, "Elusive Organization of 'Identity.'"

3   As is well known, the concept of transculturation was first coined by Fernando Ortiz, who employed it to describe the making of Cuban culture from its distinct European and African elements. See his *Cuban Counterpoint,* 97–98. While most scholars employ the term to describe the creation of new Afro-American cultures from its European and African components (such as Cuban culture), I use it here to describe the creation of new Afrodiasporic cultures from two or more already existing Afro-American cultures.

4   The literature on gender in the UNIA has demonstrated the hierarchal vision of the Garveyite model of nationhood. See, e.g., Bair, "True Women, Real Men"; Taylor, *Veiled Garvey;* Summers, *Manliness and Its Discontents,* 66–110; Mitchell, *Righteous Propagation,* 218–39; and Stephens, *Black Empire.* For an interpretation of Garveyism as a form of "black fascism," see Gilroy, *Between Camps,* 135–237.

5   Diamond, *Performance and Cultural Politics,* 1.

6   Here I am following Richard Schechner's notion that performance is "always subject to revision" because it is never performed by the same performer in the same way nor for the same audience in the same moment. As Schechner observes, performance is "never for the first time . . . [but instead] for the second to the nth time" and thereby always and already repetition with a (critical) difference. Schechner, *Between Theatre and Anthropology,* 36. Similarly, Diana Taylor argues that performance is an "act of transfer" that transmits social knowledge, cultural memory, and identities in the Americas. See Taylor, *Archive and the Repertoire,* 2.

7   On the U.S.–Caribbean world formulation, see Guridy, *Forging Diaspora.* On U.S. interventionism in the Caribbean and Central America in this period, see Schmidt, *United States Occupation of Haiti*; Calder, *Impact of Intervention*; Pérez, *Cuba under the Platt Amendment*; Gobat, *Confronting the American Dream.*

8   On Afro-Caribbean migration throughout the region, see Newton, *Silver Men*; Conniff, *Black Labor on a White Canal*; Watkins-Owens, *Blood Relations;* James, *Holding Aloft the Banner of Ethiopia*; Chomsky, *West Indian Workers*; McLeod, "Undesirable Aliens," 4; and Putnam, *Company They Kept,* 25–75. West Indian migrants were joined by approximately 183,000 migrants from Haiti.

9   The "Great Migration" scholarship is voluminous. For a useful overview, see Trotter, *Great Migration in Historical Perspective.*

10 The notion of "outpost" Garveyism was first employed by Emory Tolbert in his book *The UNIA and Black Los Angeles.* For another recent study of the UNIA in a local context, see Rolinson, *Grassroots Garveyism.*

11 On the complexities of identity formation among West Indian migrants in Cuba, see Giovannetti, "Elusive Organization of 'Identity.'"

12 Eduardo Morales to Emmett J. Scott, May 6, 1910, Reel 319, Booker T. Washington Papers.

13 On Morales's and Stoute's activities in Panama, see Burnett, "Are We Slaves or Free Men?," 68, 88. Burnett provides the most detailed analysis of Morales's activism in Panama. He eventually becomes UNIA "high commissioner" in Cuba in 1921. For an example of the comparative race relations model in the context of Caribbean activism, see James, *Holding Aloft the Banner of Ethiopia*.

14 On Afro-Cuban associational traditions, see Guridy, *Forging Diaspora*, 71–82, 117–24.

15 Hill, *Marcus Garvey and Universal Negro Improvement Association Papers*, 1:274–75. On the Garveyite version of racial uplift, see ibid., 1:xxxv–xc. On the religious character of the UNIA, see Burkett, *Garveyism as a Religious Movement*.

16 "Regalmento de la División #55, de la ciudad de Sagua la Grande; de la Asociación Universal para el Adelanto de la raza negra," legajo 77, no. 558, Archivo Histórico Provincial de Villa Clara.

17 On "racial *regeneración*," see Morrison, "Civilization and Citizenship."

18 "Opiniones," *Alma Joven* (n.d.): 3.

19 "Alma Joven," *Alma Joven* 3 (August 15, 1923): 2.

20 Deschamps Chapeaux, *El Negro en el periodismo cubano*; Scott, *Slave Emancipation in Cuba*, 268–78; Rushing, "*Cabildos de Nación*"; Hevia Lanier, *El Directorio Central de las Sociedades Negras de Cuba*, 43–60; Howard, *Changing History*, 172–205; Ferrer, *Insurgent Cuba*, 128–38.

21 On the ways African Americans turned segregation into "congregation," see Lewis, *In Their Own Interests*.

22 Hill, *Marcus Garvey and Universal Negro Improvement Association Papers*, 2:315.

23 *Negro World*, August 20, 1927.

24 The "African Police" was likely some version of the Universal African Legion.

25 *Negro World*, March 19, 1921. On the importance of translation across linguistic differences in Afrodiasporic encounters, see Edwards, *Practice of Diaspora*.

26 Hill, "Making Noise"; Abrahams, *Man of Words in the West Indies*.

27 Martin Summers has highlighted the similar discourses of black manliness between the UNIA and Prince Hall Freemasons. See Summers, *Manliness and Its Discontents*, 77, 97.

28 *Negro World*, April 16, 1921.

29 On UNIA auxiliaries, see Summers, *Manliness and Its Discontents*, 93–101, and MacPherson, "Colonial Matriarchs."

30 Hill, "Making Noise," 199–200.

31 *Marcus Garvey: Look for Me in the Whirlwind*.

32 Ibid.

33 Hill, *Marcus Garvey and Universal Negro Improvement Association Papers*, 2:209–10.

34 *Negro World*, March 19, 1921. I want to thank Frances Sullivan for bringing this reference to my attention.

35 *Negro World*, April 16, 1921.

36   Mulzac, *A Star to Steer By,* 79, 80.

37   The limits placed on Afro-Cuban activism during this period are clear in the repression of the Partido Independiente de Color (Independent Party of Color) in summer 1912. The party was banned by a constitutional amendment in 1910 and crushed by the Cuban government two years later. See Helg, *Our Rightful Share,* 165–226.

38   On the dynamics of racial segregation in Cuba during this period, see Guridy, "Racial Knowledge in Cuba," chapter 3. Unlike in the U.S. South, racial segregation was not backed by a legal structure. In fact, the 1901 Cuban Constitution stipulated that "all Cubans would be equal before the law." Yet racial segregation was a routinely practiced "custom" throughout this period.

39   *Negro World,* September 20, 1924.

40   Taylor, *Archive and the Repertoire,* 2. On the question of "translation" in Afro-diasporic encounters, Brent Edwards's work showed how translation shaped these textual encounters. However, a focus on the production and interpretation of embodied practices enables us to examine how connections happen in ways that they might not in literary practices. See Edwards, *Practice of Diaspora.*

41   Hill, *Marcus Garvey and Universal Negro Improvement Association Papers,* 2:277.

42   "Copia de unos programas publicados en inglés y español," legajo 77, no. 558, Archivo Histórico Provincial de Villa Clara. The importance of music to the UNIA can be seen in the budget figures of the Black Star Line compiled by the U.S. government in its investigation of Garvey and the steamship company. Between 1919 and 1920, music was among the highest stock selling expenses for the company, constituting $10,518.20, a shade less than the costs of travel ($10,649.26). See Hill, *Marcus Garvey and Universal Negro Improvement Association Papers,* 2:689.

43   Rubiera Castillo, *Reyita,* 23.

44   Ibid., 24.

BIBLIOGRAPHY

Abrahams, Roger D. *The Man of Words in the West Indies: Performance and the Emergence of Creole Culture.* Baltimore: Johns Hopkins University Press, 1983.

Archivo Histórico Provincial de Villa Clara. Santa Clara, Cuba.

Bair, Barbara. "True Women, Real Men: Gender, Ideology, and Social Roles in the Garvey Movement." In *Gendered Domains: Rethinking Public and Private in Women's History,* edited by Dorothy Reverby and Susan Reverby, 154–66. Ithaca, N.Y.: Cornell University Press, 1992.

Booker T. Washington Papers. Library of Congress, Washington, D.C.

Burkett, Randall K. *Garveyism as a Religious Movement.* Metuchen, N.J.: Scarecrow Press and American Theological Library Association, 1978.

Burnett, Carla. "Are We Slaves or Free Men? Labor, Race, Garveyism and the 1920 Panama Canal Strike." PhD diss., University of Illinois at Chicago, 2004.

Calder, Bruce J. *The Impact of Intervention: The Dominican Republic during the U.S. Occupation of 1916–1924.* Austin: University of Texas Press, 1984.

Chomsky, Aviva. "'Barbados or Canada?' Race, Immigration, and Nation in Early-Twentieth-Century Cuba." *Hispanic American Historical Review* 80 (August 2000): 415–62.

———. *West Indian Workers and the United Fruit Company in Costa Rica, 1870–1940.* Baton Rouge: Louisiana State University Press, 1996.

Conniff, Michael. *Black Labor on a White Canal: Panama, 1904–1981.* Pittsburgh, Pa.: University of Pittsburgh Press, 1985.

Deschamps Chapeaux, Pedro. *El Negro en el periodismo cubano en el siglo XIX.* Havana: Ediciones R, 1963.

Diamond, Elin, ed. *Performance and Cultural Politics.* London: Routledge, 1996.

Edwards, Brent Hayes. *The Practice of Diaspora: Literature, Translation, and the Rise of Black Internationalism.* Cambridge, Mass.: Harvard University Press, 2003.

Ferrer, Ada. *Insurgent Cuba: Race, Nation, and Revolution, 1868–1898.* Chapel Hill: University of North Carolina Press, 1999.

Gilroy, Paul. *Between Camps: Nations, Cultures, and the Allure of Race.* London: Routledge, 2004.

Giovannetti, Jorge L. "Black British Subjects in Cuba: Race, Ethnicity, Nation, Identity in the Migratory Experience, 1898–1938." PhD diss., University of North London, 2001.

———. "The Elusive Organization of 'Identity': Race, Religion, and Empire among Caribbean Migrants in Cuba." *Small Axe* 10 (2006): 1–27.

Gobat, Michel. *Confronting the American Dream: Nicaragua under U.S. Imperial Rule.* Durham, N.C.: Duke University Press, 2005.

Guridy, Frank Andre. *Forging Diaspora: Afro-Cubans and African-Americans in a World of Empire and Jim Crow.* Chapel Hill: University of North Carolina Press, 2010.

———. "Racial Knowledge in Cuba: The Production of a Social Fact, 1912–1944." PhD diss., University of Michigan, Ann Arbor, 2002.

Helg, Aline. *Our Rightful Share: The Afro-Cuban Struggle for Equality.* Chapel Hill: University of North Carolina Press, 1995.

Hevia Lanier, Oilda. *El Directorio Central de las Sociedades Negras de Cuba, 1886–1894.* Havana: Ciencias Sociales, 1996.

Hill, Robert A. "Making Noise: Marcus Garvey's Dada, August 1922." In *Picturing Us: African American Identity in Photography,* edited by Deborah Willis, 181–205. New York: Free Press, 1994.

———, ed. *The Marcus Garvey and Universal Negro Improvement Association Papers.* 7 vols. Los Angeles: University of California Press, 1983–90.

Howard, Philip A. *Changing History: Afro-Cuban Cabildos and Societies of Color in the Nineteenth Century.* Baton Rouge: Louisiana State University Press, 1998.

James, Winston. *Holding Aloft the Banner of Ethiopia.* London: Verso, 1998.

Lewis, Earl. *In Their Own Interests: Race, Class, and Power in Twentieth Century Norfolk.* Berkeley: University of California Press, 1991.

Locke, Alain, ed. *The New Negro.* New York: Albert and Charles Boni, 1925.

MacPherson, Anne. "Colonial Matriarchs: Garveyism, Maternalism, and Belize's Black Cross Nurses." *Gender and History* 15 (2003): 507–27.

Marcus Garvey: Look for Me in the Whirlwind, DVD. Directed and produced by Stanley Nelson. Arlington, Va.: PBS Home Video, 2001.

McLeod, Marc C. "Garveyism in Cuba, 1920–1940." *Journal of Caribbean History* 30 (1996): 132–68.

———. "Sin dejar de ser cubanos: Cuban Blacks and the Challenges of Garveyism in Cuba." *Caribbean Studies* 31 (2003): 75–104.

———. "Undesirable Aliens: Race, Ethnicity, and Nationalism in the Comparison of Haitian and British West Indian Immigrant Workers in Cuba, 1912–1939." *Journal of Social History* 31 (Spring 1998): 599–623.

Mitchell, Michele. *Righteous Propagation: African Americans and the Politics of Racial Destiny after Reconstruction.* Chapel Hill: University of North Carolina Press, 2005.

Morrison, Karen Y. "Civilization and Citizenship through the Eyes of Afro-Cuban Intellectuals during the First Constitutional Era, 1902–1940." *Cuban Studies* 30 (2000): 76–99.

Mulzac, Hugh. *A Star to Steer By.* New York: International, 1963.

Newton, Velma. *The Silver Men: West Indian Labor Migration to Panama, 1850–1914.* Mona: University of the West Indies Press, 1984.

Ortiz, Fernando. *Cuban Counterpoint: Tobacco and Sugar.* 1947. Reprint, Durham, N.C.: Duke University Press, 1995.

Pérez, Louis A. *Cuba under the Platt Amendment, 1902–1934.* Pittsburgh, Pa.: University of Pittsburgh Press, 1986.

Putnam, Lara. *The Company They Kept: Migrants and the Politics of Gender in Caribbean Costa Rica, 1870–1960.* Chapel Hill: University of North Carolina Press, 2003.

Rolinson, Mary G. *Grassroots Garveyism: The Universal Negro Improvement Association in the Rural South, 1920–1927.* Chapel Hill: University of North Carolina Press, 2007.

Rubiera Castillo, Daisy. *Reyita, sencillamente.* Havana: Instituto del Libro Cubano, 1997.

Rushing, Fannie T. "*Cabildos de Nación* and *Sociedades de la Raza de Color:* Afro-Cuban Participation in Slave Emancipation and Cuban Independence, 1865–1895." PhD diss., University of Chicago, 1992.

Schechner, Richard. *Between Theatre and Anthropology.* Philadelphia: University of Pennsylvania Press, 1985.

Schmidt, Hans. *The United States Occupation of Haiti, 1915–1934.* New Brunswick, N.J.: Rutgers University Press, 1971.

Scott, Rebecca J. *Slave Emancipation in Cuba: The Transition to Free Labor, 1868–1899.* Princeton, N.J.: Princeton University Press, 1985.

Stephens, Michele. *Black Empire: The Masculine Global Imaginary of Caribbean Intellectuals in the United States, 1914–1962.* Durham, N.C.: Duke University Press, 2005.

Summers, Martin. *Manliness and Its Discontents: The Black Middle Class and the Transformation of Masculinity, 1900–1930.* Chapel Hill: University of North Carolina Press, 2004.

Taylor, Diana. *The Archive and the Repertoire: Performing Cultural Memory in the Americas*. Durham, N.C.: Duke University Press, 2003.

Taylor, Ula Y. *The Veiled Garvey: The Life and Times of Amy Jacques Garvey*. Chapel Hill: University of North Carolina Press, 2002.

Tolbert, Emory. *The UNIA and Black Los Angeles: Ideology and Community in the American Garvey Movement*. Los Angeles: University of California Press, 1980.

Trotter, Joe William, ed. *The Great Migration in Historical Perspective: New Perspectives on Race, Class, and Gender*. Bloomington: Indiana University Press, 1991.

Watkins-Owens, Irma. *Blood Relations: Caribbean Immigrants and the Harlem Community, 1900–1930*. Bloomington: Indiana University Press, 1996.

8

Reconfiguring the Roots and Routes of New Negro Activism: The Garvey Movement in New Orleans

CLAUDRENA HAROLD

Late in fall 1946, W. E. B. Du Bois delivered a moving address at the Southern Negro Youth Congress in Columbia, South Carolina. In it he positioned the U.S. South as a key battleground not only in African Americans' revolutionary quest for political empowerment but also in the global struggle to free all oppressed nations. The South, Du Bois informed his captivated audience, "is the firing line not simply for the emancipation of the American Negro but for the emancipation of the African Negro and the Negroes of the West Indies; for the emancipation of the colored races; and for the emancipation of the white slaves of modern capitalistic monopoly."[1] Frequently, when engaging this particular passage from Du Bois's poignant speech, "Behold the Land," my thoughts turn to a lesser known activist, John B. Cary, who, during an earlier period in African American history, harbored similar thoughts about the South's radical potential. A New Orleans–based trade unionist actively involved in New Negro era politics, Cary believed strongly that the native sons and daughters of the "Black South" had a pivotal role to play in securing a more empowering modernity for the world's dispossessed. To realize his political goals, he invested a tremendous amount of time and energy into the organization that, in his view, best embodied the independent spirit of the New Negro: Marcus Garvey's Universal Negro Improvement Association (UNIA).

Occupying several leadership positions within the New Orleans UNIA during the 1920s, Cary regarded the regional expansion of the Garvey movement from the Northeast to the Jim Crow South as a critical development in African Americans' ongoing fight against racial capitalism and American imperialism. His deep commitment to the organization's pan-African agenda was readily apparent in his organizing work in New Orleans as well as in his vital role in establishing UNIA chapters in the states of Alabama and Mississippi. Notwithstanding his extensive involvement in the UNIA, Cary remained an active participant in local trade union politics. In fact, he envisioned his activist work with both the UNIA and the New Orleans Carpenters Union as complementary components of his larger political agenda of improving the lives of "those of the rank and file who labor with their hands and thereby produce the wealth of the land."[2]

If nothing else, Cary's organizational profile underscores a theme articulated throughout this volume: the ideological complexity and diversity of New Negro activism. Not exclusively beholden to any one political movement, Cary embraced organizations viewed by several theorists of the New Negro era as possessing diametrically opposed political sensibilities and goals. In the pages of *The Messenger,* for example, A. Philip Randolph routinely denounced the UNIA for distracting black laborers from serious engagement in working-class politics: "The whites in America don't take Garveyism seriously," noted Randolph. "They dub Garvey a 'Moses of the Negro' in order to get Negroes to follow him, which will wean them away from any truly radical economic program. They know that the achievement of his program, the redemption of Africa is unattainable, but it serves the purpose of engaging the Negroes' brains, energy and funds in a highly nebulous, futile and doubtful movement so far as beneficial results to Negroes are concerned."[3] If we accept Randolph's assessment of the UNIA's influence on black workers as accurate, then how do we make sense of the fact that the labor organizer Cary was a key player in the expansion of the UNIA throughout the U.S. South? How do Cary's political alliances and their implications force us to rethink New Negro politics in the age of Jim Crow? To be more precise, what does Cary's simultaneous embrace of labor politics and black nationalist organizing tell us about the transformed psychology that permeated the New Negro masses?

With an eye toward these and other questions, this essay centers its focus on southern-based activists, such as John Cary, who endorsed the pan-African agenda of the UNIA as a viable strategy of racial uplift and economic advancement. Sensing that the political moment was ripe for revolutionary change, thousands of black southerners embraced the opportunity to ally themselves with politically engaged blacks in other parts of the world.[4] "There is one way," reasoned one southern Garveyite, "in which we can improve ourselves, and take our place beside other races of the earth, and that is to develop our full power by uniting our forces and bringing about unity of action among the Negro peoples of the world. We must draw together our scattered and divided forces into one gigantic organization and act as one solid body all over the world for the amelioration and ultimate emancipation of the race."[5]

Statements such as this one not only remind us that the UNIA's influence extended beyond the vibrant community of Harlem but also force us to grapple with the U.S. South's significance as an important incubator of black political insurgency during the interwar period. Operating in a variety of political arenas, from labor halls to college campuses, southern New Negroes struggled mightily to put an end to state-sanctioned forms of racial apartheid as well as undermine capital's expanding power. Their struggles significantly informed how blacks in other parts of the country, including the international capital of the pan-African world (New York), imagined, constructed, and performed in material and textual sites of political contestation.

By tracing the history of the UNIA in one of its major southern strongholds, New Orleans, Louisiana, this essay explores how the trajectory of New Negro thought and politics was shaped not only by activists based in New York but also by people, ideas, and organizations rooted in the South. It unpacks the ways in which working women and men in the Garvey movement relied on the politics of statecraft, cooperative economics, and locally based initiatives to facilitate the creation of a self-reliant, democratic laboring class capable of transforming the local terrain and the capitalist world economy. In my view, the political engagements of New Orleans Garveyites reflected not only a rising racial militancy within African American communities but also the southern black majority's determination to play a crucial role in the making of a New Negro modernity.[6] Thus it is not my intention simply to provide the reader with a regional variation on the familiar tale of the UNIA's meteoric rise and catastrophic fall. Instead, my analysis foregrounds the fascinating story of southern Garveyism within the larger context of the inner lives, cultural realities, and political sensibilities of local people. It proceeds from the premise that grasping the many complexities of one of the most dynamic political moments in American history requires that we take seriously the southern roots and routes of New Negro activism and its various ideological outlets. To limit our analysis of the New Negro movement to black intellectuals, activists, and artists based in New York City is to obscure the complexity of a historical moment in which black southerners provided exciting organizational models of grassroots labor activism, assisted in the revitalization of pan-African black nationalism, and challenged the governance of historically black colleges in ways that occasioned new perspectives on the potential sites of black radical activity. The point here is not simply to make a case for the existence of a New Negro political culture in the South but also to demonstrate how this evolving culture influenced black activists in the North.

Not at all oblivious to the political and intellectual undertakings of black activists and writers who maintained their southern residencies during the Great Migration era, New Negroes in the North followed closely the labor struggles of African American trade unionists in the coastal cities of New Orleans, Norfolk, and Charleston, mulled over the political implications of black southern youths' collective struggles against the authoritarian policies of white college administrators during the mid-1920s, and featured some of the South's brightest minds, most notably Abram Harris and James Ivy of Virginia Union, in leading New Negro publications such as *The Messenger* and *Opportunity*. Turning our analytical gaze to the U.S. South does much more than expand the geographical boundaries of New Negro studies, a field whose transnational reach has broadened significantly in the past decade.[7] It also allows for a nuanced understanding of how black activists throughout the United States and the larger African diaspora arrived at certain theoretical positions regarding nation, class struggle, democracy, and international politics. Particularly with respect to the UNIA, extending our analysis beyond the political community of Harlem and the dominant figure of Garvey, as Frank Guridy[8] has done in his fascinating work on the New Negro politics of Afro-Cubans, constitutes an important step in challenging personality-driven narratives that frequently overlook the institutional arrangements, collective endeavors, and quotidian activities that gave both the UNIA and the New Negro movement their intellectual dynamism and political breadth.

THE RISE OF THE GARVEY MOVEMENT IN THE JIM CROW SOUTH

The UNIA solidified its presence in rural and urban communities throughout the South between 1918 and 1922. Similar to New Negro moderns in other parts of the country, southern Garveyites hoped to create a mass movement that would push their communities toward a new political maturity. Above all else, they aspired to secure the essential attributes of modernity: self-possession, economic independence, cultural capital, and political power. Nowhere in the South was this modernist quest more visible than in the birthplace of southern Garveyism: Hampton Roads, Virginia. On the eve of the close of World War I, this politically volatile community became the first major UNIA stronghold in the South. If one takes into account the growing militancy of the local black community during World War I, the UNIA's initial success in Hampton Roads should hardly surprise us. Wartime strikes initiated by black workers, combined with local activists' unrelenting critiques of the racist policies of the American Federation of Labor, sparked a firestorm of controversy over the contested meanings of democracy, the role of African Americans in the political economy, and the immediate need to abolish labor systems and arrangements responsible for unimaginable levels of human suffering.[9] Moreover, key developments in the labor arena, particularly the formation of such independent black labor unions as the National Brotherhood Workers of America, disposed many African American workers toward a nationalist orientation.

Such developments rendered Hampton Roads an ideal recruiting ground for the UNIA. On his first visit to Newport News in September 1918, Garvey convinced one hundred women and men to become members of the newly formed

Newport News division. "Continuously thereafter," Henry Vinton Plummer later recalled, "members were enrolled to the extent of three or four thousand in less than six months."[10] To sustain the interest of its swelling membership, the Newport News division established a paramilitary group (the African Legions), organized a Black Cross Nurses auxiliary, and gained quite a reputation for hosting some of the most passionate political meetings in the area. Not to be outdone by their Newport News neighbors, blacks in Norfolk also organized a vibrant division that became fully integrated into the social, political, and cultural fabric of the local community. Spirited discussions on a wide range of political issues, uplifting music from the division's jazz band, and special appearances from Garvey, socialist Hubert Harrison, and local leaders such as P. B. Young ensured a diverse audience for the local division. Not only the politically engaged but scores of black pleasure seekers became permanent fixtures at the UNIA's weekly meetings, which were held at the local Negro Longshoremen Hall on Princess Anne Avenue.

The UNIA also attracted followers as a result of its economic agenda. A recurrent theme in many of Garvey's writings was the importance of the race developing its own bases of economic power. "If we are to rise as a great people," Garvey advised his followers, "we must start business enterprises of our own; we must build ships and start trading with ourselves between America, the Caribbean, and West Africa. We must put up factories in all the great manufacturing centers of this country, to give employment to the thousands of men and women who will be thrown out of work as soon as the nation takes on its normal attitude."[11] To solidify the UNIA's economic foundation, Garvey organized the Black Star Line Steamship Corporation (BSL) in summer 1919. The BSL's agenda was ambitious yet straightforward: to facilitate the creation of an integrated community of consumers, workers, and businesses strapped with the necessary funds, knowledge, and vision to transform patterns of capitalist ownership within the larger society and thereby secure a brighter future for people of African descent. Though Garvey and his associates were novices to the shipping industry, hundreds of black workers in Hampton Roads rallied behind the BSL. On his tour of Virginia in July 1919, Garvey marveled at Afro-Virginians' fervor for the line:

> I have been lecturing through the state of Virginia for fourteen days, and I must say that the people all through have been the most responsive to the new doctrine being taught, that of preparation and action in this, the age of unceasing activity. The great enterprise of the Black Star Line is receiving great support in Virginia, and I feel sure that by the splendid start by the people in [this section] that our steamship line will become one of the most prosperous ones afloat after October 31.[12]

Enmeshed as they were in a local economy dominated by the shipping industry, many Virginia Garveyites upheld the BSL as key to the race's continued modernization. One such individual was Walter Green, a labor activist widely respected for his involvement in the American Federation of Labor, along with his organizing work for the National Brotherhood Workers of America. Insisting that black workers must continue their activist work in the labor arena while assisting in the creation of race-based economic cooperatives, Green championed the BSL as "a great boon and benefit to the race in the future."[13]

Thanks in large part to the confidence Green and other black Virginians placed in the BSL and the UNIA, Garvey developed a new appreciation for the revolutionary possibilities in the U.S. South. "Away down in Virginia," Garvey informed his New York supporters,

> I have discovered that the Negro of the South is a new and different man to what he was prior to the war. The bloody war has left a new spirit in the world—it has created for all mankind a new idea of liberty and democracy, and the Southern Negro now feels that he has a part to play in the affairs of the world.[14]

Inspired by the UNIA's success in Virginia, Garvey pushed for greater influence in other parts of the South. Toward this end, he assigned some of his most able recruiters—Reverend James Walker Hood Eason, T. C. Glashen, Arnold S. Cummings, George Tait, Jacob Slappey, and Adrian Johnson—to the region in early 1921. Not long thereafter, notices of thriving UNIA branches in Nashville, Tennessee, Raleigh, North Carolina, Charleston, South Carolina, Brunswick and Waycross, Georgia, and Miami and Key West, Florida, among other southern locales, dominated the headlines of the *Negro World*.

Of the new recruiting hotbeds in which UNIA organizers performed remarkably well, no area attracted greater praise from Parent Body officials than New Orleans.[15] Seemingly overnight, Dixie's largest city emerged as one of the most dynamic UNIA strongholds in the world. Much of this had to do with the recruiting talents of Adrian Johnson. Navigating the political terrain of black New Orleans was no easy task, but Johnson received tremendous support from the New Orleans division's founder, Alaida Robertson, its president, Sylvester Robertson, and its treasurer, Maime Reason. Recognizing the necessity of forging amicable relationships with community leaders, Johnson preached a message of unity without uniformity. Speaking before members of the West Indian Seaman Society, the charismatic newcomer insisted that "all Negro organizations should take up the fight for a better day for the race by uniting their efforts, without losing their specific identity."[16] Owing in part to Johnson's remarkable service, membership in the New Orleans division of the UNIA (NOD) swelled from seventy persons in February 1921 to nearly four thousand people by October of the same year.[17] "When I arrived in New Orleans," Garvey boasted in summer 1921, "I found hundreds of loyal men—good men and true men—who were waiting to receive me through the great work that Johnson had done preparatory to my getting there."[18]

Lest my focus on Johnson's remarkable talents be misconstrued as privileging a top-down perspective on the UNIA's explosive growth, it is important to acknowledge the ways in which local dynamics also influenced the movement's success in the Crescent City. Specifically within the organizational matrix of uptown New Orleans, the vibrant world of black labor activism provided institutional support, political language, and a highly trained leadership class from which the NOD derived great support in its formative years. Not only did the Negro Longshoremen Hall function as the principal meeting place for the UNIA but the International Longshoremen Association and the Carpenters Union supplied the local division with some of its most able leaders (most notably T. A. Robinson, vice president of the International Longshoremen's Association, and the previously mentioned John Cary).

On their arrival to New Orleans from New York, UNIA organizers discovered a black working class with not only a deep commitment to improving their economic condition and an unwavering confidence in their leadership abilities but also a pro-black perspective that meshed perfectly with the racial message of the UNIA. Thus another significant factor in the UNIA's expansion in New Orleans was its ideological similarities with preexisting philosophical perspectives within the local community. To further illustrate this point, let us turn to social worker Millie Charles, who, in 1994, reminisced on why her grandmother, a domestic worker, proudly "donated her dollar" to the Garvey movement: "The whole movement back to Africa was what intrigued her and that kind of philosophy caught her fancy because she always had a sense of curiosity about where she came from and that sort of thing. Even though she worked for whites, she was a proud black woman." Moving away from her grandmother's experience and looking at the movement more broadly, Charles also believed that the city's cultural and spatial dynamics, particularly the division between uptown blacks and downtown Creoles of color, factored significantly in the UNIA's expansion during the early 1920s: "It was kind of easy that a movement such as that would take hold, especially uptown. I am *not* talking about downtown."[19] Far from being in need of a savior to lead them out of political darkness, many "uptown blacks" already possessed a strong ontological foundation regarding their relationship to the pan-African world. Strong evidence of this can be found in the reflections of Carlise Arsenburg, a New Orleans Garveyite who situated the formation of his pan-African vision within the context of his family's political sensibilities: "I am greatly enthused over the movement with its great cause and success. I had been taught about Africa since I was fourteen years old by my mother, and I had always lived in hopes that the time would come that her words would come to pass. Surely that time has come. It is now."[20] Here Arsenburg is clearly referring to the UNIA's resettlement plans in Liberia.

As many readers are well aware, the necessity of strengthening Liberia's economic and political standing in the international arena constituted a principal theme in many of Garvey's writings, which routinely drove home one important point: until the West African country maximized its potential for self-governance and embraced its political mission of leading the pan-African struggle against European colonialism, political liberation for blacks in the Caribbean, the Americas, and Europe would remain an elusive dream. The seriousness in which the UNIA regarded its responsibility of assisting Liberia in fulfilling that particular mission became quite apparent in summer 1920, when the UNIA sent Elie Garcia to the capital city of Monrovia. The purpose of Garcia's trip was threefold: to (1) familiarize Liberian officials with the UNIA's political objectives; (2) negotiate a land deal in which the UNIA could establish a settlement in Liberia comprising enterprising black women and men from the West, primarily the United States and the West Indies; and (3) evaluate the Liberian elite's relationship with nearby indigenous groups.

If entry into modernity required a demonstration of one's readiness to engage in the politics of statecraft, then many within the NOD fulfilled the necessary qualifications. On the pages of the *Negro World* and at their weekly meetings, New Orleans Garveyites repeatedly stated their desire to transform Liberia into a political and economic force in world politics. "The time has come," Elenore Brown, a domestic worker, declared in October 1921, "for every nation to look to his own country for a place of safety. We are looking forward to our home, 'Africa for the Africans.' We are proud of the Messiah that God has sent us, and the message of the Great Marcus Garvey is come home; where we shall no longer possess the name nigger, but we shall be a nation respected by the world."[21]

Unfortunately for Brown and other Crescent City Garveyites, the UNIA was no closer to achieving its political goals than it had been at the time of its formation. One major stumbling block for the organization was the BSL. So much of the UNIA's initial success in the South had been built on the enthusiasm generated by the BSL, but as the line entered its third year of operation, fiscal difficulties forced BSL officials to cut their losses.[22] On February 20, 1922, Elie Garcia, treasurer of the BSL, ordered all divisions to cease the sale of BSL shares. Several weeks later, the *Negro World* announced the line's suspension.[23] To add insult to injury, the UNIA's relationship with the Liberian government had become increasingly strained. Worried about the negative impact their connection with the Garvey movement might have on their already fragile relationship with the governments of England, the United States, and France, Liberian officials, particularly President C. D. B. King, backed away from their initial endorsement of the UNIA's colonization plans.[24]

Notwithstanding these and other challenges, UNIA divisions in New Orleans managed to weather the storm. To the astonishment of many, Garveyites in these areas still held weekly meetings, continued their subscriptions to the *Negro World,* and remained committed to Garvey's message of race pride, group unity, and African redemption. On a brief sojourn in New Orleans during summer 1922, Garvey experienced firsthand his organization's continued popularity among New Crowd Negroes. Converging en masse on South Rampart Street, five thousand women and men assembled at the Negro Longshoremen Hall in a moving display of solidarity for their embattled leader. The prevailing mood was one of optimism and confidence in the eventual triumph of the UNIA's agenda. In response, Garvey proudly noted that "the Universal Negro Improvement Association is anchored forever, as far as its dignity and honor are concerned, in the city of New Orleans."[25]

To understand why UNIA divisions in New Orleans and elsewhere stayed afloat during this difficult period, it is necessary to remember that *local Garveyism* had a validity and vitality of its own. So much more than an institutional appendage of the parent body in New York, local UNIA branches provided an institutional and discursive space in which laboring people could forge a movement culture, engage in lengthy discussions on the viable political solutions, and criticize the ways of white folks and the black elite without fear of reprisal. Moreover, the division's democratic structure offered working women and men a critical space for political development. Largely denied access to the formal political arena, routinely marginalized in the American labor movement, and devalued in many elite-controlled black institutions, a significant number of African American workers appreciated greatly the leadership opportunities available in the UNIA. Since extensive formal education, occupation, and social background were not determining factors in an individual's eligibility for office in the UNIA, working women and men frequently held positions of authority within their local divisions and their various auxiliaries.[26] Such opportunities were increasingly important as class tensions within the black community became more pronounced.

Especially as social uplift ideology lost currency among many black workers during the New Negro era, a critical mass of UNIA followers not only contested the power and paternalistic policies of the white ruling elite but also railed against a brokerage form of racial politics[27] in which decision-making power rested in the hands of a select few. Taking notice of this development, John Cary applauded the growing political independence of "the common people of the Negro race," who are beginning to realize that they must think and act for themselves. The Negroes have been so often deceived by their supposed leaders that they have reached a conclusion not to be fooled any longer. During the World War they were told by those who represented selfish interests that the war would make the world safe for Democracy. Have such promises benefited the Negro? With the ending of war practically all the liberties of the Negro people have been taken away. Big business and professional politicians, supported by faithless clergy, have fastened the shackles upon the Negro people, and we continue to suffer under the terms of our deceptors.[28]

Owing in no small part to their growing frustration with established black leaders, Cary and other workers valued the UNIA for providing an institutional space in which they could articulate their political concerns, engage in meaningful debate, and develop the leadership skills needed to realize their political goals. In fact, a persistent theme in the reflections of many Garveyites was each local UNIA's importance in their intellectual–political maturation. Long after the Garvey movement's demise, Communist activist Sylvia Woods celebrated the NOD as an egalitarian space that opened up its followers to new ways of envisioning their place in the world. Though only eleven at the time of the division's founding, Woods had fond memories of the leadership lessons provided by the movement, particularly the women who constituted its backbone:

I'll never forget, there was a little woman there and she used to speak every Sunday. When that woman got up to talk, my father would just sit thrilled and then he'd look at me: "Are you listening?" I'd say, "I'm listening." "I want you to hear every word she says because I want you to be able to speak like that woman. We have to have speakers in order to get free." And when we got home he would say, "Now what did she say?" I could say it just like her, with her same voice, all of her movements, and everything. This would please him [to] no end.[29]

Obviously for this activist family, which had strong ties to the local labor movement, the UNIA's significance derived from its role as an important incubator of *political being and becoming.*

Only through an analysis of how Garveyism manifested itself at the local level can one understand the UNIA's survival without reducing the movement's working-class constituency to misguided dupes. The decentralized nature of the Garvey movement in New Orleans and other parts of the South afforded working women and men opportunities for leadership and advancement within the organization that were not always available in more centralized locations like New

York and Philadelphia. Of course, the UNIA's resiliency in the face of enormous odds also had a great deal to do with the political intelligence and perseverance of the organization's rank and file. Years of organizational experience had instilled within many a revolutionary patience that proved sustaining during difficult times. So although the UNIA encountered its share of setbacks, its most loyal followers remained committed to the organization and their embattled leader.

Buoyed by his followers' unwavering confidence in the righteousness of the UNIA's political cause, Garvey refused to retreat from his nationalist position. To detractors and admirers alike, he framed his organization's current difficulties as temporary inconveniences rather than signs of deep structural problems. Thus Garvey proceeded with plans to strike a deal with the Liberian government and revitalize his pan-African agenda. Toward the end of 1923, he dispatched three of his most trusted associates, Robert Lincoln Poston, Henrietta Vinton Davis, and J. Milton Van Lowe, to Monrovia, Liberia, where they negotiated with state officials over the acquisition of territory near the Cavalla River in Maryland County.[30] To complement his endeavors in Liberia, Garvey also organized the Black Cross Navigation and Trading Company (BCNTC) in March 1924. This newly constituted line, Garvey promised, would transport "the first organized group of colonists to Liberia," while additional vessels would be acquired for the purpose of establishing a "trade relationship between Negroes of Africa, the United States of America, the West Indies, and South and Central America."[31] Upon news of the BCNTC's formation, UNIA branches throughout the nation experienced something on the order of a political revival. Thanks to support from blacks throughout the South and the larger pan-African world, the BCNTC acquired its first and only vessel, the SS *General Goethals,* in fall 1924. Several months later, on January 10, 1925, the *Goethals* embarked on its first voyage to the West Indies and Latin America.

One important factor in the marketability of the UNIA's latest economic venture was the mounting concern of black workers over the consolidation of corporate capital, the accelerated rate of mechanization, and the ubiquitous problem of labor redundancy in many parts of the urban South. "The modern inventions," Henry Harrison of Norfolk, Virginia, wrote in 1925, "have the greatest tendency to obstruct the earning power of the Negro people, as the majority of our race depends upon the white race for their livelihood."[32] The resultant surplus of unemployed workers, he elaborated, "makes labor so cheap that it is impossible to get a salary at a rate in which we can live comfortable." These circumstances, in Harrison's opinion, left workers with no choice but to support the "commercial and industrial enterprises of the UNIA."[33] Unfortunately for Harrison and others, who pinned many of their economic dreams on the Garvey movement, the industrial enterprises of the UNIA, particularly the undercapitalized BCNTC, were in no position to solve the race's economic woes. Only five months after its first voyage, the mechanically troubled and financially insolvent *Goethals* suspended operations.

The colossal failures of the organization's most ambitious projects—the Liberian colonization scheme, the BSL, and the BCNTC—brought some to the conclusion that the movement was in desperate need of radical restructuring. Moreover, internecine battles among parent body leaders in New York after Garvey's incarceration for mail fraud in 1925 severely undermined the movement's ability to mount a united front in the face of intense public scrutiny. Saddled by an array of political problems within and outside the UNIA, Garveyites in New Orleans confronted the complex question of "where do we go from here?" Was the movement even salvageable given Garvey's imprisonment, or were there competent leaders in New York capable of steering the UNIA in the right direction? And if so, should local branches remain loyal to the stated objectives of Garvey? Or did the times mandate greater political independence on the part of local branches?

Faced with these and other pertinent questions, the New Orleans UNIA increasingly shifted its focus to local issues as the further decentralization of the national movement created new opportunities for enterprising branches. Framing its new initiatives as integral components of the Garvey movement's overall project of racial modernization, the NOD organized a free medical clinic, set up an adult night school for leadership training and educational enhancement for black workers, and augmented the division's social welfare programs. These community outreach programs assisted blacks in better handling the stresses and demands of everyday life in the Jim Crow South as well as legitimized the UNIA in the eyes of many who had previously dismissed Garveyism as a utopian movement detached from the *real* concerns of local people.

If queried on whether this new emphasis on "community issues" represented a departure from their division's earlier agenda of assisting the southern black majority in fashioning new political selves, New Orleans Garveyites would have probably responded in the negative. Solving the problems of black workers' social alienation, material deprivation, and political powerlessness still animated the political choices and commitments of Garveyite women and men. Moreover, local leaders hardly abandoned their ambitious dream of creating a self-reliant democratic laboring class in control of its political destiny. To be sure, a shifting political terrain meant that UNIA followers could no longer pursue the politics of racial modernization through pan-African empire building. Nonetheless, many Garveyites believed strongly that local resources and infrastructures could be harnessed to advance one important aspect of the political project of New Negro modernity: the redemption of the African American body politic.

Critical inquiry into two of the division's most impressive endeavors, the Free Community Medical Clinic and its adult night school, proves this point. Simultaneously servicing the community, the race, and the New Negro movement, these institutional cornerstones did much more than distribute services to disadvantaged groups on the dark side of modernity. On the cultural and political front, they posed great challenges to dominant representations of black working-class humanity as physically and morally degenerate, socially pathological, intellectually inferior, and incorrigibly uncivilized. Maybe no aspect of the UNIA's social welfare program demonstrates this more than New Orleans Garveyites' endeavors in the field of public health.

On January 21, 1928, the NOD informed the public of its plans to open up a medical clinic in the back of the division's Liberty Hall, a mid-sized building purchased by the NOD in late 1926. "Within the next few days," Lillie Jones announced in the *Negro World,* "we shall open a first-class medical clinic for the poor of our community."[34] To say that such an endeavor was desperately needed in the South's largest city would be an understatement. Of the nation's urban centers with a population of over one hundred thousand, New Orleans claimed the distinction of having the highest black morbidity and mortality rate.[35] Framing the health crisis within the black community as a behavioral rather than a structural issue, the city's white population pointed to what they viewed as African Americans' deviant behavior, medical negligence, cultural backwardness, and general unfitness for urban life as the primary reasons for the race's health problems. Such claims would not go unchallenged within black activist circles. Noting that the problematic health of black folk could not be treated as an isolated phenomenon, African Americans drew attention to the limited medical facilities and health services available to the city's black population, the inefficient manner in which the local government distributed municipal services, and elected officials' general disregard for the medical needs of its impoverished residents (white and black).[36]

Identifying the city's health crisis as an issue of great import, Garveyites implemented several programs to fight against the community's climbing mortality and morbidity rate. Central to its efforts was the UNIA Free Community Medical Clinic, which opened in fall 1928. Logan Horton, a young African American doctor in the city, directed the clinic, while the division's Black Cross Nurses focused on patient care. Precisely because the city's public health services had routinely maligned the black poor, New Orleans Garveyites guaranteed first-rate service to uptown's most marginalized citizens. "Courtesy and efficient care will always be given to everyone," division leaders promised the community.[37] Thoroughly impressed by the NOD's latest endeavor, community leaders applauded Garveyites for their ambitious work. In fact, an editorial in the *Louisiana Weekly,* the city's black newspaper, challenged other organizations to follow in the division's footsteps: "Too much credit cannot be given to this organization for its forward step towards the uplift of fallen humanity. This city and State needs many such clinics to cope with the rising death rate of the colored group in this section."[38]

None of the NOD's success would have been possible without the dedicated service of the Black Cross Nurses, which, in addition to serving the clinic, coordinated other aspects of the UNIA's health service program. Using strategies employed by thousands of black women in urban centers across the country, the Black Cross Nurses disseminated information on disease prevention, promoted and observed National Negro Health Week, and sponsored weekly symposiums on diet, sanitation, and other disease-prevention measures.[39] It was quite clear that the NOD believed that any movement committed to racial modernization must attend to the physical well-being of the black body politic.[40]

A corollary requirement for those seeking to enjoy the benefits of modernity, according to the NOD, was a sound political mind. Coupled with their efforts to save black bodies, New Orleans Garveyites also deemed it their responsibility to provide working-class women and men with a strong intellectual foundation to minimize their need for political representation from above. Toward this end, the division established an adult night school on October 21, 1928.[41] Surviving well into the New Deal years, the night school offered classes in reading, writing, and arithmetic as well as special seminars for working women and men actively involved in the associational lives of their communities. "A course in public speaking and leadership," according to Doris Busch, targeted "those whose abilities and fraternal and social connections warrant the need of the course."[42] A recurrent theme at the adult night school was the need for working-class people to possess the ability to identify problems and construct effective solutions to generate social change. Leadership training and intellectual stimulation should not be confined to the educated elite. "Everyone," Lucille Hawkins announced in an advertisement for special programs taking place during the division's "Education Month," "is expected to make a special study of race problems."[43]

Working women and men with a thirst for intellectual exchange appreciated the opportunity to engage in critical discussions on the strengths and limitations of the UNIA's nationalist orientation, the most reasonable time table for an improvement in the association's relationship with Liberia, and the necessity of forging links with other organizations within the black community. With the purpose of creating a thriving democratic culture marked by spirited exchange and self-criticism, the division embraced controversial topics that pushed its members beyond their political comfort zones. One forum, for example, broached the following questions:

1. Is Garvey a Thief?
2. Is Garvey crazy?
3. Is Garvey a fake?
4. Is Garvey diplomatic?

5. How can Negroes build for themselves a mighty nation?

6. Isn't the Negro's progress in the Western world a sufficient indication that he is going to enjoy equality with the white people within the next few years?[44]

To the outside world, the New Orleans UNIA put forth, as objects of both analysis and admiration, politically sophisticated black workers who were intellectually prepared to engage in complex discussions on how the modern black subject should navigate the cultural, social, and political terrain. Far from being in need of intervention and guidance from the black cultural elite, the self-reliant black laborer was more than ready to assert herself on the world stage as a political actor.

Understandably proud of their accomplishments, New Orleans Garveyites wasted no time in updating the pan-African world on their endeavors. "Great things are being carried on by the New Negroes in this section. . . . We are constantly on the firing line—the line that leads to true and lasting emancipation."[45] Indeed, during the second half of the 1920s, the NOD made significant progress in terms of expanding its political program and deepening its relationship to the broader community. Undoubtedly the social services provided by the adult night school and the free medical clinic factored significantly in the story of the NOD's growth; however, brief attention should also be given to how the division's willingness to involve itself, if only sporadically, in civil rights issues also improved its standing in black New Orleans. To prove this point, our attention turns to the division's involvement in the Eros murder case.

Truly one of the most horrific reminders of the fragility of black life in the Jim Crow South, the Eros murder case involved a black sharecropper whose two daughters had been brutally murdered by a group of drunken white men in Eros, Louisiana, on Christmas Day 1928.[46] Suspecting that "the conviction of these cold blooded murders could have a profoundly salutary effect not only upon Louisiana but throughout the South," Walter White ordered the president of the New Orleans NAACP, George Lucas, to initiate an intensive fund-raising drive for the case.[47] Obliging White's request, Lucas sought financial assistance from local clubs, churches, labor unions, mutual aid and benevolent societies, and civic organizations. It is impossible to gauge the full extent of White's familiarity with the internal politics of black New Orleans, but one suspects that he was probably surprised by Lucas's notification of the UNIA's contribution to the sharecropper's defense fund. "Have received a few dollars from local sources," Lucas informed White, "among which is a check for twenty dollars from the local Branch of the U.N.I.A., and they promise more help."[48] At first glance, the UNIA's modest contribution to the local branch's defense fund may strike us as insignificant. However, if viewed in light of Marcus Garvey's contentious relationship with the NAACP, the NOD's public gesture of support for the branch's litigation efforts takes on greater political meaning for two important reasons: (1) it reminds us of the important collaborative projects occurring in black communities throughout the South and (2) it demonstrates the willingness of local Garveyites to pursue a course of action independent of the parent body in New York. Though Garvey and several of the NAACP's prominent leaders, namely, W. E. B. Du Bois and Robert Bagnall, engaged in some of the most vitriolic exchanges of the 1920s, UNIA leaders in New Orleans discovered a common ground on which they could collaborate with NAACP leaders in their community.

The independence displayed by New Orleans Garveyites underscores the depths of the self-determinist spirit that guided their political utterances and actions within the local community and the broader black world. Even more, their political engagements remind us that Garvey's imprisonment in 1925 and subsequent deportation in 1927 hardly marked the movement's end in many communities. Confronted with the challenge of ensuring the viability of the movement, Garveyites in New Orleans anxiously grasped at the opportunity to impose their will on the current political landscape. To their credit, they constructed a vibrant social movement that legitimized the UNIA in the eyes of many detractors who believed the organization to be all flash and no substance.

Ultimately, however, the New Orleans UNIA experienced a precipitous decline as the harsh economic conditions of the Depression era transformed the ideological commitments and political loyalties of many African Americans. The material deprivation brought about by the collapse of the capitalist world economy not only limited Garveyites' ability to maintain the NOD's local initiatives but also caused many to question the organization's self-help philosophy.

Notwithstanding its relatively short existence as a thriving institution, the New Orleans UNIA occupies an important place in the memory of quite a few local activists, including the noted black arts movement writer Kalamu ya Salaam, whose 1978 poem "Whirlwind Storm Warning UNIA" provides a thought-provoking take on the historical links between New Negro era politics and Black Power activism. In particular, Salaam's assertion that "garvey meant us / when he said the whirlwind"[49] resonated deeply among many activists for whom the southern wing of the UNIA played a decisive role in their politicization. The names that loom largest among this distinguished group include Randolph Blackwell, future director of the Voter Education Project, advisor to Martin Luther King Jr., and founding president of the Rural Action Poverty Program; Virginia Collins, a key leader in the Louisiana division of the Southern Conference for Human Welfare; Audley "Queen Mother" Moore, the pioneering black nationalist whose organizational affiliations ranged from the Communist Party to the Republic of New Africa; and Sylvia Woods, an active organizer for the Congress of Industrial Organizations and the Communist Party from the 1930s to the 1970s. These former Garveyites provided theoretical insight, exemplary leadership, and dedicated service to numerous political movements. Thus to engage the distinguished careers of these and other activists is to recognize the importance of the New Negro era in understanding the ways in which the intergenerational transmission of political knowledge and experience informed the "long" black freedom struggle.

Beyond the question of the political legacy of the UNIA, the scholarly significance of the Garvey movement lies in the ways in which it challenges the regional biases in much of the scholarship on the New Negro. If nothing else, the history of southern Garveyism reminds us that the Jim Crow South—as a geographical and metaphorical space—occupied an important place in New Negroes' historic quest for political empowerment, ontological clarity, and existential freedom. Long before terms such as *Global South* captured the imagination of the scholarly community, UNIA followers like John Cary envisioned themselves as performing a decisive role in the struggle for the creation of a more humane world devoid of racial oppression, dehumanizing labor practices, and colonial subjugation. If scholars in the fields of Africana studies, American and African American history, and new southern studies devote more attention to the incredibly rich history of southern Garveyism, they will undoubtedly gain a deeper appreciation for the centrality of the U.S. South in the making and remaking of New Negro modernity.

NOTES

1 Du Bois, "Behold the Land," 545.

2 *Negro World,* November 17, 1927.

3 *The Messenger,* January 1923.

4 Several scholars have challenged the common portrayal of Garveyism as a northern, urban-based movement. See Bair, "Renegotiating Liberty," 220–40; Bair, "Garveyism and Contested Political Terrain," 227–49; Vought, "Racial Stirrings in Colored Town," 56–76; Rolinson, *Grassroots Garveyism*; and Duncan, "Efficient Womanhood."

5 *Negro World,* November 27, 1926.

6 Significant insight into how black southerners were influenced by and involved in the New Negro movement can be found in Arnesen's *Black Protest and the Great Migration.*

7 In recent years, many scholars working in the field of New Negro studies have built on previous studies on black diasporan politics in the Atlantic world while carving out new research questions based on black activists' trans-Pacific entanglements. See Onishi, "New Negro of the Pacific," 191–213, and Makalani, "Internationalizing the Third International," 151–78.

8 Guridy, *Forging Diaspora.*

9 For more information on black activism in Virginia during the World War I period, see Lewis, *In Their Own Interests,* 46–58, and Foner and Lewis, *Black Worker,* 417–27.

10 *The Spokesmen,* May 1927.

11 Hill, *Marcus Garvey and Universal Negro Improvement Association Papers,* 1:352.

12 Ibid., 1.452.

13 Ibid., 2.366.

14 Ibid., 2.121.

15 See *Negro World,* February 19, 1921, June 25, 1921, October 29, 1921, February 4, 1922, and March 11, 1922.

16 *Negro World,* April 12, 1921.

17 For details on New Orleans UNIA's membership growth, consult *Negro World,* April 12, 1921, August 20, 1921, and October 29, 1921; Agent J. M. Toliver to Bureau, July 16, 1921, case file 198140-198, Record Group 59, Department of State, National Archives; Harry Gulley to Bureau, January 24, 1923, case file 61-50-195, Federal Bureau of Investigation–Freedom of Information Act.

18 Toliver to Bureau, July 16, 1921, 198140-198, Record Group 59, Department of State, National Archives.

19 Felix Alexander interview with Millie Charles, July 12, 1994, Behind the Veil History Project, Special Collections Department, William R. Perkins Library, Duke University.

20 *Negro World,* December 20, 1924.

21 *Negro World,* October 29, 1921.

22 For more on Black Star Line's demise, consult Stein, *World of Marcus Garvey,* 61–107; Martin, *Race First,* 151–73; and Bandele, *Black Star.*

23 Hill, *Marcus Garvey and Universal Negro Improvement Association Papers,* 4:529.

24 See Sundiata, *Brothers and Strangers.*

25 Hill, *Marcus Garvey and Universal Negro Improvement Association Papers,* 4:694.

26 *Negro World,* March 11, 1922.

27 My reading of brokerage racial politics draws heavily from Reed's *Stirrings in the Jug.*

28 *Negro World,* November 17, 1927.

29 Lynd and Lynd, *Rank and File,* 114.

30 See Sundiata, *Brothers and Strangers,* 32–36.

31 *Negro World,* March 22, 1924.

32 *Negro World,* March 21, 1925.

33 *Negro World,* March 21, 1925.

34 *Negro World,* January 21, 1928.

35 U.S. Bureau of the Census, Department of Commerce, "Mortality Rates, 1910–1920, with Population of the Federal Censuses of 1910 and 1920 and Intercensal Estimates of Population" (Washington, D.C.: U.S. Government Printing Office, 1923), 268; *Louisiana Weekly,* September 22, 1928.

36 See George Lucas to Robert Bagnall, December 14, 1926, Box G-81, NAACP Papers; *Louisiana Weekly,* September 22, 1928.

37 *Negro World,* September 15, 1928.

38 *Louisiana Weekly,* September 22, 1928.

39 *Negro World,* March 9, 1929.

40 For more on how the Garvey movement dealt with this issue, see Mitchell's *Righteous Propagation,* 219–39.

41 *Negro World,* November 3, 1928. Garveyites in Port Limon, Costa Rica, Colon, Panama, and New York City also built schools in their respective communities.

42 *Negro World,* November 23, 1929.

43 *Negro World,* March 9, 1929.

44 *Negro World,* January 12, 1929.

45 *Negro World,* March 9, 1929.

46 *New Orleans States,* December 31, 1928.

47 Walter White to George Lucas, letter undated, box G-81, NAACP Papers.

48 Thanks to the work of the NAACP, the white men responsible for the death of the two women were found guilty and sentenced to life in prison. George W. Lucas to Walter White, April 22, 1929, box G-81, NAACP Papers.

49 Salaam, "Whirlwind Storm Warning UNIA."

BIBLIOGRAPHY

Alexander, Felix. Interview with Millie Charles, July 12, 1994, Behind the Veil History Project, Special Collections Department, William R. Perkins Library, Duke University.

Arnesen, Eric. *Black Protest and the Great Migration: A Brief History with Documents.* Boston: Bedford/St. Martin's, 2002.

Bair, Barbara. "Garveyism and Contested Political Terrain in 1920s Virginia." In *Afro-Virginia History and Culture,* edited by John Sailant, 227–49. New York: Garland, 1999.

———. "Renegotiating Liberty: Garveyism, Women, and Grassroots Organizing in Virginia." In *Women of the American South: A Multicultural Reader,* edited by Christine Anne Farnham, 220–40. New York: New York University Press, 1997.

Bandele, Ramla. *Black Star: African American Activism in the International Political Economy.* Urbana: University of Illinois Press, 2008.

Du Bois, W. E. B. "Behold the Land." In *W. E. B. Du Bois Reader,* edited by David Levering Lewis, 545–50. New York: Macmillan, 1995.

Duncan, Natanya. "The 'Efficient Womanhood' of the Universal Negro Improvement Association: 1919–1930." PhD diss., University of Florida, Gainesville, 2009.

Foner, Philip S., and Ronald Lewis. *The Black Worker from 1900 to 1919.* Vol. 5. Philadelphia: Temple University Press, 1980.

Gilmore, Glenda Elizabeth. *Defying Dixie: The Radical Roots of Civil Rights, 1919–1950.* New York: W. W. Norton, 2008.

Guridy, Frank Andre. *Forging Diaspora: Afro-Cubans and African-Americans in a World of Empire and Jim Crow*. Chapel Hill: University of North Carolina Press, 2010.

Harold, Claudrena. *The Rise and Fall of the Garvey Movement*. New York: Routledge, 2007.

Hill, Robert A., ed. *The Marcus Garvey and Universal Negro Improvement Association Papers*. Vols. 1–4. Los Angeles: University of California Press, 1983–85.

Lewis, Earl. *In Their Own Interests: Race, Class, and Power in Twentieth-Century Norfolk, Virginia*. Berkeley: University of California Press, 1991.

Lynd, Staunton, and Alice Lynd, eds. *Rank and File: Personal Histories by Working-Class Organizers*. Boston: Beacon Press, 1973.

Makalani, Minkah. "Internationalizing the Third International: The African Blood Brotherhood, Asian Radicals, and Race, 1919–1922." *Journal of African American History* 96, no. 2 (2011): 151–77.

Martin, Tony. *Race First: The Ideological and Organizational Struggles of Marcus Garvey and the Universal Negro Improvement Association*. Westport, Conn.: Greenwood Press, 1976.

Mitchell, Michelle. *Righteous Propagation: African Americans and the Politics of Racial Destination after Reconstruction*. Chapel Hill: University of North Carolina Press, 2004.

NAACP Papers. Library of Congress.

Onishi, Yuichiro. "The New Negro of the Pacific: How African Americans Forged Cross-Racial Solidarity with Japan, 1917–1922." *Journal of African American History* 92, no. 2 (2007): 191–213.

Reed, Adolph. *Stirrings in the Jug: Black Politics in the Post-segregation Era*. Minneapolis: University of Minnesota Press, 1999.

Rolinson, Mary. *Grassroots Garveyism: The Universal Negro Improvement Association in the Rural South, 1920–1927*. Chapel Hill: University of North Carolina Press, 2007.

Salaam, Kalamu ya. "Whirlwind Storm Warning UNIA." New Orleans, La.: Ahidiana, 1978.

Stein, Judith. *The World of Marcus Garvey: Race and Class in Modern Society*. Baton Rouge: Louisiana State University Press, 1986.

Sundiata, Ibrahim K. *Brothers and Strangers: Black Zion, Black Slavery, 1914–1940*. Durham, N.C.: Duke University Press, 2004.

U.S. National Archives and Records Administration. College Park, Md.

Vought, Kip. "Racial Stirrings in Colored Town: The UNIA in Miami during the 1920s." *Tequesta* 60 (2000): 56–76.

IV
ENGENDERING THE EXPERIENCE

9

Black Modernist Women
at the Parisian Crossroads

JENNIFER M. WILKS

In her 1932 essay "Eveil de la Conscience de Race" ("Awakening of Race Consciousness"), Martinican intellectual Paulette Nardal (1896–1985) not only predates Frantz Fanon's assertion that, for the colonized Francophone individual, travel to Paris spurs the onset of racial consciousness. She also extends the claim by arguing that the construct of gender is as important as geography and nation in the articulation of racial identities. In an oft-cited passage explaining the genesis of *La Revue du monde noir (The Review of the Black World),* the bilingual publication that she cofounded and coedited, Nardal writes,

> Pourtant, parallèlement aux efforts isolés cités plus haut s'affirmaient chez un groupe d'étudiantes antillaises à Paris les aspirations qui devaient se cristalliser autour de la Revue du Monde noir. Les femmes de couleur vivant seules dans la métropole moins favorisées jusqu'à l'Exposition coloniale que leurs congénères masculins aux faciles succès, ont ressenti bien avant eux le besoin d'une solidarité raciale qui ne serait pas seulement d'ordre matériel . . .
>
> (The aspirations which were to be crystallized around "The Review of the Black World" asserted themselves among a group of Antillian [*sic*] women students in Paris. The coloured women living alone in the metropolis until the Colonial Exhibition [,] have certainly been less favoured than coloured men. . . . Long before the latter, they have felt the need of a racial solidarity which would not . . . be merely material.)[1]

This essay examines how Nardal's critical triumvirate of gender ("women students"), geography ("Paris"), and nation ("metropolis") operates in her work as well as in that of her U.S. contemporary Jessie Redmon Fauset (1882–1961). How—or why—does Paris serve as a narrative, social, or personal catalyst for Nardal's and Fauset's respective autobiographical and fictional personae? What role does the French capital play for Fauset's African American women that the U.S. urban centers featured in her work cannot?

The goal is to consider Paris not as a nonracialized site of escape—a myth that has been carefully debunked by other scholars—but as an instrumental modernist crossroads where, through geographic and cultural dislocation, black women writers, such as Nardal and Fauset, negotiated intersecting categories of identity in their own lives as well as in those of their characters. As a means of building on the excellent comparative studies of African American and Francophone culture that have preceded my work—particularly Michel Fabre's *From Harlem to Paris* (1991), Tyler Stovall's *Paris Noir* (1996), and Brent Hayes Edwards's *The Practice of Diaspora* (2003)—the "ground of comparison" that undergirds my reading is the absence of a meeting between Nardal and Fauset: although both writers lived in Paris at one time or another, there is, to my knowledge, no record of these two black modernist intellectuals actually meeting.[2] Likewise, in keeping with Cheryl Wall's *Women of the Harlem Renaissance* (1995), T. Denean Sharpley-Whiting's *Negritude Women* (2002), and, again, Edwards's *The Practice of Diaspora,* I am interested in how African diasporic intellectuals incorporated gender into their understandings of modern black identities in ways that challenged the masculinism of the Harlem Renaissance and Negritude. The "crossroads" of my title is one that Nardal and Fauset explored independently of one another but that was similarly informed by an interwar black internationalism that, through its circulation of cultural objects, facilitated diasporic exchanges and, through its interrogation of social categories, paved the way for conversations about gender and class as well as about race.

I have explored the masculinist underpinnings of black modernism in greater detail elsewhere, but they warrant revisiting here because questions of gender and mobility were central to the two figures around which those foundations were constructed: the Negritude hero and the New Negro. In Aimé Césaire's *Cahier d'un retour au pays natal* (*Notebook of a Return to the Native Land*; 1939), Léon-Gontran Damas's *Pigments* (1937), and Léopold Sédar Senghor's *Chants d'ombre* (*Shadow Songs*; 1945) and *Anthologie de la nouvelle poésie nègre et malgache de langue française* (*Anthology of New Black and Malagasy Poetry in French*; 1948), the personae exploring and articulating their blackness, which is often brought into focus by real and imagined travels, are almost exclusively male. The women featured in this poetry are often mythic or static beings: they represent an ideal, such as Africanness or motherhood, more than an individual, and they represent a fixed attitude, whether affirmative or negative, toward racial identity. As a result, the philosophical, physical, and political journeys of canonical Negritude are coded as primarily male endeavors.

Similar limitations characterize the centrality of the New Negro within African American modernism. As sketched by philosopher Alain Locke, the New

Negro is a diasporic, dynamic, and, again, implicitly male figure. He is also inextricably linked to New York City through Locke's declaration of Harlem as the modern black capital. When women are mentioned vis-à-vis the New Negro, as is the case in *The Messenger*'s special number on the New Negro woman, they are often positioned as secondary figures whose primary function is to support the work of the New Negro.[3] In addition to their masculinist outlook, such perspectives are limiting in their implication that the most groundbreaking intellectual work of early-twentieth-century African American culture was that produced in New York and in their assumption that women would want to serve "the race" as an extension of their domestic caretaking duties. Writer Marita Bonner, who was born in Boston, worked in Washington, D.C., and lived in Chicago, contests both assertions in her 1925 essay "On Being Young—a Woman—and Colored." Travel was neither an easy nor a common undertaking for many African Americans in the 1920s and 1930s, and, given the gender conventions of the day, having ample financial means did not necessarily facilitate matters for women: "You hear that up at New York this is to be seen; that, to be heard. [Yet] you know that—being a woman—you cannot twice a month or twice a year, for that matter, break away to see or hear anything in a city that is supposed to see and hear too much. . . . That's being a woman. A woman of any color."[4] Bonner addresses expectations of racial uplift earlier in the essay, where she challenges the injunction to help "her" people. Although the aforementioned New York– and androcentric constructions of black modernism account for differences in socioeconomic, generational, and even national perspectives, they do not account for questions such as those raised by Bonner and other women writers who considered or found themselves on the margins of New Negrohood.

Nardal's and Fauset's depictions of black modernist women in Paris are important, then, not simply as catalogs of their travels as "refined black women."[5] The literal removal of their bodies and imaginative transposition of their characters from their respective homes to France enable readers to contemplate examinations of race that are voiced by engaged, mobile black women rather than dependent on silent, static ones. Nardal's and Fauset's writings provide literary venues where the questions posed by Bonner are integral instead of anomalous. Though the conclusions that Nardal and Fauset reach are not uniformly progressive, the intellectual ground they cover nonetheless encourages constructive reconsiderations of gender, location, and race in Negritude and the Harlem Renaissance.

PAULETTE NARDAL AND THE AWAKENING OF RACE CONSCIOUSNESS

For Nardal, who, like many of her Francophone peers, traveled to the metropole to pursue a university degree, Paris was a site of opportunity and *dépaysement* (disorientation): opportunity in the form of the institutions of higher learning that were as yet unavailable in her native Caribbean and disorientation in the geographic shift from Martinique to France. The actual experience of living in the French capital, however, gave new meaning to both terms. In Paris Nardal found herself disoriented not only by the cooler weather but also by the chilly reception with which she and other students of color were greeted: they were caught in the apparent contradiction of having a "Negro soul" *(une âme nègre)* and a "Latin education" *(formation latine).*[6] In short, in being perceived as not French, Nardal and her peers experienced a type of intranational *décalage,* which Brent Edwards describes as "the received biases that refuse to pass over when one crosses the water," "the work of 'differences within unity.'"[7] Although Edwards uses *décalage* to discuss cultural exchange across African diasporic communities, the term is applicable here given the dynamic of familiarity and foreignness likewise at play in interactions between the Caribbean French and their metropolitan counterparts. It is out of this disconnect that the second meaning of *opportunity* emerged for Nardal: in conjunction with interwar Paris's status as a cultural crossroads, the limits of French nationalism encouraged citizens from the country's overseas colonies to see their identity through other lenses, most notably those of diaspora and transnationalism.

Nardal charts the negotiation of opportunity and disorientation in "Eveil de la conscience de race." A comparative reading of African American and Francophone Caribbean literary history, the essay uses African American intellectual development as a barometer against which to measure the progress of Antillean thinkers. Nardal attributes the lapse between the New Negro movement and the as-yet-unnamed Negritude to differing sociopolitical climates in the United States and France. Sharpley-Whiting summarizes the differences as follows: "French racism could generally be characterized as paternalistic, whereas American racism seesawed between stamping out the very existence of African Americans (via lynching) and reducing them to social outcasts dispossessed of human and civil rights."[8] Accordingly, the French policy of assimilation encouraged upwardly mobile Martinicans, Guadeloupeans, and Guyanese of color to fold their racial identities into their national ones: to "become" French was to cease "being" black. Citing the work of German author Friedrich Sieburg, Nardal explains that "l'absence du préjugé de couleur chez les Français provient de leur certitude de faire du Noir, en un temps relativement court[,] un vrai Français" (the lack of colour prejudice among the French is due to the fact that they are certain to transform the mind of any coloured man into a truly French one in a comparatively short time).[9] It is important to note that, whereas the English translation refers to transforming minds, the original French actually speaks of refashioning one type of person ("faire du Noir") into another ("un vrai Français"), a nuance that more accurately reflects the philosophy behind assimilation: the absorption of the Other into French culture. Nardal concludes that, given this promise of incorporation and the mixed-race heritage of most Antilleans, the turn toward European culture was a natural one for Caribbean intellectuals.

Yet if the transformation "of any coloured man into a truly French one" was desired in theory (or, one might say, in absentia, i.e., in the colonies), its desirability was less certain, if not impossible, when put into practice. For although Nardal describes the embrace of "Latin culture" as a natural part of Antillean intellectual formation, her subsequent reference to the 1931 Exposition coloniale internationale (International Colonial Exposition) indicates that there was no seamless incorporation of Antilleans into metropolitan French society. Indeed, held amid the exoticist vogue of the interwar period, events such as the exposition highlighted the limits of assimilation. "The most enduringly popular features of the colonial exhibitions," writes historian Elizabeth Ezra, "were their human exhibits," which "were designed to convey the look and feel of a native village."[10] Exoticism's penchant for conflating bodies of color resulted in additional affronts to the Caribbean students, who saw themselves alternately associated with the "natives" in the exhibition and represented by someone without any ties to France and its empire: in a controversial decision that was later reversed, African American Josephine Baker was appointed the exposition's Queen of the Colonies. In addition to representing "the colonies" writ large in her temporary position, on stage and screen, Baker stood in for women from specific French colonial sites: she was a lovelorn Vietnamese woman while performing the song "La Petite Tonkinoise," a lovesick Caribbean *métisse* in the 1927 film *La Sirène des tropiques (The Siren of the Tropics)*, and a North African urchin in the 1935 movie *Princesse Tam-Tam*. Regardless of one's educational, national, or socioeconomic background, to be a person of color was to be "exotic." With some French citizens of color regarded as curiosities and others displayed as objects, the contradictions born out of the intersection of geography, race, and nation became real in Paris in a way that they had not, or perhaps could not, in Fort-de-France, Pointe-à-Pitre, or Cayenne.

Nardal raises the question of the exposition's impact on black women students because, as exemplified by the early years of Baker's career, modernist explorations of race and identity were inextricable from questions of gender. In the 1931 short story "Histoire sans importance" ("A Thing of No Importance"), Guyanese author Roberte Horth creates the character of Léa, a young Caribbean woman who, once transplanted to Paris, realizes how stereotyped images of women of color predetermine how others perceive her: "Elle ne sera jamais dans ce pays une femme comme toutes les autres femmes ayant droit à une bonheur de femme car elle ne pourra jamais effacer pour les autres le non-sens de son âme occidentale vêtue d'une peau scandaleuse" (In this country, she will never be a woman like the others, with a right to a woman's happiness, because she will never be able to blot out, for the others, the absurdity of her soul fashioned by Occidental culture but concealed by an objectionable skin).[11] Unlike the fictional Léa, Josephine Baker seized on the attention paid to her skin color and, in so doing, transformed that which was formerly "objectionable" into an object of desire. Bennetta Jules-Rosette argues that, through "a conscious and repeated process of identity reconstruction," Baker traded on the familiarity of stereotypes "to surmount cultural barriers."[12] This observation echoes Jane Nardal's remarks in "Pantins exotiques," which credits Baker with helping to associate blacks with modernism, even if she did so while "dressed in feathers and banana leaves" ("vêtue de plumes ou de feuilles de bananes").[13] Thus, while the complications of gender could not be escaped, they could be appropriated in black modernist women's efforts to articulate their sense of themselves and to control their respective images.

In keeping with her focus on Antillean women students, Paulette Nardal uses "Eveil de la conscience de race" to chart a transnational turn not to stereotype but to scholarship. For it is to intellectual work, she explains, that she and her peers turned their attention when confronted with the limitations of their society and of their male peers:

> Au lieu de mépriser leurs congénères attardés ou de désespérer de voir jamais la race noire arriver à égaler la race aryenne, elles se sont mises à l'étude. . . . Pour la première fois, au diplôme d'études supérieures d'anglais, l'une d'elles opta pour «L'œuvre de Mrs Beecher Stowe (1° La Case de l'Oncle Tom ; 2° Le puritanisme dans la Nouvelle Angleterre)[»] . . . Une étudiante de français a exprimé le désir d'analyser l'œuvre de John Antoine Nau ou encore les Mémoires du Père Labat.
>
> (Instead of despising their retarded brothers or laying aside all hope . . . about the possibility of the black race ever being on a par with Aryans, they began to study. . . . For the first time, one of them took "The Life and Words of Mrs. Beecher Stowe (*Uncle Tom's Cabin*—Puritanism in New England) ["] as a subject for the Diplôme d'Etudes supérieures anglais. . . . A student of French selected the poems of John Antoine Nau, and the Works of the R. F. Labat.)[14]

Nardal posits the aforementioned student work as poised to fill the void in Caribbean students' knowledge of diasporic history in general, represented here by the thesis on American writer Stowe, and of Francophone Caribbean history in particular, which is represented by the research on white French authors Nau and Labat. Nardal's insistence on specifying the gender of these newly conscientized students indicates the "nascent feminism" within her "evocation of an emergent black cultural internationalism."[15] When Nardal cites the poems of Jamaican American Claude McKay and of African American Langston Hughes, she does so not simply as a Martinican intellectual but also as a middle-class woman who has found in African American literature the racial self-acceptance and valorization that were only just beginning to be embraced in her social milieu.

The sense of *dépaysement* that Nardal felt in Paris facilitated transnational connections that crossed class lines as well as linguistic ones. Much has been said, and rightfully so, of the elitist tinge of some of Nardal's positions. When assuring readers that her stance on race consciousness is moderate, she writes, "Nous avons pleinement conscience de ce que nous devons à la culture blanche et nous n'avons nullement l'intention de l'abandonner pour favoriser je ne sais quel retour à l'obscurantisme" (We are fully conscious of our debts to the Latin culture and we have no intention of discarding it in order to promote I know not what return to ignorance).[16] With this statement, Nardal counters any suspicion that she is advocating sociopolitical upheaval and does so in language that suggests that any mind devoid of Latin culture is a deficient or uninformed one. However much she is inspired by the work of Hughes and McKay, Nardal does not advocate a radical break with polite society, as both men do in their respective work.

Yet, in the 1935 story "Guignol Ouolof" (Wolof clown), which appeared in the journal *L'étudiant noir (The Black Student),* Nardal creates a scene of diasporic solidarity that transcends economic distinctions. The vignette imagines a brief exchange between an Antillean *bourgeoise* and a Senegalese peanut vendor who find themselves in the same Parisian café. The former is there to eat before going to the theater; the latter is there to ply his wares. The vendor's outlandish dress underscores the social difference indicated by the characters' respective positions as customer and worker, insider and outsider: "Costume de général d'opérette. Drap noir sur lequel éclatent des brandebourgs imposants, épaulettes, casquette plate d'officier allemand, galonnée d'or et de rouge, et détail encore plus inattendu, monocle à cordonnet noir, encastré dans l'arcade sourcillière [*sic*] gauche." (A general's costume from the operetta. Black cape on which imposing brandenburgs glitter, epaulettes, the flat cap of a German officer, trimmed with braid of gold and red, and an even more unexpected detail, a monocle attached to a black cord, set in courtly arch to the left.)[17] Although disgusted by the contrast between the Senegalese man's costume and the subdued attire of his white colleague, the Caribbean woman is also aware of the interest that the café's white customers have taken in this encounter. Up until this moment, "Guignol Ouolof" appears to foreshadow the famous streetcar scene in Aimé Césaire's *Cahier d'un retour au pays natal,* in which the speaker encounters—and refuses to identify with—a "gangly," disheveled black man on a streetcar.[18] Offering an alternative vision of cross-class, intradiasporic interaction, Nardal's fictional episode closes with the Caribbean woman and the African man experiencing a moment of mutual recognition in spite of those waiting to see how the collision of race and class will affect them. She asks the man if wearing such a "uniform" bothers him; he responds that he enjoys dressing in clownish garb "as much as being unemployed, or living off women."[19] His words suggest a previously unappreciated subjectivity, a quality that allows his middle-class interlocutor to see the humanity beneath his gaudy exterior. The interaction recalls Edwards's description of Nardal's race consciousness as "not predetermined 'solidarity' but a hard-won project only practiced across difference, only spoken in ephemeral spaces."[20] It is a project that, throughout her work, Nardal uses to explore how questions of gender, geography, and nation intersect with those of class and race and, subsequently, how such crossings can transform cultural disorientation into diasporic connection.

JESSIE FAUSET AND THE SEARCH FOR LIBERTÉ

If, in Nardal's writing, Paris functions as a site of disorientation (from the Caribbean) and contextualization (of colonial politics), it is largely in the former, deterritorializing vein that the French capital and France at large operate in the work of Jessie Fauset. In Fauset, however, *dépaysement* serves as a means of clarifying, not complicating, one's national identity. One of the New Negro movement's many Francophiles, Fauset studied at the Sorbonne in 1914, attended the Second Pan-African Congress in Paris in 1921, and returned to Paris for additional study in 1924–25; in 1919, she completed the MA in French at the University of Pennsylvania. As a result, Fauset's relationship to France was, one might argue, more akin to Martinican Nardal's than to that of African Americans who idealized the country as a color-blind haven. This is not to say that Fauset did not experience race differently in France, for she did, and she notes as much in her travel writing. On the contrary, it is to say that when Fauset wrote about France, she did so as an informed observer cognizant of how colonial politics circumscribed the lives of France's residents of color even as African Americans found themselves enjoying new freedoms once outside of the United States.

Although Fauset leaves the question of gender relatively unexplored in "Impressions of the Second Pan-African Congress" (1921) and "Yarrow Revisited" (1925), the two essays foreshadow her use of international travel as a narrative catalyst in her novels. In "Impressions," Fauset reports details from congress sessions in London, Brussels, and Paris and, in the process, reveals the at times uneasy intersection of colonial politics and diasporic activism. What begins in London as an apparently seamless realization of diaspora—"Not one of us but envisaged in his heart the dawn of a day of new and perfect African brotherhood"—becomes a more complicated negotiation as the congress moves to its French-speaking sites.[21] Fauset illuminates the political differences between European and American delegates by comparing their rhetorical styles:

> The contrast between the speakers of the Eastern and Western hemispheres with but two exceptions was most striking. Messieurs Diagne and Candace gave us fine oratory, magnificent gestures—but platitudes. But the speeches of Dr. DuBois [*sic*], of Edward Frazier, of Walter White, of Dr. Jackson, of a young and fiery Jamaican and of M. Bellegarde, gave facts and food for thought. The exceptions were the speeches of M. Challaye, a white member of the Society for the Defense of African Natives, and those of the grave and courtly Portuguese, Messieurs Magahaens and Santos-Pino.[22]

The rhetorical differences that Fauset distills as "platitudes" versus "facts and food for thought" reflect the political fissures that emerged in Brussels and Paris; as members of the French legislature, Senegalese Blaise Diagne and Guadeloupean Gratien Candace were reluctant to criticize either the colonial enterprise of their own government or that of Belgium; during the congress, the two men sought to temper rather than join any incisive critiques of colonialism. The experience led Fauset to deduce "that the black colonial's problem while the same intrinsically, wore on the face of it a different aspect from that of the black American."[23] As Paulette Nardal would surmise eleven years later in "Eveil de la conscience de race," Fauset concludes that the path to diasporic solidarity, to a "new and perfect African brotherhood," cannot be successfully charted without attention to cultural specificity.

Such attention does not prevent Fauset from acknowledging—and relishing—the new opportunities that travel to France opened up for African Americans. Fauset builds the essay "Yarrow Revisited," published four years after her reflections on the Second Pan-African Congress, to a climax by recounting the perspectival shift induced by her Parisian sojourn:

> In the beginning I said that life in Paris is the same as life in the civilized world over but that there was one exception. In Paris I find myself more American than I ever feel in America. I am more conscious of national characteristics than I have ever been in New York. When I say: "We do that differently in America," I do not mean that *we* do that differently in Harlem, or on "You" street in Washington, or on Christian Street in Philadelphia. I mean that Americans white and black do not act that way.[24]

Not only is the Paris she encounters under the "drab" skies of early fall different from the tourist mecca more often visited during the "golden weather" of summer;

the realities of its everyday life also differ from the conditions of daily life in U.S. cities.[25] In keeping with the Wordsworth poem from which she takes her title, Fauset explores Parisian "life as she is" and shares experiences of cultural disconnect, such as her ongoing frustration with French hotel proprietors reluctant to turn on the heat.[26] Even her compliment of French industriousness is couched in terms of national difference: "I have never seen people [work] so hard in my life nor with such seriousness! It is true that they lose the time from twelve or twelve-thirty until two every day."[27] At the same time that Fauset praises French labor, she casts a critical eye on taking an extended lunch, a practice cherished in Europe but discouraged in the United States. The most important distinction that Fauset makes between French and American life comes in the essay's final sentences, when she declares her intention to "have tea . . . *at the first tea room which takes my fancy*"; in other words, she intends to satisfy her appetite without worrying about encountering racial discrimination.[28] She is decidedly American, but she is also free to avail herself of the social opportunities offered by "French 'life as she is.'"[29] Where the *dépaysement* of Paris leads Nardal and her characters, legally French but not uniformly recognized as such, to reconsider their national identity, disorientation reaffirms Fauset's Americanness.

In Fauset's fiction, this affirmation of national culture seems unachievable in major U.S. cities, such as New York and Philadelphia. As Deborah McDowell notes, Philadelphia carries the weight of the past in Fauset novels, where the city's colonial landmarks and elite African American community of "Old Philadelphians" denote a history that is venerable and omnipresent.[30] Although Fauset paints New York, with its promise of economic opportunity and self-reinvention, as exemplified by Wall Street, Broadway, and Striver's Row, as less tradition bound, the commercial center does not assure her characters an easy negotiation of either their Americanness or their blackness because of the discriminatory practices that take place there as well. Indeed, Fauset continually refers to racial prejudice as a national problem that her characters cannot escape as long as they are within the geographic boundaries of the United States. In novels such as *Plum Bun: A Novel without a Moral* (1929) and *Comedy: American Style* (1933), it is Paris that provides the backdrop against which the identities of Fauset heroines and antiheroines are crystallized.

Fauset's second novel, *Plum Bun,* chronicles the coming of age of Angela Murray, a fair-skinned young woman who leaves her sister and her past in Philadelphia to pass for white and study art in New York City. Angela begins passing as a young girl accompanying her equally light-skinned mother on Saturday shopping expeditions; the source of Mattie Murray's amusement develops into a single-minded pursuit for her daughter, whose youth is marked by repeated episodes of forging interracial social ties that inevitably unravel when her racial identity is revealed. After her parents die, Angela, now in her early twenties, decides to pass definitively, to use her inheritance to strike out on her own in a city where no one knows her. The decision necessitates a break with her younger sister, Virginia, who has inherited their father's darker skin. Angela departs Philadelphia as an African American and arrives in New York City as the putatively white Angèle Mory, but she discovers that, even in the "absence" of racial issues, gender and (social) geography continue to impact her life.

References to French culture appear throughout the novel, but Fauset casts Francophilia as a commodity more than an ideal. If any aspect of the French republican motto of "*Liberté, égalité, fraternité,*" often cited to vaunt French liberalism, is part of Angela's consciousness early in the novel, it is *liberté* (freedom), but not in the collective spirit of the French Revolution so much as in an individual one. School-age Angela labors over her French homework because "there was an element of fine ladyism about the beautiful, logical tongue that made her in accordance with some secret subconscious ambition resolve to make it her own."[31] The passage's association of French with both culture and acquisition prefigures Angela's goals upon arriving in New York: to pursue "her Art" and to secure the "power of a certain kind" that women can exercise.[32] Well aware of "the structural inequalities" circumscribing her dreams—she knows that women are expected to preside in salons, not boardrooms—Angela nonetheless feels that her new "white" life promises a level of personal freedom unattainable for African Americans.[33] Fauset brings the development of Angela the French student into Angela the urban adventurer full circle by having her protagonist adopt a Franco-Spanish pseudonym, "Angèle Mory," for her new existence.[34] Neither an affectation nor a purely aesthetic matter, French culture serves instead as an echo of, and instrument in, Angela's plans for self-reinvention.

These early scenes prepare the reader for Fauset's discussion of gender, geography, and nation in the remainder of the novel. Angela's cultural pragmatism gestures toward the strategic interest in foreign locales that emerged among early twentieth-century African Americans. In the de facto salon that the Murray sisters hold in their home before Angela's departure, their friends discuss expatriation as one method of escaping racial discrimination. Arthur Sawyer, an aspiring engineer, shares the following vision of his postgraduate life: "When I get through, if this city has come to its senses, I'll get a big job with Baldwin. If not, I'll go to South America and take out naturalization papers."[35] To the reader, the jump from Philadelphia to South America may seem drastic, but Sawyer's estimation of his options makes sense in Fauset's vision of U.S. racial dynamics. Her African American characters experience estrangement from their white peers in ways similar to the metropolitan-based Caribbean students featured in Paulette Nardal's work and elsewhere in *La Revue du monde noir*. Indeed, before being apprised of

Angela's racial identity, one of her white Philadelphian classmates confesses that she "never think[s] of darkies as Americans."[36]

In keeping with Fauset's assertion of race and nationality as interrelated nodes of identity, Angela's geographic shift to New York City fails to provide her with a problem-free space in which to remake herself. The inability to forget her African American heritage makes her sensitive to the ways in which her new acquaintances echo the despair and prejudice expressed by her Philadelphian friends. Rachel Powell, the openly African American woman in Angela's Cooper Union art class, dreams of studying in France so that her success abroad might prove the irrationality of U.S. racism. The epithet-laden outbursts of Roger Fielding, Angela's wealthy white suitor (who does not know that she is passing), recall her former classmate's inability to view African Americans as equal, worthy members of the body politic. Accordingly, a dinner date turns sour when Roger explains his reaction to seeing black patrons in the restaurant:

> Roger came back, his face flushed, triumphant, "Well, I put a spoke in the wheel of those 'coons'! They forget themselves so quickly, coming in here spoiling white people's appetites. I told the manager if they brought one of their damned suits I'd be responsible. I wasn't going to have them here with you, Angèle. I could tell that night at Martha Burden's by the way you looked at that girl that you had no time for darkies."[37]

However "free and . . . full" Angela's new life is, she cannot escape antiblack prejudice.[38] As McDowell contends, Fauset's protagonist "recognizes [the gendered and racialized] relations of power" at play in U.S. society but overestimates her ability to manipulate them.[39] New York cannot serve as an unfettered "land of opportunity" as long as Angela continues to confront the social limitations of being a woman and to bear the emotional "burdens of [her] mixed-race heritage," burdens whose psychic toll mounts the longer she allows racist statements such as Roger's to go unchallenged.[40] It gradually dawns on Angela that it will take more than a financial inheritance and train ticket to facilitate her modernist self-fashioning.

Yet Angela does not pursue expatriation until after the dissolution of her relationship with Roger. Even upon realizing that she does not feel the same love for him that she feels for Anthony Cross, another Cooper Union classmate, Angela holds fast to the idea that her association with, if not marriage to, Roger will secure her position in American society and the power she desires. This conviction spurs Angela to dismiss Anthony's suggestion that she apply for a scholarship to study in France at Fontainebleau: "She only smiled wisely; she would have no need of such study, but she hoped with all her heart that Miss Powell would be the recipient of a prize which would enable her to attend there."[41] Fauset deploys a double, almost contradictory narrative move to restore France to a place of prominence in Angela's mind. First, Fauset sets Roger's idea of "free love" on a collision course with Angela's individual quest for "freedom"; because he is unwilling to risk the *mésalliance* of marrying someone from a lower social station, Roger engages Angela in a relationship that, as McDowell and other critics have noted, is little more than an early-twentieth-century version of concubinage. Angela is not liberated from rituals of courtship and marriage so much as she is removed from their sphere altogether. The second move undertaken by Fauset is the rehabilitation of convention in Angela's eyes: as she realizes that Roger's assertion of his independence requires the suppression of hers, Angela begins to think that perhaps independence is not what she seeks after all. After once plotting her future around the dissolution of communal ties, Angela now reconsiders: "And she began to see the conventions, the rules that govern life, in a new light; she realized suddenly that for all their granite-like coldness and precision they also represented fundamental facts; a sort of concentrated compendium of the art of living and therefore as much to be observed and respected as warm, vital impulses."[42] Spurred by her newfound respect for "the art of living" and her rededication to "Art," Angela applies for a scholarship to Fontainebleau.

Like her contemporary Marita Bonner, Fauset charts an "alternative modernist cartography" by routing the end of Angela's journey away from New York, through France, and, by implication, back to the United States.[43] Paris enters the narrative in "Market Is Done," *Plum Bun*'s final section. Along with Miss Powell, Angela successfully applies to the School for Americans at Fontainebleau; however, any hopes Angela has of escaping to France are dashed when Miss Powell's scholarship is revoked. The ensuing controversy compels Angela to reveal her racial identity, and although she eventually makes her way to the French capital, she arrives not with a sense of triumph but with resignation. As summer fades, so do the charms of Paris:

> Paris, so beautiful in the summer, so gay with its thronging thousands, its hosts bent on pleasure, took on another garb in the sullen greyness of late autumn. The tourists disappeared and the hard steady grind of labour, the intent application to the business of living, so noticeable in the French, took the place of a transient, careless freedom.[44]

The City of Light is ultimately redeemed from this somber portrait just as it is in "Yarrow Revisited": Angela's liberation from the American variant of racism allows her to tap into her artistic potential. True to Fauset's interest in the formation and reconstitution of family units, the character also develops a greater appreciation for the priority that her parents and sister once placed on creating domestic refuges from the pressures of the world. Marriage no longer strikes Angela as a means of scaling the social ladder or changing races; instead, she seeks in such commitment "a practical foundation on which a smart, ambitious woman might build a life."[45] In the novel's final scene, Angela is "rewarded" for her epiphany with a reunion with Anthony, who has revealed his African American heritage and whom she has come to recognize as her true love. Rather than leave the reader with the impression of Paris as a site of permanent escape, Fauset depicts the French capital as a site where an early-twentieth-century African American can rediscover her identity and, consequently, fortify herself for her eventual return to the United States.

In *Comedy: American Style,* Fauset's last novel, Paris witnesses no such happy ending. The story of Olivia Blanchard Cary's efforts to whiten her family through psychological manipulation, social engineering, and interracial marriage, *Comedy* largely associates Europe with Olivia's racial mania. Like Angela the daughter of a fair-skinned mother and brown-skinned father, Olivia initially considers passing when an elementary school teacher assumes she is white. As an adult, Olivia sends her two oldest children, Teresa and Christopher, both light skinned like their parents, away to boarding school to recast them as white. Because this stratagem is impossible with Olivia's youngest child, the delicate, bronze-skinned Oliver, she alternately ignores him, sends him to live with his grandparents, and dresses him up like a servant. The result is a family home that is as cold and alienating as Angela Murray's childhood home in *Plum Bun* is cozy and inviting. Olivia's self-hatred is so destructive that it eventually tears her family apart; although the novel concludes with Christopher and his wife happily married in Philadelphia, where he plans to practice medicine with his father, the other members of the Cary family meet far grimmer fates: Olivia is exiled and impoverished in Paris, Teresa is unhappily married to a racist white Frenchman in Toulouse, France; and Oliver is dead from a self-inflicted gunshot wound.

The meditations on home and exile that punctuate the story foreshadow this tragic turn of events. Contrary to the ideal of the New Negro woman as an extraordinary nurturer, Olivia renders any residence in which she is present uncomfortable, if not toxic. When she is young, her parents' idyllic marriage seems troubled only by their child's cold behavior: "in those brief interims when they were not completely engrossed in the wonderment of their perfect companionship, they fell to considering [Olivia] with a mingling of amazement and wistfulness, of a somewhat wry humor and of no little chagrin."[46] As an adult, Olivia has the same chilling effect on her family's Philadelphia house. Her refusal to welcome their African American playmates discourages Christopher and Teresa from socializing at home, and when Oliver is permitted to return, he is struck, even while fairly young, by "the frigid sterility of the house."[47]

By contrasting the unhappiness of the Cary residence with the contentment found in other dwellings, Fauset links the concept of "home" to racial identity as well as to physical space. For the places where the Cary children do find warmth and acceptance are those where race is not a point of contention. In Philadelphia, Teresa gravitates to the house of her childhood friend Marise, whose comfort in her brown skin is later mirrored in Alicia Barrett, Teresa's boarding school classmate. Oliver, in turn, basks in the "breadth and . . . brightness" of his Grandmother Blake's home in Boston and discovers "a vast, enveloping love and a strange, palpitating pride" with his Cary grandparents in Philadelphia.[48] Although all four grandparents are fair enough to pass for white, they embrace their African American heritage and their darker-skinned grandson. Olivia is "an anti-race woman," then, in that she not only deprives her children of a loving home but also fails to provide them with a stable foundation on which to build their identity.[49]

France becomes a potential alternative homesite after Teresa's thwarted engagement with the visibly African American Henry Bates. Having lost Henry because she put Olivia's prejudice before their happiness, Teresa begins to rebuild her shattered sense of self through her knowledge of the French language. She successfully tutors Christopher's college classmates in French and, to her surprise, is revived by dreams of entrepreneurship:

> The work had taken her out of herself, completely absorbed her. . . . It was rather nice to make even the scanty dollars which they had been able to pay. . . . Wouldn't it be rather wonderful, she thought to herself, to earn her living in this pleasant way? Not only need she be of no additional expense to her father, she could take herself completely off his hands. . . . Why she would be a business woman, like Phebe and Marise! Here was a calling right to her hand which she could pursue until she married.[50]

The passage reflects Teresa's first expression of initiative since her breakup with Henry, and the absence of any mention of her mother suggests growth on the young woman's part—an ability, at last, to conceive of a future without her mother's interference. Teresa's subsequent trip to France, where she travels to increase her teaching prospects through additional study, promises still greater expansion of the character's stifled spirit: "She liked the sea-trip. She liked the free-masonry which it engendered; she liked to watch the amazing lack of restraint which young America displays when she gets on, so to speak, her sea-legs."[51] Teresa seems poised to join Angela Murray in finding contentment on the other side of her Parisian sojourn.

If Angela's time abroad affirms her African American identity and precedes her reintegration into U.S. society, however, Teresa's stay devolves from an opportunity to reconnect with herself into a period of semipermanent exile. Fauset forecasts a future filled with disorientation, inauthenticity, and suffocation through the character's first impressions of Paris. Upon her arrival, Teresa finds the city "too full of the remembered noise and traffic of New York, too cosmopolitan, not enough French and far, far too hot."[52] When Olivia encourages her daughter's marriage to a University of Toulouse professor, Teresa becomes a "fragmented expatriate."[53] Traumatized in the United States by her mother's zealous pursuit of whiteness, Teresa now finds herself mired in the racially charged colonial politics of interwar France. At the end of the chapter dedicated to her story line, Teresa is isolated in Toulouse with a disagreeable mother-in-law and a husband, Professor Aristide Pailleron, whose vision of France is as insular—and racist—as Teresa's is expansive and diverse. After Teresa admires Senegalese soldiers quartered in nearby Toulon, Aristide calls the men *"ces vilains noirs"* (these black villains).[54] Shortly thereafter, Teresa's dream of giving her brother Oliver a home is dashed by the realization that Aristide's racism is not limited to French colonial subjects but includes African American men as well: "I do not like any of them. I saw them in the war, *les Américains noirs,* neither black nor white. Our women liked them too well."[55] With these words, Teresa, who has not revealed her racial background to Aristide, becomes a woman without a family as well as one "without [a race and] a country."[56]

The curtain of *Comedy: American Style* falls on Olivia alone in Paris, where her only pleasure comes from witnessing the tender exchanges between a mother and son who live across the hall in her cheap Parisian hotel. The "slender, rather tall lad" reminds her of Oliver, the child whom she despised when he was alive yet remembers fondly after his death.[57] The conclusion is one of the bleakest in Fauset's oeuvre, in which happy reunions far outnumber unhappy separations. The characters who do fare well in *Comedy*—Teresa's brother Christopher, their father, and Christopher's wife, Phebe—do so because they, like *Plum Bun*'s Angela Murray and Anthony Cross, ultimately prioritize integrity over illusion and community over individualism. In Fauset's fictional worlds, the road from Philadelphia to Paris can lead to personal bliss rather than tragic irony, but only if one travels not to escape "home" and identity but to rediscover and restore them.

CONCLUSION

Whether politically engaged or socially estranged, the women featured in the work of Paulette Nardal and Jessie Fauset reflect the myriad complications behind archetypes such as the Negritude hero and the New Negro as well as those that exist behind the idealization of cities such as New York and Paris. Through their actual travel and the imagined journeys of their characters, Nardal and Fauset provided alternative ways of mapping the ideological crossroads of black modernism. What were the particular challenges of being a black woman in the 1920s and 1930s? How did travel reveal or remove the social obstacles faced by those who, because of their gender and race, were doubly marginalized? What were the stakes of claiming one's national identity when such an act was not always comfortable for oneself or accepted by others? Midway through the story "Guignol Oulof," Nardal's unnamed *bourgeoise* wonders what ties her to the title character: "Il y a cependant, entre nous et lui, à défaut de solidarité réelle, celle apparente de la couleur" (Meanwhile, there is between us, in the absence of real solidarity, the apparent solidarity of skin color).[58] Forgoing the pitfalls of racial essentialism, Nardal locates "real solidarity" in the cultural exchange, diasporic connection, and intellectual work that being in Paris fostered for her and others. By relocating—or, better yet, dislocating—her characters in the same city, Fauset spurs them to discover, or mourn, the substantive bonds that connect them to the families and communities they have left behind. In neither case is the City of Light an idyllic location; it is, instead, a site for change and growth, one where authors and characters navigate the shoals of affiliation and alienation, home and exile, self-esteem and self-effacement.

NOTES

1 Nardal, "Eveil de la conscience de race," 347.
2 Cheah and Culler, "Grounds of Comparison," 3.
3 "The New Negro Woman," editorial, *The Messenger* 5 (1923): 757.
4 Bonner, "On Being Young," 4–5.
5 Edwards, *Practice of Diaspora*, 185.
6 Nardal, "Eveil de la conscience de race," 343.
7 Edwards, *Practice of Diaspora*, 14.
8 Sharpley-Whiting, *Negritude Women*, 30.
9 Nardal, "Eveil de la conscience de race," 344. See Sieburg, *Gott in Frankreich?*
10 Ezra, *Colonial Unconscious*, 22, 23.
11 Horth, "Histoire sans importance," 120.
12 Jules-Rosette, *Josephine Baker in Art and Life*, 71.
13 Jane Nardal, "Pantins exotiques," *La Dépêche africaine* 8 (October 1928): 2. Translated as "Exotic Puppets" by T. Sharpley-Whiting and Georges Van Den Abbeele in Sharpley-Whiting, *Negritude Women*, 109.
14 Nardal, "Eveil de la conscience de race," 348.
15 Edwards, *Practice of Diaspora*, 122, 123.
16 Nardal, "Eveil de la conscience de race," 349.
17 Nardal, "Guignol Ouolof," *L'Etudiant noir*, 4. Translation in Edwards, *Practice of Diaspora*, 183.

18 Césaire, *Cahier d'un retour au pays natal (Notebook of a Return to the Native Land)*, in *Aimé Césaire: The Collected Poetry*, 62/63.

19 Nardal, "Guignol Ouolof," 184.

20 Edwards, *Practice of Diaspora*, 186.

21 Fauset, "Impressions of the Second Pan-African Congress," 370.

22 Ibid., 377–78.

23 Ibid., 376.

24 Fauset, "Yarrow Revisited," 355; emphasis in original.

25 Ibid., 349.

26 Ibid., 350.

27 Ibid., 354.

28 Ibid., 355; emphasis in original.

29 Ibid.

30 Deborah McDowell, "Introduction: Regulating Midwives," in Fauset, *Plum Bun*, xix.

31 Fauset, *Plum Bun*, 37.

32 Ibid., 93, 88.

33 McDowell, "Introduction: Regulating Midwives," xvi.

34 Fauset, *Plum Bun*, 94.

35 Ibid., 69.

36 Ibid., 70.

37 Ibid., 133.

38 Ibid., 92.

39 McDowell, "Introduction: Regulating Midwives," xix.

40 Wall, *Women of the Harlem Renaissance*, 75.

41 Fauset, *Plum Bun*, 208.

42 Ibid., 228.

43 Wilks, *Race, Gender, and Comparative Black Modernism*, 93.

44 Fauset, *Plum Bun*, 376.

45 Wall, *Women of the Harlem Renaissance*, 78.

46 Fauset, *Comedy*, 10.

47 Ibid., 142.

48 Ibid., 138.

49 Wall, *Women of the Harlem Renaissance*, 81.

50 Fauset, *Comedy*, 114–15.

51 Ibid., 120.

52 Ibid., 122.

53 Cherene Sherrard-Johnson, introduction to Fauset, *Comedy*, xxiii.

54 Fauset, *Comedy*, 133. See Sherrard-Johnson for an explanation of the multiple translations possible for "*ces vilains noirs*" (266n44).

55 Ibid.

56 Ibid., 69.

57 Ibid., 235.

58 Nardal, "Guignol Ouolof," 4/183.

BIBLIOGRAPHY

Bonner, Marita. "On Being Young—a Woman—and Colored." 1925. In *Frye Street and Environs: The Collected Works of Marita Bonner,* edited by Joyce Flynn and Joyce Occomy Stricklin, 3–8. Boston: Beacon Press, 1987.

Césaire, Aimé. *Aimé Césaire: The Collected Poetry.* Trans. and with an introduction by Clayton Eshleman and Annette Smith. Berkeley: University of California Press, 1983.

Cheah, Pheng, and Jonathan Culler, eds. "Grounds of Comparison: Around the Work of Benedict Anderson." Special issue. *diacritics* 29, no. 4 (1999).

Edwards, Brent Hayes. *The Practice of Diaspora: Literature, Translation, and the Rise of Black Internationalism.* Cambridge, Mass.: Harvard University Press, 2003.

Ezra, Elizabeth. *The Colonial Unconscious: Race and Culture in Interwar France.* Ithaca, N.Y.: Cornell University Press, 2000.

Fauset, Jessie Redmon. *Comedy: American Style.* 1933. Edited and with an introduction by Cherene Sherrard-Johnson. New Brunswick, N.J.: Rutgers University Press, 2010.

———. "Impressions of the Second Pan-African Congress." 1921. In *The Chinaberry Tree and Selected Writings,* 367–82. Boston: Northeastern University Press, 1995.

———. *Plum Bun: A Novel without a Moral.* 1929. With an introduction by Deborah McDowell. Boston: Beacon Press, 1990.

———. "Yarrow Revisited." 1925. In *The Chinaberry Tree and Selected Writings,* 349–55. Boston: Northeastern University Press, 1995.

Horth, Roberte. "Histoire sans importance" [A Thing of No Importance]. *La Revue du Monde Noir* [The Review of the Black World]: *1931–1932, Collection complète no. 1 à 6,* 118–20. Paris: Jean-Michel Place, 1992.

Jules-Rosette, Bennetta. *Josephine Baker in Art and Life: The Icon and the Image.* Urbana: University of Illinois Press, 2007.

Locke, Alain. "The New Negro." In *The New Negro,* edited by Alain Locke, 3–16. 1925. Reprint, New York: Touchstone, 1997.

Nardal, Paulette. "Eveil de la conscience de race" [Awakening of Race Consciousness]. *La Revue du Monde Noir* [The Review of the Black World]: *1931–1932, Collection complète no. 1 à 6,* 343–49. Paris: Jean-Michel Place, 1992.

———. "Guignol Ouolof." *L'Etudiant noir* 1 (1935): 4–5.

———. "Guignol Ouolof," translated by Brent Hayes Edwards. In *The Practice of Diaspora: Literature, Translation, and the Rise of Black Internationalism,* 182–84. Cambridge, Mass.: Harvard University Press, 2003.

Sharpley-Whiting, T. Denean. *Negritude Women.* Minneapolis: University of Minnesota Press, 2002.

Sieburg, Friedrich. *Gott in Frankreich? Ein Versuch.* Frankfurt am Main, Germany: Frankfurter Societäts-Druckerei, 1929.

Wall, Cheryl A. *Women of the Harlem Renaissance.* Bloomington: Indiana University Press, 1995.

Wilks, Jennifer M. *Race, Gender, and Comparative Black Modernism: Suzanne Lacascade, Marita Bonner, Suzanne Césaire, Dorothy West.* Baton Rouge: Louisiana State University Press, 2008.

10

A Mobilized Diaspora: The First World War and Black Soldiers as New Negroes

CHAD WILLIAMS

By the time he arrived in London, Claude McKay was a rising star. The Jamaica native left for the United States in 1912, attending the Tuskegee Institute and Kansas State University, eventually settling in Harlem. A budding poet who had experienced moderate success, McKay burst onto the literary and political scene with the July 1919 appearance of "If We Must Die," written in the midst of the summer's torrent of racial violence. Originally published in the socialist newspaper *The Liberator* and reprinted in black periodicals throughout the country, "If We Must Die" served as a rallying cry for a postwar generation of African Americans and other peoples of African descent committed to challenging racial injustice. With McKay's newfound notoriety came an opportunity to travel to London, and, eager to escape America's volatile racial climate, he departed in fall 1919.

McKay did not initially enjoy London, but his comfort level increased when a West Indian student from Oxford introduced him to a local club for black soldiers. "There were a host of colored soldiers in London," McKay later wrote. They came mostly from the "West Indies and Africa," although the group included "a few colored Americans, East Indians, and Egyptians." He regularly frequented the club, listening to the soldiers "telling tales of their war experiences in France, Egypt, and Arabia." "Many were interested in what American Negroes were thinking and writing," McKay remembered, and he fulfilled their curiosity by giving them copies of various militant African American publications—*The Crisis, The Messenger,* the *Negro World,* the *Pittsburgh Courier,* and the *Chicago Defender.* Inspired by his interactions, McKay penned a series of articles about the soldiers and their meeting place for his friend Hubert Harrison, the legendary Harlem activist and editor of Marcus Garvey's *Negro World.* In this small London basement in Drury Lane, black soldiers from throughout the African diaspora fraternized, exchanged ideas, and, in the process, further shaped the radical consciousness of one of the leading figures in a globally expanding New Negro movement.[1]

The close relationship between Claude McKay, soldiers of African descent from the First World War, and the New Negro is not an anomaly. The New Negro was a diasporic figure, and the propagation of this trope directly correlated to the wartime militarization of black communities across the globe. Historian Joseph Harris, in his seminal essay "Dynamics of the Global African Diaspora," posits the emergence of a "mobilized" modern African diaspora, coinciding with the early-twentieth-century apex of European colonialism, comprising "descendant Africans with a consciousness of the identity of their roots, occupational and communication skills, social and economic status, and access to decision-making bodies in their host country."[2] Harris conceptualizes mobilization in terms of collective political organization around issues of race and ethnicity. But thinking about a different type of mobilization—the mobilization of material, ideas, and, most significantly, men for employment in the First World War—allows for a broader historical understanding of the modern African diaspora. The war set millions of descendant Africans in motion through the demands of combat and labor, bringing them into contact with one another and fundamentally transforming the demographic, ideological, and imaginative contours of the diaspora.

Reframing the meaning of *mobilization* also provides a theoretical entryway into rethinking how we historicize and conceptualize the New Negro of the interwar period. In this essay, I examine the impact of the war on soldiers of African descent and their place, as both symbols and historical actors, in the New Negro movement. Until relatively recently, scholars have examined the New Negro largely as a cultural product, the work of artists, poets, novelists, photographers, and a select group of white and black intellectuals invested in portraying a reconstructed vision of modern blackness. More narrowly, the New Negro is often posited as a distinctly American creation, inextricably linked to the so-called Harlem Renaissance. Fortunately, historians and literary theorists have increasingly begun to challenge these assumptions by placing the New Negro in the context of various social, political, and cultural movements during the war and postwar periods that reached beyond the narrow confines of Harlem and America itself.[3] Such an interdisciplinary and geographically broadened approach also allows for an alternative exploration of the symbolic and historical significance of black soldiers during this period.

World War I is traditionally cast as a Eurocentric event. Scholars remain captivated by the bloody drama that played out between the Allied forces and Central powers on the French western front between August 1914 and November 1918, effectively relegating other participants, and other theaters, to marginal roles. To the contrary, people of color, and peoples of African descent in particular, shaped the history of the war in profound ways. The imperial powers of Germany, France, and Great Britain utilized over two million men from Africa, as both workers and combatants, in Europe and on the African continent itself. They fought in battles ranging from Verdun to the German East Africa campaign and labored from Cape Town to St. Nazaire. Upward of 25,000 black troops served from the various islands of the British and Francophone Caribbean, several thousand black soldiers came from Canada, and some 380,000 African American troops—200,000 of whom traveled overseas to France—donned the uniform of the U.S. Army.[4] As these numbers attest, the exigencies of war uprooted and dispersed servicemen of African descent from all corners of the diaspora, a process of social, political, and economic upheaval that directly contributed to the transnational emergence of the New Negro.

Focusing on the experiences of various soldiers of African descent in the First World War, as well as on the personal and political impact of their service, demonstrates that the New Negro was not only a diasporic figure but one that black soldiers uniquely encapsulated. The New Negro, as Henry Louis Gates and others have argued, was in part a symbolic creation, a "trope" to signify a black modernist cultural aesthetic and political sensibility.[5] It was highly gendered as well, conveying, in its male incarnation, an ideal of modern black manhood. These traits are indeed applicable to the idea and imagery of the black veteran, who in the newspaper editorials, plays, artwork, and literature of the Harlem Renaissance conveyed a resurgent masculinist spirit of militancy and commitment to combat global white supremacy. The New Negro, however, was just as much an historical figure as a metaphorical product, and this extended well beyond the borders of the United States. Although their experiences varied widely, as did the particular aspects of their lives, servicemen of African descent shared a common internalized and imposed identity as veterans, a status that was at once highly personal and deeply political. They had traveled widely, witnessing firsthand both the harsh realities and incongruities of white supremacy. They had encountered people of different backgrounds, languages, and beliefs. And many came away from the war with a new self-consciousness, a new sense of manhood, a new broadened, more critical awareness of the world in which they lived, one in which radical social and political change was indeed possible. Through their symbolism and historical experiences, these soldiers and veterans, these New Negroes, profoundly shaped the cultural, social, and political tenor of the postwar era and determined to make their world anew.

The life and work of Claude McKay vividly illustrates the importance of black soldiers and veterans in the cultural and historical formation of the New Negro. Perhaps more than any other individual, McKay stands as the key literary architect of the New Negro as a modern, diasporically situated, transgressive figure. McKay's personal biography is itself transgressive, as he resided at various times in the United States, England, the Soviet Union, France, Spain, and Algeria. Informed by his remarkable lived experiences, McKay's literature aimed to spark the radical imaginations of readers by alerting them to the complex relations and shared struggles of African-descended peoples. But despite the wealth of scholarship devoted to the internationalist dimensions of McKay's work, and his novels in particular, the centrality of the black soldier and veteran in his writings has received little attention.[6]

The main characters of *Home to Harlem* (1928) and *Banjo* (1929), McKay's first two novels, are former soldiers. Both Jake and Banjo epitomize McKay's vision of, as Michelle Stephens writes, the "New Worldly Negro." Jake, the central protagonist of *Home to Harlem,* is a veteran of the U.S. Army who, "disappointed" with his service in a labor battalion in Brest, France, goes AWOL.[7] He lives in London until the armistice, questioning why he bothered to mix himself "up in a white folks' war," before deciding to return to Harlem.[8] There he joins other working-class New Negroes in rebelling against the bourgeois social, cultural, and political norms of postwar America. But Jake, as McKay's working-class hero, exhibits a restlessness with Harlem and imagines a world of broader possibilities. His relationship with and admiration for Ray, a Haitian-born railroad worker, speak to his nascent diasporic sensibilities. McKay's second novel revolves around the adventures of "Banjo," an African American veteran who served in the Canadian Army. Unlike Jake, Banjo is an explicitly transnational figure who shatters any attachment to the American nation. Lamenting his role as a soldier in making a "wul' safe foh crackerism," he immerses himself in "the seaman's dream port" of Marseilles.[9] In Marseilles, Banjo encounters seamen, dockworkers, and ex-soldiers from throughout the African diaspora, similarly engaged in a life of vagabondage, and establishes a musical band to express his freedom dreams. Jake and Banjo represent a strategic decision by McKay to construct his vision of postwar radicalism, black masculinity, and African diasporic community around the symbolic figure of the former soldier.

For Jake and Banjo, their identity as veterans is crucial. McKay links them through a cultural trope of the disillusioned veteran of African descent and a unique black cosmopolitanism. Military racism, in its nationalist and imperialist manifestations, circumscribes the freedom of McKay's protagonists, who come to symbolize the futility of black participation in a white supremacist war. Instead of heroic combat, Jake is reduced to a laborer and ultimately rejects the army; instead of returning home a decorated hero, Banjo mocks the very idea of democracy and remains in France. The destructive forces of war effectively alienate them from the white Western world, at first glance suggesting the limitations of cosmopolitanism for black soldiers and for peoples of the African diaspora more broadly. But McKay uses his black veterans to offer an alternative model of cosmopolitanism, one rooted in an African diasporic sensibility forged in the mobilizing dimensions of the war.[10] While Jake and Banjo denounce their military service, it nevertheless imbues them with both skills and status. Having acquired knowledge of modern warfare, traversed the Atlantic, visited major European cities, and interacted with peoples of various nationalities and cultures, Jake and Banjo, whether in Harlem or Marseilles, navigate a mobilized diaspora and emerge for McKay as emblematic "New Worldly Negroes." As McKay demonstrates, the trope of the black veteran occupies an important place in the global New Negro cultural moment.[11]

McKay and his work serve as a useful conceptual bridge between a symbolic, metaphorical New Negro and a New Negro rooted in the diverse range of historical experiences of peoples of African descent during the war and postwar periods. Indeed, World War I had a far-reaching impact on the African diaspora. As W. E. B. Du Bois articulated in the landmark 1915 essay "The African Roots of War," the origins of the global maelstrom lay in the furious competition between the major Western powers for imperial control of Africa's material and human resources.[12] Africa and its peoples figured prominently in how Europe mobilized for and waged war. Over two million Africans served, and the continent itself became a key battlefront, with France and Great Britain taking aim at Germany's colonial possessions.[13] The most extensive campaign occurred in German East Africa, where the British Army employed thousands of troops from Kenya and its other east African colonies, many of whom fought in the King's African Rifles, while Germany relied almost exclusively on African colonial servicemen.[14] Beyond the continent, imperial racial ideologies shaped the decisions of the warring nations to use black soldiers on the European front. Great Britain and Germany, most notably, asserted that soldiers of African descent had no place on the battlefield with white troops. Germany only used colonial troops in the African theater, whereas the British consigned the vast majority of African and West Indian soldiers to labor duties, remaining consistent with their view of colonized people of color as an easily exploitable and ultimately expendable workforce.[15]

France, however, made full use of its African subjects, including in combat. Devastating casualties at the war's onset prompted French military officials to expand the use of their colonial soldiers beyond the African continent. While a significant number of soldiers from France's Caribbean possessions, such as Guadeloupe, fought in the war and served in metropolitan forces, the vast majority of France's colonial soldiers came from Africa.[16] France undertook a massive recruitment campaign throughout its African colonies, and by the end of the war, some 450,000 colonial Africans had traveled to Europe to fight for the tricolors.[17] France raised over two hundred thousand troops from its North African colonies of Algeria, Morocco, and Tunisia, who participated in several major battles, including Verdun and the crucial battle of the Marne.[18] The most well-known troops were the *tirailleurs sénégalais,* a generic label applied to all colonial soldiers from the French West African Federation (AOF). Over 140,000 conscripted West Africans fought on the western front during the war, frequently serving as the first wave of assault or counterattack against German positions.[19]

The forces of nationalism and imperialism dictated how various racialized groups and subject populations participated in the war. It is important to acknowledge the broad diversity of experience in how black soldiers individually and collectively experienced the war and responded to their new condition. There was the rural sharecropper from the American South who, instead of fighting to make the world "safe for democracy," spent the war laboring night and day in a stateside training encampment.[20] There was the Nandi recruit from Kenya who approached service in the King's African Rifles as an opportunity to express traditional cultural beliefs, such as land cultivation and cattle acquisition, previously circumscribed by British colonial pacification.[21] There was the Jamaican volunteer who protested the exclusion of black men from the British West Indian Regiments (BWIR) and demanded the right to fight for the Crown.[22] There was the Senegalese conscript, impressed into duty against his will, who, as he crossed the Mediterranean, packed into a French cargo hold, feared he was instead really being shipped across the Atlantic into a life of slavery.[23] These war experiences represented the diversity of the diaspora and the tensions, fissures, and historical incongruities embedded within it.[24]

It is possible, however, to identify certain commonalities pointing to a shared diasporic condition between various soldiers of African descent that allows us to situate them within the context of the emerging New Negro movement. Most glaring was the ubiquitous presence of racial discrimination in the militaries of the United States and the warring European nations. White supremacy has functioned as a powerful force in the creation of the modern African diaspora and, more specifically, in the development of a unifying diasporic consciousness.[25] The racism endured by soldiers of African descent in the war represented a significant moment in this formative process. Although some West African and Antillean soldiers fought in the integrated metropolitan French army, the vast majority of black soldiers remained segregated in their respective armies. For example, the experience of black servicemen from South Africa, who traveled to France as part of the South African Native Labour Contingent (SANLC) and were essentially quarantined by the British to restrict their access to the civilian population, paralleled that of the French *tirailleurs sénégalais,* who were also heavily policed for similar reasons.[26] Racialist thinking on the part of European and American military officials likewise had direct bearing on the employment of black troops. Only 40,000 out of 380,000 African American soldiers actually engaged in combat, just as only one battalion of the BWIR took up arms, and not on the western front. Seen as mentally and physically inferior, the vast majority of African American and Caribbean soldiers toiled in labor battalions, loading and unloading ships and carrying shovels instead of rifles.[27] Conversely, for the French, a belief in the inherent warrior-like nature of their West and North African colonials translated into using them overwhelmingly as shock troops, resulting in disproportionately high casualty rates.[28] Often more destructive than German assaults, Allied racism targeted the dignity and, frequently, the very humanity of soldiers of African descent.

The belief that black soldiers posed a sexual threat to white French women constituted a powerful force in shaping the military policies of France, Great Britain, and the United States. Black masculinity and sexuality figure prominently in cultural representations of the New Negro, just as they do in the history of black military service. The presence of thousands of black soldiers fraternizing with a largely female French civilian population raised the specter of interracial sexual contact and the more explosive concern of rape. Throughout the course of the war and its aftermath, various soldiers of African descent thus became linked by a discourse of black servicemen as a danger to white womanhood, with the potential to disrupt the stability of the global color line. As contingents of black South Africans prepared to depart for France, many whites worried that, as one commentator remarked in October 1916, "every black man will have a woman on each arm" and, upon their return home, corrupt the minds of the native population.[29] Following the armistice, James Vardaman, a former U.S. senator from Mississippi, warned his fellow white southerners to watch for "French-women-ruined" black veterans who, in his imagination, jeopardized the region's racial order.[30] The New Negro as a hypersexualized black soldier raised the anxieties of white supremacists across the globe.

The actual treatment of black soldiers reflected these fears. The British Army developed a compound system to strictly segregate black troops of the SANLC, in large part to guard against possible interaction with French women.[31] For African American soldiers, their oftentimes cordial interactions with French civilians, and women in particular, had severe consequences. The American Expeditionary Forces high command went to great lengths to educate their French hosts on American racial customs, specifically concerning the risk black men posed to white women. The "Secret Information on Black American Troops" memorandum, issued on August 7, 1918, warned French officers to "make a point of keeping the native cantonment population from 'spoiling' the Negroes," as African American troops had allegedly "given rise to as many complaints for attempted rape as all the rest of the army."[32] These wholly unsubstantiated rumors of sexual assaults dogged black soldiers throughout their time in France. As a result, American military leaders successfully pressured Allied commander Ferdinand Foch to prioritize the return of African American troops back to the United States immediately following the armistice, with one prominent white officer arguing that "no man could be responsible for the acts of these Negroes toward Frenchwomen."[33] The French likewise took extraordinary measures to keep their colonial soldiers isolated from white civilians to prevent sexual liaisons, both consensual and violent. But unlike their African American counterparts, large numbers of North and West African troops remained in Europe after the war, with upward of 45,000 serving in the French forces occupying the Rhineland in 1920 and 1921. A humiliated Germany turned the association between France's African soldiers and rape into an international affair, propagandizing wild stories of German women being terrorized by sex-crazed African "savages" that generated considerable attention and sympathy, especially in the United States.[34] The idea of soldiers of African descent as a "black horror," however, extended beyond the Rhine and reflected a broader transnational perception by white supremacists of the New Negro black servicemen as a social and sexual menace.

The shared struggles against and memories of nationalist and imperialist racial oppression, while significant, did not totally define black soldiers' experiences during the war. The global maelstrom broadened the social, cultural, political, and spatial horizons of black servicemen, exposing them to new lands, new people, and new ideas. On a personal level, for the majority of soldiers of African descent, whether they traveled to France or Great Britain, German East Africa or the Middle East, military service entailed a process of dislocation from their prewar identities, spheres of comfort, and geographic zones of familiarity. Black troops from the New York 369th Infantry Regiment, for example, trained in the heart of white supremacist South Carolina, then boarded ships to France, where they encountered North and West African soldiers who had similarly been uprooted from their native homes by the demands of military service.[35] The overseas experience proved especially enlightening. In the trenches, on the docks, and in the streets, soldiers of African descent tested the legitimacy of notions of "democracy" and "self-determination" through their oftentimes dramatic introduction to people of different cultures and beliefs.[36] For individual servicemen, the results of these encounters could be profound. Following the war, African American veteran Lemuel Moody reflected that his experience "changed my outlook on life. I see things now with different eyes."[37] A former member of the SANLC similarly remarked after the war, "My head is full up with new things and the wonders of the world."[38] The son of a former Senegalese *tirailleur* recalled of his father, "When [my father] came back, he had learned many things from the war and [about] the 'white' man.... He had gained more understanding about the kinds of ways officials should [behave]."[39] Such sentiments, however deeply internalized, did not necessarily translate into explicit acts of resistance or sustained revolt. But they do reflect how many soldiers saw themselves in a new light, with a broadened consciousness, and subsequently grappled with the social, political, and psychological dislocations of their experience.

The personal transformations experienced by individual soldiers mirrored broader transformations occurring in black communities throughout the African diaspora. The forces of war and revolution unleashed powerful social, political, and economic tensions, informed by the racialized nature of European imperialism and Wilsonian rhetoric of self-determination.[40] The national and imperial obligation of sacrifice in the forms of both voluntary and compulsory support for the war effort facilitated a heightened political consciousness and expectations for increased citizenship rights, economic freedoms, and even independence on the part of the colonized and racially oppressed. The major Western powers, in response to such aspirations, feared a weakening of their political authority and its white supremacist ideological underpinnings. In major American and European cities, African, African American, West Indian, and Asian workers and discharged soldiers were viewed as a source of competition for scarce jobs and social resources, while in the colonies, subjected peoples tested the boundaries of imperial legitimacy with acts of resistance, both small and large in scale.[41] Whereas white government and military leaders sought to stabilize a racial and social order seemingly turned upside down, peoples of African descent approached the postwar moment emboldened with aspirations for fundamental change.[42]

As black people, individually and collectively, began to challenge the color line, white people recoiled and determined to maintain their global supremacy. Racial and political violence erupted throughout the diaspora. In the United States, the infamous Red Summer of 1919 was marked by a dramatic spike in lynchings and dozens of race riots, most notably in Elaine, Arkansas, Washington, D.C., and Chicago.[43] Beyond America's borders, bloody disturbances occurred in Egypt, India, the United Kingdom, South Africa, and Sierra Leone. The worldwide outbreak of violence stemmed from multiple sources. Some incidents, such as the Amritsar, India, massacre in which British colonial forces killed 369 men, women, and children in cold blood, had their roots in overt political demands for expanded civil rights and independence.[44] Many conflagrations revolved around labor, which included competition between black and white workers for scare postwar jobs as well as white resistance to black workers' desire for greater economic freedom.

Black veterans represented another important generative force of postwar violence and diasporic racial militancy more broadly. Walter Loving, a highly valued African American agent in the U.S. Military Intelligence Division, directly attributed the Red Summer riots to "the awakened spirit of the Negro soldier returning from France full of bitter resentment," which "set the spark that has released the pent up feelings of the masses."[45] Loving's assessment speaks to the metaphorical potency of black veterans as symbols of both fear and inspiration. In the United

States, many white Americans clung to an image of black ex-servicemen as vectors of radicalism and inevitable racial turmoil based on their overseas experience and internalization of the war's democratic ideals. American military intelligence officials identified returning black servicemen as one of the greatest threats to domestic racial tranquility, with several reports falsely suspecting that soldiers were "returning from France with army pistols or revolvers" and, inspired by black newspapers openly advocating for "race war and violence," could possibly use them "in the future in race or radical movements."[46] The famed University of Chicago sociologist Robert Park echoed the thoughts of an anxious white population when he forebodingly wondered, "What is going to happen when the negro troops return from France?"[47] African Americans pondered the same question, as well, but instead viewed the return of black soldiers as a moment of triumph and hope. African American journalists, intellectuals, and civil rights activists skillfully constructed and embraced a heroic black veteran, one who embodied the highest attributes of manhood, leadership, and dedication to racial progress. Following the February 17, 1919, homecoming of the Eighth Illinois National Guard to Chicago, an editorial in the *Defender* declared,

> We are loath to believe that the spirit which "took no prisoners" will tamely and meekly submit to a program of lynching, burning and social ostracism as has obtained in the past. With your help and experience we shall look forward to a new tomorrow, not of subserviency, not of meek and humble obeisance to any class, but with a determination to demand what is our due at all times and in all places. You left home to make the world a safer place for democracy and your work will have been in vain if it does not make your own land a safer place for you and yours.[48]

Similarly, W. E. B. Du Bois, in his May 1919 *Crisis* rallying tour de force "Returning Soldiers," avowed that the "Soldiers of Democracy" who sacrificed in the war would now *"return fighting,"* symbolically linking African American veterans with a renewed commitment on the part of the race to make the democratic aspirations of the war a reality. The image of the black veteran loomed large for black and white people alike as the notion of a postwar New Negro began to form in the domestic and global consciousness.

Though Du Bois may have been figurative in his construction of the New Negro, and intelligence officers were gripped by paranoia, soldiers of African descent did in fact stand at the center of postwar social and political upheaval. Although the impact of the war on New Negro soldiers was highly personal, and the transformations in consciousness were often subtle, military service did have a clear radicalizing effect on many troops of African descent. In trying to make sense of the explosive racial climate in the American South following the armistice, Dr. Josiah Morse, a native of South Carolina, informed his colleagues of the YMCA Interracial Committee, "We have a new Negro with us, he has come back from the world war changed."[49] Aspirations of equal citizenship versus the realities of Jim Crow, dreams of heroic combat contrasted to the indignities of forced labor, expectations of gratitude juxtaposed against the postwar horrors of lynching and race riots, caused numerous veterans to return from service highly disillusioned and, in some cases, committed to revolutionary change. "I regret to say that I have come home from France with a feeling of intense bitterness towards white men," African American lieutenant James H. N. Waring angrily told the Baltimore *Afro-American* in March 1919.[50] He would become a member of the League for Democracy, the most militant postwar organization specifically for ex-servicemen. Another African American officer, William Colson, joined the staff of A. Philip Randolph and Chandler Owen's radical journal *The Messenger,* penning a series of explosive articles, including one titled "The Immediate Function of the Negro Veteran." In this December 1919 essay, Colson proclaimed, "The returned Negro veteran, by virtue of his service and experience, has a certain special function which he cannot afford to fail to press to the limit. . . . Let them neither smile nor sleep until they have burned into the soul of every Negro in the United States. an unquenchable desire to tear down every barrier which stops their onward march."[51] Colson's words echoed the actions of black veterans in the Chicago race riot and other violent clashes, where their military training and leadership proved vital in providing communal defense and, in several instances, pressing the offensive.[52] African American veterans upheld themselves as the New Negro personified, emboldening other black people in the process.

A similar development occurred throughout the African diaspora. The war and military service did not necessarily create a radical mass of ex-soldiers committed to destroying European imperial rule. Indeed, the vast majority of veterans attempted to readjust to postwar life as best as possible or, having experienced firsthand the devastating military capabilities of the colonial powers, accepted the futility of outright revolution. Nevertheless, government leaders, state intelligence agencies, and colonial officials expressed deep concern over the return of black servicemen to their respective societies and their potentially disruptive impact on the racial status quo. At the same time, many soldiers of African descent acted on the socially broadening and, in some instances, politically enlightening aspects of their war experience to contest the legitimacy of empire in ways both subtle and dramatic. As Gregory Mann demonstrates, the roughly two hundred thousand returning West African *tirailleurs,* expecting both material and immaterial recognition for their service, presented AOF administrators with a host of challenges concerning demobilization, employment, political patronage, and disability benefits. Taking advantage of a discourse of mutual obligation and refusing to discard their old uniforms, these "unruly clients" tested the limitations of the colonial bureaucracy and, by their very presence, the stability of West African societies.[53] In South Africa, black veterans of the SANLC may not have ushered in a sustained wave of resistance to white domination, but some did exhibit a new self-confidence and restlessness with their social status that translated into everyday acts of defiance.[54]

The situation was more acute in the British West Indies, where the return of black soldiers had discernable social, political, and economic reverberations. An October 10, 1919, report produced by a British intelligence agent acknowledged the pressing matter of "negro unrest throughout the world" and its implications for "the large colored population in the colonies of the British Empire." "It was hardly to be expected," the officer wrote, "that coloured troops could be employed in France without stirring up race-consciousness among the returning soldiers."[55] This unease was hardly unfounded. Many soldiers of the BWIR emerged from the war profoundly disillusioned and highly radicalized.[56] In the wake of a four-day mutiny at Tarranto, Italy, in December 1918, sixty noncommissioned officers secretly met to plan the formation of the "Caribbean League," envisioned as a vehicle for the promotion of pan-Caribbean political unity and black self-determination. Although the Caribbean League never materialized as a formal organization, the men and ideas behind its conception contributed to the wave of radical activism that swept the Caribbean following the war. Returning soldiers of the BWIR, "imbued with revolutionary ideas," as one British official wrote, were seen as a source of potential unrest and racial discord.[57] Ex-servicemen from Grenada, Barbados, Jamaica, and British Honduras demanded recognition of their service, employing tactics ranging from petition writing to violent protest to achieve their aims. On the night of July 18, 1919, Jamaican veterans in Kingston, some screaming "kill the whites," took to the streets and attacked a group of white sailors and civilians, while in December of the same year, the Trinidad Workingmen's Association, dominated by former soldiers and led by BWIR captain Arthur Cipriani, organized a series of protests against unfair wages and poor labor conditions.[58]

The activities of veterans from the British West Indies point to the involvement of many former soldiers in various radical working-class movements that contributed to the emergence of the postwar New Negro and a politically mobilized African diaspora. In the wake of the Bolshevik Revolution, government and military officials focused much of their attention on the specter of communism and its potential attraction to peoples of African descent. While fears of black soldiers returning to their homes contaminated with Bolshevist propaganda were wildly exaggerated, the diasporic, left-leaning nature of some veterans' political sensibilities did in fact make the Communist Party (CP) an attractive organizational and ideological home for translating postwar disillusionment into structured activism.[59] Black people used the CP, and the African Blood Brotherhood (ABB) in particular, to fuse anticapitalist Marxism with pan-African anticolonialism to challenge the roots of black racial oppression across the diaspora.[60] The ABB structured and promoted itself as a clandestine paramilitary organization, with calls for "membership by enlistment" and recruits "willing to go the limit" appearing in the pages of *The Crusader*.[61] This self-conscious appropriation of black soldiers as symbols of New Negro militancy not only shaped the tenor and structure of the ABB but influenced its membership as well. Trace historical evidence strongly suggests that ex-soldiers constituted a significant portion, if not the core, of the organization's participants. One of these men was Harry Haywood, who joined the ABB in 1922 on the recommendation of his brother Otto Hall, also a veteran. "In the years since I had mustered out of the Army," Haywood reflected in his autobiography, "I had come from being a disgruntled Black ex-soldier to being a self-conscious revolutionary looking for an organization with which to make revolution."[62]

The participation of former servicemen in the CP extended beyond the United States. A small number of West African veterans became active in the CP, the most prominent being Lamine Senghor. Disillusioned by his war experience, Senghor joined the French CP in 1924. After leaving the CP in 1926, he founded the Comité de Défense de la Race Nègre and the short-lived newspaper, *La Voix des Nègres*. Through his newspaper, Senghor argued for the liberation of "le race nègre" from French imperial rule. He used the war and the sacrifices of black soldiers like himself to highlight the limitations of Frenchness and the hypocritically oppressive nature of colonialism.[63] In the March 1927 issue of *La Voix des Nègres*, Senghor astutely wrote, "When one needs us to make us kill or make us work, we are of the French; but when it is a question of giving us rights, we are not any more of the French, we are negroes."[64] While Harry Haywood and Lamine Senghor represented only a small fraction of the millions of veterans of African descent, the vast majority of whom did not become unabashed radicals, they and other black servicemen, on one hand, occupy an important place in the history of a global New Negro movement and, on the other, demonstrate how the symbol of the black veteran as New Negro was rooted in the experiences of actual individuals.

No one individual and no one organization more effectively mobilized the symbolic potency and physical presence of black soldiers than Marcus Garvey and the Universal Negro Improvement Association (UNIA). The UNIA was the largest and most far-reaching organization of the New Negro movement. Marcus Garvey founded the UNIA in Jamaica in 1914. By the early 1920s, the organization had established branches throughout the African diaspora and boasted of a worldwide membership in the millions. Garvey inspired black people throughout

the diaspora with his uplifting vision of black nationhood, economic independence, and racial pride.

The phenomenal growth of the UNIA was in part attributable to Garvey's
ability, through a unique combination of pageantry and oratorical flair, to make
use of the symbolic meaning and participatory presence of black veterans. Garvey employed a host of rhetorical strategies to demonstrate the commonalities
between black people across the globe, one of the most effective being the use
of the recent world war as a shared struggle for self-determination as well as a
demonstration of black manhood and martial heroism. Immediately following
the November 1918 armistice, Garvey consistently invoked the fresh historical
memory of soldiers of African descent and their military service in the war to both
popularize the UNIA and signal the readiness of black people to emerge victori-
ous in a future worldwide conflict between the races.[65] On July 24, 1921, Garvey
thrilled an enthusiastic crowd, declaring, "They talk about the New York 15th;
that was only an experiment in warfare. . . . They talk about the Illinois 8th; that
was only a pastime for the boys. They talk about the prowess of the West Indian
regiments; those fellows were only having a picnic; it was a gala day. No man
has ever yet seen the Negro fighting at his best, because the Negro has never yet
fought for himself."[66] Garvey continued this theme in a January 15, 1922, address
before a packed audience at New York's Liberty Hall. "I say this positively," Garvey
boomed, "the morale of the New Negro cannot be broken." "The morale of the
Negro American soldier in France," Garvey continued, "the morale of the Negro
West Indian soldier in France, the morale of the Negro African soldier in France
was unbroken and the morale of the soldiers of the bloody war of 1914 to 1918 is
the morale of Negroes throughout the world."[67] As black people throughout the
diaspora flocked to the UNIA in unprecedented numbers, Garvey grounded the
militarism of the organization in the history of the war and the service of soldiers
of African descent.

The issue of racial leadership operated at the core of Garvey's conception
of the New Negro. Black soldiers represented not only the frontline defenders
of Garvey's envisioned black empire but, because of their war experiences, its
future leaders as well. "Out of this war we have produced the American, or the
West Indian, or the African Napoleon who will ultimately lead the 400,000,000
black people of the world to Victory," Garvey exhorted in a 1919 address.[68] Black
veterans, as New Negro leaders, stood poised to supplant bourgeois "old Negro"
leaders whom Garvey deemed obsolete. "We are not depending on the statesmanship of fellows like Du Bois to lead this race of ours," Garvey announced in an
August 1921 speech, "but we are depending on the statesmanship of fellows like
the New York Fifteenth, the West Indian regiments and the Eighth Illinois, who
fought their way in France."[69]

This call for racial leadership constituted part of a mutually reinforcing bond between the UNIA and former servicemen of African descent. A number of African American soldiers joined the UNIA and became key leaders within the organization. They included men such as Clarence Benjamin Curley, a former officer of the Ninety-Second Division who fought in France and served on the board of directors of the Black Star Line; J. Austin Norris, a veteran and prominent attorney who represented the UNIA in Philadelphia; and William Clarence Matthews, who spearheaded the organization's efforts in Boston. Likewise, a significant number of ex-soldiers from the British West Indies joined the UNIA and became prominent members. Barbados native Arnold Ford, who served in the British Royal Navy during the war, became the UNIA's musical director and composed the "Universal Ethiopian Anthem." Samuel Haynes, a veteran of the BWIR, earned the position of general secretary of the UNIA's British Honduras chapter.[70]

The Universal African Legions, the paramilitary wing of the UNIA, functioned as the primary avenue for black veterans to join the organization and make use of their military training. Garvey based much of the structure, organization, and drill regulations of the African Legions on the U.S. Army, making the presence of African American and other veterans of African descent, already familiar with the rules and conventions of military life, extremely valued.[71] African American veteran Emmett L. Gaines held the powerful position of minister of the African Legions. Similarly, Wilfred Bazil, a native of St. Lucia and a commissioned officer in the U.S. Army during the war, served as commander of the Brooklyn Division African Legion.[72] Veteran James B. Nimmo, who was born in the Bahamas and migrated to the United States, began his service with the UNIA as colonel of the Miami African Legion and eventually became the division's vice president.[73] West Indian veterans led the African Legions in Cuba and, on October 10, 1921, marched in celebration of Cuban independence day.[74] The pageantry of the African Legions, instrumental in conveying the strength and aspirations of the UNIA, drew on both the memory and the actual physical presence of black servicemen.

While in Marseilles during the mid-1920s, Claude McKay became enamored with the Vieux Port, the seedy waterfront section of the city populated by sailors, dockworkers, prostitutes, hustlers, and criminals from throughout the African diaspora, all "swarming, scrambling and scraping sustenance from the bodies of ships and crews."[75] It was here that McKay forged, as Wayne Cooper writes, a "sense of kinship" with a "small, transient international community of black men from Senegal, South Africa, Dahomey, Morocco, the West Indies, and the United States."[76] McKay struck up a friendship with, as McKay described him, a "quiet, level-headed, shrewd" former Senegalese sergeant named Pierre M'Baye, owner of a popular café. M'Baye had traveled to the United States following the war, temporarily operating a boardinghouse for African Muslim immigrants in New York City. After amassing enough money, he returned to France and bought a bar in the Vieux Port.[77] At his café, which became, in Brent Edwards's words, "the center of radical activity in the port," M'Baye introduced McKay to another war veteran, the Communist leader Lamine Senghor.[78] The two men immediately bonded, with Senghor showing great interest in McKay's writings and encouraging him to "write the truth about the Negroes in Marseilles."[79] Indeed he did. The New Negroes so vividly brought to life in *Banjo* are inspired by McKay's experiences in the Vieux Port and, most importantly, his close personal interactions with former soldiers. Senghor is in fact briefly mentioned in the novel, and M'Baye's bar serves as the model for Banjo's Café Africain.[80]

The Vieux Port of Marseilles and Claude McKay's experiences are a microcosm of a broader phenomenon that occurred across the African diaspora. The First World War caused peoples of African descent, in the United States and beyond, to ponder the dimensions of their social, political, and racial identities; the nature of their relationships to one another; and, ultimately, their collective future in a modern world in the throes of profound change. If the war constituted the engine of mobilization setting the diaspora into motion, soldiers of African descent represented the vectors of connectivity and transmission that made the process of diaspora alive with radical possibility. In reconsidering the global dimensions of this era, and concomitantly moving beyond a U.S.-centric conception of the New Negro, the war and the experiences of black soldiers must remain front and center. Their legacy speaks to the dynamic nature of this moment. Their legacy speaks to the dynamic history of the New Negro.

NOTES

1   Cooper, *Claude McKay,* 107–10; Tillery, *Claude McKay,* 42; McKay, *A Long Way from Home,* 66–68.

2   Harris, "Dynamics of the Global African Diaspora," 15.

3   Notable examples of this emerging scholarship include Baldwin, *Chicago's New Negroes*; Edwards, *Practice of Diaspora*; Runstedtler, "Visible Men"; Stephens, *Black Empire*; Whalan, "Only Real White Democracy."

4   Historian Morrow, *Great War,* provides the most comprehensive overview of the imperial dimensions of the war and the broad participation of peoples of color in it. For key studies of African American participation in World War I, see Barbeau and Henri, *Unknown Soldiers*; Lentz-Smith, *Freedom Struggles*; Williams, *Torchbearers of Democracy.*

5   Gates, "Trope of a New Negro."

6   Key scholarship on Claude McKay and the internationalist dimensions of his work include Cooper, *Claude McKay*; Cooper, "Claude McKay"; Edwards, *Practice of*

Diaspora; James, *A Fierce Hatred of Injustice*; Stephens, *Black Empire*; Whalan, *Great War*.

7   McKay, *Home to Harlem*, 4.

8   Ibid., 8.

9   McKay, *Banjo*, 11, 193–94.

10 Key historical and literary works that specifically interrogate the concept of black cosmopolitanism include Gillett, "Jazz and the Evolution of Black American Cosmopolitanism"; Nwankwo, *Black Cosmopolitanism;* Stovall, *Paris Noir,* 129.

11 Scholars who have recognized the connections between McKay's work and World War I include Davis, "World War I, Literary Modernism, and the U.S. South"; Stephens, *Black Empire*; Whalan, *Great War*.

12 Du Bois, "African Roots of War."

13 Page, "Black Men in a White Man's War," 14.

14 Key studies of the East Africa campaign include Anderson, *Forgotten Front*; Miller, *Battle for the Bandu*; Paice, *World War I*; Samson, *Britain, South Africa, and the East Africa Campaign*. On the King's African Rifles, see Page, *A History of the King's African Rifles*; Parsons, *African Rank-and-File*.

15 Howe, *Race, War, and Nationalism*; Joseph, "British West Indies Regiment"; Grundlingh, "Impact of the First World War on South African Blacks," 56–58.

16 Jennings, "Monuments to Frenchness?," 562.

17 Clayton, *France, Soldiers, and Africa*; Andrew and Kanya-Forstner, "France, Africa, and the First World War," 16.

18 Ruedy, *Modern Algeria*, 111; Gershovich, *French Military Rule in Morocco,* 171.

19 Key studies of the *tirailleurs sénégalais* include Fogarty, *Race and War in France*; Lunn, *Memoirs of the Maelstrom*; Michel, *Les Africains et la Grande Guerre*; Balesi, *From Adversaries to Comrades-in-Arms*; Echenberg, *Colonial Conscripts*.

20 For discussion of African American labor troops who remained in the United States, see Williams, *Torchbearers of Democracy*, 108–11.

21 Greenstein, "Nandi Experience in the First World War."

22 For discussion of the Jamaican experience in World War I, see Smith, *Jamaican Volunteers in the First World War*.

23 Lunn, *Memoirs of the Maelstrom*, 47–49, 100–3.

24 Edwards, "Uses of *Diaspora*"; Hall, "Cultural Identity and Diaspora"; Lewis, "To Turn as on a Pivot."

25 Gomez, *Reversing Sail,* 2; Palmer, "Defining and Studying the Modern African Diaspora."

26 Grundlingh, *Fighting Their Own War,* 100–14; Fogarty, *Race and War in France.*

27 Williams, *Torchbearers of Democracy,* 119–43; Joseph, "British West Indies Regiment."

28 The subjects of France's use of West African colonial soldiers as "shock troops" and disproportionate casualty rates have generated considerable scholarly debate. See Balesi, *From Adversaries to Comrades-in-Arms*; Echenberg, *Colonial Conscripts*; Fogerty, *Race and War in France*; Lunn, *Memoirs of the Maelstrom*; Michel, *Les Africains et la Grande Guerre.*

29   Quoted in Grundlingh, *Fighting Their Own War,* 47.

30   "Put the Blame Where It Belongs," *Vardaman's Weekly* 11, no. 51 (August 28, 1919).

31   Grundlingh, *Fighting Their Own War,* 101–3.

32   L. Linard, "Au sujet des troupes noires américaines," *Août* 7 (1918), 17N 76, Service Historique de l'Armee de Terre.

33   General John Pershing to Marshal Ferdinand Foch, November 26, 1918, in Nalty and MacGregor, *Blacks in the United States Armed Forces,* 257; Pershing to Foch, November 30, 1918, ibid., 258; Bullard, *Personalities and Reminiscences of the War,* 297.

34   Michel, *Les Africains et la Grande Guerre,* 233–39; Nelson, "Black Horror on the Rhine."

35   For histories of the 369th Infantry Regiment, formerly the New York 15th National Guard, see Little, *From Harlem to the Rhine*; Harris, *Hellfighters of Harlem*; Nelson, *A More Unbending Battle*; Slotkin, *Lost Battalions*; Fogarty, *Race and War in France*; Lunn, *Memoirs of the Maelstrom,* 91.

36   For discussion of how Woodrow Wilson's articulation of international self-determination became a rhetorical and ideological catalyst for postwar nationalist and anticolonial movements in Egypt, India, China, and Korea, see Manela, *Wilsonian Moment.*

37   Lemuel Moody, Virginia War Historical Commission, Library of Virginia, http://www.lva.lib.va.us.

38   Quoted in Grundlingh, *Fighting Their Own War,* 59.

39   Lunn, *Memoirs of the Maelstrom,* 192.

40   See Manela, *Wilsonian Moment.*

41   For discussion of racial tensions in war and postwar France, see Stovall, "Color Line behind the Lines," 737–69.

42   Morrow, *Great War,* 299–314.

43   Key studies of the Red Summer of 1919 include McWhirter, *Red Summer*; Tuttle, *Race Riot*; Voogd, *Race Riots and Resistance*; Waskow, *From Race Riot to Sit-In.*

44   Manela, *Wilsonian Moment,* 159–75; Sayer, "British Reaction to the Amritsar Massacre."

45   Walter Loving to Director of Military Intelligence, "Final Report on Negro Subversion," August 6, 1919, 10218-337, MID, RG 165, U.S. National Archives and Records Administration (hereafter NARA).

46   M. Churchill, Director of Military Intelligence, to intelligence officer, Newport News, Virginia, April 28, 1919, 10218-329, MID, RG 165, NARA; Colonel John M. Dunn to M. Churchill, Director of Military Intelligence, April 25, 1919, 10218-329, MID, RG 165, NARA.

47   Chicago Urban League, *Second Annual Report for the Fiscal Year Ended October 31, 1918,* cited in Waskow, *From Race Riot to Sit-In,* 40.

48   "Welcome, Eighth!," *Chicago Defender,* February 22, 1919.

49   Minutes of the Meeting of the Inter-Racial Committee, Atlanta, September 17, 1919, Colored Work Department Records, box 9, Kautz Family YMCA Archives, University of Minnesota, Minneapolis.

50 "Lieuts. Tell of Raw Deals from Superiors," *Afro-American*, March 14, 1919.

51 William N. Colson, "The Immediate Function of the Negro Veteran," *The Messenger*, December 1919; for further discussion on African American veteran participation in the League for Democracy and on the staff of *The Messenger*, see Williams, "Vanguards of the New Negro."

52 Williams, *Torchbearers of Democracy*, 248–60.

53 Mann, *Native Sons*, chapter 2.

54 Grundlingh, *Fighting Their Own War*, 122–41.

55 Elkins, "Unrest among Negroes."

56 Joseph, "British West Indies Regiment," 114–17.

57 Quoted in Howe, *Race, War, and Nationalism*, 180.

58 Ibid., 192, 197. Joseph, "British West Indies Regiment"; Singh, *Race and Class Struggles in a Colonial State*; James, *Life of Captain Cipriani*.

59 Kornweibel, *"Seeing Red."*

60 Makalani, *In the Cause of Freedom*; Hill, introduction to *The Crusader*.

61 *The Crusader*, October 1919, 27.

62 Haywood, *Black Bolshevik*, 117.

63 Dewitte, "La dette du sang," 8–11; Edwards, *Practice of Diaspora*, 28–34, 51; Conklin, *A Mission to Civilize*, 302; Lunn, *Memoirs of the Maelstrom*, 202–5.

64 *La voix des nègres*, mars 1927, cited in Dewitte, "La dette du sang," 8–11; Williams, *Torchbearers of Democracy*, 271.

65 Stephens, *Black Empire*, 37–38.

66 Speech by Marcus Garvey, July 24, 1921, in Hill, *Marcus Garvey and Universal Negro Improvement Association Papers*, 3:551.

67 Speech by Marcus Garvey, January 15, 1922, *Negro World*, January 21, 1922.

68 Hill, *Marcus Garvey and Universal Negro Improvement Association Papers*, 1:331–33.

69 "Opening Speech of the Convention by Marcus Garvey," August 1, 1921, in ibid., 3:577.

70 Williams, *Torchbearers of Democracy*, 291–92.

71 "Rules and Regulation for Universal African Legions of the U.N.I.A. and A.C.L.," Hill, *Marcus Garvey and Universal Negro Improvement Association Papers*, 3:755; Hill, *Marcus Garvey Life and Lessons*, 419.

72 Stein, *World of Marcus Garvey*, 174; "Report of Brooklyn UNIA Meetings," *Negro World*, February 4, 1922.

73 Vought, "Racial Stirrings in Colored Town," 56–76; Hill, *Marcus Garvey and Universal Negro Improvement Association Papers*, 7:167.

74 Smith, *Jamaican Volunteers in the First World War*, 165–66.

75 McKay, *A Long Way from Home*, 277.

76 Cooper, *Claude McKay*, 228–29.

77 McKay, *A Long Way from Home*, 278.

78 Edwards, *Practice of Diaspora*, 227; McKay, *A Long Way from Home*, 278.

79 McKay, *A Long Way from Home*, 278.

80 Edwards, *Practice of Diaspora*, 227–29.

BIBLIOGRAPHY

Anderson, Ross. *The Forgotten Front: The East African Campaign 1914–1918*. Stroud, U.K.: Tempus, 2004.

Andrew, C. M., and A. S. Kanya-Forstner. "France, Africa, and the First World War." *Journal of African History* 19 (1978): 11–23.

Baldwin, Davarian L. *Chicago's New Negroes: Modernity, the Great Migration, and Black Urban Life*. Chapel Hill: University of North Carolina Press, 2007.

Balesi, Charles. *From Adversaries to Comrades-in-Arms: West Africa and the French Military, 1885–1918*. Waltham, Mass.: Crossroads Press, 1979.

Barbeau, Arthur E., and Florette Henri. *The Unknown Soldiers: African American Troops in World War I*. Philadelphia: Temple University Press, 1974. Reprint, New York: Da Capo Press, 1996.

Bullard, Robert Lee. *Personalities and Reminiscences of the War*. New York: Doubleday, Page, 1925.

Clayton, Anthony. *France, Soldiers, and Africa*. London: Brassey's Defence, 1988.

Colson, William N. "The Immediate Function of the Negro Veteran." *The Messenger*, December 1919.

Conklin, Alice L. *A Mission to Civilize: The Republican Idea of Empire in France and West Africa, 1895–1930*. Stanford, Calif.: Stanford University Press, 1997.

Cooper, Wayne F. "Claude McKay and the New Negro of the 1920s." *Phylon* 25 (1964): 297–306.

———. *Claude McKay: Rebel Sojourner in the Harlem Renaissance*. Baton Rouge: Louisiana State University Press, 1987.

Davis, David A. "World War I, Literary Modernism, and the U.S. South." PhD diss., University of North Carolina, 2006.

Dewitte, Philippe. "La dette du sang." *Hommes et Migrations* 1148 (November 1991): 8–11.

Du Bois, W. E. B. "The African Roots of War." *Atlantic Monthly* (May 1915): 707–14.

Echenberg, Myron. *Colonial Conscripts: The "Tirailleurs Senegalais" in French West Africa, 1857–1960*. Portsmouth, N.H.: Heinemann, 1991.

Edwards, Brent Hayes. *The Practice of Diaspora: Literature, Translation, and the Rise of Black Internationalism*. Cambridge, Mass.: Harvard University Press, 2003.

———. "The Uses of *Diaspora*." *Social Text* 19, no. 1 (2001): 45–73.

Elkins, W. F. "A Source of Black Nationalism in the Caribbean: The Revolt of the British West Indies Regiment at Taranto, Italy." *Science and Society* 34 (Spring 1970): 99–103.

———. "'Unrest among Negroes': A British Document of 1919." *Science and Society* 32, no. 1 (1966): 66–79.

Fogarty, Richard S. *Race and War in France: Colonial Subjects in the French Army, 1914–1918*. Baltimore: Johns Hopkins University Press, 2008.

Gates, Henry Louis, Jr. "The Trope of a New Negro and the Reconstruction of the Image of the Black." *Representations* 24 (Autumn 1988): 129–55.

Gershovich, Moshe. *French Military Rule in Morocco: Colonialism and Its Consequences*. London: F. Cass, 2000.

Gillett, Rachel. "Jazz and the Evolution of Black American Cosmopolitanism in Interwar Paris." *Journal of World History* 21, no. 3 (2010): 471–96.

Gomez, Michael A. *Reversing Sail: A History of the African Diaspora*. Cambridge: Cambridge University Press, 2005.

Greenstein, Lewis J. "The Nandi Experience in the First World War." In *Africa and the First World War*, edited by Melvin E. Page, 81–94. New York: St. Martin's Press, 1987.

Grundlingh, Albert. *Fighting Their Own War: South African Blacks and the First World War*. Johannesburg: Ravan Press, 1987.

———. "The Impact of the First World War on South African Blacks." In *Africa and the First World War*, edited by Melvin E. Page, 54–80. New York: St. Martin's Press, 1987.

Hall, Stuart. "Cultural Identity and Diaspora." In *Identity: Community, Culture, Difference*, edited by Jonathan Rutherford, 222–37. London: Lawrence and Wishart, 1990.

Harris, Bill. *The Hellfighters of Harlem: African-American Soldiers Who Fought for the Right to Fight for Their Country*. New York: Carroll and Graff, 2002.

Harris, Joseph E. "Dynamics of the Global African Diaspora." In *The African Diaspora*, edited by Alusine Jalloh and Stephen E. Maizlish, 7–21. College Station: Texas A&M University Press, 1996.

Haywood, Harry. *Black Bolshevik: Autobiography of an Afro-American Communist*. Chicago: Liberator Press, 1978.

Hill, Robert A. Introduction to *The Crusader*. New York: Garland, 1987.

———, ed. *Marcus Garvey Life and Lessons*. Berkeley: University of California Press, 1987.

———, ed. *The Marcus Garvey and Universal Negro Improvement Association Papers*. 7 vols. Berkeley: University of California Press, 1983–90.

Howe, Glenford D. *Race, War, and Nationalism: A Social History of West Indians in the First World War*. Kingston: Ian Randle, 2002.

James, C. L. R. *The Life of Captain Cipriani*. Nelson, U.K.: Coulton, 1932.

James, Winston. *A Fierce Hatred of Injustice: Claude McKay's Jamaica and His Poetry of Rebellion*. London: Verso, 2000.

Jennings, Eric T. "Monuments to Frenchness? The Memory of the Great War and the Politics of Guadeloupe's Identity, 1914–1945." *French Historical Studies* 21, no. 4 (1998): 561–92.

Joseph, C. L. "The British West Indies Regiment 1914–1918." *Journal of Caribbean History* 2 (May 1971): 94–124.

Kornweibel, Theodore, Jr. *"Seeing Red": Federal Campaigns against Black Militancy, 1919–1925*. Bloomington: Indiana University Press, 1998.

Lentz-Smith, Adriane. *Freedom Struggles: African Americans and World War I*. Cambridge, Mass.: Harvard University Press, 2009.

Lewis, Earl. "To Turn as on a Pivot: Writing African Americans into a History of Overlapping Diasporas." *American Historical Review* 100 (June 1995): 765–87.

Linard, L. "Au sujet des troupes noires américaines." Août 7, 1918, 17N 76, Service Historique de l'Armee de Terre, Paris.

Little, Arthur. *From Harlem to the Rhine: The Story of New York's Colored Volunteers.* New York: Covici Friede, 1936.

Lunn, Joe. *Memoirs of the Maelstrom: A Senegalese Oral History of the First World War.* Portsmouth, N.H.: Heinemann, 1999.

Makalani, Minkah. *In the Cause of Freedom: Radical Black Internationalism from Harlem to London, 1917–1939.* Chapel Hill: University of North Carolina Press, 2011.

Manela, Erez. *The Wilsonian Moment: Self-Determination and the International Origins of Anticolonial Nationalism.* New York: Oxford University Press, 2007.

Mann, Gregory. *Native Sons: West African Veterans and France in the Twentieth Century.* Durham, N.C.: Duke University Press, 2006.

McKay, Claude. *Banjo: A Story without a Plot.* New York, 1929.

———. *Home to Harlem.* 1928.

———. *A Long Way from Home.* New York: L. Furman, 1937.

McWhirter, Cameron. *Red Summer: The Summer of 1919 and the Awakening of Black America.* New York: Henry Holt, 2011.

Michel, Marc. *Les Africains et la Grande Guerre: L'appel à l'Afrique (1914–1918).* Paris: Karthala, 2003.

Miller, Charles. *Battle for the Bandu: The First World War in East Africa.* London: McDonald, 1974.

"Minutes of the Meeting of the Inter-Racial Committee," Atlanta, September 17, 1919, Colored Work Department Records, box 9, Kautz Family YMCA Archives, University of Minnesota, Minneapolis.

Morrow, John H., Jr. *The Great War: An Imperial History.* New York: Routledge, 2004.

Nalty, Bernard C., and Morris J. MacGregor, eds. *Blacks in the United States Armed Forces: Basic Documents, Vol. 4.* Wilmington: Scholarly Resources, 1977.

Nelson, Keith. "The 'Black Horror on the Rhine': Race as a Factor in Post–World War I Diplomacy." *Journal of Modern History* 42, no. 4 (1970): 606–27.

Nelson, Peter. *A More Unbending Battle: The Harlem Hellfighter's Struggle for Freedom in WWI and Equality at Home.* New York: Basic Civitas Books, 2009.

Nwankwo, Ifeoma Kiddoe. *Black Cosmopolitanism: Racial Consciousness and Transnational Identity in the Nineteenth-Century Americas.* Philadelphia: University of Pennsylvania Press, 2005.

Page, Malcolm. *A History of the King's African Rifles and East African Forces.* London: Leo Cooper, 1998.

Page, Melvin. "Black Men in a White Man's War." In *Africa and the First World War,* edited by Melvin Page, 1–27. New York: St. Martin's Press, 1987.

Paice, Edward. *World War I: The African Front: An Imperial War on the African Continent.* New York: Pegasus Books, 2010.

Palmer, Colin A. "Defining and Studying the Modern African Diaspora." *Perspectives* 36 (September 1998): 22–25.

Parsons, Timothy H. *The African Rank-and-File: Social Implications of Colonial Military Service in the King's African Rifles, 1902–1964.* Portsmouth, N.H.: Heinemann, 1999.

Ruedy, John. *Modern Algeria: The Origins and Development of a Nation.* Bloomington: Indiana University Press, 1992.

Rundstedtler, Theresa. "Visible Men: African American Boxers, the New Negro, and the Global Color Line." *Radical History Review* 103 (Winter 2009): 59–81.

Samson, Anne. *Britain, South Africa, and the East Africa Campaign, 1914–1918: The Union Comes of Age*. New York: St. Martin's Press, 2006.

Sayer, Derek. "British Reaction to the Amritsar Massacre 1919–1920." *Past and Present* 131 (May 1991): 130–64.

Singh, Kelvin. *Race and Class Struggles in a Colonial State: Trinidad 1917–1945*. Calgary, Alb.: University of Calgary Press, 1994.

Slotkin, Richard. *Lost Battalions: The Great War and the Crisis of American Nationality*. New York: Henry Holt, 2005.

Smith, Richard. *Jamaican Volunteers in the First World War: Race, Masculinity, and the Development of National Consciousness*. Manchester, U.K.: Manchester University Press, 2004.

Stein, Judith. *The World of Marcus Garvey: Race and Class in Modern Society*. Baton Rouge: Louisiana State University Press, 1986.

Stephens, Michelle Ann. *Black Empire: The Masculine Global Imaginary of Caribbean Intellectuals in the United States, 1914–1962*. Durham, N.C.: Duke University Press, 2005.

Stovall, Tyler. "The Color Line behind the Lines: Racial Violence in France during the Great War." *American Historical Review* 103 (June 1998): 737–69.

———. *Paris Noir: African Americans in the City of Light*. Boston: Mariner Books, 1996.

Tillery, Tyrone. *Claude McKay: A Black Poet's Struggle for Identity*. Amherst: University of Massachusetts Press, 1992.

Tuttle, William M., Jr. *Race Riot: Chicago in the Red Summer of 1919*. New York: Atheneum, 1970.

U.S. National Archives and Records Administration. College Park, Md.

Voogd, Jan. *Race Riots and Resistance: The Red Summer of 1919*. New York: Peter Lang, 2008.

Vought, Kip. "Racial Stirrings in Colored Town: The UNIA in Miami during the 1920s." *TEQUESTA: The Journal of the Historical Association of Southern Florida* 60 (2000): 56–76.

Waskow, Arthur Ocean. *From Race Riot to Sit-in, 1919 and the 1960s: A Study in the Connections between Conflict and Violence*. Garden City, N.Y.: Doubleday, 1966.

Whalan, Mark. *The Great War and the Culture of the New Negro*. Gainesville: University Press of Florida, 2008.

———. "'The Only Real White Democracy' and the Language of Liberation: The Great War, France, and African American Culture in the 1920s." *Modern Fiction Studies* 51 (Winter 2005): 775–800.

Williams, Chad L. *Torchbearers of Democracy: African American Soldiers in the World War I Era*. Chapel Hill: University of North Carolina Press, 2010.

———. "Vanguards of the New Negro: African American Veterans and Post–World War I Racial Militancy." *Journal of African American History* 92, no. 3 (2007): 347–70.

11

Climbing the Hilltop: In Search of a New Negro Womanhood at Howard University

TREVA LINDSEY

> Regardless of the wish of many parents that their daughters become adjuncts of "man," modern life forces them to be individuals in much the same sense as men are individuals.
>
> —Lucy Diggs Slowe

In 1922, Lucy Diggs Slowe became the first official dean of women at Howard University in Washington, D.C.[1] The newly created position, approved in 1920 by university president J. Stanley Durkee, mirrored the dean of men position that President Durkee had approved a year earlier. Prior to accepting this position, Slowe met with and wrote a detailed letter to Durkee to discuss her expectations regarding the offer to serve the university in an administrative capacity. In a letter dated May 31, 1922, Slowe listed the conditions under which she would accept the position. She requested a salary of thirty-two hundred dollars, a professorship in English through the School of Education, and a full-time office assistant.[2] She also stated that "all policies pertaining to the women of the University shall emanate from my office with the approval of the President."[3] This particular point of negotiation specifically unveiled Slowe's desire to become a primary figure in the shaping of women's experiences at Howard University. Before accepting the dean position, Slowe recognized that Howard had institutionalized a relatively conservative view regarding "women's place" through its policies. Consequently, Slowe understood that expansive administrative latitude was vital to her ability to prepare female students for modern life. This letter of negotiation established both a foundation on which a culture of New Negro womanhood could emerge at Howard and a figuration of modernity that developed among African American women.

This article explores the challenges, setbacks, and achievements of Dean Slowe during her storied fifteen-year career at Howard.[4] Furthermore, I discuss how her story connects to a broader cultural current that evolved among African

American women during the early to mid-twentieth century: New Negro woman-hood. The combination and reimagination of ideas from rhetoric about the New Woman and the New Negro among black women communities resulted in the materialization of New Negro womanhood in the early twentieth century. The melding of cultural, social, and political currents captured the challenges black women faced in achieving both racial and gender equality. This amalgamation also arose out of a desire among some African American women to attain authorial control over their bodies, their identities, and their aspirations. The assertion of New Negro womanhood challenged black women's exclusion from and/or limited participation in contemporaneous political and cultural currents. At the core of New Negro womanhood was the movement of black women into a wider array of economic, political, social, and cultural possibilities available in the public sphere. Within the public sphere, and in particular at Howard University during Slowe's tenure, some African American women attempted to etch out the parameters of individual and collective aspirations and desires within a modern world in which they were treated as third-class citizens.[5]

Slowe embraced a form of New Negro womanhood as a conduit to the "modern world." At an institution lauded for its progressive politics, its nurturing of black intellectuals, and its involvement in the black cultural explosion of the early twentieth century, Howard provided a distinct space in which African American women could strive to become full participants in the modern life that Slowe described in her writings. Michael Hanchard asserts that blacks "create[d] a form of relatively autonomous modernity distinct from its counterparts of Western Europe and North America."[6] During the New Negro era, blacks developed technologies, discourses, and institutions that expressed their perspectives, preferences, and desires. For African Americans, the path to the "modern world" significantly differed from the path for whites. Jim Crow laws, de facto segregation, employment and housing discrimination, and white supremacist ideology obstructed the passageway to the modern world. The obliteration of racist attitudes and practices was essential to blacks accessing the promises of the modern world. Black modernist sensibilities, therefore, included the political, economic, and social activism of African Americans attempting to achieve racial equality.

Still, African American women formed autonomous modernities distinct not only from whites but also from African American men. At the core of New Negro womanhood is a specific understanding of the modern world. Slowe often discussed the necessity of preparing African American women for the modern world and imparted this vision onto Howard's female population. Slowe conceived of the modern world as a place in which all people, regardless of race or gender, strove for professional achievement and personal fulfillment. What distinguished New Negro womanhood from other black modernist modalities was not simply its primary focus on African American women. New Negro women such as Slowe confronted gender norms and conventions that produced an intraracial hierarchy. The African American women's community at Howard during Slowe's tenure exemplifies the presence of a burgeoning New Negro women's community.

Through a brief history of Howard University and African Americans in the nation's capital, a close examination of Slowe's life, and a discussion of Howard's campus culture during the 1920s and 1930s, this essay uncovers the contours of the modern world for which Slowe sought to prepare her African American female students. Slowe and Howard women of the early twentieth century contributed to the New Negro movement through challenging and reshaping the institutional culture of the nation's leading institution of higher learning for black students. Furthermore, under the leadership of Slowe, Howard University became a unique space for black women to define themselves as New Negroes and to redefine the New Negro experience on their own terms.

AFRICAN AMERICANS IN WASHINGTON, D.C., AND THE RISE OF HOWARD UNIVERSITY

Washington, D.C., had a substantial population of African Americans, particularly of African American women, during the early twentieth century. Between 1860 and 1930, the population of black women in the District of Columbia increased by over 800 percent. The federal census of 1860 reported a total of 8,402 black women in Washington, D.C. In 1890, the federal census counted 41,581 black women in the nation's capital; by 1930, there were 69,843 black women.[7] African American migration to Washington, particularly among black women, occurred largely between 1860 and 1900. African Americans were spread throughout the city in racial enclaves such as Georgetown, Anacostia, Southwest, Le Droit Park, and the U Street Corridor, which were primarily self-sufficient and self-governing. Each community had religious institutions, black-owned businesses, and civic and social institutions that served a rapidly growing black population. Howard University, however, emerged as a preeminent black institution that anchored a collective sense of progress and achievement among blacks in Washington, D.C.[8]

Howard University is located in the Northwest quadrant of the city just outside of the predominantly black Shaw neighborhood. Chartered by Congress on March 2, 1867, Howard emerged as the leading postsecondary institution for African Americans by the 1900s. Although attending college was a privilege for any person in the United States during the late nineteenth and early twentieth centuries, it was far more rare for an African American, particularly an African American woman. For example, in 1908, the year in which Lucy Diggs Slowe graduated from Howard and forty academic years after the school's chartering, only nineteen African American students graduated, eleven men and eight wom-en.[9] During the late nineteenth century, only a handful of colleges and univer-sities educated blacks and trained them for careers predominated by whites. One of the founders of Howard University noted that an institution such as this

> was demanded by the necessities of the great educational movement which was inaugurated among the freed people at the close of the late war. When primary, secondary and grammar schools were being opened throughout the South, for the benefit of a class hitherto wholly deprived of educational advantages, it became evident that institutions of a higher grade were needed for the training of the teachers and ministers who were to labor in this field. It was with this view of supplying this need that Howard University was founded.[10]

Before officially becoming Howard University, it was decided that this school would have an open admissions policy. The university garnered the distinction of being a pioneer in higher education because of its lack of restrictions based on race, sex, creed, or color. The early to mid-twentieth century was a substan-tial growth period for Howard University. Throughout this period, the school experienced physical expansion, a student body on the rise, increased financial investment from the federal government and private donors, and an intellectual diversification of the curriculum. The heightened prestige of the faculty, staff, and administration also contributed to the university's prominence among blacks throughout the United States.[11]

The Hilltop, as Howard was and is affectionately known by those familiar with the institution, offered a space in which black women could excel in previously unimaginable ways. At Howard, however, like many other institutions within African American communities during the early to mid-twentieth century, African American women were marginalized and had to fight against a gender structure that perpetuated gender inequities.[12] In many ways, campus policies regarding women reflected broader social expectations and mores within black communi-ties. Slowe, during her tenure at Howard, stated that "frequently, Negro college women come from homes where conservatism in reference to women's place in the world of the most extreme sort exists."[13] Many women came to Howard ex-pecting to become servants of their communities, primarily as educators, wives, and mothers. These professional and personal paths reflected an adherence to a black conservatism that relegated black women to particular positions within the modern world. Climbing the Hilltop for New Negro women required combating the prevalence of gender inequities and of narrowed expectations of postgraduate achievement at Howard and, more broadly, in their respective communities. The expectations Howard women confronted were indicative of an institutional culture that perceived women at Howard through a lens that did not fully recognize them as equal participants in the modern world. Slowe explicitly challenged the status quo upon her arrival as dean of women at Howard and sought to create an institutional space for African American women to reconsider how they could engage in the modern world.

LUCY DIGGS SLOWE: EARLY YEARS ON THE HILLTOP

After graduating second in her class from Colored High School in Baltimore, Slowe enrolled at Howard University on an academic scholarship. She became the first female graduate of her school to enroll at Howard and was the first student from her school, male or female, to receive an academic scholarship there. Upon her arrival on the Hilltop, Slowe involved herself in nearly every aspect of the university, from musicals to athletics. She served as president of the women's tennis team, sang in the university choir, and was the first president of Alpha Kappa Alpha Sorority Incorporated, a Greek letter sorority for black women. Respected and lauded by the university's faculty, administrators selected Slowe to chaperone other Howard women on off-campus shopping trips—a responsibility only bestowed on select individuals whom the university deemed of sufficiently high moral character.[14] Slowe appreciated the university's praise of her moral character during her time as a student; however, during her eventual tenure as an administrator at Howard, she openly criticized "the assignment of chaperons to women students as paternalistic and demeaning."[15]

After graduating from Howard in 1908 as class valedictorian, she accepted an English teaching position at Douglass High School in Baltimore. Several black women who received college degrees and remained unmarried pursued teaching as a career. In October 1915, she received a master's degree from Columbia University's Graduate School of Arts and Science. With her degrees from Howard and Columbia, Slowe began a teaching stint at one of the three black high schools in Washington, Armstrong Manual Training School. She eventually became "lady principal" at Armstrong. During her time at Armstrong, her title "lady principal" became "dean of girls." This title change represented a shift in her role from that of a matron to that of a student services administrator. Slowe was one of the main organizers of the first African American junior high school in the Washington area, Shaw Junior High School. In addition to organizing Shaw, which would later become one of the most well respected and widely recognized African American educational institutions, Slowe served as the school's principal until 1922.

Beyond Slowe's academic and professional achievements within the field of higher education, she enjoyed and excelled at many other activities. In 1917, she became the first African American woman to win a national title in any sport: she garnered the first women's title at the American Tennis Association's national tournament in Baltimore. Prior to the association's founding, African Americans in the urban upper South and New England competed in invitational and interstate tournaments but could not aspire to the prestige that accompanied a national title until Slowe's victory in 1917. Slowe also sang in local choirs to fulfill her interest in vocal performance. Being well rounded was of great importance to Slowe and proved foundational to her mentoring and nurturing of the multiple talents her African American women students embodied.

Her accomplishments as an administrator, particularly as one who worked with women, made her a particularly attractive candidate for the newly created position of dean of women at Howard. Slowe had a stellar reputation in black Washington, D.C., and President Durkee saw the impending resignation of Helen Tuck as an opportunity to recruit Slowe to the rapidly growing institution. In summer 1922, Slowe officially accepted the dean of women position. After her appointment, Slowe studied the responsibilities, practices, and procedures of women deans at other universities, regardless of differing racial demographics. "She was guided in the establishment of the office of the Dean of Women at Howard University by Dr. Romiett Stevens at Columbia University, who gave the first course for Deans of women in the United States."[16]

In 1923, Slowe founded and became president of the National Association of College Women (NACW), an organization for African American women alumnae of accredited colleges and universities.[17] In the broadest sense, Slowe viewed the NACW as a way to promote racial and gender equality and to spark important conversations about how to dismantle racial tensions. "If there are to be peace and harmony," Slowe explicated, "among the races in the United States the trained men and women of both races must take the lead in bringing this about. . . . The colleges of the land ought to open and keep open eternally their doors to men and women of good character and mental capacity regardless of race, in order that there may be a common meeting ground where each race can learn and appreciate that which is fine and worthy of the other."[18] Although Slowe worked on a predominantly black campus, she recognized the importance of promoting interracial conversations about race and of trumpeting higher education as a means of recognizing the humanity of all people.

As an organization specifically committed to the strivings of black women in higher education, the NACW promoted the growth of the number of black women on college campuses and sought to support black women students, faculty, staff, and administrators at all institutions educating African American women beyond the high school level. This support included raising the standards in colleges for black women, developing and providing resources for black women faculty and administrators, and securing scholarships and other forms of financial support for African American women. Of particular importance to NACW was the appointment of women deans at African American colleges and universities. Slowe exemplified what NACW envisioned as the ideal women's dean: an education professional, not a matron or caretaker. Through the NACW and her role as dean of women at Howard, Slowe sought to refashion the role of women deans from policing black women's activities on college campuses to developing the intellectual, social, and cultural capacities of African American women college students.

One of Slowe's main goals as a dean was increasing possibilities for her African American women students. Although Slowe served as teacher for over a decade before becoming an administrator, she expressed concern regarding the large number of college-educated African American women who became teachers. She did not discourage African American women from pursuing a career in education, but she vociferously advocated for the diversification of career aspirations among African American women college students. For Slowe, to equip black women for the modern world meant exposing African American women to disciplines such as psychology, economics, and sociology. "The curriculum which is pursued by students in college must," Slowe asserted,

> take account of the fact that they will, upon leaving college, enter a world torn by the most profound upheaval in history. The women students, particularly, must be prepared to shoulder the responsibility first of all for making a living because they are definitely committed in the modern world to developing their own individual talents and of being responsible for their own lives.[19]

Slowe's perspective on the modern world was connected to her understanding of the political, social, and cultural realities that inscribed the lives of this particular historical era. Describing the specificity of the historical moment in which she worked at Howard, Slowe explains that, "living as we do in an industrial democracy, the college woman has a right to expect also some guidance toward the choice of her life's work."[20] Slowe viewed her role as dean of women as one of guidance for female students. She also openly criticized Howard and other predominantly black colleges and universities for not addressing the new needs of women. In a piece titled "The Colored Girl Enters College. What Shall She Expect?," in the *Opportunity Journal of Negro Life*, Slowe affirms that

> one of the most serious defects in the Negro college is the slowness with which it has recognized this need. . . . This guidance is even more important for Negro women than it is for white women because the former have to be

guided not only with reference to their aptitude, but because of racial identity, also, with reference to possible opportunities for work. Negro women
cannot assume that because they are prepared efficiently as individuals they
will receive the same consideration as others when they apply for work. In
every Negro college a woman has a right to expect a well established guidance office where she can secure dependable information on the work.[21]

Slowe explicitly recognized the unique challenges African American women faced
during the New Negro era and demonstratively spoke out about the importance of
African American women being equipped to enter the modern world as workers
in any and all fields of endeavor.

In addition to attempting to expand career possibilities for her black female students, Slowe also contested an institutional policy that dictated that, once married,
African American women should resign from their careers and relinquish their
professional aspirations. This ideology was deeply ingrained in the university's
policies. In 1913, Howard's board of directors voted that, "any female teacher who
thereafter married while teaching at the university would be considered as having resigned her position."[22] While this policy at Howard and in African America
more broadly did not deter African American women from participation in the
African American public sphere through social, civic, and, in some cases, political arenas, it effectively rendered African American women dependent on men
(primarily African American men) for financial sufficiency in the modern world.
Throughout her tenure as dean of women, Slowe opposed the institutionalized
gender structure that prevented African American women from attaining full autonomy through her mentoring of students and through her work with the NACW.

In 1923, when addressing the NACW, Slowe stated that, "if a college accepts
women students and employs women faculty, it should give them the same
status as it gives male students and male teachers respectively."[23] Concerning
African American women faculty, equal pay became a prominent issue for Slowe
and the NACW. "So far as women members of college faculties are concerned,"
Slowe argued, "they should have the same opportunities for advancement that
male members have and should receive equal pay for equal services rendered."[24]
To achieve equal status with African American male students at Howard, Slowe
asserted the necessity of a women's campus. Most colleges, regardless of racial
composition, required that women live off-campus during this era. Leading women
authorities on student personnel, largely white women until the ascendance of
Slowe, believed that residential housing for women functioned as a site for the
development of women students and their leadership abilities. Slowe further
elaborated on this idea by emphasizing that "adequate housing should be made
available for . . . women students for their physical and social development, as

well as for the training of their minds."[25] Although hesitant during the first few years of Slowe's tenure, Howard's administration recognized the growing need for female housing and campus life. Slowe argued that "proper housing is one of the most potent influences in the education of college students." She continued, "Dormitories designed and furnished in accordance with decent standards of living, and presided over by members of the faculty trained in their supervision can be and should be valuable adjuncts to the academic life of a student"; her arguments resonated with many within Howard's administration, including then president Mordecai Johnson.[26] In 1931, Slowe's tireless efforts resulted in the establishment of a "female" campus. Three dormitories for women composed the women's campus that resulted from Slowe's efforts. On the day on which the women's campus officially opened, Slowe stated,

> The great purpose of this educational institution—the awakening of a new spirit of mind, a new mode of thought, a new standard of life, a new vision of light—can be achieved only by putting in place in the life of each student the corner stone of unselfishness, generosity, of truthfulness, courage, righteousness, and high endeavor. It is for us, the faculty, to lay our spiritual and intellectual corner stone in the lives of the students of Howard University as artistically, as durably, as this stone is laid today. To that great task we take joy in addressing ourselves.[27]

Slowe took great pride in establishing the women's campus at her alma mater. Through these residence halls, Slowe and faculty and staff who supported the agenda of preparing African American women college students for the modern world cultivated an environment in which women students engaged in cultural, social, and political activities. Only a year after the formal founding of the "female" campus, Slowe's efforts were heralded by the African American press in Washington, D.C. The *Washington Afro-American* published an article titled "Howard Women Run Themselves in New Dorms" that highlighted the self-governance of the dormitories, the social and cultural activities led by black women students, and the rigor of the intellectual discussions occurring in women's residences. The women's campus provided tangible evidence of African American women's capacity to fully participate in all arenas of public life.

Furthering her investment in African American women's possibilities, Slowe stressed the detrimental effects of differing expectations for male and female students at Howard University. Slowe questioned, "Have those who formulate policies of institutions of higher learning where Negro women study surveyed our changed modern life and consciously attempted to prepare Negro college women for intelligent participation and leadership in it?"[28] When Slowe returned to her alma mater as a dean, she recognized a hunger for leadership opportunities and intellectual, social, and cultural stimulation outside of the classroom among African American women students. "Whether or not Negro college women will be able to take their places as leaders in their communities, depends," Slowe articulated, "to a large extent, upon the opportunities offered them for exercising initiative, independence, and self-direction while in college."[29]

Of particular importance to the surge of women seeking leadership roles during the New Negro era was the issue of women's suffrage, in particular, voting rights for African American women. For example, as the first public act of the founders of a black women's sorority at Howard University, Delta Sigma Theta Sorority, Incorporated, the organization participated in the March 13, 1913, women's suffrage march held in Washington, D.C. African American women at Howard perceived their academic and extracurricular accomplishments as vital to a historical moment in which new ideologies about women and African Americans formed. The women's suffrage movement and the presence of women's activism in the nation's capital ignited a passion among many Howard women between 1900 and 1940. Slowe capitalized on this political energy when she became dean of women and continuously led and supported efforts to formalize leadership development for African American women students. The zeal among black women students Slowe witnessed in the 1920s and 1930s stemmed from the emergence of new opportunities for women and from the convergence of New Negro era political and cultural currents such as black radicalism, pan-Africanism, black and interracial labor movements, black internationalism, American militarism and imperialism, and jazz and early blues culture.

What Slowe came to realize more insightfully throughout her tenure as a dean was that "the university, tolerant of radical ideas when it came to race, was way behind when it came to the social freedoms of its female students or even the rights of its women on the faculty."[30] Her experience as an undergraduate introduced her to the restrictions and gendered expectations Howard imposed on women. As a dean, she faced strong opposition and numerous policies that attempted to maintain a racialized gender hierarchy. In response to Howard's stated and unstated gender structure that policed African American women's participation in all facets of modern life, Slowe continued to demand the fuller participation of women in public arenas.

THE SLOWE AND JOHNSON YEARS: CONTESTING AFRICAN AMERICAN GENDER IDEOLOGY IN THE NEW NEGRO ERA

Opposition to debunking Howard's institutionalized gender ideologies reached its peak during the tenure of Howard's first African American president, Mordecai

Johnson. He arrived in 1926, only four years after Slowe's appointment as dean of women and at the height of New Negro era intellectual and cultural currents converging on the Hilltop.

A graduate of the all-male Morehouse College and an ordained Southern Baptist preacher, Mordecai Johnson arrived at Howard University with a vision for the future of the nationally renowned institution in the nation's capital. His religious background influenced his views on education and his thoughts pertaining to "appropriate" behavior and career paths for African American women. Hiring African American women as faculty at Howard and establishing the women's campus was the extent of his engagement with women's concerns about equality in higher education. At the time when Johnson assumed leadership of Howard University, Slowe had made numerous efforts to provide African American women students with unparalleled opportunities for leadership, social and cultural exploration, and career-oriented education. Slowe explicitly critiqued African American churches and social conservatism, to which many black families adhered. Slowe publicly acknowledged that

> much of the religious philosophy upon which Negro women have been nurtured has tended toward suppressing in them their own powers. Many of them have been brought up on the antiquated philosophy of Saint Paul in reference to women's place in the scheme of things, and all too frequently have been influenced by the philosophy of patient waiting, rather than the philosophy of developing their talents to their fullest extent. Under these conditions, it is inevitable therefore, that the psychology of most of the women who come to college is the psychology of accepting what is taught without much question; the psychology of inaction rather than that of active curiosity.[31]

Johnson, as a Baptist minister, embraced the religious philosophy that Slowe denounced.[32] Because of their substantially differing viewpoints regarding the roles of African American women in the modern world, Slowe and Johnson and his all-male administration maintained a contentious relationship that lasted until Slowe's untimely death in 1937.

Throughout his presidency, Johnson's administration rescinded many of the new opportunities Slowe established for African American women students. Under Johnson, Slowe lost her position as a member of the President's Council of deans and her management role in the women's residence halls. Johnson demanded that Slowe move to Howard's campus to supervise the African American women on campus. This shifted Slowe's role as a manager and a leader of women on campus to that of a matron. When Slowe received her initial offer to serve as dean of women, she requested that she not be required to live on campus.[33] This request stemmed from a belief that her role as an administrator would shift to that of a matron for Howard's female students. On most college and university campuses during this era, women administrators did function in a matronly capacity. Slowe strongly opposed the matron role as both demeaning and regressive; it undermined the general thrust of much of her work at Howard, which tried to dismantle policies based on the assumption that African American women required more supervision and restrictions and less leadership development than their male counterparts. Additionally, Slowe shared a house with a noted woman playwright, Mary Burrill. The implications of two unrelated, single, adult women living together contradicted the university's values surrounding "appropriate" gender and sexual roles and relations, as it was widely known that Burrill and Slowe were in an intimate, romantic relationship.[34]

Her new role as matron exacerbated existing tensions between Slowe and Howard's all-male leadership. Furthermore, in 1933, the women's program, which included career guidance for female students as well as female leadership programs, was dismantled. Although the trustees and the administration proffered the decision as one of economic necessity, many African American women and white women supporters external to Howard firmly believed that the dismantling of the women's program signaled a devaluation of equal opportunities for women in higher education. When the university dismantled the women's program, Slowe responded with ferocity. She remarked, "When the trustees, in the interest of the economy, wiped out of the women's department every person except for two . . . they destroyed, in one day, practically everything that I had built up over a period of eleven years."[35] The frustration expressed by Slowe also stemmed from the fact that only the dean of women was required to live on Howard's campus. The dean of men was permitted to reside in his own home in Washington, D.C. The implications of necessitating supervision for female students, faculty, and staff and not male students, faculty, and staff were particularly hurtful to African American women at Howard, who could interpret these policies as a reflection on their character and potential. This requirement also hinted toward the administration's discomfort with Slowe and Burrill's relationship.

Her confrontation with gender inequity for African American women students and faculty, however, extended beyond educational issues. Slowe also sought to redefine relationships between men and women in higher education in an attempt to curb the exploitation of New Negro women in collegiate and professional spheres. She was concerned with the daily treatment of women on college campuses and in black communities more generally. Her concern for African American women's experiences at Howard became blaringly evident in her handling of a complaint made by women students at Howard about a male professor in

1927. This complaint sparked a chain of events that highlighted the lack of power women students, faculty, and staff possessed at the university. The stark contrast between Howard's racial progressivism and its adherence to traditional gender roles, expectations, and relations provided women at Howard with a seemingly insurmountable obstacle in achieving fuller equality during the New Negro era.

Slowe received an initial complaint about Professor Clarence Harvey Mills from a parent in 1927. The letter accused Professor Mills of using "improper and sometimes vulgar language in his class room with women students present."[36] Seeking to "avoid a public controversy, Slowe arranged to speak privately with Mills about the allegations."[37] Slowe noted that Mills responded positively to their meeting and actually thanked Slowe for bringing it to his attention without involving the administration. The following day, however, Slowe received a letter from Mills, which she described as "vile." This letter accused the female student of hypocrisy, of spending time in brothels, and of pretending to be offended by the vulgar language Mills allegedly used in the classroom. His written reaction to the accusations attacked not just the character of his accusers but also Slowe, in her position as dean. Of Slowe, Mills wrote, "You forget that you are merely the Dean of Women and not the custodian of morals of the male teachers of Howard University."[38] He also suggested that, if Slowe had the same responsibilities as her male counterparts, she would not be a receptacle for "ridiculous" complaints lodged against respected male faculty members. After receiving this letter, Slowe felt compelled to share what had transpired from the initial complaint to this point with Dudley Weldon Woodard, professor of mathematics and dean of the School of Liberal Arts, and President Mordecai Johnson.

Woodard and Johnson agreed that both the parent's complaint and Mills's fiery letter to Slowe warranted serious action. During a meeting with Mills, it was decided that Mills would be dismissed at the end of the term, that no public discussion would accompany the administration's decision, and that Mills must apologize to Dean Slowe for his scathing remarks about her. Inevitably, however, Mills finished the entire year at Howard and was granted a leave of absence with partial salary during the next academic year. During his leave of absence, Mills finished his doctoral degree at the University of Chicago and continued a career in education unmarred by his alleged behavior toward Howard women. Mills's eventual departure from Howard was more voluntary than punitive. Slowe's relationship with Howard's male administrators, particularly President Johnson, further deteriorated because of her insistence on Professor Mills's termination and her advocacy against Howard women being subjected to gender-based harassment.

The consequences Slowe endured did not deter her from remaining outspoken about a campus culture that silenced the voices of women and condoned an intraracial gender hierarchy at both the student and faculty and staff levels. Her 1927 "Memorandum on the Mills Case" conveyed a profound sense of disappointment and frustration with Howard University and its attitudes and policies toward African American women. This memorandum affirmed her commitment to ensuring that Howard's administration evaluate the experiences of women at the university. In addition to drafting one of the first known memos about the gender harassment of African American women in the academy, Slowe used this memo to critique gender inequity more broadly at Howard. She explained,

> From the time this case happened down to the present, I have not had the cordial support of the President. When the time came to raise salaries, he raised mine $200 and raised other Deans with qualifications no better than mine in amounts ranging from $850–$1150. He, without explanation, excused me from his conferences with the Academic Deans, although prior to 1930, the Dean of Men and the Dean of Women had sat with the Board of Deans. He has never sympathetically studied the real work of the Dean of Women, and still seems to have a wrong conception of her function sponsored by the Department of the Dean of Women, and cannot have first hand knowledge of her work. I have tried in every way to correct this but can get no co-operation from the President.[39]

Slowe utilized the Mills case and its aftermath to highlight her struggles as a dean and the resistance she encountered in her efforts to achieve gender equity for Howard women. Sexual harassment, the university's prioritizing of black male leadership, the paternalistic and patriarchal perspectives and policies of Howard's predominantly male administration, and the lack of suitable and intellectually, culturally, and socially stimulating living conditions for women students became visible through Slowe's response to the Mills case. The setbacks only further encouraged Slowe and African American women at Howard to continue to push for gender equity and to address women's exclusion from leadership and women's underrepresentation in the student population and on the faculty.

SLOWE'S LEGACY: MOVING FORWARD WITH A NEW NEGRO CONSCIOUSNESS

Religion did not play an integral role in Slowe's educational philosophy, although it played an important role in her life. Slowe openly criticized black men and women who placed any limitations on what black women could achieve and/or aspire to in areas outside the home. Slowe fought for and with black women to secure not just a place but an equal place in American higher education. Her politics reflected a different consciousness that specifically addressed the needs and burgeoning aspirations of black women, using education as a means for greater visibility in the public sphere.

As president of the NACW, Slowe achieved national attention because of her commitment to black women's education in all U.S. institutions. Slowe articulated how injustices against black women signaled a broader injustice to humankind. Although Slowe was not the first to connect the inequalities faced by African Americans to a broader understanding of inequality, she was among the first to associate the educational achievements of black women to a fuller realization of American democracy. The broadened "justice" lens Slowe engaged added a distinctly New Negro woman's component to her activism. Slowe embodied a commitment to eradicating racial and gender oppression and almost exclusively focused on the plight of African American women. During her tenure as a member and leader of the NACW, the organization formulated its purpose and publicly circulated it. "The organization has devoted itself to the study of living conditions for women and college students and to the raising of educational standards in colleges, with special emphasis upon the introduction into the curricula of courses to meet the needs of modern life," she wrote.[40] Recognizing the potential for black women to become leaders in all fields of human endeavor, Slowe used her position at Howard as a dean, in conjunction with her professional organizations, to forward an agenda that honored black women's distinct potential. Slowe viewed Howard as an institution that could lead the way in harnessing the gifts of African American women and training them for the modern world.

CONCLUSION

African American women at Howard in the early twentieth century were participants and catalysts of debates about the role of black women in the modern world. Black women attending institutions of higher learning were equipped with skills and bodies of knowledge that were nearly unattainable for their mothers and most of their peers. Consequently, a realm of possibility opened to black women who desired to pursue professional aspirations. Black college-educated women began to branch out into other career fields. Their defiance of the status quo met with substantial backlash from Howard's administration. At Howard, however, African American women students had an ally in Slowe. Their talents and ambitions were nurtured by a woman who viewed higher education as a springboard to racial and gender equality. Slowe and her Howard students during the 1920s and 1930s built on a variety of political and social movements occurring during this era and formulated a unique political agenda that heralded gender equity as a top priority.

Joyce Hanson argues that most African American women activists of this era grounded their political standpoints in a "confidence in women's higher moral capacity, the power of educational advancement, Christian responsibility, and community activism."[41] These ideologies permitted race women to strategically advocate for African American women from the standpoint of black respectability. In her personal life, Slowe rejected gender and sexual mores and expectations by engaging in a romantic and intimate relationship with a woman. Professionally, she pushed back against a New Negro ethos that emphasized masculinity by openly contesting gender structures that limited the strivings and possibilities of African American women. Slowe's story sits on the axes of modernity, New Negro–ness, sexuality, and African American social structures, particularly gender norms and conventions.

Johnson arrived at Howard at the height of black women students' activism. Upon his arrival, he enacted policies that affirmed that, "as elsewhere on black college campuses, black women were subjected to strict rules and regulations regarding their behavior and movement on and off campus."[42] Slowe guided African American female Howard students in challenging the viability of these rules and regulations and openly decried the sexism that motivated their enforcement at such a "progressive" institution. She led Howard's women in confronting sexist attitudes and practices and in demanding that the progressive vision for Howard encompass racial and gender equality.

The personal relationships Howard women formed with Slowe and other members of the women's campus staff resulted in a community of highly educated women interrogating the validity of racial progress movements and organizations that did not critique gender inequality and the relegation of African American women to particular career paths and the domestic sphere. Women such as Thelma Preyer Bando, who became a dean of women and a departmental head, cited Slowe as an influence on her life and became the "modern" woman Slowe envisioned every African American woman could be. Bando was a leader as a student at Howard, and because of Slowe's efforts and the women's campus staff, she fulfilled the promise of African American possibility that New Negro womanhood offered to black women in higher education.

Howard women confronted issues of sexual harassment, a paternalistic and socially conservative administration and board of trustees, and the national image of Howard as a progressive institution. They organized and led discussions about the inseparability of women's rights from racial progress. Notably, New Negro women at Howard challenged the status quo of male dominance on campus through seeking leadership positions in campus clubs, taking classes in all disciplines, and initiating programming that examined the accomplishments of African American men and women. Howard administrators rejected many of the changes African American women students, faculty, and staff sought to institutionalize and rescinded many of the strides these women made in the early twentieth century. Howard female students and faculty and staff confronted a contentious space in which competing ideals for black women's public behavior intersected. The university, however, could not suppress the New Negro ethos that developed among Howard women. Lucy Diggs Slowe played an integral role in preparing Howard's New Negro women for making history as activists, professionals, intellectuals, and pioneers in numerous fields of human endeavor. Slowe thrived as a New Negro woman through transforming one of the premier black institutions of the twentieth century.

NOTES

1   Prior to Slowe's appointment in 1922, the current president of Howard University, J. Stanley Durkee, PhD, approved the establishment of the position "dean of women." From 1920 to June 1922, Helen Tuck served as acting dean of women at Howard. The role and responsibilities of the dean of women, however, were not solidified until the appointment of Slowe to the newly established administrative position.

2   Letter from Lucy D. Slowe to Dr. J. Stanley Durkee, May 31, 1922, in Lucy Diggs Slowe Papers, box 90-2, folder 51, Manuscript Division, Moorland-Spingarn Research Center, Howard University (hereinafter Slowe Papers).

3   Ibid.

4   A handful of scholars, including Linda Perkins, Sharon Harley, Rosalyn Terborg-Penn, and Carolyn Terry Bashaw, examine Slowe's life and career as an educator and an administrator. See Perkins, "Lucy Diggs Slowe"; Harley, Terborg-Penn, and Porter, *Afro-American Woman*; Bashaw, "Slowe, Lucy Diggs," 375–77. While Perkins, Harley, and Terborg-Penn approach Slowe as a dynamic historical subject, Bashaw focuses on Slowe as a pioneer for women in higher education. My exploration of Slowe differs in that I use her story to introduce how African American women uniquely engaged with New Negro womanhood.

5   My focus in this essay is African American women. Although other women of African descent were present at Howard during the 1920s and 1930s, the predominant constituency of women that matriculated at Howard throughout the Slowe years were African American women born and raised in the United States.

6   Hanchard, "Afro-Modernity," 247.

7   Bureau of the Census, *United States Census of Population: 1860*, 588; *United States Census of Population: 1890*, Table 22; and U.S. Department of Commerce, *Fifteenth Census of the United State*, Table 2, 99.

8   Howard University was central to political, intellectual, and cultural strivings of blacks locally, nationally, and globally. Its physical location in Washington, D.C., however, gave many Washingtonians a physical symbol of black progress during the New Negro era.

9 Logan, *Howard University.*

10 Howard, *Annual Report.*

11 Zora Neal Hurston, Thurgood Marshall, Alain Locke, Carter G. Woodson, E. Franklin Frazier, Kelly Miller, Sterling Brown, Patricia Roberts Harris, and James Farmer Sr. were among those who called Howard home at some point in their exemplary careers as leaders, writers, intellectuals, activists, innovators, and pioneers.

12 This gender structure embodied both intra- and interracial expectations for the roles of women in both private and public spheres. Although my focus is primarily on how African American men's and women's experiences differed at Howard University, it is important to note that gender ideology at Howard regarding the role of women in modern life often mirrored that of white institutional communities, particularly predominantly white colleges and universities.

13 Slowe, "Higher Education of Negro Women," 356.

14 During the early to mid-twentieth century, women students could not leave the campus without university-sanctioned supervision. A policy grounded in the widespread belief that the city was a dangerous place for a woman traveling alone, it restricted women's mobility and demanded that women's bodies be policed in the public sphere in a way to which their male counterparts were not subjected.

15 Perkins, "Lucy Diggs Slowe," 90.

16 "Dean Lucy D. Slowe," Slowe Papers, box 90-11, folder 207.

17 Bashaw, "Slowe, Lucy Diggs," 375–77.

18 Lester A. Walton, "Negro Women Seek to Better College Living," *The World,* April 25, 1926, in Slowe Papers, box 90-11, folder 207.

19 Lucy D. Slowe, "The College Woman and Her Community," opening speech presented at the National Association of College Women, Atlanta, Georgia, April 1934, in *Howard University Alumni Journal,* Slowe Papers, box 90-6, folder 120.

20 Lucy D. Slowe, "The Colored Girl Enters College," *Opportunity,* 278, Slowe Papers, box 90-6, folder 121.

21 Ibid.

22 Logan, *Howard University,* 170.

23 Lucy Diggs Slowe, *The Hilltop,* May 14, 1931.

24 Ibid.

25 Lucy Diggs Slowe, *The World,* April 25, 1926.

26 Lucy Diggs Slowe, "The Dean of Women in a Modern University," in *Howard University Alumni Journal,* December 1933, 10, Slowe Papers, box 90-6, folder 125.

27 "Speech by Lucy D. Slowe, Dean of Women, Howard University on the Occasion of the Cornerstone of the Women's Dormitories at Howard University, June 5, 1931," Slowe Papers, box 90-6, folder 123.

28 Slowe, "Higher Education of Negro Women," 334.

29 Ibid., 335.

30 Giddings, *When and Where I Enter,* 43.

31 Slowe, "Higher Education of Negro Women," 357.

32 McKinney, *Mordecai*.

33 Letter from Lucy D. Slowe to Dr. J. Stanley Durkee, May 31, 1922, Slowe Papers, box 90-2, folder 51.

34 The relationship between Slowe and Burrill is not entirely clear from an archival standpoint, but many scholars acknowledge the intimacy of their relationship as well as the historical context in which their relationship existed. Therefore *lesbian* or *same-sex* would not be an historically grounded term to use regarding what was a romantic relationship.

35 Lucy Diggs Slowe to Howard University Board of Trustees, April 26, 1933, Slowe Papers, box 90-2, folder 52.

36 Lucy Diggs Slowe, "Memorandum on the Mills Case," January 11, 1927, Slowe Papers, box 90-2, folder 51.

37 Bell-Scott, "To Keep My Self-Respect," 72.

38 Letter from Clarence Mills to Lucy Diggs Slowe, January 13, 1927, Slowe Papers, box 90-2, folder 51.

39 Slowe, "Memorandum on the Mills Case."

40 *National Association of Women's Deans and Advisors of Colored Schools Calls to Convention*, 1930, Slowe Papers, box 90-6, folder 120.

41 Hanson, *Mary McLeod Bethune.*

42 Perkins, "Lucy Diggs Slowe," 96.

BIBLIOGRAPHY

Bashaw, Carolyn Terry. "Slowe, Lucy Diggs. Dean of Women at Howard University (1922–1937)." In *Historical Dictionary of Women's Education in the United States,* edited by Linda Eisenman, 375–77. Westport, Conn.: Greenwood Press, 1998.

Bell-Scott, Patricia. "To Keep My Self-Respect: Dean Lucy Diggs Slowe's 1927 Memorandum on the Sexual Harassment of Black Women." *NWSA Journal* 9, no. 2 (1997): 70–76.

Bureau of the Census. *United States Census of Population: 1860, Population: Vol. 3, Population, by States.* Washington, D.C.: U.S. Department of the Interior.

———. *United States Census of Population: 1890, Population: Vol. 2, Population by States.* Washington, D.C.: U.S. Department of the Interior.

———. *United States Census of Population: 1930, Population, Vol. 4, Occupations, by States.* Washington, D.C.: U.S. Department of Commerce.

Giddings, Paula. *When and Where I Enter: The Impact of Black Women on Race and Sex in America.* New York: Bantam Books, 1984.

Hanchard, Michael. "Afro-Modernity: Temporality, Politics, and the African Diaspora." *Public Culture* 11, no. 1 (1999): 245–68.

Hanson, Joyce A. *Mary McLeod Bethune and Black Women's Political Activism.* Columbia: University of Missouri Press, 2003.

Harley, Sharon, Rosalyn Terborg-Penn, and Dorothy Porter. *The Afro-American Woman: Struggles and Images.* Baltimore: Black Classic Press, 1997.

Howard, Oliver O. *Annual Report of the President of Howard University*. Washington, D.C.: Howard University, 1869.

Logan, Rayford W. *Howard University: The First Hundred Years, 1867–1967*. New York: New York University Press, 1969.

Lucy Diggs Slowe Papers. Manuscript Division, Moorland-Spingarn Research Center, Howard University.

McKinney, Richard I. *Mordecai, the Man and His Message: The Story of Mordecai Wyatt Johnson*. Washington, D.C.: Howard University Press, 1997.

Perkins, Linda M. "Lucy Diggs Slowe: Champion of the Self-Determination of African-American Women in Higher Education." *Journal of Negro History* 81, no. 1 (1996): 89–104.

Slowe, Lucy Diggs. "The Higher Education of Negro Women." *Journal of Negro Education* 2 (July 1933): 352–58.

12

New Negro Marriages and the Everyday Challenges of Upward Mobility

ANASTASIA CURWOOD

We might be forgiven for thinking of New Negroes as merely race men and women, with no concerns save those that might advance the race. But New Negroes were also complex human beings, with identities as husbands, wives, and other family members. Just as it is important to expand the conversation on New Negroes geographically and beyond the arts and letters, scholars must reckon with the full subjectivity of black historical actors in the early twentieth century. Private life, through the lens of marriage, documents both New Negroes' powerful visions of the marriages that they hoped would advance the race and their individual struggles to realize those marriages.

One defining aspect of the New Negro moment was the contested meaning of gender roles within class identity. New Negroes felt the pull of the old politics of respectability, which had been one strategy to combat racism, mixed with the desire to remake a modern black middle class that dealt more frankly with both politics and sexuality. Although matters of taste and culture divided black elites, one thing on which many middle-class or aspiring middle-class New Negroes agreed was the need to distance themselves from the behaviors of poor and working-class black people. Gender roles were a key differentiator of class status for New Negroes. Nowhere was this more pronounced than in tensions over spouses' roles in marriage. Specifically, the ideal that men would make enough money to be family breadwinners while women would inspire and support New Negro manhood collided with the reality of New Negro women's own career and activism ambitions. Furthermore, as the 1920s gave way to the Great Depression, uncertain employment, low wages, and women's participation in paid labor chipped away at the ideal of a male breadwinner. However, many New Negroes clung to the male breadwinner ideal and predicated racial status on gender role hierarchy.

That the New Negroes saw class and gender identities as central to the racial project has begun to be incorporated into scholarship of the era. However, the realities of living those identities, on the level of marriage relationships, are far less explored. In this essay, I examine the ideal of male breadwinning among New Negroes and then turn to the realities: I describe a marriage between two upwardly mobile spouses who confronted divergent visions of gender roles in marriage. My grandparents Sarah and James Curwood, who have left evidence of their marital discussions in hundreds of letters, were New Negroes because they participated in the aggressive racial self-definition—his as a cosmopolitan male breadwinner and hers as a professional, financially independent race woman— that characterize these historical actors.[1] Like other New Negroes, the Curwoods were caught up in a movement toward self-determination through racial pride and upward mobility. But, simultaneously, they experienced painful negotiations over evolving gender roles. Their divergent expectations are particularly revealing in that they embody the competing tensions over husbands' and wives' roles in the early twentieth century. The story of their marriage shows the impact of cultural expectations within the most intimate of human relationships, an impact that they were certainly not alone in feeling.

HUSBANDS, BREADWINNING, AND EVERYDAY COUPLES

Gender role ideals for marriage conflicted with each other and were difficult to implement—and that left individual couples to work out the marital divisions of labor for themselves. Most tried to maintain a male breadwinning model, especially if they saw themselves as leaders within the race: Marie Brown Frazier herself had given up her career as a writer to be a proper faculty wife to the sociologist E. Franklin Frazier, and Fisk president Charles S. Johnson's wife spent much of her time worrying about and buttressing her husband's reputation.[2] However, especially after 1929, everyone also had to consider economic reality and the individual situations of each partner. Some husbands could not find or hold jobs that paid a family wage; some wives strongly desired a career or had skills that could bring in significant income. Thus conforming to the male breadwinner ideal was often difficult. Even for members of the middle class, financial concerns arose from the common expectation that husbands had to be the sole breadwinners.

Marital problems often arose when men did not fulfill their economic role or when wives took on too much economic independence for their husbands' liking. Then and now, finances and financial trouble were extremely frequent as sources of conflict within marriage. Amy Jacques Garvey, who carefully outlined men's and women's responsibilities in her *Negro World* writings, was deeply disappointed when her husband, Marcus Garvey, failed to provide adequately for her and her children. Moreover, as the marriage went on and the couple's children encountered medical problems, his financial instability had devastating effects on the family's health and well-being. Garvey had, in part, married her not only to manage the household's income but to help him oversee the Universal Negro Improvement Association as well. In practice, this working partnership caused considerable stress for Amy as she struggled to make financial ends meet while taking orders from a husband who tolerated no dispute of his authority.[3]

The Garveys were not the only couple who had to work at maintaining a gendered division of labor. The New York journalist and diplomat Lester Walton was determined that both his wife and daughter would always be able to rely on a husband as a provider. He himself knew that this could be very difficult. In 1930, he was between jobs and struggling to support his family. Encouragement came from his own mother. "*Remember this,*" she wrote, "you are the bread winner [*sic*] and would be most miserable should you have to depend on Gladys and the girls for help."[4] Several years later, Walton sought to make sure that his daughter's husband would be able to provide financially for her. When his daughter Gladys the younger ("Sister") unexpectedly fell in love and got engaged in 1937, his first concern was that her fiancé (Charles) was able to support a wife.

After receiving two airmail letters from the starry-eyed couple at his diplomatic post in Liberia, Walton telegraphed, "I feel it is my duty to learn more about a prospective son-in-law before conscientiously giving approval. Is he in a position to support a wife? Is he steadily employed with an assured income or is he building air castles? If he can provide you with a comfortable home of his own I do not oppose marriage." However, Walton was not at first convinced that this was the case. When he was told that Sister's fiancé sold class pins, he wondered how he was supporting himself during summer vacations.[5] In response, Walton's wife and Charles sent a telegram that was essentially a résumé and description of business prospects. Gladys wrote, "You should know that I would not give my consent to Sister's marrying unless I had proof that Charles could support her[.] He is connected with Loverture jewelry manufacturing company of New York of which Kenneth Bright that owns Lafayette Property is President[.] He is not selling pins during time schools are closed but already has contracts for graduation pins from schools in his territory[.] You need have no fear for your daughter's future at any time[.]" Charles, Sister's fiancé, wrote in the same telegram, "Aware of the implications of marriage[.] Love Gladys too much to take unnecessary risks[.]" He went on to give the occupations of his parents: his mother was head of the English department at a high school in Houston, whereas his father was a school principal in the same city. He also described his own educational background (Fisk College) and his previous employment history with the Works Progress Administration.[6] In response to this satisfactory information, Lester Walton gave his consent. He cabled back his instructions for how to word the wedding invitations, along with a list of those to be invited; it included the Beardens, the

Du Boises, the Powells, Mary McLeod Bethune, and other prominent African Americans.[7] To him, the top priority was to marry his daughter off to an appropriately middle-class man, with the appropriate accoutrements for the wedding.

In some cases where husbands were able to fulfill the breadwinning role, problems arose when husbands and wives differed over how much paid work wives should do. The actress Fredi Washington and her husband Lawrence Brown hit a snag early in their marriage when Washington was filming on location in Jamaica. The producers of *Run Little Chillun,* a play in which she had already starred in New York, sent her a telegram saying that the show would open in Boston immediately upon her return. Anticipating Brown's dismay, she wrote, "Steady your nerves now, I've got to tell you something which I'm afraid you're not going to like so well but I'm in it and there's nothing I can do about it since it involves my word and my honor." As she explained, she felt an obligation to the rest of the play's cast and crew to appear in the show because their sacrifices had advanced her career: "I owe something to those people who worked so faithfully in the show last season. Sometimes they only received two or three dollars a week when I received my full salary."[8] Although Brown's response does not survive, Washington's next letter to him indicates that he was indeed very angry. Apparently, he asked her why the show needed her and could not use another actress and said that distance could ruin marriages. He also chided her for making a decision without him, saying that he would not do the same to her. Washington remained steadfast. She reminded him that she had signed a contract for the show before they were married, and as for his fear that their relationship would suffer from the distance, she replied, "I expect your love and mine to be strong enough, enduring enough to bring us out on top. Its [sic] only lukewarm love that spoils with the slightest opportunity." Finally, she reminded him that she would have plenty of time on her hands to spend with him after this final obligation. Cleverly, she cast her actions in terms of her own personal integrity and desire to do what was best for their marriage as well as herself.[9]

At least two of Zora Neale Hurston's three marriages and several romances ended because her career ambitions were her first priority. Hurston deeply loved Herbert Sheen, a medical student in Chicago, but once she exchanged vows in May 1927, she second-guessed her decision. She spent a scant three-day honeymoon before starting back to work and sending Sheen back to Chicago. Hurston was interested in her writing and research activities, not in fulfilling the role of a doctor's wife. They divorced in 1931. Many years later, Hurston wrote to her ex-husband that she believed marriage to be a protective institution for mothers and children and that she had had no desire for this protection when they were married.[10] Hurston also appears to have been more invested in her research and writing activities than in the financial stability that marriage might bring;

though her education and occupation made her middle class, she was poor at the end of her life.

Hurston fell in love again several years later, with Percival Punter, whom she met in 1932 and began to see romantically in 1935. He was a twenty-three-year-old graduate student, and Hurston was forty-four (although she claimed to be ten years younger). Her relationship with Punter was more passionate than it had been with Sheen, but if anything, she experienced an even greater tension between her career ambitions and his demands on her. Punter was heavily invested in the masculine ideal of the provider and, as Hurston put it, "stood on his own two feet so firmly that he reared back." On one memorable occasion, he became irately offended because Hurston offered to lend him a quarter and thus inadvertently insulted his manhood, implying that he could not "do for a woman." On another, he walked out in anger when Hurston had to cut a date short because of a literary obligation. He pleaded with Hurston to stop working and become his housewife and was mystified when she would not. In turn, she could not fathom why Punter could not see that she could love him and continue her career at the same time. "My career balked at the completeness of his ideal," she recalled. "I really wanted to conform, but it was impossible. To me there was no conflict. My work was one thing, and he was all the rest. But, I could not make him see that. Nothing must be in my life but himself."[11] Hurston took several leaves of absence from the relationship, only to return each time to find that the conundrum still remained. Eventually the two lovers split permanently in 1944.[12]

In contrast, some women willingly discontinued their own careers. Isabel Washington Powell, Fredi Washington's sister, was pursuing a career in show business when she met her husband, Adam Clayton Powell. She had been a chorus girl at the popular Harlem nightclub Connie's Inn, had a lead in a Broadway show, and, in 1929, had costarred with Bessie Smith in *St. Louis Blues* (she played Smith's husband's mistress). She then had moved up to lead chorus girl at the famous Cotton Club, where she met Powell in 1930. At that point, she was offered a leading part in the traveling company for *Showboat* but turned it down because of her marriage. Although Powell left her in 1944 for another woman, Mrs. Powell claimed that she had no regrets about giving up her career for marriage and had had an exciting life.[13]

However, some couples discovered that blending responsibilities was a practical way to make ends meet and allow each spouse to fulfill his or her desires. Marriages could resemble a cooperative economic effort. One striking example of such an arrangement was the marriage of Robert and Katherine Stewart Flippin. The Flippins adjusted gender roles to make their marriage work economically—not only for survival but also to create a respectable middle-class lifestyle in their own generation. The Flippins married during the Great Depression and were forced to grapple with economic necessity. While Robert, a college graduate, was underemployed in a series of service jobs, Katherine found steady work in a department store. As newlyweds, the couple lived in an apartment owned by Katherine's mother and shared it with Robert's mother. Robert Flippin did not seem to fear for his manhood when the young couple moved into his mother-in-law's house. The couple simply seemed to see this fact as an indication of the difficulties that black people had finding housing in San Francisco. Also, Robert owed his career advancement to Katherine's connections: his job as director of the Booker T. Washington Community Service Center was facilitated by his relationship with Katherine's mother, a founder of the center.

Katherine's breadwinning role and her family's help in finding a prestigious job for Robert indicate both the importance of extended family relations and the problems that educated black people faced in finding full employment. Furthermore, their material needs caused the Flippins to place emphasis on egalitarianism and on mutual, complementary contributions. Among their social elite peer group in San Francisco, Katherine's education and civic activities were as salient as those of her husband, Robert. Also, the Flippins did not have children or confront the additional financial burden that childrearing would have imposed. It is unclear whether they avoided having children by choice or whether they were not able to have them. The fact of childlessness could well have affected Katherine's choice to work outside the home.[14]

Rather than attempt to fit their lives into a rigid economic template, the Flippins seemed to turn financial necessity into an opportunity for growth for themselves, their relationship, and their community. Their joint community service raised their status in the eyes of the community. Katherine's paid labor during the 1930s gave Robert the resources to advance his own career, thus increasing the couple's stature in the 1940s. Throughout the rest of their marriage, they continued the pattern of dual careers that they developed over the first two decades. In some respects, their married lives reflected a pattern of spousal cooperation in community work that had been more common at the turn of the century.[15]

JAMES AND SARAH THOMAS CURWOOD

Sarah and James Curwood's struggles with upward mobility were fraught with conflicting ideals of husbands' and wives' roles. While James wanted to be the sole breadwinner and decision maker, Sarah's ambition and the couple's precarious financial position stymied his efforts. James was likely attracted to Sarah because of her solid middle-class family, and the higher status that her light skin might have signified for him, but she did not fit the ideal of a helpmate wife.

The Curwoods probably entered their marriage in 1936 with what they thought were common goals for their socioeconomic advancement. They sought to serve as exemplars for their race through designing a comfortable middle-class lifestyle at home and through launching their well-educated children into the world. Unfortunately, structural factors—such as James's lack of earning power—exposed the fact that the Curwoods differed bitterly over how to prioritize these goals. To James, these goals were to be accomplished through his financial support of the family and his masculine authority over his wife and children. Sarah thought she could accomplish their dreams through her three kinds of service: to her family, to her race, and to her own self-sufficiency.[16] Sarah intended to advance her own career at the same time that she gave adequate, but only part-time, care to her husband and children. When the Curwoods married, these differences in the means to an end seemed small or even nonexistent. As the marriage went on, however, the fault lines of gender and work divided them.

James and Sarah were two very different individuals from two very different worlds. Sarah was the more middle-class partner and the one who actually inhabited the world of black intellectuals—a world of education and learned life. Whereas James was an autodidact who read voraciously and developed a library of the New Negro thinkers of his time, it was Sarah who met them as an intellectual equal. While James shared E. Franklin Frazier's contempt for striving wives,[17] Sarah saw through this prescription. She knew from personal experience that those striving wives were crucial to race advancement. James's resentment of Sarah's education and ambition and her resentment of his stifling desire for her to be an obedient housewife did tremendous damage to their relationship.

Some of the damage came from the couple's inability to reconcile their different class backgrounds. The Curwoods embodied the fact that intraracial differences profoundly affected the public and private lives of African Americans. First, the couple differed in age. Sarah was born in 1916 and was nineteen at the time she met James. James was born in or around 1908 and was twenty-seven. Second, they grew up in different areas of the country: Sarah in a German immigrant neighborhood in Binghamton, New York, and James in Houston, Texas. Third, in their different worlds, Sarah was familiar with and friendly with white people as neighbors and classmates, whereas most of James's contact with white people came from serving them. Fourth, Sarah had considerably lighter skin than James, much as other middle-class black wives had lighter skin than their husbands. Finally, and very importantly, they were from different socioeconomic classes. Sarah's family of origin was middle class, and James's was poor or lower working class.

This class difference is evident in the availability of archival material for each partner. Sarah's life, especially before she met James, is copiously documented in comparison with that of her husband, who left behind very little about his origins. Sarah Ethel Thomas was born January 23, 1916, in the middle-class home of her maternal grandparents in Binghamton, New York. Sarah described her family of origin by remembering, "We were the 10%," alluding to Du Bois's Talented

Tenth.[18] Her grandparents, George and Ella Nora Coakley Dorsey, had met in Washington, D.C., and moved to Utica, New York, before settling in Binghamton. Once there, they had moved from a mostly Irish and black section of the town into the German immigrant neighborhood, and they had bought a house with weekly payments. There her grandfather and his brother worked as chefs in hotels and managed their own catering business. Sarah's mother, Sarah ("Sadie") Elizabeth Dorsey, was the second of George Dorsey's five children.

Maurice Thomas, Sarah's father, descended from a family in southern Ohio. His father had been a racehorse timer and a cobbler but had died when Maurice was two years old. After high school, Maurice realized that his only employment in Ohio would be menial. He moved east and tried to earn money for medical school. He met and married Sadie Dorsey, instead, and put his accumulated savings into establishing a middle-class household. Eventually he became a building contractor. The Thomases enjoyed a stable economic situation, thanks to Maurice's business and real estate investments, his ownership of a fleet of taxicabs, and his new position working in a unionized job for American Railway Express. He was able to spend significant amounts of time with his family because he worked an overnight shift. Sadie, who had had three years of high school, stayed at home and enjoyed small luxuries: three diamond rings and a fur coat.[19]

When Sarah was born, Maurice and Sadie already had two daughters: six-year-old Elizabeth ("Betty") and four-year-old Elnora ("Nony"). Sadie bore Sarah in her parents' house because the house that Maurice had built for his young family had been damaged by racially motivated arson. The house had burned just before the young family was to move in. As Sarah recalled, "Mother refused to live in the 'damaged' house because she did not like things that had been repaired and also because she feared that the fire, which had been set, might be evidence of anti-Negro feelings." Maurice sold it at a profit, and the family bought another. This time they acquired the new home through white friends Maurice knew through his real estate dealings, although when the Thomases moved in, the white neighbors on either side moved out. The white neighbors who remained when the Thomases moved into the new neighborhood eventually became friendly.[20]

Though they endured harassment from whites and isolation from other black people, the Thomas family did enjoy a supportive extended family and friends. Guests often visited. Thanksgiving included copious amounts of food, and Christmas meant many gifts and guests. Sarah and her sisters were the only black children in the same school that their mother had attended. Outside of school, Sarah participated in many extracurricular activities, including a Catholic Girl Scout troop. She and her sisters had plenty of friends, many of them Jewish, inside and outside of school.[21]

Sarah's parents demanded proper decorum but offered conflicting advice on the role of proper middle-class femininity. On one hand, her father had demanded "ladylike behavior" from her.[22] Sarah's mother, Sadie, however, demonstrated autonomy and strong views to her daughter. While Sadie seemingly surrendered power to her husband, whom Sarah acknowledged as strong and controlling, she actually combined deference and self-assertion. Her husband was an atheist and frowned on her attending church, so she brought a member of the church into her home for regular study sessions. Her husband discouraged her from voting, but she joined the Woman's Christian Temperance Union and Margaret Sanger's birth control movement. She owned boxes full of the Little Blue Books from the Haldeman-Julius publishing house in Girard, Kansas.[23] Sadie's Little Blue Books testify to her active and independent interest in radical politics.

Maurice Thomas died in 1930, when Sarah was fourteen. He had lost much of his wealth in the financial crash of 1929 so that even had he lived, the family's financial status still would have deteriorated. When Maurice died, Sadie and Sarah's older sisters showed Sarah that "ladies" could also be self-sufficient, provided they were educated. Sadie decided that Sarah must finish school. Nony and Betty, "who had finished high school the previous year, gave up plans for college, took domestic jobs, partly live-in, and supported mother and me." At first, Sadie worked for pay, too. The sisters became concerned, however, because Sarah, who could not cook herself a proper meal, usually arrived home from school to an empty house. Therefore, Sarah wrote later, "my sisters decided it was wiser for mother to remain home." The sisters were compensated financially, with legal ownership of the family home.[24] In the meantime, Sarah performed some household duties, such as shopping for food. During this period, she and her mother became very close.

Thus Sadie Thomas started Sarah on the path of education and taught her the value of female self-sufficiency. Sadie doubtless wanted to ensure that her youngest daughter would not have to work in domestic service. When Sarah received a Cornell scholarship, Sadie must have been delighted and relieved. Stephanie Shaw has documented the childrearing practices that parents of early-twentieth-century black professional women employed. These parents wanted their daughters to acquire education that would provide alternatives to service work. Chief among these was instilling a culture of achievement, self-confidence, and community responsibility.[25] Bart Landry agrees that it was a feature of middle-class black women's culture—a culture that they themselves designed and transmitted to each other—that pushed Sarah into professional work and shaped her desire to work for her family, her career, and civil rights. As Landry found, the higher the class status within the black middle class, the more likely it was that wives worked.[26]

Sadie's sacrifice of Nony and Betty's education paid off in Sarah's academic success. Graduating as valedictorian of her high school class, Sarah earned a scholarship to Cornell University from the Harvard Club of Binghamton. Sarah was well aware that this achievement came on the backs of her sisters. She also knew that, for a respectable black woman, femininity encompassed self-sufficiency. Her enrollment at Cornell was welcome as the symbol of how well she had utilized her costly academic achievement and as the means to educated autonomy in the future.

At Cornell, Sarah had her first significant contact with other African Americans besides members of her family. Many of the other black students at Cornell were graduate students from the South, and Sarah was startled by the hatred that one of her peers felt toward white people. For the first time, she was aware of her membership in an African American group. Becoming aware of racial issues, she began to take an interest in economics and sociology. She also began to think of her conduct and achievements as a reflection not only of herself or her family but also of her responsibility toward other members of her race. Prejudiced teachers, the denial of a scholarship she merited, and the request that she enter a sorority through a back door all made her conscious of racial prejudice directed toward her. Her private life also changed. At home in Binghamton, the four women in Sarah's family had typically done their hair together. But at Cornell, Sarah feared that using a hot comb would create an odor and offend the white families with whom she boarded because she was barred from the women's dormitories. She was forced simply to brush and oil her hair until she went home on vacations.[27]

James Curwood's early childhood was very different, with less money, education, and status. From an early age, he came into contact with white people as their subordinate. Little is known of his origins. He was born in Houston, sometime around 1908, to a woman named Ellen (maiden name unknown) and an absentee father. He was possibly christened Edward Bonny, and it is not known whether this last name belonged to his biological father or his mother. After Edward was born, Ellen married a man whose last name was Rasmus. She bore seven more children. When he was about fourteen, James rode the train north to Chicago and somehow found his way to North Adams, Massachusetts. There he became friendly with the family of Charles Arnum, a Civil War veteran from the Fifty-Fourth Massachusetts Regiment.[28]

Somewhere between Houston and North Adams, James forged a new, more northern and urban identity, that of James Lawrence Curwood. He recast his name to be nearly identical to that of a popular author at the time, James Oliver Curwood, because James aspired to be a writer. He invested time and effort in remaking himself into a handsome, cosmopolitan, middle-class gentleman. The "man" in gentleman was operative: to complete the picture, he sought a proper lady to be his wife. A refined woman in his life would, perhaps, prove to other men that he had arrived.[29]

From North Adams, James found his way to Ithaca, where he found work within student housing in some sort of service capacity. Before meeting Sarah, James had not yet completed the eighth grade. After meeting her, he moved to Rome, New York, for a year and completed his junior high school diploma while working two jobs.[30] He was determined to acquire an educated, middle-class identity—emulating the leisure class for whom he worked. His behavior echoes the theories of Thorstein Veblen: realizing that the appearance of wealth in itself has the power to confer honor and respectability, those in the class of domestic servants (whom we call service workers) sometimes emulate the actions of their masters. Actual wealth is not available to servants, but the cultural markers—material goods and the conspicuous leisure of women—are.[31] James knew how to present a respectable image, even if he did not have the actual wealth it represented. Key to this image was his extensive library. He owned first editions of such New Negro classics as Alain Locke's *The New Negro,* Charles S. Johnson's *Patterns of Negro Segregation,* Horace Cayton and George Mitchell's *Black Workers and the New Unions,* Gunnar Myrdal's *An American Dilemma,* and Otto Klineberg's *Characteristics of the American Negro,* along with later editions of Du Bois's *The Souls of Black Folk, Dusk of Dawn,* and *Black Reconstruction in America* and James Weldon Johnson's *Black Manhattan* and *The Life and Times of Frederick Douglass.*[32] He also subscribed to *New Masses.* He was very protective of his books: when he went into the army in 1944, Sarah had to write to him to ask how to unlock his bookcase so she could look at the volumes in it.[33]

Sarah and James had met in January 1935, probably at a meeting of the black student group the Booker T. Washington Club, on the Cornell campus.[34] Sarah was a student; James was a servant. When Sarah met James, who was eight years older than she, she found him "interesting." The two met again at a club meeting the following month, a delightful evening for Sarah. They danced, an experience that Sarah described as "heaven," and James bought her candy. After that, to Sarah's happiness, he began to court her strongly and call her often, sometimes twice or three times a day. They attended the theater together, and he often walked her home in the evenings. The two even became ill at the same time and were in the Cornell infirmary together, on different floors. Visitors relayed their messages back and forth. By the end of March, they were in love, and James at least was thinking that they would marry.[35]

The fact that the older, well-traveled James was on a journey to remake himself and to leave behind his poor Texas roots interacted dramatically with Sarah's youth, her established middle-class identity and light skin, and her lack of broad experience. James and Sarah went their separate ways during the summer. He traveled to his adopted family and hometown of North Adams, Massachusetts. Sarah went home to Binghamton. After summer 1935, Sarah returned to Cornell for her junior year. James moved to Rome, New York, for school and work at a car dealership. He lived in a boardinghouse. Sarah would sometimes write to him on lined notepaper while in class, pretending to take notes. After Sarah's junior year ended in June 1936, the two made hasty plans to marry. Sarah joined James in Rome, where she expected to set up house with him and then commute to a substitute teaching job for the rest of the summer. She had begun to envision staying in Rome with her new husband and not returning to Cornell. The couple married on June 20, 1936. None of Sarah's family were present at the chapel when they married; Sarah notified her mother via a telegram that evening. Although the couple tried to live together in Rome right away, James's financial difficulties and Sarah's subsequent illness quickly made it evident that the couple was not ready to set up a household. Sarah went home to Binghamton. While Sarah had been prepared to leave Cornell, she decided instead to finish her senior year. The couple would be reunited in Boston in summer 1937, after her graduation.

Perhaps because of their respective vantage points—Sarah's middle-class upbringing in a mostly white neighborhood and James's seeming awe of black people who had personal and physical capital—the appearance of respectability was less consuming for Sarah than it was for James. Indeed, in some ways, Sarah's middle-class family intrigued him. She observed that "many of the things I took for granted, things that my father had done, [material] things that my mother had, my husband viewed as constant prods for him also to not only achieve, but to surpass." Whereas her father had given her mother modest, living plants on her birthday and their anniversary, James would give huge bunches of cut flowers to Sarah on every conceivable holiday. Later on, she would have to find money in the household budget to cover his delinquent accounts at the florist.[36]

On the part of Sarah's family, no evidence of conflict over her choice of mate survives, but it is clear that James's financial problems embarrassed Sarah herself. In summer 1936, Sarah's mother, sisters, and extended family subsidized the new couple after they married hastily, Sarah became ill, and the couple found themselves without enough money to set up their household. James found a job as a butler for a Jewish family in the Jamaica Plain neighborhood in Boston, but he continued to struggle to make ends meet. Sarah, facing the inquiries of family, continued to push James to repay his debts so that they could set up a household together. "Aunt Blanche is wondering what kind of husband I have that sends me home to be supported by mother when I am ill," she wrote, and then, "I may also add that Mother expects you will help me with my expenses at school this year and I can't tell her you have nothing to help with." When her mother discovered a large unpaid bill in one day's mail, Sarah went so far as to refuse to write letters until James proved to her that he was making payments on the debt. She hoped that by repaying his debts and helping with expenses, he would regain "some standing" in her family's eyes.[37]

James and Sarah Curwood also encountered the effects of colorism within their intimate lives. Like the Garveys mentioned earlier in this essay, and discussed by Ula Taylor in *The Veiled Garvey*, though in a less prominent way, the Curwoods were concerned with racial advancement. Unlike the Garveys, their goal was assimilation, not black nationalism or separatism. But they held in common with the Garveys a recognition that authentic blackness was politically ideal. For example, when Sarah wrote to her husband about a summer job at the Boston Urban League in 1937, she wrote excitedly that the director was "a real brown skin."[38] It is clear that Sarah saw this as a good thing, that the director's racial allegiances were on the correct side of the struggle.

However, within their own marriage, the Curwoods did not discuss skin color. Within the couple, Sarah was a light tan color and James a medium brown. When Sarah's darker maternal grandfather had married her light maternal grandmother from a prominent Washington, D.C., family, the couple had left Washington because her grandfather would not fit in with her grandmother's social set there. Still, James might well have thought that Sarah's light skin solidified his ascendance to the ranks of the middle class. In letters, James often extolled Sarah's beauty, describing how he found her features and her picture enticing. It was important to James to marry a beautiful woman, and that beauty was connected to the color of her skin.

In his letters, especially the early ones, James often alluded to his admiration of Sarah's beauty and his lack of social position. Several months after they met, he showed her picture to other residents of his boardinghouse, one of whom reportedly said, "You can see that she is a fine girl." In the same letter, he anxiously predicted that "there is more than a little liklihood [sic] that you will meet among your associates, some one nearer your equal socially than I am, one you can respect as well as love, for it takes a combination of things to evoke true happiness."[39] Two days later, he was explaining his lack of material achievement, saying, "You have not known the man I used to be, but all my earlier life was spent in the clouds, that accounts for my being so far behind now." Not long after this anxious letter, he was again praising her beauty, delighting in the fact that "those lovely lips are mine to kiss, and that beautiful hair is mine to play with." Sarah, by her own description, had "good hair." He wrote, "I think I have told you—I love your hair. It's so, oh, I don't know, It's just sweet, and pretty, and soft, and, long."[40]

Although little direct evidence exists of how Sadie felt about James, she did seem to worry about his lack of financial independence. Sarah herself recalled that James was constantly competing with Sarah's family of origin in terms of class status—he bought them grandiose and expensive gifts.[41] Importantly, no correspondence survives that directly addresses their class differences in terms of color. This suggests that the fact was so unremarkable, or so unmentionable, that it went unspoken.

The middle-class respectability that Sarah took for granted was crucial to James, who took advantage of every indicator of middle-class status available to him, such as marriage to Sarah. His ambition helps to explain his intense dislike of her getting a job and his lack of imagination regarding her potential career choices. He tried to get her to cook and clean and do little else, provoking conflict that emerged in the early years of their marriage. Sarah came from a family that

James thought would have taught her the proper roles of femininity. But in his eyes, she seemed not to understand the importance of a dependent role. In fact, though she protested otherwise, she valued her career development at least as much as her role as wife and helpmate.

On the surface, Sarah and James shared similar values, especially their enjoyment of and belief in the importance of learning and literature, their self-definition as middle class, and their hopes for racial advancement. In a journal entry of 1968, Sarah remembered the pretense and the reality of their relationship:

> My upbringing made me an ideal wife for my husband. What he viewed mainly as my acceptance of his greater years and wider experience was in reality my acceptance of masculine superiority, especially in the field of family support and decision making affecting the welfare for the family. I was well versed in many of the womanly arts . . . I could sew very well, bake, cook, play the piano, entertain properly. My liberal arts education had equipped me well to become a volunteer worker in various fields and I did so. But slowly it dawned on me that though I was the type of wife my husband said he wanted, in reality I was a disaster.[42]

What she meant by "disaster" was that James got more than he bargained for. She was ambitious, as was he, but their ambitions did not match. Sarah sought to contribute to her race through her work outside the home in economics and sociology. James sought to contribute to his race through his identity as a respectable New Negro in a solid, middle-class household and his full participation in the American dream. Like other New Negroes, James thought that this dream had to rest on patriarchal authority.

In spring 1937, Sarah graduated from Cornell, and James lost the butler's job that he had held for the past year. He found new employment at the Roseledge estate, in Cohasset, Massachusetts, an hour from Boston by train. Although Sarah had moved to Boston, the two now lived at least an hour away from each other. They once again stayed in contact via mail and met once a week on James's day off. Now that Sarah had graduated, the couple had to decide how to make the gendered balance of power work within their marriage. James's absences for most of each week helped make the summer a rocky one. Up until now, the Curwoods had lived together only in their imaginations and had seen each other little during the year. Sarah had still been at school, a state of affairs that had been nonnegotiable and that James accepted as a matter of course. Now Sarah took a volunteer job at the South End settlement house run by the Boston Urban League.

James was unhappy with this new job because Sarah was associating with men he did not know, she had represented herself as single to get the job, and she was not spending enough time cleaning their room at a nearby boardinghouse.

He seemed uncomfortable with this career-oriented job and stated that he actually preferred that she work in domestic service if she needed additional money. To justify her work at South End House to her husband, Sarah cleverly did so in terms of service and not in terms of money. "I want to spend my life in bettering the race," she wrote, "i.e. bettering possibilities of the race—spiritually, economically, politically, etc.—I now have a chance to work on the economic aspect; later with you on the spiritual."[43] She very likely used a similar justification when she took a position at a progressive, interracial nursery school. In James's view, her working for the betterment of the community was more palatable than working to advance her career. She also refrained from pointing out that James's income could not support both of them. While engaging in the sorts of activities that her husband came to accept as more permissible (getting more education and teaching), she was indeed increasing her economic power. But her efforts did not protect James from his insecurity. Her career moves became less attractive to James as his illness and alcoholism eroded his own earning power.

Conversely, James's letters indicate his growing anxiety. The more professional autonomy Sarah claimed, the more he worried about her contact with other people, especially men, and he constantly reassured her of his own fidelity, of his eyes for no one but her, and of his awe of her beauty. He wanted to control Sarah's life totally, and he seemed to live in fear that he would lose her if she engaged in activities unrelated to him or outside their home. James was unhappy about her independence. At least once over the summer, he believed that the marriage was over and made preparations to break up with her. The Curwoods did stay married, however. Throughout the 1940s, Sarah steadily advanced her career in early childhood education, while James attempted to run a home cleaning business. But he also drank heavily, gambled compulsively, behaved abusively, and was hospitalized several times for psychiatric illness, making it difficult for the business to succeed. By December 1949, the cleaning business had gone bankrupt. James committed suicide, leaving Sarah a single mother of their by then two children.

At the same time that the Curwoods' experiences show the power of the male breadwinner ideal, so, too, do they show that wives' competing claims to public careers caused no small amount of conflict. As a case in point, James paid a price for his expectations regarding Sarah's behavior. Aspiring to become a bona fide member of the middle class, James was more aware of a white model of middle-class women's leisure, for he had little firsthand contact with professional black women. He was baffled and dismayed by his ambitious, career-oriented wife. Whereas her ambitions were part of an emerging model of New Negro womanhood—one that conceptualized black women as egalitarian political and economic partners in the modern race—James dreamed of white upper-class culture in which women were allowed, even required, to stay at home. In his imagination, and in the imaginations of many New Negro thinkers, a wife was to maintain a serene, sparkling home with hot dinner waiting on the table for her husband when he returned from his well-paying job.[44] But, as Sarah herself wrote in her memoir, she was a disaster at subservient domesticity. Ideals differed, and reality did not match either set of ideals in the Curwood marriage. The best way to avoid conflict, Sarah found, was to get James to comply with her wishes if she framed them in terms of a project for bettering the race.

In the realm of race work, too, James faced a double bind. On one hand, he needed Sarah's credentials to boost his own status and give him access to the world of middle-class New Negroes he idolized, as evidenced by his book collection. But on the other hand, he pushed back against the idea of women's public roles and agreed with many of his New Negro peers that he should be the thinker, writer, and earner in his home. He wanted to emulate those public intellectuals who had maintained a male breadwinning model, such as E. Franklin Frazier and Charles S. Johnson. But James did not have the luxury of such an arrangement. He was in the ironic position of gaining middle-class status through his wife, without being able to live his middle-class dream of patriarchy. The Curwoods thus confronted their divergent versions of reality and experienced anger and disappointment. In the Curwoods' case, the sharp disjuncture between Sarah's and James's visions of the responsibility of their family to their race, and the pressure caused by their inability as a couple to live up to gendered ideals, was never resolved. Instead, the marriage ended in the tragedy of James's suicide, which left Sarah a single mother.

The Curwoods' story is a vivid illustration of how the New Negroes' middle-class ideals collided with changing gender roles. Whereas some New Negroes saw upward mobility as contingent on a male breadwinner ideal, some New Negro women challenged such gendered expectations. The disjuncture between class and gender expectations could, as the Curwoods demonstrated, lead to conflict on the level of personal relationships. This history of private life exposes a major fissure in the construction of New Negro identities.

NOTES

1   Sarah Thomas Curwood Papers, Schlesinger Library on the History of Women in America, Radcliffe Institute, Cambridge, Mass. (hereinafter Curwood Papers).

2   Nell Painter interview with Marie Brown Frazier, 1975. Nell Irvin Painter Papers, Special Collections, Duke University Library.

3   Garvey, *Philosophies and Opinions*, 1023; Garvey, *Garvey and Garveyism*, 162, 164–68; Taylor, *Veiled Garvey*, 90, 189–90.

4   Mrs. [first name unknown] Walton to Lester A. Walton, July 4, 1931. Lester A.

Walton Papers, box 1, folder 9, Schomburg Center for Research in Black Culture, New York Public Library (hereinafter Walton Papers).

5   Lester A. Walton telegraph to Gladys ["Sister"] Walton, circa July 22, 1937, Walton Papers, box 1, folder 13.

6   Gladys Walton and Charles W. L. Johnson telegram to Lester A. Walton, July 30, 1937, Walton Papers, box 1, folder 13.

7   Lester A. Walton telegram to Gladys Walton, circa August 2, 1937, Walton Papers, box 1, folder 13.

8   Fredi Washington to Laurence Brown, October 10, 1933, Fredi Washington Papers, box 1, folder 1, Schomburg Center for Research in Black Culture, New York Public Library (hereinafter Washington Papers).

9   Fredi Washington to Laurence Brown, October 26, 1933, Washington Papers, box 1, folder 1.

10 Boyd, *Wrapped in Rainbows,* 149–50, 224–25.

11 Hurston, *Dust Tracks on a Road,* 183–88 (quotation on 184); Boyd, *Wrapped in Rainbows,* 272–74.

12 Boyd, *Wrapped in Rainbows,* 373.

13 Polly Woollcott Murphy, "Adam Powell's Ex-Bunny Girl Isn't Forgetting or Regretting," *Vineyard Gazette* (Martha's Vineyard), October 31, 1975, clipping in Isabel Washington Powell Papers, Schomburg Center for Research in Black Culture, New York Public Library.

14 Statistics show that 40 percent of black upper-middle-class wives with children were employed in 1940, whereas nearly 60 percent of childless upper-middle-class black women were. Landry, *Black Working Wives,* 200, Figures B3 and B4.

15 Curwood, *Stormy Weather,* 22–28.

16 Landry, *Black Working Wives,* 92.

17 Curwood, "A Fresh Look," 325–37; Curwood, *Stormy Weather,* 60–70.

18 Sarah Thomas Curwood Memoir, Curwood Papers.

19 Sarah T. Curwood Manuscript, 1967–68, Curwood Papers (dated November 1967 and Fall 1968). Manuscript entries were all written between 1967 and 1968; where she dated an entry, I have included her dates.

20 Ibid. (including dated entry of January 28, 1968).

21 Ibid.

22 Ibid.

23 These books cost five or ten cents each and contained what the publishers hoped was an education in socialist ideas for working-class men and women. See website for the Debs Collection, Indiana State University, http://library.indstate.edu/about/units/rbsc/debs/bluebook.html.

24 Sarah T. Curwood Manuscript (including entries from "Easter 1968" and November 1967), Curwood Papers.

25 Shaw, *What a Woman Ought to Be and Do,* 13–16, 35–38.

26 The opposite was true for white middle-class marriages, in which economic necessity trumped a desire for professional service to communities. Landry, *Black Working Wives,* 30–31.

27 Sarah T. Curwood Manuscript, Curwood Papers.

28 Author interview with Sarah E. Curwood, April 23, 2003. James likely had a sexual relationship with Charles's daughter Charlietta, or "Chas" (he told Sarah that Chas was his aunt). He also adopted another woman as his mother, identified only as Mrs. Horace V. Hill and "Mother" in his correspondence.

29 For a discussion of the self-made man in America and men's desires to appear powerful in the eyes of other men, see Kimmel, *Manhood in America*, 6–10.

30 "Jr. High Promotes Its Largest Class," June 20, 1936, newspaper unknown, enclosed with Sarah E. Thomas Diary 1932–36, Curwood Papers.

31 See Veblen, *Theory of the Leisure Class*, 29–32, 57–58, 242–43; Richard Bushman has documented the growing use in the eighteenth and nineteenth centuries of less expensive alternatives to architectural and wearable finery among what he calls the "vernacular gentility," nonmembers of the middle class who wanted to appear respectable. People without good taste, he suggests, were thought of as lower in the progression of civilization. See Bushman, *Refinement of America*, xiii, 207–9.

32 Volumes cited are in possession of author. I have identified them as belonging to James Curwood by the presence of bookplates bearing his name. It is interesting to note, however, that the 1940 edition of *The Negro Family in the United States* was Sarah's own. It has her personalized label on its endpaper. I do not know whether James ever read *The Negro Family in the United States,* but a copy was in his house.

33 Sarah Curwood to James Curwood, April 19 and 27, 1944, Curwood Papers.

34 Booker T. Washington Club minute book, 1934–35. Archives 37-6-3516, Kroch Library Rare Books and Manuscripts, Cornell University, Ithaca, N.Y.

35 Sarah E. Thomas Diary, January 12, 1935, February 9 and 19, 1935, April 3, 1935, May 20, 1935; James Curwood to Sarah Thomas, March 27, 1935, Curwood Papers.

36 Sarah T. Curwood Manuscript, Curwood Papers.

37 Sadie Thomas to Sarah T. Curwood, July 9, 1936; Sarah T. Curwood to James L. Curwood, July 30, August 16, and August 31, 1936, Curwood Papers.

38 Indeed, if the same person had remained at the helm of the Boston Urban League since 1931, a photograph of him exists in *Opportunity* magazine and shows him to have medium-brown skin tone. Photograph of George S. Goodman, Executive Secretary, Boston Urban League. *Opportunity* 9, no. 7 (1931): 213.

39 James Lawrence Curwood to Sarah Ethel Thomas, September 3, 1935, Curwood Papers.

40 James Curwood to Sarah Thomas, September 5 and September 9, 1935; March 7, 1936, Curwood Papers. Sarah's description of her hair is in her memoir manuscript, Curwood Papers.

41 Sarah T. Curwood Manuscript, Curwood Papers.

42 Ibid.

43 Sarah Curwood to James Curwood, July 1, 1937, Curwood Papers.

44 Curwood, *Stormy Weather,* 83–91.

BIBLIOGRAPHY

Boyd, Valerie. *Wrapped in Rainbows: The Life of Zora Neale Hurston*. New York: Scribner's, 2003.

Bushman, Richard. *The Refinement of America: Persons, Houses, Cities*. New York: Alfred A. Knopf, 1992.

Curwood, Anastasia C. "A Fresh Look at Frazier's Sexual Politics in *The Negro Family in the United States*," *Du Bois Review* 5, no. 2 (2008): 325–37.

———. *Stormy Weather: Middle-Class African American Marriages between the Two World Wars*. Chapel Hill: University of North Carolina Press, 2010.

Frazier, E. Franklin. *The Negro Family in the United States*. Chicago: University of Chicago Press, 1939.

Fredi Washington Papers. Schomburg Center for Research in Black Culture, New York Public Library.

Garvey, Amy Jacques. *Garvey and Garveyism*. New York: Octagon Books, 1978.

———. *Philosophies and Opinions of Marcus Garvey*. New York: Arno Press, 1968.

Hurston, Zora Neale. *Dust Tracks on a Road*. 1942. Reprint, New York: Harper Perennial, 1996.

Kimmel, Michael. *Manhood in America: A Cultural History*. 2nd ed. New York: Oxford University Press, 2006.

Landry, Bart. *Black Working Wives: Pioneers of the American Family Revolution*. Berkeley: University of California Press, 2000.

Lester A. Walton Papers. Schomburg Center for Research in Black Culture, New York Public Library.

Murphy, Polly Woollcott. "Adam Powell's Ex-Bunny Girl Isn't Forgetting or Regretting." *Vineyard Gazette* (Martha's Vineyard), October 31, 1975, clipping in Isabel Washington Powell Papers, Schomburg Center for Research in Black Culture, New York Public Library.

Painter, Nell. Interview with Marie Brown Frazier, 1975. Nell Irvin Painter Papers, Special Collections, Duke University Library.

Sarah Thomas Curwood Papers. Schlesinger Library on the History of Women in America, Radcliffe Institute, Cambridge, Mass.

Shaw, Stephanie. *What a Woman Ought to Be and Do: Black Professional Women Workers in the Jim Crow Era*. Chicago: University of Chicago Press, 1996.

Taylor, Ula. *The Veiled Garvey: The Life and Times of Amy Jacques Garvey*. Chapel Hill: University of North Carolina Press, 2002.

Veblen, Thorstein. *The Theory of the Leisure Class*. 1899. Reprint, Fairfield, N.J.: Augustus M. Kelley, 1991.

V

CONSUMER CULTURE

13

"You Just Can't Keep the Music Unless You Move with It": The Great Migration and the Black Cultural Politics of Jazz in New Orleans and Chicago

CHARLES LESTER

> What seems to me most important about these mass migrations was the fact that they must have represented a still further change within the Negro as far as his relationship with America is concerned. It can be called a psychological realignment, an attempt to reassess the worth of the black man within the society as a whole, an attempt to make the American dream work, if it were going to.
>
> —Amiri Baraka, 1963

Later in life, Louis Armstrong wrote about his first journey to Chicago in 1922, reflecting on his motivations for the trip. "Hillare and the rest of us kids who turned out to be good musicians, migrated from New Orleans—to Chicago, when times were real good. There were plenty of work, lots of *Dough* flying around, all kinds of beautiful women at your service. A musician in Chicago in the early twenties were treated and respected just like—some kind of a God."[1] Armstrong's brief recollection reflects the dream of Chicago as a land of hope and opportunity for African Americans during the First Great Migration. For jazz musicians in particular, South Side Chicago presented unique avenues to openly ply their trade, advance careers, organize collectively, and achieve a social standing and a kind of respectability unattainable in the South (certainly the black elite would find little, if anything, respectable about jazz north or south). The cabarets and theaters of Chicago's black entertainment district, known as "the Stroll," acted as incubators that nurtured jazz from its infancy to adolescence. Here the music matured into a distinct Chicago style that blended southern and northern influences, cultures, and personalities to create a national, and uniquely American, musical art form.

Louis Armstrong's mentor, Joe "King" Oliver, left for Chicago in 1918. With his encouragement and assistance, Armstrong finally set out for Chicago. As Armstrong explained of Oliver, "He kept sending me letters and telegrams telling me to come up to Chicago and play second cornet for him. That, I knew, would be real heaven for me. I had made up my mind that I would not leave New Orleans unless the King sent for me. I would not risk leaving for anyone else."[2] Cleary Armstrong thought long and hard about his decision to leave New Orleans based on a variety of factors. Ultimately, he was swayed based on the advice of a close confidant. Though this particular element of Armstrong's story is telling, it is far from unique.

By 1924, Armstrong would bring the Chicago style to New York City, intent on leaving his own mark on the brand of jazz that was beginning to take Harlem by storm. For Armstrong and fellow musicians, the migration experience opened new avenues for political activism unavailable in the South. In the 1920s and 1930s, the young trumpet impresario became a dues-paying member in both the Chicago and New York musicians locals, and though he projected an apolitical persona to the general public, he quietly channeled funds to civil rights organizations such as the NAACP as his income grew more secure.[3]

Armstrong's migration story challenges popular narratives about jazz that center on Harlem as *the* nodal point of black cultural production in the first decades of the twentieth century.[4] Among Armstrong's belongings that he brought north was the cultural baggage of New Orleans jazz. He checked that baggage and augmented it in Chicago *before* making his way to Harlem. Once in New York, he was less than impressed with the music scene there. After joining Fletcher Henderson's band (one of the biggest and most sought after acts in the city), he found the group lacking the discipline and dynamism of its Chicago counterparts. "I stayed and tolerated them cutting up on the bandstand instead of playing the music right. . . . The fellows in Fletcher's band had such big heads . . . such big heads until—even if they miss a note 'So what.'" Furthermore, he believed Henderson cared little for his innovative style: "Fletcher only let me play third cornet in his band the whole time I was in his band—dig that shit. . . . Fletcher was so carried away with that 'society' shit and his education he slipped by a small timer and a young musician—me—who wanted to do everything for him musically."[5] Armstrong returned to Chicago within the year. Louis Armstrong's story also indicates that jazz musicians were a central but distinct component of the Great Migration. Additionally, because of their experiences as both labor activists and performing artists, jazz musicians remain a crucial yet underappreciated strain within the larger narrative of the New Negro experience.

Between 1915 and 1930, well over one million African Americans left the South for the urban North.[6] The net effect of this Great Migration was an explosion of African American culture and entrepreneurship concentrated in places like Chicago's South Side and Harlem. Jazz made its own Great Migration on the backs of a cadre of grassroots musician leaders whose political awareness has yet to be fully appreciated. As clarinetist Sidney Bechet explained in 1960, "You know, there's this mood about the music, a kind of need to be moving, . . . You just can't keep the music unless you move with it."[7] This essay is an effort to shed new light on the development of jazz, the Great Migration, and the New Negro aesthetic by examining the political activism of musicians in New Orleans and Chicago. Certainly the New Negro aesthetic as an ethos encompassed an array of activities that included politic activism and cultural production, but it was not limited to these endeavors. Furthermore, it was not defined solely by what happened in the limited geographic space on the northern corner of Manhattan Island.[8] By casting a wider net on the political and artistic achievements of the period, the New Negro of jazz broadens our understanding of New Negro activism so closely associated with the visual and literary artists of the Harlem Renaissance. All too often, the accomplishments of the musicians of the period are relegated to a supporting role in the cultural and political activism of the New Negro movement.[9] Additionally, when historians and cultural critics make the connection between music and the Harlem Renaissance, Harlem jazz is the beginning and end of the conversation. These considerations indicate that a deeper analysis of jazz, the Great Migration, the Harlem Renaissance, and the political activism of musicians beyond 135th Street and Lenox Avenue is necessary to uncover the New Negro of black popular music.

OUR WORLDS WERE FAR APART

Overemphasizing the role of Harlem jazz in the cultural flourishing of the New Negro movement is nothing new. This misconception emerges not from cultural critics of a later generation but from contemporary admirers and practitioners of the Harlem arts scene. In 1930, James Weldon Johnson wrote of the centrality of Harlem to the jazz craze enthralling the nation in the 1920s and 1930s, saying that "New Yorkers and people visiting New York from the world over go to the night-clubs of Harlem and dance to such jazz music as can be heard nowhere else; and they get an exhilaration impossible to duplicate."[10] Certainly Harlem was a crucial center for the early development of jazz, but Johnson's assessment is overstated. By 1930, Harlem was emerging as one of the nation's jazz capitals, but it was not unrivaled or wholly unique in that regard.

Thanks to works like David Levering Lewis's *When Harlem Was in Vogue* and Nathan Irvin Huggins's *Harlem Renaissance,* the political activism of the black intelligentsia and literary components of the Harlem Renaissance is well known. Together, Lewis and Huggins clearly demonstrate the connection between politics and artistic expression as embodied in the Harlem Renaissance. Both men argue that the goals of the New Negro movement, which sought to harness black art as a means of effecting social change, were a failure.[11] Failure, however, is in the eye of the beholder, as neither author devoted considerable attention to the effect jazz had on American society and culture. In fact, jazz fostered social interaction across racial boundaries, and in this respect, it embodied the goals of the New Negro movement, which utilized black cultural production to effect social change.

Certainly jazz stood at the forefront of innovative forms of black cultural expression in the 1920s and 1930s. Yet opinions vary widely as to the extent jazz played in the Harlem Renaissance. When Alain Locke announced that a new day dawned for African Americans with the 1925 volume *The New Negro,* little coverage was devoted to jazz and the blues. J. A. Rogers's essay "Jazz at Home" was the lone exception, but his take on jazz reflected an elitism that associated the new music with vice, immorality, and primitivism. Rogers's final assessment advocated reforming rather than eradicating jazz: "It has come to say, and they are wise, who instead of protesting against it, try to lift and divert it into nobler channels."[12] Locke's own essay on black folk music focused entirely on the spirituals, which he dubbed "the most characteristic product of the race genius as yet in America."[13] At the height of the Jazz Age, it is striking that Locke overlooked the genius of jazz musicians or popular music in general.

In 1936, Locke published a follow-up volume that sought to widen the lens of black cultural achievement in music. In *The Negro and His Music,* while discussing jazz and the blues in greater detail than in *The New Negro,* Locke retained a qualified view of jazz and jazz musicians. His taste for music excellence was rooted in European standards that placed high value on the classics, thus his analysis is more akin to the proverbial comparison between apples and oranges. For example, Locke is complimentary of Louis Armstrong, but his praise is tempered by claiming that the trumpeter's music appealed to a "racier taste."[14] Contrast this with his analysis of Duke Ellington, whose refined manner and middle-class upbringing more closely fit Locke's mold for the New Negro. He declared that singular praise of Ellington "becomes something quite different when echoed here and there independently by the most competent European and American critics and composers. . . . Duke Ellington is the pioneer of super-jazz and one of the persons most likely to create the classical jazz toward which so many are striving."[15] By basing his assessment of jazz on European aesthetics, Locke failed to judge jazz on its own merits.

The elitism reflected by Rogers, Locke, and other figures of the Harlem Renaissance was not lost on jazz musicians. The saxophone player, bandleader, and composer Benny Carter believed jazz was not entirely accepted by the literary and artistic community as an art form in its own right during the Harlem Renaissance: "I wasn't, I feel, involved in it. . . . I think the people . . . that were involved in the Renaissance; I think jazz was looked down upon. . . . I think they felt it lacked dignity." Though Carter and his fellow musicians were well aware of the burgeoning artistic and political achievements of the New Negro movement, they were given little respect for their own contributions: "We in music knew there was much going on in literature, for example, but our worlds were far apart. We sensed that the black cultural as well as moral leaders looked down on our music as undignified."[16] Though jazz stood at the vanguard of black cultural innovation in this period, owing to the lack of recognition for the artistry of jazz musicians, the music played second fiddle to the more "acceptable" artistic contributions of black writers and visual artists.[17]

While jazz was relegated to the supporting cast of artistic achievement, by insisting on the centrality of Harlem to the music, cultural observers such as James Weldon Johnson devalued the vitality of jazz in regions outside New York. To be certain, Harlem was an emerging center of jazz innovation by 1930, but in the 1910s and 1920s, New York jazz was busy playing catch-up to the dynamic brand of jazz first developed in New Orleans and refined in Chicago.[18] In the decades preceding the 1930s, Harlem was one of many sites of black cultural exchange that lent its character to the development of jazz. Therefore it is important to direct much-needed attention to other locales of innovation and artistic mastery as key nodal sites in the making of a black modernity, particularly New Orleans and Chicago.

THE GUYS NEVER TRIED TO CUT EACH OTHER'S THROAT

In 1896, the Supreme Court's decision in the landmark *Plessy v. Ferguson* case gave legal sanction to the American system of apartheid known as Jim Crow. Just four years after the pivotal decision was handed down, several days of racial violence swept over New Orleans. The riots began when Robert Charles, an African American, resisted a beating at the hands of the police. He fought back and killed several would-be assailants over the course of four days, before being killed himself. His refusal to submit touched off days of white-on-black violence in the streets, and when it finally ended, a dozen African Americans lay dead. The violence sent a plain message to the African American community in New Orleans that anyone who challenged Jim Crow would be dealt with with lethal force. It also made clear that not only would individuals be held accountable for any perceived threats against the system but so would entire communities at large. In such a hostile environment to African American independence, open and overt challenges of white power were simply too dangerous.[19]

The lack of overt political activism did not signal that black New Orleanians were uninterested in public protest or in challenging the oppressive mechanisms of southern life. Rather, it meant that acts of protest manifested themselves in covert ways on the contested streets of the city. It also meant an increased reliance on self-help strategies and on limited attempts at economic cooperation. Ultimately, African Americans in New Orleans utilized grassroots networks of like-minded individuals to "uplift" the race from within. These networks became instrumental in challenging Jim Crow in New Orleans, launching the Great Migration, and spreading jazz to the far reaches of the country in the early 1900s.

In his 1994 study of black working-class culture and politics, *Race Rebels,* Robin D. G. Kelley argues that, all too often, conventional scholarship only views "legitimate" forms of protest and resistance as those that take place within the parameters of civil rights organizations or trade unions. Kelley asserts that by doing so, scholars diminish disparate viewpoints within these groups and downplay resistance that takes place outside these institutions. Instead, Kelley advocates redrawing the map of political discourse by questioning common notions of what constitutes "legitimate" protest and resistance. He rejects "the tendency to dichotomize people's lives, to assume that clear-cut 'political' motivations exist separately from issues of economic well-being, safety, pleasure, cultural expression, sexuality, freedom of mobility, and other facets of daily life. Politics is not separate from lived experience or the imaginary world of what is possible; to the contrary, politics is about these things."[20] Viewed in this light, the story of the development of jazz in New Orleans, and the subsequent migration of black musicians out of that city to northern locales, is one ripe with political overtones. This is particularly true given the contested nature of urban space in New Orleans and the prevalence of benevolent and mutual aid organizations in the black community.

Just one year after the Supreme Court decided the *Plessy* case, the City Council of New Orleans enacted an ordinance that legalized prostitution within the confines of a regulated red-light district.[21] Named after New Orleans city councilman Sidney Story, who proposed the measure, the district offered a number of employment opportunities to aspiring musicians. Though it remained largely off limits for African Americans, a few light-skinned Creole musicians, such as Jelly Roll Morton, did find limited employment in Storyville. At roughly the same time, an all-black red-light district developed in the uptown African American ghetto known as "Back O' Town" (located across Canal Street from the French Quarter), where black musicians found jobs playing in working-class saloons and dance halls known as honky-tonks.[22] The honky-tonks where early jazz developed became, in essence, "free spaces"[23] where African Americans could openly express themselves culturally. Honky-tonks represented a space where African Americans could freely intermingle, dance, discuss the latest news of the day, drink, and, of course, listen to jazz. It was in the honky-tonks that African Americans found alternative modes of expression and tested the boundaries of covert political resistance.[24] In addition, given the extensive reach of Jim Crow in this period, these establishments represented some of the few places where black residents could spend their leisure-time dollars.

While the honky-tonks and dance halls represented free spaces where early jazz was nurtured, the streets of New Orleans were contested spaces among the city's citizenry, black and white. New Orleans has a long tradition of brass bands marching through the city streets on Sundays, holidays, and when it just simply looked like a good day for a parade. This dynamic developed following the Civil War, when scores of musical instruments were left in the city by military marching bands during the occupation of New Orleans.[25] By the turn of the twentieth century, this tradition was fully in place. By marching through city streets with trumpets, drums, and trombones blaring, African Americans claimed a virtual stake in the future of the city for themselves. Though disenfranchised and relegated to the status of second-class citizenry, black musicians still maintained control of the aural foundations of city life. It was one area where African Americans could assert their agency and dignity in a public setting in New Orleans.

With these brass bands in the lead, the parade following the music was known as the second line. Simply put, if the band represented the first line of individuals in the parade, members of the second line were average citizens following the parade. The second line comprised New Orleanians who danced, sang, and played improvised rhythms to the beat of the brass band. This grouping of the black working class was composed of neighborhood children, day laborers, street vendors, music admirers, and anyone else with a spare moment, which could sometimes number in the hundreds. Louis Armstrong had fond memories of second lining (parading) as a child through the uptown neighborhood known as "the Battlefield," where he grew up.[26] Together with the marching brass band, the second line formed a popular front challenging Jim Crow for the aural control of city streets. As Sidney Bechet recalled, the members of the second line would "take off shouting, singing, following along the sidewalk, going off on side streets when they was told they had no business being on the sidewalks or along the kerbs [sic] like that, or maybe when the police would try to break them up. Then they'd go off one way and join the parade away up and start all over again."[27] Thus the second line was both a celebration of cultural expression and a means of staking a claim to contested ground in the city.

The contested nature of the city's streets can be seen in the prevalence of "cutting contests" or "bucking contests," which were musical battles between rival bands. As Sidney Bechet explained, "one band, it would come right up in front of the other and play at it, and the first band it would play right back, until finally one band just had to give in. . . . It was always the public who decided. You was always being judged."[28] At times, these contests pitted black groups against one another as each was parading through the streets. Jelly Roll Morton recalled an African American band literally drawing a line across which a rival band was not supposed to step. A fight soon ensued that required an ambulance: "The fact of it is, there was no parade at no time you couldn't find a knot on somebody's head where somebody got hit with a stick or something."[29] The contested nature of public streets often had violent consequences.

African Americans in New Orleans also turned to an increased reliance on self-help strategies and on small-scale efforts of economic cooperation based on communal networks. These networks centered less on large-scale mobilization and more on grassroots organization. Instrumental in this organizing push was a focus on black-run enterprises and benevolent societies. New Orleans boasted black-run benevolent societies as early as the eighteenth century.[30] These organizations served a number of organizing capacities. Members were provided health care, insurance policies, burial services, and education. Social and pleasure clubs formed in a similar manner in this period, but unlike benevolent societies, they were devoted to celebrating the joys in life rather than planning for the unexpected. At the turn of the twentieth century, these disparate organizations began to serve essentially the same functions, and jazz musicians enthusiastically created and supported their own benevolent societies and social and pleasure clubs.[31]

In many respects, the benevolent societies for black musicians mirrored early attempts to unionize musicians nationally. Generally, these organizations more closely resembled labor exchanges than modern unions. Musicians networked with fellow members to find employment, and these organizations provided prospective employers with a mechanism for hiring bands.[32] There are several explanations for why black New Orleans lacked a standard union in this period. First, the long tradition of benevolent and pleasure societies meant that there was a level of familiarity and an existing framework for collective action. Second, it reflected a national trend of reluctance on the part of musicians to be recognized as workers rather than as artists.[33] Finally, organizing a union was a very dangerous proposition, especially for African Americans, in New Orleans in this period. In the Depression years of the 1890s, labor strife turned particularly violent, and a number of bloody riots erupted in the city over the issue of the unionization and segregation of dockworkers and roustabouts.[34] Given the preceding considerations, creating a formal union was not at times as viable an option as maintaining and strengthening the existing organizations that protected the interests of musicians. Though unionization was not always a viable option, black New Orleanians continued to pursue the creation of a musicians local, and they were finally successful in 1926.[35]

Although a formal union did not protect black musicians before the Great Migration, jazz artists did manage to assert themselves collectively through grassroots networks and benevolent societies in a manner that very much resembled union activity. Pops Foster explained, "The colored musicians in New Orleans didn't have no union, but man, we stuck together. . . . The guys never tried to cut each other's throat; it was better in those days without no union."[36] These organizations also served as an integral instrument for collective action among the city's black community. Clarinetist Louis Cottrell remembered that "an organization in 1932 . . . a benevolent association in New Orleans was the big reason and the big step forward what brought on in 1940, '41, Negroes registered to vote in the city of New Orleans through these organizations."[37] Even after the successful unionization of black musicians, the prevalence, persistence, and activism of benevolent societies speaks to their ability to address the needs and aspirations of the black community.

Grassroots networking[38] was instrumental for musicians seeking employment. Similar networks also facilitated small-scale efforts for economic cooperation that attempted to keep black leisure dollars in the black community. Jazz was an essential component that attracted patrons to places like fish fries and lawn parties. While many of the honky-tonks catered to African American clientele, very few, if any, were black-owned establishments. Pops Foster explained, "In those days the Italians owned nearly all the grocery stores and saloons. When I worked doing longshore work we used to hang out at Tony's Saloon at Celeste and Chapatula. It was strictly for colored."[39] Not only did African Americans have a finite number of leisure options available to them under Jim Crow but there were also few avenues to property ownership. Consequently, would-be black entrepreneurs employed a number of creative strategies to provide venues for entertainment and draw profits from these enterprises. .

Two such enterprises, fish fries and lawn parties, were spaces of urban sociability, but they also provided labor for black musicians. These were closely related ventures, though drummer Paul Barbarin noted that fish fries usually occurred on Saturday evenings, whereas lawn parties took place on Sundays.[40] These social gatherings were semi-public affairs where guests paid a small admission fee to listen and dance to music and eat home-cooked food, drink spirituous beverages, and socialize. The trombone player Edward "Kid" Ory began holding fish fries as an entrée into professional music: "Well, I couldn't get a job [playing music], so I started to promoting fish fries."[41] Pops Foster explained, "All over New Orleans on Saturday night there'd be fish fries. . . . To advertise, you'd get a carriage with the horses all dressed up, a bunch of pretty girls, and then the musicians would get on, and you'd go all over advertising for that night." Foster further revealed, "The wife usually did the cooking in the morning. She'd fry catfish, cook gumbo, make ham sandwiches, potato salad, and ice cream to sell. The man would get the beer, wine, and whiskey. When it got toward dark, you'd hang a red lantern out on the front door to let anybody going by know there was a fish fry inside and anybody could go in." Foster concluded, "The fish fry that had the best band was the one that would have the best crowd."[42] Louis Armstrong remembered a woman named Mrs. Cole who threw lawn parties two or three nights a week. He believed she was successful, in part, because she employed Kid Ory's band, which was one of the most popular in the city.[43] Not only did these parties provide entertainment that kept black dollars in the black community but they also helped the hosts pay the bills. This tradition was also carried north during the Great Migration. In Chicago and New York City, these social events were referred to as "rent parties" because the proceeds often meant the difference between having the rent and being short for that month.[44] Because the built environment in both Chicago and New York was much more heavily congested than it was in New Orleans, the social dynamics and the music were also very different. Fish fries and lawn parties featured jazz ensembles and large crowds. Rent parties, on the other hand, were often crowded and more intimate affairs because of the lack of space. Consequently, they employed small combos or sometimes simply a piano player. This meant that the brand of jazz played at these social engagements differed from one urban setting to the next.

Musicians also utilized grassroots networks to aid fellow musicians in need. When Louis Armstrong's first wife fell ill, Joe Oliver offered his assistance. "'You need money for a doctor? Is that it?' he said immediately. 'Go down and take my place at Pete Lala's for two nights. . . . ' In two nights I would make enough money to engage a very good doctor and get Irene's stomach straightened out." Armstrong made sure he returned the favor by feeding Oliver when he was unemployed just weeks later.[45] Pops Foster remembered, "If a guy was building a house, we'd show up and play and help him build it. When we were playing we were having fun; the pay sometimes just made it a little bit sweeter."[46] Though competition remained a very real part of a musician's life in New Orleans, the preceding recollections attest to the strength of the grassroots networks employed when a fellow musician was in need. It was these networks that proved vital in facilitating the northern exodus of musicians during the Great Migration.

IT GOT SO HOT IT HAD TO BURST OUT

While jazz saw its fair share of criticism in the first decades of the twentieth century, it also enjoyed immense national popularity beginning in the 1920s. This popularity was due, in part, to the effect the Great Migration had on American society and culture. As recent scholarship suggests, the Great Migration that witnessed the exodus of more than one million African Americans out of the South before, during, and after World War I was a crucial period of black activism. The causes of the movement have been the subject of much debate among historians both then and now, but more recent studies argue that an array of factors led to the mass exodus.[47] Like their migratory counterparts, musicians came to Chicago during this period for a variety of reasons. James Lincoln Collier argues that the closing of the New Orleans red-light district of Storyville in 1917 coupled with the expanding vice and entertainment district in South Side Chicago forced black jazz musicians to migrate.[48] Thomas Brothers, conversely, notes that recent historians are divided about the effect of Storyville's closing on migration. But he does admit that the closing "must have caused more than a few musicians to search for greener pastures."[49] Yet the story is actually far more complex.

To be certain, economic opportunities were a significant contributing factor to musicians journeying to Chicago. However, just as is the case with broader interpretations of the Great Migration, a focus on primarily economic motives diminishes the agency (the decision-making capacity) of jazz musicians themselves. Indeed, jazz musicians have a history of grassroots networking with colleagues to find work. The link between southern musicians and their counterparts in Chicago during this period is no exception.[50] While previous studies only offer an incomplete explanation for why musicians left New Orleans, they also fail to address the contributions of individuals that made the jazz exodus possible. For example, trumpeter Natty Dominique left New Orleans a few years before the closing of Storyville to work as a cigar maker. Dominique had a job lined up before he left, thanks to a friend named Casino. "He said you want to come to Chicago? . . . I said, all right, I'll get ready. I got ready too, had my clothes, had my trumpet, and I got to Chicago." Dominique utilized the kind of grassroots support common to the movement to enable his journey to Chicago.[51] Like Jelly Roll Morton, Sidney Bechet, Paul Barbarin, and many others, Dominique left New Orleans before the closing of Storyville.[52]

The clarinet player Albert Nichols first left for Chicago in 1923, after being offered a job in Joe Oliver's band. Along with the opportunity to play in Oliver's band and the economic lure of Chicago, Nichols remembered that racial discrimination in New Orleans when he left "used to be brutal." In 1924, Nichols found himself once again in New Orleans, but thanks to a job offer from Kid Ory, he returned to Chicago. While on tour in 1937, he returned for a brief visit to his hometown before leaving once more, certain that he did not "care if I never saw the place again."[53] For Nichols, the combination of assistance from colleagues, economic opportunity in Chicago, and racial discrimination in New Orleans meant that the decision to leave his hometown was an easy one.[54]

It is no mere coincidence that Oliver and Ory were the ones encouraging Nichols to leave; they facilitated the migration of dozens of individuals, including Baby Dodds, Pops Foster, and Barney Bigard.[55] In this vein, the work of Ory and Oliver mirrors the efforts of those in the larger migrant community that enabled others to leave the South. Historian James R. Grossman points to the tradition within African American communities of mobility as an assertion of agency. Following emancipation, Grossman contends, blacks found spatial mobility to be of the utmost significance, and from here a grassroots network of information and leadership emerged that was essential to the movement.[56] A key component of the musicians' network was providing employment. This network also often provided musicians with train fare to leave New Orleans, a place to stay upon arrival, and food to ease the transition to a new home.[57] The cost of travel was not cheap, so help in offsetting expenses was particularly important. While most jazz migrants traveled a direct line from New Orleans aboard a car on the Illinois Central Railroad to Chicago, those most destitute could also make their way north via riverboat to places like Davenport, Iowa, before the final trek to Chicago. The most famous musician to take advantage of this network was Louis Armstrong, who made his own journey to Chicago with the assistance and encouragement of Oliver.[58] Armstrong's account reveals that, as a result of economic considerations and the aid of grass-roots networks, the cornet player decided Chicago was the right fit for his future.

The first-person accounts of Dominique, Nichols, and Armstrong illustrate that a variety of considerations played a part in the decision to leave New Orleans in search of greener pastures. Musicians were not pushed out of the South due only to economic considerations any more than the African American community at large was pushed north during the Great Migration. Rather, musicians actively chose to improve their conditions on their own volition. To pursue that end, many utilized the kind of grassroots networks employed by scores of African Americans across the South during this period. But unlike their counterparts of the larger migration, these musicians left their homes because of both the lack of creative outlets in the South and the opportunity for creative expression in the North. The added incentive of finding greater avenues for creative expression set them apart from other migrants and made their story unique.

Thanks to the innovation of New Orleans jazz pioneers and the Great Migration, the music seemingly burst onto the national stage in the 1920s. It soon became a cultural force to be reckoned with, culminating in F. Scott Fitzgerald famously dubbing the decade the "Jazz Age."[59] As Armstrong put it, "The men I knew as a boy started it all. Whatever it's good for, and however long it will live, swing music was born in my country; it seeded there in New Orleans and grew there, and there it got so hot it had to burst out and it did, and spread to the world."[60] Part of the attraction of the new music was the blending of highbrow and lowbrow influences that made it appealing to both black and white audiences. In a number of ways, this appeal opened the door for limited social change. Once in Chicago, the grassroots network that facilitated the jazz migration continued to work on behalf of musicians based on a foundation of mutual cooperation.

The musicians network helped newcomers like multi-instrumentalist George Dixon. He received tutelage, advice, and encouragement from bandleaders Dave Peyton and Erskine Tate.[61] Ikey Robinson, a banjo player from Virginia, recalled a jazz promoter named "Stomp King" who helped a number of musicians. Stomp King not only fed and housed musicians in his South Side apartment but also helped them find work. "He had a list that was calling him for jobs, you know. He would call you up today and be working tonight."[62] Not every migrant found full-time employment as a musician. Natty Dominique, for instance, supplemented his income working in a cigar factory, and Paul Barbarin worked in Chicago's stockyards.[63] Other musicians worked grueling schedules to avoid another line of work. At times it was necessary to begin the workday playing in a theater pit orchestra for a matinee show, followed by an evening shift in a restaurant or dance hall, before finishing the night in an after-hours club that stayed open until after dawn. Given these difficulties, the musicians network proved as important in the North as it was enabling individuals to leave the South.

Grassroots musicians' networks not only aided with housing, meals, education, and employment but also helped pay the bills. Just like fish fries and lawn parties, northern rent parties employed musicians and provided spaces for urban sociability. In Chicago, because of limited space, the music was restricted to one piano player or a small combo. The brand of jazz played at rent parties was considered a lower grade than that played in dance halls because of the lack of instrumentation and refined arrangements. Despite this perception, rent parties remained popular among Chicago's black working class, and owing to their charisma and promotional skills, a select group of women ran the most successful parties. Danny Barker remembered that one successful business lady was very popular because she supplied great entertainment, good whiskey, and excellent food.[64]

Jazz musicians also organized collectively in the black musicians' union. Based on the tradition of collective action on the part of musicians in New Orleans, it is no coincidence that the first successful attempt to unionize black musicians in Chicago was spearheaded by New Orleans transplants. Charles Elgar joined Chicago's Local 208 of the American Federation of Musicians not long after arriving from New Orleans: "Ah, this local-208, had just been given a charter . . . July of that year [1902]. And this picture you see up there is a picture of all the presidents [of the union]. The man in the upper left hand corner was the first president; his name was Alexander Armand, originally from New Orleans himself."[65] Barney Bigard was also active in Local 208.[66] The local was formed because Chicago's Local 10 refused to admit African American members. By the early 1920s, Local 208 had purchased a three-story building on South State Street to serve as the union's offices and meeting place. Local 208 soon exerted enough clout to force club owners to accept wage scales for member musicians. Between 1918 and 1929, the local's membership more than doubled from three hundred to over six hundred. The rolls of dues-paying members read as a veritable who's who of early jazz innovators, including Barney Bigard, Joe Oliver, and Louis Armstrong.[67]

The union was rather adept at protecting the interests of its members and its economic turf. Bandleader and longtime union officer William Everett Samuels described the successful attempt of the local to block the replacement of live musicians with recorded music in South Side theaters.[68] He was also involved in a strike of the Vendome Theater because the owner refused to sign a contract with Local 208. Samuels recalled, "We had a quick small strike and he fell in line.

After the union showed its strength—that's what did it. It also helped member-ship."[69] Local 208 was also well versed in getting its message out. The activities of the union were advertised in the *Chicago Defender*. "There was no problem in getting the Black musicians to see the need for the union. We didn't have that problem. They wanted to join. They knew what the problems were," according to Samuels.[70] Though Local 208 remained an advocate for jazz musicians throughout the 1910s, 1920s, and 1930s, it should also be noted that some musicians were critical of what they saw as elitism on the part of the local regarding proficiency standards to obtain a union card that were based on the union's perception of what constituted "acceptable" music.

The camaraderie of the informal musicians network and Local 208 coalesced into a form of emerging "race" consciousness in that certain musicians, such as Charles Elgar, felt a sense of responsibility to help fellow black musicians in need.[71] This emerging consciousness was also evidenced by the fact that Joe Oliver, Dave Peyton, and other Chicago musicians began playing events for civil rights groups like the NAACP in the 1920s. Peyton, the *Defender* music journalist, often promoted the accomplishments of black musicians as both artists and community activists with an air of racial pride in his weekly columns: "All factions are functioning 100 percent for a progressive future. When it comes to music and musicians Chicago leads." On another occasion, after an extended discussion of the black national anthem "Lift Every Voice and Sing," Peyton turned his attention to the accomplishments of black musicians through their work with Local 208: "The Chicago musicians are away ahead of musicians of our group in other cities of the country. Their achievements have been wonderful. They own their own building . . . for the organization that is officered entirely by members of the Race. Musicians in other places should follow the Chicago gang. Wake up and do something. Let us make the world respect us. Ours is an art. Organize yourselves. . . . Work together, acquire real estate and then you will be independent."[72] Musicians also engaged in consciousness raising through their art.[73] For example, the lyrics to the 1926 song "The Bridwell Blues," by Nolan Welsh and Louis Armstrong, tell the tale of a man wrongfully detained by the Chicago police. The narrator paints a picture of his experience in an unjust legal system that resulted in an extended sentence at a penal farm:[74]

> And they sent me to the stone quarry
> I'm standin' in the door
> It's just that way people, you know I've been here before

Welsh and Armstrong's song about the harsh conditions at Chicago's Bridwell Prison and the overt lack of equity for blacks in the American legal system re-minded jazz and blues listeners of the injustices faced in their own lives. In that vein, the call and response between the artist and listener served as a theoretical call for further action in combating repression during the age of the New Negro.

The popularity of jazz also opened the door for limited social change in the North. The interracial "black and tan" clubs in Chicago's South Side actively courted white patrons, and quite often their dance floors were the only socially acceptable locales for blacks and whites to interact. Consequently, South Side black and tans acted as incubators for limited social change as white gawkers and admirers flocked to see the latest innovations in dance and music. Black and tans pursued varying policies of segregation. Some smaller black-owned cabarets admitted white customers but largely served the local African American community. Some of the largest black and tans were specifically designed for interracial clientele, whereas a few white-owned clubs employed black musicians but catered to white customers. Some clubs maintained strict segregation in seating arrangements, and others simply ignored such social conventions. The degree of integration or segregation was left to the whim of the individual club owner, and these whims changed from week to week and from one establishment to the next.[75] Clubs like the Dreamland, Sunset, and Royal Gardens "specialized in presenting unprecedented spectacles of interracial contacts in social dancing," according to historian William Howland Kenney.[76] The taboo-breaking atmosphere of black and tans constituted the city's only leisure space to experiment with both racial and sexual boundaries.[77] Certainly not every white customer was an altruistic reformer. Many whites viewed an evening at a black and tan as a form of intracity tourism, where they could experience a night of "primitive" entertainment. In the Progressive era, venues that hosted interracial entertainment were increasingly concentrated in black neighborhoods and were considered immoral by elitist reformers, and often these establishments were the focus of antivice campaigns. Such establishments were generally tolerated so long as they adhered to a strict racial double standard regarding their clientele. This meant that interracial dancing was tolerated if a white man danced with a black woman, but not vice versa. Therefore, based on the racial fears of the period, external forces governed the level of interracial mingling in these clubs.[78]

Many white musicians, including the famous Austin High Gang, ignored racial norms altogether and sought advice and camaraderie from black musicians working in the South Side.[79] As a result, black and white musicians interacted not just in cabarets but after hours as well. Bassist Milt Hinton recounted such meetings:

Well the rule said that we could not play together . . . but it had nothing to do with our respect for each other as musicians. So after hours, when the clubs would close the musicians, black and white, would get together. . . . We would trade choruses, and we would get some of the academics from the white musicians, and they'd get some of the creativity from the black musicians. . . . We'd have this big jam session going on. This is why Chicago was the basis for really putting this together, because we found out that music was in all our hearts. We didn't care what color you were, or where you came from, it's how you sound.[80]

The interracial camaraderie of black and white musicians was often motivated by artistic, not political, concerns, and few white musicians from the early period of Chicago jazz became civil rights advocates. However, such associations, and the musicians that courted them, signaled the emergence of the biracial swing era a generation later.[81]

Although jazz musicians were not zealous reformers seeking to tear down all barriers of injustice, jazz retained some power to effect limited social change. In an era when the dominant portrayal of African Americans in pop culture was the minstrel show, the emergence of national black celebrities leading jazz bands was groundbreaking. Ethel Waters, the famous jazz and blues singer, believed black performing artists retained the power to affect public opinion from the stage. "I realize the good work that I and all of us colored artists have been doing. Many white people who would not listen to any other side of Negro life will gladly hear a Negro jazz artist or blues singer. All that helps pave the way by making them more sympathetic to our race."[82] Though his talent was only just being recognized by white America in 1929, Louis Armstrong's status as the best musician in the country was not something the black community took lightly. To black residents of New Orleans and Chicago in particular, he was a hero, and at a time when there were no nationally recognized black celebrities, Armstrong's influence was tremendous. While elitist critics of jazz believed the new music violated traditional American tastes and sensibilities, the unsurpassed talents of jazz artists slowly gained wider recognition and praise. The appreciation of black genius—moving beyond just the admiration for talent—was something altogether new in American society.[83]

Although Lewis and Huggins argue that the Harlem Renaissance did not progressively alter American society, the accounts of Louis Armstrong, Ethel Waters, Milt Hinton, and Dave Peyton and the work of black activists in New Orleans and Chicago tell a different story. African American art retained the power to effect change. Though American society was not transformed overnight, jazz helped pave the way for future progress. Furthermore, by decentering Harlem as *the* site of cultural innovation, it is clear that jazz was a truly national phenomenon, thanks in no small part to the Great Migration. Scores of musicians across the country contributed to a flourishing of African American culture that introduced the New Negro of jazz to the world. Most importantly, it was the activism of the migration experience that informed subsequent activism in new locales, and in this regard, jazz musicians were just as politically active as other black artists of the period. But jazz musicians were not content to wait for their reward in heaven. When the rate of progress was too slow, they took matters into their own hands. From small-scale economic efforts like fish fries, lawn parties, and rent parties to organizing efforts like forming benevolent societies in New Orleans or unionization in Chicago, black musicians actively sought to "make the American dream work," in the words of Amiri Baraka. When the American dream was not working, they pursued greener pastures during the Great Migration and brought America swinging into the Jazz Age.

NOTES

1   Armstrong, "Armstrong Story," in Brothers, *Louis Armstrong in His Own Words,* 74 . The epigraph appears in Baraka, *Blues People,* 95–96.

2   Armstrong, *Satchmo,* 226.

3   Louis Cottrell, interview transcript, March 14, 1978, Hogan Jazz Archive, Tulane University, New Orleans (hereinafter HJA).

4   There are several recent works on early jazz that expand the narrative focus beyond Harlem. For a few examples of this development, see Driggs and Haddix, *Kansas City Jazz*; Hersch, *Subversive Sounds*; Kenney, *Chicago Jazz*. Notwithstanding the work of the preceding scholars, the general tendency remains to situate Harlem at the center of black cultural, economic, political, and artistic production in this period.

5   Louis Armstrong, Armstrong Tapes, CD 426, disc 1, track 7, Louis Armstrong Collection, Louis Armstrong House Museum Archives, Queens College, New York.

6   Arnesen, *Black Protest and the Great Migration,* 1.

7   Bechet, *Treat It Gentle,* 95.

8   For a more detailed analysis of the New Negro movement in a broader social, political, and geographic context, see Baldwin, *Chicago's New Negroes.*

9   This is not to suggest that the scholarly community has ignored the work of jazz artists in the political arena. Rather, the efforts of jazz activists have not received the level of attention that literary activists have long enjoyed.

10   Johnson, *Black Manhattan,* 160.

11   For Huggins's assessment on the success or failure of the Harlem Renaissance, see Huggins, *Harlem Renaissance,* 7–12. Huggins also argues that the black elite relegated jazz to a supporting role in the Renaissance, but he does not explore, in depth, the effect jazz and jazz musicians had on American society through their activism. For Lewis's take on the movement, see Lewis, *When Harlem Was in Vogue,* xxi–xxiv. Jon Michael Spencer refutes the interpretation that the Harlem Renaissance was a failure. For a more detailed discussion of his critique, see Spencer, *New Negroes and Their Music.*

12   Rogers, "Jazz at Home," 224.

13   Locke, "Negro Spirituals," 199.

14   Locke, *Negro and His Music,* 98.

15   Ibid., 99.

16   Benny Carter, interview transcript, October 13, 1976, Institute of Jazz Studies, Rutgers University, Newark, N.J. (hereinafter IJS); Benny Carter, liner notes for *Benny Carter: Harlem Renaissance.*

17   Recently a number of authors have reassessed the role music, and jazz in particular, played in the Harlem Renaissance. A collection of essays edited by Samuel A. Floyd Jr. initiated a long overdue scholastic dialogue on the influence of music on the period. For a more thorough analysis, see Floyd, *Black Music in the Harlem Renaissance.* Since the publication of the preceding volume, Paul Allen Anderson has taken up the mantle for an expanded dialogue of the music of the period. For the complete analysis, see Anderson, *Deep River.*

18   Baraka, *Blues People,* 151.

19   Thomas, *Plessy v. Ferguson*; Wells, *Mob Rule in New Orleans,* in Royster, *Southern Horrors and Other Writings,* 158–208.

20   Kelley, *Race Rebels,* 4, 9–10.

21   Rose, *Storyville, New Orleans,* 1.

22   Armstrong and Meryman, *Louis Armstrong,* 12–13.

23   Francesca Polletta, "Free Spaces," notes that the notion of "free spaces" has been used by a number of sociologists, political scientists, and historians to describe "small-scale settings within a community or movement that are removed from the direct control of dominant groups, are voluntarily participated in, and generate the cultural challenge that precedes or accompanies political mobilization" (1). For more information on free spaces and political activism, see ibid., 1–38. Charles Hersch argues that honky-tonks resembled what Michel Foucault calls "heterotopias," where politically marginalized groups find sanctuary from and modes to express resistance to the mechanisms of repression. For a more detailed analysis of Foucault's heterotopias, see Hersch, *Subversive Sounds,* 35.

24   Hersch, *Subversive Sounds,* 35.

25   For more information on the development of brass bands in New Orleans, see Turner, *Jazz Religion*; Ellison, "African American Music and Muskets," 285–319.

26   Armstrong, *Satchmo,* 24.

27   Bechet, *Treat It Gentle,* 62.

28   Ibid., 63, 65.

29   Morton and Lomax, *Mister Jelly Roll,* 13.

30   Jacobs, "Benevolent Societies of New Orleans," 22.

31   Turner, *Jazz Religion,* 110.

32   Kraft, "Artists as Workers," 516, 524–26.

33   Ibid., 524–26.

34   Arnesen, "Turning Points," 450–500.

35   The first attempt at the unionization of black musicians in New Orleans occurred in 1902, but the local soon collapsed, though the specific cause of the collapse is unclear. In 1926, a number of activists were successful in creating a lasting local that protected the interests of the city's black musicians. Fischer, "American Federation of Musicians," 2.

36 Foster and Stoddard, *Autobiography of Pops Foster,* 69.

37 Cottrell, HJA.

38 Charles M. Payne has pointed out that grassroots organizing consists of more than helping others find employment or education. Often, efforts that provide an economic base within an oppressed community, or efforts that offer food and shelter to those in need, are overlooked. For more information on Payne's analysis, see Payne, *I've Got the Light of Freedom,* 276. My definition of grassroots networks takes into account this deficiency.

39 Foster and Stoddard, *Autobiography of Pops Foster,* 71.

40 Paul Barbarin, interview digest, December 23, 1959, HJA.

41 Edward "Kid" Ory, interview transcript, April 20, 1957, HJA.

42 Foster and Stoddard, *Autobiography of Pops Foster,* 16.

43 Armstrong, *Satchmo,* 30.

44 Foster and Stoddard, *Autobiography of Pops Foster,* 16.

45 Ibid., 102–4.

46 Ibid., 65.

47 Grossman, *Land of Hope*; DeSantis, "Selling the American Dream Myth."

48 Collier, *Louis Armstrong,* 70–71, 86.

49 Brothers, *Louis Armstrong's New Orleans,* 256.

50 Grossman, *Land of Hope,* 95.

51 Natty Dominique, interview transcript, October 24, 1981, Chicago Jazz Archive, University of Chicago (hereinafter CJA).

52 Morton and Lomax, *Mister Jelly Roll,* 45; Bechet, *Treat It Gentle,* 115; Paul Barbarin, interview digest, December 23, 1959, HJA.

53 "Jazz Scene," 16.

54 Albert Nichols, interview digest, June 26, 1972, HJA.

55 Dodds and Gara, *Baby Dodds Story,* 33; Bigard, *With Louis and the Duke,* 26; Foster and Stoddard, *Autobiography of Pops Foster,* 53.

56 Grossman, *Land of Hope,* 66–97.

57 Bigard, *With Louis and the Duke,* 26–30; Armstrong, *Satchmo,* 234.

58 Armstrong, *Satchmo,* 226–28.

59 Fitzgerald, *Tales of the Jazz Age.*

60 Armstrong, *Swing That Music,* 28.

61 George Dixon, interview transcript, August 15, 1990, CJA.

62 Ikey Robinson, interview transcript, July 25, 1988, CJA.

63 Dominique, CJA; Barbarin, HJA.

64 Kenney, *Chicago Jazz,* 13–14; Barker, IJS.

65 Charles Elgar, interview transcript, May 27, 1958, HJA.

66 Bigard, *With Louis and the Duke,* 32.

67 Halker, "A History of Local 208 and the Struggle for Racial Equality," 211–12.

68 Donald Spivey interview with William Everett Samuels, in Spivey, *Union and the Black Musician,* 38.

69 Ibid., 53.

70 Ibid., 119.

71   Danny Barker, interview transcript, April 1980, IJS.

72   Dave Peyton, "The Musical Bunch," *Defender,* July 3, 1926, 6; June 19, 1926, 6; July 31, 1926, 6; June 12, 1926, 6.

73   Here I am borrowing the analytical framework for studying the consciousness-raising effects of blues lyrics as articulated by Angela Davis. For a more detailed explanation of this method, see Davis, *Blues Legacies and Black Feminism,* xi–xiv, 54–57.

74   Nolan Welsh with Louis Armstrong, "The Bridwell Blues," Okeh Records, 1926. This song title can be found today on Armstrong, *Portrait of the Artist As a Young Man* (New York: Sony Records, 1994). Many thanks to Will Buckingham from Tulane University's School of Music for bringing this song to my attention and for providing me with an MP3 file of the tune and a transcription of the music and lyrics.

75   Kenney, *Chicago Jazz,* 17.

76   Ibid., 24.

77   Bachin, *Building the South Side,* 279–80.

78   Mumford, *Interzones,* 20, 26–27, 30–32.

79   Peretti, *Jazz in American Culture,* 58.

80   Milt Hinton, in Burns, *Jazz.*

81   Peretti, *Jazz in American Culture,* 58.

82   Ethel Waters, as quoted in J. A. Rogers, "Ethel Waters Selected as First Subject from Pen of Gifted Writer and Author," *New York Amsterdam News,* November 27, 1929, 9.

83   For a more complete analysis of jazz genius, see Griffin, *If You Can't Be Free,* 15–16.

BIBLIOGRAPHY

Anderson, Paul Allen. *Deep River: Music and Memory in Harlem Renaissance Thought.* Durham, N.C.: Duke University Press, 2001.

Armstrong, Louis. *Satchmo: My Life in New Orleans.* New York: Da Capo Press, 1954.
———. *Swing That Music.* New York: Da Capo Press, 1936.

Armstrong, Louis, and Richard Meryman. *Louis Armstrong—A Self Portrait.* New York: Eakins Press, 1966.

Arnesen, Eric, ed. *Black Protest and the Great Migration: A Brief History with Documents.* New York: Bedford/St. Martin's Press, 2003.
———. "Turning Points: Biracial Unions in the Age of Segregation, 1893–1901." In *The Louisiana Purchase Bicentennial Series in Louisiana History Volume XI: The African American Experience in Louisiana Part B: From the Civil War to Jim Crow,* edited by Charles Vincent, 490–500. Lafayette: University of Louisiana Press, 2000.

Bachin, Robin F. *Building the South Side: Urban Space and Civic Culture in Chicago, 1890–1919.* Chicago: University of Chicago Press, 2004.

Baldwin, Davarian L. *Chicago's New Negroes: Modernity, the Great Migration, and Black Urban Life.* Chapel Hill: University of North Carolina Press, 2007.

Baraka, Amiri (LeRoi Jones). *Blues People: Negro Music in White America.* Westport, Conn.: Greenwood Press, 1963.

Bechet, Sidney. *Treat It Gentle: An Autobiography.* New York: Twayne, 1960.

Bigard, Barney. *With Louis and the Duke: The Autobiography of a Jazz Clarinetist*. Edited by Barry Martyn. New York: Oxford University Press, 1980.

Brothers, Thomas, ed. *Louis Armstrong in His Own Words: Selected Writings*. New York: Oxford University Press, 1999.

———. *Louis Armstrong's New Orleans*. New York: W. W. Norton, 2006.

Burns, Ken. *Jazz*. Hollywood: PBS Home Video, 2000.

Carter, Benny. Liner notes to *Benny Carter: Harlem Renaissance*. Ocean, N.J.: Music Masters Jazz Label, 1992.

Chicago Jazz Archive, Illinois Oral History Collection, University of Chicago.

Collier, James Lincoln. *Louis Armstrong: An American Genius*. New York: Oxford University Press, 1983.

Davis, Angela Y. *Blues Legacies and Black Feminism: Gertrude "Ma" Rainey, Bessie Smith, and Billie Holiday*. New York: Pantheon Books, 1998.

DeSantis, Alan D. "Selling the American Dream Myth to Black Southerners: The Chicago *Defender* and the Great Migration of 1915–1919." *Western Journal of Communication* 62, no. 4 (1998): 474–511.

Dodds, Warren "Baby," and Larry Gara. *The Baby Dodds Story*. Los Angeles, Calif.: Contemporary Press, 1959.

Driggs, Frank, and Chuck Haddix. *Kansas City Jazz: From Ragtime to Bebop—A History*. New York: Oxford University Press, 2005.

Ellison, Mary. "African American Music and Muskets in Civil War New Orleans." *Louisiana History* 35, no. 3 (1994): 285–319.

Fischer, Sue. "American Federation of Musicians Locals 174 and 496 Records at the Hogan Jazz Archive." *Jazz Archivist*, 2005–6, 1–7.

Fitzgerald, F. Scott. *Tales of the Jazz Age*. New York: Scribners, 1922.

Floyd, Samuel A., Jr., ed. *Black Music in the Harlem Renaissance*. Westport, Conn.: Greenwood Press, 1990.

Foster, George "Pops," and Tom Stoddard. *The Autobiography of Pops Foster: New Orleans Jazzman*. San Francisco: Backbeat Books, 1971.

Griffin, Farah Jasmine. *If You Can't Be Free, Be a Mystery*. New York: Free Press, 2001.

Grossman, James R. *Land of Hope: Chicago, Black Southerners, and the Great Migration*. Chicago: University of Chicago Press, 1989.

Halker, Clark. "A History of Local 208 and the Struggle for Racial Equality in the American Federation of Musicians." *Black Music Research Journal* 8, no. 2 (1998): 207–22.

Hersch, Charles. *Subversive Sounds: Race and the Birth of Jazz in New Orleans*. Chicago: University of Chicago Press, 2007.

Huggins, Nathan Irvin. *Harlem Renaissance*. New York: Oxford University Press, 1971.

Institute of Jazz Studies, New Jersey Oral History Collection, Rutgers University, Newark.

Jacobs, Claude F. "Benevolent Societies of New Orleans Blacks during the Late Nineteenth and Early Twentieth Centuries." *Louisiana History* 29, no. 1 (1988): 21–33.

Johnson, James Weldon. *Black Manhattan*. New York: Alfred A. Knopf, 1930.

Kelley, Robin D. G. *Race Rebels: Culture, Politics, and the Black Working Class*. New York: Free Press, 1994.

Kenney, William Howland. *Chicago Jazz: A Cultural History, 1904–1930*. New York: Oxford University Press, 1994.

Kraft, James P. "Artists as Workers: Musicians and Trade Unionism in America, 1880–1917." *Musical Quarterly* 79, no. 3 (1995): 512–43.

Lewis, David Levering. *When Harlem Was in Vogue*. 1979. Reprint, New York: Penguin Books, 1997.

Locke, Alain. *The Negro and His Music*. New York: Associates in Negro Folk Education, 1936.

———. "The Negro Spirituals." In *The New Negro: Voices of the Harlem Renaissance*, edited by Alain Locke, 199–213. New York: Albert and Charles Boni, 1925.

Morton, Ferdinand "Jelly Roll," and Alan Lomax. *Mister Jelly Roll: The Fortunes of Jelly Roll Morton, New Orleans Creole and "Inventor of Jazz."* Berkeley: University of California Press, 1950.

Mumford, Kevin J. *Interzones: Black/White Sex Districts in Chicago and New York in the Early Twentieth Century*. New York: Columbia University Press, 1997.

Payne, Charles M. *I've Got the Light of Freedom: The Organizing Tradition and the Mississippi Freedom Struggle*. Los Angeles: University of California Press, 1995.

Peretti, Burton W. *Jazz in American Culture*. Chicago: Ivan R. Dee, 1997.

Polletta, Francesca. "'Free Spaces' in Collective Action." *Theory and Society* 28 (1999): 1–38.

Rogers, J. A. "Jazz at Home." In *The New Negro: Voices of the Harlem Renaissance*, edited by Alain Locke, 216–24. New York: Albert and Charles Boni, 1925.

Rose, Al. *Storyville, New Orleans: Being an Authentic, Illustrated Account of the Notorious Red-Light District*. Tuscaloosa: University of Alabama Press, 1974.

Royster, Jacqueline Jones, ed. *Southern Horrors and Other Writings: The Anti-lynching Campaign of Ida B. Wells, 1892–1900*. Boston: Bedford/St. Martin's Press, 1997.

Spencer, Jon Michael. *The New Negroes and Their Music: The Success of the Harlem Renaissance*. Knoxville: University of Tennessee Press, 1997.

Spivey, Donald, ed. *Union and the Black Musician: The Narrative of William Everett Samuels and Chicago Local 208*. Lanham, Md.: University Press of America.

Thomas, Brook, ed. *Plessy v. Ferguson: A Brief History with Documents*. Boston: Bedford/St. Martin's Press, 1997.

Turner, Richard Brent. *Jazz Religion, the Second Line, and Black New Orleans*. Bloomington: Indiana University Press, 2009.

Welsh, Nolan, with Louis Armstrong. "The Bridwell Blues." Okeh Records, 1926.

William Ransom Hogan Jazz Archive, Louisiana Oral History Collection, Tulane University, New Orleans.

14

New Negroes at the Beach: At Work and Play outside the Black Metropolis

ANDREW W. KAHRL

On May 10, 1921, a ship carrying bananas from Jamaica docked at the port of Baltimore. Among its passengers was Austine Scarlett, a young Jamaican man who had stowed away in the ship's hull. Liberated from his native island's colonial-ruled peonage economy and dropped onto the streets of this burgeoning black metropolis, Scarlett steadily—and ruthlessly—built his own underground empire on the profits of the city's "numbers" trade, rising to become, by the 1940s, one of the city's most powerful, feared, and despised urban kingpins and a major dealer in real estate in black Baltimore. Eight years after Scarlett arrived in the United States, William L. Adams, a fifteen-year-old sharecropper's son from the cotton fields of eastern North Carolina, boarded a train bound for Baltimore. Like Scarlett, Adams's journey from the fields to the streets began on the Baltimore waterfront, where, as a teenager, he worked various odd jobs on the docks, carefully saving what little earnings he could muster and plotting his entry into the city's thriving numbers trade. Within years, the kid from Carolina had become "Little Willie," the numbers bookie, nightclub owner, prolific buyer of slum real estate, and invisible ruler over a vast network of businesses in northwest Baltimore.

No sooner had Scarlett and Adams conquered the city streets than they cast their eyes toward the country, specifically, the rolling hills and quiet shores of rural Maryland. In 1944, Adams's syndicate began acquiring real estate on a small peninsula near Annapolis, Maryland, where they constructed rustic summer cabins for themselves and invested heavily in the commercial development of Carr's Beach, a small, family-owned beach resort that catered to African American groups and families denied access to other spots along the shore. Scarlett, meanwhile, purchased 123 acres of farmland near the sleepy village of Westminster, in Carroll County, Maryland, in 1947, where, along with tending to a working farm consisting of sixty-two milking cows and herds of pigs and hogs, he invested over one hundred thousand dollars toward the construction of a swanky country club for the East Coast's select set, and where he began making plans to retire from the streets and become a "gentleman farmer." Both were confident of the lucrative potential of their enterprises and of their ability to attract urban black pleasure seekers to spend their weekends (and their leisure dollars) in rural Maryland.

And both numbers kings left behind a trail of paper slips that, until now, historians have neglected to follow. During the 1930s, operators of illegal lotteries made significant investments in black-owned businesses and fledgling institutions that were struggling to weather the Great Depression and circumvent the institutionalized discrimination of lending institutions. As they did, numbers kings became prominent businessmen and celebrated race leaders. By the early 1940s, Baltimore's major numbers kings had a financial stake in numerous black-owned businesses as well as residential and commercial properties in the city. Their increasingly diverse business portfolios spoke to numbers kings' dreams of transitioning into legal, and respectable, enterprises. But whereas they had carried these dreams with them on their journey from the country to the city decades earlier, it was not until the postwar years that the profits accumulated from illicit economies began to extend outside the city, as the changing tastes and outlooks of a critical mass of urban black consumers made large-scale investments in rural real estate and commercial enterprises seem profitable, and as federal, state, and local anticrime and anti-vice waves hastened urban kingpins' efforts to launder their earnings and transition (at least publicly) into "legitimate" trades.

The reintegration of "the countryside" (as both place and idea) into our understanding of "the city" in twentieth-century America is long overdue. As the historians Andrew Needham and Allen Dieterich-Ward note, "for most urban historians, even those interested in the development of the suburbs, rural areas remain undifferentiated 'green spaces' on the map that are of little importance until they are suddenly transformed into full-fledged members of the metropolis by the arrival of the first subdivision."[1] With rare exceptions, these rural landscapes barely register at all in scholarship on and popular culture representations of the twentieth-century African American experience.[2] Instead, the dusty, country roads of rural America usually figure (if at all) as merely a foil for the bustling streets of the city. For early-twentieth-century migrants, it was the site of their ancestors' literal and their own virtual enslavement, a place where generations of black Americans learned, as Eldridge Cleaver famously put it, "to hate the land" and from which they sought deliverance in the slums and ghettoes of northern cities.[3] Or, conversely, the rural South conjured a set of comforting images that assuaged, if only momentarily, feelings of dislocation, as when Ralph Ellison's invisible man is transported back to his homeland by the whiff of hot yams being sold by a New York City street vendor.[4] For mid-twentieth-century white liberals searching for ways to alleviate the "urban crisis" that African Americans' mass exodus from the rural South had supposedly wrought, the countryside was the land of "fresh air," where the hardened souls of urban black youth could be rejuvenated for a few weeks each summer before being deposited back in dying cities. Today, if popular culture is any guide, rural America might as well be a foreign country to many urban black youths, a place many only come to know through the caged windows of a bus on their way to a state or federal penitentiary. Two scenes from the acclaimed series *The Wire* capture popular understandings of urban blacks' relationship with the lands beyond the urban core well. In one episode, a character is assigned a job that requires him to drive from Baltimore to Philadelphia, during which he is surprised to learn that Baltimore radio signals fade as one leaves the city, himself having never left Baltimore in his life. In another episode, a police lieutenant relocates a teenager whose cooperation in a drug investigation makes him a target of gang members to his grandmother's house in rural Prince George's County. For the character, the prospect of being felled by an assassin's bullet on the streets seems almost preferable to dying of boredom out in the country. "The air down here all sticky. Worse than Baltimore, yo. And these crickets, louder than a motherfuck. Can't get no sleep. I don't think I'm cut out to be no country-ass nigga, man."[5]

Black Baltimoreans' investment in and relationship with Maryland's rural countryside, in the age of the New Negro, challenge such static, one-dimensional depictions of the country in the city—and the city in the country. It also forces a more fundamental reassessment of the cultural politics associated with the Harlem Renaissance and the New Negro. The seeming incongruity of New Negroes of the black metropolis in the countryside (both then and now) has tended to be replicated in the historical record, where the term *New Negro* and the Harlem Renaissance phenomenon have become synonymous with urbane lifestyles, radical politics, and a more fundamental rejection of a culture of American capitalism that had locked persons of color in a vicious cycle of deprivation and ostracism for centuries. In this reading, persons such as Scarlett and Adams curiously figure as exemplars of resistance to that order, their lives held as examples to both contemporaries and future generations of the alternatives to wage labor awaiting those urban migrants with the pluck and guile to thumb their noses at both the law and self-proclaimed black cultural authorities and to stake out their own paths to liberation.

This essay traces African Americans' attempts to develop rural black beaches, country clubs, and leisure-based enterprises in and around the Baltimore metropolitan area from the 1920s to post–World War II. In so doing, it offers a different reading of urban black Americans' evolving relationship with American capitalism during a time when the nation's economy was undergoing its own transformation—from one grounded in industrial production to one increasingly geared toward facilitating and servicing pleasure and consumption. From this vantage, Scarlett and Adams can be understood to exemplify, without contradiction, the New Negro generations' new visions of blackness and efforts to claim a new place in a global community as well as the values, markers of success, and notions of the "good life" normally associated with upper-class white America at this time—among others, a spacious country estate, membership in a country club, and a summer cottage on the shore. Rather than the world of "make-believe" E. Franklin Frazier disparaged in his polemic *The Black Bourgeoisie,* these places and the people who made them were the product of a ruthless culture of acquisitive capitalism forged on the streets of the black metropolis and conducted via informal economies that operated on the margins of the law and "respectable," middle-class black society.[6] By interrogating the origins of the enterprises and institutions that nourished the rise of a postwar black middle class—by, in other words, following the money—we can begin to see that the New Negro of the 1920s and 1930s did not succumb to the forces of a more consumption-oriented and "moderate" black politics in the postwar era but, in many respects, laid the groundwork and provided the institutional foundations for it to flourish.

In early-twentieth-century cities, one of the clearest indicators of class status in the black community was the ability to *leave* the city during the summer months. Although churches and social clubs arranged annual train and riverboat excursions that temporarily removed passengers from the city and briefly reunited some of them with family members back home, extended sojourns into the rural countryside were a pleasure enjoyed by a select few black Americans. Being able to spend time in quiet rustic retreats, and being there as vacationers and not as laborers, was often cited by leading race men and women as a telltale sign of a rising race. The acquisition and use of rural lands for the pleasure of black Americans were treated both as a racial imperative and, for rural black landowners, as a potentially profitable venture.[7] A southern border city, Baltimore, Maryland, had one of the nation's largest urban black populations throughout the late nineteenth and into the early twentieth centuries. As late as 1930, Baltimore had the fourth largest urban African American population in the nation, behind only New York, Chicago, and Philadelphia. For many newcomers to Baltimore and other burgeoning black metropolises, the ability to travel outside of the city, and to venture into the country as a visitor and under one's own volition, was fundamental to their process of becoming free and, by extension, becoming urban. As a result, black-owned and operated summer boardinghouses and sea- and lakeside resorts grew during these years, especially in the mid-Atlantic and Chesapeake states, which had both a comparatively large number of urban African American communities and black rural landowners. Along with summer seaside villages founded by

Washington's and Baltimore's "aristocrats of color" along Maryland's western shore were African American owners of property in ideally situated spots in the mountains or by the Chesapeake, who turned their homes into makeshift hotels during the summer months. In a tucked-away section of Maryland's western shore known as Shadyside, for instance, lived a cluster of black landowners whose presence in the area dated back to the early days of freedom. By the early 1900s, this area had emerged as a popular destination for black travelers, in the process turning struggling, mostly subsistence farm families into part-time hoteliers and incorporating them, albeit slightly, into emergent leisure market economies.[8]

The acquisition and commercial development of rural leisure spaces came to occupy a prominent place in early-twentieth-century black capitalist ideology and an urban spatial imaginary.[9] In Baltimore and other mid-Atlantic cities, scores of entrepreneurial black men acquired excursion steamboats and real estate hugging the shores of the Chesapeake and Potomac, where they worked to build business empires on the pennies of pleasure seekers who were segregated from white-owned commercial amusements.[10] The extent of black investment in real estate and recreation and amusement enterprises offered a telling snapshot of the state of black business as a whole. Seeking to take advantage of the opportunities created by a Jim Crow marketplace, and lacking the capital, connections, or market to sustain large-scale commercial and industrial development, real estate speculation and amusement enterprises, as Abram Harris, in his 1936 study *The Negro as Capitalist,* found, served as two of the main arenas of black business activity. At the same time, real estate and recreational enterprises constituted much of the capital assets held by fledgling black-owned lending institutions such as Baltimore's Taylor and Jenkins Bank.[11]

The sorry state of black-owned banks and the skewed, limited nature of black business activity were two related and reinforcing manifestations of African Americans' lack of capital and unequal access to credit. From this void, operators of illicit trades emerged to become prominent businessmen and increasingly exalted figures of the black metropolis. Though its name and the rules governing its operation varied by city (in Chicago it was called "policy," in Miami "*bolita*"), the core characteristics of the "numbers" was fairly consistent across urban America and differed only in degree from what Americans today call the "lottery."[12] Each morning, numbers runners passed through barbershops, beauty salons, groceries, and other storefronts in black neighborhoods, collecting nickels and quarters from bettors wagering on three-number combinations. To avoid charges of tampering, the more reputable books pegged winning numbers to the Federal Reserve daily closing number or another published figure.[13]

The popularity of lotteries in urban centers long predated African American urbanization. Lotteries were a common and popular feature of nineteenth-century working-class and immigrant urban neighborhoods and, like today, offered struggling individuals hope of instant material gain at little cost, even as it steadily drained them of their earnings. More than a pastime, playing the numbers became, for many living paycheck to paycheck, an investment strategy. In their appropriation of numbers generated by stock exchanges and other formal outlets of economic activity, urban lotteries were similar to other contemporary forms of gambling, such as the ubiquitous "bucket shops" that were located in the shadows of the Chicago Board of Trade and New York Stock Exchange, where individuals who did not possess the capital to invest in stocks wagered on the price movements of stocks and commodities.[14] Given the volatility and endemic corruption of stock exchanges during this era, the line separating real and fictitious investments was, for most, indistinct, which made, as Ann Fabian notes, the stigmatization of lotteries and off-the-books speculation an important aspect of the domestification of modern capitalism.[15]

By the 1890s, most states had outlawed lotteries. The suppression of nonsanctioned forms of gambling was one manifestation of a broader set of Progressive reforms sweeping across urban America. As other scholars have argued, early-twentieth-century urban Progressivism did not so much neglect the needs of black migrant communities as construct them as the contrast by which white ethnic immigrant assimilation would be gauged. What the historian Khalil Gibran Muhammad called the "condemnation of blackness" found its clearest expression in the spatial confinement of African Americans to racially defined sections of the city through public policy and private real estate industry practices and, moreover, the concentration and tacit acceptance of vice in these sections of the city.[16] Progressive reforms set in motion self-perpetuating stigmas of ghettoized urban African Americans that would come to profoundly shape the struggle for equality in twentieth-century America. The convergence here between race and urban space also indelibly reshaped the structure of black urban economies—creating opportunities for ambitious and entrepreneurial black businessmen and businesswomen to amass profits from illicit trades, generating numerous jobs and facilitating the extension of credit to fledgling black-owned businesses—and the culture of black urban life. In their monumental study of black Chicago, the sociologists St. Clair Drake and Horace R. Cayton noted that, in 1938, three of the city's numerous black-run policy companies generated an average of $3,023 in weekly profits, while dispensing $25,885.25 in weekly wages to a vast army of employees that included clerks, pickup and delivery men, doormen, bookkeepers, and bouncers.[17] The game's popularity also spawned subsidiary industries in fortune-telling and dream books.[18] And in times of official repression, operators of illegal lotteries fled into the countryside, beyond city limits, to conduct their trade. In Chicago, for instance, policy drawings were often conducted, as Drake and Cayton found, "in the open fields and woods in the suburbs of the city."[19]

As the profits illegal urban lotteries generated grew alongside urban populations in the early twentieth century, their operators increasingly came out of the woods (both literally and figuratively). By the 1920s, the larger numbers books in many northern cities had become what Drake and Cayton described as "protected businesses." While illegal, the game operated "under the benevolent patronage of the city political machines." This was certainly the case in Baltimore, where the city's large Roman Catholic and immigrant population blunted the more repressive excesses of Progressivism (indeed, the state of Maryland openly flaunted Prohibition and established its own agency to regulate liquor sales) and contributed to a cozy relationship between public officials and vice peddlers.

One of Baltimore's first, and most powerful, African American numbers kings was Thomas R. Smith. Smith's entry into the business was facilitated by his work as a loyal operative for the state's Democratic Party. After serving a prison sentence for tampering with ballot boxes in the 1895 election, Smith was awarded control over a numbers book by his friends in City Hall, which he continued to operate with impunity in exchange for helping to depress African American turnout for Republican candidates each election season.[20] With his earnings and access to power, Smith invested in hospitality and real estate, opening, in 1913, a twenty-six-room hotel on Druid Hill Avenue and, in 1921, founding the Smith Realty Company.

Investment in slum properties had a metastasizing effect on Smith and future numbers kings' wealth. With the introduction of racial zoning and neighborhood covenants during the earliest waves of black migration into Baltimore, a "dual housing market" took shape, forcing African Americans to pay grossly inflated rents on inferior housing. The private and loosely coordinated actions of early-twentieth-century real estate markets were, in the New Deal era, incorporated into federal policy, leading to the formation of what Arnold Hirsch called the "second ghetto." In both the first and second ghettoes, owners of slum properties amassed fortunes from these structural inequalities.[21] The historian N. D. B. Connolly estimates that in Jim Crow Baltimore, an investor in slum real estate could expect between a 27 and 60 percent annual return on an investment.[22] Numbers kings and black capitalists who accumulated profits from urban vice were among the earliest, and most extensive, African American owners of slum real estate. Their exploitation of the black working poor through slum real estate was less an indicator of lack of conscience and more a product of the nature of their business, which required the quick laundering of profits through investment in illiquid assets. Given that African American owners of real estate in slum districts were often buying property from whites and second-generation immigrants, their accumulation of property (and the largesse that flowed from it) were seen by many as ironic, but nevertheless positive, developments in the struggle for economic empowerment and cultural self-determination.

While Smith built a part of his fortune from poor housing stock in the city, he gratified his achievements out in the country. In 1917, Smith purchased several acres and built a country home outside the city on Reisterstown Road.[23] There he and his wife, Jessie, hosted elaborate parties, in which guests came "attractively attired in picture hats and gaily colored afternoon frocks, [and] played Auction Bridge on the spacious lawn."[24] Upon his death in 1938, over fifteen hundred people flocked to the country estate for his funeral, which was held inside the mansion and broadcast over a loudspeaker to an overflow crowd situated on the front lawn. U.S. senator George Radcliffe, Democrat of Maryland, delivered Smith's eulogy. The spectacle of hundreds of automobiles parked alongside a rural country road to mourn one of the city's leading black figures overshadowed the fact that only on the outskirts of the racially zoned and covenanted city could Smith have hoped to live in such luxury.[25]

Of more immediate significance than their symbolic stature as successful black businessmen was the financial support numbers bankers provided to others. As their profits mounted, numbers kings dispensed loans to black-owned businesses turned away by discriminatory lending institutions and made donations to fraternal orders, churches, and charitable institutions. "Access to black policy dollars," Juliet E. K. Walker, the foremost scholar on African American business history, notes, "provided black communities with a privately funded, informal cash subsidy, which was used as venture capital in the promotion and support of black business."[26] The most admired numbers kings earned a reputation for generosity and race loyalty that transcended cold economic calculations. In Baltimore, Smith was rumored to have owned mortgages on over 50 percent of the city's African American churches and kept deposits in unsteady black-owned banks long after others had withdrawn their savings. Indeed, the nickels and quarters bettors handed over to numbers runners recirculated back into local communities and touched every facet of urban social and institutional life.

This was never more true than as the nation slid into the Great Depression. As unemployment soared in the early 1930s, undercapitalized African American businesses and institutions desperately clung to life. In many urban black neighborhoods, only the depression-proof numbers game continued to generate healthy profits and provide jobs and hope for workers and players alike. Black capitalists and entrepreneurs turned to numbers kings for loans to keep their fledgling enterprises afloat. As baseball historian Adrian Burgos Jr. noted, numbers kings almost single-handedly kept Negro League baseball franchises in operation during the 1930s.[27] The Great Depression augmented numbers kings' power and stature within the black metropolis, provided them with the opportunity to expand their business holdings into the licit economy, and furthered their quest to become respectable businessmen.[28] Indeed, persons who had once operated in the shadows, on the margins of society, were by the 1930s feted as local heroes and called on to officiate ceremonies, march in parades, and toss out the opening pitch at Negro League baseball games.[29]

Shortly after Thomas R. Smith's death, his brother Wallace, who inherited his numbers book and other enterprises, was gunned down in front of one of his storefronts on Druid Hill Avenue. Wallace's short reign and violent end were indicative of the increased competition that accompanied the growth of the city's African American population and black commercial sector during these years. By the late 1930s, the growing number of storefronts, bars, nightclubs, and social institutions that lined black Baltimore's Main Street, Pennsylvania Avenue, were effectively funded by numbers dollars and operated by a host of competing syndicates. In Baltimore, the New Negro was coming into her and his own—culturally and economically—during a time that historians often label as the twilight of the Harlem Renaissance. The rise of William L. "Little Willie" Adams signaled their arrival. At the time of Smith's death, Adams had accumulated enough income running a small numbers book to open a tavern on Druid Hill Avenue. Following Smith's death, Adams worked to consolidate control over portions of Smith's former turf. He successfully repelled the incursion of white mobsters from Philadelphia, withstanding the bombing of his tavern in 1938 and apparently retaliating in kind. In the years that followed, he quickly expanded his gambling operations, putting several smaller books out of operation or bringing their operators under his control. At its height, Adams's syndicate handled daily receipts well in excess of five thousand dollars (Figure 14.1).[30]

Adams dexterously used the power of his purse to consolidate his control over commerce in northwest Baltimore. A master of the Jim Crow marketplace, Adams dangled before black men and women denied loans from formal lending institutions the opportunity to access the capital necessary to start or grow their own businesses. In return, borrowers handed Adams a 51 percent stake in their companies.[31] "He gave out lots of loans" to fledgling black-owned businesses, one person said of Adams. "But [before long] he owned the place."[32] By the late 1940s, Adams's effective control over black-owned businesses in west Baltimore was extensive—and virtually untraceable. As one chronicler of black Baltimore wrote, while "hardly a black-owned tavern in west Baltimore was not part of [Adams's] empire . . . all his properties were listed in someone else's name."[33] By the postwar years, Adams's syndicate had an ownership stake in several nightclubs and saloons along Pennsylvania Avenue, most prominent among them the celebrated Club Casino.

FIGURE 14.1. William L. "Little Willie" Adams (third from right) and a group of associates leaving a Baltimore police station following the bombing of his tavern in 1938. Courtesy of the Afro-American Newspapers Archives and Research Center.

Adams was a cool, unassuming, and ruthlessly skillful black capitalist who embodied the more rural, southern inflection of Baltimore's urban culture. In contrast to popular depictions of urban gangsters, Adams exhibited little desire to take part in the high-rolling, big-timing lifestyle and instead conveyed a more gentlemanly, chivalrous manner. He dressed conservatively, drove a modest automobile, married a schoolteacher, and was rarely seen out on the town. Perhaps most importantly, while many of these new "barons blew their wealth bigtiming," the *Baltimore Afro-American* wrote, Adams "profited by others' experiences. [He] invest[ed] in property[.]"[34] Land records from the city of Baltimore during the 1940s indicate an almost direct relationship between Adams's ascendance to the top of the city's numbers business during these years and his investment in real estate in the predominantly black neighborhoods of the city's northwest.[35] For most black Baltimoreans, how Adams earned his money paled in comparison to what his success symbolized—and the tangible benefits it provided. Describing public attitudes toward Adams, *Afro-American* columnist Early Byrd wrote, "What we had in common is that we all wanted to be independent of a racist white society. That's why we admired men like 'Little Willie.'"[36]

Adams's business investments helped bring to Baltimore the styles, consumer tastes, and cultural aesthetics that had characterized black life in Harlem and other northern cities over the previous decades. In 1948, Adams and his partners opened the Charm Center on Pennsylvania Avenue, the first high-end clothing store in the city where black women could try on the latest fashions and be treated with dignity and respect. Previously, black Baltimore women traveled as far north as Philadelphia and New York to shop in style. His wife, Victorine, managed the store and taught classes on social graces and etiquette to young black women. Some of Adams's other business investments contributed to the commercial commodification of black celebrities and entertainers, such as the Joe Louis Bottling Company, a line of soft drinks featuring the heavyweight champion and Adams's close friend and golfing partner.

The rise of mass culture, communication, and transportation not only linked black Baltimore to national and increasingly global networks but quite literally facilitated its expansion outside the physical boundaries of the metropolis. By the 1940s, the ability of black urbanites to leave the city was matched only by the relative dearth of places to which they could freely travel. Indeed, over the previous decades, exclusive black vacation retreats, such as Highland Beach, located outside Annapolis, Maryland, had waged an annual war against a seemingly endless parade of trucks and automobiles packed with "common" black folks from the city attempting to sneak onto "their" private beaches and enjoy an afternoon in the sun.[37]

As early as the 1930s, numbers of African Americans owning beachfront property in proximity to urban centers opened their property to visitors and hosted outings for various churches and civic groups from the city. For blacks living in Washington, D.C., and Baltimore, the Carr family's coastal property, located on the Annapolis Neck peninsula in Anne Arundel County, offered such an outlet for pleasure and relief. After inheriting the family's farm following their father's death in 1928, sisters Elizabeth Carr and Florence Sparrow began advertising summer boarding accommodations at the family's farmhouse and scheduling outings on their beach. Events at Carrs and Sparrows Beaches were enormously popular. On summer weekends, crowds swarmed around the charter buses that transported groups to the rural resort; by noon, the neighborhood associated with a certain group's outing fell silent and took on the resemblance of a ghost town. The beach steadily transitioned from group events to general admission and booked local and touring jazz bands and musicians for Sunday afternoon shows on the beach's pavilion.[38]

It would not take long before the property's commercial potential caught the attention of a major capital investor such as Adams. In 1944, Adams and business partners Chandler Wynn, Askew Gatewood, John Neal, and Littleton Gamby formed the Oak Grove Beach Company and acquired several acres of waterfront property adjacent to the Carr family's tract, where each built his own summer cabin. Called Elktonia Beach, the exclusive summer community signaled the arrival of black Baltimore capital on Anne Arundel County's shore. Following the death of Elizabeth Carr in 1948, Adams convinced Carr's son Frederick and his wife, Grace, to partner with Adams's syndicate in expanding the beach's commercial operations. Adams and his business partners subsequently formed the Carrs Beach Amusement Company and embarked on massive capital investment in the grounds. By 1951, the Carrs Beach Amusement Company had spent over $150,000 in improvements to the site, which included a covered, open-air concert pavilion, the Club Bengazi nightclub (named after a well-known club in Washington, D.C., and managed by Chandler Wynn Jr., the son of one of Adams's closest associates), and a midway.[39]

Similar to the storefronts that lined Pennsylvania and Druid Hill avenues, Adams had a financial stake in virtually every company conducting business on the beach and profited from every aboveboard transaction—from the gate receipts to the slot machines to the concessions. Adams's syndicate owned the music and entertainment equipment company that provided the nightclub and midway with vending machines, jukeboxes, pinball machines, and nickelodeons. It was his liquor wholesale business that stocked the bars at the music pavilion and nightclub. The Southern Maryland Novelty Company, another Adams-controlled enterprise, provided the rows of slot machines that lined the grounds and drew crowds by the busload.[40]

By the early 1950s, Carrs Beach attracted a steady stream of big-name and local jazz and R&B acts for Saturday evening and Sunday afternoon shows. As the dollars of Baltimore's informal economy were invested in this rural outpost, the seasonality and spatiality of black cultural production changed. A distinctly black and urban summer culture took shape here, its production, dissemination, and commercialization closely tied to the situation of audience and performer outside of the city. This distinct rural habitus reverberated back into the city. On Sunday afternoons in the summer, Annapolis deejay Hoppy Adams broadcast live on WANN-AM in Annapolis, whose fifty-thousand-watt tower carried as far west as Ohio. At three o'clock in the afternoon on Sundays, Adams stepped onto the stage at Carrs Beach's pavilion while reaching the front stoops of homes, row houses, and public housing in Washington, D.C., Annapolis, and Baltimore.

The beach became not only a place but a disposition. It served as both a site and a symbol of pleasure, pride, and community and as a visible rebuke, inscribed in sand, of the markers of inferiority that polluted the landscape of Jim Crow America. It not only provided a new outlet but also gave new meaning to the cultural aesthetics of the New Negro. Whereas a generation earlier, adventurous whites went slumming into urban black districts seeking a glimpse of "the

Negro" in his "natural" habitat (in the process reinforcing notions of race, space, and blacks' proper "place"), rural beaches attracted large crowds of urban blacks into settings (and, more specifically, burgeoning real estate markets) that white landowners and coastal developers were anxious to color as "white." In a narrow sense, Carrs Beach posed little challenge to segregation, narrowly defined. (And indeed, segregationists would later point to these venues as evidence of blacks' desire for "separation.") But in a broader sense, it subtly and indirectly struck at the very foundations of white supremacy (grounded in notions of privilege that were quite literally written onto the landscape). The earnings generated and dreams of freedom hatched on the streets of Baltimore in the interwar years became the infrastructure and inspiration for the post–World War II freedom struggle. At Carrs Beach, urban blacks came to understand themselves as a people through pleasure and consumerism, and through claiming space outside of the metropolis. Both culturally and financially, the New Negro renaissance of the 1920s and 1930s was a living presence in the postwar metropolis.

Violent suppression of economic competition and strategic exploitation of African Americans' consumer habits were as much a product of the race-conscious, leisure-based marketplaces of the New Negro metropolis as notions of political solidarity and economic cooperation. And in this respect, others were less subtle than Adams in their adherence to the "dog eat dog" maxim of the streets. After arriving as a stowaway from Jamaica, Austin Scarlett fought his way to the top of northwest Baltimore's numbers business, along the way earning a reputation as arrogant, impetuous, and violently unpredictable (Figure 14.2). Whereas Adams was small, quiet, and unassuming, Scarlett was large (weighing over 250 pounds), loud, and intimidating. One profile described him as "perhaps the most disliked gambler ever to rise to power in Northwest Baltimore."[41] Scarlett came to "the land of the fast buck," as he called the United States, to satisfy a thirst for material gain denied in his native homeland. The collapse of the British colony's sugar industry due to increased global competition in the late nineteenth century led to a massive exodus of workers to the Panama Canal Zone and the United States, followed shortly by the island's economic reorientation around the cultivation and shipment of bananas to markets on the U.S. East Coast. As international fruit magnates consolidated control over the land and established large-scale plantations, the Jamaican peasantry became increasingly trapped in debt peonage, with few prospects to own land or become economically independent of the island's system of wage slavery.[42] By the early 1920s, worker riots sporadically erupted, while desperate conditions led to a flood of refugees sneaking onto outbound ships. Scarlett was one of untold numbers of Jamaicans who arrived in the United States via the port of Baltimore as a stowaway about a cargo ship. By the 1920s,

FIGURE 14.2. Austine Scarlett, one of the kingpins of black Baltimore's informal economy. Courtesy of the Afro-American Newspapers Archives and Research Center.

the capture and detainment of stowaways aboard ships bearing bananas and other produce from the West Indies had become so common that the *Baltimore Afro-American* commented, "All Jamaica seems to be trying to come to Baltimore[.]"[43]

In Baltimore, Scarlett worked the streets but dreamed of the countryside. In 1947, he seemed to have turned the corner from gangster to businessman and from businessman to "gentleman farmer." After years of building wealth from investing in real estate in Baltimore's slums, Scarlett purchased a country estate near the small town of Westminster, in Carroll County, Maryland, located twenty-eight miles from Baltimore. The 123-acre property included a working dairy farm and came equipped with a swimming pool and horse stables. That fall and winter, Scarlett spent over one hundred thousand dollars on improvements to the house and grounds. The following spring, Scarlett's "lavish grounds . . . and swank country club" opened to the public.[44] In photographs of Scarlett's Country Club,

FIGURE 14.3. View of the grounds of Austine Scarlett's Country Club. Courtesy of the Afro-American Newspapers Archives and Research Center.

fashionably dressed young women dip their toes in the club's swimming pool (Figure 14.3). Groups of young black men lounged under the umbrella-covered tables or gathered on the back porch that looked out on the rolling countryside. Others played badminton on lawn tennis courts or rode bikes around the property. A couple from Camden, New Jersey, enjoyed their honeymoon there, decamping in one of the "finely-appointed guest houses" on the ground.[45] It quickly became a chief summer destination for high rollers on the East Coast. On weekends, one visitor later described, "the familiar rattle of the dice could be heard in the night. Shooting craps," the writer added, "was Scarlett's first love."[46] Scarlett seemed intent on making the estate multifunctional and appealing to both the Saturday night high rollers and Sunday afternoon picnic crowds. After opening, Scarlett announced plans to open a summer youth camp that would afford urban kids the chance to spend a few days playing in the countryside, learning to milk cows, and other wholesome activities. Eventually, he also hoped to open a retirement home facility on the grounds.[47] The extent to which Scarlett's Country Club was simply a front for his numbers business, affording him a means of laundering his earnings, is unclear, although the ties between his legitimate and illicit business activities were evidenced by the club's staff, which consisted of business associates who would later be arrested on racketeering charges.[48]

Whether blacks were rolling dice or riding bikes there, small-town and rural white neighbors in Carroll County did not welcome their presence and were alarmed at Scarlett's grandiose plans for the country club's future growth and development. No sooner had the ink dried on the deed than neighbors and local officials began applying pressure on Scarlett to abandon the venture and sell the land. Among them was reportedly a wealthy neighbor whose close relative was a Baltimore police commissioner.[49] First, it seemed, they applied gentle pressure to the brash sportsman. Almost daily, Scarlett later said, neighbors or persons in the town of Westminster approached him and asked, "Scarlett, why don't you sell your farm?" and "Scarlett, you want to sell your farm?"[50] He later described having been subject to constant harassment by "white interests" who were irritated by "the presence of colored residents in the tiny town, living in such sumptuous quarters[.]"[51]

After Scarlett roundly rejected their entreaties, more forceful measures ensued. The opening of Scarlett's Country Club coincided with a wave of investigations into organized crime and racketeering in Baltimore and on the federal level, culminating in the formation of the Senate Special Committee to Investigate Crime in Interstate Commerce (aka the Kefauver Committee) in 1950.[52] In a city (and state) where official corruption was endemic and the influence of organized crime on elected officials ubiquitous, it should come as no surprise that Baltimore's early 1950s antiracketeering hysteria resulted in selective investigations and targeted operations, with Scarlett at the top of vice squads' hit lists. In 1950, he was arrested and charged with criminal racketeering after a raid on the home of small-time numbers runner Rodger Wilkes turned up slips of paper bearing Scarlett's name. (On the basis of this flimsy evidence, Scarlett was subsequently acquitted of the charges.)[53] In 1951, the state's attorney, Anselm Sodoro, launched a grand jury investigation into organized crime in Baltimore, with the predominantly African American northwest section of the city at the center of the probe. All but six of the thirty-three persons summoned before the jury that summer were African American. Along with Scarlett, Willie Adams and several of his associates were called to testify. The city's black newspaper, the *Afro-American,* was quick to note that the racially biased nature of the city's investigation into organized crime paralleled that of other cities, "where the only individuals indicted as a result of the Senate probes have been colored operators[.]"[54]

In particular, the paper highlighted the real estate acquisitions by both Scarlett and Adams that preceded their arrests. In November 1949, Adams challenged the city's residential color lines with his purchase of a modest home in the all-white Forest Hill neighborhood. Shortly thereafter, he was arrested as he approached the house of associate Walter Rouse two hours after police had commenced a raid on the home. (Adams, like Scarlett, escaped conviction of this charge.)[55] "It is no secret that white residents in the Carlisle Ave. section resented the Adamses moving into their neighborhood," the *Afro-American* wrote. "Also it is no secret that the white citizens, both in the county and the city, resented the fact that Austin Scarlett purchased the rolling farm lands in Westminster where he operates his exclusive country club, the only one of its kind in Maryland for colored citizens."[56]

In September 1951, both Adams and Scarlett were charged by a Baltimore grand jury for operating an illegal lottery. Before his trial got under way, Adams secured a deal with federal prosecutors to testify before the Kefauver Committee in exchange for immunity from prosecution. Before the Senate committee, Adams claimed to have retired from the numbers trade and entered solely into legitimate business enterprises. Along with his extensive real estate holdings, Adams informed the committee of his ownership stakes in several black-owned businesses, including the Carr's Beach Amusement Park. (Following Adams's testimony, he was reindicted and convicted by a Baltimore jury; the U.S. Supreme Court, however, overturned the decision.) The large profits and enormous popularity of Carrs Beach throughout the 1950s and early 1960s exemplified Adams's successful transition from gangster to legitimate and respected businessman, while underscoring the role of real estate and commercial enterprises located outside urban ghettoes in facilitating the rise of urban black capitalists and, by extension, the making of black popular culture.

Scarlett was not as fortunate as Adams. In August 1951, police arrested one of Scarlett's underlings, Horace Cann, on charges of operating an illegal lottery in an attempt to compel him to testify against his boss. Cann refused and was sentenced to six months in prison. In exchange for his silence, Scarlett promised to pay Cann's wife forty dollars a week during his imprisonment. When Scarlett failed to keep his promise, Cann contacted the state's attorney's office and said he was ready to "talk."[57] On the basis of Cann's testimony, Scarlett was convicted of numbers conspiracy in December 1951.[58] In June 1952, Scarlett was sentenced to seven years in the state penitentiary, a decision Judge E. Paul Mason said aimed to convey to the city's criminal syndicates that "big fish are beginning to fall into the net."[59] (The decision came two days after Adams's conviction.)

Following his conviction, the federal government seized Scarlett's assets, including the country club, for back taxes totaling more than sixty-five thousand dollars and quickly moved to sell the estate at public auction.[60] In response, Scarlett, according to a U.S. Treasury official, began "moving heaven and earth to keep the place[,]" calling on "a group of East Coast sportsmen" to round up the cash necessary to successfully bid on the property at public auction. The extensive coverage Scarlett's feverish attempts to save the country club received in the local black press suggests the extent to which this rural retreat was seen as intimately tied to a broader struggle for spatial self-determination and, as a place of pleasure and business (and the business of pleasure), was part of a larger web of social and economic relations.[61] At auction, Scarlett's attorney, R. Palmer Ingram, purchased the sixteen acres that comprised the main buildings and swimming pool for thirty-four thousand dollars. Joseph Starner, described as a "prominent white Westminster cattleman," bought the eighty-two-acre farm for

352 ANDREW W. KAHRL

twelve thousand dollars.[62] The following week, over fifty bidders flocked to the auctioning of Scarlett's personal effects. On the front lawn of the former country club, cases of expensive whiskeys, high-end furniture, refrigerators, and electrical appliances were "sold for a song." A piano that Count Basie and Mary Lou Williams, among others, had played for summer crowds at the estate sold for two dollars. An "ultra-modern bedroom suite" that included a bed, vanity chest, bureau, and night table received the day's highest bid: $154. The auctioneer even sold the house's kitchen sink—for ten cents. Several African American nightclub and tavern owners were in attendance; all walked away with new furnishings for their establishments at deep discounts.[63]

After exhausting his appeals, on May 20, 1953, Scarlett surrendered to Baltimore County sheriffs and began serving his seven-year sentence. Months later, he was given the option of serving his entire sentence or being deported to his native Jamaica. Scarlett chose the latter. An account of the former kingpin's swift fall from grace said of its sad conclusion, "Scarlett, with dreams of his country club . . . yearned for the wide open spaces without bars or guards. He's going to get his wish, but he has got to go home to get it."[64]

The determined effort to drive Scarlett and his well-heeled black clientele from Carroll County resembled countless numbers of cases over the previous decades of rural whites applying intimidation and brute force to drive out "uppity" Negroes and expropriate their property holdings. Black-owned commercial beaches and resorts, in particular, had been a specific target over the years. On one hand, the seizure of Scarlett's property and liquidation of his assets by the federal government reflected the evolution of land-based racism from crude acts of terrorism conducted by torch-bearing night riders to dispossession through the courts via tax law enforcement and selective criminal investigations. On the other hand, the concerted effort to keep New Negroes and the profits of urban informal economies out of Carroll County reflected more recent changes in the political economy of race and rural real estate. Such practices also foreshadowed the emergence of new rationales for black exclusion in a suburbanizing nation. Indeed, the exponential growth of suburbia in post–World War II America not only turned farmlands into planned subdivisions but introduced legal and institutional mechanisms of racial exclusion into rural areas that had once offered prospective African American landowners freedom from the restrictions and physical confinement of the city. The closure of Scarlett's Country Club, in this respect, was not so much a product of the landscape of Jim Crow in rural America as it was a sign of a new culture of whiteness taking shape outside America's cities.

The New Negro embodied a broader set of aspirations rooted in a desire for cultural and economic self-determination. Much of this struggle took shape in the interwar years and took place in the city. It would be a mistake, though, to assume that those dreams extended only to the city's edge or that the cultural production associated with the New Negro renaissance was primarily an urban phenomenon grounded in the urban experience of the pre–World War II metropolis. As this essay demonstrates, the urban experience itself is inseparable from ideas about and interactions with the rural.

That the rich and revealing history of African Americans from the city who sought pleasure and pursued opportunities in the country throughout the first half of the twentieth century has been virtually unexamined by scholars is a testament to the insidious and far-reaching effects of the state-sanctioned real estate practices that worked to spatialize race in the second half of the twentieth century. The relocation of black populations to spatially confined urban ghettoes has tended to be replicated in the histories of black people more generally. Just as African American landowners in Maryland's suburbanizing countryside found themselves subject to removal and their lands targeted for expropriation in the decades following World War II, so, too, have the dreams and dollars this generation of enterprising, newly urbanized black Americans carried with them to bucolic, rolling hills and undeveloped shores outside the city been written out of the history of the long black freedom struggle. Indeed, one would be hard-pressed to find in the literature on race and civil rights in the twentieth century any mention of African Americans and country clubs that did not center on struggles to integrate these all-white citadels. This reflects a broader tendency among both scholars and the public to treat the twentieth-century black experience as a journey from the rural, plantation South to the industrial North. Despite the proliferation of important, revelatory scholarship on the hard work that went into making suburbs white, and the urban core black, we still know little about the social construction of those lands that lie far beyond the outer belt, where divided highways become single-lane roads and where the history of race in America generally ends. We must look anew at the quiet streets of Westminster, Maryland (whose African American population remains as miniscule today as it was when Scarlett arrived on the scene), or within the wealthy gated community that stands on the site of the former Carr's Beach, with an eye also cast on the devastated streets of black Baltimore, where figures like Adams and Scarlett once amassed wealth from the rent checks and spare pennies of working persons and families. Here we will find a new genealogy of the New Negro and gain a new perspective on the constitutive role of land (as physical space) and landscapes (as imagined space) in shaping understandings of race and determining categories of power—then and now.

NOTES

1   Needham and Dieterich-Ward, "Beyond the Metropolis," 947.

2   See Wiese, *Places of Their Own*.

3   Cleaver, "Land Question and Black Liberation," 57.

4   Ellison, *Invisible Man*, 261–95.

5   "Ebb Tide," *The Wire*, season 2, episode 1, directed by Steve Shill, aired June 1, 2003 (New York: Home Box Office, 2003); "The Hunt," *The Wire*, season 1, episode 11 , directed by Steve Shill, aired August 18, 2002 (New York: Home Box Office, 2002).

6   Frazier, *Black Bourgeoisie*.

7   See Kahrl, "Political Work of Leisure," and Gatewood, *Aristocrats of Color*.

8   See "Annapolis," *Baltimore Afro-American*, August 21, 1926; "Camp Bay Breeze Now Open at Shadyside, Md.," *Baltimore Afro-American*, July 9, 1932; on black coastal landownership and rural real estate development, see Kahrl, *Land Was Ours*.

9   Use of the term *spatial imaginary* comes from Lipsitz, *How Racism Takes Place*.

10 See Kahrl, "Slightest Semblance of Unruliness."

11 Harris, *Negro as Capitalist*.

12 See Wolcott, "Culture of the Informal Economy"; Connolly, "Games of Chance"; White et al., *Playing the Numbers*; and Baldwin, *Chicago's New Negroes*.

13 See Drake and Cayton, *Black Metropolis*, 470.

14 Hochfelder, "Where the Common People Could Speculate."

15 See Fabian, *Card Sharps, Dream Books, and Bucket Shops*, 2–3.

16 See Muhammad, *Condemnation of Blackness*.

17 Drake and Cayton, *Black Metropolis*, 479–82.

18 See Wolcott, *Remaking Respectability*.

19 Drake and Cayton, *Black Metropolis*, 472.

20 See Pietela, *Not in My Neighborhood*, 116–18.

21 For an introduction, see Hirsch, *Making the Second Ghetto*; Freund, *Colored Property*; Satter, *Family Properties*.

22 See Connolly, "We Are Exactly What We Seem."

23 Lillie M. Young to Thomas R. Smith, mortgage, June 2, 1917, Baltimore County Land Records, book 510, page 536. Accessed at http://mdlandrec.net/.

24 "Mrs. T. R. Smith Entertains at Lawn Party," *Baltimore Afro-American*, July 23, 1927.

25 "1500 Persons at Smith Funeral," *Baltimore Afro-American*, August 20, 1938.

26 Walker, *History of Black Business in America*, 238.

27 See Burgos, *Cuban Star*. See also Lanctot, *Negro League Baseball*.

28 Wolcott, "Culture of the Informal Economy," 56.

29 In Chicago, Drake and Cayton found, the Great Depression "weakened the legitimate Negro business institutions, the symbols of financial control and stability in Bronzeville. The policy kings emerged as one group who could point to the thousands of workers still employed by The Race. They were thus able to assume

the role of Race Leaders, patrons of charity, and pioneers in the establishment of legitimate business." See Drake and Cayton, *Black Metropolis,* 486.

30 In 1951, Adams told members of the Senate Special Committee to Investigate Crime in Interstate Commerce (aka the Kefauver Committee) that his numbers lottery generated one thousand dollars in daily revenue. Given rampant discrepancies between Adams's reported and actual income, this figure was likely far less than his actual daily intake.

31 See Pietela, *Not in My Neighborhood,* 118.

32 Zastrow Simms, interview with Andrew Kahrl, November 23, 2010.

33 Pietila, *Not in My Neighborhood,* 118.

34 Louis Lautier, "Capital Spotlight," *Baltimore Afro-American,* September 2, 1944.

35 See http://mdlandrec.net/.

36 Quoted in Luke, *Baltimore Elite Giants,* 78.

37 See Kahrl, *Land Was Ours,* 86–113.

38 See ibid., 178–209.

39 "The New Carr's: Playground of the East," *Baltimore Afro-American,* June 9, 1951.

40 "Thrown from 'Caterpillar,'" *Baltimore Afro-American,* July 8, 1950.

41 "Downfall: Owned Half Million, Digits Banker Broke," *Baltimore Afro-American,* March 19, 1955.

42 See James, *Holding Aloft the Banner of Ethiopia,* 9–49.

43 See *Baltimore Afro-American,* May 5, 1925.

44 Ibid., April 12, 1952.

45 *Philadelphia Tribune,* July 5, 1949.

46 *Baltimore Afro-American,* March 19, 1955.

47 Ibid., July 31, 1948.

48 Ibid., January 5, 1952.

49 Ibid., June 14, 1952.

50 Ibid., April 12, 1952.

51 "Scarlett, Resort Owner, Gets 7 Years for Numbers," ibid., June 7, 1952. See also "Scarlett Cites Persecution for Lavish Country Club," ibid., April 12, 1952.

52 On the Kefauver Committee hearings, see Bernstein, *Greatest Menace,* 61–83.

53 *Baltimore Afro-American,* January 6, 1951.

54 Ibid., August 11, 1951.

55 "Club Operator Is Object of Probe," ibid., September 1, 1951.

56 "Gambling Crackdown Followed Expansion of Adams, Scarlett," ibid., September 1, 1951.

57 Ibid., January 5, 1952.

58 Ibid.

59 Ibid., June 7, 1952.

60 "Seize Resort for Back Taxes," ibid., September 20, 1952.

61 "May Not Sell Swank Country Club After All," ibid., November 1, 1952; "Sportsman May Save This Resort from the Auction Block," ibid., November 1, 1952.

62 "Scarlett's Sold for $34,000," ibid., November 15, 1952.

63 "Sportsman's Expensive Effects 'Sold for a Song,'" ibid., November 22, 1952.
64 Ibid., March 19, 1955.

BIBLIOGRAPHY

Baldwin, Davarian L. *Chicago's New Negroes: Modernity, the Great Migration, and Black Urban Life.* Chapel Hill: University of North Carolina Press, 2007.

Bernstein, Lee. *The Greatest Menace: Organized Crime in Cold War America.* Amherst: University of Massachusetts Press, 2002.

Burgos, Adrian, Jr. *Cuban Star: How One Negro-League Owner Changed the Face of Baseball.* New York: Hill and Wang, 2011.

Cleaver, Eldridge. "The Land Question and Black Liberation." In *Eldridge Cleaver: Post-prison Writings and Speeches,* edited by Eldridge Cleaver and Robert Scheer, 57. New York: Random House, 1969.

Connolly, Nathan D. B. "Games of Chance: Jim Crow's Entrepreneurs Bet on 'Negro' Law-and-Order." In *What's Good for Business: Business and Politics since World War II,* edited by Julian E. Zelizer and Kimberly Phillips-Fein, 140–56. Oxford: Oxford University Press, 2012.

———. "We Are Exactly What We Seem: Notes on Interpreting a Black Property Rights Movement." Talk given at University of Michigan, November 2010.

Drake, St. Clair, and Horace Cayton. *Black Metropolis: A Study of Negro Life in a Northern City.* 1945. Reprint, Chicago: University of Chicago Press, 1993.

Ellison, Ralph. *Invisible Man.* 1947. Reprint, New York: Vintage, 1995.

Fabian, Ann. *Card Sharps, Dream Books, and Bucket Shops: Gambling in Nineteenth-Century America.* Ithaca, N.Y.: Cornell University Press, 1990.

Frazier, E. Franklin. *The Black Bourgeoisie.* Glencoe, Ill.: Free Press, 1957.

Freund, David M. P. *Colored Property: State Policy and White Racial Politics in Suburban America.* Chicago: University of Chicago Press, 2007.

Gatewood, Willard B. *Aristocrats of Color: The Black Elite, 1890–1920.* Bloomington: Indiana University Press, 1990.

Harris, Abram L. *The Negro as Capitalist: A Study of Banking and Business among American Negroes.* College Park, Md.: McGrath, 1936.

Hirsch, Arnold R. *Making the Second Ghetto: Race and Housing in Chicago, 1940–1960.* Chicago: University of Chicago Press, 1983.

Hochfelder, David. "'Where the Common People Could Speculate': The Ticker, Bucket Shops, and the Origins of Popular Participation in Financial Markets, 1880–1920." *Journal of American History* 93 (September 2006): 335–58.

James, Winston. *Holding Aloft the Banner of Ethiopia: Caribbean Radicalism in Early Twentieth-Century America.* London: Verso, 1998.

Kahrl, Andrew W. *The Land Was Ours: African American Beaches in the Jim Crow and Sunbelt South.* Cambridge, Mass.: Harvard University Press, 2012.

———. "The Political Work of Leisure: Class, Recreation, and African American Commemoration at Harpers Ferry, West Virginia, 1881–1931." *Journal of Social History* 42 (October 2008): 57–77.

————. "'The Slightest Semblance of Unruliness': Steamboat Excursions, Pleasure Resorts, and the Emergence of Segregation Culture on the Potomac River, 1890–1920." *Journal of American History* 94 (March 2008): 1108–37.

Lanctot, Neil. *Negro League Baseball: The Rise and Ruin of a Black Institution*. Philadelphia: University of Pennsylvania Press, 2004.

Lipsitz, George. *How Racism Takes Place*. Philadelphia: Temple University Press, 2011.

Luke, Bob. *The Baltimore Elite Giants: Sport and Society in the Age of Negro League Baseball*. Baltimore: Johns Hopkins University Press, 2009.

Muhammad, Khalil Gibran. *The Condemnation of Blackness: Race, Crime, and the Making of Modern Urban America*. Cambridge. Mass.: Harvard University Press, 2010.

Needham, Andrew, and Allen Dieterich-Ward. "Beyond the Metropolis: Metropolitan Growth and Regional Transformation in Postwar America." *Journal of Urban History* 35 (November 2009): 943–69.

Pietela, Antero. *Not in My Neighborhood: How Bigotry Shaped a Great American City*. Chicago: Ivan R. Dee, 2010.

Satter, Beryl M. *Family Properties: Race, Real Estate, and the Exploitation of Black Urban America*. New York: Metropolitan, 2009.

Walker, Juliet E. K. *The History of Black Business in America*. New York: Macmillan, 1998.

White, Shane, Stephen Gartson, Stephen Robertson, and Graham White. *Playing the Numbers: Gambling in Harlem between the Wars*. Cambridge, Mass.: Harvard University Press, 2010.

Wiese, Andrew. *Places of Their Own: African American Suburbanization in the Twentieth Century*. Chicago: University of Chicago Press, 2004.

Wolcott, Victoria W. "The Culture of the Informal Economy: Numbers Runners in Interwar Black Detroit." *Radical History Review,* no. 69 (Fall 1997): 46–75.

————. *Remaking Respectability: African-American Women in Interwar Detroit*. Chapel Hill: University of North Carolina Press, 2001.

VI

HOME TO HARLEM

15

"Home to Harlem" Again: Claude McKay and the Masculine Imaginary of Black Community

THABITI LEWIS

When Claude McKay first set foot in Harlem, he was far from naive or new to America. In fact, when this twenty-one-year-old arrived in the United States from Clarendon Hills, Jamaica, in August 1912, not only was he a fairly well traveled and well educated man of peasant origins but he brought with him a distinct outsider perspective. This worldly intellectual man of working-class sensibilities possessed not only a global black diasporic perspective of the world but an interest in what he termed "the lust to wander and wonder." After a stay in the Midwest, he set out for New York City, pursuing business opportunities (owning a restaurant) he felt existed there. The failure of McKay's business venture and marriage cleared space for him to devote attention to his art. To support himself while he wrote, he worked a series of odd jobs available to black men in American cities, such as a porter, janitor, bar boy, coal shoveler, houseman, butler, and waiter. McKay later wrote that he "waded through the muck and scum" so that he could become a writer. So from 1914 to 1919, McKay's "leisure was divided between the experiment of daily living and the experiment of essays in writing,"[1] and these experiences not only shaped his political radicalism but also provided ample material for his first novel, *Home to Harlem* (1928), which targeted the common man.

This essay discusses McKay's *Home to Harlem* with an eye toward the predominately masculine lens through which he explores the variety and scope of black urban diasporic life—its global and multiregional perspectives. McKay's depiction of black life and notions of community in 1920s black America examines the wonder, excitement, and limits of Harlem through recognition of alternative locations where black community thrived. In the spirit of this collection, I am reading *Home to Harlem* as a literary depiction of an expansive African diasporic reality in the early twentieth century. McKay's complicated and primarily masculinist presentation of modern industrial life focuses on proletarian characters that map out the divergent diasporic routes of the New Negro reality and Renaissance.

His global and working-class perspective in *Home to Harlem* is unique and stems from his Caribbean roots and peasant origins to reveal black space, place, and cultural production in the person of the "common man" (who is also decidedly his own man). This approach is a subtle alternative to the official Renaissance and its focus on either pastoral notions of "folk" or the "Talented Tenth." Thus this essay explores McKay's novel as an alternative or a renewed understanding of the New Negro. To be sure, it is an "understanding" that attempts to engage a culturally diverse notion of African American community while expanding notions of race by traveling through the divergent contours of urban space and the folk inhabiting these oppressive spaces.

Home to Harlem is dynamic in its range of perspectives and experiences from which to explore African American notions of beauty, politics, and cultural production of the New Negro. Indeed, McKay is interested in a wider lens through which to view the New Negro—one that embraced a working-class perspective and an individual sense of respectability. The novel does more than capture Harlem's creativity; it also embraces the jazz of black culture. Indeed, it captures the wretchedness, crime, poverty, unemployment, and overcrowding of Harlem that forced people to alternate locations such as Brooklyn, Pittsburgh, Chicago, and Philadelphia. Harlem is essentially one nodal point in the protagonist Jake Brown's navigation of a wider black experience. His tour of black life in low places throughout the African diaspora in multiple cities is a riff on the jazz of black culture. For McKay, the New Negro is both international and regional; he is individual soloist and a representative of communal aspects of black life.

McKay's narrative, adroitly powered by jazz, the meanderings of a soldier, and the locomotive symbolism of a train, reflects his modernist proclivities toward fragmentation that delicately balances the communal and individualism. The rhythms of black life are diverse in this story. Thus McKay effectively absorbs a popular symbol of black progress during this era—the black soldier—to show the myriad ways in which masculinity imagines and performs community. *Home to Harlem* is a novel that has several tentacles. Its plot feels episodic and lost at sea as Jake Brown meanders from the backside of World War I to Harlem, then from woman to woman, job to job, and city to city. However, to view *Home to Harlem* this way is a mistake. What feels like a disjointed narrative is a virtual jazz piece that is cogent for it riffs on the notion of global, multiregional, black diasporic life. And, like jazz, McKay's narrative resists being static or compromised because it ruptures the elite brokerage politics that sought to limit New Negro era notions of masculinity and black culture.

The story begins with the protagonist Jake, who has just deserted the military during World War I over his disgust at being excluded from participating in battle. Jake is "disappointed" because he "had enlisted to fight," but black men were discriminated against and therefore relegated to domestic chores. Soon after his desertion, he spends some time living with an English woman in London before heading back to a Harlem that he is impatient to reach. Soon upon arriving, Jake visits a cabaret and meets the beautiful Felice, with whom he spends one glorious night, instantly falling in love. However, he soon loses contact with her. After an unsuccessful search for Felice, he shacks up with the cabaret singer Congo Rose in Brooklyn. He works briefly as a longshoreman but quits when he discovers that he is being accused of scabbing—crossing the picket line to work (and many times the only way black laborers gained access to factory work). Jake then hangs out with his new friend Zeddy, who embraces the "sweet life" (also known as "sweetbacking" or being kept by a woman in exchange for sexual services or companionship). When Congo Rose wants Jake to be her sweetback, he refuses (because he is an independent, "respectable" man) and leaves her to work and live away from Harlem as a laborer on the Pennsylvania Railroad. From here the plot makes several episodic stops and starts in cities such as Philadelphia, Pittsburgh, and Washington, D.C., during Jake's service on the railroad. However, Jake eventually returns to New York, where he miraculously finds his lost love Felice, gets into a brawl over her, avoids a violent outcome, and then finally flees with Felice to escape the chaos and danger threatening him in Harlem.

It is important to note that despite its provocative treatment of everyday black life, McKay saw his novel as situated somewhere in between the more sensational primitivism of Carl Van Vechten's provocative *Nigger Heaven* and the "cultured" literary respectability of New Negro leaders, urging for civility and decorum in all things black. To be sure, McKay's goal was not to correct or replicate the primitivism found in Van Vechten's novel. As Marlon Ross correctly discerns in *Manning the Race: Reforming Black Men in the Jim Crow Era,* McKay sought to distinguish his approach from the "footloose . . . [of] Van Vechten's treatment of these topics. Instead of merely pandering to commercial tastes or conforming to primitivists' vogue, McKay has a genuine interest in the sociopolitical potential of these unconventional sexual relationships."[2] Though the focus here is not unconventional sexual relationships, Jake's rejection of racial stereotypes and middle-class masculine convention deserves intense discussion. McKay understood that the acceptance from many white reviewers of both his novel and Van Vechten's stemmed from a comfort with caricatures of black laziness, hypersexuality, and violence.[3] Moreover, as Nathan Huggins suggests in *Harlem Renaissance,* McKay was perhaps disappointed that many of these same reviewers of his novel missed his intent to convey a sense of "gentility and propriety" in black folk beyond the middle class "that was absent from *Nigger Heaven.*"[4]

The larger racial backdrop, of course, troubles McKay's narrative decisions in *Home to Harlem* to examine the so-called underside of black life. The novel received mixed reviews, ranging from intense condemnation to intense praise.[5] Although McKay's treatment of Harlem may have made W. E. B. Du Bois feel "unclean," the writer was unfazed. Rather than bitterness, he felt pity and sympathy for Du Bois, who seemed to be "forced by circumstances into the role of racial propagandist," which limited his "contact with real life."[6] Others, such as Langston Hughes, wrote to McKay praising the work as "the finest thing we've done yet. . . . Your novel ought to give a second youth to the Negro Vogue . . . and even those who dislike it say it is well written."[7] Even James Weldon Johnson, a member of the older generation, thought it was a "wonderful book."[8]

McKay's aim, absent from what many of the critics suspected, was to tap into the unworked mines of black life to produce literature that reflected a more complex portrait of that life. He locates black humanity, heroism, culture, and artistry in the image of the rank and file, which differed from what the black elite advocated. Indeed, as literary scholar Jerry Ward Jr. points out, "McKay was writing about normal ordinary people. Van Vechten was writing about talented savages."[9] McKay's desire to write about ordinary people endeared him to younger Renaissance era artists. His decision to produce an art more broadly representative of mass desires is largely what made Home to Harlem extremely popular—even in controversy.[10] From the shores of France, McKay enjoyed the attention his novel received back home.

His choice of a soldier as the central protagonist is also not incidental to the masculine lens through which he explores black community. Military men were central physical and symbolic figures in the larger New Negro struggle for black humanity in the early twentieth century. Jake Brown's desertion because of the military's racial discrimination rejects, if not directly challenges, the military as an acceptable space to cultivate black masculinity in America. The World War I promise of equality elided blacks as whites, angered by the sight of black soldiers, violently upheld racist notions of separation. Thus Jake's desertion demonstrates an alternate expression of courage and defiance against militarist representations of black manhood within New Negro fiction.

The presence of the black soldier during this era was thorny at best. Though often depicted in mainstream fiction as disappointed, dejected, isolated, angry, disillusioned, rejected, docile, and dangerous, black men's participation in the U.S. military, alongside being coercive or demeaning, played a central role in working through ideas of both race pride and national belonging. Many soldiers reported experiencing a sense of manhood for the first time while in France, when soldiers and citizens abroad treated them with a relative level of respect and fairness.[11] This was starkly different from treatment back home in the United States, where World War I black soldiers returned home expecting a hero's welcome but received a rude awakening. Instead, these veterans were often greeted with violence and ingratitude. Racial tensions were high because many whites feared that African Americans would return home demanding equality and would try to attain it by employing their military training. During summer and fall 1919, antiblack race riots erupted in twenty-six cities across America. The lynching of blacks also increased from fifty-eight in 1918 to seventy-seven in 1919. At least ten of those victims were war veterans, and some were lynched while in uniform.

Despite this treatment, African American men continued to enlist in the military. And as historian Sarah-Jane Mathieu points out, "the specter of the black soldier cast a shadow over African Americans' cultural, social, and political lives."[12] McKay was acutely aware of the military's impact. Like many black writers, he chooses a soldier as his heroic protagonist. However, his protagonist is antithetical to the notion of soldier as loyal follower of an organization or as willing to serve. On the contrary, Jake Brown deserts limiting racial and social politics and demands equality. Thus he explains to Felice that he left Brest because the military wanted black men as servants instead of soldiers. Moreover, he represents a brand of New Negro heroism and respectability committed to serving self and community. The armed service experience in Europe undermines his manhood and hence his humanity rather than elevating it.

Although McKay's deserter soldier may seem antiheroic, or an odd choice when so much black hope during the early twentieth century hinged on heroic black soldiers, the prideful deserter is a powerful alternative symbol of black manhood. Jake is independent and unreconstructed, which represents a different brand of heroic black masculinity and respectability that is divergent from the black soldier seeking approval. The emergence of an uncompromising soldier impatient with the pace of change, honest about the shortcomings of America, and critical of the military's insufficient horizon of change for black Americans is important. Although impatient, Jake is not immoral, docile, or dangerous. On the contrary, the thing that most angers him or makes him somewhat dangerous is the military's failure to deliver its promised democracy. "Jake was disappointed. He had enlisted to fight. For what else had he been sticking a bayonet in the guts of a stuffed man and aiming bullets straight into a bull's-eye? Toting planks and getting into rows with White comrades at Bal Musette were not adventure. . . . They didn't seem to want us niggers foh no soldiers. We was just a bunch a despised hod-carriers."[13] This New Negro soldier–hero is unconcerned with being a neat, uncomplicated symbol of black progress. Thus he rejects the unfairness and disrespect black soldiers face by abandoning the military as a viable option for exerting his manhood.

Despite his complex circumstances, what Jake desires is quite simple. As he explains in the first few pages of the narratives, he merely desires an opportunity to prove himself a man by getting "a crack at the Germans,"[14] just like the other men fighting for their country. However, discrimination strips Jake of this opportunity. What is interesting about the language in the opening scene is that Jake's use of the term *comrade* makes clear that he sees himself as equal to his fellow white soldiers—even if the whites running the military do not treat him as such. Jake's status as military man who will not accept unethical or unfair orders foreshadows McKay's personal belief that progress for black folk required a desertion of sorts from conventional approaches to equity, democracy, notions of community, and even gender. Jake's desertion of Europe also foreshadows the primacy of only his own culture (Harlem and other enclaves) as a suitable route to the prideful masculine existence he desires.

McKay is not keen on the notion of the military providing the New Negro with opportunity, equity, or status as American. On the surface, though McKay follows the convention of using Great War veterans as heroes, his narrative does not neatly fit the mode of African American unsung heroes representing humanity through military sacrifice, tenacity, and strength.[15] And he conveys this to readers early on, when Jake complains about patiently waiting two years for an opportunity to fight and prove his manhood. We are immediately introduced to an angry and disillusioned Jake, a man unwilling to make any more sacrifices and regretting his decision to join the military: "Why did I ever enlist and come over here? Why did I want to mix myself up in a white folks' war?"[16] The point here is that although African Americans were earning higher positions in the army, that did not necessarily mean they were getting equal treatment. Black draftees endured extreme hostility from white men refusing to salute black officers, while black officers were often barred from the officers' clubs and quarters. The War Department's refusal to intercede to halt discrimination caused extreme frustration, compelling men like Jake to desert the military for alternative routes to masculinity and humanity—separate from white norms and social structures.

Even Jake's eagerness to return to the creative expressiveness of black culture in Harlem can be read as a rejection of stifling black conservatism in favor of the jazz nature of notions of blackness. Hence we are informed that Jake's "steel-gray English suit" fits him "loosely and well."[17] McKay's decision to drape Jake in a loose "steel-gray English suit" suggests black humanity with space to move freely in one's own personal and cultural aesthetics. This idea is punctuated in Jake's exclamation, upon boarding a ship that will take him out of Europe, "Harlem for mine! . . . Take me home to Harlem, Mister Ship."[18] Moreover, the looseness of Jake's suit is a metaphor for his willingness throughout the narrative to grow, to discover and explore alternative sites of black cultural production for the New Negro. Jake's rebellion bucks norms, while also positioning him as a new variant on the black hero soldier; he is a combatant in the war against racism and narrow notions of black representation.

Therefore Jake's chant of "Take me home . . . Mister Ship! Take me home to the brown girls waiting for the brown boys"[19] as he is fleeing Europe serves two functions. It positions Harlem's black culture and women as a partial salve for his wounded masculinity, and it poses a critical question that the narrative attempts to answer:

> Jake danced with the girl. They shuffled warmly, gloriously about the room. He encircled her waist with both hands, and she put both of hers up to his shoulders and laid her head against his breast. And they shuffled around. "Harlem! Harlem!" thought Jake. "Where else could I have all this life but Harlem? Good old Harlem! Chocolate Harlem! Sweet Harlem!"[20]

Jake's revelry in the sounds and sights of black folk when he returns to Harlem soothes his soul, which undergoes a rebirth. The blues music, Harlem, a beautiful woman, and "sweet liquor" wash the anger from Europe and at the military away. This scene is essential for framing the question, "Where else could I have all this life but Harlem?"[21]

But Jake soon learns that "all this life" in Harlem is not sweet and good, as he experiences several obstacles. Jake embodies notions of individualism and independence that influenced the spirit of defiance that World War I black soldiers brought back with them from abroad and cast into African American life. Jake's attempt to define and express his masculinity as a longshoreman is as unsatisfactory as his military experience and relationship with a white woman in Europe. When he learns that his job is considered scabbing, he initially defends his manhood by asserting his honesty and work ethic. His sense of masculine pride compels him to tell the white man confronting him, "I've don worked through a tur'lble assortaments o' jobs in mah lifetime, but I ain't nevah yet scabbed on any man."[22] Jake's code of personal integrity is rooted in a masculine sense of honesty and integrity but also independence and social consciousness. However, he lacks faith in white integrity, which is why he tells the union recruiter, "I ain't no joiner kind of fellah. . . . I ain't no white folks' nigger and I ain't no poah white's fool. . . . No, pardner, keep you' card. I take the best I k'n get as I goes mah way."[23] This is an important scene, for it captures the essence of Jake's prideful and independent "mah way" mantra. He rejects alliances with whites because his history with the military has taught him to distrust them, or as Jake explains to the union man, "Things ain't none at all lovely between white and black in this heah Gawd's own country."[24] Still, despite Jake's distrust and hostility, his sense of honor and pride keep him from "scab[bing] on . . . even the orneriest crackers."[25] Decency, honesty, independence, and pride personify McKay's black imaginary. Unfortunately, the expression of these traits is too often reserved for the novel's male characters.

BLACK MASCULINITY AND WOMEN

Jake's sense of pride and honor compels him to leave the longshoreman job. Once again, he seeks Harlem's nightlife for refuge. The Harlem cabaret scene that Jake enters is a colorful and expansive space representing a divergent diasporic black reality. Far from a static space, it is vibrant with "Dandies and Pansies, chocolate, chestnut, coffee, ebony, cream, yellow, everybody . . . teased up to the high point of excitement."[26] Jake is smitten by a "moaning" saxophone "and feet and hands and mouths were acting it. Dancing. Some jigged, some shuffled, some walked, and some were glued together swaying on the dance floor,"[27] being driven crazy by the energy in the room. The atmosphere is blissful, disrupted only by a wild and angry woman "jazzing" a table "into the drum," knocking down the cabaret singer and ending the entertainment for the evening.[28] McKay's Harlem scene has two significant roles in the story: not only is Harlem the standard by which other cities are compared but it also foreshadows the problematic place women occupy in McKay's imaginary of black life and culture.

Jake's return to the familiar sights and sounds of Harlem is an important step toward establishing his sense of respectability and masculinity but also echoes McKay's personal belief in privileging the beauty found in black life and culture. It is easy to surmise this because, early in the novel, Jake informs the reader that the English woman with whom he lives after his military desertion is not ample salve for his wounded masculinity: "Jake's woman could do nothing to please him now. She tried hard to get down into his thoughts. . . . But for Jake this woman was now only a creature of another race—of another world. He brooded day and night."[29] McKay suggests that neither Europe nor sex across the color line will heal racial wounds or appease his aesthetic sensibilities.

After reconnecting to the jazz and revelry of black culture found in Harlem, which includes Jake's evening with Felice, the soldier's wounded manhood begins to mend. After an evening with her, "he woke up in the morning in a state of perfect peace. . . . He was satisfied. . . . He sniffed the fine dry air. Happy, familiar Harlem."[30] Felice is his felicity, bringing him joy; she is an elixir that restores him. He is so blissful that he muses, "I ain't got a cent to my name, but ahm as happy as a prince, al the same."[31] Felice more so than Harlem seems to have restored his sense of pride and manliness. His interaction with her allows him to stroll down Lennox Avenue in ecstasy, feeling a "handful o' luck shot stright outa heaven."[32] This is in stark contrast to his intimacy with the anonymous English woman he deserted. She, like the military, did not fulfill his sense of manhood. However, his encounter with Felice has him floating inside the "bear" Harlem.[33]

The restorative encounter with Felice foreshadows a trend in the novel whereby black women are, for the most part, minimized as tools or props against which

New Negro manliness is measured, satisfied, or finds expression. Perhaps this explains why Jake spends the bulk of the novel passively searching for Felice and in the blissful company of males. Although Felice offers him something that a "creature of another race"[34] (the woman in England) cannot, she is noticeably absent in the narrative until the very end. Like the other female characters, her presence is peripheral.

McKay is not shy in his pronouncement that there is no space for New Negro women in conversations about black humanity. The pattern for women in this narrative is that they are a bothersome but necessary impediment men must endure while trying to discover their individual identities:

> [Jake] had concluded that a woman could always go farther than a man in coarseness, depravity, and sheer cupidity. Men were ugly and brutal. But beside women they were merely vicious children. Ignorant about the aim and meaning and fulfillment of life; uncertain and indeterminate; weak. Rude children who loved excelling in spectacular acts to win the applause of women.[35]

He offers excuses for the behavior of men. Women, Jake informs us, are "the real controlling force of life," the reason "men fought, hurt, wounded, killed each other."[36] The men of the narrative are but innocent "victims of sex . . . foolish apelike blunderers in their pools of blood,"[37] unaware of the cause of battle, "except it was to gratify some vague feeling about women."[38] McKay sacrifices female characters to expand the scope of black humanity and community. In McKay's New Negro world, women serve as mere allegories for larger ethical decisions. They are either obstacles or pawns for masculine elevation and personal fulfillment.

More often than not, the function of all the women characters is to appease or assist the exertion of McKay's masculine imaginary—tools for solidifying prideful masculine existence. Despite his search for Felice, Jake seems to desire male companions most. Although black women offer what the "creature of another" race cannot, their true value is specious; there is not enough to convince the reader that their value is more than sexual or that they function as a contrast to male humanity. Women are usually disruptive forces that must be tolerated. In an early scene, after a fight closes a club, Jake stands on the sidewalk with his pal Zeddy and shares his opinion of women: "Sometimes they turn mah stomach, the womens. . . . Ain't no peace on earth with the womens and there ain't no life anywhere without them."[39] And while the women in the novel are part of the life of the story, their role is always to function as contrasts that resituate and propel Jake toward pursuing higher levels of masculine integrity and security.

BLACK LIFE BEYOND HARLEM

While Jake is elated with the sights, sounds, and smells of Harlem, McKay is adroit enough to explore Brooklyn as a black spatial alternative to Harlem. Brooklyn, New York, represents a domestic alternative space where black community is performed. Jake, who is open to "any little thing for a change,"[40] allows Zeddy to take him there. It is not as commercial, fast paced, or appealing, but Myrtle Avenue in Brooklyn is not without some luster. As their pal Strawberry Lips explains, "Myrtle Avenue used to be a be-be itching of a place," with a cabaret that was "running neck and neck with Marshall's in Fifty Third Street."[41] McKay, who initially chose Brooklyn to live and grow a business, makes clear that Harlem was not the only space black people desired, nor the only place where they thrived. This is important because often discussions of black America (particularly its literary history) in the 1920s begin and end with a claustrophobic picture of Harlem.

The differences and similarities between Harlem and Brooklyn in this text immediately emerge in the interior of the Myrtle Avenue gin-fest hosted by Miss Curdy and Miss Susy. Like in Harlem, there is dancing, gambling, jazz and blues music, drinking, and a sexual atmosphere on Brooklyn's Myrtle Avenue. However, the wild and vibrant nature of the scene in Brooklyn pales in comparison to the one in Harlem:

> The phonograph was discharging its brassy jazz notes when they entered the apartment. Susy was jerking herself from one side to the other with a potato-skinned boy. Miss Curdy was half-hopping up and down with the only chocolate that was there. Five lads, ranging from brown to yellow in complexion, sat drinking with jaded sneering expressions on their faces.[42]

The Brooklyn gin-fest party hosted in Susy's apartment is a calm, smaller, more intimate space that offers free gin, music, gambling, and fun. The music, though jazz and blues, is produced through a phonograph, whereas in Harlem, it is a live production. But unlike the women dancing in Harlem, Susy is "jerking herself from one side to the other," and Miss Curdy is "half-hopping up and down" with another man.[43] Brooklyn's level of reverie and excitement does not compare to Harlem's, where nearly all are on their feet or swaying to the music. In the Brooklyn apartment, the "desultory dancing . . . dice . . . Blackjack . . . Poker"[44] and the "jaded sneering expressions" the men exude suggest they are displeased with the circumstances of being relegated to two unattractive, older women. The description of the apartment is complicated, at once an intimate and humane "close, live, intense place" but also a "jungle atmosphere driven by two women savagely" searching the "eyes of males"[45] hoping for sexual liaisons. Here a "savage" woman "jerking herself" around is contrasted against calm, dapper male characters. The preceding is another example of McKay following Western culture's use of women to position male figures as desirable, humane, civilized figures.

The topic of Brooklyn rivaling Harlem as an alternative black space emerges when Miss Curdy interrupts two chaps arguing about celebrities to inform them that Harlem is not that big a deal and, moreover, is full of fake people. McKay lets us know that the Brooklyn folk are also worldly as Miss Curdy tells them, "I knew Bert Williams and Walker and Adah Overton and Editor Tukslack and all that upstage race gang that wouldn't touch Jack Johnson with a ten foot pole. I have lived in Washington and had Congressmen for my friends. . . . Why you can get with the top-crust crowd at any swell ball in Harlem. All you need is the clothes and coin. I know them all, yet I don't feel a bit haughty mixing here with Susy and you all."[46] In many regards, Miss Curdy is a subtle critique of Renaissance era life in Harlem as lacking substance. She even uses famous boxer and non-Harlemite Jack Johnson (who hails from Chicago) as the ultimate yardstick for her discussion about respectability and consciousness. Her discussion reminds the reader of the multiregional urban reality of black life. Thus, when Zeddy wants to go to Harlem to hang out with Jake, Susy protests with an unflattering depiction of the Harlem scene that raises the status and safety of her Brooklyn apartment gin-fest. She chides Zeddy and others who might consider Harlem *the* urban pastoral reality for black folk: "What makes you niggers love Harlem so much? Because it's a bloddy ungodly place."[47] Interestingly, McKay has a female character live in an alternative space and make this powerful statement against Harlem as the *only* preferred place.

In the Harlem buffet flat, Jake had entered a much larger space churning out blues music in a room filled with "couples . . . dancing, thick as maggots in a vat of sweet liquor."[48] Though it lacks the intimacy of Myrtle Avenue, the Harlem space is crowded, residents are anonymous, and it is filled with strangers. Also, the food and drink are not free. Finally, while Jake is offered free sex from Miss Curdy, in Harlem he gives Felice "all" the money he "has left in the world."[49] The scenes in Brooklyn and Harlem offer similar things, but McKay suggests that the costs associated with the less intimate space in Harlem are much higher.

Indeed, Harlem has a heavier cost attached to it, reflecting a warning that, although Harlem is electric, it is "ungodly" and not the only location producing vibrant black culture and life. What McKay describes in the cabarets of Harlem is an atmosphere more deadly, chaotic, full of pretensions, and thick sexual intensity. It includes a Fiddler, saxophonist, drummer, and cymbalist, who inspire and catch "inspiration from him."[50] This frenzied music compels Rose to dance in "rhythmical exactness for two" and compels her to "lift[] high her short skirt and show[] her green bloomers."[51] But such sexual electricity also provokes violence that does not exist in Brooklyn.

On one level, the dialogue between Miss Curdy and Susy in the Harlem cabaret best articulates McKay's belief in the richness of alternative locations of black culture. Unimpressed with the Harlem cabaret, Curdy tries to convince Susy to leave: "Lesh git furthest away from this low-down nice hole. . . . I never did have any time for Harlem."[52] She goes on to remind Susy that Washington preceded Harlem as a vibrant center of black cultural production: "When I was high up in society all respectable colored people lived in Washington."[53] With this Susy concurs: "There was no Harlem full a niggers then. . . . I should think the nigger heaven of a theater downtown is better than anything in this heah Harlem."[54] In addition, Susy declares Brooklyn as a heavenly alternative to Harlem. McKay distances his depiction of black life from Carl Van Vechten's depiction when Susy adds, "It's good and quiet ovah in Brooklyn. . . . This here Harlem is a stinking sink of iniquity. Nigger hell."[55] Though some critics thought otherwise, McKay clearly offers an alternative to navel-gazing authors like Van Vechten. McKay avoids a caricatured portrait of black life; this is a comprehensive picture of the daytime struggles, the good-time nightlife, and the alternatives to the vaunted Harlem.

Perhaps McKay is a poor "Talented Tenth" representative—a member of the elite black educated and professional class—a bad New Negro, because he embraced the values found in black diasporic folkways where good and bad are visible and morality is not black and white. McKay, critical of the educated folk and the racial obsession with "civilization," has Ray instruct Jake "to get something new, we Negroes . . . get our education like our houses. When the whites move out, we move in and take possession of the old dead stuff. Dead stuff that his age has no use for. . . . And civilization is rotten. We are all rotten who are touched by it. . . . All men have the disease of pimps in their hearts. . . . I have seen your high and mighty civilized people do things that some pimps would be ashamed of."[56] This is not only a direct challenge to the civilized establishment folk of the Harlem Renaissance era but also McKay's way of directing the New Negro to look inward for morality and valuable cultural models. McKay favored an artistic philosophy that literary scholar Brent Hayes Edward describes as an ethic of "mobility" and "footlooseness."[57] For him, fresh models of cultural representations exist within black culture. As a result, McKay rejects narrow and pretentious notions of respectable black life that are outside of or limit the terms of black possibility for standards for "high culture" or "uplifting channels," which he deems nothing more than "old dead stuff."

Because McKay's sense of black culture is not relegated to a single space or model, it is not surprising that he sets the wandering Jake aboard a train fleeing Harlem and the immoral demands of a woman. Jake's adventure among a diverse group of black men aboard the train extends his self-directed, free vision of black life and black masculinity. The train becomes a powerful locomotive republic of black male fraternity full of dandies, professors, cooks, and roundabouts from across the diaspora, confined in a single space, boarding and exiting at different black urban locations. The second part of *Home to Harlem* begins with a description of a train as an animate character—"a huge black animal" snorting and roaring through the heart of Pennsylvania, "packed with people and things, trailing on the blue-cold air its white masses of breath" where the chef, cooks, and waiters make the train function.[58] This imagery is striking as the mobile republic moves between various spaces throughout the black urban diaspora, from dining car to kitchen, from fresh linens to outhouses. The train rolls in that indeterminate space between racial respectability and primitivism, between middle class and working class, highly educated and illiterate. McKay implodes the notion of a monolithic black male or black community aboard the train.

While imploding notions of monolithic black culture, *Home to Harlem* also privileges individualism, bonds between black men, and the symbolism of the dynamics surrounding these masculine bonds, suggesting larger possibilities for ideal black community formation. But in an interesting gender twist, McKay explores the complex status of black community as masculine fraternity on the train via a movable kitchen—a space traditionally considered the domain of women. It can be argued that the symbolic importance of the train and kitchen suggests the moveable feast of creative and intellectual black life and community during the Harlem Renaissance era. The pecking order of the workers on the train represents diverse black masculinity, modernity, and racial contradictions of progress in the 1920s. McKay achieves this by relegating black men, regardless of their education or skills, to roles of service traditionally held by women in domestic settings. Perhaps the Chef put it best that "this heah white man's train service ain't no nigger picnic."[59] Indeed, modernity is no "picnic" for black Americans, as evidenced by Jake's numerous disappointments; modernity consistently fails to deliver the social progress and opportunity it promised. Even modern America relegated black men to the kitchen as cooks and waiters. Therefore the black men aboard the train, whether highly educated or working class, are literally in the backrooms providing service, and McKay's narrative wants to expose this tragedy.

Despite this flaw, aboard the train, Jake's masculinity is at ease among the diverse display of black manhood. He finds himself in the neutral space of third cook, whose duty is to "hand out the orders."[60] This is a step forward from his previous position as a soldier who was expected to be loyal and follow orders. His position as third cook elides a binary; it is a jazzlike existence that grants him space to formulate his own sense of what it means to be a black man. In this setting Jake's masculine reality "rubbed smoothly along with the waiters . . . he remain[s] himself and [does] not [try] to imitate the chef."[61] As he had done ever since leaving Europe, Jake seeks a comfortable, individual sense of manhood—one void of mimicry or soldiering.

For McKay, black masculinity is akin to the complicated jazz existence Jake experiences aboard the train. Such existence is also as diverse as the black communities the train visits. Some of the cooks and waiters only spent time together gambling. The "older men were dignified"; the "light-skinned" fellows only hung with their kind in stopovers, while the steward and chef kept distance from them all.[62] Aboard the train, there is no singular way of being male. Some are well educated, others are uneducated and irresponsible, and some are notable family men. There are also men from the South and the Caribbean. Nevertheless, what they share in common is the impact of racism, which cramps them all together in a pecking order working on the railroad. Similarly, the salient issue for black men is navigating being *men* in America.

McKay even inserts a lesson about black diasporic race pride through the Haitian character Ray, who informs the waiters about Haiti and men like Toussaint L'Ouverture and Dessalines. The history Ray shares compels Jake to feel pride as a black man: "He felt like a boy who stands with the map of the world in colors before him, and feels the wonder of the world."[63] As Jake learns about Dessalines and Toussaint L'Ouverture and that "Africa was not the jungle as he had dreamed of it, nor slavery the peculiar role of black folk,"[64] his pride swells. This masterful education is meant to deflate popular stereotypes about black culture but is another unfortunate example of narrow masculine imaginary about men told among men. Female humanity and heroism are once again absent. On the train, McKay offers a powerful vision of modern black masculine possibility that unintentionally but noticeably renders women invisible.

What is visible is the symbolism of the railroad, which links and extends diasporic connections as well as notions of modern black community in *Home to Harlem*. Indeed, "these men claimed kinship. . . . They were black like him. . . . They were chain-ganged together and . . . counted as one link."[65] The reader can literally track connections between Baltimore, New York, and Philadelphia in the same way that tracks connect trains to different cities. The cities hum salient themes but have distinct personalities. On each stop during Jake's railroad adventures, McKay unwraps regions filled with colorful characters, rituals, and innovative music similar to but also different from those of Harlem. For example, Pittsburgh serves as a rich alternative black experience, a thriving cultural space that, like Harlem, has poolrooms, pimps, prostitutes, jazz and blues music, saloons, drugs, gambling, and basement restaurants. However, in Pittsburgh, the poolroom "was a sort of social center for the railroad men and the more intelligent black workmen of the quarter."[66] Meanwhile, in Philadelphia's buffet flat parties, jazz and blues set the pace, just as they do in Harlem and Brooklyn.

McKay's contention is unabashedly that black people and their behaviors are valuable cultural products ripe to be picked or mined. Moreover, his narrative riffs that black people are far from monolithic. Ray, Jake, and the diverse group of men aboard the train and in numerous cities along the rail lines are iterations of vibrant, progressive black culture existing and thriving in cities outside of Harlem—a point McKay emphasizes by featuring the character Ray, who is from "Hayti" and in possession of "another language and literature."[67] The motif of progressive black cultural production and diverse black reality moves throughout the narrative from the beginning to the very end but is primarily channeled through male bodies or varied perspectives. In Jake's words, "We may all be niggers aw'right, but we ain't nonetall all the same."[68] Ray's railroad soliloquy echoes McKay's embrace of the beauty of black diasporic culture as *the* standard of respectability over education, which Ray calls "a prison with white warders."[69] To be sure, the content of *Home to Harlem* plays on this point to entice middle-class folk to embrace the diversity and beauty of black humanity as an authentic and rich cultural subject.

McKay has been called an internationalist because he unapologetically bathed in the beauty and complexity of black diasporic culture. Brent Hayes Edwards, in his successful book *The Practice of Diaspora,* tags McKay a "vagabond international" aware of the significant role of blacks in the "logic of modern civilization."[70] And though Du Bois may have felt he needed a bath after reading *Home to Harlem,* quite possibly he felt equally unclean about vying for "respectability" at the expense of black music, dance, and art produced by working-class folk representing the other 90 percent of black communities in major cities like Harlem, Washington, D.C., or Pittsburgh. To be clear, McKay's novel demands a rupture from middle-class mimicking of white culture. A great example of this celebration of black life and culture occurs when Jake visits a Philadelphia house party and describes what he sees there as "black lovers of life caught up in their own free native rhythm, threaded to a remote scarce-remembered past, celebrating the midnight hours in themselves, for themselves, of themselves."[71] Of course, the passage echoes Langston Hughes's famous 1925 essay "The Negro Artist and the Racial Mountain" but also captures the impetus of *Home to Harlem.*

Certainly the portal through which McKay views black life is wider than a work like *Nigger Heaven.* Although his perspective is profoundly limited by its gendered vision of black community, his diverse assemblage of black male characters is quite dazzling. And given the struggle to express the frustrations of black masculinity in America at that time, his shortcomings regarding women are somewhat understandable. The characters here challenge the hard lines between respectability and sensationalism set up by Harlem Renaissance artists and intellectuals on both sides of the color line. Indeed, not only does McKay orchestrate a jazzlike rupture from notions of Harlem Renaissance location but he also ruptures past perceptions of black male representation, shaping his own iteration of New Negro reality.

As *Home to Harlem* hurtles toward its conclusion, it selects an alternative space for masculine safety. New York becomes increasingly unsafe, so Jake escapes to Chicago. McKay's decision to shift the location at the end is important. It cautions readers against stifling notions of the New Negro by relegating them to New York or America. One thing his novel shows is that, although Harlem is a significant black cultural breeding ground for 1920s and 1930s blacks, it was hardly utopic or the only location. Hence the narrative introduces the reader to the cultural bounty of New Negro life in Haiti, in Africa, and in cities such as Pittsburgh, Washington, D.C., and Chicago.

A February 2011 story in the *Wall Street Journal* proclaimed Harlem "The Mecca of Black America" and rightfully lauded Harlem as the site of enormous artistic and political energy "for black America."[72] However, *Home to Harlem* is a gentle reminder that Harlem "ain't" necessarily the only site for rich artistic and political energy in black America past or present. As McKay's novel reveals, Harlem offered cramped quarters and limited opportunity. This is a striking point that cannot be ignored because Jake, who could not wait to get to Harlem, flees it twice in search of safety or better opportunity. What does it mean that a novel featuring the name "Harlem" in the title concludes with its protagonist indefinitely headed "foh a little while"[73] to Chicago for refuge? Jake remarks to Felice at the conclusion, "This heah country is good and big enough for us to git lost in. You know Chicago? . . . Why, le's go to Chicago . . . I hear it's a mavhelous place foh niggers."[74] With this, McKay is reminding readers that the wealth of black cultural production does not end in Harlem. We trust Jake's insights because we know he has traveled to several urban black locations where black artistic and political life is thriving. Felice punctuates this point at the end, instructing readers to follow her, when she concurs with Jake, "Ain't nothing in Harlem holding me, honey. Come on les pack."[75]

Perhaps McKay was correct that it would take many decades for "the Negro in America to appreciate" the "spirit" of *Home to Harlem*. Not only did he open fresh areas of exploration for black literary artists but his novel stands as a testament that thriving communities and artistic production were taking place throughout the New Negro world. McKay imagines and crafts a brand of heroic masculinity whereby men like Jake fearlessly desert soldiering roles that will not let them fight to be men on their own terms. This brand of heroism rejects a litany of conscripted notions of black masculinity from scabbing to beating women. Jake is an honorable working-class New Negro hero determined to be a man on his own terms. He is the antithesis of notions of black people as brutal, lazy, violent, or hypersexual. In the end, McKay peels back the skin of his motley crew of male characters aboard trains, in bistros, at rent parties, and in backrooms to reveal a complex world of gender relations, class struggle, white primitivism, and diasporic exile and belonging. Jake rebukes white expectations and black intellectual notions of what black masculinity was or could be. And though his New Negro lens extends well beyond Harlem, it still does not extend far enough because it inadvertently excludes women from the frame, or they occupy a minor trajectory on the landscape.

Throughout *Home to Harlem*, McKay urges readers to appreciate the "peasant matrix" of black life as the model, or at least the richest element, from which to extract art and humanity. What some critics deemed a nefarious cast of characters betraying secrets McKay saw more as a celebration of the liberating reality of the rich black culture he knew and embraced. Jake, the men on the dock, the people in cabarets, and the workers on the train do not care what whites or the black middle class think. Their pleasures and obsessions are their own, unfettered by strivings to measure up for white approval of their humanity.

NOTES

1 Cooper, *Claude McKay*, 77.

2 Ross, *Manning the Race*, 334.

3 Cooper, *Claude McKay*, 238.

4 Huggins, *Harlem Renaissance*, 121.

5 Cooper, *Claude McKay*, 241.

6 Ibid., 244.

7 Ibid., 243.

8 Ibid., 243–44.

9 Quoted from Jerry Ward Jr. during a telephone conversation while he was in New Orleans about the importance of McKay's novel on July 6, 2011. Ward lauds McKay for focusing on Harlem as a great location but also as a city riddled with the same social problems blacks endured in other cities.

10 McKay explains the core of *Color Scheme* in a letter to H. L. Mencken. In this letter, he admits that the book is uneven, then he goes on to describe it as "a realistic comedy of life" as he "saw it among Negroes on the railroad and in Harlem." Although *Home to Harlem* is void of the uninhibited colloquial language that kept *Color Scheme* from being published, it includes topics from *Color Scheme*, such as blacks on the railroad and in Harlem. So although McKay may have burned *Color Scheme* after it became clear that it would not be published, he kept many embers of the ideas from it alive, using them to lay the groundwork for *Home to Harlem*. Cooper, *Claude McKay*, 221.

11   Mathieu, "Great Expectations," 411.

12   Ibid., 410.

13   McKay, *Home to Harlem*, 4, 331.

14   Ibid., 4.

15   Mathieu, "Great Expectations," 412.

16   McKay, *Home to Harlem*, 7-8.

17   Ibid., 11.

18   Ibid., 8–9.

19   Ibid., 9.

20   Ibid., 14.

21   Ibid.

22   Ibid., 45.

23   Ibid., 45–46.

24   Ibid., 46.

25   Ibid., 48.

26   Ibid., 32.

27   Ibid.

28   Ibid., 33–34.

29   Ibid., 8.

30   Ibid., 15.

31   Ibid.

32   Ibid., 16.

33   Ibid., 14.

34   Ibid., 8.

35   Ibid., 69–70.

36   Ibid., 70.

37   Ibid.

38   Ibid.

39   Ibid., 34.

40   Ibid., 65.

41   Ibid., 64.

42   Ibid., 65.

43   Ibid.

44   Ibid., 68.

45   Ibid.

46   Ibid., 67–68.

47   Ibid., 79.

48   Ibid., 14.

49   Ibid.

50   Ibid., 92.

51   Ibid., 93.

52   Ibid., 98.

53   Ibid.

54 Ibid.
55 Ibid., 98–99.
56 Ibid., 243–44.
57 Edwards, *Practice of Diaspora*, 206.
58 McKay, *Home to Harlem*, 123.
59 Ibid.,124.
60 Ibid., 125.
61 Ibid.
62 Ibid., 126.
63 Ibid., 134.
64 Ibid.
65 Ibid., 153.
66 Ibid., 142.
67 Ibid., 154–55.
68 Ibid., 159.
69 Ibid., 157.
70 Edwards, *Practice of Diaspora*, 198.
71 McKay, *Home to Harlem*, 197.
72 Edward Kosner, "The Mecca of Black America," *Wall Street Journal*, February 26, 2011, C5.
73 McKay, *Home to Harlem*, 335.
74 Ibid., 332–33.
75 Ibid., 333.

BIBLIOGRAPHY

Cooper, Wayne. *Claude McKay: Rebel Sojourner in the Harlem Renaissance.* New York: Schocken Books/LSU Press, 1987.

Edwards, Brent Hayes. *The Practice of Diaspora: Literature, Translation, and the Rise of Black Internationalism.* Cambridge, Mass.: Harvard University Press, 2003.

Huggins, Nathan Irvin. *Harlem Renaissance.* Updated ed. New York: Oxford University Press, 2007.

Lewis, David Levering, ed. *The Portable Harlem Renaissance Reader.* New York: Penguin Books, 1994.

Mathieu, Sarah-Jane. "Great Expectations: African Americans and the Great War Era." *American Quarterly* 63, no. 2 (2011): 410–17.

McKay, Claude. "Claude McKay Letters and Manuscripts 1915–1952." Schomburg Collection, Schomburg Library, Harlem, New York.

———. *Home to Harlem.* Boston: Northeastern University Press, 1987.

Ross, Marlon B. *Manning the Race: Reforming Black Masculinity in the Jim Crow Era.* New York: New York University Press, 2004.

16

Not Just a World Problem: Segregation, Police Brutality, and New Negro Politics in New York City

SHANNON KING

"The cosmopolitan atmosphere [of New York City] knows less of color prejudice than probably any other city in the United States," optimistically opined George Edmund Haynes in 1921.[1] Haynes, founder of the National Urban League, and the first black man to graduate from Columbia University with a PhD in the new discipline of sociology, envisioned Harlem as an exemplar of interracial comity. Gotham's cosmopolitanism was predicated on blacks' reported full integration into the city's political life. This, Haynes believed, "indicate[d] a liberal feeling on the part of the white voters." Accordingly, Haynes conceived of Harlem as a model of interracial relations that blacks of the United States and across the globe should follow. "For, both directly and indirectly," opined Haynes, "the mental feeling, attitudes, and thoughts of the Negroes of the nation, as well as other parts of the world in their . . . relations with their white neighbors are influenced by the Negroes of New York as by those of no other city."[2] As far as race relations were concerned, New York was exceptional. White supremacy was, in response to W. E. B. Du Bois's insights, a world problem, yes, but not a New York problem.[3]

By proffering Harlem as a panacea for all ills of white supremacy across the black world, Haynes deftly distinguished black New Yorkers' experience of race as an anomaly to the threat of white supremacy repressing and subjugating black-occupied spaces in the United States and around the globe. Black reformers and their depictions of New York and Harlem as exceptions challenged both scientific and popular charges of blacks people's inherent criminality and intellectual inferiority. Yet this utopian version of Harlem—a sort of reactionary form of resistance, generally devoid of political conflict and, especially, violence—has overshadowed the black experience of racism, segregation, and violence that engulfed New York City at the height of the New Negro era. While faithfully acknowledging the notorious 1900 race riot that rocked Gotham, black reformers and civil rights leaders ignored the cycle of white mob attacks and police brutality that continued to rampage black neighborhoods around New York throughout the first three decades of the twentieth century. Yet since first settling in the white-ethnic communities around the city, blacks continued to wage defiant battles over territorial spaces where whites remained committed to delimiting black settlement.

This chapter argues that black self-protection activity in Harlem operated as a rejection of "white definitions of black rights, opportunities, and sociability" in residential and public places. In these politicized urban spaces, New Negroes actively asserted their "claims to citizenship and equal civil and political rights with whites."[4] This chapter juxtaposes the trope of Harlem as the "Negro mecca" with the lived experiences of Harlemites waging physical battle over urban space in the first three decades of the twentieth century. The cojoined forces of racial violence and black self-protection practices allow us to further interrogate the still prevalent conceptualization of interwar Harlem as primarily a site of New Negro cultural and intellectual production and even as a model of racial comity. Most scholars of the period now even claim that the New Negro of Harlem marked a moment of black political decline, with an increased focus on culture.[5] But in fact, self-protection activities powerfully demonstrate that the political radicalism of New Negro politics persisted throughout the 1920s and 1930s.

Harlem was a site of white civilian and state-sanctioned violence, reflecting black New Yorkers' shared *condition* with Africa and its diaspora.[6] In this sense, this chapter "escapes from New York" by providing a more complicated and undeniably violent narrative of the city's history before the Harlem riot of 1935. This essay broadens the range of political activities constituting the New Negro movement, foregrounding self-protection activity—specifically the individual and collective self-defense efforts posed against racial violence and residential containment—as a key generative force of New Negro politics.[7] Whereas most studies frame the New Negro movement as a product of the Great War, I locate the initial stirrings of New Negro ferment before the war in interracial struggles over residential and public places, where blacks first demanded respect and equal treatment either through legal means or through violent and, sometimes, armed resistance. Throughout the period covered in this chapter, black leaders, radicals, and journalists persistently followed police brutality and self-protection in New York City. Before the war, race leaders criticized blacks arming themselves. But by the Great War, New Negroes rebelling and protesting clamorously on the streets and in print media against police brutality awakened the *New York Amsterdam News,* compelling it to speak out forcefully against police brutality throughout the interwar period.

In the early postwar period, white supremacy—in the guise of white mobs in the U.S. South, U.S. Marines in Port-au-Prince and the Asian Pacific, and British stevedores along the docks—reasserted itself, combating the rising tide of race consciousness and protest thriving both at home and abroad.[8] As hopeful African American migrants flooded industrial centers of the Northeast and the Midwest, they quickly learned that "the whole [world] [wa]s southern."[9] Blacks encountered racism in all areas of society and sectors of the state. Police malfeasance, especially, hit national and international headlines as state actors joined forces with white mobs in wreaking havoc on black communities across the nation, from East St. Louis, Elaine, Arkansas, and Houston, Texas, to Chicago and Washington, D.C., among other cities. As white domestic terrorism ascended, white conservative and even liberal social scientists explained increasing black incarceration, child delinquency rates, and ghetto formation as the product of black inferiority.[10] Even as some liberal segments of the scientific community proclaimed that blacks were not inherently inferior to whites, many, nonetheless, incriminated black culture. In this context, black criminality and culture became a proxy for racism. Accordingly, black and white reformers targeted black pathology rather than structural forces shaping black urban communities in the North.[11]

But New York City seemed to be different—especially the burgeoning black neighborhood of Harlem. By the early 1920s, black leaders had christened Harlem as a beacon of hope for the black world. In 1925, James Weldon Johnson, native Floridian, diplomat, and executive secretary of the National Association for the Advancement of Colored People, chronicled the cultural and political significance of the black district in his essay "The Making of Harlem."[12] Johnson remakes Harlem as the "greatest Negro city in the world," displacing primitivist caricatures of Harlem too often made by the "sight-seer" and the "pleasure-seeker."[13] More importantly, in describing blacks' movement into the district, he spotlighted that "Harlem was taken over without violence." As he recalled, "not since the riot of 1900 [Tenderloin district] has New York witnessed, except for minor incidents, any interracial disturbances."[14] Closer inspection of black New Yorkers' violent encounters with the police and whites, however, disproves Johnson's characterization of race relations in the city and therefore challenges any notion of New York's exceptionalism. On the contrary, blacks in New York City, like blacks throughout the diaspora, violently suffered at the hands of white supremacy.

During the prewar period, blacks incessantly confronted belligerent whites and malfeasant police in New York City. In the aftermath of the 1900 pogrom in the Tenderloin district, blacks stormed the San Juan district and Harlem. As historian Marcy S. Sacks has shown, blacks from the South, blacks from the Caribbean, and black New Yorkers settling in Harlem consistently collided with white supremacy.[15] The constant flows of blacks to Harlem precipitated white violence and police brutality. While some blacks met violence with violence, other blacks formed ad hoc associations demanding the enforcement of the law.

This strategy, known as legalism, demonstrated the black community's respect for law and order, though it often led black leaders to label acts of self-defense as criminal activity.[16] The *New York Age,* subsidized by Booker T. Washington and edited by Fred Moore, best represents this leadership style.

On Christmas Day in 1901, interracial violence erupted in Harlem. A horde of Irish youths stoned a drunken black man on 130th Street between Amsterdam and Broadway avenues. As three white men came to the black man's aid, three black men, Burley May, Wallace Bird, and William Jones, all intoxicated, "overtook the trio near Amsterdam Avenue, and either believing them to be the offenders or not caring, started to punch them." Interracial conflict, as this case indicates, was not necessarily predestined. But once the fighting began, combatants drew sides along racial lines. According to the *New York Times,* blacks "rushed out of the tenements" and "revolvers began to crack and razors flash." One black man "who had his head and face cut with a clasp knife" ran into B. B. Myers's drugstore. The white mob threatened to hang the man if they got in, and once they did, only the presence of the police led them to flee.[17]

Yet despite whites' participation in the melee, the police targeted black perpetrators. The stoning of the drunken black man by Irish "hoodlums" played no role in the police roundup of entrants. Instead, the police safeguarded the three white men and redirected their attention to tracking down blacks involved in the riot. To catch black rioters, the police searched tenements where "negroes were pulled out from under beds, in closets, and one was found in a wash tub."[18] By the end, the police apprehended almost two dozen men, all black. Rather than arresting all perpetrators, the police exacted justice by detaining blacks for audaciously fighting whites and protecting members of their own race.

August 4, 1907, another melee erupted on 136th Street and Madison Avenue, "the worst block of Harlem," according to the *New York Times.* After a baseball game between two white teams, a white man and a black man argued over the payment of a bet on the game, attracting a large crowd. Once the black man struck the white man, "there was a rush made for him. Immediately the street was in an uproar." Blacks unequivocally resisted whites' attacks and diligently defended the black-tenanted buildings. According to the *Times,* "razors and baseball bats were wielded. Negroes who had been leaning out of windows came rushing into the street, and joining the fray, and colored women hurled dishes from the windows on the heads of the fighters."[19]

Once again, the police searched only black-tenanted buildings. As the *New York Times* reports, "Inspector Thompson and Acting Captain Jackson ordered the men to patrol the streets and see that the negroes were kept within doors." By targeting blacks in the exclusive surveillance of their buildings, the police tacitly legitimized white violence directed at blacks. But the police were not alone in incriminating black self-defense activity. The *New York Times* also reinscribed the trope of black criminality on black enclaves in Harlem and sanctioned the police targeting of black combatants. Yet these alleged criminal and violent representations of blacks also reveal an open rejection of the legitimacy of police violence as well as a critique of criminal representations of black people found in popular media.

While Johnson remade Harlem as the "Negro mecca," white ethnics and the police department singled out blacks in the streets of New York. Black New Yorkers, nonetheless, defiantly battled white mob and police violence, reflecting the spirit of the New Negro and its ethos of self-determination and self-defense.[20] This strand of New Negro political consciousness began *before* the Great War, developing over time in the face of white supremacy in the city. These ubiquitous skirmishes prodded black leaders to demand the police to protect black civil rights, but it also prompted them to discipline black self-protection activity.

In 1909, following several incidents of interracial conflict across black Manhattan, the *New York Age* criticized blacks' reprisals against the police. "We have not one word to say in defense or extenuation of the disgraceful outbreakings of the Negroes in Harlem against the police," lamented the *Age*. The paper encouraged respectable blacks to "crusade against" black criminality. The black elite wavered between characterizing police brutality as an isolated incident or as an integral part of black people's daily experience. "Doubtless," the *Age* admitted, "there is an occasional policeman over-meddlesome, mean and authoritative, that in no wise justifies the mobilizing of Negroes to vent their rage upon him." Despite the irrefutable archive of police brutality, the *Age* believed, blacks should always uphold the law. Describing police behavior as "occasional" and "meddlesome," the black weekly masked the institutional and daily character of police violence.[21] By May 1914, the *Age*'s rhetoric changed. Although the *Age* disagreed with violence, the black weekly began to acknowledge the black community's reasons for self-defense: "Where Negroes are concerned in Negro districts they [police] are ready to shoot when ever there is a disturbance of any sort, and, because they are, those who know that the police are disposed to give them no quarter are also ready to shoot and do shoot."[22] The *New York Age*'s editorial suggests a departure, though brief, from its usual practice of censuring blacks' retaliation against the police, suggesting the growing influence of black recriminations against police misconduct on the conservative black weekly. In the midst of World War I and the 1920s, the black search for better living conditions and greater economic opportunities in New York City, as well as alternative viewpoints showcased in various forms of media, all in different ways, reinvigorated earlier waves of New Negro protest.

During and after World War I, black southerners and Afro-Caribbeans arrived in a community already enveloped in a debate on racial violence and police brutality. In the short period between 1910 and 1930, New York City's black population surged from 91,709 to 327,706, while the Caribbean population represented approximately 25 percent (39,833) of Harlem's black population.[23] The community also expanded geographically. In 1920, the majority of the black population lived between 131st Street and 144th Street, between Lenox and Seventh avenues. By 1928, Harlem had expanded south and north, from 110th Street and Central Park East to 159th Street to the Polo Grounds, and west to east, from St. Nicholas Avenue to the Harlem River.[24]

While black Harlem's ostensible autonomy operated as a powerful symbol of race achievement, blacks' rising expectations collided with a shrinking but hostile white community of residents, proprietors, and workers aggressively holding on to public and residential space in the city. White proprietors openly practiced de facto segregation. Even in Harlem, segregated housing and public places shaped black daily life. Segregation represented white struggles to recoup and contain public and residential spaces now teeming with blacks. Blacks, nonetheless, demanded fair treatment from white proprietors and the protection of their civil rights from city officials. But to no avail, discrimination, racial violence, and the degradation of black humanity prevailed. Subways, restaurants, and especially the streets operated as theaters of war, where blacks defended themselves, reclaiming public and residential space as their own. In so doing, New Negroes discursively deconstructed criminality and reformulated their acts of self-protection as expressions of citizenship.[25]

In the fateful Red Summer of 1919, for example, a waiter refused to serve Miss Olyve Jeter, a black woman, at a restaurant on East 42nd Street near Grand Central Station. After Jeter wrote a letter to the restaurant owner, the Childs Company, the establishment assured her that the matter would be addressed. When she entered a restaurant in Harlem, 272 West 125th Street, owned by the same company, the manager told a waitress to inform Jeter that if she wanted to be served, she would have to "sit in a back seat." Steadfast, Jeter held her ground, requesting to "see the manager, whereupon they were permitted to remain where they were."[26] Despite the existence of New York State civil rights law prohibiting segregation in public places, black patrons had to demand equal treatment from white businesses to pry open restaurants to black patrons, even in Harlem. So with a defiant resoluteness, as well as considerable patience, some blacks ate where they wanted.

These individual struggles were ultimately limited, however. Circumstance, particularly the disposition of the manager and the staff, determined how blacks were treated in restaurants and other consumer spaces. In many cases, whites rejected or ignored blacks or offered them inferior service. In September 1919, Jessie Fauset, novelist and the literary editor of the NAACP magazine *The Crisis*, waited patiently over half an hour before she was served in the lunchroom of

Gimbel Brothers. Dissatisfied with the service, and offended by being "served by the 'bus-boys' rather than by the usual attendants," Fauset wrote a letter to Gimbel Brothers' general manager requesting that he explain the department store's policy "with reference to serving colored patrons" in the lunchroom.[27] Fauset explained that she "like[d] a statement from [him] letting myself and other colored people in New York know." Anticipating later consumer-based protest strategies, such as the "Don't Buy Where You Can't Work" campaign of the 1930s, Fauset expected businesses to be responsible to their patrons. But the Gimbel Brothers' management did not reply. As Fauset wrote to John R. Shillady, an official of the NAACP, "I have been waiting vainly for an answer . . . from Gimbels and [the] general manager."[28] Gimbels' nonresponse reflected white businesses' indifference to the concerns of black consumers. By openly disregarding the state's civil rights laws, white proprietors, in some cases, completely excluded blacks from public places.

In restaurants and other public places, blacks often won minor victories, receiving a semblance of fair treatment. But in theaters, black civil rights efforts generally foundered. On November 30, 1921, James Weldon Johnson wrote a letter to Mr. Marcus Loew, of Loews Theatres, explaining that the Victoria Theatre on 125th Street excluded black patrons from the orchestra seats, even when they were sold tickets for that area. Reminding the theater owner of New York State's civil rights law, amended April 13, 1918, Johnson admonished Loew to "correc[t] this flagrant violation of the law before we take legal steps to correct this condition."[29] In a short letter, Loew's Incorporated replied, "We are thoroughly aware of the existence of the Civil Rights Law. Employees of theatres, in which we are interested, are instructed by their respective managements to afford equal accommodations to all persons, irrespective of race, creed, or color." But without the enforcement of the law, Loew's acknowledgment meant little to black patrons.

Pervasive racism in New York City prompted some blacks to compare de facto segregation in the city to de jure segregation in the South.[30] In 1929, Jacob Brigman, of the NAACP, wrote to Mayor James J. Walker, inquiring if the manager at the same Victoria Theatre had the right to prohibit blacks from sitting in the orchestra or if the theater was "taking the law in their own hands." Brigman suggested sardonically that "it would be more honest to Colored people to place a sign in the box office with the lettering (merely as a suggestion) words 'NO COLORED PEOPLE ALLOWED IN THE ORCHESTRA OF THIS THEATRE' with such a sign the Colored people would feel less embarrassed."[31] Like Fauset before him, Brigman highlights black indignation in the face of de facto segregation. The hypocrisy and complicity of the city government legitimized the racist practices of white proprietors, reinforcing segregation as an insidious feature of New York City. The sporadic and inadequate protection of the law, as well as the limited pressure of the NAACP, exacerbated blacks' already heightened frustration with discrimination in public places.

Black demands for equal public accommodations and equal protection under the law often triggered white residents and the police to further disrespect, harass, and sometimes violently pummel blacks in public places. In 1920, at the elevator station on the corner of 130th Street and 8th Avenue, a ticket chopper assaulted Maude P. LaVann, a black woman. According to M. Waller French, the secretary of the New York City branch of the NAACP, "there [was] . . . an unusual amount of unnecessary roughness on the part of the elevator and subway guards in the Harlem District."[32] These seemingly trivial exchanges often developed into outright physical confrontations. In 1919, two white men, according to Dr. M. L. Ogan, an eyewitness, beat up a black man in the subway near 142nd Street. The police arrested the black man, who had allegedly called the white men names after they stepped on his feet. Dr. Ogan's wife explained that her husband and she "d[id] not believe this man should suffer; the others appearing as aggressors." Enveloped in the brutality of the Red Summer, she warned that "the city might be plunged into a so-called 'race riot' by just such unpunished conduct." Gauging the ire of the black community correctly, Ogan argued that the white men, "not the colored man, should be 'made an example of,' as the magistrates are so fond of handing to the Negro."[33]

Several years later, three Harlemites refused to give up their seats in spaces of public transportation. In 1922, a day after the Fourth of July, Frank Morris, Frances Tarris of 64 West 129th Street, and Flora Bryant of 225 West 140th Street rejected a white man's request that they "remove some of their belongings from one of the seats, so that an elderly white woman might sit down." Appalled, an unidentified white man "told the negroes they would not dare act as they were acting if they were in the South." When patrolman McGough arrived in response to the whistle-blowing of a motorman, he found black women and men "threatening the other occupants."[34] They refused to allow white people to demarcate the boundaries of their freedom. Instead, they claimed public spaces as their own, defending their own right to sit wherever they chose.[35]

These small skirmishes also spilled out onto the streets. Like previous cases of interracial violence, these conflicts sprung from black and white daily interactions and tensions, which residents enacted and settled on the streets and in public places in Harlem. In late May 1917, a black gang and black passersby battled the police in the streets of Harlem. In a saloon on 137th Street and Lenox Avenue, Walter Clark protested against the price of liquor and threatened the saloon's employee with a razor. While walking outside with his daughter, James Mohan, an off-duty police officer, overheard cries in the saloon. He ran into the saloon, commanding Clark to give up the weapon. Clark told the officer that his gang would not allow the entire police force to take his razor.[36] Daily occurrences of police brutality and interracial battles certainly influenced Clark's actions. Mohan grabbed Clark and led him down the block. When the police arrived, they found over two hundred blacks trying to release Clark from Mohan. With their nightsticks, the officers scattered the crowd and arrested Clark and another black man, William Grant.

These cases of New Negro self-protection activity reflect the rising and unmet expectations of black residents as they clashed with white ethnics over the use and control of residential areas and public places in Harlem and throughout the city. In the 1920s, key elements of an antipolice brutality campaign converged, as black journalists described, interpreted, and articulated the grievances of many black New Yorkers who had publicized their discontent through acts of self-defense.

Throughout the 1920s, stories of police brutality punctuated the front pages of New Negro organs and black newspapers. The black community specifically targeted the third degree, an interrogation method that the police deployed to coerce blacks in custody either to admit to a crime or to supply them with information about a criminal case. In 1922, this issue made national news when Luther Boddy, a black man, murdered two white police officers to avoid the third degree.[37] Marcus Garvey's *Negro World* warned the police that mistreating black prisoners made their "work dangerous." A black person's criminal status, the *Negro World* suggested, was no excuse for police misconduct. "Those that practice it," forewarned the *Negro World*, "are a menace to the lives of other men on the force." If the police desired to work in safe conditions, then they had to respect the lives of blacks, even criminals, for their lives were as valuable as the police officers, suggested the *Negro World*.[38] The *Amsterdam News*, in 1926, described the third degree as "nothing more nor less than an indoor lynching, or near-lynching, . . . sanctioned openly by authority." In comparing the third degree to lynching, the *Amsterdam News* reconfigured Harlem as an extension of the South. Concluding that violence begot violence, the black weekly justified the slaughter of policemen, stating, "We are not surprised that six police officers have been shot down by gunmen in New York City since the first of the year."[39]

Two years later, Harlemites "staged a little riot with the police."[40] On the evening of July 22, 1928, after seven o'clock, "Harlem citizens," described the *Amsterdam,* defended themselves against 150 police on 139th Street and Lenox Avenue. Harlemites retaliated after witnessing a police officer smack a black woman, who courageously scolded four police officers assaulting Clarence Donald, a black man. As reserves from different precincts arrived, Harlemites threw bricks, dishes, and chairs from their windows. The riot persisted for an hour, until the presence of the emergency squad, armed with machine guns and a fire truck, finally subdued the crowd. Harlem had mobilized to protect itself from police brutality. Harlemites refused to accept the claim that gangsters or hoodlums were responsible for the antagonistic relationship between blacks and the police. As the editor of the *Amsterdam News* wrote, "Three thousand people can't be wrong."[41]

In the ensuing days of the riot, the *New York Amsterdam News* staged its own war against the police department. On the front page, this black newspaper charged, "Brutality, not brains, seems predominant in the mind of the average white police officer in Harlem," warning that "unless something is done about it immediately by Police Commissioner Warren and others who exercise direct authority over the police force, consequences of a serious nature are compelled to follow."[42] The black weekly condemned the entire police force—whites and blacks. "The police force in Harlem must be rid of both white and colored officers who use their uniforms as a cloak behind which to commit assault and murder," demanded the *Amsterdam News*.[43] By specifying black and white officers, the black weekly described brutality as an accepted policy of the police department, not the individual act of police officers. That some police officers were black had no bearing on their actions as part of the police force, for they represented and perpetuated the police department's pattern of brutality toward black people.

The *Amsterdam News* also emboldened blacks to take action. In an editorial titled "Police Terrorism," the *Amsterdam News* encouraged Harlemites to follow Jersey City's black community as a model for community mobilization. According to the *Amsterdam News,* fifteen hundred Jersey City denizens attended a public trial, where the police commissioner dismissed the offending officer from the police force. The *Amsterdam News* charged the people to "get together in Harlem as they did in Jersey City and demand the dismissal of policemen who abuse the privileges of their uniform." To rally support for their campaign, but also to warn the police department, the *Amsterdam News* urged Harlemites to raise their own expectations of themselves by way of declaration, announcing that the people "will soon put a stop to police brutality in Harlem."[44]

The "little riot" of July 1928 was the culmination of previous black battles with the police in public places and on the streets. More importantly, these conflicts served as dress rehearsal for the Harlem race riot of 1935. The *New York Amsterdam News*'s advocacy of the Harlem rebellion in 1928 signaled the black community's shift from an episodic condemnation of individual police officers to a sustained critique of the police department as a symbol of white supremacy. The *Amsterdam News* conceptualized black residents as *citizens* precisely because they defended their civil rights, exposing the criminal aggression of the police department. The *Amsterdam News*'s campaign against police brutality and more broadly state-sanctioned violence reflected the incorporation of New Negro politics on the ground with the broader insights of race consciousness among New Negro organizations. By the end of the 1920s and throughout the 1930s, the *Amsterdam News's* critique became the dominant viewpoint of Harlem regarding police brutality.

During the early 1930s, empowered by their own efforts, such as the national "Don't Buy Where You Can't Work" campaign, alongside growing convergences between black radicalism and communist internationalism, blacks and now white activists coordinated their efforts to attack a range of issues, especially police brutality, demanding not only the enforcement of the law but also the accountability of public officials at the highest levels—the police commissioner and the mayor. In late March 1934, as people gathered to attend a Scottsboro meeting on 126th and Lenox, the police threw tear gas and firebombs into a crowd. The police, complained the *Amsterdam News,* "acted with vicious, wanton and uncalled-for brutality in dispersing an innocuous gathering." Days after, Mayor LaGuardia ordered Chief Inspector Lewis J. Valentine to conduct an investigation of this alleged case of police misconduct. In its March 24 editorial titled "It's Time to Act," the *Amsterdam News* agreed that the investigation was necessary but, more imperatively, that "it must be followed by disciplinary action by Police Commissioner O'Ryan and Mayor LaGuardia."[45] The police department charged two police officers, one black, Charles Brown, and one white, Joseph Pappace, with police brutality. Six months later, an exasperated Harlem community learned that both cases were closed and that no action would be taken.

Incensed, the *Amsterdam News's* September 15 issue featured an editorial titled "O'Ryan Must Go." Despite admitting that Officer Brown lied during both the investigation and the trial, O'Ryan stated flippantly that he was "not going to ruin the record of good men by putting marks against their records on such minor charges," adding as an afterthought that "if they get in serious trouble... [he was] going to sock them plenty." The *Amsterdam News* demanded O'Ryan's dismissal. As the black daily explained, "We have not allowed ourselves to be swayed in this belief by the oft-raised issue of race prejudice. But at the same time, we have not been able to ignore the fate of the Negro, as a minority group, under your police commissioner." The *Amsterdam News* reminded Mayor LaGuardia that it had questioned O'Ryan's competence months before, mentioning the "slaying of a religious leader in Brooklyn by two officers, . . . [and] the brutal attack by a uniformed patrolman on an 18-year-old girl in a municipal park and other similar incidents." The black weekly then told the mayor, "We know that you must realize that your obligation [is] to the people who elected you . . . we cannot longer remain silent on this vital issue which affects us all."[46]

One week later O'Ryan resigned, citing the mayor's "'interference' with police discipline."[47] The *Amsterdam News* graciously thanked the "mayor for his timely announcement of the resignation of Police Commissioner O'Ryan and congratulate[d] him upon the appointment of Chief Inspector Valentine to the post."[48] O'Ryan's resignation was not solely the outcome of the *Amsterdam News*'s demands. Nevertheless, it demonstrates the heightened expectations of the black community and their demands for governmental accountability with specific regard to policing. Throughout fall 1934 and spring 1935, the *Amsterdam News* reported many cases of police malfeasance. Despite his promise to bring a semblance of civility to the New York Police Department, new Police Commissioner Lewis J. Valentine upheld his officers' excessive abuse of both the criminal offenders and the innocent. In late February 1935, less than a month before Harlem's first large-scale race riot, Valentine congratulated patrolman Isadore Astel for shooting to death Andrew Barnes, a twenty-three-year-old, in a darkened basement in a grocery store. "We want you to know," said the commissioner to his officers, "that we appreciate your work and I want to congratulate you." This recent killing of Barnes by Astel was one link in a chain of killings where minor crimes resulted in the murder of an alleged criminal offender. As the *Amsterdam News* lamented, for blacks, "burglary becomes a capital offense—in Harlem."[49]

To be sure, Mayor LaGuardia held an early record of liberal relations with the black community. But on the issue of police brutality, he failed to protect blacks from police aggression and to censure Commissioner Lewis J. Valentine for validating their behavior. The rebellion on March 19, 1935, may have shocked the nation but not Harlemites. It was long overdue. From the turn of the twentieth century to the explosion of the 1935 rebellion, black people persistently combated police brutality, contributing to a range of self-protection efforts that collectively highlighted the normalcy of state-sanctioned violence directed at black people in Harlem and throughout New York City. Despite the distinctiveness of the Big Apple, white mob attacks and state violence were not just a world problem but a New York problem.[50]

During the first four decades of the twentieth century, black New Yorkers understood city streets as theaters of war. Although these small, deadly battles rarely resulted in full-blown race riots, they nonetheless incited an intransigent New Negro spirit well before World War I. This social movement, a countermeasure to white resistance against black settlement of urban communities and public places, emerged in the face of white mob aggression and police violence. Through these efforts, New Negroes incessantly questioned the sacred liberal creed of "law and order" and tested the shibboleth that New York was an exception to the rest of the world, where people of African descent were persistently objects of white violence. In the midst of the World War I era, New Negro intellectuals and organizations promulgated ideas of self-defense and militancy that black New Yorkers, alongside countless others, had already staged on the streets and in public places throughout the city.

In Harlem, and perhaps other communities, black self-defense activity preceded and arguably extended black radical critiques of white mob violence and police brutality. Beginning in the 1920s, the *New York Amsterdam News* articulated the grievances of victims of police brutality and repositioned black collective acts of self-defense as an antipolice brutality campaign. Through the efforts of the *Amsterdam News,* critiques of police brutality operated as a bridge for New Negro protest from the early to the middle decades of the twentieth century.[51] Although this essay focuses on Harlem, it also suggests that New Negro politics on the national and international scene emerged alongside and in convergence with the daily battles of black folks in public and residential spaces undergoing urbanization across the nation. These sites of discrimination and self-protection activity functioned as theaters of war, where blacks resoundingly broadcast their political grievances through public actions.

NOTES

1   George E. Haynes, "Impressions from a Preliminary Study of Negroes of Harlem, Borough of Manhattan, New York City, 1921," George E. Haynes Papers, box 1, folder "Report: Impressions from Preliminary," 104, Schomberg Center for Research in Black Culture, New York Public Library.

2   Ibid., 8.

3   Du Bois, "Color Line Belts the World," 42.

4   Kelley, "We Are Not What We Seem"; Dailey, "Deference and Violence in the Postbellum Urban South," 555.

5   Foley, *Spectres of 1919*; Gates and Jarrett, *New Negro,* 6–7.

6   Historians Patterson and Kelley describe diaspora as a *condition* that "exists within the context of global race and gender hierarchies which are formulated and reconstituted across national boundaries," though "the arrangements that the hierarchy assumes may vary from place to place." Patterson and Kelley, "Unfinished Migrations," 20.

7   For a sample of scholarship on the origins of the New Negro movement, see Gates and Jarrett, *New Negro,* 1–20. For sampling of this literature on the New Negro movement, see Locke, *New Negro*; Vincent, *Voices of a Black Nation*; Favor, *Authentic Blackness*; Foley, *Spectres of 1919*; Caroll, *Word, Image, and the New Negro*; Baldwin, *Chicago's New Negroes*; Perry, *Hubert Harrison*. For scholarship on self-defense, see Cha-Jua, "Warlike Demonstration"; McLaughlin, *Power, Community, and Racial Killing*; McLaughlin, "Ghetto Formation and Armed Resistance"; Umoja, "Eye for an Eye"; Tyson, *Radio Dixie*; Nelson, *Police Brutality*; Hill, *Deacons for Defense*; Strain, *Pure Fire*.

8   Johnson, "Self-Determining Haiti," four articles reprinted from *The Nation* embodying a report of an investigation made for the National Association for the Advancement of Colored People together with official documents; Zack-Williams, "African Diaspora Conditioning"; Elkins, "Unrest among the Negroes." For a sampling of the riot literature on Harlem, see *Complete Report of Mayor LaGuardia's Commission*; Osofsky, "Race Riot, 1900"; Shapiro, *White Violence and Black Response*; Greenberg, *"Or Does It Explode?,"* esp. "The Politics of Disorder"; Johnson, *Street Justice*; Sacks, *Before Harlem*. See also Sandburg, *Chicago Race Riot*; Shogan and Craig, *Detroit Race Riot*; Tuttle, *Race Riot*.

9   Payne, "Whole United States Is Southern!," 91; Kelley, "Slangin' Rocks," 23–24.

10 Muhammad, *Condemnation of Blackness*, 51.

11 Ibid., 98–145.

12 First in Locke, "Harlem: Mecca of the New Negro," and in the expanded volume *New Negro*.

13 Johnson, "Making of Harlem," 635.

14 Johnson, *Black Manhattan*, 155–56; Osofsky, *Harlem*, 46–49.

15 Sacks, "To Show Who Was in Charge."

16 For a detailed example of legalism, see Cha-Jua, "Warlike Demonstration," esp. 603–6.

17 "Fierce Race Riot in Upper New York," *New York Times*, December 26, 1901, 1.

18 Ibid.

19 "Race Riot Rages in Harlem Streets," *New York Times*, August 5, 1907, 1.

20 For a pre–World War I history of black self-defense rhetoric, see Strain, *Pure Fire*, 20–24. Strain begins with T. Thomas Fortune, first editor of the *New York Age* before Bookerite Fred Moore takes over as editor, and the black radical Ida B. Wells-Barnett. As Wells-Barnett explains in 1892, "a Winchester rifle should have a place of honor in every black home." Quoted from Strain, *Pure Fire*, 21.

21 *New York Age*, August 5, 1909, 4.

22 *New York Age*, May 28, 1914, 1; June, 1914, 4.

23 Osofsky, *Harlem*, 129–31.

24 New York Urban League, Report 1920, 5; New York Urban League, "A Challenge to New York," Annual Report, Year 1927, 6.

25 Makalani, *In the Cause of Freedom*; James, *Holding Aloft the Banner of Ethiopia*; Solomon, *Cry Was Unity*.

26 Letter to Childs Company from the National Association for the Advancement of Colored People, June 14, 1919, Papers of the NAACP, Part 11, Series A, Reel 21.

27 Jessie Fauset, letter to General Manager of Gimbel Brothers, September 12, 1919, Papers of the NAACP, Part 11, Series A, Reel 21.

28 Jessie Fauset, letter to John Shillady, September 18, 1919, 2, Papers of the NAACP, Part 11, Series A, Reel 21.

29 James Weldon Johnson to Marcus Loew, November 30, 1921, Papers of the NAACP, Part 11, Series A, Reel 28.

30 For a sampling of scholarship reconsidering the role of the state in the urban north,

see Biondi, *To Stand and Fight*; Muhammad, *Condemnation of Blackness*; Lassier and Crespino, *Myth of Southern Exceptionalism*.

31 Jacob Brigman to Honorable James J. Walker, Mayor, December 10, 1929, Papers of the NAACP, Part 11, Series A, Reel 28.

32 M. Waller French to Rev. F. A. Cullen, December 20, 1920, Papers of the NAACP, Part 12, Series B, Reel 4.

33 Mrs. M. L. Doran J. Ogan to Mr. Spingarn, October 11, 1919, Papers of the NAACP, Part 12, Series B, Reel 4.

34 "Race Row on Elevated," *New York Times,* July 6, 1922, 7.

35 Kelley, "We Are Not What We Seem."

36 *New York Times,* May 31, 1917, 18.

37 *New York Times,* January 21, 1922, 6.

38 *Negro World,* January 21, 1922, 11.

39 "Third Degree," *New York Amsterdam News,* August 18, 1926, 20.

40 "Why 3,000 Harlem Citizens Rebelled against the Authority of the Police Department," *New York Amsterdam News,* July 25, 1928, 1.

41 Ibid.

42 Ibid.

43 Ibid.

44 *New York Amsterdam News,* March 13, 1929, 16.

45 "It's Time to Act," *New York Amsterdam News,* March 24, 1934, 1.

46 "O'Ryan Must Go," *New York Amsterdam News,* September 15, 1934, 1.

47 "General O'Ryan's Statement on Difference with Mayor," *New York Times,* September 25, 1934, 16.

48 "Thank You, Mr. Mayor," *New York Amsterdam News,* September 29, 1934, 8.

49 "Crime and Punishment," *New York Amsterdam News,* February 23, 1935, 8.

50 Malcolm X, "Not Just an American Problem, but a World Problem," circa 1964.

51 L. D. Reddick, "Guest Editorial," *New York Amsterdam Star-News,* November 22, 1941, 8; according to journalist Elmer Carter in his editorial "Plain Talk" and the NAACP's Roy Wilkins's "The Watchtower" in *New York Amsterdam News,* August 14, 1943, 10–11, respectively; Biondi, *To Stand and Fight,* chapters 3 and 9.

BIBLIOGRAPHY

Baldwin, Davarian L. *Chicago's New Negroes: Modernity, the Great Migration, and Black Urban Life.* Chapel Hill: University of North Carolina Press, 2007.

Biondi, Martha. *To Stand and Fight: The Struggle for Civil Rights in Postwar New York.* Cambridge, Mass.: Harvard University Press, 2003.

Caroll, Anne E. *Word, Image, and the New Negro.* Bloomington: Indiana University Press, 2005.

Cha-Jua, Sundiata Keita. "Warlike Demonstration: Legalism, Violence, Self-Help, and Electoral Politics in Decatur, Illinois, 1894–1898." *Journal of Urban History* 26, no. 5 (2000): 581–629.

The Complete Report of Mayor LaGuardia's Commission on the Harlem Riot of March 19, 1935. New York: Arno Press, 1969.

Dailey, Jane. "Deference and Violence in the Postbellum Urban South: Manners and Massacres in Danville, Virginia." *Journal of Southern History* 63, no. 3 (1997): 553–90.

Du Bois, W. E. B. "The Color Line Belts the World." In *W. E. B. Du Bois: A Reader,* ed. David Levering Lewis, 42–43. New York: Holt, 1995.

Elkins, W. F. "'Unrest among the Negroes': A British Document of 1919." *Science and Society* 32, no. 1 (1968): 66–79.

Favor, J. Martin. *Authentic Blackness: The Folk in the New Negro Renaissance.* Durham, N.C.: Duke University Press, 1999.

Foley, Barbara. *Spectres of 1919: Class and Nation in the Making of the New Negro.* Urbana: University of Illinois Press, 2003.

Gates, Henry L., Jr., and Gene Andrews Jarrett, eds. *The New Negro: Readings on Race, Representation, and African American Culture, 1892–1938.* Princeton, N.J.: Princeton University Press, 2007.

Greenberg, Cheryl. *"Or Does It Explode?": Black Harlem in the Great Depression.* New York: Oxford University Press, 1991.

Hill, Lance. *The Deacons for Defense: Armed Resistance and the Civil Rights Movement.* Chapel Hill: University of North Carolina Press, 2004.

James, Winston. *Holding Aloft the Banner of Ethiopia.* New York: Verso, 1998.

Johnson, James Weldon. *Black Manhattan.* New York: Atheneum, 1975.

———. "Making of Harlem." *Survey Graphic, Harlem, Mecca of the New Negro* 6, no. 6 (1925): 635–39.

———. "Self-Determining Haiti." In *Speech and Power,* vol. 2, edited by Gerald Early, 92–97. Hopewell, N.J.: Ecco Press, 1993.

Johnson, Marilynn. *Street Justice: A History of Police Violence in New York City.* Boston: Beacon Press, 2003.

Kelley, Robin D. G. "'We Are Not What We Seem': Rethinking Black Working-Class Opposition in the Jim Crow South." *Journal of American History* 80, no. 1 (1993): 75–112.

———. "'Slangin' Rocks . . . Palestinian Style': Dispatches from the Occupied Zones of North America." In *Police Brutality: An Anthology,* edited by Jill Nelson, 21–59. New York: W. W. Norton, 2000.

Lassier, Matthew D., and Joseph Crespino. *The Myth of Southern Exceptionalism.* New York: Oxford University Press, 2010.

Locke, Alain, ed. "Harlem: Mecca of the New Negro." Special issue, *Survey Graphic* 6, no. 6 (1925).

———. *New Negro: Voices of the Harlem Renaissance.* New York: Atheneum, Macmillan, 1992.

Makalani, Minkah. *In the Cause of Freedom: Radical Black Internationalism from Harlem to London, 1917–1939.* Chapel Hill: University of North Carolina Press, 2011.

McLaughlin, Malcolm. "Ghetto Formation and Armed Resistance in East St. Louis, Illinois." *Journal of American Studies* 41, no. 2 (2007): 435–67.

———. *Power, Community, and Racial Killing in East St. Louis*. New York: Palgrave Macmillan, 2005.

Muhammad, Khalil G. *The Condemnation of Blackness: Race, Crime, and the Making of Modern Urban America*. Cambridge, Mass.: Harvard University Press, 2010.

Nelson, Jill. *Police Brutality: An Anthology*. New York: W. W. Norton, 2000.

Osofsky, Gilbert. *Harlem: The Making of a Ghetto*. Chicago: Ivan R. Dee, 1996.

———. "Race Riot, 1900: A Study of Ethnic Violence." *Journal of Negro Education* (Winter 1963): 16–24.

Papers of the NAACP, Schomburg Center for Research in Black Culture, New York Public Library.

Patterson, Tiffany R., and Robin D. G. Kelley. "Unfinished Migrations: Reflections on the African Diaspora and the Making of the Modern World." *African Studies Review* 43, no. 1 (2000): 20–45.

Payne, Charles. "'The Whole United States Is Southern!': *Brown v. Board* and the Mystification of Race." *Journal of American History* 91, no. 1 (2004): 83–91.

Perry, Jeffrey. *Hubert Harrison: The Voice of Harlem Radicalism, 1883–1918*. New York: Columbia University Press, 2009.

Sacks, Marcy S. *Before Harlem: The Black Experience in New York City before World War I*. Philadelphia: University of Pennsylvania Press, 2006.

———. "'To Show Who Was in Charge': Police Repression of New York City's Black Population at the Turn of the Century." *Journal of Urban History* 31, no. 6 (2005): 799–819.

Sandburg, Carl. *The Chicago Race Riot*. New York: Harcourt, Brace, and World, 1969.

Shapiro, Herbert. *White Violence and Black Response: From Reconstruction to Montgomery*. Amherst: University of Massachusetts Press, 1988.

Shogan, Robert, and Tom Craig. *The Detroit Race Riot: A Study in Violence*. Philadelphia: Chilton Books, 1964.

Solomon, Mark. *The Cry Was Unity: Communists and African Americans, 1917–1936*. Jackson: University Press of Mississippi, 1998.

Strain, Christopher. *Pure Fire: Self-Defense as Activism in the Civil Rights Era*. Athens: University of Georgia Press, 2005.

Tuttle, William M., Jr. *Race Riot: Chicago in the Red Summer of 1919*. New York: Atheneum, 1970.

Tyson, Timothy. *Radio Free Dixie: Robert F. Williams and the Roots of Black Power*. Chapel Hill: University of North Carolina Press, 1999.

Umoja, Akinyele K. "Eye for an Eye: The Role of Armed Resistance in the Mississippi Freedom Movement." PhD diss., Emory University, 1996.

Vincent, Theodore. *Voices of a Black Nation: Political Journalism in the Harlem Renaissance*. Trenton, N.J.: Africa World Press, 1973.

Zack-Williams, Alfred B. "African Diaspora Conditioning: The Case of Liverpool." *Journal of Black Studies* 27, no. 4 (1997): 528–42.

VII

SPEAKEASY: REFLECTING ON THE NEW NEW NEGRO STUDIES

17

The Conjunctural Field of New Negro Studies

MICHELLE ANN STEPHENS

The New Negro is here. Perhaps no more courageous than the Old Negro who dropped his shackles in 1863, and fought against ignorance, propaganda, lethargy and persecution, but better informed, privy to his past, understanding of the present, unafraid of the future. . . . He is aware that the balance of power is shifting in the world and so are his cousins in Africa, in India, in Malaysia, the Caribbean and China.

—George Schuyler, *Crisis*, 1938

In the decades since the 1988 publication of Henry Louis Gates Jr.'s influential essay "The Trope of a New Negro and the Reconstruction of the Image of the Black," his notion of the *trope* of a New Negro has come under quite a bit of critical scrutiny.[1] At the same time, some of Gates's key claims have since become canonical. The first was that the New Negro was engaged primarily in a politics of visual re-presentation. The trope of the New Negro was literally "an image of the black," blackness itself the product of an act of self-reconstruction performed in the face of a racializing (white) gaze. Gates justified this claim by placing print cartoons and portrait photography demonstrating how African Americans chose to represent themselves visually, alongside a "visual essay" of racist images that circulated in various popular cultural forms throughout the 1890s and the first decades of the twentieth century. These included postcards with photographs of lynchings, of black Americans stereotypically dressed as "ole time niggers," racist cartoon caricatures found on "coon song" sheet music, magazine covers, and advertisements, and the cover of a popular children's board game. Here and in his preface for Thelma Golden's *Black Male: Representations of Masculinity in Contemporary American Art*, Gates describes the force of this visual archive in overdetermining African American conceptions of black identity at the turn and in the early decades of the twentieth century.[2]

Gates's second insight is historical; he points to the trajectory of the New Negro movement as beginning in 1895, well before the peak of the Harlem Renaissance in the mid-1920s, and entailing a shift from politics to aesthetics. This leads him to the argument that is the most problematic for the authors included in *Escape from New York*, namely, that the "'New Negro,' of course, was only a metaphor . . . a rhetorical figure" who existed only in "the non-place of language."[3] For the cultural, social, and political historians included in this collection, Gates's second claim reflects both the strengths and the weaknesses of his location as a literary and cultural studies scholar for whom, by the 1920s, the New Negro movement had narrowed into the more purely aesthetic Harlem Renaissance. As heralded in its title, the greatest critique *Escape from New York* offers is that, when we collapse the New Negro movement into the artistic Harlem Renaissance, this ties the New Negro as a trope inescapably to Harlem, and vice versa—with Harlem as the focus, the New Negro becomes a purely aesthetic category.

In contrast, the essays in *Escape from New York* reenact on a broader scale the insights of historian Ernest Allen Jr. in an essay productively placed in dialogue with Gates's text. In "The New Negro: Explorations in Identity and Social Consciousness, 1910–1922," Allen usefully fleshes out a political New Negro of the 1910s and 1920s, expanding on Gates's sense of the New Negro as a purely rhetorical figure.[4] Allen's New Negro of the 1920s sets the stage for the proletarian turn of post-Depression works such as Richard Wright's *Native Son*.[5] Notably, however, Allen's political New Negro was as internally contradictory as the one split between the forces of the aesthetic and the political in Gates's account. Allen describes a group, "torn between bourgeois nationalist and bourgeois assimilationist proclivities" and split along a "nationalist/socialist divide in which questions of social identity and of envisioned social structure both played a role."[6] For a previous generation of scholars and critics on the New Negro, Robert A. Hill exemplary among them, it was this line between different ideological visions, rather than the one between art or culture and political processes, that most clearly defined the period.[7]

In their introductions and afterwords to George Schuyler's *Black Empire* and *Ethiopian Stories*, Hill and Kent Rasmussen took literary form and rhetorical devices seriously in providing an alternative imaginative space for the articulation of a new black transnational consciousness emerging as part of the New Negro movement.[8]

Despite his political conservatism, as a journalist, even George Schuyler could not ignore the brewing of some new world sensibility, a shifting toward what Tiffany Ruby Patterson, Robin Kelley, and Brent Hayes Edwards have all described as a black globality.[9]

How does *Escape from New York* help us to understand some of these tensions and contradictions, both within the movement itself and in the study of the New Negro by scholars of the 1980s and 1990s? First I want to suggest that by broadening into the realm of social and cultural history, the authors in this collection link, in an even more systematic way, the political and the aesthetic to a terrain of struggle broader than each. This field of struggle revolves around the questions of race and representation emerging in the wake of communist revolution, imperial decline, and world war. The broader historical contours of this terrain do begin in the late nineteenth century, as Gates argued, but they also extend well into the twentieth century. In this ideological and cultural field, the problem of representation emerges both as an artistic problem of modern black identity—"The Negro in Art—How Shall He Be Portrayed?," as *The Crisis* asked in 1926—and as a question concerning the race's political representation in the new structures and discourses of nationhood and self-determination that usher in the new century.

The political, experienced as individual and private or in sociocultural terms, is no less political. Language itself has commonly served as a bridging medium between the discourses of the everyday that structure social life and the more refined—as in cultivated, manufactured, worked over, and produced—discourses of art, poetics, and culture. Older scholarly discourses on the New Negro that bridged the gap between history and literature by linking them through the lens of a radical black politics demonstrated the ways in which individual subjects are interpellated by the social and the historical and then express or perform those interpellated selves creatively in the cultural, social, and political realms. What Louis Althusser described as interpellation—the individual's self-construction within parameters defined by society and the state—Stuart Hall also described as a form of "articulation" whereby "the different levels of a social formation as an articulated hierarchy [with] no perfect replication, homology of structures, ex-pressive connexion—between these different levels [form instead] as an 'ensemble of relations.'" In this ensemble, "there will be structured relations between its parts," or as Hall quotes Althusser, "a 'complex unity, structured in dominance.'"[10] Hall's elaboration of Althusserian interpellation in terms of race points to what Antonio Gramsci, another historical materialist important for Althusser and Hall, thought of at a macro level as the conjunctural, that is, as the articulation of multiple points of contradiction within a given mode of production, to each other but in ways that cannot be reduced to each other. The conjunctural defines a field or terrain of struggle in which systemic contradictions in a mode of pro-duction emerge in the realm of culture, in civil society, and in political ideology.

By describing the New Negro as a purely rhetorical figure, one misses what was new and distinctive about the real-life experiences of African Americans during this period and the ways those experiences were shaped by much broader historical forces and global processes that extended well beyond Harlem and into the mid- to late twentieth century. However, by delinking the historical from the discursive, from the "non-space of language" important to Gates, one also misses the ways in which the trope of a New Negro was itself an interpellating discourse articulated both to the social and the everyday, and to the broader, conjunctural terrain of struggle defined by the political issues of representation raised globally by revolution and world war. Instead, together, the discourse of the New Negro and the experiences of New Negro men and women form a global ensemble of relations linked under the tropological sign of the New Negro and played out on the conjunctural field of the New Negro movement as a historical formation.

With this ensemble of the new World Negro in mind, one could say that the line being drawn consistently in *Escape from New York* between the tropological and historical experience is drawn a little too harshly. From a more materialist literary perspective, a trope is nothing but the rhetorical trace of the discursive and epistemological context in which historical actors find themselves. Above and beyond its fictive, constructed nature, the trope of a New Negro set a standard to live by. Instead, then, what seems to me to be the most important point behind this collection's emphasis on black historical experience is the paradigm-shifting observation about the deeper hegemonic crisis that the study of the New Negro reveals, as a conjunctural epiphenomenon articulated to the literary, the artistic, the cultural, the social, the private, the psychological, the economic, the military, and the political simultaneously, in an ensemble of geohistorical relations that come to a head at the turn and in the early decades of the twentieth century.

The New Negro as an ensemble of relations marks a much deeper organic crisis that extends from 1865, with the emancipation of the slave and the granting of his right to citizenship during Reconstruction, through the restoration of Jim Crow segregation, the expansion of women's suffrage, and the role of education in preparing a multiracial citizenry for civic participation, through world war, European immigration, black southern migration and West Indian immigration, world war again, and continued U.S. economic expansion and imperialism, and continuing into the era of Third World decolonization. In his introduction, Davarian L. Baldwin announces the emergence of a "Renaissance" in New Negro studies, emphasizing the collection's reorientation around place: "the more well-known literary and visual art expressions most associated with Harlem are situated within a broader range of social movements, popular culture, and public behavior that spanned the globe from New York and New Orleans to Paris, the Philippines, and beyond." This respatializing of the New Negro Renaissance, however, also occurs very much with an eye backward to 1865 and forward to the 1940s and 1950s. In other words, it is because the essays in *Escape from New York* situate their subjects within a deeper genealogical and reperiodizing project that the new spatial dimensions of the New Negro movement and trope become clear.

In offering his genealogy of a later period, the "new cultural politics of difference" that emerged in the 1980s and 1990s, Cornel West identified three key
historical coordinates: colonial modernity (the *longue durée* of 1492 to 1945), the
American Century (the United States' emergence as a global superpower in the
1940s and 1950s), and decolonization (beginning in 1955 with Bandung).[11] This
later period in the study of black consciousness maps back onto the earlier one, in
which the New Negro movement and cultural formation of the 1920s lie. Like the
late-twentieth-century framing of blackness in terms of a cultural politics of difference, the New Negro moment also shares some of this deeper backward genealogy
in colonial modernity, while looking forward to a much longer span of conjunctural effects that continue to have an impact in the mid- to late twentieth century.

Escape from New York describes a period of organic, historical development
and crisis, occurring within the context of a U.S. *empire* rather than nation, that
has two intrawar dynamics or waves. The first begins with the Spanish–American
War in 1898 and culminates, with the end of World War I, in Woodrow Wilson's
"Fourteen Points" speech delivered to a joint session of Congress on January 8,
1918. Works that identify the 1910s as a key decade for New Negro studies miss
the longer and deeper historical context in which the varying events and crises
of the second decade of the twentieth century occur.[12] Only a longer view allows
us to articulate the crises and events of the 1910s to prior dynamics emerging in
the specific context of the United States in the 1890s, but with broader implications for the transition from a colonial to a global modernity.

In both Jeanette Eileen Jones's and Teresa Runstedtler's essays, which open
parts I and II of the collection, respectively, cross-cultural relationships between
African Americans and Africa, on one hand, and the Philippines, on the other,
occur in the shadow of black soldiers' participation in the Spanish–American
War. As Jones demonstrates, both the image of Africa in the African American
imagination and pan-Africanist sentiment more broadly are wielded in black political ideologies that cross the spectrum from "the missionary and emigrationist
pan-African movements of the late nineteenth century," many of them colonialist
in inclination, to the militant nationalism of Garvey's "Africa for Africans" movement, to the radical internationalism of Cyril Briggs and the Communist African
Blood Brotherhood. What Jones's narrative makes clear is that, while certainly
contradictory, the changing political trajectories of pan-Africanism over time are
animated by a shared historical consciousness of the black Atlantic diaspora—the
displacement of Africans to the New World and the colonization of Africa—as
somehow foundational to a countercultural history of modernity and the future
condition of black and colonial subjects across the globe in the twentieth century.
It is precisely this political realization about Africa's centrality at the level of the
world system, Minkah Makalani argues, that informs James's much later turn to

the continent, rather than the Caribbean, in articulating an anticolonial politics from England during the 1930s.

Similarly, the kind of subaltern solidarities Runstedtler recovers between Filipino and African American boxers, almost impossible to imagine, only make sense within the rubric of a broader awareness of coloniality which, in the late twentieth and early twenty-first century, we now call the Global South (itself an updating of the postcolonial framework articulated more properly to the mid- to late-twentieth-century wave of decolonization and the cultural politics of difference). In another instance of cross-racial alliance, dialogues between African Americans and the Japanese in the context of World War I find their logic in an imagined subaltern solidarity shaped by colonial modernity. Yuichiro Onishi is very clear to point out that this alliance around a "space of resistance" that African Americans shared with the "New Negro of the Pacific" rested on the key evasion of Japanese imperialism. Nevertheless, as in earlier and contemporaneous pan-Africanist discussions, this alliance created a cognitive map of the existing world system as organized "in racial terms," thereby offering "a countermap of Wilsonian liberal internationalism" as an "international politics promoting white supremacy."

If the first intrawar wave the essays cover ends with World War I, the second picks up in the years leading to World War II, the intrawar years of the Jazz Age and the Depression. The majority of the essays in the collection cover this period, and for reasons that I believe are crucial, many of them bring gender relations to the forefront. The advantage of attending to the New Negro as a historically specific ensemble of relations articulated to the conjunctural moment is that this methodology provides a rigorous way of linking broader political developments, such as the international consciousness of the radical New Negro, to the specifically gendered expressions of New Negro consciousness that shaped notions of black manhood and femininity at the turn of the century.

Despite our criticisms of his description of the New Negro as a semiotic unit—a mere sign, signifier, or metaphor—in his essay, Gates did identify and emphasize the specifically gendered nature of the New Negro trope and cultural formation as it emerged in the late nineteenth century and evolved into the 1920s. In *Righteous Propaganda,* Michele Mitchell expands on his insight and provides a crucial backstory for the essays included in *Escape from New York.* The gender performances and relations between New Negro men and women in the 1920s and 1930s are themselves related to dynamics that governed the perception of black people as a racial collective in the 1890s. Locating her work very much in a social and historical archive, Mitchell offers us a deep historicizing of the very specific ways in which *race as a politico-historical discourse,* encapsulated in the narrative of a racial destiny (itself an articulation of the limits of American citizenship left unresolved after emancipation and further complicated by the

Spanish–American War), becomes articulated to *race as a social performance*, with the regulation of black masculinity, femininity, and sexuality conceived as the path toward full citizenship.

Mitchell describes the 1890s, the beginning decade of the conjuncture *Escape from New York* describes, as the moment when African Americans developed a particular sense of themselves as a "collective whose destiny would be either exalted or debased, depending on the actions of its members."[13] Since the success of this collective project depended on the behavior of its members, between 1890 and 1900, "African American ideas about racial destiny turned inward as black activists focused upon changing individual and collective habits."[14] In other words, since a shared sensibility concerning the collective relied and focused on the individual's participation, "the concept of racial destiny, then, politicized the most private aspects of black life."[15] This "inward" turn would take the "black interior," in both senses of the word, as its ideal space for social engineering and personal reconstruction.[16]

Thus simultaneous with the respatialization outward—from Harlem to the rest of the territorial United States to the territories of the U.S. empire to the rest of the world—this period also started with a respatialization inward, to the private and domestic spaces in which black subjects' individual, imaginary, and interpersonal relations were constructed and interpellated during the New Negro era. Gender is of particular concern, both in this collection and in this period, not only because it represents the social aspects of the private that link a black interior to the aesthetic and the political. More importantly, gender is the very feature of New Negro identity and culture that sits in this fraught space *between* the tropological and the historical. In other words, as many of these essays make clear, whether in the form of New Negro heterosexuality or in figures such as the black soldier, the Garveyite, the New Negro woman, or the bad New Negro, gender is the primary mediating modality between the tensions of constructing and performing an individual black identity and negotiating one's ties to a more collective sense of self based on the race's status and fate.

Anastasia Curwood's study is singular in this regard perhaps because she recovers African Americans struggling not only with their own individuality but also with their relational subjectivities in the context of the intimate space of black marriages. For heterosexual New Negro couples, the trope of the New Negro operates as a real historical and ideological force shaping the intimate lives of black subjects struggling with the New Negro as an impossible ideal. Rather than a mere rhetorical device manufactured by a black elite, in Curwood's essay, but also in Treva Lindsey's account of the life and career of the first dean of women at Howard University, the ideal of the New Negro has real weight in shaping the lives and actions of historical figures such as Sarah Curwood and Lucy Diggs Slowe.

Focusing on the large increase of African American women in Washington, D.C., between 1860 and 1900, Lindsey identifies the college-educated black woman as a new social type in the broader "cultural current" of "New Negro womanhood" that emerges during the early to mid-twentieth century. She was different from the "race woman" of a previous generation precisely because she not only fought on behalf of black women but also challenged intraracial sexism as it emerged from the racial and gender ideologies of the moment. As Curwood also describes, for black women in New York, this "emerging model of New Negro womanhood . . . conceptualized black women as egalitarian political and economic partners in the modern race." The New Negro woman becomes a complex trope and historical identity, however, for middle-class black women who "felt the pull of the old politics of respectability, which had been one strategy to combat racism, mixed with the desire to remake a modern black middle class that dealt more frankly with both politics and sexuality."

Regardless, as Lindsey recounts, by openly contesting the limits placed on striving African American women, Curwood and Slowe pushed back against the politics of black respectability. On the other side of the Atlantic, as Jennifer Wilks describes, black modernist women of Paris, such as Paulette Nardal, were struggling to define themselves in relation to another masculine trope of the 1930s, that of the "Negritude hero," created by male poets and writers such as Aimé Césaire, Léon-Gontran Damas, and Léopold Sédar Senghor. Together with Jesse Fauset, Zora Neale Hurston, and Amy Jacques Garvey, Nardal, Curwood, and Slowe joined a cohort of New Negro women for whom black middle-class female ambition, self-sufficiency, and sexual autonomy, all the modern traits of the New Negro woman, contradicted the competing discourse of domesticity and respectability by which she was still bound.

On the other side of the gendered color line, New Negro men, such as James Curwood, were also struggling to conform to the image of the "handsome, cosmopolitan, middle-class gentleman" prized in certain visions of New Negro masculinity. A number of essays in the collection provide nuanced accounts of the layers of issues complicating black masculine performances in the period, the first one being that of class. For James Curwood, his own working-class condition prevented him from fully achieving the standard of masculinity set by the New Negro ideal, resulting in his tragic suicide. Jazz men such as Louis Armstrong, however, migrating to Chicago in the 1910s and 1920s, as Charles Lester describes, used their very different art and location to carve out an alternative performance of New Negro working-class masculinity distinct from the "Talented Tenth" models provided by such Harlem literati as W. E. B. Du Bois and Alain Locke.

Claude McKay also rejected New Negro "masculine convention," using his fiction to represent "the 'common man' (who is also decidedly his own man) as a subtle alternative to the official Renaissance." Thabiti Lewis describes "McKay's desire to write about ordinary people," good or bad, as resulting in a "bad New Negro," that is, a different type of soldier hero, one "unconcerned with being a neat, uncomplicated symbol of black progress." Chad Williams also uses McKay's work as a "conceptual bridge between a symbolic, metaphorical New Negro" and the real-life experiences of New Negro soldiers in the years during and between the two world wars. For Williams, the Negro soldier's wartime mobility not only freed him from prescribed New Negro masculine ideals but also gave him a particular purchase on the global forces surrounding him. If Lewis's reading of *Home to Harlem* contextualizes the character Jake's status as one kind of bad New Negro male, Williams's discussion of the novel's other soldier–hero, Ray, offers an even deeper historical perspective on McKay's ability to cognitively map the context of world war and the United States' invasion of Haiti onto the history of hegemonic crisis catalyzed by the Haitian Revolution.

If deeper historical questions were consolidated in a very particular way in the figure of the Harlem New Negro as the age's most idealized "image of the black," in real-life terms, this figure traveled with myriad black subjects, who carried this imaginary form in their heads as a marker to measure themselves against, either in rebellion or in despair. Emily Lutenski rereads Jean Toomer's later writings less as a simple rejection of his blackness than as an attempt to find other tropes or meanings for blackness and Americanness when tied to different landscapes. Lutenski argues, for example, that Toomer continued to discuss race in his writings based in the Southwest, but in a different way than in his writings set in the rural South and the urban North. Lutenski's argument concerning Toomer's engagement with discourses of *mestizaje* more particular to the Southwest highlights a central tenet of the collection as a whole. Not only did the idea of the New Negro travel beyond Harlem but also, when it did, it was transformed in turn by interactions with alternative discourses of race specific to geohistorical landscapes both within and without the United States.

In his study of the New Negro movement, Cuban *Negrismo*, and Mexican *Indigenismo* in the 1920s, David Luis-Brown finds that the discourse of primitivism, much maligned as a racist and racializing aesthetic discourse of white modernists, can also be rethought, in an admittedly counterintuitive but productive move, as a form of "black diasporic vernacular expression" when seen from the vantage point of black aesthetic movements in the Americas. For Luis-Brown, primitivism is actually "the chief discursive commonality linking the nationalisms and transnationalisms of . . . the 'darker peoples' in the Americas." As such, it can be read as one of the semiotic elements by which all three movements were articulated to a conjunctural, global field of struggle, one that includes white modernists responding to shared historical conditions. Furthermore, in his reading of *Home to Harlem,* Luis-Brown also argues that the discourse of primitivism "can be viewed as constructing a postcolonial sensibility. McKay searches for the methods of decolonization among the black proletariat, allegedly endowed with the imprimatur of racial authenticity." This idea, that one of the primary dynamics shaping the New Negro movement and the circulation of the trope was its dialogic relationship to other discourses of colonialism, race, labor, and exploitation scattered across the globe, shapes the ways in which Claudrena Harold and Frank Guridy position the Garvey movement and its spread into the South and the Spanish Caribbean, a kind of precursor to the alliances and affiliations we now see in the Global South.

By the latter end of its second, intrawar wave in the late 1930s and 1940s, the trope of the New Negro continued to shape discourses of coloniality and blackness that would be crucial for the beginning of a new conjuncture, the era of decolonization, whose transformative implications for the world system would first be glimpsed in the 1955 meeting of African and Asian leaders in Bandung. Andrew Kahrl's and Shannon King's essays explore in political economic terms the urban geography of the New Negro movement itself, shattering assumptions about both the confinement of black subjects to urban landscapes and the mystification of an earlier Harlem as a Negro mecca. On one hand, King demonstrates with some irony how the intellectuals reconstructing the capital of the black world as a paradise exempt from racialized urban violence escaped imaginatively without ever really having to leave Harlem.

In a contrasting vision of black urban space, Andrew Kahrl demonstrates how the stories of perhaps the two "baddest" New Negroes in *Escape from New York,* Baltimore numbers runners, black market entrepreneurs, and real estate magnates Austine Scarlett and William L. Adams, force us to rethink our approaches to the political economy of urban geographies writ large. Not only did the dynamics that led to both men's initial success and ultimate downfall encompass a black Baltimore landscape that included both the rural and the urban. In addition, Baltimore, Maryland, serves as a microcosm of forces shaping race and place across the globe, throughout the twentieth century and into the twenty-first. As Howard Winant reminds us in *The World Is a Ghetto,* the black urban ghetto is as "cosmopolitan" a space as the most sophisticated global city, and both city and country, cities and suburbs, in First and Third World locations, are subject to the intersecting racial and politicoeconomic dynamics that shape our current moment of globalization.[17] As the scholars who contributed to *Escape from New York* turn our attention backward, to the New Negro movement as a historical formation but also to the deeper structures of colonial modernity to which the New Negro as a trope was articulated, one finds oneself wondering what conjunctural epiphenomenon this renaissance in the field of New Negro studies itself heralds. In the wake of President Barack Obama's election and Kenneth Warren's provocation regarding the end of African American literature, are we at the end of a period of organic crisis organized around issues of race and representation?[18] Or could postblackness herald not the end of race but finally the recognition that race was always already more than simply a cultural identity or discourse, even as it is irreducibly cultural since that is the realm to which it articulates itself most vividly, in the visual and rhetorical forms that structure our historical experiences?

NOTES

1   Gates, "Trope of a New Negro," 129–55.

2   Henry Louis Gates Jr., preface to Golden, *Black Male*, 11–16. This archive also shaped African Americans' sense of themselves as consumers, as Michele Mitchell relates: "Many black women and men felt the need to counteract offensive images and objects with items that promoted pride, self-love, and black consciousness." Mitchell, *Righteous Propagation*, 175–76. It was this commercial context that produced the first black children's dolls in the United States, setting the stage for a material counterculture of black consumer products meant to promote black racial pride in the face of white stereotypes.

3   Gates, "Trope of a New Negro," 132.

4   Allen, "New Negro," 48–68.

5   Wright, *Native Son*.

6   Allen, "New Negro," 54.

7   This is also why the New Negro tends to figure prominently in a cross-disciplinary field studying oppositional black radicalism in the United States, stretching from political scientist Cedric Robinson's work on black Marxism first published in 1983 (*Black Marxism*) to the social histories of black communists in both the North and the South by Naison, *Communists in Harlem during the Depression*, and Kelley, *Hammer and Hoe*, respectively, to the cultural and literary histories of the black left we get in works by Denning, *Cultural Front*; Smethurst, *New Red Negro*; Maxwell, *New Negro, Old Left*; and Foley, *Spectres of 1919*. Much more recently, female scholars have led the charge in writing black women back into this history of black radicalism; see Davies, *Left of Karl Marx*, and Higashida, *Black Internationalist Feminism*.

8   See Robert A. Hill's introduction to Schuyler, *Ethiopian Stories*, 1–50, and his afterword, written with Kent Rasmussen, to Schuyler, *Black Empire*.

9   Patterson and Kelley, "Unfinished Migrations," 11–45, 26. Edwards et al., "'Unfinished Migrations': Commentary and Response," engage the term *globality* in their response to Patterson and Kelley in the same issue, but also earlier, in Edwards's 1997 dissertation at Columbia University titled "Black Globality."

10 Althusser, "Ideology and Ideological State Apparatuses," 152; Hall, "Race, Articulation, and Societies Structured in Dominance," 329, 325.

11 West, "New Cultural Politics of Difference."

12 World war in 1914 and the Russian Revolution of 1917 were the key initiating events in my own study of this period (see *Black Empire,* esp. the introduction and part I). For more on 1915 and the emergence of the "new" in the cultures of American modernism, see Heller and Rudnick, *1915, the Cultural Moment,* 6; for more on 1919 and the significance of international events such as the peacemaking meeting of the Council of Four, representing Britain, France, the United States, and Italy, who prepared the postwar peace treaty recommending a League of Nations, see MacMillan, *Paris 1919.* For more on the significance of national events such as the Red Summer of 1919, when race riots occurred in more than three dozen cities in the United States during the summer and early autumn, see Foley, *Spectres of 1919.*

13 Mitchell, *Righteous Propagation,* 7.

14 Ibid., 9.

15 Ibid., 12.

16 For the notion of a black interior used precisely in this sense, to connote both black subjective life and domestic space, see Alexander, *Black Interior.*

17 Winant, *World Is a Ghetto.*

18 Warren, *What Was African American Literature?*

BIBLIOGRAPHY

Alexander, Elizabeth. *The Black Interior: Essays.* New York: Graywolf Press, 2004.

Allen, Ernest, Jr. "The New Negro: Explorations in Identity and Social Consciousness, 1910–1922." In *1915, the Cultural Moment: The New Politics, the New Woman, the New Psychology, the New Art, and the New Theatre in America,* edited by Adele Heller and Lois Rudnick, 48–68. New Brunswick, N.J.: Rutgers University Press, 1991.

Althusser, Louis. "Ideology and Ideological State Apparatuses." In *Lenin and Philosophy and Other Essays,* 127–88. New York: Monthly Review Press, 1971.

Davies, Carole Boyce. *Left of Karl Marx: The Political Life of Black Communist Claudia Jones.* Durham, N.C.: Duke University Press, 2008.

Denning, Michael. *The Cultural Front: The Laboring of American Culture in the Twentieth Century.* London: Verso, 1998.

Edwards, Brent Hayes. "Black Globality: The International Shape of Black Intellectual Culture." PhD diss., Columbia University, 1997.

Edwards, Brent Hayes, Cheryl Johnson-Odim, Agustín Laó-Montes, Michael O. West, Tiffany Ruby Patterson, and Robin D. G. Kelley. "'Unfinished Migrations': Commentary and Response." *African Studies Review* 43, no. 1 (2000): 47–68.

Foley, Barbara. *Spectres of 1919: Class and Nation in the Making of the New Negro.* Urbana: University of Illinois Press, 2003.

Gates, Henry Louis, Jr. "The Trope of a New Negro and the Reconstruction of the Image of the Black." *Representations,* no. 24 (1988): 129–55.

Golden, Thelma, ed. *Black Male: Representations of Masculinity in Contemporary American Art*. New York: Whitney Museum of Art, 1995.

Hall, Stuart. "Race, Articulation, and Societies Structured in Dominance." In *Sociological Theories: Race and Colonialism*, 305–45. Paris: UNESCO, 1980.

Heller, Adele, and Lois Rudnick, eds. *1915, the Cultural Moment: The New Politics, the New Woman, the New Psychology, the New Art, and the New Theatre in America*. New Brunswick, N.J.: Rutgers University Press, 1991.

Higashida, Cheryl. *Black Internationalist Feminism: Women Writers of the Black Left, 1945–1995*. Urbana: University of Illinois Press, 2011.

Kelley, Robin. *Hammer and Hoe: Alabama Communists during the Great Depression*. Chapel Hill: University of North Carolina Press, 1990.

MacMillan, Margaret. *Paris 1919: Six Months That Changed the World*. New York: Random House, 2003.

Maxwell, William J. *New Negro, Old Left*. New York: Columbia University Press, 1999.

Mitchell, Michele. *Righteous Propagation: African Americans and the Politics of Racial Destiny after Reconstruction*. Chapel Hill: University of North Carolina Press, 2004.

Naison, Mark. *Communists in Harlem during the Depression*. New York: Grove Press, 1984.

Patterson, Tiffany Ruby, and Robin D. G. Kelley. "Unfinished Migrations: Reflections on the African Diaspora and the Making of the Modern World." *African Studies Review* 43, no. 1 (2000): 11–45.

Robinson, Cedric. *Black Marxism: The Making of the Black Tradition*. London: Zed Books, 1983.

Schuyler, George. *Black Empire*. Boston: Northeastern University Press, 1991.

———. *Ethiopian Stories*. Boston: Northeastern University Press, 1994.

Smethurst, James. *The New Red Negro: The Literary Left and African American Poetry, 1930–1946*. New York: Oxford University Press, 1999.

Stephens, Michelle A. *Black Empire: The Masculine Global Imaginary of Caribbean Intellectuals in the United States, 1914–1962*. Durham, N.C.: Duke University Press, 2005.

Warren, Kenneth W. *What Was African American Literature?* Cambridge, Mass.: Harvard University Press, 2011.

West, Cornel. "The New Cultural Politics of Difference." In *Out There: Marginalization and Contemporary Cultures*, 19–38. Cambridge, Mass.: MIT Press, 1990.

Winant, Howard. *The World Is a Ghetto: Race and Democracy since World War II*. New York: Basic Books, 2002.

Wright, Richard. *Native Son*. New York: Harper, 1940.

18

Underground to Harlem: Rumblings and Clickety-Clacks of Diaspora

MARK ANTHONY NEAL

The railroad was perhaps the most prominent metaphor of travel and movement for blacks at the dawn of the New Negro era, as Pullman porters, jazz musicians, and World War I veterans became the ambassadors for diasporic formation—if we are to consider the vast geographical difference found across the United States and North America as, ultimately, an articulation of difference that produced all the tension associated with shared national borders. Those railroads have long been romanticized as a site of black progress, even in the twentieth century, when Spike Lee reimagined, in his film adaptation of Richard Price's novel *Clockers,* the plight of a generation of black youth who could no longer look toward a promised land. At the film's resolution, we find the protagonist Strike (Mekhi Phifer) putting aside his model train set—a metaphor for the redundancy of progress for the hip-hop generation—to board a train for, literally, nowhere. And yet I'd like to argue that such a view of the promised land, whether Marcus Garvey's Africa or destinations that inspired the "great" migration, undervalues the ways that various black bodies produced community, and even notions of diaspora, in the midst of movement, relocation, and dislocation.

Those railroads were just one iteration of that movement; I like to think instead of a subway ride, which, in the early days of the system, only took you to 110th Street—areas north of that point, Harlem and the Bronx, were deemed hinterlands, apparently not fit for civilization. When enterprising developers found themselves without tenants for a New York City that they imagined would tame those hinterlands, they found willing migrants in the communities of relatively newly minted black Americans, who, given the routes they traveled—unwillingly and by force—to the so-called New World, offered little resistance to moving uptown from Lower Manhattan and the Tenderloin section of the city. As James Weldon Johnson noted in *Black Manhattan,* blacks in New York were largely relegated to what is now known as Greenwich Village and Little Italy well into the nineteenth century and were later forced uptown to the Tenderloin, San Juan Hill, and West

Fifty-Second Street. The move to Harlem, whether forced or by choice, seemed par for the course for black New Yorkers, if not for a nation of Negroes in general.

Twenty years before Jamaican-born writer Claude McKay would publish his groundbreaking novel *Home to Harlem*—his reflection on the vagabond nature of black diasporic formation—a generation of black New Yorkers were already calling Harlem home: a tethered notion of being and place that remains largely undisturbed, gentrification notwithstanding, to this day. As Thabiti Lewis writes of McKay's tome, his "narrative, adroitly powered by the meanderings of a soldier and a locomotive symbolism of a train, reflect his modernist proclivities, as well as the diverse rhythms of black life, and the myriad ways in which masculinity imagines and performs community."[1] This *home* was never static—Harlem was always already a cosmopolitan space, reflective of the overdeveloping metropolis that shared its borders (and had to build upward) but also of the comings and goings of southern migrants and Afro-Caribbean immigrants. That this place would be not only a site of becoming and coming together but also a site of departure and expansion highlights the tension between roots and routes that has always animated black life across the globe. I am imagining here Harlem as a way to rethink diaspora, as I am powerfully swayed by the work of political scientist Richard Iton, who wrestles with notions of black diaspora throughout his recent book *In Search of the Black Fantastic: Politics and Popular Culture in the Post–Civil Rights Era.*

Pushing aside concepts of diaspora that privilege the transatlantic slave trade and a rupture with Africa, on one hand, and, on the other, a seemingly inherent desire to reclaim Africa, through what Iton calls the "cycle of retaining, redeeming, refusing and retrieving" Africa, we might think of Harlem and the renaissance that called it home as a productive site of diaspora, as opposed to yet another jump-off for thinking of diaspora as a homelessness from Africa.[2] Again, Iton is useful, arguing that we might "conceive of Diaspora as an alternative culture of location and identification to the state, which would encourage a de-emphasis on the circulation and primacy of national blackness and suggest different maps and geographies."[3] Iton hints at an experience that Taiye Selasi would later coin as that of the "Afropolitan."[4] Indeed, Minkah Makalani identifies such a dynamic in the political development of C. L. R. James during his time in London in the mid-1930s and often in and around the Florence Mills Social Parlour that Amy Ashwood Garvey operated, as the city "provided James an opportunity to contemplate colonial Africa's role in world revolution," marking the "beginning of his turn from the Caribbean and toward Africa as a source of world revolution."[5]

An alternative geography might be located in the web of underground train tracks and the elevated rail system that the Interboro Rapid Transit Company and the Brooklyn–Manhattan Transit Company inhabited as early as 1904, and as late as 1940, when the two companies merged with the Independent Subway

System, forming what we now know as the New York City subway system. Decades later, young visual artists—graffiti writers—would call their tagging of the system's lines "All City," a measured articulation of globalization for a generation of folk that had never really left their boroughs. But they didn't have to; the globe came to them, literally via the everyday comings and goings of diaspora that occurred each and every time one of those subway car doors opened and closed and in the actual traveling of those diasporic bodies from the far reaches of Gun Hill Road in the Bronx to Eastern Parkway in Brooklyn.

Writing about the dynamics of Jim Crow segregation in the 1920s, critic Meta DuEwa Jones observes that "Subway Rush Hour," a piece by noted Harlem Renaissance poet Langston Hughes, "troubles the social architecture of Jim Crow segregation by placing it in an urban context. . . . The intermingling of the poem's words and lines mirrors an intermingling of social and sexual worlds—erotic tension is embedded in the poem."[6] Jennifer Wilks finds such intimacy at the "Parisian Crossroads" where the work of Paulette Nardal and Jessie Fauset "provided alternative ways of mapping the ideological crossroads of black modernism."[7] As Yuichiro Onishi suggests, these tight spaces of intermingling, writ large, enhanced the possibilities for black women's activism.[8]

While Jones's observations about Hughes's poem speak to the ways that tight urban spaces challenged the racial spatial logic, the same could be said about the construction of diaspora in such spaces, reimagining nation, if you will, on a trip uptown on the A Train—the closed, closeted spaces, marked by comings and goings in motion—a way of knowing black bodies, traveling underground (another notable metaphor), sharing the intimacy of a diaspora as much marked by national origin as it was by sexual desire and reimaginings of gender. In his essay "A Mobilized Diaspora: The First World War and Black Soldiers as New Negroes," Chad Williams makes similar observations about New Negro service in the military, noting that the "war set millions of descendant Africans in motion through the demands of combat and labor, bringing them into contact with one another and fundamentally transforming the demographic, ideological, and imaginative contours of the diaspora."[9] Keenly, Williams adds, "Reframing the meaning of 'mobilization' also provides a theoretical entryway into rethinking how we historicize and conceptualize the New Negro in the interwar period." Theresa Rundstedtler echoes this theme in her essay detailing the role of black servicemen in the rise of the sport of boxing in the Philippines, noting that the "New Negro was as much a product of these multiple and often contradictory lines of cross-national connection as it was the brainchild of black artists and intellectuals based in the United States."[10]

Such notions were not exactly lost on a figure like Duke Ellington, whose literal and musical forays into the sounds of the diaspora (thinking about "Caravan" as one small example), particularly given his proximity to New Negro veterans and those same "mobile" literary spaces that Hughes imagined, may have begun well before he recorded what would survive as the most timeless melody of that place, that space, and that era (with his most notable collaborator, Billy Strayhorn, who surely understood the importance of cultivating such intimacy in those dark, moving spaces). That melody, as much a metaphor for black movement as it was a metaphor for an urgent and incessant desire for the constitution of community (in all its flawed and frayed glory), would later find resonance in that reverbed clickety-clack of the subway, fermented initially in the sound we know as be-bop, or what might as well have been the rhythmic mimicking of those subway trains that Black Star—Mos Def and Talib Kweli—would make even more readily apparent on the track "Respiration" nearly a century later.

By the time Black Star sampled dialogue from the best visual tribute to the birth of hip-hop—Tony Silver and Henry Chalfant's *Style Wars* (1983)—it was evident that diaspora was no longer tethered to place. Indeed, Mos Def and Talib Kweli's invocation of Black Star was less a reference to Marcus Garvey's dreams of a literal return to Africa as it was recognition of the power of the dream itself; that return was always already realized in those clickety-clacks (sampled from New York City–born musician Don Randi's version of "Theme from the Fox" by producer Hi-Tek) that were at the foundation of "Respiration." As long as hip-hop continued to move, hip-hop, too, could remain a viable home—to anyone who wanted to inhabit it.

In the song "Respiration," Black Star anticipates, along with collaborator Common—who evokes his native Chicago in an act of digital diaspora making that was unfathomable in the 1920s—what Iton would later formally term the "Black Fantastic," in reference to the "minor key sensibilities generated from the experiences of the underground, the vagabond, and those constituencies marked as deviant."[11] The early New Negro conceptualizations of diaspora suggest that the Black Fantastic might have been an apt description of that moment and movement also, and that, perhaps, is ultimately the value of *Escape from New York*—the title itself seemingly being a gesture to the kinds of postapocalyptic-themed Hollywood films that became popular in the 1980s—which finds its own voice in the contexts or notions of movement and community and in the fundamental belief that the historical period defined by the Harlem Renaissance, black migration, various iterations of pan-Africanism, Garveyism, and diaspora formation is not the site of disparate and discrete scholarly interventions. For some, the refocusing of the New Negro era away from "home"—work that the volume coeditor had already broached with his important text *Chicago's New Negroes*—is tantamount to an apocalyptic vision of the Harlem Renaissance. As such, *Escape from New York* is a welcome challenge to the neatly drawn and perhaps too precise historical lines we've drawn around the period and its voices.

NOTES

1   Chapter 15, this volume.
2   Iton, *In Search of the Black Fantastic,* 199.
3   Ibid., 200.
4   Taiye Selasi, "Bye-Bye, Babar (Or: What Is an Afropolitan?)," *LIP,* March 3, 2005.
5   Chapter 3, this volume.
6   Jones, *Muse Is Music,* 41.
7   Chapter 9, this volume.
8   Chapter 5, this volume.
9   Chapter 10, this volume.
10   Chapter 4, this volume.
11   Iton, *In Search of the Black Fantastic,* 16.

BIBLIOGRAPHY

Iton, Richard. *In Search of the Black Fantastic: Politics and Popular Culture in the Post–Civil Rights Era.* New York: Oxford University Press, 2008.

Jones, Meta DuEwa. *The Muse Is Music: Jazz Poetry from the Harlem Renaissance to Spoken Word.* Urbana: University of Illinois Press, 2011.

19

The Gendering of Place
in the Great Escape

T. DENEAN SHARPLEY-WHITING

The varied historical roots and routes of black diasporic political, cultural, and literary expressivity; rhetoric; and practices of New Negro womanhood and manhood, cosmopolitanism, and internationalism are at the heart of *Escape from New York*. And as the anthology's title suggests and the volume's contributors ably verify, Harlem, New York, was but one nerve center of such frenzied creative and communal energy. Peripatetic intellectual Claude McKay attested to as much as he reflected on these strands of activity in the global hopscotching that formed the core of his autobiographical *A Long Way from Home*. Whether he foresaw the rise of noted singer Florence Mills in Harlem, only later to find the Parisian rendition of the musical *Blackbirds* starring Adelaide Hall somehow inauthentic, or threaded the needle on masculinity and diasporic confraternity in the French port town of Marseille with the novel *Banjo,* McKay himself was both participant in and chronicler of the multisited flourishings of the African diaspora from above and below.

An escape from a Harlem state of mind widens our frame to include other places and spaces where black folks sought *and* created possibilities. "The power of place," Aristotle wrote in an opening epigraph to *Physics,* "will be remarkable." For some, those remarkable places could be found in other vibrant cities in the United States; for others, the transformative catalysts of place were necessarily abroad, where a writer like Jessie Fauset offered:

I like Paris because I find something here, something of integrity, which I seem to have strangely lost in my own country. It is simplest of all to say that I like to live among people and surroundings where I am not always conscious of "thou shall not." In order to offset criticism, the refined colored woman must not laugh too loudly, she must not stare—in general she must stiffen her self-control even though she can no longer humanly contain herself. I am colored and wish to be known as colored, but sometimes I have felt that my growth as a writer has been hampered in my own country. And so—but only temporarily—I have fled from it.[1]

Gender, too, colors the power of place. In Harlem, Fauset nurtured the movement that we are now reconsidering in its plurality; she also felt hemmed in by the possibilities available to her as a "colored" woman and writer in that very evocative space, opting for a temporary rupture with America in a move to Paris.

Between the First and Second World Wars, the period that some call the Jazz Age as well as the New Negro movement more broadly, or the Harlem Renaissance, France became a place where a black American woman could realize personal freedom and creativity, in narrative or in performance, in clay or on canvas, in life and in love. Paris, as it appeared to her, was physically beautiful, culturally refined, inexpensive as a result of the war, and seductive, with its seeming lack of violent racial animus. It was also hospitable, for like the revered Harlem, there was an existent black community. As Tyler Stovall notes,

the experience of community was fundamental to the history of black Americans in the French capital. Blacks did not come to Paris as isolated individuals but generally with the encouragement and assistance of African Americans already there. Once in Paris they were able to participate in a rich community life with its own institutions, traditions, and rituals. Moreover, the creation of an expatriate black *community* played a vital role in easing the pangs of exile. Many blacks in Paris rejoiced in their escape from the United States but at the same time feared losing touch with African American culture. Informal networks enabled them to recreate a black cultural presence abroad freed from racism.[2]

Though there were very few other women writers of the era who had the wherewithal to escape from New York to Paris, art, and performance art, in particular, provided other avenues. Like Claude McKay before him, Langston Hughes did an accounting of black women performance artists' place in interwar Paris:

In Paris, within the last decade, one after another three colored women have risen to reign for a time as the bright particular stars of the night life of Montmartre. And all three of them have been American colored women. Princes, dukes, great artists, and kings of finance have all paid them homage (plus a very expensive cover charge) in brimming glasses of sparkling champagne lifted high in the wee hours of the morning.[3]

Hughes writes about Florence Embry Jones of Chez Florence fame, Ada "Brick-top" Smith Ducongé, and Adelaide Hall. Noticeably absent from Hughes's "three colored women" narrative is Josephine Baker, whose name is undeniably associated with black Americans *d'ailleurs* and the *Paris noir* cultural enclave of the 1920s and 1930s. But Baker never conquered Montmartre per se. She lived there for a time under the tutelage of the venerable Bricktop, performed at the Casino de Paris, and even opened a Chez Josephine on one of the district's tiny *rues* with her Svengali-like common law husband and manager, Pepito Abatino, in the background. However, Hughes, who had cut his own teeth in Montmartre, arrived in France's capital city when Florence Embry Jones was at her height, Bricktop was at her start, and Hall, who became the black equivalent of the Zeigfeld Follies celebrated showgirl in New York, upstaged Baker in Paris with her arrival at the Moulin Rouge.

For Hughes, who declared Harlem in vogue, Montmartre was its veritable counterpart in Paris. Weeks after his arrival in Paris, he wrote in a letter to Countee Cullen,

> I am in Paris. I had a disagreement on the ship, left and came to Paris purely on my nerve, as I knew no one here and I had less than nine dollars in my pocket when I arrived. For a week I came as near starvation as I ever want to be, but I got to know Paris, as I tramped from one end to the other looking for a job. And at last I found one and then another one and yet another!
>
> Happily . . . I have fallen into the very whirling heart of Parisian night-life—Montmartre where topsy-turvy no one gets up before seven or eight in the evening, breakfast at nine and nothing starts before midnight. Montmartre of the Moulin Rouge, Le Rat Mort and the famous night clubs and cabarets! I've just had tea over in the Latin Quarter with three of the most charming English colored girls! Claude McKay just left here for the South. Smith is in Brussels and Roland Hayes is coming.
>
> I myself go to work at eleven pm and finish at nine in the morning. I'm working at the "Grand Duc" where the culinary staff and the entertainers are American Negroes. One of the owners is colored too. The jazz-band starts playing at one and we're still serving champagne long after day-light. This is my second cabaret job within the last two weeks. I'm vastly amused. But at my first place glasses and even bottles were hurled. . . . The Grand Duc is not so wild and there our folks are quite chic. Last night we had a prince in the house and his party.[4]

Hughes describes an at times raucous yet cosmopolitan black world in Paris made up of writers, entertainers, and chic trendsetters comingling with white gentry.

Though Harlem would become Hughes's primary perch, his transnational preoccupations helped to offer a more gendered understanding of black cosmopolitanism and internationalism in the New Negro era.

As with the Harlem Renaissance, a quasi-synecdoche for the range of black productive spaces, the Harlem in Montmartre, Harlem to Paris, New York to Paris transit, too, has become a dominant jumping-off point for exploring the New Negro experience in France. And yet closer scrutiny reveals bends, detours, and backtracks, even as New York may have been the port of embarkation.

In our gendered remapping of the Harlem to Paris transit, Ada Bricktop Smith disrupts the New York/Harlem to Paris narrative. Born in "West-by God" Alderson, Virginia, she became a Chicago entertainer who had crisscrossed the United States before arriving in Harlem permanently in 1922. But it was actually while performing in Washington, D.C.—one of her favorite "chocolate cities," given its vibrant community—that she received the invite to Paris.

In the memoir *Bricktop,* the saloon keeper recalled the events that led to her voyage to Paris:

> At the time, there weren't more than eight or ten Negro entertainers in all of Paris. . . . There was exactly one female Negro entertainer. She was Palmer Jones's wife and her name was Florence. She was a sharp-dressing little girl, very haughty, and she'd been so popular at a place called Le Grand Duc that she was leaving to headline at a new place down the street.
>
> Florence's leaving gave Gene Bullard . . . the unwelcome problem of having to replace her. Florence's husband, Palmer Jones had a suggestion. "Why don't you send to New York? There's a little girl over there called Bricktop. She don't have no great big voice or anything like that, but she has the damndest personality, and she can dance. She'll be a big success here." So they cabled Sammy Richardson, who was in New York at the time and asked him to find me and make me an offer. Sammy tracked me down in Washington [D.C.] and followed me there. . . . There was nothing left to do but accept.[5]

The less than fairytale-like confection of Bricktop's arrival in Paris has been recounted multiple times, or at least the highlights of it: her utter dismay at the 52 rue Pigalle's Lilliputian cabaret and her encounter with a busboy by the name of Langston Hughes, who offered her some food as comfort on witnessing her teary outburst. In between those details are many unpromising others that would have seemed to signal that Paris was not the glamorous cure for her American ennui but rather a colossal mistake.

May 11, 1924, was gray and windy. Between seasickness from the eleven-day transoceanic journey, the loss of her purse containing her life savings totaling twenty-five to thirty dollars, and an opening night to an empty club, Bricktop's first week in Paris ended with an emergency hospitalization for an appendectomy.

Over the course of two nights, nonetheless, Eugene Bullard introduced her to Paris nightlife and the handful of Negroes in Paris, who could be found, for the most part, either performing or eating after hours in the clubs and restaurants along rue Fontaine, rue de la Trinité, rue Pigalle, and rue des Martyrs, the burgeoning heart of black Montmartre.

Montmartre, or La Butte or "hill," occupies the northern part of Paris. Situated in the eighteenth arrondissement on the Right Back, just above it sits the Sacre-Coeur Basilica at its summit. From its lofty perch, the late-nineteenth-century monument has been a witness to the many vices and artistic transformations of the district. As a quasi-outpost of Paris, the hill attracted artists, thespians, Bohemians, and those in search of more decadent offerings. While Pablo Picasso lived for a while on La Butte in an artistic colony, Toulouse-Lautrec's Moulin Rouge series of posters featuring French can-can dancers Jane Avril and La Goulue captured the irrepressible spirit of Montmartre. The trickling in of the black expatriate community added a rare and flavorful gloss to the district's distinction. An almost melodically written twenty-four-page account by British writer Henry Hurford-Janes describes Bricktop's Montmartre and the invasion of jazz on the hill:

> The second invasion of Montmartre was already underway, and little Harlem was springing up next to little Russia. Negro bands were gaining a fanatical following, and Paul Colin's witty black posters showing only white teeth, white eyes and shiny trombones drew people up the Butte to see drummers throw their sticks in the air and beat six drums at once. Trombones blared, saxophones wailed and the bands jerked up and down in fascinating rhythms. No one quite knew where the men and music had come from, but they pushed into Bricktops [sic] and Florence and Mitchell's and came away crazed with jazz. . . . Jazz was the coming thing, a compulsive beat that still hadn't found its dance.[6]

Even Hurford-Janes falls back on the Harlem in Montmartre metaphor. The passage nonetheless encapsulates Bricktop's change in luck post spring 1925. For after an uneventful spring, a chance visit to Le Grand Duc by John Dean, husband of vaudeville and silent film actress Fannie Ward, significantly changed the hostess's circumstances. Though she had been able to earn a comfortable living on the few stragglers who dropped into Le Duc, the Ward-Dean discovery of her unique performing charms bolstered Bricktop's verve. Tired of Florence Jones's antics at Chez Florence, who would "condescend to sit at their table" for hefty sums of cash, Dean and Ward steered their friends and business to Le Grand Duc, where the "pleasingly plump, freckled-face, reddish-haired young lady who sang well and danced a little . . . treated everybody so hospitably."[7]

Bricktop's sojourn to Paris by way of Washington, D.C., reconfigures the direct lines from Harlem to Paris. Settled with a small but devoted clientele, Bricky, as she was called, also began sending correspondence to the *Chicago Defender*. Unlike Alberta Hunter, another Chicago-by-way-of-Memphis transplant to New York and then Paris who sent her missives direct to the *Amsterdam News,* Brick's decision to serve as a correspondent abroad of sorts for the *Defender* undergirds the thesis of this volume—that there were black renaissances, New Negro movements, occurring domestically and internationally simultaneously, that Chicago, too, was the site of a renaissance. Indeed, in the aftermath of her debacle of a debut in New York, Josephine Baker wrote to her estranged manager Pepito Abatino in awe of black Chicago "the coloured people . . . their houses, their universities, their hospitals, everything."[8]

Bricktop's hometown black newspaper began tracking her career as early as 1916, when she was dancing and singing on the Chicago club circuit, to her engagements out west in Los Angeles in the "Entertainment" section of the paper. Her move to Paris was held up in a kind of "look at how our hometown girl" made good. Though she certainly reveled in talking up her modest success, she also used her correspondence to inform the Chicago community of artists in search of the much-ballyhooed racial and financial nirvana in Paris of the realities of post–World War I France. Bricky was earnest in her assessment of life on the ground in Paris, writing in March 1925, "I receive so many letters from different bands and entertainers inquiring about jobs over here. Please let them know through your columns that of the thousands of cabarets in Paris but very few use American entertainment. Unless one is booked through contract it is foolish for them to come. If they are booked in advance, however, the pay is good and sure."[9]

And by May 1924, Hughes was also sounding the "stay in America" alarm to Harold Jackman:

Stay home! Europe is the last place in the world to come looking for a job, and unless you've got a dollar for every day you expect to stay here, don't come. Jobs in Paris are like needles in hay-stacks for everybody, and especially English-speaking foreigners. The city is over-run with Spaniards and Italians who work for nothing, literally nothing. And all French wages are low enough anyway. I've never in my life seen so many English and Americans, colored and white, male and female, broke and without a place to sleep as I have seen here. Yet if you'd give them a ticket home tomorrow, I doubt if ten would leave Paris. Not even hunger drives them away. The colored jazz bands and performers are about the only ones doing really well here. The rest of us, with a dozen or so exceptions, merely get along.[10]

As Hughes relates, a dearth of employment and virtual poverty were not enough to make Americans, colored and white, flee Paris. Paris was still a cultural haven, an incomparable brew of cosmopolitanism and freedom that America couldn't match on any given day. And Bricktop, like Jessie Fauset, had found a place for herself in it.

They both left the thriving community of Harlem for Paris. That Paris transfer, for these black women, meant the one became the Queen of Montmartre café culture, whereas the other, between "loaf[ing] and dream[ing] and stud[ying] and writ[ing] and destroy[ing]," [11] honed her writerly skills during her eight-month stay in France in 1924–25 and eventually published her most acclaimed novel in 1929, *Plum Bun,* in which Paris, for Fauset's protagonist, the artist Angela Murray, represents an escape from New York.

NOTES

1   *Paris Tribune,* February 1, 1923, n.p.
2   Stovall, "Harlem-sur-Seine."
3   Langston Hughes, "Adelaide Hall New Star of Paris Night Life: Her 'Big Apple' Glows over Rue Pigalle," 1937, 1, unpublished essay in Langston Hughes Collection, Beinecke Library, Yale University.
4   Langston Hughes to Countee Cullen, March 11, 1924, Countee Cullen Papers, Amistad Research Center, Tulane University.
5   Bricktop, *Bricktop,* 81–82.
6   Henry Hurford Janes, unpublished account of Josephine Baker's arrival in Paris in the 1920s, Hurford-Janes-Josephine Baker Papers, James Weldon Johnson Collection, Beinecke Library, Yale University.
7   Hughes, "Adelaide Hall," 1.
8   Josephine Baker to Pepito Abatino, April 1936, Eugene Lerner Josephine Baker Collection, Department of Special Collections and University Archives, Stanford University.
9   "'Bricktop' Happy," *Chicago Defender,* March 21, 1925, 8, column 5.
10 Langston Hughes to Harold Jackman, May 25, 1924, Langston Hughes Collection, Beinecke Library, Yale University.
11 Jessie Fauset to Langston Hughes, January 6, 1925, Langston Hughes Collection, Beinecke Library, Yale University.

BIBLIOGRAPHY

Bricktop, with James Haskins. *Bricktop.* 1983. Reprint, New York: Welcome Rain, 2000.
Stovall, Tyler. "Harlem-Sur-Seine: Building an African American Diasporic Community in Paris." *Stanford Electronic Humanities Review* 5, no. 2 (1997). http://www.stanford.edu/group/SHR/5-2/stoval.html.

Acknowledgments

Often in scholarly endeavors, timing is everything. The paths of the editors of this volume crossed several times for nearly fifteen years leading up to this publication. Not only were we nearly fellow graduate students at New York University but, in different years, we each held the Erskine A. Peters Fellowship at the University of Notre Dame. In the years that followed our Peters years, we routinely saw one another at conferences, where our brief conversations revealed a shared interest in the New Negro movement, in rethinking the study of black life, arts, and politics in the 1920s and 1930s beyond the seemingly singular literary frame of the Harlem Renaissance. We met once again shortly before the publication of Davarian's *Chicago's New Negroes* (2007), when a much longer conversation about the growing number of young scholars writing on the New Negro movement convinced us both that there was a need for a collection adequately broad, thematically diverse, theoretically rich, and globally focused to capture this burgeoning field. Still, the auspicious timing of those conversations to have culminated in the volume you now have before you had less to do with us or our conversations per se than with the wealth of scholars working on this era.

We were truly honored that so many scholars, both up-and-comers and established stars, agreed to play some role in making this project possible. An important group of colleagues and friends heard, read, debated, supported, or enriched some aspect of this larger work: Shawn Alexander, Mia Bay, Corey Capers, Sundiata Cha-Jua, Jelani Cobb, Jonathan Coit, Melissa Cooper-Caraballo, Sylviane Diouf, Brent Hayes Edwards, Michael Flug, Rena Fraden, Tiffany Gill, Johnathan Gray, Richard Iton, John Jackson, Kelly Josephs, Robin D. G. Kelley, Deborah Levenson, Thabiti Lewis, Seth Markle, Carter Mathes, Quincy Mills, Jessica Millward, Mark Anthony Neal, Jeffrey O. G. Ogbar, Diana Paulin, Vijay Prashad, Samuel Roberts, David Roediger, Tracy Sharpley-Whiting, Evie Shockley, John Stauffer, Michelle Stephens, Martin Summers, Rebecca Wanzo, Fanon Che Wilkins, Mabel Wilson, Victoria Wolcott, Edlie Wong, and Susan Zeiger.

When we conceived of this project, the first press that came to mind was Minnesota, and that was because of one man: Richard Morrison. His care, focus, brilliance, and capacity to translate our greatest ambitions into a finished product made us understand the beauty of an amazing editor. His sustained efforts, alongside those of his editorial assistant, Erin Warholm-Wohlenhaus, have proven invaluable. The Dean of Faculty Office at Trinity College provided crucial funding for the completion of this project.

Early versions of the ideas assembled here were presented as a keynote address at the Triangle African American History Conference at the University of North Carolina at Chapel Hill. Colleagues were also gracious with feedback in various forums, including the Schomburg–Mellon Summer Institute, Duke University, Smith College, and two events that literally brought this whole collection together: the Harlem Renaissance Revisited conference, convened by the University of Connecticut's Institute for African American Studies (2008), and the "New Negro Reconsidered" panel, organized by Chad Williams, at the American Studies Association meeting in San Antonio, Texas (2010).

Finally, to the "little New Negroes" in our lives, we are indebted to our children, Nylan, Noah, and Ellison and Cheyenne and Yesenia, for always reminding us of what is most important. And of course, none of this could have been possible without the ones who make so much possible, Bridgette Baldwin and Delida Sanchez-Makalani.

Contributors

Davarian L. Baldwin is the Paul E. Raether Distinguished Professor of American Studies at Trinity College, Connecticut, and author of *Chicago's New Negroes: Modernity, the Great Migration, and Black Urban Life*. He is editor of the forthcoming *Encyclopedia of the Harlem Renaissance: Using the Present to Excavate the Past*. His recent projects are *Land of Darkness: Chicago and the Making of Race in Modern America* and *UniverCities: How Higher Education Is Transforming Urban America*.

Anastasia Curwood is assistant professor of African American and diaspora studies at Vanderbilt University and a visiting fellow at the James Weldon Johnson Institute for Race and Difference at Emory University. She specializes in the history of African American women, gender, and sexuality; the black family; and African American intellectual, political, and cultural history in the twentieth century. She is the author of *Stormy Weather: New Negro Marriages between the Two World Wars* and is working on a book about Shirley Chisholm.

Frank Guridy is associate professor of history and African and African diaspora studies at the University of Texas at Austin. He is the author of *Forging Diaspora: Afro-Cubans and African Americans in a World of Empire and Jim Crow,* which won the Elsa Goveia Book Prize from the Association of Caribbean Historians and the Wesley-Logan Book Prize from the American Historical Association. He is coeditor of *Beyond el Barrio: Everyday Life in Latino/a America*.

Claudrena Harold is associate professor of African American and African studies and history at the University of Virginia. She is author of *The Rise and Fall of the Garvey Movement in the Urban South* and is working on a manuscript on New Negro politics in the Jim Crow South. She is coeditor of *The Punitive Turn: Race, Prisons, Justice, and Inequality*.

Jeannette Eileen Jones is associate professor of history and ethnic studies at the University of Nebraska–Lincoln. She is author of *In Search of Brightest Africa:*

Reimagining the Dark Continent in American Culture, 1884–1936 and coeditor of *Darwin in Atlantic Cultures: Evolutionary Visions of Race, Gender, and Sexuality.*

Andrew W. Kahrl is assistant professor of history at Marquette University. He is author of *The Land Was Ours: African American Beaches from Jim Crow to the Sunbelt South.* His research focuses on the legal, economic, and environmental history of coastal real estate development, tax policy and administration, and African American property ownership in the twentieth-century United States. He is working on books on the open beaches movement in 1970s Connecticut and on the history of property assessments and tax liens in black America.

Robin D. G. Kelley is the Gary B. Nash Professor of American History at the University of California, Los Angeles. His books include *Thelonious Monk: The Life and Times of an American Original; Freedom Dreams: The Black Radical Imagination;* and *Africa Speaks, America Answers: Modern Jazz in Revolutionary Times.*

Shannon King is assistant professor of history at the College of Wooster. He is writing a book on community and working-class politics in Harlem in the early twentieth century.

Charles Lester received his PhD in history from the University of Cincinnati. His dissertation examined the role of jazz and jazz musicians in forging cultural, economic, political, and civic institutions in New Orleans, Chicago, and New York City in the first decades of the twentieth century.

Thabiti Lewis is associate professor of English, African American studies, and American studies at Washington State University Vancouver. He is author of *Ballers of the New School: Race and Sports in America* and editor of *Conversations with Toni Cade Bambara.* He is working on projects on Toni Cade Bambara's fiction and masculinity and race in American sports museums.

Treva Lindsey is assistant professor of women's and gender studies at the University of Missouri–Columbia. Her research and teaching interests include African American women's history, black popular and expressive culture, black feminism(s), critical race and gender theory, sexual politics, and African diaspora studies. Her work has been published in the *Journal of African American Studies,* the *Journal of Pan-African Studies,* and *African and Black Diaspora.* She is writing a book on New Negro womanhood in Washington, D.C.

David Luis-Brown is associate professor of English and cultural studies at Claremont Graduate University. He is author of *Waves of Decolonization: Discourses of Race and Hemispheric Citizenship in Cuba, Mexico, and the United States*.

Emily Lutenski is assistant professor of American studies at Saint Louis University. Her work in comparative ethnic literatures, modernism, and gender studies has been published in *MELUS: Multi-ethnic Literature of the United States*, *Western American Literature*, and *Studies in American Indian Literatures*.

Minkah Makalani is assistant professor of African and African diaspora studies at the University of Texas at Austin and author of *In the Cause of Freedom: Radical Black Internationalism from Harlem to London, 1917–1939*. He is working on two projects: a study of C. L. R. James's ideas about democracy and postcolonial governance while in Trinidad from 1958 to 1961 and a study of the (conflicting) vernaculars of blackness in the Dominican Republic from 1915 to 1965.

Mark Anthony Neal is professor of black popular culture in the Department of African and African American Studies at Duke University. He is the author of five books, including *Looking for Leroy: (Il)Legible Black Masculinities*. He hosts the weekly webcast "Left of Black" and is the founder and managing editor of the blog NewBlackMan. He is on Twitter @NewBlackMan.

Yuichiro Onishi is assistant professor of African American and African studies and Asian American studies at the University of Minnesota, Twin Cities. He is author of *Transpacific Antiracism: Afro-Asian Solidarity in Twentieth-Century Black America, Japan, and Okinawa*. His essays have been published in *XCP: Cross-Cultural Poetics*, *Journal of African American History*, *American Quarterly*, and *Extending the Diaspora*.

Theresa Runstedtler is associate professor of history at American University in Washington, D.C. She is author of *Jack Johnson, Rebel Sojourner: Boxing in the Shadow of the Global Color Line* and has published in *Radical History Review*, *Journal of World History*, and *Canadian Issues*. She is working on a project about the international tours of late-nineteenth-century African American performers. Her blog is available at http://www.theresarunstedtler.com/ and she is on Twitter @klecticAcademik.

T. Denean Sharpley-Whiting is the Gertrude Conaway Vanderbilt Distinguished Professor of African American and Diaspora Studies and French at Vanderbilt University. She is author and editor or coeditor of eleven books, including *Negritude*

Women (Minnesota, 2002). She is studying African American expatriate women in Paris in the jazz age.

Michelle Ann Stephens is associate professor of English and Latino and Hispanic Caribbean studies at Rutgers University–New Brunswick. She is author of *Black Empire: The Masculine Global Imaginary of Caribbean Intellectuals in the United States, 1914 to 1962*. She coedited the January 2009 special issue of *Radical History Review*, "Reconceptualizations of the African Diaspora." She is studying the film work of African American stars Paul Robeson and Harry Belafonte and the musical performances of blackface minstrel Bert Williams and reggae performer Bob Marley. She writes regularly on Caribbean art and the emerging field of archipelagic American studies.

Jennifer M. Wilks is associate professor of English and African and African diaspora studies at the University of Texas at Austin. She is author of *Race, Gender, and Comparative Black Modernism*, and her essays have been published in *African-American Review, Callaloo,* and *Modern Fiction Studies*. She is working on a history of transpositions of the Carmen story set in African diasporic contexts and on a study of representations of black masculinity in contemporary literature and culture.

Chad Williams is associate professor of African and Afro-American studies at Brandeis University. His first book, *Torchbearers of Democracy: African American Soldiers in the World War I Era*, received the 2011 Liberty Legacy Foundation prize from the Organization of American Historians and the 2011 Distinguished Book Award from the Society for Military History; it was also a 2011 CHOICE Outstanding Academic Title. His projects include an edited collection of essays on African American military service in modern U.S. history and a monograph on W. E. B. Du Bois, African American soldiers, and World War I.

Index